ANATOMY OF THE MOVIES

ANATOMY OF THE MOVIES

Editor David Pirie

Macmillan Publishing Co., Inc.
New York

Art Editor: Mel Petersen
Designer Linda Abraham
Illustrations by Jim Robins, Tony Graham, Harry Clow, Bill Sanderson, Philip Hood, Howard Levitt, John Holder
Picture research: Linda Proud

Produced, edited and designed by
Shuckburgh Reynolds Ltd,
8 Northumberland Place, London W2 5BS

Macmillan Publishing Co., Inc.,
866 Third Avenue, New York, N.Y. 10022
Collier Macmillan Canada, Ltd.

Library of Congress Catalog Card Number: 81-3690

First American Edition 1981
10 9 8 7 6 5 4 3 2 1

Printed in Hong Kong.

Contents

Contributors

The Editor
David Pirie is a film critic for London's weekly entertainment guide *Time Out Magazine* and presenter of the BBC World Service's *Soundtrack* as well as a regular contributor to other BBC and commercial radio stations. He has lectured on film at various universities and the National Film School, and has contributed to numerous film publications. His first book about the cinema *A Heritage of Horror* was published in 1972 and was described by *The Times* as one of the best media books of its year. He has since written several film books, and in 1980 published his first novel *Mystery Story*.

The Contributors
Andrew Laskos is a freelance writer based in Los Angeles who has written scripts for film and television and contributed to the *Los Angeles Times, American Classic Screen, Action, American Film, EMMY,* and other magazines. He is currently lecturing on screenwriting at California State University.

Mike Bygrave is a freelance journalist and author who lives in Los Angeles. He writes regularly for *The Observer, Penthouse, American Film* and many other American and British publications. His books include *Fuel Food* and the novel *About Time*.

Mitch Tuchman lives in Los Angeles and contributes to the *Los Angeles Times, Chicago Sun-Times, Village Voice, Esquire, The New Republic, New West* and film magazines, including *Film Comment, Take One* and *Film Quarterly*. His doctoral dissertation at Yale was on 'Structure of Cinematic Thought: American Political Films'.

B. J. Franklin is the Los Angeles-based American editor for the movie trade paper *Screen International*. She was formerly editor of *Hollywood Reporter* and an associate editor of *MAC*, the West Coast's leading advertising magazine.

Paul Kerr is currently working as a TV officer for the National Film Archive in London. He contributes regularly to *Screen, Screen Education* and *Framework* and is editor of the forthcoming British Film Institute publication *The Hollywood Film Industry*.

David Thomson is head of Film Studies at Dartmouth College, New Hampshire. His widely praised *Biographical Dictionary of the Cinema* was recently reissued in paperback; he has also written *America in the Dark: Hollywood and the Gift of Unreality* and a biography of Laurence Sterne.

Lynda Myles is curator of the Pacific Film Archive based in Berkeley, California. She ran the Edinburgh Film Festival from 1968 until 1980, during which time it built a reputation as a leading showcase of contemporary American film. She has taught at the British National Film School and co-authored numerous books on film, including *Samuel Fuller, Roger Corman* and, with Michael Pye, the critically acclaimed *The Movie Brats*.

Quentin Falk is co-editor of *Screen International* and a contributor to *Sight and Sound, New Standard* and the *Los Angeles Times*. He broadcasts frequently on film for BBC and commercial radio.

Colin Vaines is a reporter and feature writer for *Screen International* and a contributor to *Photoplay, Movie Star* and the *Daily Mirror*.

John Fleming is a freelance television writer, and a specialist writer on science fiction and special effects for several magazines.

Richard Combs is editor of the *Monthly Film Bulletin* and has written on film for *The Times, Financial Times, The Listener, Times Literary Supplement* and *Film Comment*. He is co-author of *Robert Aldrich*.

Christopher Wicking has scripted numerous films and TV series, including Hammer's *Blood from the Mummy's Tomb* and *Demons of the Mind* and AIP's *Cry of the Banshee* and *Scream and Scream Again*. More recently he has written the film adapation of *Lady Chatterley's Lover* starring Sylvia Kristel and several episodes of *The Professionals* TV series. He is co-author of the recent *The American Vein*, a widely-praised study of directors and directing in television.

Cynthia Rose is an American freelance writer living in London. She edits the 'Thrills' section of the *New Musical Express*, and writes for *Harpers and Queen, The Movie, Time Out* and *The Observer*.

Dilys Powell was film critic for *The Sunday Times* from 1939 until 1976 and continues to write on film for that paper. She has been a member of: the Board of Governors of the British Film Institute; the Independent Television Authority; and the Cinematograph Films Council. She is a regular broadcaster and among her many books are *Films Since 1939* and *An Affair of the Heart*. She was awarded the CBE in 1974.

Geoff Brown is a freelance film writer who has published three books about British film-makers, *Walter Forde, Frank Launder and Sidney Gilliat, Michael Balcon*. He has written about film for *Sight and Sound, Monthly Film Bulletin, Financial Times* and *Radio Times*.

Tom Milne is a former associate editor of *Sight and Sound* and a former editor of *Monthly Film Bulletin*. He edited the *Cinema One* series of books and writes regularly for *The Observer, Sight and Sound* and *Monthly Film Bulletin*. His published work includes studies of *Rouben Mamoulian* and *Carl Dreyer*; he edited *Losey on Losey*, and edited and translated *Godard on Godard*.

Joel W. Finler is a writer and lecturer on cinema history. His books include *Stroheim, All-Time Movie Favourites* and annotated versions of film-scripts of *The Rules of the Game* and *Greed*.

Gilbert Adair is a regular contributor to *Film Comment, Monthly Film Bulletin* and *Sight and Sound*. His book *Hollywood's Vietnam* was published in 1981.

David McGillivray is a screenwriter whose many movies include *White Cargo, Frightmare, House of Mortal Sin* and *Terror*. From 1976 until 1980 he co-presented BBC Radio London's nightly arts programme *Look, Stop, Listen*. He is currently working on a book about failures to be entitled *Flops*.

Acknowledgements

As well as the contributors, many movie producers, directors, writers and studio personnel helped in the compilation of this book. There are too many to name (and several requested anonymity), but in particular I would like to thank producers and executives: Gary Kurtz, Ned Tanen, Frank Yablans, Frank Price, Alan Ladd Jr., Gareth Wigan, David Puttnam, Sandy Lieberson, Michael Douglas, Hercules Bellville and David Barber; directors: Michael Crichton, Richard Donner, John Badham and Harley Cokliss; writers: Paul Mayersberg, John Gregory Dunne, Jimmy Sangster and Bob Mundy; publicists: Joel Kohler, John Friedkin, Gilly Hodson, Anna-Maria Geraldino and Graham Smith.

I am particularly grateful to those contributors who work inside the industry who gave time in order to tell me their own stories: Martin Scorsese, Donald Sutherland, Robert Evans, Lorenzo Semple Jr. and Robert Towne. These accounts of their life, work and views are all recent with the exception of Robert Towne's. His recollections, which have not been published before, date from 1974 while *Chinatown* was still fresh in his mind.

David Gordon, managing director of *The Economist*, whose past research for that magazine has been invaluable, has played a vital role as a consultant, especially in connection with the inflation-adjusted All-Time Hits lists and the major studios' profit chronologies. Joel W. Finler, who also helped greatly in the compilation of both the above sets of lists, was generous enough to provide data from his forthcoming *The Hollywood Studios: A Comprehensive Handbook*. Paul Taylor and Don Macpherson permitted the use of some unpublished interview material with Stanley Jaffe and Robert Benton, and Paul Taylor has performed the invaluable task of checking facts and dates. Among friends and colleagues I was especially assisted by Jude Harris, Chris Petit, Chris Auty, Lynda Myles, Cornelia Bach, Meredith Brody, Joan Goodman, Dave Perry and Christopher Wicking.

Among the many libraries and reference sources consulted, most valuable were the Motion Picture Academy of Arts and Sciences in Los Angeles and the British Film Institute Library in London, both of whose staffs proved enormously helpful. It would also be unthinkable to attempt a book of this nature without repeated reference to the most famous source of movie information and statistics *Variety* and to the *Motion Picture Almanac*. The London-based *Screen International* was also a constant help.

I am grateful to Dell Publications for permission to quote from William Goldman's *Story of A Bridge Too Far*; to *The Atlantic Monthly* and the Raymond Chandler Estate for permission to quote from Raymond Chandler's 'Ten Per Cent of Your Life'; to Farrar, Straus & Giroux for allowing me to use an extract from *The Studio* by John Gregory Dunne.

Among the numerous books that have been written about Hollywood the following have been quoted or have been of factual assistance: *United Artists*, Tino Balio; *The Warner Bros. Story*, Clive Hirschorn; *Universal Pictures*, Michael G. Fitzgerald; *Kings of the Bs*, Todd McCarthy & Charles Flynn; *The Studio*, John Gregory Dunne; *Hollywood Now*, William Fadiman; *The Movie Moguls*, Philip French; *American Film Industry*, Tino Balio; *American Film Now*, James Monaco; *History of the American Film Industry*, Benjamin B. Hampton; *International Film Encyclopaedia*, Ephraim Katz; *The Jaws Log*, Carl Gottlieb; *Story of A Bridge Too Far*, William Goldman; *Making Legend of the Werewolf*, Ed Buscombe; *The White Album*, Joan Didion; *Slouching Towards Bethlehem*, Joan Didion; *Quintana and Friends*, John Gregory Dunne; *The Hollywood Screenwriters*, Richard Corliss; *The Screenwriter Looks at the Screenwriter*, William Froug; *The Last Tycoon*, F. Scott Fitzgerald; *Hollywood Cameramen*, Charles Higham; *Hollywood and After: The Changing Face of Movies in America*, Jerry Toeplitz; *Hollywood: the Haunted House*, Paul Mayersberg.

It is difficult to exaggerate my debt to the pioneering work of Michael Pye and Lynda Myles in *The Movie Brats* and of Michael Pye in *Moguls*. Without these two books it would have been far harder to arrive at a starting-point for this one, and I was greatly helped by the investigation of MCA in *Moguls*.

Finally I would like to dedicate this book to the memory of my grandfather George Tarbat, whose film interests spread through four generations, and to three vital, and not uncritical, members of Hollywood's increasingly youthful target audience: Robin, Caroline and Victoria Goodman. I hope the film industry has more wonders in store for them and for their children.

D.P.

Dates Except where otherwise stated, the dates appended to film titles throughout this book are the dates of first release.

Abbreviation Throughout this book m. stands for million.

Introduction

There was once a time when it was thought vulgar for serious studies of film even to mention the word money, except perhaps when sneering at Hollywood producers. Film study was focused almost exclusively on the director's struggle to create art out of what was considered the debased commercial world of Hollywood, the struggle to transcend low budgets and crass material. Now that the flood of monographs on directors has slowed to a trickle it's easier to see that this was only one step, albeit an important one, in the recognition of the cultural importance of popular cinema. Increasingly the film enthusiast has been forced to confront the reality that Hollywood is, less a battlefield between artists and capitalists, than an extraordinarily diffuse cultural machine whose fuel is – and always was – money. It is that machine's fluctuating ability to respond to the demands of its audience which make its products so fascinating.

From this perspective, questions that would once have been dismissed as trivial or sensational – questions about the wheeling and dealing behind the screen – assume a new importance. But, except in the strictly topical articles of the trade press, they are rarely asked and even more rarely placed in any kind of context.

The purpose of *Anatomy of the Movies* is to lay bare the interaction of creativity and finance at the heart of contemporary movies – the power structures, the personalities, the money. It follows that we have also paid serious attention to the process by which several recent creative and commercial successes reached the screen. Who had the idea? How did it originate? How were backers persuaded? What did it cost? How was it shot? And so on. For the first time in a book about film we include exhaustive lists of the most popular movies of all time, based, not on some vague notion of their fame or fortune, but on an inflation-adjusted assessment of the money they actually earned for their distributors at the box office.

Contributors to *Anatomy of the Movies* were fortunate to be studying popular cinema at a peculiarly vital and successful moment in its history. In the early 1970s, as several of the major production companies recorded huge losses, no-one could have foreseen that Hollywood was on the verge of one of its biggest booms ever – a boom which would be based, not on television or even video, but on the oldest of all the film capital's attractions: hit movies on general release. As our charts of box office hits reveal there is no comparison here with the short-lived boom at the end of the 1960s which grew out of *The Sound of Music*. For many studios, the peak years of the 1970s compare only with the peak years of the 1940s: for example, in 1946, still remembered fondly as a boom year for world film attendance, Twentieth Century-Fox enjoyed a film revenue of $90.1 million. But, even adjusted for inflation, that figure barely matches Fox's record earnings year of 1978 when revenue from theatrical film production reached $346.6 million.

If this book had been written in 1970, it would have seemed less an anatomy than an autopsy. Indeed, at that time, one astute observer, the former studio executive William Fadiman, stated quite confidently in his book, *Hollywood Now*: 'Hollywood will survive largely as a museum of vanished glories. It . . . will never regain the prestige or worldwide acceptance it had unless drastic changes are effected in its basic structure.' No such changes were effected, but the decade which followed the publication of *Hollywood Now* produced *Jaws*, *Saturday Night Fever* and *Star Wars*, Clint Eastwood, John Travolta, Woody Allen and Robert Redford. Worldwide acceptance of Hollywood's product has rarely been so complete.

Now some of the euphoria of the 1970s is spent and the studios in the 1980s face new problems, including over-generous budgeting and an unwelcome number of expensive flops. But, unlike the late 1960s when a drastic recession followed boom, the hits have continued and most of the majors remain healthy. As yet the bubble has not burst.

Of course some people, including a section of critics, wish it would burst. They regard the recent developments in Hollywood as a shameful sell-out, and the 1970s hits as cold, inhuman money-making machines. This book is not primarily concerned with personal movie preferences, or with criticism. But, after a decade which has given us films as varied and interesting as *Close Encounters of the Third Kind*, *Chinatown* and *American Graffiti* it takes a near-comic perversity to state, as James Monaco does in his book *American Film Now*, that so far as movies are concerned 'the seventies have no culture of their own' and that Hollywood has suffered from 'a self-induced paralysis'.

After the shambles which the industry presented in the late 1960s, it is remarkable that there is any recent Hollywood history to discuss at all. The fact, not only that there is, but that it is a success story of some considerable proportions points to an uncanny resilience in the Hollywood machine. *Anatomy of the Movies* is an attempt to understand that machine a little better, and thereby to encourage realistic hopes rather than pious expectation.

THE MONEY AND THE POWER

The Hollywood Majors

Louis B. Mayer

Paramount Pictures Corporation *(left): the chief executives photographed in 1915 shortly after the formation of the company. Left to right: Morris Geste, Adolph Zukor, Cecil B. DeMille, Jesse L. Lasky and Samuel Goldfish (later Goldwyn).*

Carl Laemmle

Once, when the fragrance of magnolia trees still lingered in the Los Angeles air, some very powerful men with the instincts of killer sharks ran some very big movie studios where there were More Stars Than There Are in Heaven. Their names were Louis and Jack and Harry and Adolph and Darryl and Uncle Carl, plus a few others who rose from obscurity only to fall into oblivion. They were mostly little-educated, working class immigrants: manufacturers and salesmen who never lost the common touch. They knew exactly what movies should be. Movies were everything life wasn't. Movies were Stars. Movies were A Show. Movies were – to appropriate the novelist William Saroyan's description of the circus – 'adventure, travel, danger, skill, grace, romance, comedy, peanuts, popcorn and chewing gum.'

Each man owned a big chunk of his studio. Although he had to consult New York money men in a general sort of way, rarely did he defer to them, and he had a simple code: his studio was a kingdom with a fence around it. Inside the fence, all the employees, from stars to electricians, were encouraged to feel part of a winning team. They were supposed to obey orders – 'I pay 'em,' snapped Jack Warner. 'They do what I tell 'em.' – while, at the same time, feel like children cared for by Daddy.

Everyone outside the fence was a lesser form of mortal and an enemy. Louis Mayer complained about that gangster in the valley, and no-one needed to be told that it was Jack Warner whose ears turned red. On the main gate at Paramount, someone chalked up, 'In case of an air raid, go directly to RKO. They haven't had a hit in years.' The bosses competed ferociously for stars, writers, directors, producers and craft people – the men and women who actually made the movies. Whenever possible, they tied these talented artists down to seven-year contracts that had a habit of dragging on and on beyond seven years. Way, way

Darryl F. Zanuck

Fox Movietone Studios *in 1929 as ruled by William Fox and Winfield Sheehan. The lot became 20th Century-Fox's home in 1935 and much of it is still in use today.*

1 *Administration*
2 *Projection room*
3 *Rehearsal halls*
4 *Cutting room*
5 *Music director's hall*
6 *Stages 1 and 2*
7 *Stages 3 and 4*
8 *Apparatus building*
9 *Generator building*
10 *Machine shop*
11 *Water tower*
12 *Dressing rooms*
13 *Stage 9*
14 *Apparatus building*
15 *Stages 5 and 6*
16 *Stages 7 and 8*
17 *Space for exterior sets*

Jack Warner

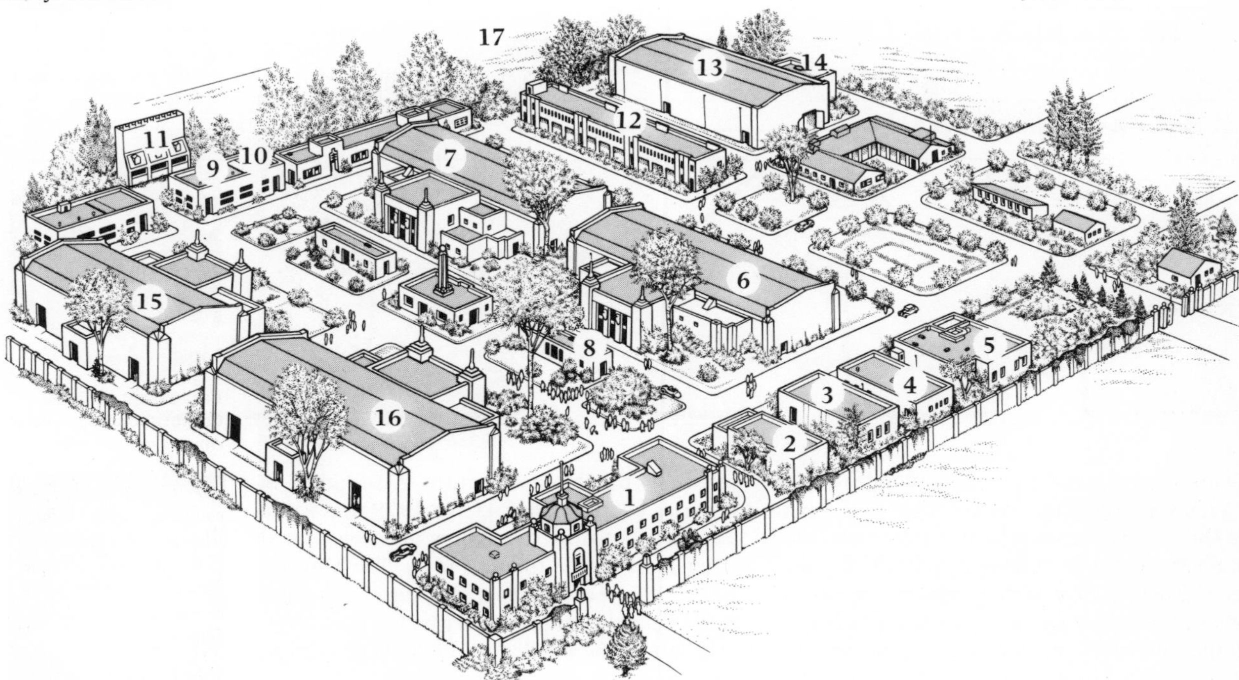

Harry Cohn

beyond. 'Some of us gave twelve or fourteen sulfurous years of our short actor's lives working off a seven-year contract,' wrote David Niven in his second book of Hollywood memories, *Bring on the Empty Horses*.

The moguls relished the pleasure of their own company. 'They owned polo ponies and racing stables and chauffeur-driven Rollses,' remembered Budd Schulberg, whose father, B.P., ran Paramount between 1925 and 1932, the time of Clara Bow, Cary Grant, Gary Cooper, Marlene Dietrich, and *Wings* (1927), the winner of the first best-picture Oscar. 'They chain-smoked expensive Havana cigars, and flamboyantly gambled thousands of dollars on the turn of a single card.' Other than a general desire to eat each other alive, the attitude of these men towards each other was neatly put by Harry Cohn of Columbia: 'I never want to see you again until I need you.'

Which is a bit too crude a style for the studio system of the 1980s. Today, Louis B. Mayer, Jack Warner, Harry Cohn, Adolph Zukor, Darryl Zanuck and Carl Laemmle probably wouldn't make it past the guards at the front gates of M.G.M., Warner Brothers, Columbia, Paramount, Twentieth Century-Fox and Universal – the studios they helped found. If they did get inside, and tried to make pictures, they'd either go at it like modern Bismarcks, snorting blood and iron, and devour everyone in sight – or, more likely, themselves be marshmallowed to death by the new generation of studio executives. The same old manipulations and lies and power plays and false friendships are endemic, of course, but the new style at the studios is to be open and flexible and interactive, achieving the appearance of instant intimacy. This is especially true among that group of younger executives dubbed the 'baby moguls' by *New West* magazine. As they rise, so does mellowspeak take hold. Never again will Harry Cohn be heard 'storming through the halls, bawling out employees,' as Frank

	U.S. & Canada	The rest of the World	Total (millions)
1969	$ 375	$340	$ 715
1970	443	355	798
1971	402	340	742
1972	500	389	889
1973	471	415	886
1974	649	470	1,119
1975	752	579	1,331
1976	698	547	1,245
1977	926	535	1,461
1978	1,215	750	1,965

Estimated Total Film Rentals *(left) for the seven major film companies plus Walt Disney and American-International from 1969 to 1978. Remarkably the American market expanded more than twice as fast as the rest of the world, so by 1978 it was worth almost twice as much. Hence the movie producers' obsession with US audience taste.*

The majors' box-office share *during the late 1970s (below). All the majors did reasonably well. Warners rose from the dreaded sixth position (during chairman Ted Ashley's sabbatical year of 1975) to a coveted 20% of the market in 1979. Fox and* Star Wars *achieved 20% in 1977, and Paramount had an unprecedented 24% in 1978, largely due to* Saturday Night Fever *and* Grease. *Columbia fought their way back to health from a very shaky 1976. Universal's success in 1980 was due to several hits including* The Jerk *and* The Blues Brothers, *while United Artists' poor performance reflects the fact that it had not a single movie in* Variety's *top twenty.*

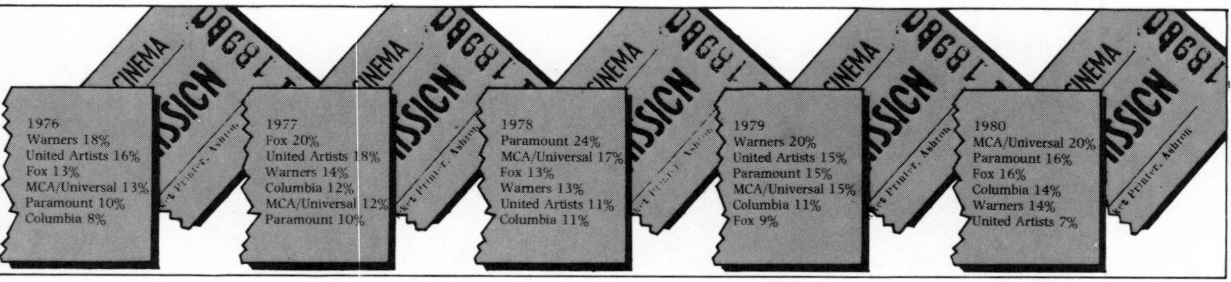

Capra remembered him, and yelling to Capra, 'Why, you little Dago bastard. I got half a mind to throw you out on your ear right now!' Nor is Sherry Lansing, president of Fox's film division, likely to deal with producers by sinking to her knees and weeping like Louis B. Mayer, despite her early days as an actress (she was the girl who blasted bad guy Mike Henry, then lent her shoulder to help John Wayne hobble away at the end of Howard Hawks' *Rio Lobo*, 1970).

Different people, different worlds. But the generations are linked by the legacy bequeathed by the old guard moguls. Their six studios, and United Artists, still dominate international film production, albeit in a different form. The studios now focus on financing and distributing films, rather than actually producing them, and, through diversification, most of them could survive quite nicely, even if they were to abandon film-making altogether. In fact, 'studios' is something of a misnomer, though everybody still uses the word. United Artists owns no physical plant, while Warners and Columbia have set up their Burbank Studios as an autonomous profit-making unit.

Together, the big seven companies finance and distribute over a hundred new movies each year, including a handful of negative pickups (films purchased for release after they have been completed). Although the number of features rated by the Motion Picture Association of America board totalled 412 in 1979, it was the 123 distributed by the majors that constituted what most people thought of as 'The Movies'. And so it is, year after year, despite vast changes in the motion picture industry and its audiences, and despite the predictions of doom levelled at the majors scarcely a decade earlier.

How well are the majors doing? During the 1970s, at least, very well. In 1979, 86 per cent of the American market share went to the big seven. Two smaller producer-distributors, Walt Disney and American International (since absorbed by Filmways), together accounted for another nine per cent, leaving a thin six per cent for such minor distributors as Avco, New World, Cannon, AFD, World Northrop, Crown International, Compass, and the International Picture Show Company.

The 1979 domestic box-office gross was about $2,821m. improved from $1,294m. in 1969. On average, 60 per cent of that gross stayed in the hands of exhibitors, leaving 40 per cent in rentals. Most of that 40 per cent went to the big seven.

At the end of the 1960s, scarcely one movie in ten made a profit, but now 'about three in seven prosper,' according to Mike Medavoy, executive vice-president of Orion Pictures (see page 27), formed by ex-United Artists executives in 1978. During the 1960s only five

Alan Hirschfield, *leading executive at Warner Bros, Columbia and currently Twentieth Century-Fox.*

Movies which made more than $10m. *In the 70s 220 movies earned more than $10m. in rentals, and a lot more in most cases from ancillary markets. This is an almost fourfold increase over the 60s, and reflects much more than just the effect of inflation. As audiences built up after the slump around 1970, the studios began to make fewer, but more expensive, movies and to spend more on marketing. However, many of the big earners were unexpected low-budget successes. In the decades prior to the 60s a greater proportion of movies made a profit, but there were few real blockbusters.*

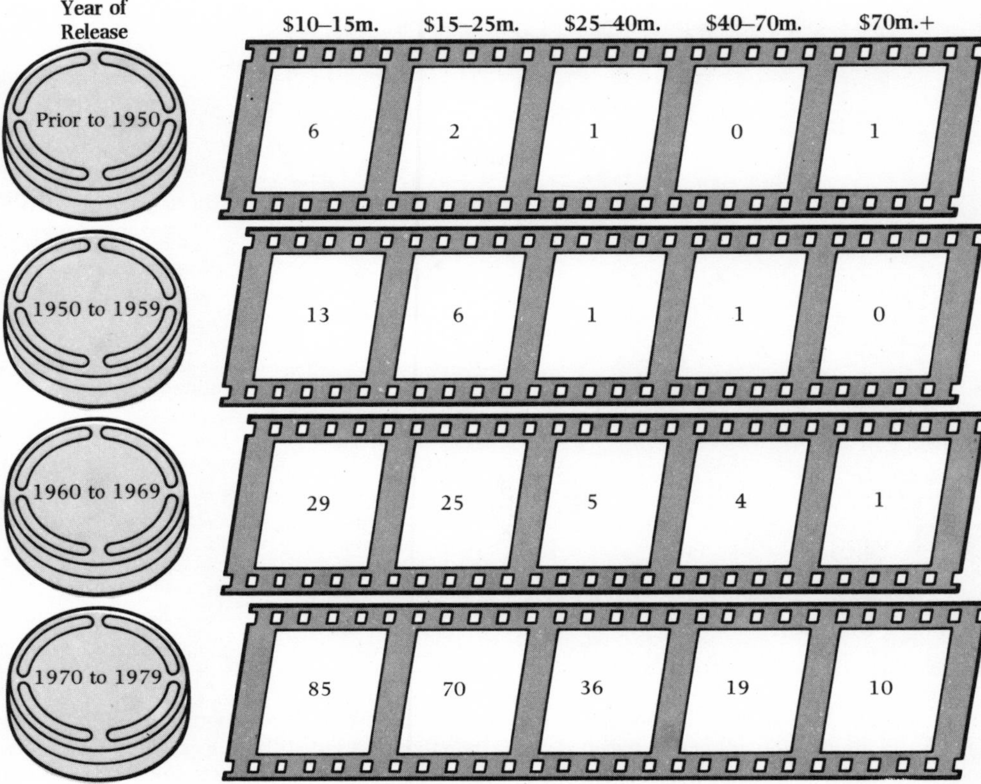

David Begelman, *one of the architects of 1970s Hollywood, who helped rebuild Columbia and survived scandal to take over MGM.*

movies made over $40m. in rentals, yet in 1979 alone, four movies (*Superman, Every Which Way But Loose, Rocky 2,* and *Alien*) cracked that barrier, which implies that profitability was increasing around four times faster than inflation. Whereas it used to be a rough rule of thumb that the worldwide box office yielded a maximum of about two billion (two thousand million) dollars, give or take for inflation, and that that was pretty much *that* for the movie industry's earning potential, nowadays revenue from such ancillary markets as TV, music and publishing can be added in, and the two billion dollar ceiling is definitely a thing of the past.

Columbia Pictures: rescued by tax shelters

Perhaps the most dramatic success story of the 1970s was that of Columbia Pictures. In 1973, the company was in debt to the tune of $223m. But within five years, under the leadership of David Begelman and Alan Hirschfield, the company reduced that debt to $35m., while increasing net worth (the value of its shares) from $6m. to $140m. Earnings bounded back from a $50m. deficit to a $80m. surplus as Columbia released a slate of successful films, including *Shampoo, Taxi Driver, The Deep* and *Close Encounters of the Third Kind.*

The idea that saved Columbia seems to have come from Chicago tax attorney Burton Kanter, who first conceived of adapting real estate investment principles to the movies. His idea: service corporations would channel outside money into production, offering individual investors the chance to write off far more than they invested against taxes. The system worked as follows: an individual with a high tax bill was offered the chance to invest, say, $10,000 in a movie. A bank then invested some larger sum, say $40,000, but the deal was constructed in such a way that the original investor was deemed to have invested $50,000. If the movie made money, the investor and the bank made money. If it lost money, the investor still paid far less tax than was originally owed. Columbia's legal division used this notion to obtain badly needed production finance and, at the same time, to offset the gamble involved in film investment while keeping Columbia's hungry distribution circuit fed with movies. The plan probably saved the company from going under.

Among outside producers, Richard Bright and Lester Persky assembled the most ambitious tax shelters. Their 1975 packages for Columbia and United Artists included *The Man Who Would Be King, The Front, Sinbad and the Eye of the Tiger, Harry and Walter Go to New York, Gator, The Missouri Breaks* and *From Noon Till Three.* According to entertainment attorney

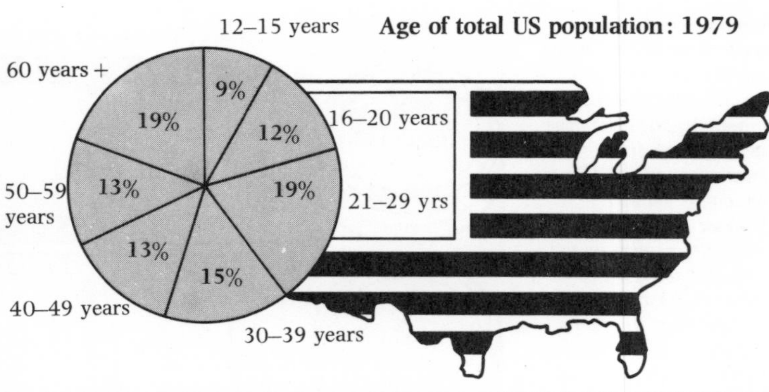

Age of movie-going population								
Age Group	1969	1970	1972	1973	1975	1976	1977	1979
12 to 15 years	18%	16%	13%	14%	14%	14%	16%	20%
16 to 20 years	31%	27%	30%	29%	32%	31%	25%	29%
21 to 29 years	28%	29%	30%	30%	28%	31%	33%	27%
30 to 39 years	10%	12%	11%	13%	12%	13%	13%	11%
40 to 49 years	6%	8%	10%	8%	8%	5%	6%	6%
50 to 59 years	3%	6%	4%	4%	3%	3%	4%	5%
60 years and older	4%	2%	2%	2%	3%	3%	3%	2%
12 to 17 years	–	–	–	–	19%	20%	26%	31%

Age of the US movie audience *(above); age statistics are a producer's bible and the rationale behind countless youth projects. The US audience is overwhelmingly weighted to teens and twenties with the under-twenties consistently making up well over 40% of the total audience.*

Kramer vs. Kramer *(above left), surprise hit, of Christmas 1979–80, despite the fact that the story had no obvious appeal to the all-important 12 to 20-year-old age group.*

Tom Pollock, tax shelters 'probably added $150m. in production money between 1971 and 1976'. After five years, the federal government squelched such shelters, but by that time the industry was far more healthy and an investment boom was almost under way.

1980: A boom in production

In 1980, reflecting a production surge throughout the industry, Columbia announced 20 features to roll through the middle of the following year for a total budget exceeding $125m. That schedule was a dramatic increase from the 14 Columbia features released in 1978, and the 10 in 1977. Columbia's reinvigorated production activity was consistent with an industry trend that saw production at the big seven majors rise 21 per cent between 1978 and 1979, from 88 features to 107, exclusive of negative pickups.

MGM, following a series of losses and flops like *The Boy Friend* (1971) and *Pat Garrett and Billy the Kid* (1973), had put its distribution arm into hibernation in 1973, subsequently releasing through United Artists. But in 1980 the lion rediscovered his roar under new film division president David Begelman. In less than five months, after coming aboard in early 1980, Begelman was planning movie versions of John Steinbeck's novel *Cannery Row*, Brian Clark's play *Whose Life Is It, Anyway?*, Gerald Ayres' *Rich and Famous*, an updated version of the old Bette Davis movie, *Old Aquaintance*, and several other important productions. In 1983, MGM reactivates its distribution arm. Significantly the film division of MGM is not liable for the disastrous fire in 1980 at the MGM Grand Hotel in Las Vegas.

MGM's re-emergence, and the ambitious plans of the smaller production companies without a distribution arm, reflected the extent of the production boom. The majors wanted product to cash in on the lucrative ancillary markets and improved box-office. 'You need a large spread of films because, let's face it, not every one performs well,' explains Mike Medavoy. 'But one hit pays for all the misses.' Before *The Godfather*, *The Sting* and *The Exorcist*, few people believed you could make a string of pictures, year after year, that would gross $100m. and more in worldwide rentals (*Gone with the Wind* and *The Sound of Music* were separated by decades), but now, if *Star Wars* (1977) or *The Empire Strikes Back* (1980) don't crack the half billion dollar mark, something else soon will. United Artists production chief, Steven Bach, calls that figure 'the Holy Grail we're all chasing now'. (Not that anyone ever *knows* which pictures will succeed and which will fail. 'If I discover that one of my men believes he knows which film will make money and which will lose,' movie-banker A. H. Howe told Michael Pye and Lynda Myles in their book, *The Movie Brats*, 'I say he has "gone Hollywood" and I fire him.' Howe was vice-president of Bank of America's National Division, in charge of motion picture credit activity.)

Even the most unassuming project can

Airplane *(right) and* **Urban Cowboy** *(far right) were Paramount's two top pictures of 1980. But in book-keeping terms the similarity ends there:* Airplane *was made for a fraction of* Urban Cowboy's *cost.*

break through. MGM's Frank Davis is just one of the Hollywood executives who was amazed by the success of Columbia's *Kramer vs. Kramer* (1979): 'Who could have predicted the runaway success just by reading the original novel, or even the screenplay? Even those people who saw the film in its early screenings, did they visualize its potential? The story hardly seemed to appeal to the 12–20-year-old age group that makes up half the movie audience. Robert Benton is a distinguished director, but had no great commercial successes behind him. And even Dustin Hoffman had faltered commercially with his two previous films. Yet everyone who saw the film loved it. That it broke away to such an extent – that's what keeps us in there fighting and scratching to get our pictures made.'

The box-office results of 1980 proved similarly unexpected. Presumed blockbusters like Warners' *The Shining* and *Bronco Billy*, starring Jack Nicholson and Clint Eastwood respectively, disappointed, while Paramount did very well from cheap trifles like the comedy *Airplane* and the formula horror picture *Friday the 13th*. Paramount's major movie of the summer season, *Urban Cowboy* with John Travolta, was successful but will probably not generate nearly as much profit for the company as *Airplane* and *Friday the 13th*; yet the cost of both these films added together was less than the cost of the closing credit titles of the expensive science fiction movie *Star Trek* (1979). Low budget films are fashionable again.

'You never know where the audience should be and you should never try to figure it out,' commented Paramount's President Michael Eisner to *Variety*. '*Urban Cowboy* is an example of a picture we did everything right on. . . . We bought rights to an article in *Esquire* that we loved . . . attracted a top producer and a top director . . . got a script written that was excellent. Only then did we attract Travolta . . . we didn't buy a hyped-up commodity; we followed the creative process . . . but it won't be a big hit, although it will be successful.'

By comparison Paramount's creative input into *Friday the 13th* was almost zero: 'We took a look at the film and though I don't like violence myself it has some of the most creative killings I've ever seen on screen . . . and it only cost us $1.5m. to buy. So here we were spending $10m. here and $5m. there. What was $1.5m?' By the late summer of 1980 *Friday the 13th* had earned a gross rental of nearly $17m.

Broadening the market and spreading the risk

But, for the moment, movies as cheap as that are the exception. In general, production budgets have risen so that movies must earn more just to break even. Paramount's *Star Trek* and United Artists' *Heaven's Gate* (1980) cost about $40m. each. The combined budget for Warner's *Superman I* (1978) and *II* (1980) was in the region of $50m. However, there is a difference between the financial risks incurred by these big-budget pictures and those of earlier years. When Paramount's *Paint Your Wagon* (1969), *Darling Lili* (1970) and *On a Clear Day You Can See Forever* (1970) posted budgets between $15m. and $22m. during the 1960s, they had little guarantee that any of that money would ever be returned. If the films flopped at the box-office, as all these did resoundingly, they entered the red, and that was that. Television sales were inevitably adjusted downwards.

But today, those financing many of the big-budget pictures hedge their bets in various ways. Sometimes, two majors will share financing, as with *Popeye* (Paramount and Disney, 1980), *1941* (Universal and Columbia, 1979), *All that Jazz* (Columbia and Fox, 1979), *The Electric Horseman* (Universal and Columbia, 1979), *Sorcerer* (Universal and Paramount, 1977) and the first major collaboration between studios *The Towering Inferno* (Fox and Warners, 1974). One major will release the film domestically in the US, the other will handle foreign release. On *Apocalypse Now* (1979), UA bought only domestic distribution rights; total financing for Coppola's $31m. epic came from UA, foreign pre-sales, and the director's own assets. In addition, exhibitors are increasingly forced

The TV Sales Bonanza: Gone with the Wind *went to NBC for $5m. and then to CBS for $35m. for 20 showings.*

American Gigolo *beat* Gone with the Wind's *initial TV sales figure by a million even before production began.*

to pay enormous guarantees for the films they screen – guarantees which are almost certainly not refunded by the majors should their product flop. *1941*, for example, reputedly hit break-even as a no-win, no-lose picture for Universal and Columbia. Ned Tanen, Universal's president, put break-even at about $60m. in rentals. But nowhere near that amount was generated by *1941*'s box-office performance. Most of the rentals came from upfront, non-refundable guarantees from exhibitors, who then proceeded to eat their losses.

Ancillary markets also help reduce – and sometimes eliminate – what the industry calls 'downside risk': these include sales to the television networks, cable TV, video cassettes and discs (including RCA's SelectaVision), syndication, and soundtrack and publishing tie-ins. That these markets could generate big money became apparent when NBC paid $5m. for the television premiere of *Gone with the Wind*, for which CBS subsequently subscribed $35m. for 20 airings over 20 years. ABC licensed the TV rights to Paramount's *American Gigolo* (1980) for over $6m. for three runs. Production costs were about $5m. (Had the film starred John Travolta, as originally planned, instead of Richard Gere, ABC was prepared to pay between $7m. and $7.5m.) Fox licensed its low-budget ($2.5m.) *Breaking Away* (1979) to NBC for $4.5m., and even its box-office loser, *Butch and Sundance: The Early Days* (1979), recovered $6.5m. of its approximately $10m. budget in a pre-release sale to television. The result? Movies that stumble at the box-office now have more opportunities to break even or reach profit. And if a movie *is* a loser, its losses are spread among the major, the numerous exhibitors, the TV network, the cable people, and so on.

'Nobody ever realized the value of ancillary rights before the mid-1970s,' says UA's Steven Bach, who also produced *Butch and Sundance* for Fox. 'I remember being in an office at Paramount ten years ago, and seeing a framed xeroxed check for ten million dollars. Very impressive. It was for the sale of the entire pre-1948 Paramount feature library to Universal-MCA. But who ended up with the better deal? Ten million dollars isn't worth ten million dollars any more, but the value of film libraries has skyrocketed. Who do the networks and cable people and videodisc people come to for the best libraries? Of course – the majors.'

Ned Tanen, *President of Universal Pictures, and one of the key patrons of the 'movie brats'.*

The golden years: 1913–1945

So why were so many people expecting the earth to swallow up the majors less than a decade ago? In 1971, when Jack Warner quit the studio he founded in 1923 with brothers Albert, Harry and Sam, to enter independent production (*Dirty Little Billy, 1776*), Old Hollywood finally appeared ready to keel over after three decades of atrophy. Between 1969 and 1972, the seven major studios lost over $250m., the pioneer moguls were dead or ousted, audiences plummeted, and economic disaster loomed. The big seven seemed to be no longer the *big* seven.

To understand what had happened it is necessary to understand Hollywood's past. The earlier, golden years had begun in 1913, when Cecil B. De Mille descended on rural Hollywood to shoot *The Squaw Man* for a group of investors who would later form Paramount Pictures. Then, in 1915, the federal courts dissolved the General Film Company, the distribution subsidiary of the infamous Motion Picture Patents Company, the east coast organization whose prime intention had always been to monopolize the young movie industry for itself. A second court order, in 1917, dissolved the MPPC itself, opening the floodgates to those men, like De Mille and Adolph Zukor, who opposed the monopoly.

In 1919, Zukor was the first to consolidate production with distribution on a large scale in Hollywood, by purchasing theatres across the United States – theatres in which he could screen his Paramount 'photoplays'. By the early 1920s, the vast majority of American movies were shot in Los Angeles, under the leadership of men whose names are now so

Elizabeth Taylor *(right) in the most expensive movie ever made,* Cleopatra.

Cecil B. DeMille *(far right) christens Hollywood in* The Squaw Man *(1913). This was the first movie made in Hollywood.*

Cleopatra $105.6m. (1962, $44m.)
Waterloo $50m. (1969, $25m.)
Mutiny on the Bounty $48m. (1962, $20m.)
Hello Dolly $48m. (1969, $24m.)
Tora! Tora! Tora! $47.5m. (1970, $25m.)
The Fall of the Roman Empire $46m. (1964, $20m.)
The Greatest Story Ever Told $46m. (1965, $20m.)
Dr Dolittle $44m. (1967, $20m.)
Star Trek $42m. (1979, $42m.)
Darling Lili $41.8m. (1970, $22m.)
Paint Your Wagon $40m. (1969, $20m.)
The Bible $39.6m. (1966, $18m.)
Superman $38.5m. (1978, $35m.)
Ben Hur $37.5m. (1959, $15m.)
Lawrence of Arabia $36m. (1962, $15m.)
Raise the Titanic! $36m. (1980, $36m.)
Heaven's Gate $36m. (1980, $36m.)
The Ten Commandments $35.1m. (1956, $13m.)

The most expensive movies of the blockbuster era. *For ease of comparison real costs have been adjusted for inflation, using the US government's cost of living index. Dates and real costs appear in parentheses.*

burdened with the aura of legend that it's difficult to imagine how they must have been when confronted simply across a desk, rather than in the pages of movie history books: Marcus Loew, Adolph Zukor, Louis B. Mayer, William Fox, Samuel Goldfish (Goldwyn), Jesse Lasky, Cecil B. De Mille, Joe and Nick Schenck, the Warner brothers, Carl Laemmle, Lewis Selznick, and Irving Thalberg.

Vertical integration – controlling every aspect of the industry, from production to consumption – was their driving objective, with each major vying for the best production facilities and personnel, and for the best theatres. Over the next couple of decades, the studio system basked in its own power: the majors owned most of the key first run theatres (owning the *most* theatres was less important than owning the *best* ones; during the early 1930s, the five biggest vertically integrated companies – Paramount, MGM, RKO, the Fox Film Corporation, and Warner Brothers – controlled only about an eighth of all theatres, but they were the key houses in all the major cities). The creative talent in Hollywood worked under long-term employment agreements, and most of those contracts were dictated by studio business affairs departments. 'All Louis B. Mayer had to negotiate was how much Clark Gable would get per picture for the next seven years, what his billing was, and when he would turn up for work,' recalls the veteran movie lawyer Martin Gang who still works close to the site of his original 1930s office on Hollywood and Vine. 'As long as this system prevailed, talent had no muscle to negotiate.'

The 'talent' weren't the only ones without muscle. The majors were also able to control the market and limit competition to such an extent that, in 1938, the Justice Department filed against the five big majors plus Columbia, Universal and United Artists, citing them for conspiracy to restrain trade in production, distribution and exhibition, and for attempting to monopolize trade within the national movie industry.

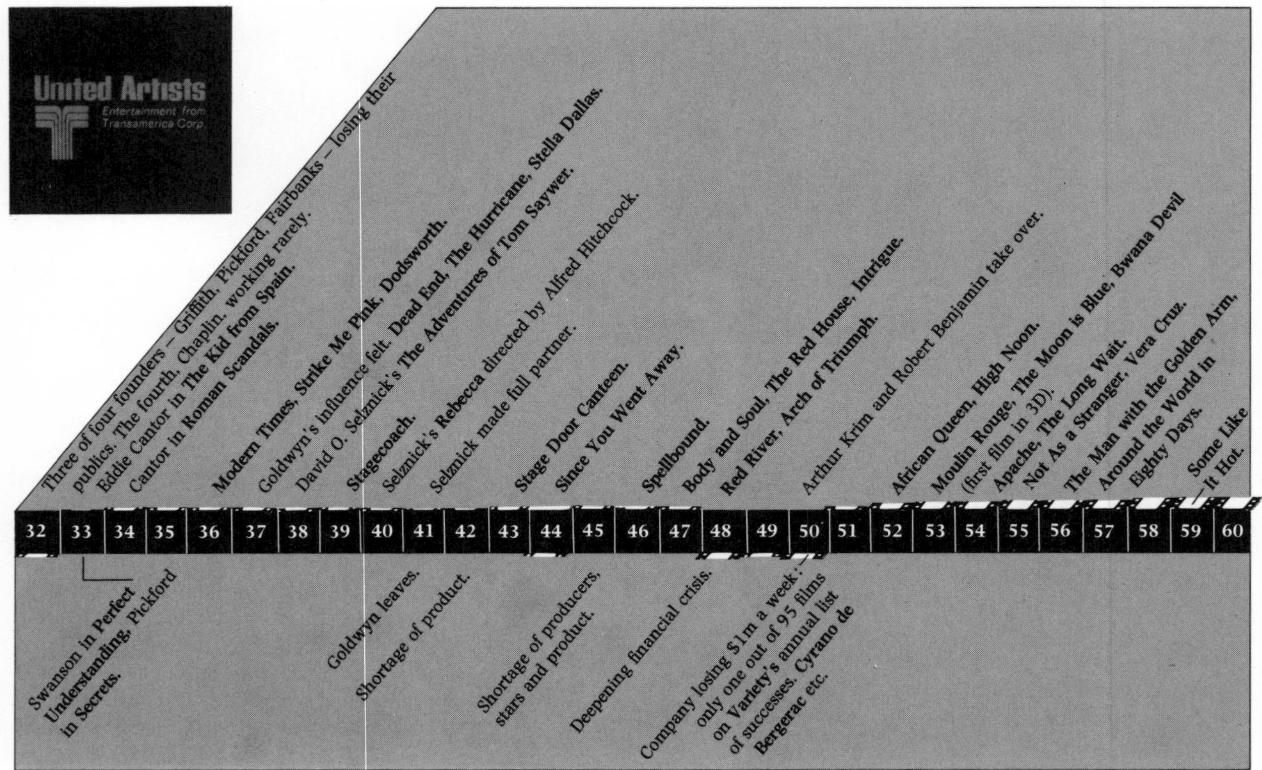

The end of the studio system

But if the studio system began to crack in the late 1930s, its decline is most clearly dated from the de Havilland case of 1945. 'Jack Warner had loaned Olivia de Havilland to David Selznick for *Gone with the Wind*,' Martin Gang explains. 'But after she returned to Warners, he kept offering her the usual junk roles. She turned him down, so Warner suspended her.' 'Suspension' was one of the studio bosses' most vicious tools. It meant that a star under contract who refused any role – even the most wretched one – was obliged to sit around unpaid for, say, four months while the picture was shot and then half of that time again as a punishment. Worse, the time they had been suspended was then added on to their contract so players could be trapped for ten or fifteen years, working off a seven year contract. De Havilland was particularly anxious about the time that kept being added on to her contract. Warners was becoming a prison, with no remission in sight. She decided to sue her employer – and Martin Gang made movie history by winning her case for her. Thereafter, studio contracts were limited to seven consecutive years, no matter what suspensions were incurred along the way. Contracts were more frequently negotiated, the studios competed for talent more furiously than ever, and Louis and Jack and Harry and Darryl began to lose more than a little of their power. But Hollywood never forgets and, according to David Niven in his autobiography, Olivia de Havilland's career suffered as a result.

The majors lost even more power when the Anti-trust Division of the US Department of Justice took their conspiracy case against the eight majors to the Supreme Court, which, in 1948, upheld a lower court decision that 'two price-fixing conspiracies existed – a horizontal one between all the defendants (and) a vertical one between each distributor-defendant and its licensees.' This decision was written by Associate Justice William O. Douglas in what became known as the Paramount consent decree case. The ruling was aimed directly at Paramount, but also, by implication, at the other majors. Production and distribution were from then on separated from theatre ownership, or exhibition. The majors could no longer count on automatic playdates for their pictures. Each one had to be sold on its box-office merits.

The combined impact of the de Havilland and Paramount decisions was to allow independent producers larger slices of the market and to increase their bargaining power, a situation exploited by attorneys Arthur Krim and Robert Benjamin, who assumed command of United Artists in 1951. 'More than anyone, Krim and Benjamin stimulated the quick rise

Profit and loss histories of the major studios *(above and following pages).*
The charts illustrate the histories of the major movie companies in terms of their corporate earnings and their hits and flops. Profits and hits appear above the line; losses and flops below the line. Every effort has been made to secure figures which reflect revenue from movie production and distribution rather than from other activities; consequently the operating income (i.e. pre-tax profit) from a conglomerate's movie division is sometimes used. Despite the majors' efforts to juggle figures in order to disguise years in which their product has performed badly, the balance sheets frequently echo the commercial strength of a year's output, and notorious flops will often visibly accompany a plunge into the red. It should, however, be remembered that a block-

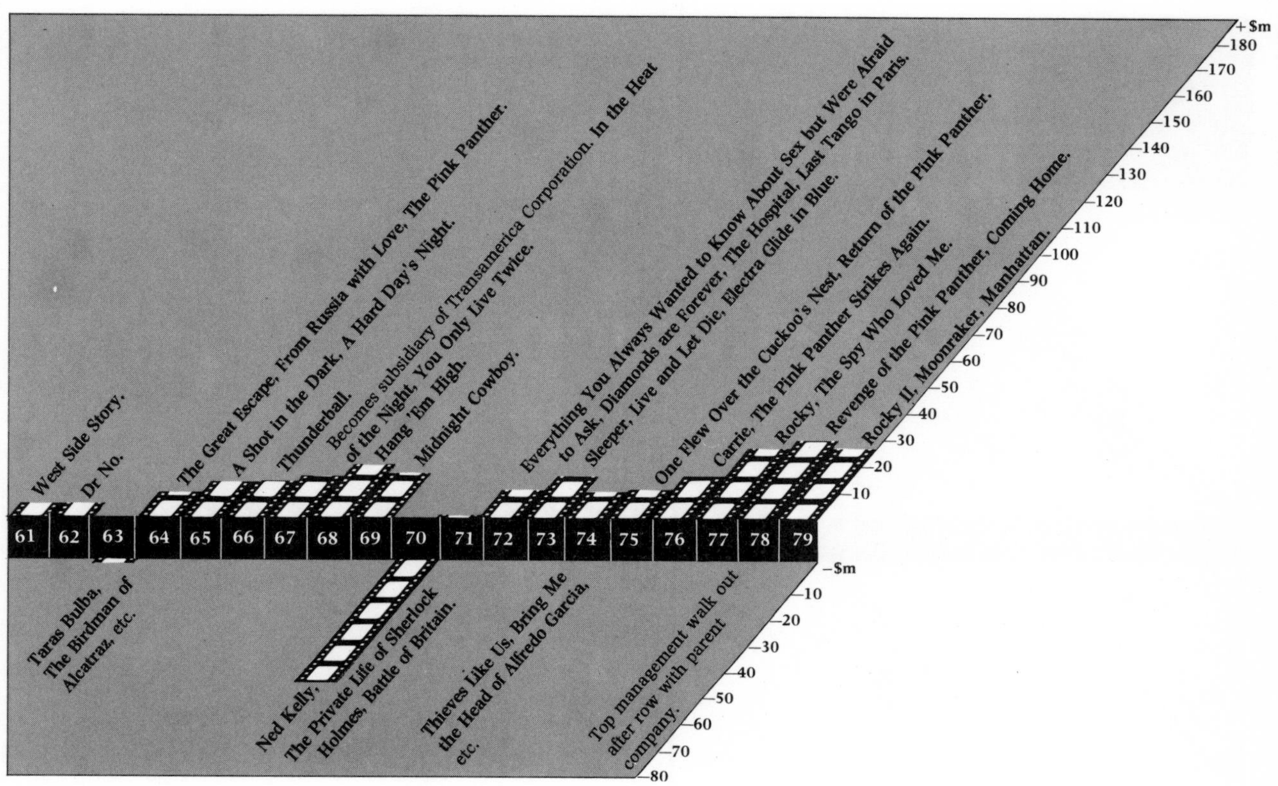

busting success can generate immense income for a studio for a period of months (and in some cases years), following its first US premier, as overseas and reissue rentals pour in.

of independent producers,' another veteran movie lawyer Leon Kaplan points out. It was Kaplan who drew up the contract transferring control of UA from Charles Chaplin and Mary Pickford. Kaplan's client, financier Walter E. Heller and Company, put up the initial $6m. to launch the Krim-Benjamin venture. The two new UA bosses worked out a simple principle for their operation: no studio plant, no overhead charges, no contract artists. The company would simply provide financing and distribution for independent producers.

A new era of deal-making followed. New kinds of contracts were devised for producers like Walter Mirisch, Stanley Kramer and the team of Harold Hecht, James Hill, and Burt Lancaster, who made single-picture or multiple-picture deals with United Artists. Profit definitions became even more important, and lawyers and agents and accountants worked overtime as never before. All of which drained power from the other studios, who failed to perceive the storm warnings and kept on going with more of the same old business.

1950–1970: decline of the majors

Simultaneously, television began siphoning audiences away, as did other forms of leisure activity like sport and crafts that began to tempt the prosperous new suburban class. Audience attendance plunged from 1946's peak of 4,060 m. to 1971's all-time low of 820 m. The majors slashed their payrolls and began selling some of their property: most of Fox's picturesque backlot of old movie sets and waterways was sold off to become the sterile Century City office complex. Between 1969 and 1972 virtually every major, including UA, bathed in red ink. Fox lost $36,800,000 in 1969, another $77,400,000 in 1970. The majors were being forced to shoulder massive long term bank debts at the very moment that production costs were starting to soar and advertising campaigns were demanding more and more expenditure. There was also some serious misinterpretation of public demand; by producing expensive but dull variations on the two big hits of the 1960s, *The Sound of Music* and *Easy Rider*, the majors effectively alienated their audiences. One major, MGM, stayed afloat throughout the 1970s only because of its profitable Grand Hotels in Las Vegas and Reno.

Gareth Wigan, formerly a production executive with Fox and now with the Ladd Company, was one of the executives who helped to reverse the process of decline, and he looks back on that time as a useful shake-up: 'The amateurism of the movie industry finally caught up with itself. Look at the history of movies. You see how it began with fur merchants and people

Continued on page 26

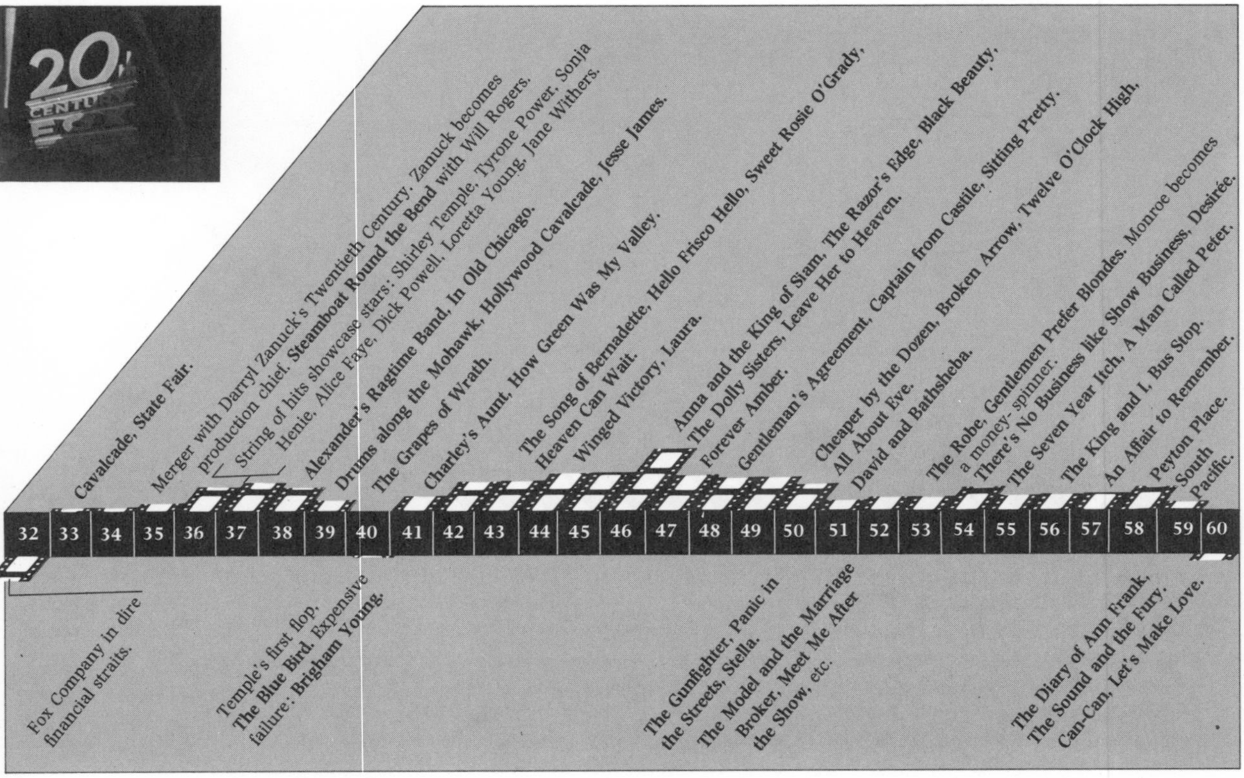

32	33	34	35	36	37	38	39	40	41	42	43	44	45	46	47	48	49	50	51	52	53	54	55	56	57	58	59	60

Fox Company in dire financial straits.

Cavalcade, State Fair.

Merger with Darryl Zanuck's Twentieth Century. Zanuck becomes production chief. **Steamboat Round the Bend** with Will Rogers.

String of hits showcase stars: Shirley Temple, Tyrone Power, Sonja Henie, Alice Faye, Dick Powell, Loretta Young, Jane Withers.

Alexander's Ragtime Band, In Old Chicago.

Drums along the Mohawk, Hollywood Cavalcade, Jesse James.

Temple's first flop, **The Blue Bird.** Expensive failure: **Brigham Young.**

The Grapes of Wrath.

Charley's Aunt, How Green Was My Valley.

The Song of Bernadette, Hello Frisco Hello, Sweet Rosie O'Grady, Heaven Can Wait.

Winged Victory, Laura.

Anna and the King of Siam, The Razor's Edge, Black Beauty, The Dolly Sisters, Leave Her to Heaven.

Forever Amber.

Gentleman's Agreement, Captain from Castile, Sitting Pretty.

Cheaper by the Dozen, Broken Arrow, Twelve O'Clock High, All About Eve.

David and Bathsheba.

The Gunfighter, Panic in the Streets, Stella. The Model and the Marriage Broker, Meet Me After the Show, etc.

The Robe, Gentlemen Prefer Blondes. Monroe becomes a money- spinner.

There's No Business like Show Business, Desirée.

The Seven Year Itch, A Man Called Peter.

The King and I, Bus Stop.

An Affair to Remember.

Peyton Place.

South Pacific.

The Diary of Ann Frank, The Sound and the Fury. Can-Can, Let's Make Love.

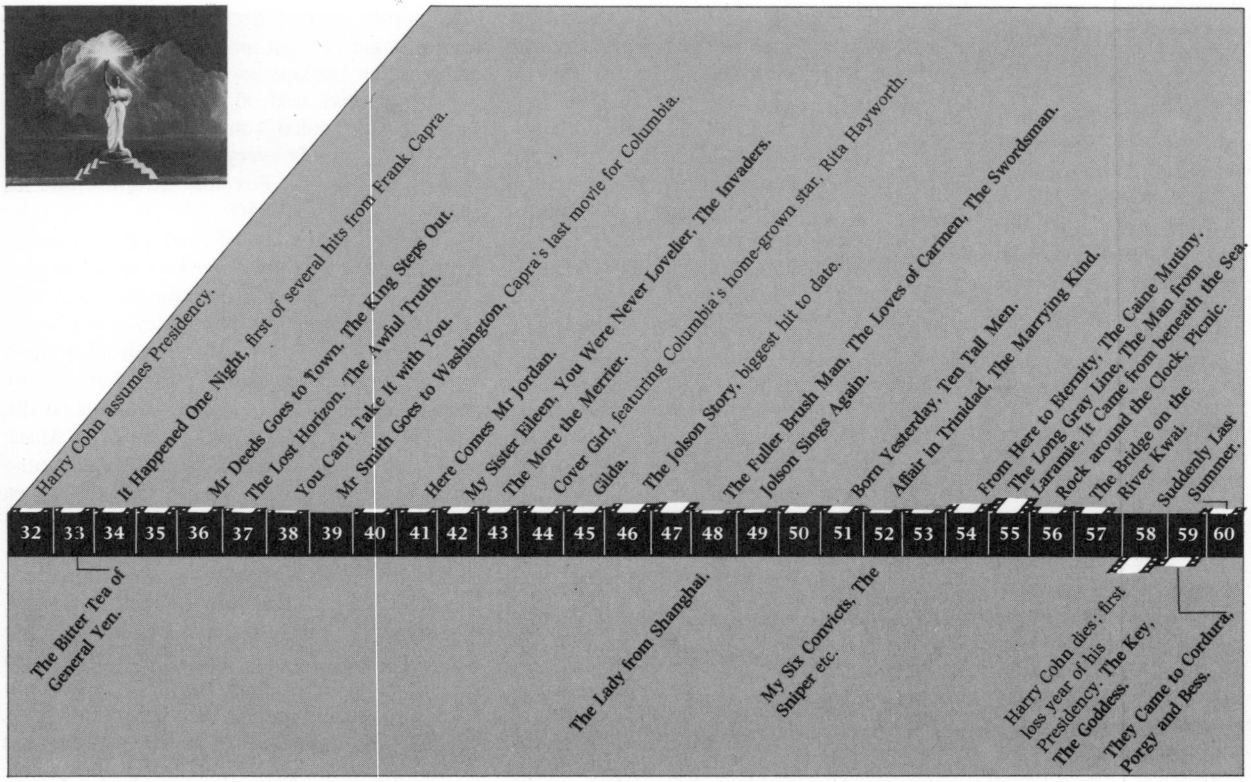

32	33	34	35	36	37	38	39	40	41	42	43	44	45	46	47	48	49	50	51	52	53	54	55	56	57	58	59	60

Harry Cohn assumes Presidency.

The Bitter Tea of General Yen.

It Happened One Night, first of several hits from Frank Capra.

Mr Deeds Goes to Town, The King Steps Out.

The Lost Horizon, The Awful Truth.

You Can't Take It with You.

Mr Smith Goes to Washington, Capra's last movie for Columbia.

Here Comes Mr Jordan.

My Sister Eileen, You Were Never Lovelier, The Invaders.

The More the Merrier.

Cover Girl, featuring Columbia's home-grown star, Rita Hayworth.

Gilda.

The Jolson Story, biggest hit to date.

The Lady from Shanghai.

The Fuller Brush Man, The Loves of Carmen, The Swordsman.

Jolson Sings Again.

My Six Convicts, The Sniper etc.

Born Yesterday, Ten Tall Men.

Affair in Trinidad, The Marrying Kind.

From Here to Eternity, The Caine Mutiny.

The Long Gray Line, The Man from Laramie, It Came from beneath the Sea.

Rock around the Clock, Picnic.

The Bridge on the River Kwai.

Harry Cohn dies: first loss year of his Presidency. **The Key, The Goddess.**

Suddenly Last Summer.

They Came to Cordura, Porgy and Bess.

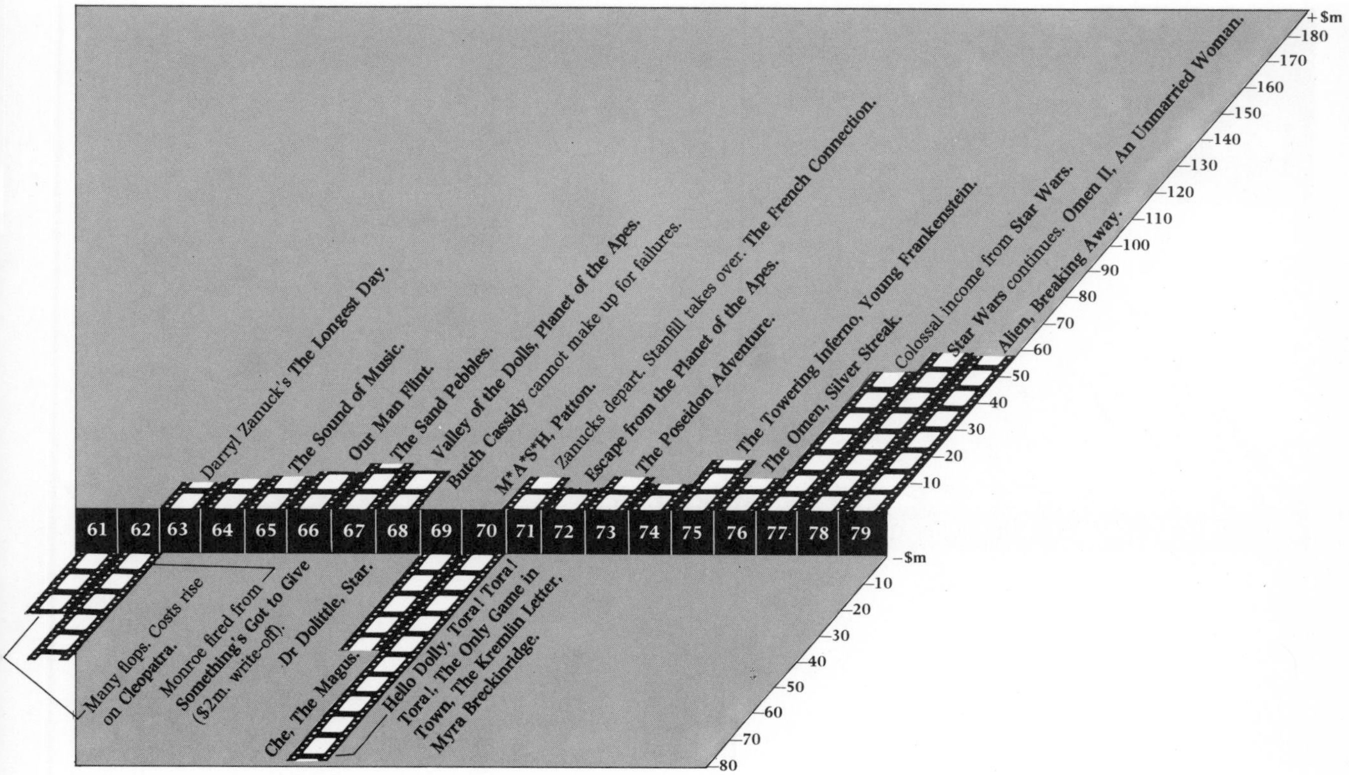

+ $m
180
170
160
150
140
130
120
110
100
90
80
70
60
50
40
30
20
10
Darryl Zanuck's The Longest Day.
The Sound of Music.
Our Man Flint.
The Sand Pebbles.
Valley of the Dolls, Planet of the Apes.
Butch Cassidy cannot make up for failures.
M*A*S*H, Patton.
Zanucks depart. Stanfill takes over. The French Connection.
Escape from the Planet of the Apes.
The Poseidon Adventure.
The Towering Inferno, Young Frankenstein.
The Omen, Silver Streak.
Colossal income from Star Wars.
Star Wars continues. Omen II, An Unmarried Woman.
Alien, Breaking Away.
61 62 63 64 65 66 67 68 69 70 71 72 73 74 75 76 77 78 79
– $m
10
20
30
40
50
60
70
80
Many flops. Costs rise on Cleopatra.
Monroe fired from Something's Got to Give ($2m. write-off).
Dr Dolittle, Star.
Che, The Magus.
Hello Dolly, Tora! Tora! Tora!, The Only Game in Town, The Kremlin Letter, Myra Breckinridge.

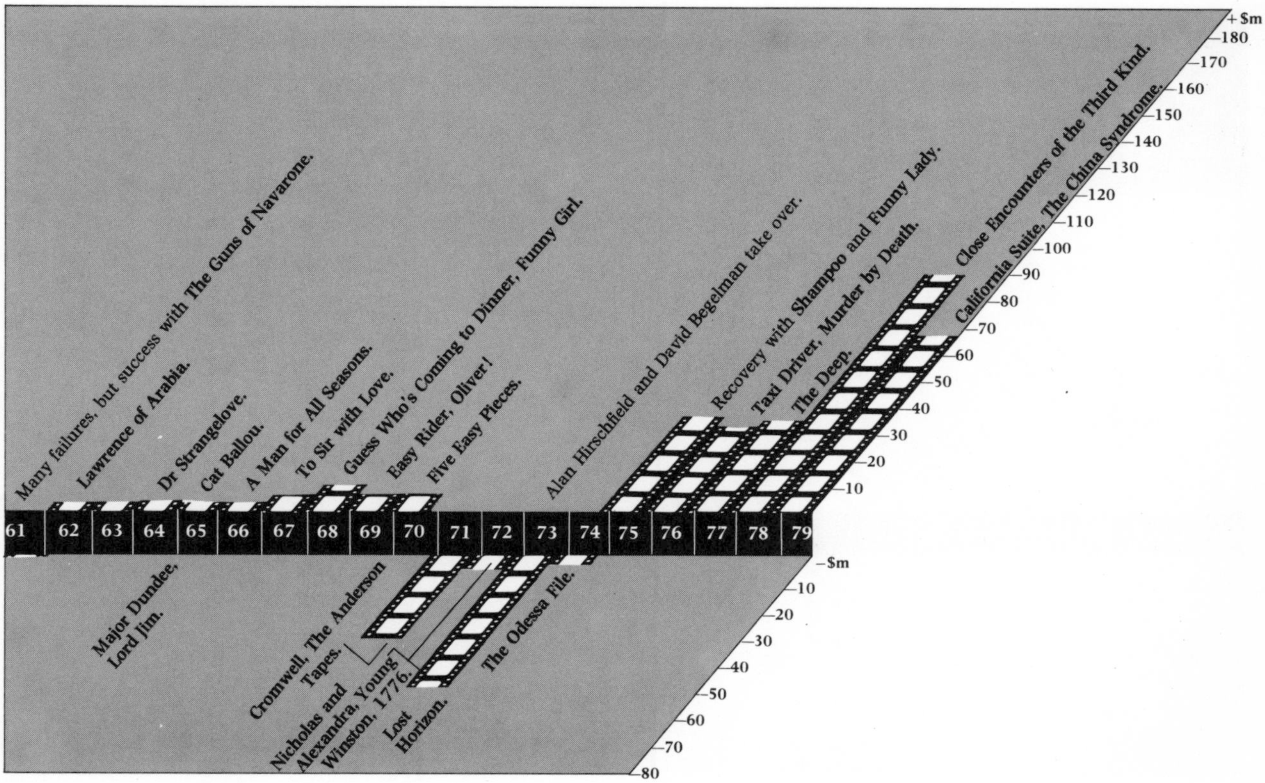

+ $m
180
170
160
150
140
130
120
110
100
90
80
70
60
50
40
30
20
10
Many failures, but success with The Guns of Navarone.
Lawrence of Arabia.
Dr Strangelove.
Cat Ballou.
A Man for All Seasons.
To Sir with Love.
Guess Who's Coming to Dinner, Funny Girl.
Easy Rider, Oliver!
Five Easy Pieces.
Alan Hirschfield and David Begelman take over.
Recovery with Shampoo and Funny Lady.
Taxi Driver, Murder by Death.
The Deep.
Close Encounters of the Third Kind.
California Suite, The China Syndrome.
61 62 63 64 65 66 67 68 69 70 71 72 73 74 75 76 77 78 79
– $m
10
20
30
40
50
60
70
80
Major Dundee, Lord Jim.
Cromwell, The Anderson Tapes.
Nicholas and Alexandra, Young Winston, 1776.
Lost Horizon.
The Odessa File.

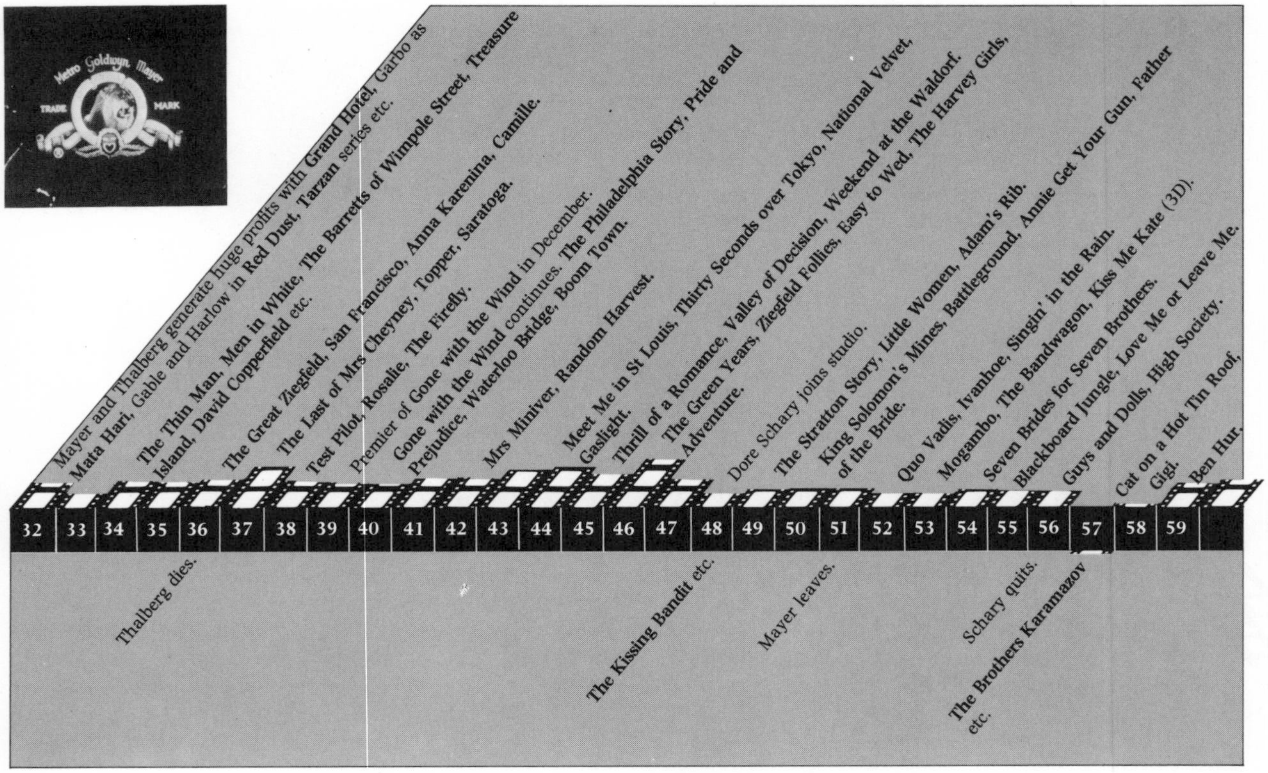

Mayer and Thalberg generate huge profits with **Grand Hotel**, Garbo as **Mata Hari**, Gable and Harlow in **Red Dust**, **Tarzan** series etc.

The Thin Man, Men in White, The Barretts of Wimpole Street, Treasure Island, David Copperfield etc.

The Great Ziegfeld, San Francisco, Anna Karenina, Camille.

The Last of Mrs Cheyney, Topper, Saratoga.

Test Pilot, Rosalie, The Firefly.

Premier of **Gone with the Wind** in December.

Gone with the Wind continues. **The Philadelphia Story, Pride and Prejudice, Waterloo Bridge, Boom Town.**

Mrs Miniver, Random Harvest.

Meet Me in St Louis, Thirty Seconds over Tokyo, National Velvet, Gaslight.

Thrill of a Romance, Valley of Decision, Weekend at the Waldorf.

The Green Years, Ziegfeld Follies, Easy to Wed, The Harvey Girls, Adventure.

Dore Schary joins studio.

The Stratton Story, Little Women, Adam's Rib.

King Solomon's Mines, Battleground, Annie Get Your Gun, Father of the Bride.

Quo Vadis, Ivanhoe, Singin' in the Rain.

Mogambo, The Bandwagon, Kiss Me Kate (3D).

Seven Brides for Seven Brothers.

Blackboard Jungle, Love Me or Leave Me.

Guys and Dolls, High Society.

Cat on a Hot Tin Roof, Gigi.

Ben Hur.

32 33 34 35 36 37 38 39 40 41 42 43 44 45 46 47 48 49 50 51 52 53 54 55 56 57 58 59

Thalberg dies.

The Kissing Bandit etc.

Mayer leaves.

Schary quits.

The Brothers Karamazov etc.

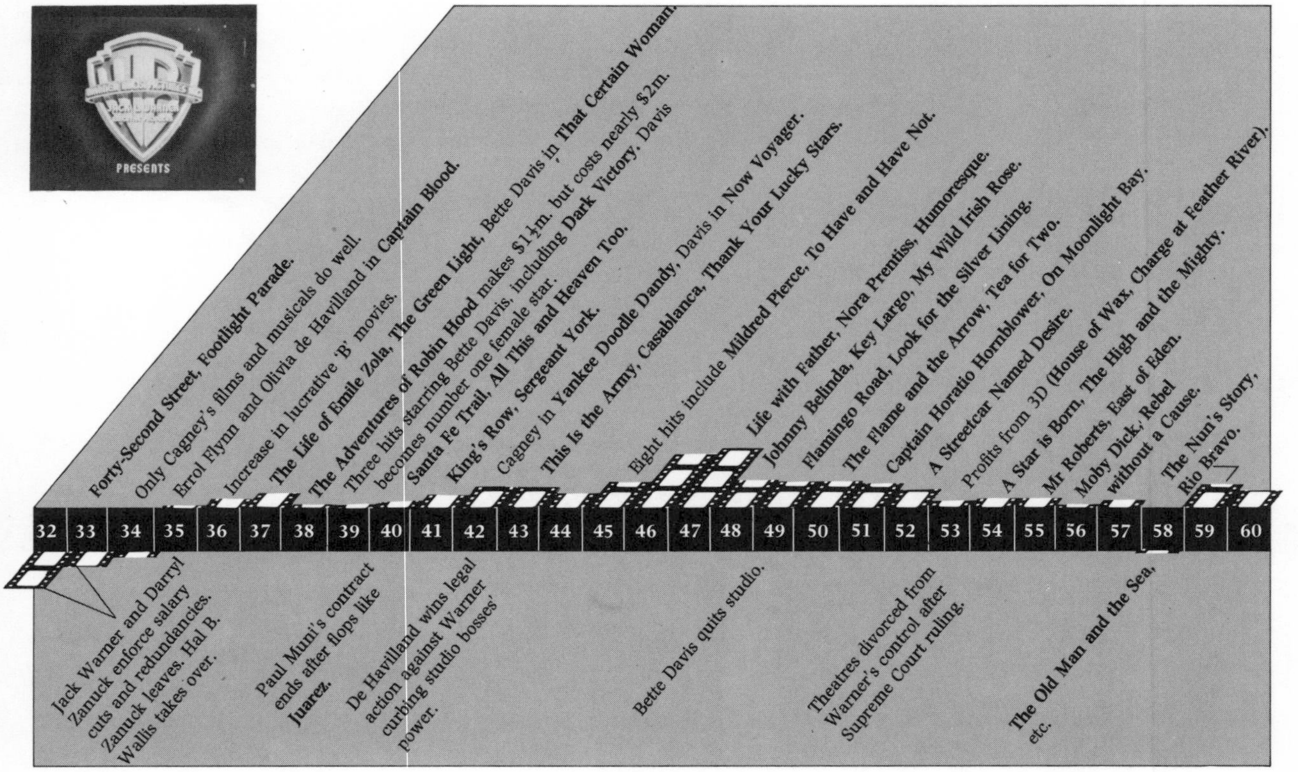

Forty-Second Street, Footlight Parade.

Only Cagney's films and musicals do well.

Errol Flynn and Olivia de Havilland in **Captain Blood.**

Increase in lucrative 'B' movies.

The Life of Emile Zola, The Green Light, Bette Davis in **That Certain Woman.**

The Adventures of Robin Hood makes $1½m. but costs nearly $2m.

Three hits starring Bette Davis, including **Dark Victory.** Davis becomes number one female star.

Santa Fe Trail, All This and Heaven Too.

King's Row, Sergeant York.

Cagney in **Yankee Doodle Dandy,** Davis in **Now Voyager.**

This Is the Army, Casablanca, Thank Your Lucky Stars.

Eight hits include **Mildred Pierce, To Have and Have Not.**

Life with Father, Nora Prentiss, Humoresque.

Johnny Belinda, Key Largo, My Wild Irish Rose.

Flamingo Road, Look for the Silver Lining.

The Flame and the Arrow, Tea for Two.

Captain Horatio Hornblower, On Moonlight Bay.

A Streetcar Named Desire.

Profits from 3D (**House of Wax, Charge at Feather River**).

A Star is Born, The High and the Mighty.

Mr Roberts, East of Eden.

Moby Dick, Rebel without a Cause.

The Nun's Story, Rio Bravo.

32 33 34 35 36 37 38 39 40 41 42 43 44 45 46 47 48 49 50 51 52 53 54 55 56 57 58 59 60

Jack Warner and Darryl Zanuck enforce salary cuts and redundancies. Zanuck leaves. Hal B. Wallis takes over.

Paul Muni's contract ends after flops like **Juarez.**

De Havilland wins legal action against Warner curbing studio bosses' power.

Bette Davis quits studio.

Theatres divorced from Warner's control after Supreme Court ruling.

The Old Man and the Sea, etc.

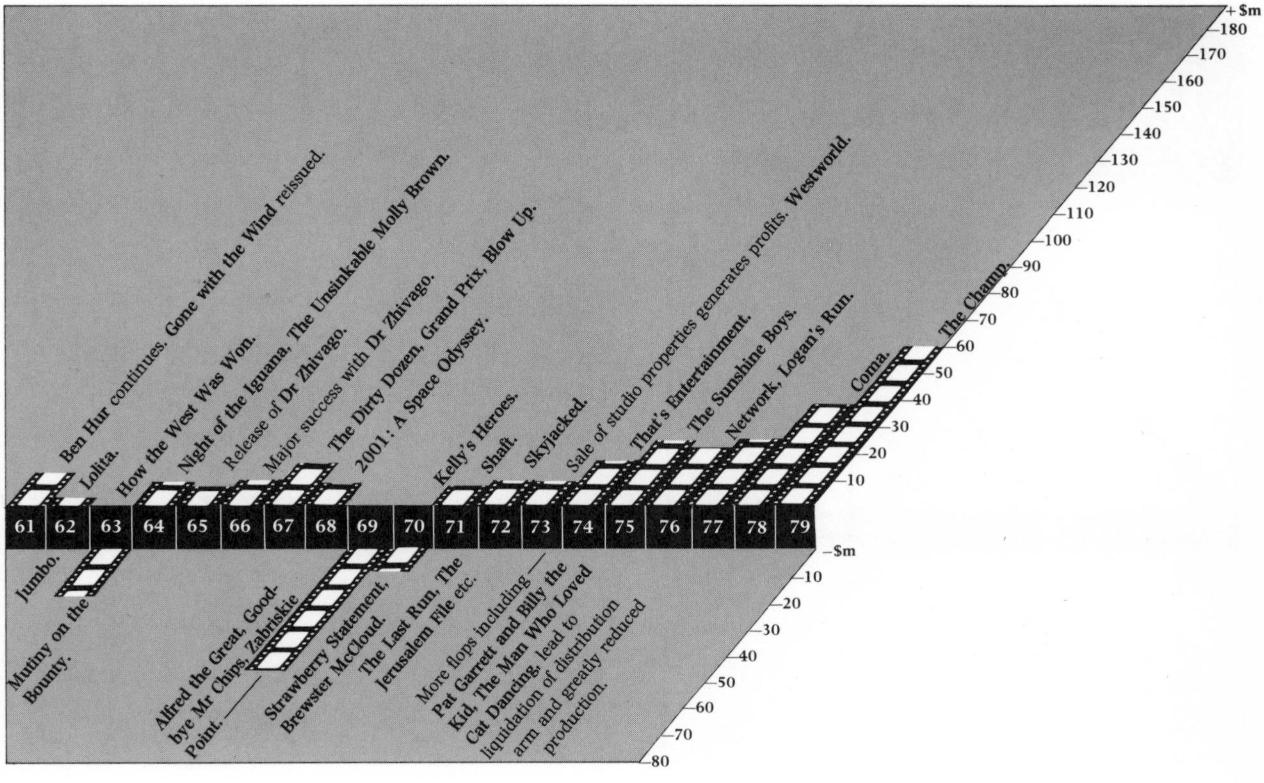

+$m 180 170 160 150 140 130 120 110 100 90 80 70 60 50 40 30 20 10 –$m 10 20 30 40 50 60 70 80

61 62 63 64 65 66 67 68 69 70 71 72 73 74 75 76 77 78 79

Ben Hur continues. Gone with the Wind reissued.
Lolita.
How the West Was Won.
Night of the Iguana, The Unsinkable Molly Brown.
Release of Dr Zhivago.
Major success with Dr Zhivago.
The Dirty Dozen, Grand Prix, Blow Up.
2001: A Space Odyssey.
Kelly's Heroes.
Shaft.
Skyjacked.
Sale of studio properties generates profits. Westworld.
That's Entertainment.
The Sunshine Boys.
Network, Logan's Run.
Coma.
The Champ.
Jumbo.
Mutiny on the Bounty.
Alfred the Great, Goodbye Mr Chips, Zabriskie Point.
Strawberry Statement, Brewster McCloud.
The Last Run, The Jerusalem File etc.
More flops including — Pat Garrett and Billy the Kid, The Man Who Loved Cat Dancing, lead to liquidation of distribution arm and greatly reduced production.

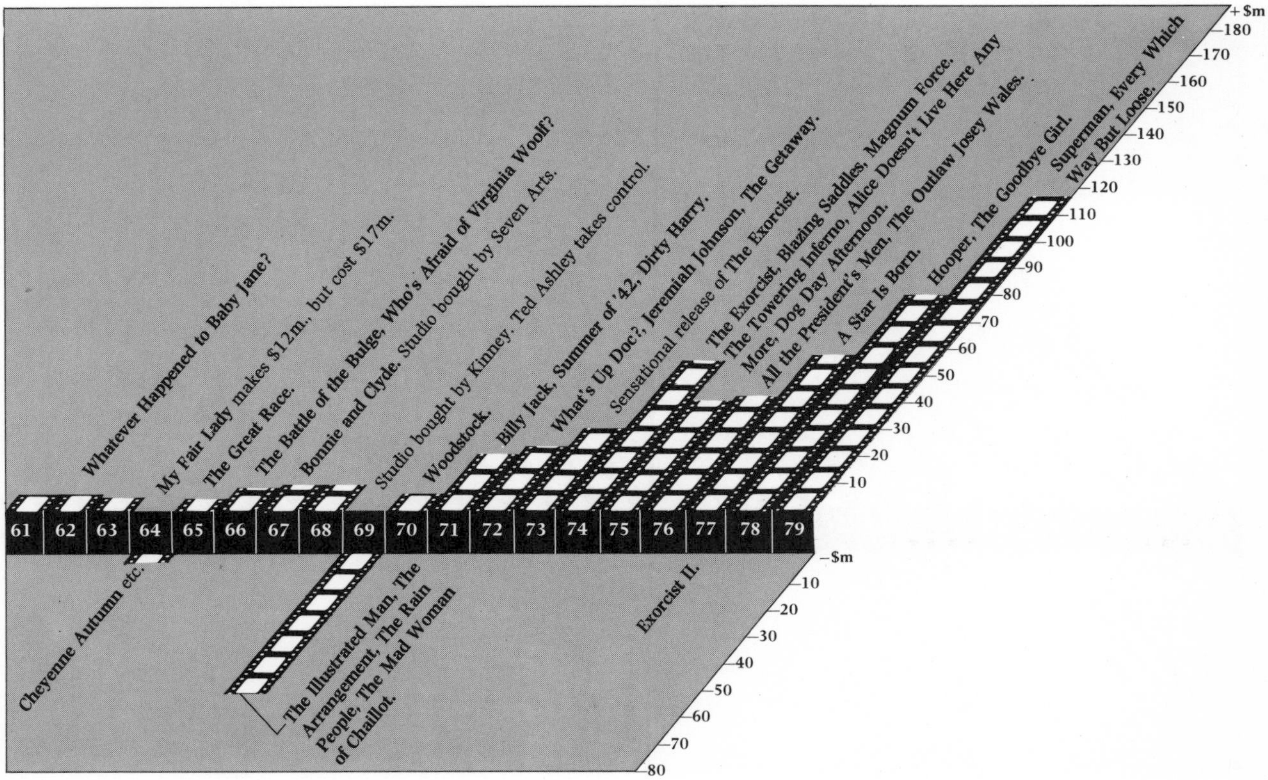

+$m 180 170 160 150 140 130 120 110 100 90 80 70 60 50 40 30 20 10 –$m 10 20 30 40 50 60 70 80

61 62 63 64 65 66 67 68 69 70 71 72 73 74 75 76 77 78 79

Whatever Happened to Baby Jane?
My Fair Lady makes $12m., but cost $17m.
The Great Race.
The Battle of the Bulge, Who's Afraid of Virginia Woolf?
Bonnie and Clyde. Studio bought by Seven Arts.
Studio bought by Kinney. Ted Ashley takes control.
Woodstock.
Billy Jack, Summer of '42, Dirty Harry.
What's Up Doc?, Jeremiah Johnson, The Getaway.
Sensational release of The Exorcist.
The Exorcist, Blazing Saddles, Magnum Force.
The Towering Inferno, Alice Doesn't Live Here Any More, Dog Day Afternoon.
All the President's Men, The Outlaw Josey Wales.
A Star Is Born.
Hooper, The Goodbye Girl.
Superman, Every Which Way But Loose.
Cheyenne Autumn etc.
The Illustrated Man, The Arrangement, The Rain People, The Mad Woman of Chaillot.
Exorcist II.

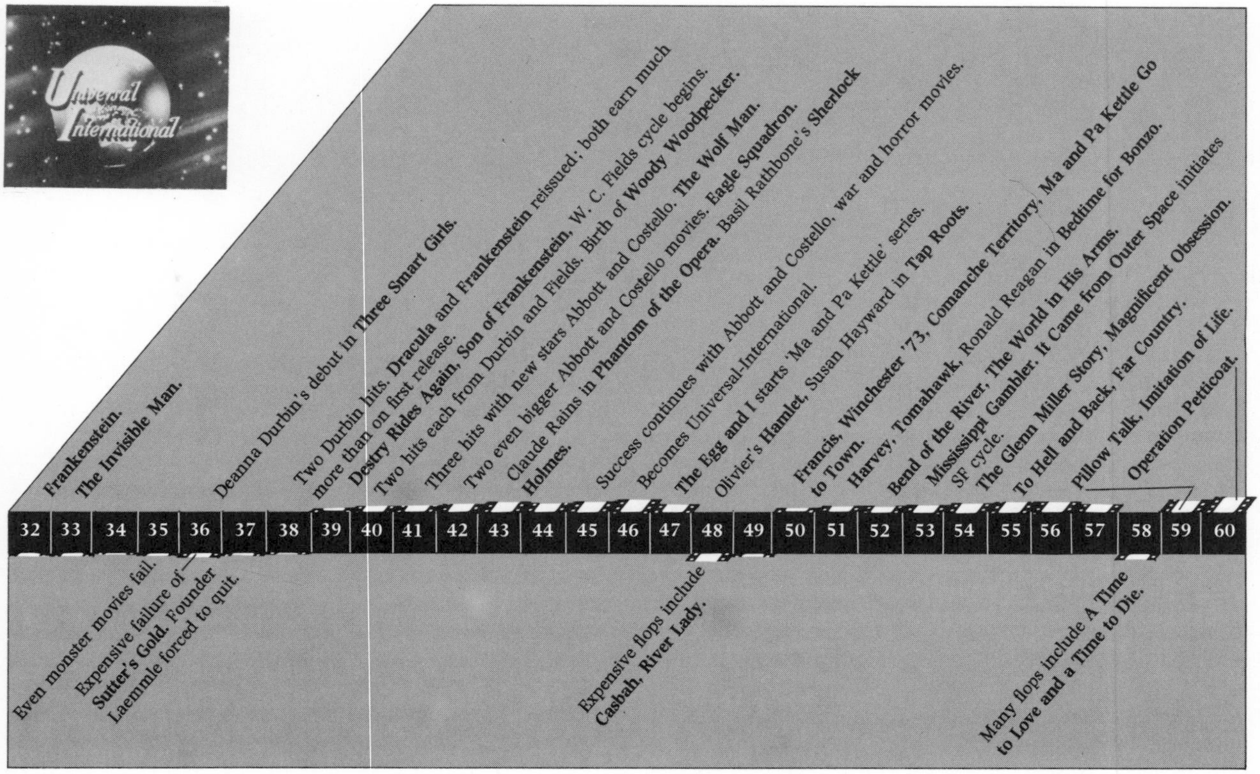

Universal International

32 **Frankenstein.**
33 **The Invisible Man.**
34 Even monster movies fail.
35 Expensive failure of **Sutter's Gold.** Founder Laemmle forced to quit.
36 Deanna Durbin's debut in **Three Smart Girls.**
37 Two Durbin hits. **Dracula** and **Frankenstein** reissued; both earn much more than on first release.
38 **Destry Rides Again, Son of Frankenstein,** W. C. Fields cycle begins.
39 Two hits each from Durbin and Fields. Birth of **Woody Woodpecker.**
40 Three hits with new stars Abbott and Costello. **The Wolf Man.**
41 Two even bigger Abbott and Costello movies. **Eagle Squadron.**
42 Claude Rains in **Phantom of the Opera.** Basil Rathbone's **Sherlock Holmes.**
43 Success continues with Abbott and Costello, war and horror movies.
44 Becomes Universal-International.
45 **The Egg and I** starts 'Ma and Pa Kettle' series.
46 Olivier's **Hamlet,** Susan Hayward in **Tap Roots.**
47 Expensive flops include **Casbah, River Lady.**
48 **Francis, Winchester '73, Comanche Territory, Ma and Pa Kettle Go to Town.**
49 **Harvey, Tomahawk,** Ronald Reagan in **Bedtime for Bonzo.**
50 **Bend of the River, The World in His Arms.**
51 **Mississippi Gambler. It Came from Outer Space** initiates SF cycle.
52 **The Glenn Miller Story, Magnificent Obsession.**
53 **To Hell and Back, Far Country.**
54 **Pillow Talk, Imitation of Life.**
55 Many flops include **A Time to Love and a Time to Die.**
56 **Operation Petticoat.**

32	33	34	35	36	37	38	39	40	41	42	43	44	45	46	47	48	49	50	51	52	53	54	55	56	57	58	59	60

Paramount (A Gulf+Western Company)

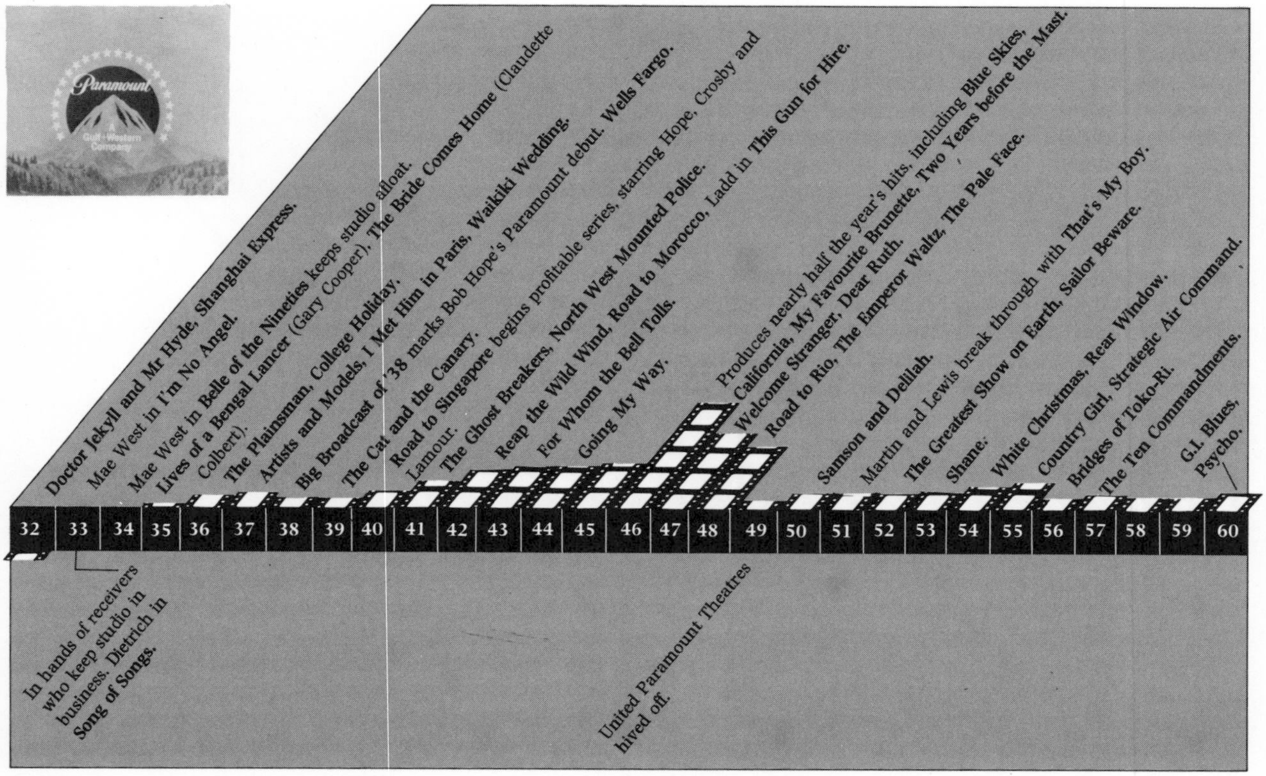

Doctor Jekyll and Mr Hyde, Shanghai Express.
In hands of receivers who keep studio in business. Dietrich in **Song of Songs.**
Mae West in **I'm No Angel.**
Mae West in **Belle of the Nineties** keeps studio afloat.
Lives of a Bengal Lancer (Gary Cooper), **The Bride Comes Home** (Claudette Colbert).
The Plainsman, College Holiday.
Artists and Models, I Met Him in Paris, Waikiki Wedding.
Big Broadcast of '38 marks Bob Hope's Paramount debut. **Wells Fargo.**
The Cat and the Canary.
Road to Singapore begins profitable series, starring Hope, Crosby and Lamour.
The Ghost Breakers, North West Mounted Police.
Reap the Wild Wind, Road to Morocco, Ladd in **This Gun for Hire.**
For Whom the Bell Tolls.
Going My Way.
Produces nearly half the year's hits, including **Blue Skies, California, My Favourite Brunette, Two Years before the Mast, Welcome Stranger, Dear Ruth.**
Road to Rio, The Emperor Waltz, The Pale Face.
United Paramount Theatres hived off.
Samson and Delilah.
Martin and Lewis break through with **That's My Boy.**
The Greatest Show on Earth, Sailor Beware.
Shane.
White Christmas, Rear Window.
Country Girl, Strategic Air Command.
Bridges of Toko-Ri.
The Ten Commandments.
G.I. Blues, Psycho.

32	33	34	35	36	37	38	39	40	41	42	43	44	45	46	47	48	49	50	51	52	53	54	55	56	57	58	59	60

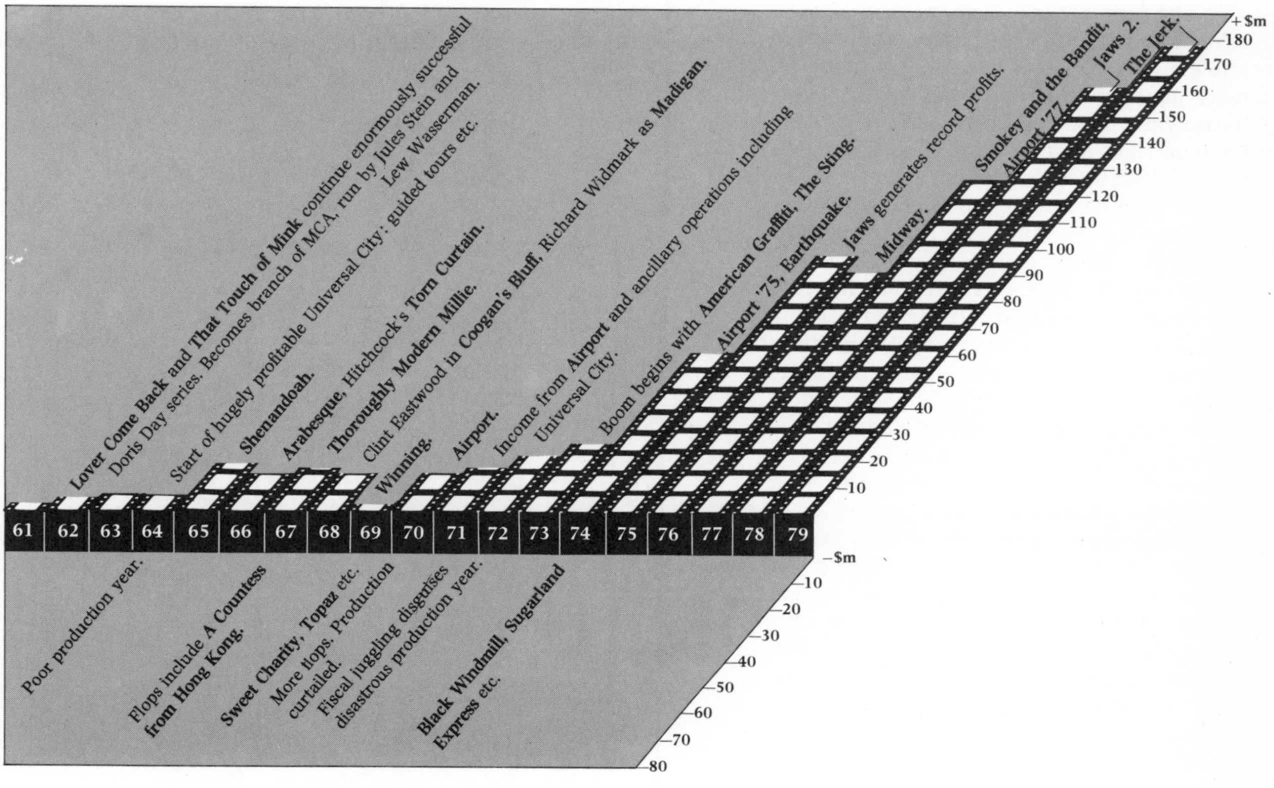

Lover Come Back and That Touch of Mink continue enormously successful Doris Day series. Becomes branch of MCA, run by Jules Stein and Lew Wasserman.
Start of hugely profitable Universal City: guided tours etc.
Shenandoah.
Arabesque, Hitchcock's Torn Curtain.
Thoroughly Modern Millie.
Clint Eastwood in Coogan's Bluff, Richard Widmark as Madigan.
Winning.
Airport.
Income from Airport and ancillary operations including Universal City.
Boom begins with American Graffiti, The Sting.
Airport '75, Earthquake.
Jaws generates record profits.
Midway.
Smokey and the Bandit, Airport '77.
Jaws 2.
The Jerk.
+$m
180
170
160
150
140
130
120
110
100
90
80
70
60
50
40
30
20
10
61
62
63
64
65
66
67
68
69
70
71
72
73
74
75
76
77
78
79
–$m
10
20
30
40
50
60
70
80
Poor production year.
Flops include A Countess from Hong Kong.
Sweet Charity, Topaz etc. More flops. Production curtailed.
Fiscal juggling disguises disastrous production year.
Black Windmill, Sugarland Express etc.

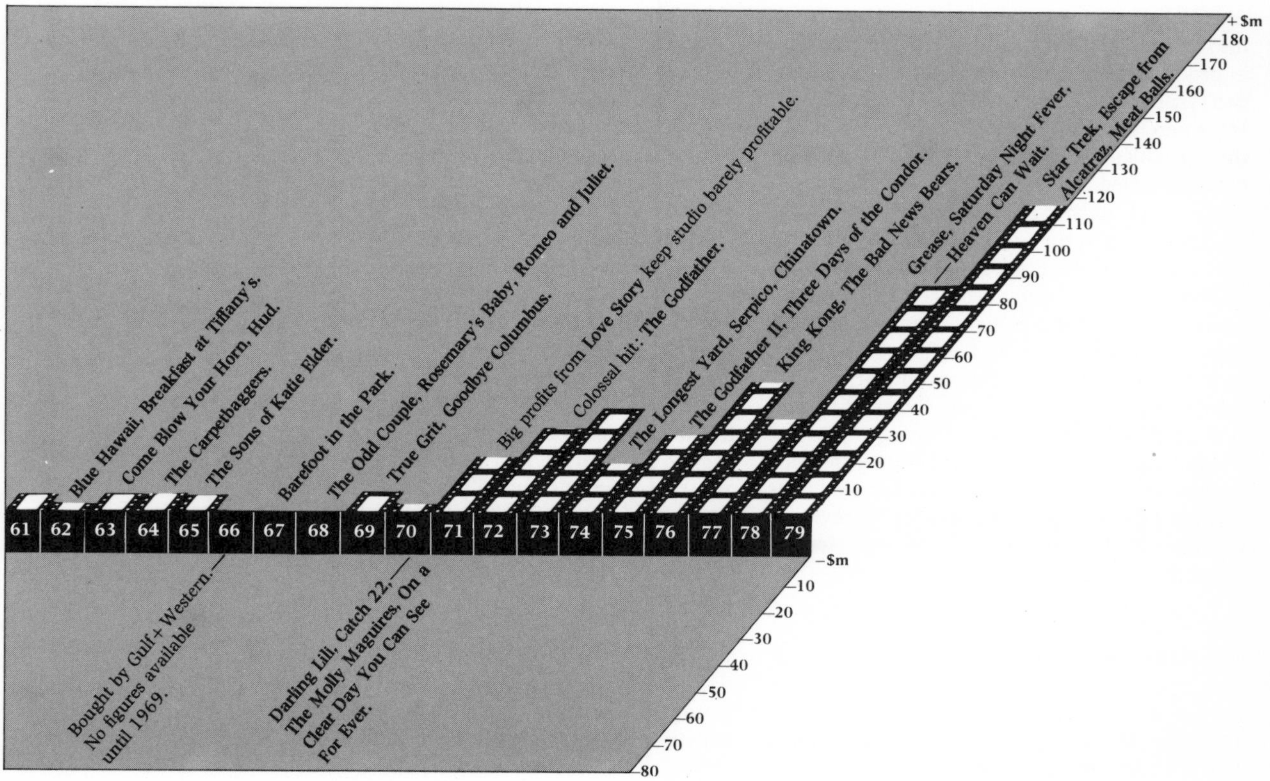

Blue Hawaii, Breakfast at Tiffany's.
Come Blow Your Horn, Hud.
The Carpetbaggers.
The Sons of Katie Elder.
Barefoot in the Park.
The Odd Couple, Rosemary's Baby, Romeo and Juliet.
True Grit, Goodbye Columbus.
Big profits from Love Story keep studio barely profitable.
Colossal hit: The Godfather.
The Longest Yard, Serpico, Chinatown.
The Godfather II, Three Days of the Condor.
King Kong, The Bad News Bears.
Grease, Saturday Night Fever.
Heaven Can Wait.
Star Trek, Escape from Alcatraz, Meat Balls.
+$m
180
170
160
150
140
130
120
110
100
90
80
70
60
50
40
30
20
10
61
62
63
64
65
66
67
68
69
70
71
72
73
74
75
76
77
78
79
–$m
10
20
30
40
50
60
70
80
Bought by Gulf+Western. No figures available until 1969.
Darling Lili, Catch 22, The Molly Maguires, On a Clear Day You Can See For Ever.

who had little patience with rigorous notions of management. The old guard, which lasted into the 1960s, took the attitude, "Nobody can tell us how to do business!" One year, they may have gone broke, but the next year they bounced right back. Somehow, their instincts were brilliant enough. And the audiences were always there, demanding a flow of new pictures every week. So when the warning bells sounded – "Television will cut your audiences! People will enjoy their cars and skiing holidays and football games and records and dancing instead of movies!" – the moguls and their immediate successors just said, "Bullshit!" That was their undoing.'

For a long time, the majors thought they could buy their way out of trouble, spending more on big budget pictures. The problem with that kind of thinking was pinpointed by A. H. Howe, the leading film investment banker at the Bank of America. In 1971, he wrote in the *Journal* of the Producers Guild of America that the world box-office gross could yield only about $2,000m. of which about $600m. (roughly 30 per cent) came back to US distributors as rentals. Of those rentals, only about $240m. was left after expenses, to cover the production costs of making more movies in the following year.

But, complained Howe, during the 1960s each of the big seven majors (RKO, the eighth, was sold by Howard Hughes to the General Tire & Rubber Company in 1955; a year later, it had ceased to exist as a producer-distributor) fell into the habit of investing over $50m. annually in production: a total of $350m. Other American companies, including Disney and American International, usually risked another $50m. on their productions. That meant total production costs exceeded $400m. a year. But the market could yield only $240m. Who could make profits from a return-on-investment ratio like that? Budgets were way too high, financial controls slight. Equally troublesome was the prime lending rate, which began its deadly climb from 6 per cent in 1969 to 12 per cent in 1974 to a high of 20 per cent in early 1980. By the late 1960s, the movie industry was in real trouble. But there was help waiting in the wings. Like politics, movies have glamour appeal, and outside money was waiting for its chance to take over. The majors were weak enough to fall victim, one by one, to a series of conglomerate take-overs.

The conglomerates move in

Universal was acquired by Decca Records in 1951; in 1962 the giant entertainment empire, Music Corporation of America (see page 42), bought Decca and, with it, Universal. Eliot Hyman's Seven Arts (a middle man buyer of old movies) bought Warner Brothers in 1967, merging two years later with Kinney National Services to become Warner Communications, Inc., with its parking lots and funeral parlours, cable TV, *Mad* magazine, Coca Cola franchise, electronic toys and games, Elektra, Atlantic and Asylum Records, Cosmos football team, Bausch & Lomb, and Panavision equipment. That same year, Transamerica Corporation (car rentals, computer services, finance loans, life insurance, moving and storage, Trans-International Airlines) took over United Artists, while Paramount went to Gulf and Western Industries (publishing, Madison Square Garden, manufacturing companies, paper and building products, auto replacement parts, financial services). It's not easy to find Paramount in Gulf and Western's annual report. It's buried in the 'Leisure Time' group which constitutes a mere 14 per cent of the company's assets. In 1968 Las Vegas financier Kirk Kerkorian purchased control of MGM for $80m., then sold off $60m. worth of studio assets, including most of the famous costume department, to help finance his new $110m. MGM Grand Hotel in Las Vegas, relegating movie-making to such a secondary activity that MGM closed down its distribution network.

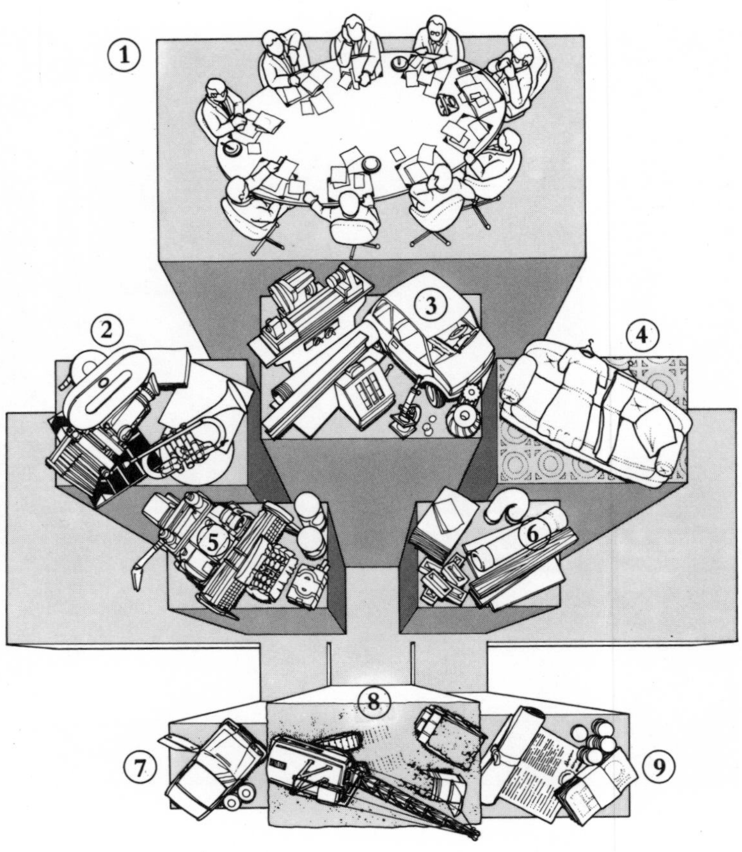

1 *Gulf + Western Industries, Inc., the parent company.*

2 *Leisure Time, 14 per cent of total assets, including Paramount, Madison Square Garden Corporation, Famous Players and Simon and Schuster.*

3 *Manufacturing, 14 per cent, including automotive, capital goods, energy products, metals, engineering, coin-operated amusement games.*

4 *Apparel and Home Furnishings, 14 per cent, including Kayser-Roth and Simmons.*

5 *Consumer and Agricultural Products, 11 per cent, including G + W Americas, G + W Food Products, Consolidated Cigar, and Schrafft Candy.*

Hal Ashby *(right) addresses his naval cast in* The Last Detail. *The film was only a modest box-office performer.*

Annie Hall *(far right), with Woody Allen starring and directing, earned $20m., but some complained it was the lowest grossing film to win the Academy's Best Picture Award.*

Gulf+Western *(left), the group structure of the conglomerate which owns the Paramount Picture Corporation. Paramount is just a part of the Leisure Time group, which in its entirety constitutes only 14 per cent of Gulf +Westerns assets. Figures are derived from* 1979 Fact Book, Gulf+ Western Industries, Inc.

6 *Paper and Building Products, 8 per cent, Brown Company.*

7 *Automotive Replacement Parts, 4 per cent, A.P.S., Inc.*

8 *Natural Resources, 14 per cent, including Marquette, New Jersey Zinc, Jersey Miniere Zinc.*

9 *Financial Services, 11 per cent, including Associates First Capital, Providence Capitol International Insurance.*

Fox and Columbia? They weren't actually absorbed by conglomerates, but rather became diversified corporate giants themselves, no longer dependent solely upon movies for their profits. In 1979, the percentages of earnings from film activities by Columbia, MCA (Universal), MGM, Fox and Warners were 75, 77, 44, 59 and 50 per cent respectively.

The majors are now controlled by a new generation of professional managers who could as well run a shoe company as a movie studio. Of Fox's 14,000 stockholders, one, Cede & Co, a grouping of bankers and stockbrokers, controls over 51 per cent of voting stock. Perhaps only Universal, part of the giant MCA entertainment group, could be said to remain under the leadership of an elder statesman, in the person of Lew Wasserman, its long-serving chairman of the board and chief executive officer.

Conflict: businessmen vs. film-makers

The arrival of the businessmen means that virtually every film is aimed at what Steven Bach called 'the Holy Grail' of stratospheric box-office returns. 'The businessmen in this town really don't like film-makers like Woody Allen or Hal Ashby,' screenwriter/producer Gerald Ayres mourns. 'They make infinitely interesting movies that stretch the syntax of film and make modest profits. But that's not enough! I heard one executive complain that *Annie Hall* was the lowest grossing picture ever to win the Academy Award for Best Picture. But it made nearly $20m. in rentals! Most of the people at the studios, especially the marketing departments, would rather not bother with pictures like *Annie Hall.*' However, some smaller, yeastier pictures are getting through, and they are successful. Lorimar's David Picker claims: 'Films are just more interesting now. Any year that offers *Being There, Kramer vs. Kramer, All That Jazz, Breaking Away, Manhattan, Norma Rae,* plus half a dozen others, is a vintage year. And most of the recent years have been vintage ones.'

As the money men moved into areas traditionally ruled by more movie-oriented executives, blood began to flow. 'Suddenly, you had to adjust your policies to accommodate companies and financial managers whose backgrounds were in other businesses,' says David Picker. As president of United Artists (1969–73) and Paramount (1975–77), Picker had to deal with the conglomerates Transamerica, and Gulf and Western, respectively. 'They wanted instant success. They felt that manpower could be replaced by manpower, that no executive was a unique asset. And if their other divisions were performing poorly, they tried to force the movie company to generate profits to compensate, distorting the whole way of doing business.' But the more violent conflicts between the movie people and their conglomerate parents seem to have been over incentive schemes and bonuses, rather than over what films to make and how to make them. The conglomerates dislike the movie industry's traditionally generous treatment of successful executives.

Mass resignations at UA and Fox

In January 1978, differences between the United Artists team and parent Transamerica led to an unprecedented series of resignations from the movie company: chairman, Arthur Krim; finance committee chairman, the late Robert S. Benjamin; president, Eric Pleskow; west coast production chief, Mike Medavoy; senior vice-president for business affairs, William Bernstein; and many others. Krim, Benjamin, Pleskow, Medavoy and Bernstein hardly paused to take a breath before resurfacing as an instant new mini-major, Orion Pictures, with a $150m. line of credit from ten banks, plus Warner Communications, in for a third. The Orion executives are careful to point out that their deal is with the Warner conglomerate parent, not Warner Brothers itself. 'We are masters of our own fate,' says Mike Medavoy. 'We finance and make our own

The studio bosses

Job titles in Hollywood were, and are, notoriously misleading: sometimes the owner of a studio was actively involved in production decisions; sometimes the important decisions were taken by the President or the production head and sometimes by two or three people together. The lists which follow name one or more (though not necessarily all) of those who supervised their studio's output of movies during the period stated. Where two or more names occur, they are in order of rank but not necessarily of creative importance. It is important to bear in mind that promotion frequently deprived studio executives of creative control as effectively as dismissal, while on the other hand studio owners sometimes moved in and out of production according to whim or to their confidence in the individual or team below them.

United Artists

1924–35	Joseph Schenck
1935–36	Mary Pickford
1936–38	Samuel Goldwyn/A. H. Giannini
1938–41	Samuel Goldwyn/Murray Silverstone
1941–47	Edward C. Raftery
1947–50	Gradwell Sears
1950–51	Frank L. McNamee
1951–69	Arthur B. Krim/Robert S. Benjamin
1969–73	David Picker
1973–78	Eric Pleskow
1978–81	Andy Albeck
1981–	Norbert Auerbach

Note: Because it was created as a producer/star co-operative, United Artists had no production bosses in any real sense until the 1950s. With the exception of Joseph Schenck in the early days, Samuel Goldwyn (who tried to wrest control of the company in the 1930s) and Mary Pickford, those named prior to 1951 were principally concerned with financial administration.

movies, then we tell the Warners marketing organization how to distribute them.' (The term mini-major usually describes those organizations which have sufficient finance to produce several pictures each year, but have no distribution arm.)

Money was the primary reason for the UA-Transamerica break. 'James Harvey, Transamerica's chief operating officer, just couldn't decide how each of us should be compensated,' recalls Medavoy. 'He felt, as most conglomerate executives do, that anybody can do the job I do, that Bill Bernstein does, that Eric Pleskow does.' Did Harvey actually say that to Medavoy? 'No, not to me directly,' says Medavoy, 'but Transamerica made its feelings known. To them, we weren't indispensable, even though we had an outstanding record – perhaps the best in the business.' Medavoy argues that conglomerates fail to understand that the movie industry always shifts in terms of profit and loss each year, that no major can predict, say, a 15 per cent profit margin for the coming twelve months, as an auto manufacturer might. 'The essence of this business is people,' maintains Medavoy. 'Relationships. We are unique because we have the best relationships with the best film-makers; that's what we should have been compensated for; that's why we were assets. Transamerica just didn't agree.'

The UA exodus was curious because a pre-eminently successful group quit, a stark contrast to the usual pattern of resignations in the movie industry. But a similar incident occurred in June 1979, when the three top production executives left Fox: the extremely successful and much respected team comprising: President, Alan Ladd, Jr.; and vice-presidents, Gareth Wigan and Jay Kanter. Twentieth Century-Fox is not a conglomerate, but an independent major studio. What caused Ladd, Wigan and Kanter to exit? Again it came down to money: Dennis Stanfill, Fox's board chairman, one of the new breed of corporate finance specialists and a former investment banker for Lehman Brothers, became impatient with the freewheeling ways of the film business. Much to the irritation of the Ladd team, Stanfill had a habit of circulating forms requesting their 'management objectives'.

The confrontation between the systems-oriented Stanfill and the more informal Ladd centred around two financial points: Ladd's insistence on additional compensation for himself, Kanter and Wigan, commensurate with the success of their pictures (*Star Wars*, *The Turning Point*, *An Unmarried Woman*, *Silent Movie*, *Norma Rae*, *Julia*, and, of course, *The Empire Strikes Back*, 1980's Fox bonanza); and Ladd's desire to initiate a bonus scheme covering middle-management executives. In neither case could agreement be reached with Stanfill. 'I got very passionate with management,' remembers Gareth Wigan. 'In the year 1977–78, every executive in the film division could have gone home during September, October, November and December, and done not a scrap of work, yet we would have been entitled by contract to receive maximum bonus. But what about the lower level people? They didn't have any such bonus system. Yet, you could have gone to Fox every night and seen them working late at night. They worked like that because they believed in, and enjoyed, their work. Those people *deserved* to be rewarded with a bonus.

'Yet what did management say? They complained that our lower level people never did much of anything *unless* they were paid bonuses! I was furious. I told them, "You don't understand what motivates creative people in this business. You never will." I believe it's close to the kind of feeling that drives people to write books and direct movies. We are not artists, but we are cousins to artists. The

Eric Pleskow *(above), top production brain at United Artists in the 1960s and 70s who took his team to found Orion in 1978. UA has not prospered since.*

Frank Price *(above), Columbia boss, managed to keep the hits coming despite many resignations. 1980 alone saw* Kramer vs. Kramer, Blue Lagoon, The Electric Horseman *and* Stir Crazy.

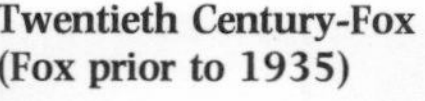

Twentieth Century-Fox (Fox prior to 1935)

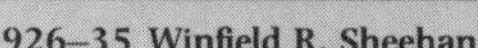

1926–35	Winfield R. Sheehan
1935–42	Darryl F. Zanuck
1942–43	William Goetz (Zanuck on military assignment)
1943–56	Darryl F. Zanuck
1956–60	Spyros Skouras/Buddy Adler
1961–62	Spyros Skouras/Peter G. Levathes
1962–71	Darryl F. Zanuck/Richard Zanuck
1971–74	Dennis C. Stanfill/Gordon Stulberg
1974–76	Dennis C. Stanfill/Alan Ladd Jr.
1976–79	Alan Ladd Jr.
1979–80	Dennis C. Stanfill/Sandy Lieberson
1980–	Alan Hirschfield/Sherry Lansing

Columbia

1924–58	Harry Cohn
1958–63	Abe Schneider
1963–67	Leo Jaffe/Mike Frankovich
1967–73	Leo Jaffe/Stanley Schneider
1973–78	Alan Hirschfield/David Begelman
1978–	Frank Price

Alan Ladd Jr. *(above), wonderboy of Fox in the 1970s, who steered the company to the triumph of 1977 and* Star Wars*, then left to found The Ladd Company.*

Sherry Lansing *(above), a former actress, became the first woman head of production in Hollywood history in 1980. But she must report to Alan Hirschfield and ultimately to Fox chairman Dennis Stanfill.*

greatest thrill for all of us is to be involved with the making of a film and to see that film be successful and popular. The accountants never understood what I was trying to say.'

The new executives

A more pliable group of executives replaced the Ladd team at Fox. 'I had dinner the other night with Sherry Lansing, David Field and Claire Townsend,' recalls screenwriter-producer Gerald Ayres, referring to the top ranking production team installed at Fox in early 1980. 'They are all charming, gracious, mild-mannered people who attend Sunday brunches in each other's homes. But I had to pinch myself to remember which studio they worked for because I had had dinner with them all only months earlier, when they had all been at different studios. This is the new generation of production executives – in their late twenties to mid thirties, moving from studio to studio, never lingering long enough to stamp their personalities on their movies, hugging each other, working and living and soaking in hot tubs together like family.

'Not one of them would chop up mother. They'd do something much more lethal – complain about her to their therapist.'

Despite the mild manners of the new executives, animosities still thrive. Bad blood exists between the Ladd team and Dennis Stanfill, and between Orion and United Artists. But these are hardly bitter, long-term vendettas, and will probably smooth out over the years. A more difficult situation exists in the wake of the so-called 'Begelman affair' of 1977 in which Columbia's successful and respected production chief, David Begelman, pleaded *nolo contendere* (i.e. that he would not contest the charge) to grand theft of $40,000 in studio funds, having forged checks to actor Cliff Robertson, director Martin Ritt, and Los Angeles restaurateur Pierre Groleau, and then cashed them for his own benefit. A string of harsh squabbles ensued, leaving scars that still burn: Columbia's then president, Alan J. Hirschfield, successfully pressed for Begelman's resignation, but was himself fired by Columbia's board. Hirschfield told *Variety* that his firing was a 'direct consequence of the David Begelman affair'.

Now that Hirschfield is entrenched at Fox as vice-president and chief operating officer, and has built his new team via heavy talent raids on Columbia executives, the Hollywood gossip mill churns with tales of bad blood between Hirschfield and Begelman, who finally emerged from limbo to become president of MGM's feature division, and between Hirschfield and producer Ray Stark, considered something of an *eminence grise* at Columbia. At this point, neither Fox nor Columbia, where production chiefs Frank Price and John Veitch have seen their best executives stolen away, feel terribly kindly towards each other.

But sagas like this are rare and unlike the rivalries of Old Hollywood, where the men who built the studios clung to power for decades, sniping at each other all the while. Louis B. Mayer's intervention as an investor led to William Fox being ousted from his own Fox Film Corporation before its merger with Zanuck's Twentieth Century Productions. Could there be a contemporary equivalent? For a while Kirk Kerkorian, who owns 47 per cent of MGM, also controlled 25.5 per cent of Columbia stock. His intentions towards Columbia were always unclear, and a month barely went by without the trade press speculating on Kerkorian's possible role as a spoiler at that studio. Francis Vincent, Columbia's president and chief executive, told New York security analysts that Kerkorian's shareholding constituted a 'failed partnership', forcing a 'siege mentality' on the studio. How-

MGM

Years	Head of production
1924–36	Louis B. Mayer/Irving Thalberg
1936–48	Louis B. Mayer
1948–51	Louis B. Mayer/Dore Schary
1951–56	Dore Schary
1956–58	Joseph Vogel/Eddie Mannix
1958–62	Sol C. Siegel
1962–68	Robert Weitman
1969	Herbert Solow
1969–73	James Aubrey
1973–76	Daniel Melnick
1976–79	Richard A. Shepherd
1979–	David Begelman

Warner Brothers

Years	Head of production
1923–29	Jack L. Warner
1929–33	Jack L. Warner/Darryl F. Zanuck
1933–44	Jack L. Warner/Hal B. Wallis
1945–67	Jack L. Warner (assistants included Steve Trilling, Ben Kalmenson)
1967–69	Eliot Hyman/Kenneth Hyman
1969–74	Ted Ashley/Frank Wells/John Calley
1975	Frank Wells/John Calley (Ashley on sabbatical leave)
1976–80	Ted Ashley/Frank Wells/John Calley
1980–	Robert Daly

ever, Kerkorian's Columbia holdings were finally bought out after MGM's calamitous Las Vegas hotel fire.

But the younger generation of studio executives have a long way to go before people start telling stories about them. 'They lack the instincts of killers,' observes Gerald Ayres. 'They have the instincts of manipulators, but that's not as refreshing as seeing a killer in action!' Nor can the power wielded by Sherry Lansing or her peers be compared with that of the old guard moguls. For one thing, they don't last long enough. Lansing is the fifth Fox production boss in the ten years since 1970, following the angry exits of Richard Zanuck (fired by his own father, Darryl, in 1971 in an ultimately futile attempt to shore up his own position); Gordon Stulberg (now president of Polygram Pictures); Alan Ladd, Jr.; and Sandy Lieberson. Of the big seven, only Warners and Universal entered the 1980s with roughly the same leadership as they had in the early 1970s, with Warners' Ted Ashley second only to Universal's Lew Wasserman in power and longevity.

If studio executives seem to be getting younger, so are audiences. That 1946 audience of 4,060 million admissions spanned every social and age group, but the 1979 ticket-buyers numbered a mere 113.7 million, with the 12–20 age group dominating (49 per cent). The age category 12–39 years accounted for 87 per cent of that year's admissions. The majors have turned to younger executives in the hope that they know what that audience wants to see. And, confronted by different economic realities, Lansing and the others can't run their studios as the old guard did, any more than they can impart an identifiable style or 'look' to their films, as was the case in the 1930s and 1940s. Producing is generally left to scores of independent producers; these either develop projects which they shop around among the studios for finance, or they form multiple-picture alliances with individual studios. The big seven, then, have become largely service operations for film-makers. 'We don't really make pictures,' admitted John Calley, president of Warner Brothers, to columnist Stuart Byron. 'We react to what's offered to us.'

If it isn't exactly a seller's market, Hollywood has never been more receptive to independent producers and packagers. 'The real power brokers today are the agents, not the majors,' ventures Gerald Ayres. 'Agents develop the packages of producers, directors, writers and stars that the studios need badly. That night I had dinner with Lansing, Field and Townsend, an agent was with us. He gazed across the table at these young faces and said, most pointedly, "By recent count, we have 33 markets." He meant that he, or superagents like Stan Kamen, Sue Mengers, Ben Benjamin, or those guys who look like riverboat gamblers, could call a studio boss and say, as if they were selling hot watches, "Hey, David, you want to get off to a good start at Metro? My star actress wants to do the remake of *Anna Karenina*. I can deliver her." And it's the *agent* who's negotiating from strength because if David doesn't bite, there are 32 other places to fish. But David *will* bite because he needs good pictures, and he's in competition with all the other studios in town for a relatively small number of "bankable" star talents.'

Robert Altman, *whose M*A*S*H gave some small help to Fox at a critical time in its history. The studio repaid him with numerous projects, but he never delivered them another hit and his relationship with the studio is rumoured to have ended in some bitterness.*

The majors and the independents

Where are these alternative markets? Mostly, they are mini-majors and independent producers like Lorimar, Mel Simon, Orion, the Ladd Company, Zoetrope, CBS, ABC, Hemdale, Marble Arch, EMI, Golden Harvest, Robert Stigwood, Filmways, Joseph E. Levine, and a slew of Canadians: all these not only put projects together, but have the ability to finance

Universal

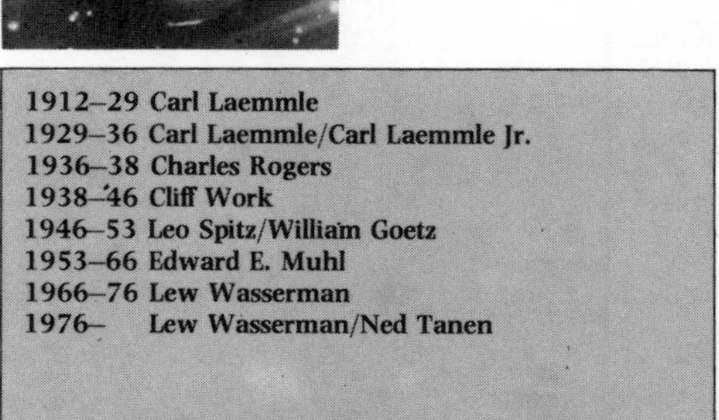

Years	Heads
1912–29	Carl Laemmle
1929–36	Carl Laemmle/Carl Laemmle Jr.
1936–38	Charles Rogers
1938–46	Cliff Work
1946–53	Leo Spitz/William Goetz
1953–66	Edward E. Muhl
1966–76	Lew Wasserman
1976–	Lew Wasserman/Ned Tanen

Paramount

Years	Heads
1916–25	Adolph Zukor/Jesse L. Lasky
1925–32	Jesse L. Lasky/B. P. Schulberg
1932–35	Emanuel Cohen
1935–36	Ernst Lubitsch
1936–41	William Le Baron
1941–44	B. G. DeSylva
1944–50	Y. Frank Freeman/Henry Ginsberg
1951–56	Don Hartman
1956–59	Jacob H. Karp
1960–64	Martin Lee Rackin
1965–66	Howard W. Koch
1966–71	Robert Evans
1971–74	Frank Yablans/Robert Evans
1974–75	Barry Diller/Robert Evans
1975–77	Barry Diller/David Picker
1977–	Barry Diller/Michael Eisner

Mel Brooks, *one of Fox's talented hit-makers, was successfully cultivated by Alan Ladd Jr. Inevitably Ladd's successors Hirschfield and Lansing were anxious to retain his services, although it is reported that only Brooks' contract stopped him leaving.*

them as well. Even when a project is cancelled by a major, it may be able to find a new home with an independent, although the independent will generally distribute through a major. When Paramount had second thoughts about their movie version of Jack Lemmon's Broadway hit, *Tribute*, and put the property into turn-around (meaning, the producers can buy it back from the major, providing they reimburse all expenses – see page 56), it was immediately snapped up by Canadian financier-producers, Joel Michaels and Garth Drabinsky, whose other credits include *The Changeling* (1980).

And Gerald Ayres' original screenplay, *Foxes*, went from Fox to Peter Guber's Casablanca FilmWorks. Fox had financed the screenplay, which Ayres was also to produce, but Gareth Wigan reacted against Ayres' script, and took the deal no further. Ayres recalls that, 'Jacques Demy, the French director, was in town sleeping on my couch that week, and he saw my long face. He suggested I meet David Puttnam, who produced Demy's *The Pied Piper* (1972). Jacques said, "He has a deal at Casablanca, so let me take you to him." So Jacques was really my agent on *Foxes*. Puttnam read the script on the plane, liked it, and called me. He then took it to Peter Guber, who had been under me at Columbia years ago, and that's how *Foxes* got made. But ten years ago, it probably would have died a lonely death after Fox passed on it. Then, the seven majors were virtually your only markets.'

Obviously, a major part of the job of any studio production boss is to woo good producers, a problem the old guard rarely had. In fact, to find a contemporary equivalent for Darryl F. Zanuck (Fox production chief 1935–56 and 1962–71) in Twentieth Century-Fox today, you would have to envision a combination of Sherry Lansing and Alan Hirschfield then subtract a little and add some. As president of Fox's feature division, Lansing is theoretically responsible for spending some \$150m. annually on about 15 films but in reality this has translated into a constant responsibility for forming alliances with key producers. For example, before Ladd, Kanter and Wigan resigned, they had assembled an enviable cottage industry of talented workers: Mel Brooks, Paul Mazursky, Jane Fonda, George Lucas, Walter Hill and David Giler, and Robert Altman. Hirschfield's responsibility, in contrast, covers Fox's business operations. 'My strength is in deal-making,' he told the *New York Times*. 'Keeping the company healthy, economically.' Hirschfield's background includes a stint as vice-president of Wall Street's Allen & Co.

Hirschfield, who hired Lansing, intends to expand Fox to a full 'entertainment' company, with its movie, TV and music divisions in the forefront of the coming age of pay-TV, cassettes and video discs. He predicts that movies will soon be released as discs and cassettes at the same time they are released in theatres. Darryl Zanuck's notion of 'entertainment,' however visionary in its day, was restricted to Fox movies screened in conventional theatres.

But Zanuck was the absolute boss. Both Hirschfield and Fox president Joseph LaBonte (responsible for the corporation's other activities, including its TV stations, Aspen Skiing Corporation, and real estate ventures) report to Fox chairman Dennis Stanfill, who continues to make his own voice heard in the production offices. For example, since the resignations of Ladd, Kanter and Wigan, Fox has become more aggressive about picking up independent films to distribute, including those made in 1980 by Mel Simon Productions (*Sam Marlowe, Private Eye*), Time-Life Films (*Fort Apache – The Bronx, They All Laughed*), and the new feature division of the ABC television network. Fox intends to pick up about 15 films a year in addition to the 15 or so it will produce itself.

'All the majors are looking to distribute

Rocky *(left), with Sylvester Stallone being playfully punched by world champion Carl Weathers, was a major contributor to United Artists' record earnings towards the end of the 1970s, and the sequel did almost as well.*

pictures made by Lorimar, Polygram, Ladd Company, Stigwood, Mel Simon, or whoever.' explains Lorimar's David Picker, 'because movie costs are extraordinarily high, and no matter how lush a major you are, if it's costing you $10m. to make a picture that used to cost $5m. you're going to look for ways to get joint financing, so that you can spread your expenditures over a much broader programme of films, and keep your international distribution machine filled with product.'

This policy of distributing films over which Fox has less control, but which keep the corporation's marketing and sales offices busy, derives as much from Stanfill as from Hirschfield, and was a source of conflict with the Ladd team. 'We tried to make only pictures we believed in,' recalls Gareth Wigan. 'We felt that the Fox name, the logo you saw on the screen, had to evoke a response in the audience – a response to quality. But management constantly complained that we didn't make enough movies for the distribution people to sell. We were told that the distribution machinery needed 20–25 pictures a year to pay for itself. We were urged to make more. Not unreasonably, perhaps. But we didn't want to make movies for the sake of making movies. And the bottom line supported us. In 1978, our leadership led Fox to its highest ever domestic and overseas gross, and we returned a record profit. We didn't need 25 films to do that.'

Middle management at the majors

Another result of the corporate changes is a morass of executives at the majors: layer upon layer of decision-making. 'Whoever you talk to at the majors, they say, "Let me think . . . maybe . . . let me check with . . . let me check with . . .,"' laments producer Gerald Ayres. 'Their wishy-washy ambivalence drives you nuts, whereas you knew exactly where you stood with guys like Harry Cohn or Mike Frankovich. They either wanted to murder you or make a hero out of you, but once they said, "Okay, you son of a bitch, we'll make that film," you knew you *would* make the film.'

Ayres was Mike Frankovich's assistant at Columbia between 1964 and 1967, after Frankovich was called back from the studio's London office to assume responsibility for worldwide production. The Frankovich era was something of a heyday for Columbia when it released *Lawrence of Arabia*, *Oliver!*, *A Man for All Seasons*, *Funny Girl*, *Guess Who's Coming to Dinner*, *The Professionals*, and *Georgy Girl*. 'I was his Bob Haldeman,' Ayres chuckles. 'But I loved those old guys. The younger executives should have to battle against conservative forces. Studios operate best on a system of checks and balances. By blocking you, the old guard forced you to examine and re-examine your motives and your projects and your budgets. But they weren't stupid. They would allow innovation. You just had to know what you were talking about.

'I remember the chairman of the board at Columbia saying, "Why we got to do Shakespeare?" and Mike and I explained that *A Man for All Seasons* wasn't written by Shakespeare, but by a modern playwright named Robert Bolt who had scored quite a success with modern audiences in London and New York. But the chairman was still dubious. "Yeah," he says, "but it's still a bunch of guys running around in their knickers." But Mike Frankovich fought for that picture all the way, just as he fought to get *Guess Who's Coming to Dinner* when the rest of Columbia's top management were terrified of it.

Heaven's Gate *(right) had a first opening which must have made United Artists yearn for the simplicities of* Rocky. *Michael Cimino's western was withdrawn after scathing notices and UA suffered their worst year in nearly a decade.*

'Today.' snorts Ayres, 'some producer or writer will say to me, "Joe Blow at Warner Brothers loves my screenplay." And I look at him with melting pity. I think for a moment: who exactly is Joe Blow? Where is he in the corporate hierarchy? Maybe he has a Mickey-Mouse title like vice-president of creative affairs, which really means he's a story editor. And maybe he's in competition with three other V-Ps, which is the way the majors operate; that is, they give one job to three people, and see who comes out a winner. Which means that Joe Blow must convince his superior to read the script. That superior will be vice-president in charge of production or an executive vice-president in charge of production, and above *them* is the president, or a couple of other titles floating around. But since the script didn't come in from a heavyweight source, like Sue Mengers, none of those people will read it until Christmas. So it's all nonsense.'

MGM's business affairs executive Frank Davis views the younger generation more kindly: 'All the majors have young, creative people stirring around town, endlessly talking to would-be writers and real writers, would-be directors and real directors, and would-be producers and real producers. They're picking up on ideas in the air. And some of those ideas come from *within* the studios. Creative young people at our studio provide a strong backbone. They're not just pretty faces.'

Doing business with the majors: controversy over the distribution fee

If the baby moguls are often the targets of unfair criticism, the real big guns are aimed four-square at studio accountants. No matter how many millions of dollars a movie makes, its producer will generally, at some point, rail against both the terms of the production-distribution agreement, and the figures as reported in the studio books.

The feeling among many producers is that the distribution fee, normally 30 per cent of incoming rentals, is a 'profit' for the majors; that it goes into stockholder dividends while holding back a picture's break-even; that it is a pool of money into which the studio may dip, yet which rightfully belongs, at least in part, to the people who made the movie; that it far exceeds the true cost of distribution. Break-even is the point at which a studio considers that a film has covered its production cost in addition to the cost of distribution and prints, advertising, interest and taxes. At this point – often calculated at around two and a half times production cost – the studio is prepared to distribute profits to the film's producers. But it is frequently difficult to determine when break-even is reached. Alfred Hitchcock once called distribution 'a freemasonry like the kitchens of a restaurant. They have deep dark secrets. I have never yet been able to discover how much it costs to distribute a film.'

Is the distribution fee fair? 'Yes,' asserts UA's Steven Bach. 'It's ridiculous to say that United Artists or any major rakes in its 30 per cent distribution fee regardless of whether a picture is profitable. We don't begin to make our 30 per cent until rentals have paid at least for prints and advertising – two incredibly expensive items. It's impossible to open a movie today, and give it a chance, for less than $2.5m. And that buys you only a moderate release. But what if the picture grosses only $500,000? Arguing about a 30 per cent distribution fee is irrelevant when we've lost $2m. right there.' Does that kind of loss occur often? 'Orion spent $7m. making *A Little Romance*

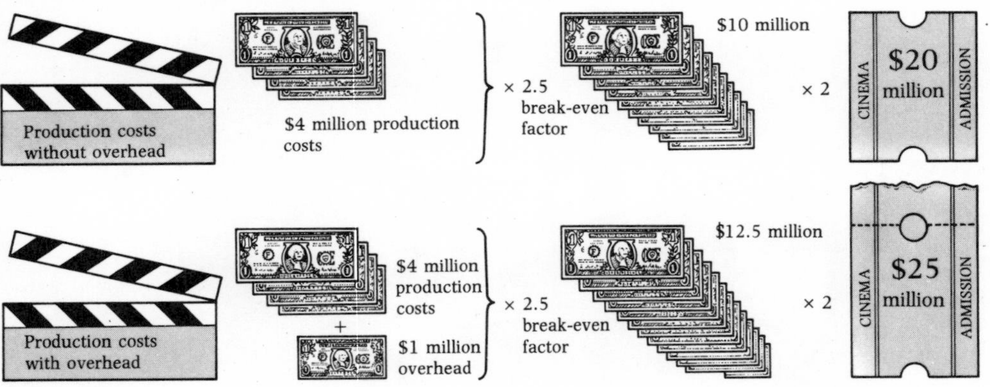

Overhead costs on a film which costs $4m.: *for every $1m. of overhead charged by the studio, $5m. more tickets must be sold to reach profit. This assumes the average break-even factor of 2.5, and a return to the distributor of 50 per cent of exhibitor's receipts.*

(1979),' Bach replies. 'It grossed $5m.'

What are the costs of prints and advertising? For the abortive first release of *Heaven's Gate* (1980), United Artists spent nearly $500,000 on prep costs alone. These are the expenses incurred when several advertising agencies compete with each other for a particular movie's account. UA and Francis Coppola went through over thirty agencies for *Apocalypse Now* before the final mix of elements was decided by taking one motif from one campaign, another from another. *Heaven's Gate* involved half a dozen agencies. But the enormous cost, which couldn't be shaved, was the cost of prints. One two-hour 35 mm print costs $1200–$1400. Since *Heaven's Gate* originally ran twice as long as most features, you might expect a print to cost about $2500. Not so. Initial openings were in 70 mm, with each print costing about $6000.

Bach admits that the studios do very nicely off the distribution fee when a movie hits big. 'When a *Rocky* (1976) makes over $100m. in rentals, then yes, we make about $30m. off the top, just for distributing the picture. But we only make that kind of money on highly successful pictures. When a movie is successful, producers have no reason to cry foul.'

But cry they do. Often with good reason. The income from a hit movie is 'a huge reservoir', claims producer Peter Guber, whose company Casablanca made *The Deep* (1977) and *Midnight Express* (1978), arguing that the majors routinely divert money due to film-makers to protect themselves against losses on less successful films. In setting up their deals, Guber claimed, the majors try 'to get you as far downstream and as far away from the reservoir as possible.'

Columbia financed *The Deep* and *Midnight Express*; in each case, Guber was highly critical of the major's book-keeping. '*The Deep* has brought in over $100m. at the box-office,' he once claimed, 'I've seen zero dollars in profitability for my company.' On the $2.6m. *Midnight Express*, Casablanca had a deal for 25 per cent of the movie's profits, but though worldwide rentals hit over $40m., Columbia assessed Casablanca's profit share at a lowly $1.4m. That share has risen since Guber's remarks, but to nowhere like the level Guber believes to be fair. He has since announced that Casablanca will in future release through Universal.

The overhead charge

Another irksome factor in studio accounting is the charge for production overhead. This is supposed to cover part of the studio expenses, not directly related to any specific project. Universal, for example, figures overhead as a straight 25 per cent of the money actually spent in production, getting a film to final negative. It's an emotional issue, fiercely disputed when production contracts are negotiated. Many producers regard the charge as a crippling, unfair drain on their profits, designed to enrich studio coffers already bloated by excessive distribution fees.

Producers may like to define negative cost (the cost of producing a movie's final negative) as real dollars expended, but most of the majors beg to differ: they include overhead as an accounting entry within negative cost. (United Artists charges no overhead because it owns no studios or equipment. Paramount recently eliminated its overhead fee, but now charges item-by-item for use of facilities that used to be offered in exchange for overhead.) While the overhead charge isn't real money paid out during production – no one signs a cheque made out to 'Overhead' – it is a real charge assessed by the studio against the profit participants, effectively pushing back the time when they collect their share of a profitable film. In many cases significantly so, especially when break-even is defined as a multiple of production cost. For a $4m. production cost, 25 per cent overhead boosts the total cost of producing the negative to $5m. If the multiple is 2.5, say, then break-even is $12.5m. (Break-even may not actually be 2.5 × negative cost, but it can be contractually defined as such for book-keeping

Swashbuckler *(right) was Universal's brave but unsuccessful attempt to revive costume melodrama.*

Ridley Scott *(far right) directing* Alien.

Division of the average movie budget *(left and below).*

Story costs

Production and direction costs

Sets and other physical properties

Stars and cast

Studio overhead

Income taxes

Net profit after taxes

purposes.) But *without* overhead, break-even is only $10m. Overhead, then, doesn't hold back break-even merely by its own dollar value, but by a multiple of that value. To trace the impact of overhead one step further: if rentals are approximately half the box-office take, then $5m. worth of tickets must be sold to pay off a $1m. overhead charge. Small wonder the participants in the profits get upset about the outcome.

Producer Robert Solo (*Invasion of the Body Snatchers*) headed Warners' foreign production programme during the mid-1970s. 'In all my years as a studio executive,' he candidly admits, 'I could never, in my heart of hearts, justify what we charged for overhead. What did we give the producers? Virtually nothing. They still had to pay for all their labour and materials. Where's the logic?'

The majors, of course, dismiss such rhetoric. Their logic is simple: every film made with studio backing (though not films they merely distribute) should contribute revenue to meet such relatively fixed costs as land taxes; interest on past borrowings; operating commissaries and accounting; legal and production departments; salaries for the likes of Lew Wasserman, Frank Wells, Barry Diller, and the janitors who clean their offices, and the guards at their gates, and the plumbers who unclog their johns and so on *ad infinitum*. These are costs that would continue to be incurred even if production ceased. Other overhead costs will vary directly from year to year according to the volume of production: lighting and power, repairs and repair materials, and indirect labour are all examples of such variable overhead costs.

That's an intimidating jumble of costs, but someone has to pay them. Since many of these costs are impossible to analyze item-by-item for every film, the majors have traditionally lumped them together as a percentage of actual production costs, then added on that percentage to arrive at final negative cost.

In return, producers benefit from studio facilities placed at their disposal. Financed by Universal, *The Sting* (1973) paid no sound stage rental fee for shooting on the lot. That studio's wardrobe department also gave *Swashbuckler* (GB: *The Scarlet Buccaneer*, 1977) the run of its pirate costumes (although it did not provide those tailored expressly for the leading actors). And when *Foul Play* (1978) needed stages, offices, parking, telephones, carbon arcs, incandescent lights, stands, cameras, grip equipment, sewing machines, and editing rooms, Paramount offered everything it had on hand. The only 'fee': 25 per cent overhead charge. (*Foul Play* was made just before Paramount eliminated overhead fees.)

'Paying overhead is like paying taxes,' insists Fox studio administrator Bernard Barron. 'I'm goddamned glad my country fought a war for me in 1942, and had the money to pay for ships, planes and bombs so that I didn't end up in the hands of the Germans or Japanese. I'm goddamned glad my city has money to pay for streets, hospitals, schools and fire departments. That's what my taxes pay for. Well, that's all studio overhead is.'

But do studios give producers goods and services equal in value to the overhead charge? 'No,' states Rob Cohen, who directed *A Small Circle of Friends* (1980) and produced *The Wiz* (1978). 'Ask any producer who's made a $3m. studio picture: when they got done charging you $750,000 overhead, did you get $750,000 worth of equipment and labour out of them? Almost always, the answer is *no*, especially if it was a location picture where you end up paying twice for the same items.' A small, but telling, example of paying more than twice for an item was cited by Beverly Hills business manager and accountant Nathan Cohen. He told the *New York Times*' Aljean Harmetz about a production where a bottle of beer, required for a scene, was missing from the set. The studio dispatched a car and driver to a supermarket to buy another beer. The driver's time was charged against the film, as was car rental. In addition, overhead was assessed on those charges. The final cost of a single bottle of beer was $300.

Statement of Participation, period ended Dec. 29, 1979	
GROSS RENTALS	Cumulative to Dec. 29, 1979
Domestic	
Theater rentals	$37,070,693
Non-theatrical rentals	312,379
Foreign	
British Territory and Continental Europe	3,918,875
International territory	7,012,111
Net trailer revenue	9,,857
TOTAL GROSS RECEIPTS	48,411,915
*Less total distribution fees	15,489,344
BALANCE	32,922,571
LESS DISTRIBUTION EXPENSES	
Taxes, duties and governmental fees	914,063
Checking and collection costs	235,353
Trade association fees and assessments	229,144
Advertising costs	15,703,841
Foreign version costs	312,486
Prints and re-editing costs	3,116,674
Shipping/delivery costs	167,853
Miscellaneous	226,993
TOTAL DISTRIBUTION EXPENSES	20,906,407
NET RECEIPTS	12,016,164
LESS:	
Interest on negative cost	1,731,104
Negative cost	10,791,734
Agreed over budget deduction	1,900,753
	14,423,591
NET PROFITS (LOSS)	(2,407,427)

**Fox distribution fees are expressed in percentages and range from 30 to 40% of each category in gross rentals.*

Alien *(above left); the battle over its disputed profits as seen by* Los Angeles Times *cartoonist Richard Fletcher. The paper also published a rare glimpse of the film's balance sheet (above).*

Alien: a case in point

The studios like to keep their books under wraps unless a profit participant demands the right to audit them. However, some figures concerning Fox's *Alien* (1979) came before the public when the *Los Angeles Times* published the picture's Statement of Participation, dated for the period ending December 29, 1979. At that point, *Alien* had returned over $48m. in rentals worldwide. *Alien* continued to generate income beyond 1980, of course, but, as with most films, the bulk of its earnings occurred in the first six months of release.

Alien cost Fox $10,791,734. Yet even with $48m. in rentals at the end of 1979, a loss of $2,407,427 was declared.

The *Los Angeles Times*' Charles Schreger broke down the figures: 'First, distributing and marketing films is expensive. Fox, contemplating a hit, spent a fortune on *Alien*'s release. It claims that the advertising costs – which includes everything from network TV spots, newspaper ads, trailers, posters, publicity junkets and promotional schemes – came to $15.7m.

'Then there is the distribution fee, which Fox, like all the studios, takes off the top . . . Total distribution fees for *Alien* add up, so far, to nearly $15.5m. In addition, Fox claimed that it spent $3.1m. to make prints for the film, including 70 mm Dolby prints used during the initial release in May and June. Today, the average 35 mm print costs about $1400. At the time *Alien* hit the theatres, the price was $1000. On the other hand, 70 mm prints in 1979 cost about $8000 each, and Fox, according to DeLuxe General, the company's processing lab, ordered 110 70 mm prints of *Alien*.

'So, for the 70 mm prints, the tab was nearly $900,000. That leaves $2.2m for the 35 mm prints. It is considered extraordinary to strike more than 1000 prints of any film. But, according to the producer's statement, Fox had spent enough on prints to make nearly 2200 35 mm copies.

'Add nearly $1m. for various taxes and duties charged by governments around the world, $150,000 for shipping and delivery of prints and other materials, $312,000 to dub and subtitle the foreign versions and more than $225,000 for various trade association fees. And don't forget another quarter-million for "miscellaneous expenses".

'In addition, the producers were penalized $1.9m. because they went over budget during production. This is one point under fierce dispute. Also, while a movie is recouping its costs – both production and distribution expenses – interest is charged, generally at the rate of 125 per cent of prime. The prime rate is the interest rate banks charge their most credit-worthy customers, who usually include movie studios. With the prime at 20 per cent

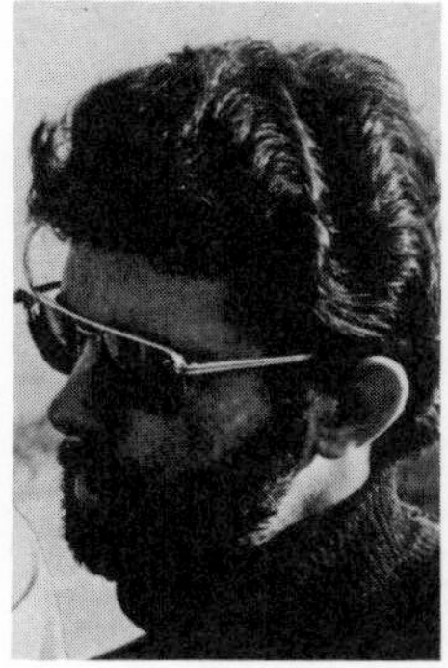

George Lucas *(above) and* **Steven Spielberg** *(right) who made more money for the majors in the 1970s than any other two directors. This put them in a unique position when dealing with Paramount on* Raiders.

during March, that meant *Alien* was sometimes being charged 25 per cent interest. Interest charges for *Alien*, per the most recent statement, come to $1.7m.

'And then, because some theatre owners don't pay their bills on time – maybe even try to cheat Fox – there is an item in the producer's statement for "checking and collection". Cost: $229,144.'

For those people owning *Alien* points there was no participation in profits, as of the end of 1979, despite rentals totalling nearly $50m. 'It scares the hell out of me,' co-producer Ronald Shusett told Schreger. 'Here I hit the jackpot and haven't seen any money.'

More to the point was the observation of entertainment lawyer Tom Pollock, whose clients include top film-makers George Lucas and Ridley Scott: 'You can't win under the rules that they are playing with.' Pollock's 'they' are the big seven majors.

Independent finance

The *Alien* figures are significant not merely for their insights into Fox book-keeping (profit participants did finally start receiving cheques in 1980 when the July financial statement announced a $4m. profit on $61.4m. rentals), but for the way they illustrate a basic fact of movie-making: the high cost of doing anything connected with moving a film from idea to script to production to screen. Traditionally, only the majors have had the resources to meet those expenses. Only if a producer can arrange his or her own financing can book-keeping begin to seem more favourable. An independently financed picture is still most often distributed by a major, but the deals are different. Expenses are recorded and approved by both the major and the producer as they are incurred, and the bottom line profit or loss is far less of a surprise.

For example, in 1980, Polygram Pictures had over $110m. in available production funds from its parent, the Dutch entertainment conglomerate Philips Seaman Polygram. The company came into being after the Polygram Group acquired Casablanca Records and FilmWorks from Peter Guber and his partner Neil Bogart. Polygram Pictures will distribute its films initially through Universal, which will finance or co-finance some of the films. But with that $110m. to play with, Polygram can exact far better terms from Universal than the *Alien* team could from Fox. For *Raiders of the Lost Ark* (1981), the combined clout of George Lucas and Steven Spielberg enabled them to negotiate distribution fees with Paramount far below the standard domestic 30 per cent, and Lucas had an equally advantageous deal with Fox on the *Star Wars* sequel: *The Empire Strikes Back*.

Polygram is a new mini-major: there have

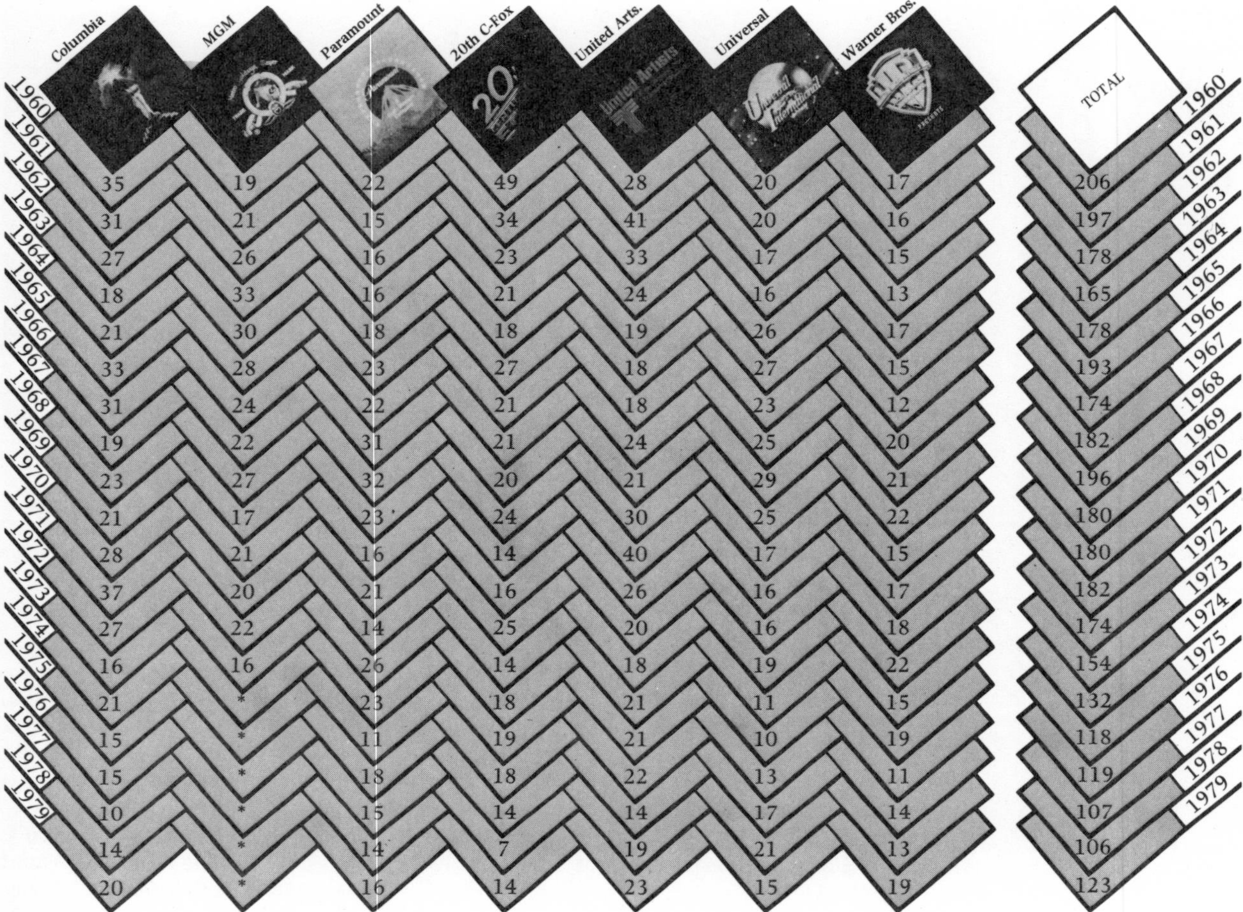

Year	Columbia	MGM	Paramount	20th C-Fox	United Arts.	Universal	Warner Bros.	TOTAL
1960	35	19	22	49	28	20	17	206
1961	31	21	15	34	41	20	16	197
1962	27	26	16	23	33	17	15	178
1963	18	33	16	21	24	16	13	165
1964	21	30	18	18	19	26	17	178
1965	33	28	23	27	18	27	15	193
1966	31	24	22	21	18	23	12	174
1967	19	22	31	21	24	25	20	182
1968	23	27	32	20	21	29	21	196
1969	21	17	23	24	30	25	22	180
1970	28	21	16	14	40	17	15	180
1971	37	20	21	16	26	16	17	182
1972	27	22	14	25	20	16	18	174
1973	16	16	26	14	18	19	22	154
1974	21	*	23	18	21	11	15	132
1975	15	*	11	19	21	10	19	118
1976	15	*	18	18	22	13	11	119
1977	10	*	15	14	14	17	14	107
1978	14	*	14	7	19	21	13	106
1979	20	*	16	14	23	15	19	123

*After 1973 MGM released through United Artists.

never been so many of these as there are today – ambitious new companies that aspire to almost the same level of financing as the big seven: Orion, the Ladd Company, Mel Simon, Robert Stigwood, ABC and CBS feature divisions, Zoetrope, Polygram, and Lorimar. These companies do not, however, generally operate their own distribution networks, preferring to rely on the existing facilities of the majors, but because they finance their movies themselves, they are likely to get better terms from the majors.

A man who has frequently challenged the traditional ways of the majors is Francis Ford Coppola. Recently, when he unveiled his ambitious plans for Zoetrope studios, *Variety* headlined it as the return of an 'old-line studio,' evoking images of Hollywood's glory days of backlot production. Coppola plans a production centre employing up to 1500 people.

'What I really want to do,' announced Coppola when he purchased the old Hollywood General Studios in March 1980, 'is develop a studio – an all inclusive gathering of talent. The studio will be their home and employ them all year round. As a writer and director, I longed for a studio like that.'

Lucy Fisher, Coppola's vice-president in charge of production, says, 'We're gathering together people who are more interested in making movies than in deals.' As someone who rose through the story departments of MGM, United Artists and Fox, Fisher compares the guiding philosophy at Zoetrope with that of the majors: 'I can't in good conscience say that any of the majors are in business solely to make great films. But that's the *only* reason we exist.'

Fisher acknowledges that Zoetrope cannot, for the present, distribute its own films. They will be released through Orion (using the marketing organization at Warners, in common with Orion's own releases), an arrangement satisfactory for both studios.

The future for the majors

After nearly a decade of very rich pickings, 1980 proved the first year in a while to generate some anxiety at the majors. With a 10 per cent overall decline in box office during its first half, and the failure of several potential blockbusters like Warners' *Bronco Billy*, Paramount's *Rough Cut*, Universal's *The Island* and UA's *Heaven's*

Rough Cut *(right) with Lesley-Anne Down and Burt Reynolds, was one of the many potential blockbusters which failed in 1980.*

Raise the Titanic *(far right) was a colossally expensive failure in 1980 for Lord Grade and AFD.*

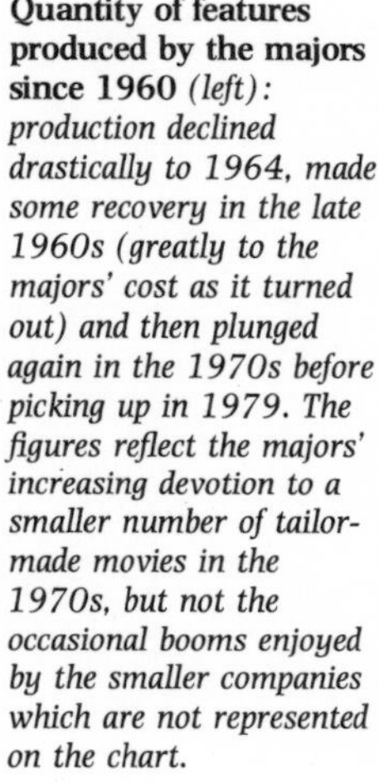

Quantity of features produced by the majors since 1960 *(left): production declined drastically to 1964, made some recovery in the late 1960s (greatly to the majors' cost as it turned out) and then plunged again in the 1970s before picking up in 1979. The figures reflect the majors' increasing devotion to a smaller number of tailor-made movies in the 1970s, but not the occasional booms enjoyed by the smaller companies which are not represented on the chart.*

Gate on top of the hostility stirred by the screen actors' strike, commentators wondered whether the euphoria of the late 1970s was going to give way to crisis. Half-way through the year *Variety* noted that even the safety-net of ancillary rights, like video and cable TV, might prove less than adequate to maintain production levels if box-office fell any further. A. D. Murphy, one of the leading experts on the film industry, wrote: 'The pre-sales market is relatively thin to begin with, which means that it can shrink alarmingly – and even dry up completely – in short order. All that any apparent boom needs to evaporate is a weakness in a primary sales market, which for theatrical feature films is the box-office.' Murphy also observed of the year in general: 'One of the truisms now in demonstration is that any sustained period of relative prosperity leads to larger, more optimistic and often poorly-supervised investments in negatives which come to market just when attendance levels decline. Phrased another way, we are currently observing that, just when Hollywood needs a box office surge, it doesn't get it.'

But, although the skies have darkened a little, it does not seem that the majors will be the ones to suffer most, even if – as is doubtful – they suffer at all. Underpinned by their distribution arms, and buttressed by the sustained profits of the past few years, many of them can sit back with anticipation: ultimately they have the ability to ride out a storm while the smaller independent producing organizations do not; many studio executives would welcome a return to the more peaceful years of the early 1970s, before the success of the movie business tempted so many other investors into production. The competition for the talent reached fever proportions in the late 1970s and in many respects the majors would love, once again, to be the only game in town. Paramount's chairman and chief executive Barry Diller, who battened down the hatches early, limiting his company's film investment in 1980 (despite blockbusters like *Reds* and *Popeye*), spells out the dangers he sees in over-competition: 'in 1980 the actual number of productions was increasing without any corresponding growth in basic theatrical or other markets . . . inevitably, the equation had only one answer: disaster, whether it would be suffered collectively, as it was in the mid-60s, or individually. We naturally wanted the least damage done.'

Ultimately it is the majors' distribution arms which make them so hard for any producer to dispense with. And it is this facility, even more than the backing of the conglomerates to which they now belong, which will continue to insulate them from the rest of the industry and see them through the 1980s. Certainly even the most determined rival corporation would think hard before investing the $500m. necessary to create a rival distribution network of a similar scale. Indeed one of the organizations worst hit by the 1980 box-office slump was Lew Grade's and EMI's AFD, whose alternative distribution arm was wound up after the anticipated 1980 summer blockbusters *Can't Stop the Music* and *Raise the Titanic* fell flat on their faces.

For most mini-majors and independent producers, it is a lot simpler to distribute through a major. Everything is under one roof. 'You know that if your picture plays in Bangkok, it's going to be handled by the UA Bangkok manager, not some guy you've never heard of, or from whom you'll never be able to collect, or from whom you'll never be able to get information,' sums up Steven Bach at United Artists. 'It's enormously difficult for a producer to carry his film from country to country trying to make distribution deals with people he doesn't know who use funny-looking money.

'Look,' says Bach. 'A producer walks into my office, and says, "Here's a script." I say, "Terrific. Not only will I give you the money to make this into a movie, and pay you a fee for having presented me with this epic, but I will also distribute it throughout the world, and try to give you a fair accounting on the other end.

'All you have to do is go home and wait for the cheque".'

The Deal

The popular image of Hollywood has close parallels in Las Vegas or Monte Carlo, because it is, essentially, about the transformation of ordinary people into the rich and famous. There are other similarities: just as the movie industry's scandals frequently have a gambling sub-plot, its style is borrowed quite openly from the card or dice-table. The motion picture business has been described as 'the biggest crap-game in the world' by Richard Zanuck while countless other producers and Hollywood personalities employ the same image. Film people talk about 'looking for a piece of the action', 'upping the ante', 'playing against a heavy deck', 'eating their losses', 'the ace in the hole'. But most of all they talk about the deal.

Outside the film industry, everyone entertains their own notion of how or why commercial films are made. Enthusiasts champion the director or writer or some elusive combination of cultural and economic forces. But it is the deal which nowadays determines not only whether a project will be made but also most of its basic ingredients. If commercial films were less expensive to make, or were more consistently successful, then the deal would not have assumed such immense importance. The way in which a film is made is now pre-determined more than ever before, by the process of raising money to make it. In a few respects, the financial operations involved resemble the loans and guarantees necessary to build an office block or a hotel. But there is one vital difference: the final product may be worthless; no bank in the world will accept an unproven film as collateral for a loan, even from a major studio. They are too well aware that although some films make gigantic fortunes, only a few films make a profit. In their book *The Movie Brats*, Michael Pye and Lynda Myles sum this up succinctly: 'Imagine the man who put money into a restaurant and then discovered that the restaurant had crumbled, the land had flooded, the business had never been worth anything, and no customer had ever come in. That is the nature of investment in a single film.' The increasing risks of film finance have helped to inflate the importance of the deal and to place enormous emphasis on any ingredient which seems to insure a film against disaster. Talent (especially talent associated with past success) is the most obvious form of insurance, and consequently the people who represent the talent and who claim to be expert in assessing its commercial potential have assumed unprecedented power. 'Blessed are the deal-makers,' went a Hollywood aphorism of the post-war period, 'for they shall inherit the industry.' In the 1970s, as several former agents took over the running of major studios, it came true. The story of the deal is, in the first place, the story of Hollywood's post-war transformation.

Before the deal era

There was a time when the deal was much less important to Hollywood than it is now. It was a time when many more films made money, and the film-makers were cushioned against the sordid requirements of the deal by studio bosses who allowed them to make picture after picture with no more thought of how their work was being financed than any production-line worker. It was a time when the agent of a big star like David Niven could go into Samuel Goldwyn's office to try to renegotiate a contract and come out not merely empty-handed, but barred from the studio lot, with his star on 'suspension' (see page 18). In those days a studio-head could dream up the idea for a movie and walk the few yards from his office to the studio commissary where, over his lunch, he could pick out the project's producer, director, star and writer, all of them on his exclusive payroll. The studios already owned the talent to make the pictures. They did not have to go out and hire it.

The studios' metamorphosis from film factories with armies of contracted employees into bankers, picking and choosing their pictures from independent talent agencies of enormous power, was long and complicated. Historically

Jack Warner *(right) with Rosalind Russell. In 1949 Warner, the cobbler's son from Ohio who founded Warner Bros., lost a battle with the agency MCA over Bette Davis's contract.*

Bette Davis *(far right) with Joseph Cotten in* Beyond the Forest, *the film which marked the stormy end to her association with Warner Brothers.*

the new era is supposed to have dawned in 1951 when two lawyers, Arthur Krim and Robert Benjamin, took over United Artists and set up purely as financiers and distributors of other people's packaged products, becoming so successful that the remaining studios gradually followed their example.

In reality, the big talent agencies had begun to rob the studios of their power long before this move, making it increasingly difficult for them to operate in the old way. For example in 1949 Jack Warner was forced into the then unprecedented humiliation of releasing a major star, Bette Davis, from a contract which had ten years left to run. His version was that 'I told Bette I was through'. In fact, Davis's agency, MCA (probably the most powerful agency in film history, see page 42), had simply told Bette Davis to refuse to re-record the soundtrack of her current film *Beyond the Forest* until she got her release. With so much money at stake, Warner was forced to agree, but not before he had banned MCA men from his studio. His brother Harry evidently told him it would be like 'bucking a stone wall'. His words proved prophetic.

Raymond Chandler on the agencies

Among the first people to see the significance of the rise of the agent in Hollywood was the novelist and screenwriter Raymond Chandler. It is probably coincidence that for a while he was represented by one of the most powerful Hollywood agents, Ray Stark, who subsequently turned producer and became a major force at Columbia Pictures. Chandler's scathing attack on the new-style agent was published in the February 1952 edition of *Atlantic Monthly*:

> This brings me, not too eagerly, to the orchid of the profession – the Hollywood agent – a sharper, shrewder and a good deal less scrupulous practitioner. Here is a guy who really makes with the personality. He dresses well and drives a Cadillac – or someone drives it for him. He has an estate in Beverly Hills or Bel-Air. He has been known to own a yacht, and by yacht I don't mean a cabin cruiser. On the surface he has a good deal of charm, because he needs it in his business. Underneath he has a heart as big as an olive pit. He deals with large sums of money. His expenses are tremendous. He will buy you a meal at Romanoff's or Chasen's with no more hesitation than is necessary for him to tot up the commissions he has made out of you in the last six months. He controls expensive talent, since with rare exceptions he is not exclusively an agent for writers. This gives him prestige in dealing with people who are starved for talent in spite of having a great deal of money to buy it with . . .
>
> The fat profits to be made in Hollywood and in radio brought a new kind of operator into the business – a sharpshooter with few scruples, whose activities spread over the whole field of entertainment. The law allowed him to incorporate, which, in my opinion, was a fatal mistake. It destroyed all semblance of the professional attitude and the professional responsibility to the individual client. It permitted a variety of subtle manoeuvres whereby the agent could make a great deal more money after taxes, and it allowed him to slide, almost unobserved, into businesses which had nothing to do with agency. He could create packaging corporations which delivered complete shows to the networks or the advertising agencies, and he loaded them with talent which, sometimes under another corporate name, he represented as an agent. He took his commission for getting you a job, and then he sold the job itself for an additional profit. Sometimes you knew about this, sometimes you didn't. In any case the essential point was that this operator was no longer an agent except in name. His clients and their work became the raw material of a speculative business. He wasn't working for

you, you were working for him. Sometimes he even became your employer and paid you a salary which he called an advance on future commissions. The agency part of his operations was still the basic ingredient, since without control of talent, he had no bricks to build his wall, but the individual meant nothing to him. The individual was just merchandise, and the "representing" of the individual was little more than a department of an entertainment trust – a congeries of powerful organizations which existed solely to exploit the commercial value of talent in every possible direction and with the utmost possible disregard for artistic or intellectual values.

Such trusts, and it is fair to call them that regardless of whether they meet an exact legal definition, cover the whole field of entertainment. Their clients include actors, singers, dancers, mouth organ players, trainers of chimpanzees and performing dogs, people who ride horses over cliffs or jump out of burning buildings, motion picture directors and producers, musical composers, and writers, in every medium including those quaint old-fashioned productions known as books. . . . Of course you don't have to become their client, but the inducements are glittering. And if they reduce you to a robot, as eventually they will, they will usually be very pleasant about it, because they can afford to employ well-dressed young men who smile and smile.

Chandler's acid observations proved accurate. By the 1970s most of the major Hollywood studios were run by graduates of these huge enterprises, while so many agents had crossed over to produce films with their own clients that it was becoming almost impossible to tell the two functions (of agenting and producing) apart. Indeed as the industry moved into the 1980s the really successful agents were becoming increasingly reluctant to give up their agency function, even to take over a major studio. As one ex-agent pointed out: 'Who wants to give up the money and the power of representing, say, five of the biggest acts in Hollywood to try and turn round a struggling studio like United Artists?'

Jules Stein's MCA

The rise of the agencies and the men who ran them is precisely mirrored by the rise of Jules Stein's 'star-spangled octopus', the Music Corporation of America, which spread its tentacles throughout the whole US film industry until it was forced to shed its agency function by the US Department of Justice in 1962. At that time, Justice Department lawyers asked producer-director Stanley Kramer whether it would be possible for him to stop dealing with MCA and still cast his movies. Kramer replied that it would not.

MCA was founded by Jules Stein, a doctor of medicine and post-graduate in ophthalmology, in 1924, the year he published his book *Telescopic Magnifiers as Aids to Poor Vision*. His company began as a booking agency for the growing dance-band craze. By the 1930s Stein's extraordinary and sometimes ruthless capacity for business had guided MCA into a pre-eminent position in the music world and he was ready to move on Hollywood.

His assault was spearheaded by Lew Wasserman who took over as head of MCA's operation there in 1940. In Stein's own words Wasserman became the 'student who surpassed the teacher'. MCA saw the true potential power of stars long before anyone else and began recruiting them by any means available. On the one hand they bought up other agents with their clients, on the other they made determined use of inside information. For example, Stein was desperately keen to hire Bette Davis, the major female star of her time. Eventually he discovered, through his all-important network of informants, that one of her husband's closest friends, Eddie Linsk, was out of work. He immediately gave him a job at $150 a week. Davis signed with the agency a short time afterwards.

As its power grew, MCA engineered new types of deals for the artists it represented. Having forced MGM to relinquish its contract with James Stewart after his wartime service, MCA refused to let him appear in *Winchester '73* (1950), except for a substantial share of the film's profits. It was the first time such an arrangement had ever been suggested, but the company making the film felt Stewart was so essential that they agreed. As a result Stewart made $600,000. The contract is rich in retrospective irony, not merely because it marked the advent of profit-sharing, but because the company who hired Stewart's services from MCA was Universal Pictures. Eventually MCA became so rich, out of precisely this kind of deal, that they were able to swallow Universal whole.

Perhaps MCA's most spectacular coup was its move into television production in the 1950s, through its subsidiary Revue. The Screen Actors Guild prohibited agents from acting as producers by a rule dating from 1939. This was intended to prevent any single company from acting as both employer and agent, an obvious conflict-of-interest under which the Guild's members might suffer. But waivers were regularly allowed to individual producers, and in July 1952, the President of the Screen Actors

Jules Stein *the Chicago ophthalmologist who founded MCA and made it the most powerful agency in America.*

Lew Wasserman *(above), Stein's protégé, who ruled MCA in Hollywood and, later, its subsidiary, Universal. An early coup was James Stewart's profit-sharing contract for* Winchester '73 *(right).*

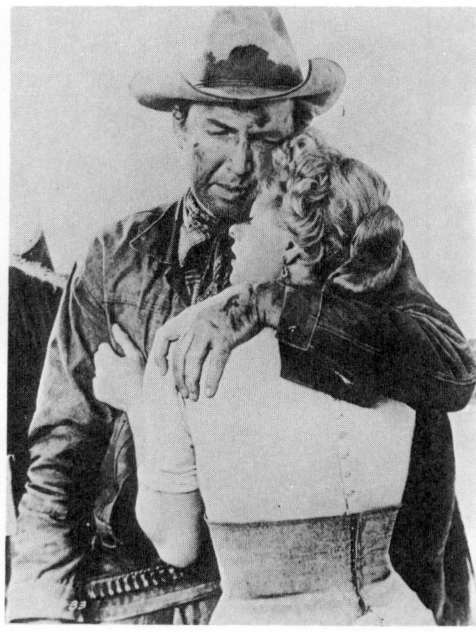

Ted Ashley, *founder of Ashley Famous and now boss of Warner Brothers.*

Guild, Ronald Reagan, granted MCA a massive seven year waiver. The company was allowed, exactly as Raymond Chandler had complained six months earlier, to act both as producer and agent in the packaging of television films. Naturally there were a few strings attached; actors did not have to pay commission to the agency side on money paid to them by the television side. Nor would MCA agents negotiate with MCA television. But the waiver remains extraordinary. It gave MCA an advantage over its television production rivals from which the latter never really recovered, and also incidentally promoted a confusion of the functions of producer and agent that exists in Hollywood to this day. Within ten years MCA's profits had soared.

Eventually, in 1962, under threat of prosecution from the Department of Justice, MCA closed down its agency and bought Decca Records and its subsidiary Universal Pictures. Stein became less involved while Lew Wasserman took up residence at Universal headquarters, the notorious Black Tower at Burbank, and went on to see his empire thrive in the wake of huge hits like *Jaws*. Ironically, considering its roots in the agency business, constant television film production allowed Wasserman to run Universal more like an old-time movie factory than any other studio in Hollywood, with strict security, some contracted employees and an impersonal, mechanistic atmosphere. But there could be no doubting its success. Wasserman was the first and most spectacularly successful agent to become a studio-head. Others would follow in a less historic, but equally determined fashion. The deal-makers were coming into their inheritance.

Ted Ashley and Ashley Famous

While the MCA story reflects Hollywood's changing economic structure, Ted Ashley's story illustrates how the deal-makers changed the business's style. Ashley's switch from agenting to movie production came five years after Wasserman's in 1967, when Ashley left his enormously successful agency business to take over Warner Bros and set about rebuilding it into one of the most successful studios in film history.

Unlike the moguls of the old days, Ted Ashley has enjoyed little publicity – indeed in his long career he appears to have given only one personality interview – but his life has all the trappings of a fairy story. He was born Theodore Assofsky on August 3rd, 1922, the son of a Russian-Jewish tailor who suffered from tuberculosis; the family lived initially in a one-room Brooklyn apartment without running water. After studying accounting at night-school, Ashley went at the age of 17 to work for the William Morris Agency, which was then as much concerned with the humble worlds of radio and vaudeville as with theatre and movies. He began in 1939 as what was virtually a messenger-boy, but soon started to handle commissions for some of the agency's scores of clients, from comics and radio announcers to tap-dancers and musicians. By 1946 he had observed that the simple function of agenting (namely, finding jobs and handling bookings) could be supplemented by the more delicate and ultimately remunerative job of personal or 'creative' management. In that year he left William Morris to set up Ashley Personal Management Associates, and he was able to persuade several of his former clients to give him ten per cent as a management fee in addition to the agency fee they were still paying William Morris. The larger agency was furious, but there was nothing they could do since Ashley could not even be accused of poaching their business; he had simply seen a gap and exploited it.

The distinction between agenting and management is as fundamental to the new Hollywood as it is mysterious to the outsider. Both jobs overlap and both are often loosely lumped under the 'agent' category, but the agent is concerned with the details of the next job and the manager is concerned (to quote a leading one) with 'the overall development of the client's career as well as who he is sleeping with, how his kids are doing in school, what's in his savings account and whether his wife is

happy.' The manager, to use a favourite Hollywood expression, is *family*. As well as an agent and a manager, some big stars have a publicity agent to handle press relations.

It is the manager, the intimate overseer of the client, whose power has burgeoned in post-war Hollywood. And part of Ashley's genius in those early days at William Morris was to spot the need for this kind of close relationship and then to build from there, while at the same time realizing the immense possibilities open to the agent who was prepared to combine clients into packages for media sale.

After leaving William Morris, Ashley began accumulating clients as fast as possible. It is recorded that every few months in those early days he would sit down at his kitchen table to add his savings to his projected profits, and work out how many new agent/managers he could hire who would bring their clients with them. By 1954 he had formed the Ashley Famous Agency and in the 1950s, as television got under way, Ashley began packaging shows featuring his clients. Ultimately he would bring to the networks such shows as *Candid Camera, Dr Kildare, The Twilight Zone* and *The Defenders*, and by an extraordinary quirk of finance, when such packages were sold to the networks, his agency collected, not merely ten per cent of the fees of those involved, but ten per cent of the whole budget. Very rapidly Ashley Famous became one of the most successful agencies in show business.

Ashley's style as a negotiator was in strict contrast to the hard-selling, table-slamming vulgarities of the old-style agent. The man who was to guide Warner Brothers into a pre-eminent position via *Summer of 42* (1971), *The Exorcist* (1973), *All the President's Men* (1976), and numerous Clint Eastwood movies is famous for his naturally subdued and pleasant manner; in fact he claims that he cannot remember ever having raised his voice. However, his toughness and shrewdness are beautifully illustrated by a rare personal recollection from his agency days which he revealed to New York Magazine in June 1974.

Ashley tells how he went into a meeting at the American television network NBC, and informed them that, after a year of discussion, Danny Kaye was prepared to go on TV but the fee for his programme would be $135,000, in those days a record. The executives were appalled, claiming no sponsor would be prepared to put up the money. Whereupon Ashley replied that he had already sold half of the programme to a tobacco firm and had their order letter in his pocket. One of the executives asked to see the letter while another tried to restrain him, saying, 'If Ted says he's got it, he's got it.' The first executive persisted. Ashley replied simply: 'I'll show it to you after I close the deal someplace else.' Shortly afterwards the deal was signed with the rival CBS network for precisely the same figure, and Ashley sent the NBC executive a copy of the tobacco company's letter, just as he had described it at the meeting. The NBC executive who had stuck up for Ashley's honesty subsequently became head of the network. History does not relate what happened to the doubter.

'What I achieved there,' says Ashley, 'and this has to do with the whole business of how you sell people – was not merely to sell Danny Kaye. I was selling one other fella. I was selling me.'

The story reveals Ashley's ambition. Making money was not, as it had been for agents in the past, the primary consideration. He was out to sell himself to an entertainment industry which badly needed a new breed of strongmen. They bought him and many others.

All the President's Men *(far left) was one of the numerous hits that steered Warners, under Ted Ashley, to a pre-eminent position in the 1970s. Clint Eastwood as cop Harry Callahan in* Dirty Harry *(left) and its sequels was also a factor, as was the nostalgic* Summer of '42 *(right).*

Creative Management Associates

Alongside Ashley Famous and MCA, the other great success story among the agents was Creative Management Associates. This was founded by Freddie Fields and David Begelman in the early 1960s to capitalize on the dissolution of MCA. It quickly amassed a stunning line-up of talent including Paul Newman, Steve McQueen, Barbra Streisand and Robert Redford. Movies packaged by the company included: *The Towering Inferno* (1974); *Dog Day Afternoon* (1975); *The Sting* (1973); and *Butch Cassidy and the Sundance Kid* (1969).

A list of CMA's former employees now in major production jobs indicates clearly the power to be derived from agenting. Besides Fields (now an independent producer – *Looking for Mr Goodbar*, 1977, *American Gigolo*, 1980) and Begelman (MGM, formerly Columbia) the list includes Alan Ladd Jr. (Ladd Co., formerly Fox), Daniel Melnick (Fox, formerly Columbia) and Mike Medavoy (Orion, formerly UA).

Freddie Fields is quite open about how he saw his role at that time: 'The studios had dropped the ball. They had become less creative and more caught up with financial considerations. My obligation was obviously to try and make things better for my clients and at the same time be more productive for the industry . . . a gap needed to be filled.'

The rise of deal-psychology

But why did a gap need to be filled? The argument is circular. The agents moved into production because their power had already changed production in such a way that agents possessed exactly the skills it required. It was no longer an assembly-line but a highly competitive market-place where the individual risks and rewards were greater than they had ever been. Each film became the product of long and frequently tortuous negotiations to establish whether, and on what terms and with whom, it would be made. The creators were as involved in these negotiations as the businessmen, since the negotiations were concerned not merely with profits and percentages but with rewrites and budgets. It was only at the end of this labyrinthine tunnel, called the deal, that the actual process of shooting could begin.

Often it never did begin. In her essay 'In Hollywood', Joan Didion describes a conversation between a film-maker and an agent in the closing stages of a deal for a picture that was about to be abandoned: 'It had been a very creative deal and they had run with it as far as they could run and they had had some fun and now the fun was over, as it also would have been had they made the picture.'

The description adeptly conveys the level of fantasy involved, the 'fun' of imaginary constructions regardless of whether they come to anything. Like any gamble, the deal feeds on its own mythology. If a picture is made and hits the jackpot, its deal, as the same essay shows, quickly becomes the stuff of legend:

> I talk on the telephone to an agent, who tells me that he has on his desk a check made out to a client for $1,275,000, the client's share of first profits on a picture now in release. Last week, in someone's office, I was shown another such check, this one made out for $4,850,000. Every year there are a few such checks around town. An agent will speak of such a check as being 'on my desk' or 'on Guy McElwaine's desk' as if the exact physical location lent the piece of paper its credibility. One year they might be the

The deal *is analogous to gambling at cards. The independent producer plays his cards, the elements in his package, and frequently loses. Occasionally, the bank (one of the major studios or a smaller production company) pays out a little in development money. More rarely the bank pays out sufficient money for the film to be made. Then the producer has a chance of hitting the jackpot.*

Frank Yablans *(right), former Paramount boss and one of Hollywood's best-known survivors. 'Film by film,' he is fond of saying, 'this business is nothing but a craps game.'*

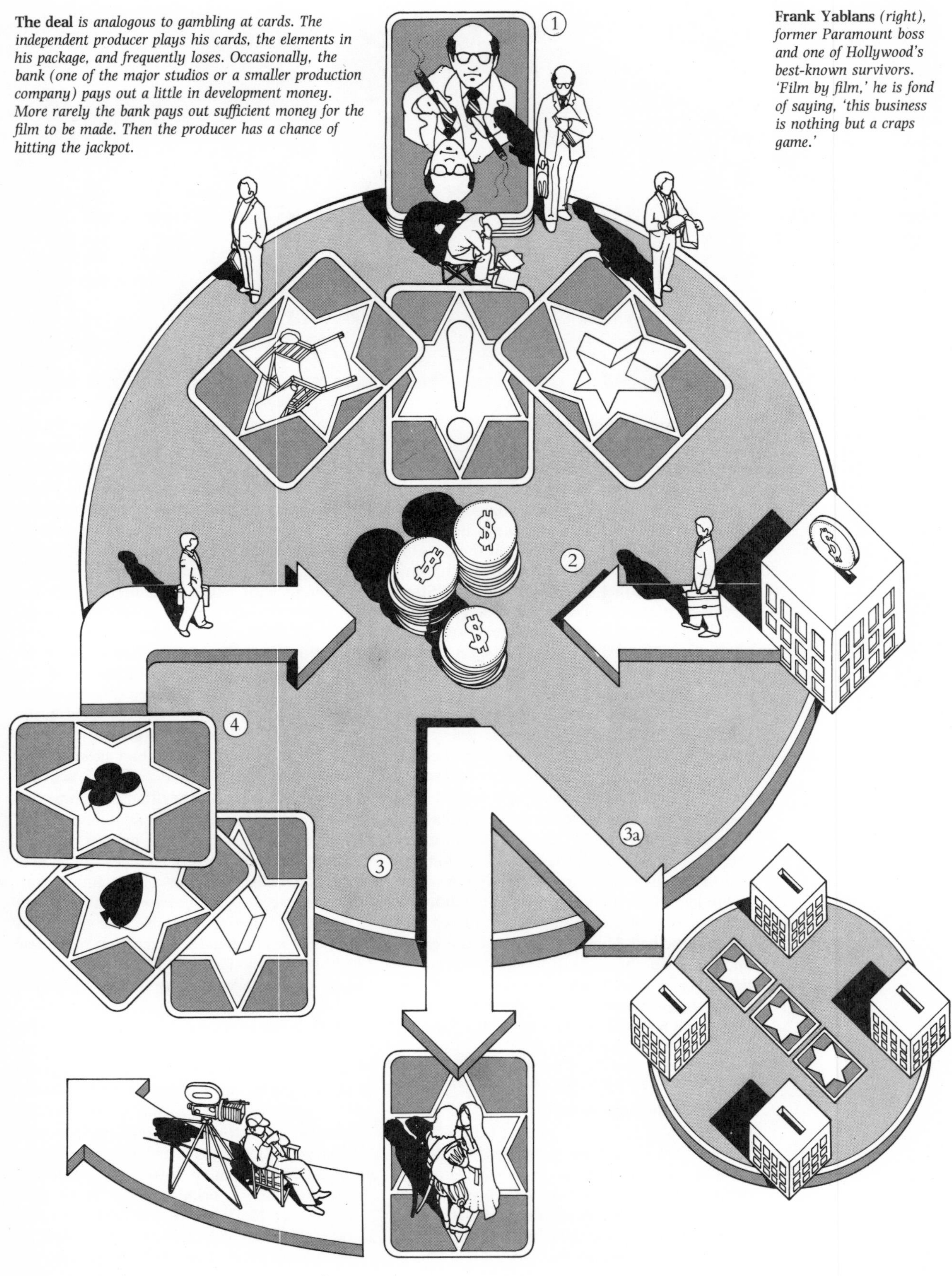

1 *The producer shows his cards. He has three elements: a successful director, a strong idea and a bankable star.*

2 *A major studio bids for the package and becomes the game's banker. The producer has won some development money.*

EITHER 3 *The studio eventually declares 'script satisfaction' and then 'election to proceed'. The budget is approved and the movie goes into production. The producer wins more money, which he will spend on making the movie.*

OR 3a *More often the studio has second thoughts and decides the cards are not worth higher stakes. The project goes into limited turn-around. The producer can lay the same cards before other studios, who can buy the hand from the banker; but the producer cannot change the cards.*

4 *Production completed, the cards turn out to be aces: the movie is a blockbusting success. The producer thinks he has won the jackpot at last, but before paying his winnings the studio deducts an overhead charge, deducts the costs of prints and promotion and extracts its distribution fee. The jackpot is smaller than the producer expected, and it is a long time before it is paid out.*

Midnight Cowboy and *Butch Cassidy* checks, another year the *Love Story* and *Godfather* checks.

In a curious way these checks are not 'real', not real money in the sense that a check for a thousand dollars can be real money; no one 'needs' $4,850,000, nor is it really disposable income. It is instead the unexpected payoff on dice rolled a year or two before, and its reality is altered not only by the time lapse but by the fact that no one ever counted on the payoff. A four-million-dollar windfall has the aspect only of Monopoly money, but the actual pieces of paper which bear such figures have, in the community, a totemic significance. They are totems of the action . . .

Didion's account is impressionistic, but it conveys a far better idea of the wish-fulfilment underlying the deal than do the turgid contracts which are the deal's end-product. Pages of tedious exposition would be necessary to explain the movie contract's legal and financial jargon (appropriately known as 'boiler-plating'): terms like 'hard floors', 'rolling break', 'cut-offs', 'conversions', 'gross participation', 'cross-collateralization' – and at the end of the exercise little of the true flavour of deal-making would be communicated. It is better to start at the beginning.

The development deal: stage one

The game usually begins with an 'independent' producer, who with a very few exceptions is someone faced with the task of selling a project to a studio. Occasionally the producer is merely another element in a lucrative agency package, and therefore comes to the project after it has been initiated by an agent. More often, he is out on his own. Attempts to define a producer's functions have filled many pages. In the old days of the studio-factories, producers acted as overseers and as liaison between the bosses and the directors who made their pictures. Within the new system, most producers became 'independent', meaning only that they must package each picture individually and hawk it around to studios for finance. Some producers may also be writers or directors or actors; some attend to each production in minute detail, while others delegate everything; but generally speaking the producer's organizational skills will lie in business and finance rather than the specialist crafts of film-making. The only real tool of his trade is the telephone: the former Paramount boss and leading independent producer Frank Yablans once joked: 'If someone could find a way of grafting a phone-jack to my ass, I wouldn't even need an office!' Many of today's producers are former agents. Producers' Association rules nominally prevent someone doing both jobs at once, but the distinction has become increasingly fine, because agenting and packaging skills are so essential in assembling the 'elements' that will satisfy a major studio.

'Elements' are fundamental to deal-making. There seems to be general agreement that two strong elements are enough to close a deal, but conflicting opinions as to what makes an element desirable. In 1980 a package floated around the Hollywood studios which linked star Jane Fonda and director James Bridges (*The China Syndrome*, 1979, *Urban Cowboy*, 1980) to the idea for an as yet unwritten script. The down-payment on that package, before a page of script was even written, was set at $2m. But nobody doubted that a development deal would be made, even if no film ever resulted from the purchase. The combination of a top box-office star and a hit director would prove irresistible to someone.

Packages of this kind are the exception, and studios will always try to avoid committing themselves to substantial expenditure upfront. But a hit star and a hit director form the perfect equation. A good script can also be a useful element as a bait for bigger fish, but generally it will need to have a star or director attached before the studio takes it seriously. An idea on its own, even a brilliant one like the recent *Escape From New York* ('1997: New York City is a maximum security prison') rarely constitutes an element. 'Ideas are like haemorrhoids' one producer observes scathingly, 'sooner or later everybody has one.' But *Escape From New York* plus director John Carpenter – the man who made *The Fog* and *Halloween* – is a different matter. It is, as David Thomson points out (see page 142), a matter of chemistry: an idea plus a name and bam!

Much of the time, the independent producer may find this chemistry difficult to achieve, and even if he succeeds in getting a development deal providing some development money, he must live with the knowledge that the majority of projects commissioned by the major studios are ultimately abandoned. Because the most expensive part of a movie's career is principal photography and distribution, any major will allow millions of dollars each year in aborted development costs – projects developed and then scrapped. This is easier to justify to their boards than spending $20m. on financing and promoting a single film that nosedives with the public.

It is this fact, more than any other, that determines what has been called the 'deal mentality'. A producer knows the chances of any deal coming to fruition are relatively slim,

Joseph E. Levine *(centre right) on location during the filming of* A Bridge Too Far, *the film in which he had to cast either* **Robert Redford** *(above) or* **Steve McQueen** *(above right) in order to raise the money to make the film at all. He had already cast* **Ryan O'Neal** *(far right),* **James Caan** *(farthest right) and*

and cannot often afford to wait around wondering whether this particular project will be 'the one'. If he or she is a former agent, his training will incline him to handle 40 deals a day rather than concentrate on one. So, in the world of production he may easily become like someone firing a starting-pistol over and over again but never looking over his shoulder to see whether the race has started. Once a studio has agreed a development deal's first stage, he moves rapidly off in search of other deals. The value of each will vary enormously, but in a $100,000 development shared between a writer, director and producer, the producer is likely to get least of all.

Consequently at the lower end of the market, the independent producer is unlikely to see much money while a project is in development. There is a celebrated Hollywood saying that a producer cannot make a living out of his job; he can only grow rich. The appearance of wealth and success is important in deal-psychology, especially for the producer, but producers' development fees are rarely substantial enough in themselves to cover the expenditure of their search for the right package. The small-time independent producer therefore has much of the desperation of a small-time casino player who has hocked everything to get into a jackpot game, where the millions appear rarely and the interim payments hardly more often. Moreover, unlike the writer or actor or director, the producer is generally an entrepreneur with skills that are hard to define and even harder to market. He is essentially a deal-maker, and stands or falls on his success in that sphere.

In the circumstances it is not surprising that there are horror stories. One writer of good reputation, who has tended to specialize in thrillers, recently sold a script option to a producer for a tiny sum. After a year the producer explained he had been unable to interest anyone in the project and asked to renew the option for a second year. A year later he wanted to renew again, but by then the writer had become suspicious. He soon discovered that the project had been sold in the first year and the producer had simply forged the writer's signature on the necessary contract and taken the money himself. Anywhere else, such patent theft would have ended up in the courts, but in Hollywood there is a mutual understanding between those who have assets at the poker-table (such as a successful writer) and those who do not (a small independent producer). In this case the writer was content simply to collect his money, though the producer had to mortgage his house in order to give it to him. A few months later they were back talking deals.

Stars and the development deal

One of the more harrowing features of the deal is inevitably the hunt for a leading player. It's sometimes forgotten that in Hollywood's so-called golden age few employees suffered more from the power-mania of the old studio bosses than the stars. The contract system with its vicious 'suspension' clause meant that a studio head could not only force stars to perform in sub-standard films, but also (with a little chicanery) lay them off for long periods unpaid when they could literally starve. The liberation from this tyranny came with the supreme court decision won by Olivia de Havilland (see page 18), and almost by way of revenge on the system that enslaved them, the stars currently exercise as much power as anyone in the industry. The result is intense competition for a comparatively static number of major talents. 'There are,' as Jack Nicholson says, 'only so many holes in the wall and everybody's pushing.' Terry Semel, an executive at Warner Brothers, has the same feeling: 'In 1970 you had about 15 important box office stars and five or six studios competing rather actively for their services. . . . Today, if you sit down to list the top stars, it is hard to come up with any more than 15, but instead of five or six companies, you can find around 15 companies fighting for the same people.'

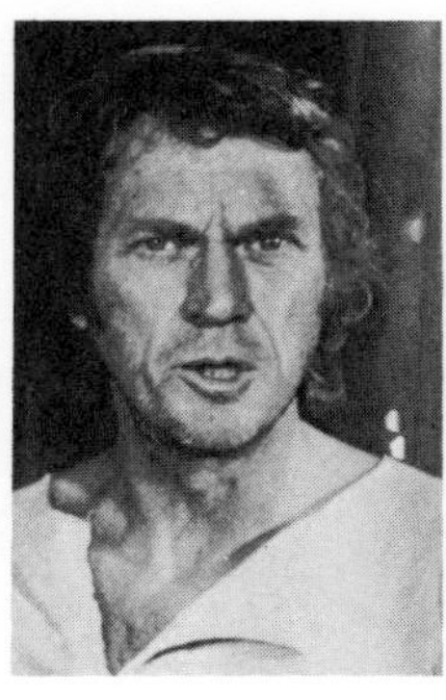

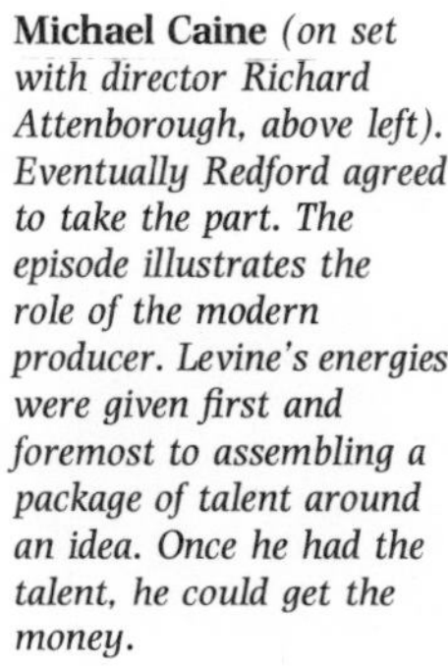

Michael Caine *(on set with director Richard Attenborough, above left). Eventually Redford agreed to take the part. The episode illustrates the role of the modern producer. Levine's energies were given first and foremost to assembling a package of talent around an idea. Once he had the talent, he could get the money.*

In order to get a major star to consider a script, the producer may very well have to find a guarantee of $1m. as some kind of insurance that the project has money behind it, and is not simply a fishing expedition. Moreover, even supposing a producer is lucky enough to have some personal relationship with a star, and the star informally reads the script and agrees to do it, that agreement may be worth almost nothing in practice. 'A true agreement only comes' says one producer ruefully 'when they're ready to go to the drafting stage. They can read something and like it, but they have an attorney, an agent, an accountant, a manager and a publicist ready to veto it.' And on top of everything, stars command such huge salaries that they have little pressing need to work unless, like Jane Fonda, they need the money in pursuit of some cause.

An entertaining account of this fraught period in a developing movie's life appears in screenwriter William Goldman's description of the making of Joseph E. Levine's blockbuster *A Bridge Too Far* (1977). In order to get the cash they needed to make the film, Levine – a notoriously shrewd producer – and director Richard Attenborough had to sign either Robert Redford or Steve McQueen, but they could offer neither actor a percentage of the profits because the film already contained other stars (James Caan, Michael Caine, Ryan O'Neal) who would certainly make similar demands. The producer finally agreed to pay Redford or McQueen half a million dollars a week. With this first problem solved, another arose from the stars' agents who demanded legal guarantees that, even if Levine did not manage to obtain backing for his film, and the project fell apart (as many expected), he would still be personally liable to pay the stars their money.

After much squabbling Levine accepted these terms and serious negotiations with the stars began. On a Tuesday McQueen turned the project down flat. With a hint of panic Levine and Attenborough met Redford the following Friday, who said he would give them an answer by Monday. Goldman takes up the story:

That weekend, McQueen came back in.

Or wanted to. But there was now only one star part left, and that had been officially offered to Redford.

The reason for McQueen's change of heart had to do with another film which had raised their money on the promise of delivering him to star. When he refused, they kept upping their offer and he kept refusing. Finally they reached three million and he said no.

Then someone got the idea of doing the two films back-to-back – McQueen insisted on both or nothing – and he would play three weeks in one, three weeks in the other.

McQueen's representatives and the other film's lawyers begin flooding Levine's hotel rooms. They explain that McQueen is now available. Levine explains that he has no part to offer. It's all up to Redford now.

'You'll never get Redford,' McQueen's people assure Levine. 'I know one thing and it's that you have no chance in this world to get Redford and I don't think you ought to take the chance of passing up McQueen.'

But there is no part to offer McQueen.

'You're not listening,' McQueen's people say. 'You will not get Redford. Not possible. Now do you want to know McQueen's terms? Three million for three weeks. He'll do the two pictures, you'll schedule them so he doesn't have any time in between, six million for six weeks.'

Anything else? Levine wonders.

'He has some people he'd like to take along.'

How much for the friends? Levine asks.

'Fifty thousand maybe.'

Levine nods.

'Then there's the house in Palm Springs.'

The what?

'Steve's house. He's got a place in Palm Springs he can't get rid of. So you'll buy that.'

That's very nice of me, Levine says. How much do I get to buy the house for?

'$470,000.'

The demands go on and on, the madness

The Missouri Breaks *(left) was one of the contractual coups of the 1970s: Jack Nicholson and Marlon Brando as co-stars.*

building, until the weekend is over and Redford says yes, he'll do *Bridge*. Levine is on the next plane out. The raid is done. He's been there for nine days, the longest stay of his career, and he's personally on the line for well into eight figures.

But he's got his cast. And now he knows, at long long last, that the picture will get made.

One of the results of the stars' extraordinary power in the setting up of movies has been a phenomenon known to the industry as a 'deal picture'. A 'deal picture' is a glittering package of talent and subject which will take months of complex negotiations to put together with shooting almost as a secondary consideration. A perfect example is *The Missouri Breaks* (1976) which set *Bonnie and Clyde*'s director, Arthur Penn, alongside Marlon Brando ($1,250,000 plus 11.3 per cent of all gross receipts over $8,850,000) and Jack Nicholson ($1,250,000 plus 10 per cent of all gross receipts over $12,500,000) playing respectively a hired gun and a horse-thief. Arthur Penn subsequently observed scathingly: 'The picture took only a few months to shoot but the deal lasted nearly a year.' Most of the lawyers and agents and accountants were perfectly satisfied with the resulting fees and percentages. The fact that the movie failed at the box office was almost a secondary consideration. One industry observer commented: 'They would have been better off filming the deal. It was more interesting.'

Directors and the development deal

The difficulty of acquiring a star is one reason why directors have assumed enormous importance in deal-making. For one thing most directors have good relationships with certain stars, and their support for a project may very well deliver the magic name. For another, contrary to the assumptions of some outsiders, the studios have considerable (in some cases even exaggerated) respect for directors. And their respect is not limited merely to those directors who have had hits. Critical notices will play a part in the studio's attitude, as will past work and the film-maker's relationships with major stars. Not a single Michael Apted movie had made any money in America when he was hired by Universal, a notoriously tough employer, to make *Coal Miner's Daughter* (1980), but his previous film *Agatha* had had reasonable notices and starred Dustin Hoffman. That, and the commercial possibilities of country singer Loretta Lynn's life-story, were enough to make a deal and the results gave Universal little cause for regret. Even more remarkable is the fact that Robert Altman had the distinction of making eleven financial turkeys in a row after *M*A*S*H* (1970), which must be something of an industry record, yet at the end of the decade he was still regarded as a marketable asset – so much so that Paramount put him in charge of their major production of 1980: *Popeye*. Prestige and cultural pretensions (often of an entirely spurious kind) can be enough to keep a player in the game for years.

Mike Nichols *(above), director of the huge 1960s hit* The Graduate. *For some time afterwards he could write his own ticket.*

'The time to hit,' says an anonymous agent, quoted in John Gregory Dunne's *The Studio*, a penetrating story of Fox under Richard Zanuck in the late 1960s, 'is before your first picture comes out. You get the word-of-mouth going. Nobody's seen the picture. It can be a piece of shit, but who knows? You get the word-of-mouth going . . . you spread the word that George Cukor loved it. Somebody tells somebody else that George Cukor loved it and pretty soon you're not in if you haven't seen it and said it was sensational. Natalie Wood, Arthur

Michael Crichton *(right) on the 'Jefferson Institute' set of his ingenious thriller* Coma *from Robin Cook's novel. After* Coma *Crichton was forced to sell his next, unwritten, script for a large sum.*

Westworld *(above), with Yul Brynner, another of Crichton's hits, was viewed with deep suspicion by MGM until it made money.*

Jacobs, they all *loved* it. Who cares if they've seen it? It's the names that count. Once the word-of-mouth momentum gets going, you move in. The guy's locked in for six pictures all over town. If the picture's good, fine, but if it stinks, he's still set up for a ton . . . Everybody's looking for the killing. So you bomb out at ten million. Well, you put together a big one, and the next time out, you might hit with one!'

Of course, if a director wants unquestioning backing from a studio for an unusual or idiosyncratic project, there are few better calling cards than a blockbuster hit. Consequently some of the follow-up movies to blockbusters make a curious study in indulgence, like William Friedkin's *Sorcerer* (GB: *Wages of Fear*) (1977), which followed *The Exorcist* (1973) and Peter Bogdanovich's *Daisy Miller* (1974), which followed *Paper Moon* (1973).

Film-maker Mike Nichols has christened this bizarre moment, when the financiers become putty in the film-maker's hands, the 'green awning effect' and goes on to illustrate what he means. After making an enormous hit, *The Graduate* (1967), Nichols is in a meeting with Joseph E. Levine, and explains to him that he wants to do a picture called 'The Green Awning'. 'What's it about?' says the producer. 'Well you know,' Nichols replies, 'there's this green awning on Fifth Avenue in New York about 63rd Street, and all those exciting people walk down Fifth Avenue but none of them walk underneath the green awning. Then there are all those interesting street characters but they don't go near it either.' 'But what's it about?' the producer repeats. 'Well it's just this green awning,' says Nichols, 'two hours of it.' So Joseph E. Levine says, 'It's unusual . . . It sounds interesting. *Let's do it.*'

This is the development deal at its most surrealistic, when it concerns projects that are no more than vague ideas in their creators' minds. Michael Crichton, who has battled his way through the Hollywood system from a highly successful career as a novelist to make two hits of considerable originality, *Westworld* (1973) and *Coma* (1978), found himself in a tangle worthy of *Alice in Wonderland* following *Coma*'s success. 'I had a verbal understanding with a studio to let them see my next film project. That was all. No money had changed hands. Not a word was written. And in time I decided to write it as a book instead, so it seemed perfectly reasonable to say to them let's just forget it. There was nothing in writing and no money involved. But the studio said we still want the project and, even though they had not seen one word of it, they seemed to think it was worth an awful lot of money. I was very uncomfortable, because I don't like to sell things before they're even written. So I said: 'But what if you don't like it?' And they said: 'That's our problem. We really feel you have an obligation.' So I had to sell them this blank page for a huge amount of money. It's very peculiar.'

Crichton's enviable predicament is not untypical of an industry which has an irresistible compulsion to gamble on past success. In the long run many of the smarter and younger directors have been able to exploit this compulsion to their advantage. But few have managed to do this with quite such startling success as George Lucas.

George Lucas's *Star Wars* deal

When he embarked on the venture that became *Star Wars* (1977), George Lucas felt that he had been abused and exploited by the studios and he was determined to get something back for himself. His first film *THX1138* (1971), a low budget science fiction drama made under the auspices of Francis Coppola's

Continued on page 54

Star Wars: the conception, production and distribution of a blockbuster. In real money terms Star Wars is far and away the most successful movie there has ever been. If inflation is taken into account, only Gone with the Wind has earned more from initial release. By the end of 1980, according to its producer Gary Kurtz, Star Wars had grossed $510m. from the worldwide box office. Star Wars' writer and director, George Lucas, was thought naively optimistic when he predicted before release that the film's rental might be between $16m. and $25m. In fact by the end of 1980 Star Wars Productions, a company formed by Lucas and Kurtz, had received $55m. as its share in profits; some of this was passed on to various unnamed profit participants and the rest was invested in the sequel, The Empire Strikes Back. Twentieth Century-Fox, who had invested $11m. to make the film and a further $16.5m. to release and promote it, had made a profit from theatrical release of $88.5m.; this was on top of their distribution fee (30 per cent of rentals) which totalled $75m. One of the stars, Sir Alec Guinness, had been granted 2.25 per cent of the profit: by the end of 1980 this was worth $3.3m. There follows a graphic representation of the biggest movie bonanza – so far.

February 1973 Lucas writes a 30 page treatment of Star Wars and produces three paintings and some drawings.

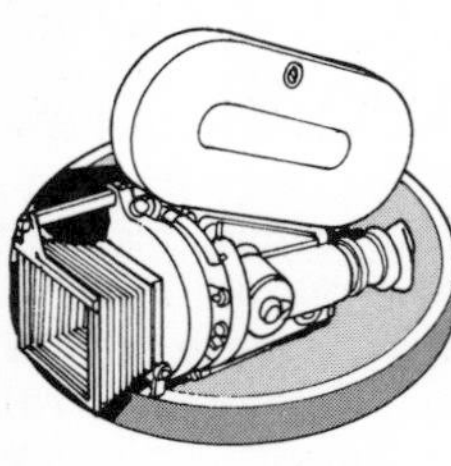

$300,000 cover stage rents, including studios, effects stages, music and post-synchronization studios, offices.

$300,000 are spent on costumes.

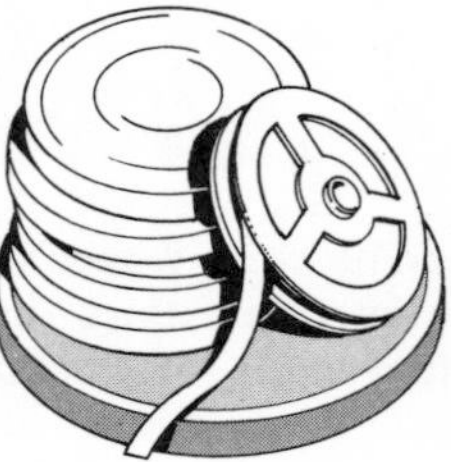

$200,000 pay for film and processing.

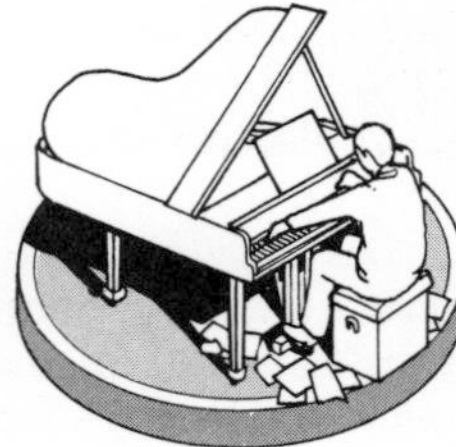

$100,000 are spent on music, including John Williams' score.

$2,100,000 covers unit salaries: production assistants, camera, sound, make-up, hair, editors, art department.

$200,000 are spent on insurance.

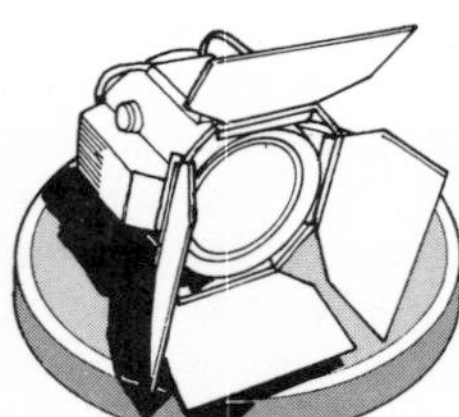

$1,600,000 go on set construction and lighting.

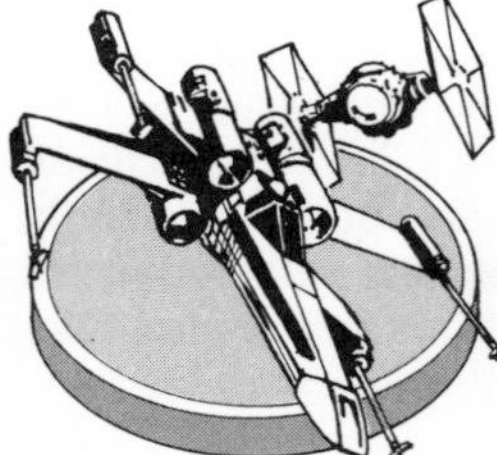

$3,900,000 are spent on special effects and models of space-ships and robots.

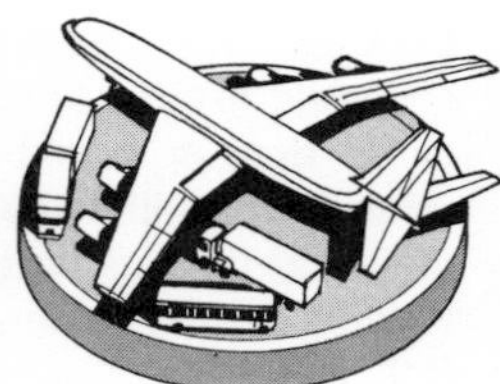

$700,000 go on transport and location costs, principally in Tunisia.

$800,000 cover the cost of finance and Fox's overhead and completion bond.

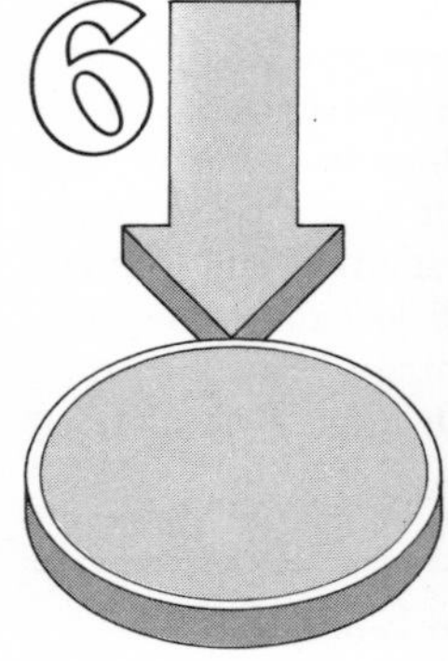

May 1977 Star Wars is premiered in Hollywood. General release follows and the film earns a rental of $3,500,000 in nine days. In two months it recoups the entire costs of production and promotion.

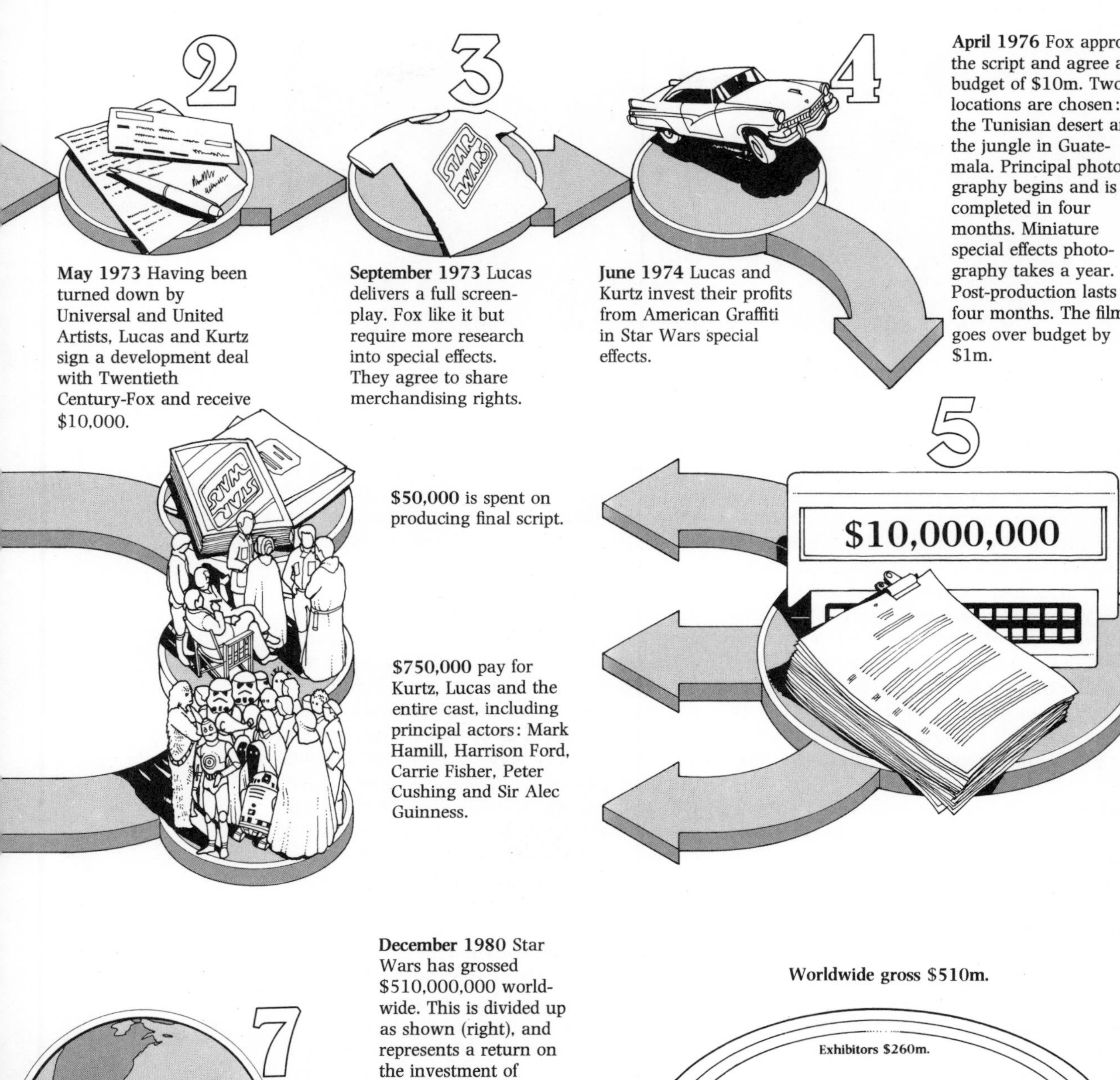

May 1973 Having been turned down by Universal and United Artists, Lucas and Kurtz sign a development deal with Twentieth Century-Fox and receive $10,000.

September 1973 Lucas delivers a full screenplay. Fox like it but require more research into special effects. They agree to share merchandising rights.

June 1974 Lucas and Kurtz invest their profits from American Graffiti in Star Wars special effects.

April 1976 Fox approve the script and agree a budget of $10m. Two locations are chosen: the Tunisian desert and the jungle in Guatemala. Principal photography begins and is completed in four months. Miniature special effects photography takes a year. Post-production lasts four months. The film goes over budget by $1m.

$50,000 is spent on producing final script.

$750,000 pay for Kurtz, Lucas and the entire cast, including principal actors: Mark Hamill, Harrison Ford, Carrie Fisher, Peter Cushing and Sir Alec Guinness.

7

December 1980 Star Wars has grossed $510,000,000 worldwide. This is divided up as shown (right), and represents a return on the investment of $27.5m. of 1855 per cent. To the profits made by Star Wars Productions must be added the immense amount made from merchandising. In one month alone, July 1977, $100,000 worth of tee-shirts and $260,000 worth of intergalactic bubblegum were sold.
Star Wars' sequel, The Empire Strikes Back, was released in 1980 and proves to be the most successful film of the year with a US rental of $124m.

Worldwide gross $510m.

Exhibitors $260m.
Negative cost $11m.
Prints, ads $16.5m.
Fox $88.5m.
Lucas, Kurtz and others $55.7m.
Fox's distribution fee $75m.
Sir Alec Guinness $3.3m.

Worldwide rental $250m.

Profit
Distribution fee
Breakeven

Star Wars *(far left), with Gary Kurtz, right, and George Lucas behind the camera.*

American Graffiti *(left) was Kurtz and Lucas's first big success, making* Star Wars *possible.*

Zoetrope company, was all but disowned by its backers Warners, and eventually appeared in truncated form. His second film *American Graffiti* (1973) nearly met the same fate at an early screening when two Universal executives described it respectively as a 'disgrace' and an 'embarrassment'. It was only because of the intervention of Coppola that the film was given a chance and became a major hit. At this point Lucas had received only $20,000 for three years' work; he was deeply in debt and claimed to have made even less money on *Graffiti* than on the flop that preceded it. However, after the success of *Graffiti* Lucas had some status as a hit-maker and he used it, first to write a deal with Fox and then to create a film that would make him a millionaire many times over.

Lucas appears to have calculated the commercial ingredients of *Star Wars* as coolly as any banker. Even the title was part of his calculation: 'The title was an insurance policy,' he has said. 'The studio didn't see it that way; they thought SF was a very bad genre, that women didn't like it . . . but we calculated that there are about eight million dollars-worth of SF freaks in the USA and they will go to absolutely anything with a title like *Star Wars*. I reckoned we should do sixteen million domestic and if the film catches right maybe twenty-five million. The chances were a zillion to one of it going further.'

When it came to the deal, Lucas's first coup was to retain all the merchandising rights for his own company. This would include: bubble gum, toys, tee-shirts, watches and breakfast cereal. Because he was more convinced than Fox that he was manufacturing a hit, he was able to persuade them to part with the merchandising rights, but perhaps his most far-sighted move was to retain virtually sole control of the *Star Wars* sequels. The majority shareholder in the sequels to one of the most profitable films in history (a film that might have been designed to inaugurate a series, so closely did it follow the old serial pattern) was George Lucas' company Star Wars Productions.

The writer and the development deal

The writer may be more closely involved in the earliest stages of the development deal than any of a film's creators, sometimes even the producer. In some respects this is an advantage. Unlike a director or a cinematographer, the writer does not have to be hired by a studio in order to go to work. But a writer may also become embroiled in all the various devices and entanglements that are a feature of an agent's or a producer's early attempts to interest a studio in a film. Sometimes an agent will 'shotgun' a script overnight to twenty of the major buyers and create an artificial deadline for them to reach a decision. This auction approach has, on a very few occasions, resulted in studios paying out huge sums for unfilmable material, but more often, according to most agents, it results in no sale at all. Recently it has proved more profitable to go the traditional producing route and match a script to a director or star, combining the suitable elements.

A harrowing aspect of the deal for the screenwriter is the numerous rewrites and changes that will inevitably be necessary before the studio and the director reach that elusive plateau known as 'script satisfaction'. Characters will be dropped, whole sequences changed and roles rewritten just to suit whoever is being wooed by the producer that week. As many as ten writers may come and go making uncredited contributions. Lorenzo Semple recalls having to rewrite the whole female lead for the remake of *King Kong* just because Barbra Streisand had expressed a passing interest, and in the event he could not be bothered to change it back. But such moments often come long after the original writer has been replaced.

Robert Benton, who had long experience as a screenwriter before he wrote and directed the hit *Kramer vs. Kramer* (1979), is particularly critical of the deal's demoralizing effects on the writer, and urges the need to experiment with ways that would turn the sheer strenuousness of the contract system to Hollywood's creative advantage: 'It has been said that every artistic

Kramer vs. Kramer *(right and far right), starring Meryl Streep and Dustin Hoffman with Justin Henry as the child, was a success partly because of writer/director Robert Benton's intense dedication to the project. He withdrew from another movie at a more advanced stage of development in order to make it.*

break-through has really consisted of somebody taking advantage of a technical break-through. For example, impressionism in painting could never have existed without tube paint. Well, I would say that the next break-through in movies might be a break-through in contract. If somebody could dream up a project structured in such a way that the writer could go away and do the 15 or 20 drafts that are necessary to make a screenplay work, then we might get a far higher proportion of filmable screenplays. At the moment the development deals work on a kind of scatter-gun theory. If you have as many people working on as many scripts as possible you hope through some blind chance to have several a year that are worth filming.'

Benton's approach may sound idealistic but, in his favour, it might be added that he defied one of the house rules of the poker-game by bowing out of a cast-iron United Artists contract with a definite start-date, even returning a large sum of money to the studio; he did this in order to begin work for Columbia on *Kramer vs. Kramer*, which was then in an early and tentative stage of development.

The development deal: stage two – drawing up contracts

Once a producer has been fortunate enough to get a studio seriously interested in a project and the major creative participants (known as 'above-the-line') have been settled, then serious negotiations can commence. At this point an awesome breed of economic and legal strategists step into the game. The people employed by the majors to negotiate and keep track of their various deals are salaried employees, not players, who consequently have everything to lose and nothing to gain from the agents and producers who congregate around them. One of these hired negotiators may be dealing with the substance of up to 50 deals every day, mostly over the telephone; he will be haggling over figures or elements, and constantly conferring with the studio president as to how each individual production is to be handled. One of the first things he will want to know is how much the participants made on their last films. There is an unwritten rule in Hollywood that no writer, director or star will work for less than they did on their previous picture, so theoretically an agent could lie to the studios about the client's previous employment in order to obtain a higher salary. In practice though, total disclosure is the rule among the employers, so a studio negotiator can very quickly check on the accuracy of what an agent tells him. With Hollywood as deal-oriented as it has been in recent years, it was only a matter of time before a studio negotiator moved over into film production, and this happened in at least one major studio, Twentieth Century-Fox, during 1980.

Because contracts run to tens of pages and are not finalized until well into a picture's production, the deal is sealed in the first place with deal-memos. These are exchanged between parties and lay out the basis of the agreement. The tortured language of the memos and the elephantine nature of the contracts reflect the fact, as actor Donald Sutherland observes, 'that so many people have taken so many unnatural liberties in the past.' Often, aware that a project has only a limited chance of ever reaching celluloid, a studio will try to negotiate a step-deal. This keeps the payments to a series of stages: assuming a writer is being offered $300,000 for a script, the studio might offer $20,000 on signature, a further $30,000 when a director is signed to the project, another $25,000 when a star is signed, $25,000 when a production date is set and the rest on completion of principal photography. Such an arrangement is favourable to the studio, because everyone knows the writer may never see anything more than the first payment. Jeff Berg, a highly successful agent, stated in *Film Comment* that he would never agree to such terms. He would either insist on all the money being paid upfront or allow the studio a short-term option so that, on expiry, the script would

Burt Reynolds *in* The End *(left), the dormant project which Reynolds' name was sufficient to reactivate.*

Cat on a Hot Tin Roof *(centre right) and* **Exodus** *(right) made a big name for Paul Newman. Consequently by the time of* **The Hustler** *(left) he was the subject of fierce studio competition. The resulting tussle had wide implications for the industry.*

revert to the writer.

If a star is involved, it becomes harder for the studio to resist making some major upfront payment and, with the competition for talent as urgent as it is, an agent frequently insists on inserting a clause into the contract known as 'pay-or-play'. At its harshest 'pay-or-play' will simply compel the studio to pay, for example, Robert Redford his full salary of, say, $2m. within a specified period whether or not they make the film: this is the deal described by Goldman for *A Bridge Too Far*. Slightly lower down the scale, with a less bankable star, the 'pay-or-play' will come into force at some specified time, for example once a start-date is agreed for shooting. When the agreed 'pay-or-play' point is reached, the director, star or writer will have to be paid in full regardless of whether a foot of film is shot.

Even the 'boiler-plated' contracts do not ensure harmony. Law-suits arising out of motion picture production fatten the pockets of the Los Angeles legal profession and in certain cases contracts are ignored altogether with little fear of legal sanction. American network television is well-known to suffer in this way. 'You sign a contract with an actor', says one TV executive, 'and if the TV series is a hit, the next year he won't even show up for rehearsal unless his contract is rewritten.' In such cases, the actor knows the TV company will probably prefer to pay up rather than risk losing a hit show in litigation.

Aborted development deals: 'Limited turn-around'

The evolution of any single motion picture deal is often sufficiently complex and dramatic to make a book in itself. At every stage of negotiation, from development to 'script satisfaction' to 'election to proceed', there are ploys and pitfalls, threats and flattery. Long delays punctuate each stage as, with dinosaur-like progress, the studio contemplates each tiny step towards production, knowing that millions of dollars may be lost if they move too fast on a project that isn't ready. 'The psychology of this whole industry is based on fear,' says one producer. 'The fear to make the film. The fear not to make it. The studios have to be constantly reassured.'

Frequently a studio will back out after a script is written and money has been invested. They will then decide to put the project into 'limited turn-around'. This means that for a limited period it can be offered to other studios, who can then buy out the original studio's interest. If the producer fails to find anyone else, the project reverts to the original studio and enters their enormous backlist of dormant properties. Occasionally a backlist property is revived; *The End* (1978) was at one stage optioned to a producer for a single dollar because it seemed so unlikely to be picked up. Then Burt Reynolds became interested and it was resurrected. But this is one of the exceptions; most dormant projects stay dormant.

Like every other part of the contract, the 'turn-around' clause has provoked much distress and huge quantities of litigation. One provision relating to it has given some agents more distress than they care to remember. Screenwriter John Gregory Dunne recalls his agent describing 'change-of-elements' as 'the worst clause in this business'.

Change-of-elements

The 'change-of-elements' clause first appeared in movie contracts during the 1960s. It means, basically, that during the one year or two year period of turn-around, when a project is on offer to other studios, it is impermissible to introduce some major change like a new script or a new star until the first studio's interest has been bought out. The difficulty appears to have originated in 1960 with *The Hustler*, a movie known to filmgoers for Paul Newman's fine performance as a pool-room hustler, but known to Hollywood for the beginning of 'change-of-elements'.

In April 1959 United Artists had announced

Robert Evans *(above), the former production head at Paramount, complains he has seen very little money from his percentages in several Paramount hits. For* **Marathon Man** *(above right) he began to receive a profit share four years after release.*

the acquisition of Walter Tevis's novel *The Hustler*, a sombre study of poolroom sharks; the film was to be produced and directed by Robert Rossen and was scheduled for principal photography that autumn. At some point in the summer UA became uneasy about what was potentially an uncommercial subject and put the project into turn-around. In October the film was re-announced by Twentieth Century-Fox with an important addition: Paul Newman, already a big star from late 1950s films like *From the Terrace*, *Cat on a Hot Tin Roof* and *Exodus*, had accepted the major part, making the project far more viable. UA suspected they had not been told the whole story when they decided to pull out, and around that time other studios began to fear that producers and agents were deliberately concealing elements during the development stage of projects, in order to raise additional development fees by shopping back and forth between studios. From this point a 'change-of-elements' clause began to be inserted into contracts.

Since no studio wants to be robbed of a major project by one of its rivals, it is easy to see the anxieties behind this precaution, but not quite so easy to see how even an unscrupulous producer can truly benefit from withholding a star's interest in a project. This may happen in a few isolated cases, but 'change-of-elements' is enormously resented by anyone trying to sell a rejected project to another studio. It literally prevents them from making any changes, and they may even feel inhibited about showing the script around. If a studio has invested money in a project (even a small amount like $50,000) and then abandoned it into turn-around, the project's creators are unable to develop it in any realistic sense until another studio has repaid all the money. The originators' predicament is worsened by the fact that an element is a vague and insubstantial thing at best. If the producers change the ending, or introduce a potential hit song, or rejig a central suspense sequence, or interest a record company in promoting the album, do any of these constitute 'change-of-elements'? They are trapped, knowing that, once in turn-around, it is almost impossible to re-interest the original studio in any changes they make, while on the other hand the alteration best designed to secure backing from another studio will probably bring the lawyers down on their heads.

Points and profits

Even after agreements are signed and production begins, problems surrounding the deal frequently continue. A source of endless dispute arises from the question of 'points', that is the percentage of the film's profits awarded by the studio to its producers and makers. Naturally the studio likes to retain as much rental revenue (the money returned to it once the exhibitors have taken their cut) as it can, and often it will refuse to part with any of it until it declares a film to be in profit, a much-disputed figure (see page 33). This practice is what producer Robert Evans has called the film industry 'vigorish', gambling slang for the betting percentage in favour of a gambling house. By various contrivances, a film has to have generated a lot of money for a studio before they will declare it in profit. 'Theoretically,' Robert Evans explains, 'the majors are in a business where they have to give away 50 per cent of the profits and yet incur 100 per cent of the losses. So the only way they can possibly keep going and cover these losses is to have a huge vigorish. Paramount have made a lot of money on every one of my pictures, but I've seen very little. I've only just started to see profits on *Marathon Man*, for example, but the company made a fortune out of it.'

Hundreds of law-suits have arisen out of this question and one American lawyer recently claimed that 'the entertainment industry is now an accountancy battlefield. . . . The whole thing is becoming one gigantic paper-chase.' Some recent cases have set disturbing precedents. *Superman* is the sixth most successful film in history according to the Variety list and

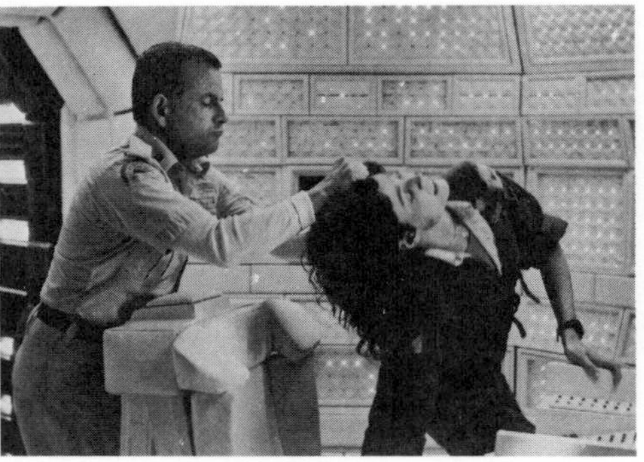

Franklin Schaffner *(far left), an outspoken critic of Hollywood's creative book-keeping, shows Lesley-Anne Down how to ride a punch while filming* Sphinx.

Alien *(left), with android Ian Holm attacking heroine Sigourney Weaver, was also the focus of accountancy battles after shooting.*

Richard Donner *(above) who made the enormously successful* Superman *is currently in litigation with its producers.*

yet its director Richard Donner has still not seen a penny from his percentage of the box office returns. The Los Angeles police have even set up a special fraud squad to look into fraud in the motion picture and TV industry.

Film-maker Franklin Schaffner, whose credits include *Patton* (1970), *Planet of the Apes* (1968), and the recent *Sphinx* (1981) likes to take his money upfront and says why with little hesitation: 'I think it is patently obvious that the exhibitors, distributors and indeed the production companies have never yet come up with a system of accountability that will persuade a star or a film-maker he isn't being constantly cheated. "They" will tell you that the budget for advertising, promotion and prints amount to, say, \$5,600,000. It may or may not be true, but it's going to take you over three years from that point to find out if it's true, plus it's going to cost a great deal of money to go to all that trouble. Now, if there was a system where there was real accountability, an awful lot of people whom, it is claimed, are demanding too much money for their above-the-line services, would reduce their position on the basis that they knew there would be a fair accounting. As it is now, everyone, with few exceptions, wants to take the money upfront and you can't really blame them. This lunacy is a response to avarice on both sides and I don't think the system's going to change – just the people.'

Some of the younger and newer film-makers like Ridley Scott, who came to prominence with the huge science fiction hit *Alien* (1979), have been horrified to discover how nakedly the odds are stacked in favour of the majors when it comes to sharing out the profits of a successful picture. *Alien* is rumoured to have made around \$50m. for Fox, but in late 1979 Scott had still seen no money, other than his director's fee (see page 36): 'It's hard enough to get lucky and have a hit,' he told *Variety*. 'So it's really a miserable state of affairs when the two writers of *Alien* and I haven't seen any money. But I do think now there is an atmosphere of change.'

Because of these practices, many of the biggest talents now demand percentages not merely of the film's profits but of its gross rentals, the money received by the distributor before it deducts its own expenses. Scott has negotiated a percentage of the gross rental of his next film *Blade Runner*, and major stars will almost always hold out for such an arrangement. If, as is reliably reported, Paul Newman had 10 per cent of *The Towering Inferno*'s gross rental, it follows that he would have received ten cents of every dollar Fox and Universal recouped from the film, before any other costs were deducted. If the figure is accurate, then Newman has made around \$10m., as well as his \$1m. salary. But in practice a percentage of the gross is more likely to mean a percentage of the 'adjusted' gross after certain indisputable costs, like advertising, have been deducted.

Why does the deal work?

The manner in which the deal conditions and determines the nature of Hollywood film production is, in many respects, pernicious. There are plenty of writers and directors who will testify to its deadening effect on creativity. Indeed in the late 1960s, before the deal-era had got under way in earnest, when the studios were facing massive losses, anyone predicting that such a clumsy and unwieldy process would result in such a high proportion of successful movies throughout the next decade would have been considered a lunatic optimist. The tone evinced in otherwise expert books published at the beginning of the decade like William Fadiman's *Hollywood Now* is extraordinarily pessimistic. Yet this laborious and haphazard system was, over the next few years, to produce *The Godfather, Jaws, Star Wars, Rocky, Close Encounters* and many other international successes. The question is how has such an apparently inefficient production process proved so successful.

The answer perhaps lies in Richard Zanuck's statement: 'You've got to gamble. The movie

Rocky *(far right) proved an enormously profitable venture for United Artists, but Sylvester Stallone, left, negotiated much more advantageous terms for its sequel.*

The Towering Inferno *(right), with Paul Newman, left, and Steve McQueen. Their income from the film was immense.*

industry isn't a slide-rule business and never will be. It's the world's biggest crap-game.' The gambling element is an integral part of the deal and lends it a certain fascination. The ramshackle nature of the process allows fantasy to flourish in a way that it never could in a bank, a canning factory, or even in a state-subsidized film foundation. Behind the elements and the money and the lawyers and accountants and agents hovers the dream, implicit in every deal, of a perfect film, a legend that will live longer and make more money even than *Star Wars* and *Gone with the Wind.* It is a seductive fantasy in which everyone participates, because an unmade film is inevitably a repository of everybody's secret hopes.

Naturally there is much to criticize in a system so oriented towards fantasy. And for almost as long as it has existed, Hollywood has been labelled a cruel, self-seeking and destructive community, founded on vulgar dreams of wealth and power. On the East coast of America, in particular, a powerful legend has grown up in which Hollywood – represented at its worst by the deal – ensnares and destroys people of great talent.

The legend is too glib. In his essay 'Pauline', screenwriter John Gregory Dunne summarizes it mischievously as 'that protocol of banality that flourishes west of Central Park – Hollywood the Destroyer', and goes on to point out that a good many talents have flourished in Hollywood. The most destructive aspect of the deal-maker's psychology is less that it is corrupting than that, like any gambling compulsion, it is obsessional – and therefore extremely monotonous for anyone not involved in the trivial day-to-day gossip of commercial film production. Plenty of creative people have plausibly claimed that the frenzied atmosphere of deal-making is invigorating and amusing for brief periods, provided there is an escape route. The most pitiful victims of the deal are not crucified artists, but those agents and producers who may not enjoy deal-making but have to survive on a diet of nothing else: from the tennis-court to the commissary to the negotiating table to the telephone on the bed or by the bath, constantly pretending to personal relationships where none exist. The true sadness behind the deal is the sadness of the salesman not of the artist.

Of course, the view that art does not suffer is challenged by those who claim to see the mechanics of the deal reflected in what they regard as the mechanical vacuousness of films like *Jaws.* Martin Ritt, who represents Hollywood's older liberal tradition with films like *Hud* (1963) and *Norma Rae* (1979), is deeply critical of the way Hollywood has developed over the past decade, and of the new breed of directors like George Lucas who seem quite as at home in deal-negotiation as on the studio floor: 'The young kids coming up,' Ritt says, 'they all seem totally into sensation. They don't have a literary tradition and they equate everything with the grosses. But it just can't go on, it just can't. You can't keep whipping that same old meringue and whipping it and whipping it and whipping it without it finally exploding in your face.'

In one sense Ritt's prophecy came true with the box-office failure of one of the biggest meringue-movies of all time, Steven Spielberg's *1941* (1979). But the failure of a comedy as expensive and as aggressively promoted as *1941* highlights the health of the system as well as its weaknesses. Like Friedkin's *Sorcerer* and Bogdanovich's *Daisy Miller, 1941* is a shining example of the 'green awning effect', a film that could only have been made by a director with two colossal hits behind him. Massive amounts of money were spent on the project and its subsequent promotion. The film was relentless, both in its willingness to entertain at all costs, and its childish delight in mass destruction. For those involved, the gamble may have seemed as safe as any they had ever made. Yet the public would not go near it. And now even Spielberg himself seems to have admitted that the public reaction was right.

The case of *1941* is important, because despite the more vulgar aspects of the deal, popular cinema emerges as a flawed but

1941 *(far left) was rejected firmly by American audiences despite saturation ads.*

Sgt. Pepper's Lonely Hearts Club Band *(left) received the same intense radio and disc promotion as* Grease *and* Saturday Night Fever, *its predecessors from producer Robert Stigwood, but no one came to see it.*

The Wiz *(above right), starring Diana Ross, which cost Universal $24m. to shoot but has so far netted only $13.6m. from the American box-office and probably far less from the rest of the world.*

vital democracy. No matter how assiduously Hollywood promotes 'deal-pictures' like *Sgt. Pepper's Lonely Hearts Club Band* (1978) and *Can't Stop the Music* (1980), or obvious errors of judgement like *Sorcerer* or *The Wiz* (1978), once the negative word spreads, the public cannot be tempted into the cinemas. Conversely films like *American Graffiti*, which have been dumped in desperation by an unenthusiastic studio, sometimes accumulate a huge and loving audience.

To assess films *simply* by how much money they have made is unrewarding to all but the deal-makers. In the first instance our response to film must be personal. However, in comparing the products of a medium we may well want to refer to some other form of arbitration besides our own individual taste. In assessing the comparative merits of films specifically designed for mass appeal, we may turn to critics' polls or Academy Awards, but these offer a far smaller sample of a popular film's impact on other individuals than the size of its audiences, especially in the later weeks of its run when this inevitably depends on positive word-of-mouth. The fact that huge numbers of people went to see *Jaws*, while equally huge numbers of people stayed away from the massively promoted *Sgt. Pepper's Lonely Hearts Club Band*, as word spread that it was poor, seems more significant than that either film was liked or disliked by Pauline Kael, won Academy Awards, received a prize from a film festival jury or came top of a New York Critics' poll.

The novelist Graham Greene, who himself worked as a film critic for a short time in the 1930s, understood this point. 'It is wrong,' Greene wrote in *The Spectator* in 1939, 'to despise popularity in the cinema – popularity there is a *value*, as it isn't in a book; films have got to appeal to a large undiscriminating public: a film with a severely limited appeal must be – to that extent – a bad film.' In a later essay 'Subjects and Stories', Greene went even further, indirectly comparing the popular cinema to poetic drama: 'The poetic drama ceased to be of value when it ceased to be as popular as a bear-baiting . . . we have got to accept (the cinema's) popularity as a virtue, not turn away from it as a vice.'

The deal's most dynamic and attractive players are not cynics manipulating the audience, but those who will stake everything, as George Lucas did with *American Graffiti* and *Star Wars*, to achieve the spark of two-way electricity, when a picture connects with the mass audience. The best kind of Hollywood gamble is the bet that your own taste coincides with everyone else's. At its barest the attempt to hit that spark may begin with a simple formula: with the notion of a man and a mysterious woman and Chinatown (*Chinatown*, 1974); with James Taylor and Carly Simon in a rock 'n' roll version of *A Star Is Born* (1976, minus the original casting dreamed up by John Gregory Dunne who had the idea); or even with a straight transposition of ideas (*Fort Apache–The Bronx*, 1981). But these are only the opening gambits in the long and complex struggle to convince yourself and your associates and backers that the public can be reached by your idea.

The spirit of gambling helps to give all the various participants in this struggle some common cause: so that accountants query the script's ending, and writers worry about the release pattern.

No book has demonstrated the nature of this better than John Gregory Dunne's *The Studio*, which exemplifies with razor-sharp clarity the economic and psychological risks run by Hollywood in the cause of success, and the atmosphere of fantasy which is necessary to sustain these risks. The fantasy runs through every stage of the deal and the making of a film – in this instance *Dr Dolittle* – reaching its climax at the film's preview when the atmosphere of suppressed hysteria and the fear of failure has become almost unbearable. Everyone who attends the ritual of mutual reassurance before the curtain goes up is a vicarious player in the game, hoping that the dice will roll well and the film will succeed. But, lurking behind each superlative, is the knowledge that, at some

Graham Greene *(above) the eminent novelist has argued forcefully that mass popularity is a virtue in the cinema.*

The making of Love Story

Love Story, a script by Erich Segal, was turned down by six of the seven major studios in 1969. Robert Evans bought an option for Paramount. His wife, Ali McGraw, was to star. Evans set Segal to work on a novel, to be published before the movie was released. Two directors, Larry Peerce and Anthony Harvey, came and went. Arthur Hiller reluctantly took over.

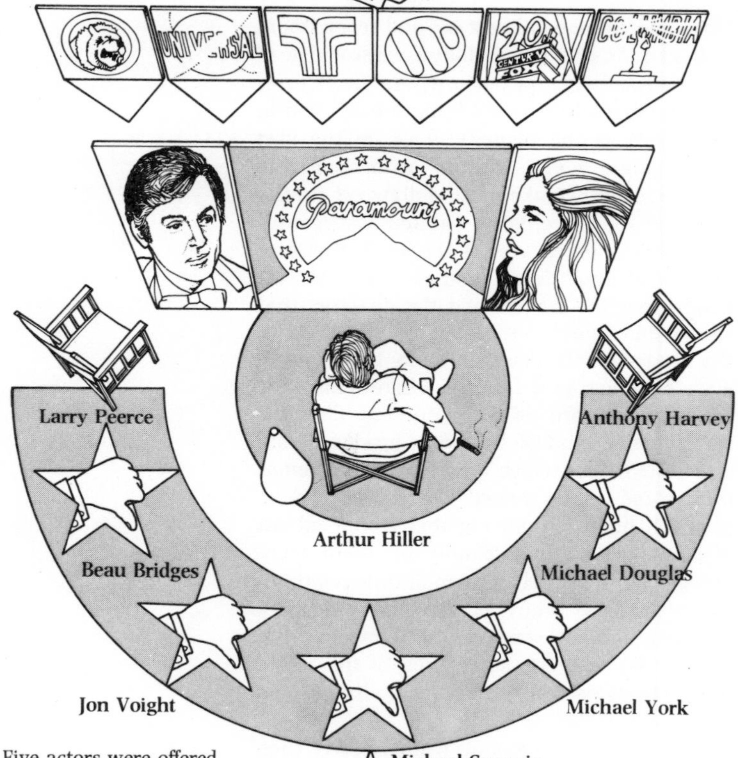

Larry Peerce
Anthony Harvey
Arthur Hiller
Beau Bridges
Michael Douglas
Jon Voight
Michael York
Michael Sarrazin

Five actors were offered the male lead, but declined despite being offered a percentage of the profits. Eventually Ryan O'Neal took the part, and shooting finished in January 1970. The book was published on Valentine's Day in an edition of 25,000 copies. Evans had persuaded the publisher to increase the printing from 5000 copies by putting up $25,000 for promotion. When the film was released in December, the book was at number one in hard and soft cover. The film grossed $50 million in the US and Canada alone.

point, even in Hollywood, reality must reassert itself; the players must face the morning outside the casino; and the film they have made must be seen and judged by its public.

'This is a real Hollywood premiere,' Bishop said. 'It's all furs and jewels and delicate hair styles, and that's just the ushers.' There was a roar of laughter. 'Here's Hank Fonda, Henry Fonda, ladies and gentlemen, Hank, I hear this is a marvellous picture, a wonderful picture.'

'A wonderful picture, Joey,' Fonda said.

'Thank you very much, Henry Fonda, ladies and gentlemen,' Bishop said. 'And here's Carol Channing. Look at those jewels.'

Carol Channing laughed and waved at the crowd.

'It's a wonderful picture, you're going to see a wonderful picture,' Bishop said.

'It's going to be a wonderful picture, Joey,' Carol Channing said.

And Rex Harrison said it was a wonderful picture and Samantha Eggar said it was a wonderful picture and Gregory Peck, who was chairman of the Motion Picture and Television Relief Fund, said he was proud that the Fund was the beneficiary of such a wonderful picture.

'And here comes Sonny and Cher, ladies and gentlemen,' Bishop said.

'Wow, look at those outfits. Sonny, Cher, come on over here.' Sonny and Cher eased their way to the microphone next to Bishop. Sonny was wearing a pale blue brocade ensemble and Cher a floor-length Russian broadtail dress.

'Those clothes are something, really something,' Bishop said. 'And I hear this picture is something, a really wonderful picture. Everyone's talking about it, and I know you're going to have a wonderful time.'

'It's going to be a wonderful picture, Joey,' Sonny said.

'So let's see the picture,' Cher said.

The New Moguls

Darryl F. Zanuck – 'Sam Goldwyn without the accent' – died on December 22, 1979 and with him died the era of Hollywood's absolute monarchs. 'The last of the moguls', they called him, this diminutive man whose career reads like a history of Hollywood. Co-founder of Twentieth Century-Fox Studios (in 1933), producer of the first talking picture, *The Jazz Singer* (1927), virtual inventor of the realistic gangster movie (with *Public Enemy* – 1931 – and others), pioneer of location shooting in Europe and of Cinemascope (*The Robe* – 1953), in later years the overseer of huge hits like *The Sound of Music* (1965) and spectacular disasters like *Dr. Dolittle* (1967). His trademarks were fat cigars and the sawn-off polo mallet he swung as he paced his office, keeping up a non-stop dialogue with himself which three secretaries simultaneously struggled to record. He went everywhere with a battalion of 'yes' men which led the comedian Fred Allen to remark, 'he should put out his hand every time he makes a right turn', and inspired Zanuck himself to rasp at an over-eager subordinate 'don't say "yes" until I've finished talking'. He was an outsize personality, a legendary figure in the tradition of Goldwyn, Harry Cohn, Louis B. Mayer, Adolph Zukor and the other pioneer moguls, with the same combination of showmanship, shrewdness and philistinism. Taking some friends to the Louvre Museum in Paris, he arrived in a taxi and kept it waiting, saying, 'we've got twenty minutes to do this joint'. He was a veteran practical joker, who had rubber chocolates made to pass out to friends and who once dressed an ape in his suit, sat the creature in his office chair and summoned his aides to a 'conference'. He made extravagantly expensive (and unsuccessful) attempts to turn girlfriends like Juliette Greco and Bella Darvi into film stars, and he appointed his son head of production at Fox (later, after a bitter boardroom battle, he fired him). When he died he was 77 years old, a sick man, living in retirement in Palm Springs, looked after by the wife he had deserted nearly 20 years before. Meanwhile, the Hollywood he knew, and a part of which he had ruled for so long, had changed almost beyond recognition.

In Zanuck's heyday, a Hollywood studio head was also its owner, or part-owner. The pictures that studio made were made 'on the lot', within 100 yards of the owner's office, in the vast sound stages which, together with their drab office buildings, make most Hollywood studios look like Air Force bases, painted, unaccountably, pink or green. Across the lot, in the commissary at lunchtime, could be found the star performers, the writers and the directors that studio had under contract. From their desks, the studio bosses could look, in their minds' eyes, back across a country where films were the universal form of entertainment, films the seven major studios financed, produced and distributed, films which then played in cinemas those same studios owned. It was a sweet deal, even if it had been put together piecemeal out of a favourable climate and an infant technology by a bunch of small-time clothing manufacturers. Many of the film industry's founding fathers were Jewish emigrés from Eastern Europe: the same area of the world that gave us modern communism also gave us Hollywood.

The power of the moguls waned slowly, then terribly fast. In the 1940s, government anti-trust legislation forced the studios to sell off their cinema chains, then altered the terms of trade between studios and theatres in favour of the theatre-owners. The labyrinthine legal and financial war between 'the producers' and 'the exhibitors' continues unabated to this day (see p. 95). Later came television. But television was as much a symptom as a cause and the moguls were slow to divine the basic change in the audience for entertainment outside the home. One by one the studios were baled out by other businesses, giant conglomerates which in turn took them over. At the same time, the 'talent' – producers, actors, directors, even writers – broke away or were let go from their contracts. Now each new picture meant a new set of deals and the agents who negotiated on behalf of 'the talent' emerged as the new ruling class. In 1971, when Zanuck was ousted

The Sound of Music, *the film that offered Hollywood a dangerously illusory formula for success.*

as Fox's Chief Executive Officer, Hollywood was the closest it had ever been to shutting its doors and hanging up the 'For Sale' sign.

'Two films nearly destroyed this industry,' says Ned Tanen, president of Universal Theatrical Pictures, 'and the first was a Zanuck film. *The Sound of Music* (1965) was a huge hit and all the studios tried to copy it. They invested in big-budget films, mainly musicals, and they were all commercial disasters. The second film was *Easy Rider* (1969) which spawned the low-budget "youth movies". The same thing happened, except most of the "youth movies" were so bad, they were never even released.'

Like the studios themselves, the new breed of moguls rose from the ashes of the old. Men like Ned Tanen, Alan Ladd Jr., Ted Ashley or Frank Price are personally conservative, financially responsible, creative businessmen, as opposed to imperious showmen. Ironically, most come from the agency business or from television, those two leeches on the body Hollywood. They are not owners, but employees of the conglomerates, salaried executives. Their power may overawe junior actors and aspiring screenwriters, but that power is sharply circumscribed. On the one hand, they must maintain the respect and approval of their corporate boards, which are made up of ordinary businessmen who dislike and distrust the film industry (but love the enormous profits a hit movie can make). On the other hand, they must maintain the respect and loyalty of 'the talent', the film-makers themselves. Since 'the talent' has no loyalty, but is touchy, egotistical, paranoid, overpaid, oversexed and probably over at a rival studio trying to get a better deal, the job of a modern studio head is a tricky one.

Making one film means a thousand and one days and nights of details, and these are details requiring sensitive negotiations not merely peremptory instructions. Making between 10 and 20 films a year (the output of the studios today) is, as Frank Yablans, ex-head of Paramount, puts it, 'purely and simply infinite aggravation'. Nor can you ever tell which films will be the hits. 'There is no formula,' says Ned Tanen. 'Everyone has tried a formula, at one point or another, and everyone has suffered for it. All you can do is make 15 films you believe in each year and hope a few of them take off. But it is never, I repeat never, the ones you think. Look at Christmas 1979. Everyone – myself included – would have told you the big Christmas pictures were going to be *Star Trek*, *1941*, and maybe *The Black Hole*. What were they? *Kramer vs. Kramer*, *The Electric Horseman* and *The Jerk*. Columbia went through agonies making up their minds even to release *Kramer* over Christmas – by all the rules, they should have got killed. But there are no rules.'

Modern film-making is a gamble played with terrifyingly high stakes. The average cost of a major studio film is around $9m. and rising, and the largest budgets are several times that. Films are made, not only by high-priced and nervously independent talent, but also mainly on location, far from the studio's physical control. They are made for an audience, the majority of which is less than 24 years old; film-goers over 30 years old are statistically insignificant. And films are made for a fickle audience which packs, say, *The Exorcist* and ignores *Exorcist II*, lines up to see Dustin Hoffman in *Kramer vs. Kramer* after rejecting him in *Agatha*. There is always the fierce competition of television, which has come up with a new form of competition in the 'TV movie'. Since a feature film takes 1½ to 2 years from idea to answer print, an enterprising TV company can get out a TV movie on the same subject far more quickly, and the network can provide virtually unlimited free advertising.

Nevertheless, the 1970s have been good for the moguls. After the disasters of the sixties, the seventies brought fat profits, full houses, even an overall increase in the audience. The studios began to extract healthy payments from network TV for their hits (Frank Yablans sold *The Godfather* to American TV for $10m. for one showing) and pretty good prices for their misses too.

With the growth of ancillary rights, the huge amounts they make from distribution and the policy of sharing the risk in the 1970s the studios became relatively secure. So how difficult is it now for a studio to lose money on a film? The current generation of studio heads disagree sharply on this. Some say it's hard, others say it's a real and ever-present danger, even a daily nightmare. All agree the status quo is threatened by rising production costs and high interest rates. Certainly, one of the biggest successes of the new breed has been to minimize the risk, just as their biggest failure, and part of the same process, has been their reluctance to take chances, to make films that seem uncommercial. They'd argue it's no part of their job in the first place. After all, the film industry is just that – an 'industry', in business to make profits. But in the very next sentence they'll tell you what they'd like to be remembered for and the answer, to a man, is 'the individual films I've made'. Having it both ways is the studio heads' most fervent wish.

Alan Ladd Jr.: the gentleman

'Laddie', son of Alan Ladd and ex-head of Twentieth Century-Fox, is one of the most respected and certainly the most liked studio heads in Hollywood. The opposite of a Darryl Zanuck in every way, he is laconic and soft-spoken. 'I sometimes think I don't shout and scream enough to be a studio head,' he says, identifying precisely the trait that endears him to most people he meets. He is also fiercely loyal, another rarity in Hollywood, where promises are often broken.

Alan Ladd Jr. took over an ailing Twentieth Century-Fox in 1976, after two years there as a vice-president. He reversed the studio's fortunes with *The Omen*, *Silver Streak*, *Young Frankenstein* and, of course, *Star Wars*. He did it by taking chances; science fiction was thought to be living death at the box office, and so were 'women's pictures' like *Julia*, *An Unmarried Woman* and *The Turning Point*. And the most impressive thing about him is that he did it by being nice, and by trusting his film-makers. 'Most studios give you ten million dollars then don't trust you,' said George Lucas. 'Laddie gave me the money and all he said was make the best movie you can. He gives positive help. He left us alone.'

However, Ladd also has his detractors. Some say he left Fox at the opportune moment, that the glow of *Star Wars* had faded and Laddie had an unpromising string of pictures in production (an argument which ignores the *Star Wars* sequel, *The Empire Strikes Back*). Besides, say the critics, Laddie had his failures too – in fact, his early days at Fox were marked by a string of losers, *The Duchess and the Dirtwater Fox*, *Lucky Lady*, *Alex and the Gypsy*. And what about Robert Altman's fateful relationship with the studio which produced failures like *Quintet* and ended in considerable bitterness, at least on Altman's side?

Like politicians and the managers of football teams, studio heads are judged by success. As Ladd himself points out: 'this is a cyclical business. Every studio has good years and years when they can't do anything right.' A studio head keeps or loses his job according to his or her choice of films, and whether they turn out hits or flops. But choosing films is only one part of a studio head's job, and it is the part that relies most on luck or, to put it another way, 'instinct'. Moreover, their choice is always limited by what's on offer. Ladd says: 'When I left Fox to form the Ladd Company, I also left a group of film-makers I'd developed relationships with and felt comfortable working with – Paul Mazursky, Mel Brooks, George Lucas, Fred Zinnemann. Of course, I'd love to have brought them with me. Fred Zinnemann wasn't signed to anything and we are going to do a couple of pictures with him. But there's no way George Lucas could bring the *Star Wars* sequels over here, unless Fox turns them down, which they're not about to do. Mel (Brooks) actually went to Fox and said to them: "Look, I made a deal with a group of people, not with a building. I want to leave." They refused. He's unhappy, but he's got to make his next film for Fox.'

'The main difference between a good studio head and a bad studio head,' Ladd continues, 'is that a bad studio head sits behind his desk and waits for calls to come in. A good studio head goes out and finds the properties, finds the people.' Where does he find them? He knows most of them already. Hollywood is a small town, a factory town, small enough for any studio head to keep a mental index of who's doing what. 'Basically, this is a business of relationships and it's relationships with people that make them bring their projects to one studio rather than another,' Ladd says. 'And from my side of the desk, too, I'm not backing films so much as people. When I made *Star*

Alan Ladd Jr.: *ex-head of Twentieth Century-Fox, now boss of The Ladd Company.*

THE UNITED

The Omen *(far left), in which Gregory Peck and Lee Remick bring up a demonic child, marked a crucial upswing in Fox's fortunes. Ladd is reputed to have closed a deal within hours of reading the script.*

Young Frankenstein *(left), devised by Mel Brooks, was another Fox hit nurtured by Ladd.*

Wars, I liked the story, I liked the idea of the film, but if it had been someone other than George (Lucas) I'm not sure I would have gone ahead. Having faith in George was the crucial element.'

Ladd smiles a lot and smokes Marlboro a lot. He is impeccably, if casually, dressed. He wears a striped, open-necked shirt, dark pants, Gucci shoes, a gold bracelet and has gold medallions around his neck. He looks very like his father, although he doesn't seem to realize this. He was overweight as a teenager and has said that he didn't have the looks to be an actor. His childhood was extraordinary. The son of Alan Ladd's first wife, his existence was kept a secret from the public for years. (Alan Ladd Senior's image had to be maintained, even to the extent that pictures of Laddie were cut out of Ladd family photographs.) However, he remains the kind of man who will never admit there is a problem. If someone behaves badly towards him, then it was his own fault. If a crisis occurs, his most violent response is to acknowledge that it exists and will be overcome. This is in part an emphasis on his own control, his own competence, in part a reluctance to put others in a poor light.

The announcement of his departure from Twentieth Century-Fox came in August 1979. It hit Hollywood like a bombshell. Studio heads simply don't fall unless they're pushed. But Ladd walked out to start his own mini-major: The Ladd Company.

'I didn't anticipate leaving Fox when I did,' Ladd says. 'It was circumstances that really forced me out. They were very good about not interfering with the films I wanted to make. But at the same time I couldn't give anyone who worked for me a five cent rise.'

Behind this rather bland statement lies Hollywood's real life 'Star Wars'. The rebels are the top studio executives. The Empire is run by the conglomerates who own the studios. The wars are, of course, financial. Independent producers get a percentage of profits from the films they make. Studio executives, making the same or identical films, do not. When a film becomes a blockbuster and its profits are shared out, the big money goes into the pockets of the independent producers. So how does a studio boss keep his top executives happy? The conglomerates would prefer to ignore the whole question. To them, the studios are just the 'film division', no different from the plastic tableware division or the canned peas division. They pay the top executives of all the divisions much the same, and that's that. They can hardly go around handing out huge bonuses to some and not to others. Understandably, the film executives feel differently. To them, the movie business is unique, with a traditional, direct relationship between an executive and the hit picture he or she backs. Since there is an equally direct and traditional relationship between an executive and his box-office flops, and the conglomerates never miss *that* one, the executives have a point. If they're going to get fired for their flops, why shouldn't they get rich (or richer) on their hits?

The executive star wars are only one of the problems the conglomerates have had in digesting the film industry, and probably not the most serious one. Even so, in recent years, the wars have wiped out the top managements of two of the six major studios overnight. First, Eric Pleskow and Arthur Krim led the walkout from United Artists – and went on to form Orion. Then Ladd and his men quit Fox. Historically, what we are seeing with the formation of Orion and the Ladd Company may be the last act in the long-running Hollywood drama – go independent and get more cash. Producers, directors, actors and writers have all done it. But whereas they all broke away because of the weakness of the major studios, the executives have been able to make the leap because of the studios' strength. It was because the studios were doing well, that Orion and the Ladd Company readily raised the cash for their brand-new 'mini-studios'.

As a boy, Alan Ladd Jr. evidently haunted cinemas. He saw just about every Hollywood movie ever made. He and his wife are reputed to be masters of that favourite Hollywood party

An Unmarried Woman *(right) was Ladd's and Fox's unexpectedly successful updated woman's picture. Here director Paul Mazursky chats to star Jill Clayburgh.*

Star Wars *(far right), Fox's and Ladd's crowning triumph in the 1970s; Alec Guinness and George Lucas on location in the desert.*

game – name the second production assistant and fourth lead actor in the 1942 chiller 'Ten Months In Turnaround'. His first business was a telephone answering service. His partners were the actors James MacArthur (*Hawaii Five-O*) and James Franciscus (*Longstreet*). Later he became an agent, later still an independent producer living in London in the 1960s. 'I thought I was a fairly good producer,' he says. 'I was fairly budget-conscious and things like that. I wasn't a successful producer in terms of hits. Had I been a studio head I'd only have done one or two of the ten pictures I did then. As a producer, you don't have much luxury of choice. You have to earn a living and you have to make films, whenever you can persuade a studio to back them. It's very insecure and you're completely in the hands of other people.

'That was the problem with Bob Altman,' he says. 'He needed money badly and I let him do too much. In retrospect, I made a wrong decision by greenlighting *Quintet* without a script. But there are other factors. It's the kind of decision I'm faced with all the time. *Quintet* depended on a certain location, the ruins of the old World's Fair in Seattle, and on a certain time of year, winter. The whole idea of the film came out of those two circumstances. It got to be winter. The script wasn't in shape. We knew they were going to knock down the World's Fair buildings the next spring. Now what do you do? Do you go ahead and shoot and hope Bob can sort out the script? Or do you cancel and look for another location, or build something in the studio?' Altman directed five films for Fox.

Like all studio heads, Ladd mitigates his isolation with a small team of aides. They are his partners really, all of them old friends – production executives Gareth Wigan and Jay Kanter, movie salesman Ashley Boone, and the London-based Sandy Lieberson. You need old friends when you're working an easy twelve hours a day, reading scripts all weekend and 'trying to see one or two films every Wednesday night and a couple more every Sunday.'

On his average day at Fox, Ladd would 'take a meeting' with a succession of producers, directors, agents and others trying to interest him in their properties. Then he would 'take another meeting' with the people promoting, marketing and distributing Fox's completed films. He took script meetings, he took editing meetings, he watched trailers, he checked posters, he oversaw salaries and administration, he travelled to cities across the US for previews. ('I always wondered,' says a friend, 'how Laddie felt in San Diego. He was there one weekend for the preview of *Rolling Thunder* and afterwards the audience literally chased him and the film-makers down the street, it was so bad. The next weekend he went back for the preview of *Star Wars*.') Occasionally, very occasionally, he gave a press interview. 'Basically, I'm shy,' he claims, 'and I don't think I talk well. I have the same problem in production meetings sometimes. I know what I think is wrong with a script but I can have difficulty articulating my points. And to this day, I hate to pick up the phone and take a call from somebody I don't know.' At the back of his mind, as he worked, Ladd knew he had to turn out 14 or 15 films every year, simply to feed Fox's distribution organization. He knew he had to originate a range of films in terms of style or subject matter, and he knew he could afford to take a real commercial risk on perhaps only two or three each year. In return for this ceaseless activity, Alan Ladd Jr. made $1,944,385 in 1978, most of it in bonuses.

'His record,' says a rival studio executive, 'is batting zero and batting 100. He batted zero as a producer and 100 with *Star Wars*. It'll be interesting to see how the Ladd Company works out. He took a lot of chances at Fox because he had to. When a studio's in that bad a shape, you're not going to get any of the hot properties; you have to take what you're offered. A lot of those guys he made it with at Fox don't need him any more. Guys like Mel Brooks are successful now. They can shop around for their deals; they don't have to go back to Laddie.'

The success or failure of the Ladd Company largely depends on whether Ladd's civilized

view of the film industry can triumph over the more popular, cynical view; whether loyalty can be as effective as selfish go-getting; and whether relationships that mean something can be as productive as relationships that are merely a veneer for ruthless self-interest.

Frank Yablans: the fighter

Frank Yablans was President of Paramount Pictures from 1971 to 1975. Working in tandem with Robert Evans (see p. 80) he turned the studio around, from heavy losses into profit. 'I was a very powerful studio head,' he says. 'Those were different days. I had pretty much total autonomy, whereas I understand the people I deal with now, as an independent producer, don't have that power. Show me a studio head in this town who has the power to commit more than $10m. of the company's money to a film. They don't have it; they have to go to their boards. We have to get away from the throwing around of titles. What is a studio head? What isn't a studio head? If you're talking about a head of production, that's a distinct job and, as far as I'm concerned, anybody can be a head of production because all you're really doing is exercising value judgements. To the extent your judgements are right, you'll be successful, and to the extent they're not, you'll generally be fired. The problem is that everybody who now becomes a studio head thinks they have instant expertise in all of the areas some of us spent 20 to 25 years cultivating and learning – like distribution and marketing. Which is basically why most of the ex-agents ultimately found that running a studio wasn't as easy as it looked. It isn't just making deals from the other side of the desk. A studio head is a very strong, renaissance man who has multi-faceted and varied aspects to his career and is capable of running the entire entity.'

Frank Yablans is a strong man, a tough guy who likes to have his own way, in stark contrast to Alan Ladd Jr. At least that's the way he was at Paramount. He says he's mellowed since, learned 'in the areas of deportment and behaviour, having a little understanding and compassion for the other guy.' He's fast, funny and open in conversation, but there's no mistaking the toughness underneath, or the restless energy. He is a short man, nut-brown, smooth-faced, with a bald dome and wings of dark hair. He pushes himself to do things, even small things: sitting in the Polo Lounge of the Beverly Hills Hotel eating a grapefruit for breakfast, he says: 'I hate grapefruit. After one of these, you don't want to eat anything else. It's

Frank Yablans: *ex-President of Paramount Pictures, now an independent producer.*

a great way to keep your weight down.'

Yablans left Paramount after falling out with conglomerate Gulf and Western's founder-owner, Charles Bluhdorn. This particular executive star war wasn't over money, as Yablans explains: 'There are two ways to fail in the movie business. One is by poor performance and one is by great performance. I think the more threatening of the two is success. Especially from the late 1960s to the mid-1970s, it was very "in" for parent companies to blame their own poor performance on the motion picture subsidiary. In those days, it was nothing for a studio to have a 60 or 70 million dollar loss one year, and two years later turn it around and have a 180 million dollar profit. Rightly or wrongly, the head of the studio bore the brunt of the frustration at company headquarters. I always thought this idea, that the parent's problems stemmed from the studio subsidiary, was a myth, and it's proved to be a myth because the movie companies have been consistently profitable for the last five years and it hasn't altered the parent companies' results to that extent.

'The other half of the story is that when you have a diversified corporation, the movie division is running against the grain of normal corporate behaviour. Our costs are outrageously high, our salaries are way out of line. So it creates tension. As a studio head, you find yourself spending more and more time justifying your costs, justifying the corporate aspects of the job and less and less time making pictures. It usually results in a collision of egos. This is not an industry for small egos. And that first blast of ego gas that comes with success is hard to contend with, particularly when you remember that most studio heads in recent years have been young men. I started that trend. I was 36 when I became President of Paramount. The irony is that, just when you begin to come to terms with it, the parent company has had enough of you.'

Gulf and Western had enough of Yablans in autumn 1974. Bluhdorn brought in Barry Diller, from ABC TV, over Yablans' head. On November 8, 1974, Yablans, Bluhdorn and the lawyers stayed at Paramount's New York headquarters until 11.30 p.m., hammering out the terms of Yablans' resignation. 'Charlie put Barry in there to embarrass me,' Yablans says. 'It was as simple as that. I screamed at Charlie Bluhdorn from the day he hired me. If I'd been Charlie, I'd have fired me long before.'

While Yablans was at Paramount, the company made *The Godfather I and II, Chinatown, The Parallax View, The Conversation, The Longest Yard, Save The Tiger* and *The Gambler*, as well

The Godfather *(far left), directed by Francis Coppola, was Paramount's biggest hit while Yablans was boss of the company.*

The Conversation *(left), also directed by Coppola, was by contrast one of Paramount's and Yablans' biggest flops.*

as the unmentionable *Little Prince* and *Jonathan Livingston Seagull.* Yablans tends to claim he was first with everything, and he was indeed one of the first 'baby moguls' and a pioneer in raising the budgets and importance of advertising and publicity to the point at which all studios now spend almost as much on selling a film as on making it.

Yablans is the marketing expert. Self-appointed, of course, as befits a self-made man. From a lower middle-class Jewish background in Brooklyn, he entered the film business as a salesman with Warners. 'I spent ten or fifteen years carrying film under my arm,' says Yablans. 'It was nothing for me to take a can of film and drive from Milwaukee to Des Moines and be away from home for three weeks selling to individual theatres. I sold them all. I was in New York, in Boston, in Chicago, in Michigan, in Minnesota. I had the entire West Coast at one time. I knew it all. I worked for Warners, Disney, I imported my own foreign films, then I went to Paramount.' So wedded was he to selling a picture that one Paramount wit described him as 'the head of distribution who also happens to be President of the studio.' Others are not so sure of his expertise. 'I thought he was a marketing genius too,' says one disgruntled publicist, 'until I worked with him. Frank is out of date – mainly he doesn't understand or like television advertising. Frank likes those big full-page ads in the newspapers which don't sell anything.'

However, Frank is sure of his expertise, and that's what matters. He's the man who turned the figures on duds like *Paint Your Wagon*, *Catch-22* and *The Great Gatsby* from red to (just) black. He's also the man who took his first independent production, *Silver Streak*, to Fox, shortly after he quit Paramount. 'That film and a Mel Brooks film carried Fox until *Star Wars* came along,' he says. 'Without either of those films, somebody other than Alan Ladd Jr. would probably have been sitting behind the desk when *Star Wars* was brought in.'

As personalities, Yablans and Ladd are worlds apart. In an ideal Hollywood, you might want Ladd and his team to pick and make your picture, Yablans to sell and market it. But that's not the way things are. 'In the case of Laddie, Jay (Kanter) and Gareth (Wigan),' says Yablans, 'from my point of view, they were close to the point of obscuring their vision. They got too incestuous. They were so locked into each others' minds, against a common enemy they perceived – chairman Dennis Stanfill and the Fox board – that they became less and less able to see the broader canvas. The secret of their success was they worked hard, did as good a job as they could under the circumstances, and they were adventurous because they had no choice but to be adventurous. Fox was a creatively bankrupt company when they took over. It's need that creates success, and greed that leads to failure.'

At Paramount, Yablans, who was based in New York, had one intimate and he was 3000 miles away on the West Coast. Robert Evans was head of production, a handsome, affable man with a string of glamorous girlfriends. The press had the two men at each other's throats, with 'hard man' Yablans envying Evans' lifestyle and his easy way with the media. Both men say the feud never happened. 'I think Frank's terrific,' says Evans. 'He's a personality. He has more balls than anyone I've ever known. He doesn't take anything from anyone. I would cringe to do the things he would do. I wouldn't have the nerve. But when you do things like that, you also make a lot of enemies. If I owned a movie company, I couldn't think of anyone I'd rather have run it than Frank. He's a dynamo. His ambition is extraordinary. He's very bright and everything he applies himself to, he does well.'

Yablans admits he had '90 days of self-examination and self-doubt' after leaving Paramount. 'You can't resign those jobs. The power is too great to give up. What you do, what I did, what all of us do, is create an atmosphere which leads to the final confrontation. And the relief you feel when it happens is incredible. Being President of a studio means being everything to everybody and nothing for yourself. Of course, after it's all over, you wonder, where do I go from here?'

Yablans was 40 when he left Paramount; he had been a supersalesman and studio head. With characteristic drive, he set out to learn a third career, as an independent producer. He's on his fifth film now, Michael Crichton's *Looker*, after *Silver Streak*, *The Other Side of Midnight*, *The Fury* and *North Dallas 40*. In *The Fury* he makes a cameo appearance as a villain who is killed when he hurtles through a car-window (it's rumoured Hollywood executives packed *The Fury* just to cheer that scene). He remains a man whom his fellows either love or hate; his saving grace is his sense of humour. While he was at Paramount, Yablans made *The Apprenticeship of Duddy Kravitz*, a Canadian film about a Jewish hustler who is funny, dynamic and warm but also ambitious, calculating and ruthless. As Frank Yablans is the first to tell you, industry insiders rapidly retitled it 'The Frank Yablans Story'.

Frank Price: the diplomat

According to Frank Yablans, 'being a studio head is all about deference. Being deferred to, in every sense. That's probably the greatest trapping of power there is. It's easier to define the destructive trapping which is insulation. One of the greatest adjustments I had to make when I left Paramount was that I didn't know how to buy an airline ticket. I didn't even know my own home phone number. It was always, get me this and get me that.'

The power Yablans sought so eagerly, the power Alan Ladd Jr. shrugs off because it makes him uncomfortable, is enjoyed with quiet satisfaction by Frank Price, President of Columbia's feature division. Most studio heads, both the traditional moguls and the new breed of creative businessmen, have been picture-makers first, deal-makers second and corporate employees a distant third. Just occasionally, a man comes along who is just as at home with high finance and boardroom politics as he is with actors, directors and producers. Such men go far – usually straight out of the film industry. They ascend to the kind of limbo America reserves for its bankers and intelligence agents. Lew Wasserman of Universal, Ted Ashley of Warners, and David Begelman of MGM (until his conviction for embezzlement) have the rare attribute of being as acceptable on Wall Street as on Sunset Strip. Frank Price is also such a man.

He dresses and looks like a banker. He is soft-spoken, diplomatic and political with a small 'p'. Indeed, he makes Hollywood seem almost respectable. He flies several thousand feet above the aspiring songwriters, nickel-and-dime drug dealers, ageing would-be screenwriters and alcoholic supporting actors who people the tatty modern apartments of Los Angeles, moving vans always at the ready in their downstairs car ports. In a city where people rent even their furniture, Frank Price represents conservatism, stability, the after-shave aura of a solid 'company man'.

Yet he began with nothing, or very little; like many of the studio heads, he is a living embodiment of the American Dream. Price sold his first script to television at the age of 20. With sheer hard work he pushed himself up through the ranks. He wrote and/or produced such classic TV series as *Matinee Theatre*, *The Virginian*, *Ironside*, and *It Takes a Thief*. He became President of Universal Television, 'the largest TV production factory in the world,' in 1974. In 1978, at the age of 48, he joined Columbia Pictures as production head. He became studio President in November 1978.

Says Price, 'I came into this job with more experience and background than anybody I can think of, because I had had thorough corporate experience. I was with MCA (Universal's parent company) for 19 years, and I was on the board of MCA. I'd run the largest and most successful division of that company, so there wasn't a lot new to me from a company standpoint.'

In other words, Price can finesse the crucial question – who runs Columbia Pictures? Yes,

Frank Price: *former President of Universal Television, now President of Columbia Pictures.*

he goes to the board for approval of the films he wants to make. But no, the board never refuses him. 'If they didn't choose to back my judgement, there wouldn't have been any point in their appointing me in the first place,' he says.

The relationship between studio head and corporate board is a grey area. What is clear cut is the relationship between studio head and everybody else. Everybody else can say 'no' to a project, or to a producer or a writer. Only the studio head can say 'yes' and mean it. If the board remains as a final court of appeal, the studio head is the trial judge.

Within the confines of his business Frank Price is a philosopher. Much of his everyday conversation could go straight into an Annual Report, and, given that restriction, he can be extremely frank. 'It's true,' he says, 'that any studio depends on one or two pictures a year for its real profits. The problem is, no one can tell which one or two films will succeed. So you try to cover the "downside" (the production costs). You have some reasonable downside protection. Under these circumstances, the worst that can happen is you break even on the ones that don't break out. With reasonable prudence ("reasonable" is one of his favourite words) it's hard to lose money on a film.'

Price's office at Columbia sits behind two sets of double doors. Between the corridor and his office is space for two secretaries, a large T-shaped area, restful and cool. Like most studio offices Price's is modern but you can tell it belongs to a top executive: there are one or two pieces of antique furniture carefully scattered about. Outside, the sun is baking the Columbia lot, but inside there is only the mechanical gush of the air-conditioning and the grey, anti-glare windows. On the wall behind Price's desk are vintage photographs of the stars – Cagney, Bogart, and others. They

Chapter Two *(right) was a successful Neil Simon original screenplay for Columbia in 1980, with Marsha Mason and James Caan.*

All That Jazz *(far right) probably turned out more prestige than it did profit. Columbia make no secret of their relief that they backed out of the project on grounds of cost.*

are signed 'To Frankie'. Price's mother collected them for him when he was a child and she was a waitress at the Columbia commissary.

'Poor but honest mother slaves to support child who will one day run the studio' – Price's life story would make one of his own movies. He came to Columbia in the wake of the David Begelman affair, the last corporate explosion to rock Hollywood before Ladd left Fox. 'Industry giant fiddles cash, gets fired, gets parole, gets rehired as head of MGM' – Begelman's story would make a movie too, and a more fashionable one than Price's, since it lacks most moral certainties. But then the two life stories interweave and the plot, proverbially, thickens.

'When I came to Columbia,' says Price, 'I said I didn't want to be part of any political faction. Obviously, there was a lot going on here. I had the inestimable advantage of not knowing a single person at Columbia. I didn't know anyone on the board. I didn't know anyone on the lot.'

A key figure in Columbia's executive star wars was Daniel Melnick. Melnick, a 46-year-old independent producer, is also an *eminence grise*, a fixer. He has been a studio head – at both Columbia and MGM – but only briefly and always reluctantly. (Like his friend, director and choreographer Bob Fosse who made *All That Jazz*, Melnick is good to his ex-girlfriends. Many of Hollywood's female executives have been linked with Melnick at one time or another, as has Tina Sinatra who once received from him a $2000 life-size doll of Melnick himself as a birthday present.) Columbia split over what to do with Begelman, the President of their motion picture and television division. On one side were independent producer Ray Stark and the board, including its most powerful member Herbert A. Allen, who wanted to keep him. On the other was the chairman Leo Jaffe, the President of Columbia Pictures Alan Hirschfield and his friend Daniel Melnick, who wanted to fire him. Begelman went. Then Hirschfield went. Melnick took over the studio as 'caretaker' head, bringing in Frank Price. Finally, with perfect symmetry, Price turned on Melnick.

'When I came here,' Price says disingenuously, 'I did what I have always done, which was to call them as I saw them. Unfortunately, in Danny's (Melnick's) case, there were certain pictures I made certain decisions on that he didn't care for.'

The 'certain pictures' comprised virtually Melnick's entire production slate with Columbia: *All That Jazz*, *Altered States*, *The First Family* and *The Four Hundred*.

'Danny wanted me to buy the novel of *The Four Hundred* for a million dollars. I said, "Danny, it's a period caper, it's going to be very expensive to make, and there's no evidence of any public appetite for that kind of subject." The novel was in London and the author's agent wouldn't bring it over to us. So I took a polar flight to London, checked into a hotel, had the manuscript sent round, read it in five or six hours, went straight back to the airport and flew home. I didn't care for it.'

Price also rejected Paddy Chayefsky's script *Altered States* and *The First Family*. 'I knew exactly what would happen with *Altered States* and it has happened. The budget is up around 20 million dollars, the writer's taken his name off it, and a 20 million dollar picture directed by Ken Russell makes me very nervous'. (Price was wrong. *Altered States* was a Christmas 1980 hit.) Columbia did make *All That Jazz*, but pulled out when the budget rose way beyond the initial $6.5m. 'I think *All That Jazz* is a superb picture.' Price says. 'I also think I made the right decision on it. Funding a six and a half million dollar personal statement is one thing, funding a 14 million dollar personal statement, which is how it's turned out, is another. You couldn't predict it would be a mass audience picture. It depended entirely on how good a job Bob (Fosse) did, and he did a wonderful job. You couldn't predict it would collect nine Oscar nominations. Even so, it cost 14 million dollars, plus another 10 million to release it and we expect it to do 18 million dollars domestic, plus an unpredictable amount in foreign. The bottom

The Electric Horseman *(far left), with Jane Fonda and Robert Redford, had a slow box-office start but became Columbia's biggest film in 1980. Its producer was veteran* **Ray Stark** *(left), who once acted as Raymond Chandler's agent.*

line is probably going to be a slight loss.'

When Columbia cut off funds for *All That Jazz*, Melnick flew to New York, assembled some rough footage, flew back to Los Angeles and raised the cash to complete from Alan Ladd at Twentieth Century-Fox, who had turned down the film at an earlier stage. *All That Jazz* is a Columbia-Fox co-production. Warner Brothers made *Altered States* and *The First Family*. Alan Hirschfield and Dan Melnick moved to Fox. Ladd is with the Ladd Company. Price is at Columbia. Begelman runs MGM. The executive star wars turned into a game of musical chairs.

And 1980 turned out to be Columbia's year. They swept the box office with *Kramer vs. Kramer*, *Chapter Two* and *The Electric Horseman* and the Oscars with *Kramer* and *All That Jazz*. 'I was particularly pleased about *Kramer*,' says Price. 'When I came to Columbia I was told, "that's really a television script". Coming from TV, I was sensitive to that jibe. But what's the difference between a good TV movie and a good movie except better production values and star casting?'

Price is dressed in a blue shirt and grey slacks. He is wearing a tie, maybe a hangover from his days at Universal, the only studio where ties are obligatory. He is smoking and figuring out how to cancel a 'substantial' bet he made with a fellow-producer over who would be the first to quit the habit. In his TV years, he racked up several 'firsts' – 665 episodes of a daily one-hour drama, *Matinee Theatre*; the first 90-minute Western to run every week, *The Virginian*; the first TV mini-series, *Rich Man, Poor Man*. For all his corporate tact, he is a film-maker at heart, committed to 'that magical moment when something works out and the whole is greater than the sum of its parts. No one can really explain that properly.'

At Columbia, he is trying to make his deals directly with the talent, rather than with independent producers or agents. He has all the *'Kramer'* people, plus Jane Fonda and others committed to projects for his studio. These are shrewd calculations in an industry riding a boom, with more and more production units chasing a finite group of actors, writers and directors.

As Frank Wells, one of the triumvirate who run Warner Bros., put it, 'we didn't realize how good we had it ten years ago when we took over at Warners. Columbia was broke, Fox was broke, Paramount was in poor shape, and we were going around making deals like drunken sailors. Now all the "majors" are healthy, plus there's Orion, Lorimar, Marble Arch, the Ladd Company and ABC and CBS films all competing for the same pool of talent.'

Price also has faith in the future. He shrugs off the multi-million dollar lawsuit Columbia faces, charging that Ray Stark and Herbert Allen 'usurped' Columbia's management and that Stark was allowed 'improperly to designate creative personnel and consultants for Columbia' – specifically Frank Price. In Hollywood, the future usually means next week, but Price sees farther than that. He doesn't believe critics who claim the industry is entering a period of inflated budgets and over-production, that the bubble could burst as dramatically as it did in 1969. 'We're seeing two important technical changes. One is pay TV, cable TV. They don't pay much for films at present, but they will be paying substantially more and they'll help take up the slack caused by network TV paying less. The second is videodiscs. Discs will be extremely good for this business. I foresee a pattern which begins with a film's theatrical release, then we put it out on discs, selling them in supermarkets. Discs are a way we can reach the over 24 audience; they relate to people getting married, having kids and staying home. These people are still interested in films, in stars; they just don't need the social act of going out to the cinema. With discs, they can watch the new films at home. After disc sales, I see cable TV, then network TV, then your ultimate syndication. There's going to be tremendous money in steps two and three – discs and cable.'

In other words, discs will be Hollywood's paperbacks in five or ten years time. In the meantime, Price will still spend his lunches and dinners with the talent, his weekends reading scripts and his days taking meetings. He'll still be persuading a Ray Stark to hire a Jane Fonda for an *Electric Horseman*, even though her salary increases the cost of the film – and hence the point at which producer Stark can start collecting his profit. Like the good company man he is, he won't scream and shout, won't show the pressure and will give only measured glimpses of his power. 'I'm in the people business' he says, with all the force of his impersonality.

Ned Tanen: the dynamo

Ned Tanen sits on the penultimate floor of the Black Tower, as Universal's office block is universally known. MCA Chairman Lew Wasserman's office is on the same floor. The penthouse, one floor above, remains at the disposal of Jules Stein (see p. 42), MCA's Chairman Emeritus. He doesn't come in to work much any more, but then he is 82 and very, very rich indeed.

If Hollywood is a factory town, Universal is the steel works. People don't much like Universal. It's too big, too rich and makes too much television. And it has the nastiest security guards in Hollywood. Its staff groan under various edicts like the one about not putting any books on office window-ledges because they spoil the lines of the Black Tower from the outside. People think a typical Universal film is *Airport '79: Concorde*. People find Universal uncreative and unadventurous – which is really saying something in Hollywood, like being a dwarf among midgets – even though Universal made *American Graffiti* and, in partnership with EMI, *The Deer Hunter*.

'The general attitude to Universal used to bother me,' says Ned Tanen. 'The Black Tower and all that stuff. But not any more. I shrug it off.' Tanen shrugs off a lot of things, and what he can't shrug off he may well shout and scream at. 'My biggest weakness is I have a very short temper,' he admits. In Ned Tanen, the ultimate entertainment bureaucracy has a resident who most resembles the volatile old-time moguls. He is blunt, outspoken and thoroughly entertaining. He gives the impression of a man who doesn't suffer fools gladly but whose job requires him to suffer them all the time. He also tells great anecdotes.

'I had Michael Cimino's first script,' he says. 'Wonderful script. Couldn't get Universal to put up the money. I went with Michael to South Dakota. We got drunk one night and went up on top of this hill called Rattlesnake Hill because thousands of rattlesnakes congregate there. We stood on this hill, picking up rattlesnakes and throwing them off the side.' Not normal behaviour for a studio head. On the other hand, maybe it's just a metaphor. Every day, Ned Tanen sits in his Universal office picking up different kinds of rattlesnakes and throwing them off the side.

Tanen has been with Universal films for almost a decade, first running production, then, since 1976, as President of Universal Theatrical Pictures. He has been with MCA, Universal's parent company, for 19 years altogether. First, he was a record executive. He took $750,000 of MCA's money and founded MCA Records; then they switched him to the film side of the business. 'I didn't want to be in the film industry,' he recalls. 'I *loved* the record business. For the first couple of years, I couldn't wait to get out of pictures. When I came here, we were in the middle of a programme of really peculiar movies. May I tell you, I still have the scars from that programme.'

It was the years after *Easy Rider* (1969) and every Hollywood studio was making 'youth movies'. 'Ours were a little different. They weren't "youth films" as such. They were Milos Forman's *Taking Off*, Dennis Hopper's *Last Movie* – there are still people wandering about the jungles and mountains of Peru who went down to work on that one – Douglas Trumbull's *Silent Running*, Peter Fonda's *Hired Hand*, John Cassavetes' *Minnie and Moscowitz*, *Diary of a Mad Housewife*, *Play It As It Lays*, *Two*

Silent Running *(right), one of Universal's ambitious late 1960s series for new directors, gave the special effects wizard of 2001, Douglas Trumbull, bending, a chance to direct. Bruce Dern starred.*

The Jerk *(far right), Universal's biggest hit of 1980, with Steve Martin.*

Lane Blacktop, Ulzana's Raid. They were all made for about one million dollars. That was tops. I was hanging in here by my thumbs trying to protect the people who were making those movies. I remember *Ulzana's Raid* ended up overrunning to $1,700,000 and I really didn't think I was going to live through it. Every day the budget went up by $20; I thought my life wasn't worth living. The only one of those pictures that made any money was *Diary*.'

Tanen's early programme included some of the more ambitious pictures of the 1970s, but 'we couldn't even get them shown, let alone get people in to see them. *Taking Off*, as good a movie as I've ever been associated with, probably ever will be associated with, ended up with 300 playdates at most. The exhibitors wouldn't book these movies. We were going for the hard eight ball [a pool-table term] every time, and you just can't do that. Today, with production costs the way they are, you'd never even contemplate such a programme.'

American Graffiti saved Tanen. It was shot in 28 nights for $743,000. 'Just for fun, George (Lucas) and I sat down the other day and did a budget for what *Graffiti* would cost if we made it today. Same number of nights, same cast and crew, no increase for George and the producers. It came out $2m. and in a couple of months it'll be $3.5m.'

'I was at a dinner party with Jack Nicholson recently, whom I don't really know. He said, "Do you remember those days when I was making *Easy Rider* and *Five Easy Pieces* and you were making all those pictures? Of all companies, for *Universal*. Of *all* companies! None of us" – he was talking about Bob Rafelson, Francis Coppola, Dennis Hopper, all the guys – "could believe you were going to live through this, because it couldn't work. God, he said, it seems like 100 years ago!"' Tanen laughs and picks up the phone which has been beeping in a subdued fashion. A tense, vibrant man, bearded and brown-shirted, he talks in full flow, immune to interruption. 'I think at Universal we are the most businesslike of the major studios,' he says. 'We approach it as a business, but we don't make the mistake of thinking it's like any other business. There is no formula! But I'll say one thing, the business projections we make for each year usually end up correct within one or two percentage points. We end up where we thought we were going to be, but we never, ever get there the way we thought we were going to get there. Christmas 1979 was the perfect example. We had *1941* which should have been huge, and did nothing. We had *The Jerk* with Steve Martin, the least expensive movie we made all year, and it's breaking 40 million dollars at the box office.'

Ned Tanen *(left): President of Universal Theatrical Pictures.*

Tanen may have smoothed out major studio economics ('one of the things we have managed to do over the years'), but he doesn't pretend that film-making itself is a smooth affair. On the contrary. His image as a studio head is of a man rolling up his sleeves, punching recalcitrant stars and directors into line, getting down to the cutting room and personally chopping up bits of film and sticking them together with glue if necessary. He doesn't do any of that, of course, although he does say, 'I stay pretty much away from all our films until I smell a problem, when I get in fast with both feet.'

He had a problem recently: *The Blues Brothers*, Universal's big-budget comedy with John Belushi and Dan Ackroyd, way over budget and still unfinished, was sitting on his back lot like a financial black hole, waiting to swallow the Black Tower, executives, producers, publicists and all. 'Putting a film into production is one thing. The real nightmare is the film that can't get out of production. All studios have them. What do you do? It's easy to talk about firing directors and closing down productions, but it's a hell of a lot harder to do it. The two leading actors have come to me and said, the day after I fire the director, they quit. So what do I do? Do I keep pumping money into the thing and pray they'll finish it? Or do I close it and take a multi-million dollar loss?'

One problem Tanen doesn't have is corporate relations. Unique among studio-owning con-

Minnie and Moskowitz *(far left), one of Universal's cheap films made at the end of the 1960s. Val Avery slugs Seymour Cassel as a distraught Gena Rowlands looks on.*

Diary of a Mad Housewife *(left), with Richard Benjamin and Carrie Snodgrass, another of Universal's low-budget series.*

American Graffiti *(right), a film which saved the careers of numerous Hollywood talents including that of Ned Tanen.*

glomerates, MCA is an entertainment giant, founded and still run by men whose roots are strictly showbiz. In fact, it's even more difficult at Universal than at other studios to see where the power lies. Lew Wasserman is the chief executive and obviously Tanen works closely with him. But Tanen claims, 'I can say "yes" to any size film budget; it really depends on how well I want to sleep at night.'

Avoiding the executive star wars may have something to do with Tanen's own character. Abrasive he may be, dissatisfied he's not. 'Most people who go into my kind of job are looking to get something else out of it,' he says. 'A very substantial group have used the job, not improperly, as a step into an independent production deal. I've never had any real interest in producing movies. It's one of the world's most tedious professions. I'd much rather be concerned with 15 films than just one. But my job is a 24-hour a day job, and it's emotionally very consuming. It's not something you walk away from easily. The problems are ever there.'

Tanen doesn't go to promotional or private screenings. It's his trademark, based on bitter experience like the 34-city previews of *Gable and Lombard* (1976) to cheering crowds – when the film opened, nobody came. He stands and pays his money along with the rest of us. The last screening he attended was *Grease* at a friend's house and the showbiz types there hated it. Tanen says he felt guilty having fun.

Tanen is the man who passed up both *Grease* and *Saturday Night Fever* for Universal, but then everybody passed up *Grease*. 'It was around for five years and they couldn't give it away. I was among the idiots who didn't get into it when I certainly could have done.' *Saturday Night Fever* was brought to Tanen by Robert Stigwood and remains 'the only movie I've ever been offered and turned down which subsequently became successful. I respect Robert Stigwood. I read that damned article (by Nik Cohn, on which the film was based) over and over again. I just couldn't see what he saw in it. There are these kids in Brooklyn, it's provincial, it won't travel well . . . I've never forgiven myself for it. I pride myself on thinking I'm in the marketplace with the people who go to see movies.'

Once a record executive, always a record executive. Of all the studio heads, Tanen is the one with his antennae most firmly fixed on the age of his audience. Generally speaking, teenagers make movies into hits. In recent years, Universal has specialized in adolescent comedies like *Animal House*, the Cheech and Chong films, *1941* and projects involving comedians like Steve Martin and members of the Saturday Night Live TV team.

'One of the biggest problems we face in this business is the producers. With few exceptions, producers have come to a sorry time. A lot of it is the fault of the studios who've given power to the directors and to a handful of stars. Producers used to be middlemen, who were able to say to the studio on the one hand and the director on the other, "you're crazy", "this is wrong". A producer was in charge, instead of being the guy who buys the rights to a paperback book and is basically in the deal-making business as opposed to the picture-making business. For the most part, when we make deals with producers we'd damn well better have our own production people on that movie. If there's a problem, don't call the producer!

He isn't even there. He's off making his other deals with three other studios. Or he's in Acapulco. Better he's in Acapulco, because then at least you hope he's having a good time, rather than wandering around the set like some kind of idiot when he's no idea what a storyboard is. It's harmed us and it's harmed the directors, because it's put the studios and the directors against one another like this.' Tanen punches his palm to make his point. 'And it's stupid. The director should be shooting a movie; that's his job, not dealing across the desk or on the phone with me.

'The hardest part of my job is to keep everybody involved on a project concentrating on the point of the whole thing – the movie we're supposed to be making. There is so much dead time. In pre- or post-production there really isn't much to do, so people create problems just to keep themselves active. You do get involved on a negative level – the aggravation, the never-ending meetings, the egos concerned. You have to keep saying: we hope we've made a movie people want to see and, if we have, how do we bring it to their attention? That's the point, but you do keep getting sidetracked with bullshit. You keep having to say: what does this have to do with our movie; how the hell did we end up over here having this conversation about the size of your dressing room or some teamster (union) problem; let's get back to where we were and what we're supposed to be doing.'

Tanen started in the mailroom at MCA when the company was still a talent agency. He's married to the daughter of veteran director Howard Hawks, and the pair of them avoid the Hollywood social scene. He's a man who seems to have succeeded in his job at the cost of losing touch with, or being cut off from, his natural allies – men like actor Peter Fonda and film-maker Monte Hellman, the rock 'n' rollers of the film world. For all the glamour and the power of his position, he still craves the immediacy and the excitement, the street energy, of the music business. When Tanen was new to Universal and Dennis Hopper was making *The Last Movie* in Peru, the production ran into problems with the Peruvian Catholic Church. The Archbishop heard that the film might be anti-clerical. Hopper was summoned to a conference in Lima. The result was a solemn agreement signed by both sides. It was only on Hopper's return to Hollywood that the director admitted to Tanen he had signed Tanen's name to the document. Says Tanen, 'as far as I know, for the last decade Universal has been owned by the Vatican.'

Power at the Hollywood studios has little to do with logic, much to do with history. As the last of the old-time moguls, the owner-operators, left the scene, every studio became a mini-bureaucracy in which individual executives gained power or lost it, gained or shed job titles. Barry Diller runs Paramount but there's a Head of Business Affairs there who is reputed to be the real authority. Sherry Lansing is head of Twentieth Century-Fox film production – the basis of Alan Ladd Jr.'s old job – but these days there's an extra 'mogul' between her and Chairman Dennis Stanfill, in the person of Vice-Chairman and Chief Operating Officer Alan Hirschfield. Hirschfield at Fox controls TV as well as films; Tanen at Universal does not.

According to director Martin Ritt, 'they say there's a shortage of executive talent in the industry and it's a big problem. But, as long as I've been in Hollywood, I've yet to figure out what studio executives really have to do with the making of a picture.' Maybe so, but at least there's one studio head in Hollywood who isn't an ex-agent or an ex-TV producer but a real live film director. If Darryl F. Zanuck was 'the last of the moguls' what does that make Francis Coppola? In the spring of 1980 Coppola, director of *The Godfather I and II* and *Apocalypse Now*, realized his dream of buying his own Hollywood studio. That makes him not just head of production, not just a conglomerate whizz-kid, but The Boss in his own right. And he started his reign in fine 'mogul' style, with sweeping plans to make feature films on video-tape, using computers. Fifty per cent of the profits, if any, of his American Zoetrope studio are to go on research and development. He intends to create a 'new talent programme' for new directors, writers and performers. Big words from a big man. Jack Warner, Louis B. Mayer and Zanuck himself would certainly have approved.

Confessions of a Kid Mogul: Robert Evans

The age of the old-time movie moguls may be long dead but if any man has kept Hollywood's fairy-tale image alive in the 1960s and 1970s it must be Paramount's boy-king Robert Evans. Presiding over the studio for a decade that began in 1966, when he was still in his mid-thirties and Paramount was in a state of near-bankruptcy, Evans weathered a shaky start, during which even Variety *predicted his dismissal, and went on to launch an unprecedented series of hits from* Rosemary's Baby *through* Love Story *and* The Godfather *to* Chinatown. *His life story is vintage Hollywood material: the son of a Manhattan dentist, Evans had spent his youth variously as a professional gambler in Havana, a child radio star, a short-lived 'discovery' of the legendary Darryl F. Zanuck and finally a senior partner in a men's clothing company. He sold his share in the company when he was in his early thirties and made his second assault on the movies, this time as a producer, eventually becoming Paramount's head of production. His marriage to Ali McGraw, the woman he built into a major star in* Love Story, *was traditional gossip columnists' fodder, but its abrupt climax (when she left him for Steve McQueen while making Peckinpah's* The Getaway) *was just one of a series of painfully colourful episodes which have made Evans' career one of the most discussed in movie history. The huge and beautiful estate in Beverly Hills, where he lives with his English butler David and a large staff, has been host to numerous international figures and showbusiness celebrities, including Henry Kissinger (who offered to fly to Texas and negotiate personally with Ali McGraw when the news of her infidelity broke), Roman Polanski (for whom Evans ringed the house with armed guards after the murder of Polanski's wife Sharon Tate in 1969) and Edward Kennedy.*

Evans' close friend Dustin Hoffman once described his lifestyle as 'a comedy of manners – cucumber sandwich reality does exist', but for all the romantic trappings of his personal life, few people have approached movie-making with more seriousness and dedication than Evans. His reputation as a painstakingly creative producer of the old school is so pervasive that when a screen adaptation was mounted of Fitzgerald's The Last Tycoon *in 1976, Evans was himself approached to play the title role (wisely he refused it in favour of Robert De Niro). Here Robert Evans looks back over his life and also talks about his two most recent films,* Urban Cowboy *and* Popeye.

Robert Evans *(left) poses for a publicity picture with Norma Shearer.*

Man of a Thousand Faces *(right) in which a nervous Robert Evans made his film debut opposite James Cagney.*

I suppose I was always a loner as a kid, and that was how I first became an actor. When all the other kids were playing hockey or softball in the street I was going down to the various agents and filling out audition blanks. While they were going to school I was getting private tutoring, and while they were attending college I was travelling in burlesque. My father was a New York dentist and many of his friends, who were professional people, criticized and even ostracized him for the way I was brought up. But my parents let me do what I wanted as long as I seemed happy. And by the age of eleven I was quite successful as a kid actor in radio.

Perhaps it was because my parents were so ready to back me – often under very strange and difficult circumstances – that in the end I didn't go the wrong way. My paternal grandfather had been a professional gambler who would go out for a night and not come back for two weeks, and my father was worried I would do the same. In fact I very nearly did. When I was 15 or so I was an understudy in the Broadway version of *Oh Mistress Mine* by Terence Rattigan starring Lynn Fontanne, the wife of Alfred Lunt. Now the Lunts' valet at that time was a black fellow who was fond of gambling, so we would go up to Harlem after the show and play poker till six in the morning. That was my first introduction to real gambling and frequently there was a lot of money on the table. Later, still in my teens, I drifted to pre-Castro Cuba as a disc jockey and began to work professionally as a gambler in Havana. All the Cleveland boys were down there at that time and I was just a kid having some extraordinary experiences. In fact I could easily have stayed there and become a professional gambler, but I think a part of me knew what my parents went through to let me do these things. If I had been on my own or if I hadn't been getting along with my parents or even if they hadn't meant a lot to me, I would certainly have been dead by now: shot. But I wanted to make them proud of me. My life has not always reflected it, but I have really come around to the idea that family is very important.

When I was 20 years old I got back into acting and did some more radio and television, but most of my time in the early 1950s as an actor I was knocking my brains out without any success at all. Then my brother Charlie came out of the army to start a men's clothing business and he offered me a partnership. I worked with him for some years but, while I was still a partner in the firm, I went back into acting more or less by accident.

I had met the actress Norma Shearer who wanted me to take a part in the film of Lon Chaney's life *Man of a Thousand Faces* (1957) chiefly because I looked so like her late husband, Irving Thalberg. And that meant that my first scene as an actor in a Hollywood movie was playing opposite James Cagney, who had always been one of my big favourites as a kid. What was even worse was that in this scene I was supposed to be teaching *him* how to act! I was so nervous and so bad in front of the camera that after about five takes Cagney told the director: 'Hold it up.' And he took me outside. He walked me round the Universal lot and he said: 'Let me tell you something kid. I'm only five foot four and when I came to Hollywood to make my first picture my first scene was with a guy who was six foot three. Well when the scene was over, I was six foot three and he was five foot four. Now come back and don't be afraid of me.' That was one of the most memorable moments of my life.

Man of a Thousand Faces was just a one-off acting job because I was still in the clothing business, but shortly afterwards there was another total accident. I was dancing in a night club and Darryl Zanuck was there. He kept looking at me and finally he asked me to come over to his table; I thought it was some kind of joke. He asked me if I was an actor and I said I wasn't but I told him the Norma Shearer story. So Zanuck asked me straight out there and then whether I would like to star opposite Ava Gardner. For the past year and a half he had been struggling to cast the part of the bullfighter Pedro Romero from Hemingway's *The Sun Also Rises* (1957). He had looked at every bullfighter and the bullfighters that spoke English didn't look like bullfighters, whereas the ones that looked right didn't speak a word of English. He said I was exactly right and asked me if I wanted the part. At that point I still thought it was a joke, but eventually I tested for the part and got it. And it led to one of the worst experiences of my life.

I had gone down to Mexico to study under the bullfighter Alfredo Leda. There was enormous pressure to have me fired and nobody in the cast would talk to me. Eventually they sent a cable to London where Zanuck was making *Island in the Sun*. It said: 'Robert Evans is wrong for the part of Pedro Romero. Everyone wants him out because if he stays the film will be ruined.' And it was signed by Ernest Hemingway, the director Henry King, Ava Gardner, Tyrone Power, Mel Ferrer and all the rest. Only Errol Flynn refused to sign it. And then I was certain I was going to be fired. I was very embarrassed and I kept thinking how my family would take it following all the build-up. But at least I learned what a real producer was. Because Zanuck took the next plane from London to Mexico and ordered me to show up

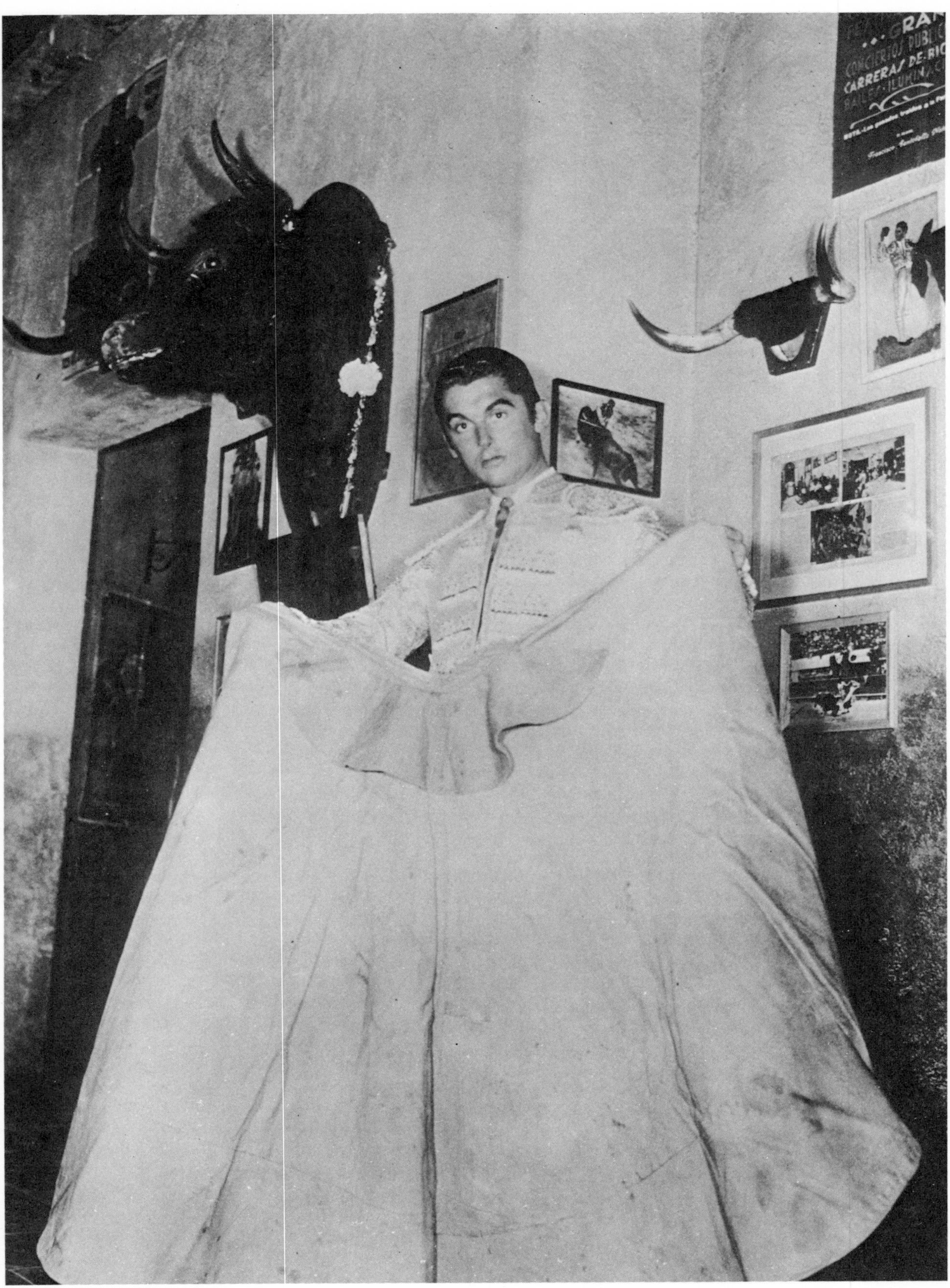
CONCIERTOS
CARRERAS DE

Robert Evans *(left) poses for a publicity shot as the matador Pedro Romero in Twentieth Century-Fox's version of Hemingway's* The Sun Also Rises.

Robert Evans *(right) chats to Barbra Streisand surrounded by the stars of Paramount's 1969 big-budget movies: Lee Marvin and Clint Eastwood (*Paint Your Wagon*); Rock Hudson (*Darling Lili*); Streisand and Yves Montand (*On a Clear Day You Can See Forever*); and John Wayne (*True Grit*). Ironically only* True Grit *made the company any money. On Streisand's left is Bernard Donnenfeld, a senior Paramount production executive.*

at the bull-ring dressed in my suit of lights. I had to go out there wearing a rubber girdle under the suit, because I was overweight at the time, and bow to him and do my *pasa dobles* and *veronicas* and place the *banderillos*. Everyone was there in the stand, even the technicians. It was a nightmarish ordeal. At the end there was a deathly silence, then Zanuck picks up his megaphone. 'The kid stays in the picture,' he bellowed, 'and anybody who doesn't like it can leave.' And then he walked out. That showed me what a producer is. There has to be one boss. But it was a hellish experience.

After *The Sun Also Rises* I went on and did some more films, and I was being billed as the next Valentino. But I really wasn't very good. There was too much hype and too little talent. Eventually my brother and his partner in the clothing business, Picone, came to me and said: 'Look you're out in Hollywood nine months in the year now but you still have a percentage of our business. So do one thing or the other, and if you decide to become a full-time actor then we'll buy you out.' It was a tough moment for me because it isn't pleasant looking at yourself in the mirror and knowing you're not that good. Perhaps I would have gone on if I had been better, but I knew deep down that I had been given the opportunity as an actor and I was underwhelming. I could remember going round filling up audition blanks as a kid and seeing men of 45 or 50 filling up their blanks, and I never wanted to become them. So I gave up and I went back to New York and the clothing business. I hated to do it because I didn't enjoy the business, but I needed the discipline and I wanted to make some money. And it proved to be the right decision because later we sold the business for a lot of money.

It was then I decided I wanted to get back into films and I knew that I didn't want to go back as an actor. I was also aware that nobody would accept a former pretty boy actor as a producer. So I stayed in New York acquiring literary properties. I had *Valley of the Dolls* for a while. That slipped away from me but then I bought *The Detective*, a book by Roderick Thorp, and arrived as a producer at Fox who eventually made the film. Shortly afterwards I was written up in the *New York Times* and I came to the attention of Charlie Bluhdorn, the chairman of Gulf and Western which owned Paramount. Eventually, to everyone's astonishment, he invited me to take over production at the studio.

When I arrived at Paramount you could have gotten three to one odds on that I would have been out in three months, six months at the latest. There were eight companies and we were eighth. In fact we were tenth, there was so much distance between the seventh company and us. But eventually, after *Rosemary's Baby* and *Love Story* and *The Godfather* and several others, we took over from Fox as the number one company and stayed there until I left. And I wanted to leave that way because in the picture business there are far too many imponderables for a string of successes like that to last.

At the time I arrived at Paramount we had got into some really expensive negative costs and things weren't good for anyone in the motion picture business. It was a very frustrating time. For example, I was desperate to do *Funny Girl* (1968) with Barbra Streisand which later became a big hit for Columbia. I was offered it by the producer Ray Stark, who had known me as an actor, but he could only give me 48 hours to come up with the money. So I called Charlie Bluhdorn and I said: 'Charlie I think it'll be a huge picture.' He asked me to let him make calls and he stayed up all night calling all around Europe. And every single person he called took the same line: 'Who wants to see a Jewish girl on the screen singing these songs? We don't want to touch it.' So Charlie came back to me and said: 'You've been here

too short a time, Bob. I can't trust you with this when no-one else wants it.' So instead we took the biggest star in the business who was Julie Andrews and we made *Darling Lili* (1970) with Blake Edwards directing. And it turned out to be the biggest box-office disaster imaginable.

A lot of stories grew out of the *Darling Lili* disaster, like the one that Blake Edwards challenged me to a fight over it. I don't know where the story came from because I backed Blake on the picture up to the point where I just about got fired myself. We were a third into the film and Bluhdorn wanted to close it down because we were hugely over budget. 'I've got a bad feeling about the picture,' I remember him saying. 'I don't like how Edwards is working. He would wait for the clouds to go by before he'll bring up a hundred planes.' I flew over to Dublin and looked at all the footage and I told Charlie that I loved the picture and I wanted to stay with it. He disagreed with me but I pleaded with him: 'Charlie let's stick with it.' So we stuck with it through millions of dollars. And when we previewed it we got a wonderful reaction. Then we opened it around the country and nobody came. We even took an ad out which began: 'It's funny when you can't give a picture away' and offered every adult the chance to bring their kids for nothing. They still didn't come, mainly because the timing was completely wrong. *Deep Throat* had just come out and sex was the name of the game. In fact *Life Magazine* had a two page spread showing lines around the block for *Deep Throat* and *Darling Lili* totally deserted.

Around the time when I first came to the studio I was hunting desperately for properties, because nobody was submitting anything important to Paramount. And I managed to persuade one agent to let me have the first crack at Nabokov's next novel. One day, in the middle of winter, I got a call from the agent and he said I could see the first typescript of *Ada*, but I had to get it from Nabokov himself. I took the polar flight from Los Angeles to Paris and went from there to Lucerne. Finally I arrived at a huge, empty hotel and entered a dining room that must have been 300 feet long. Right at the far end of the dining room, Nabokov who was then 78 years old was sitting with his wife, the two of them entirely alone. To begin with when I went up to him he wouldn't believe I *was* Robert Evans. He just looked at me like I was some little boy. Finally, after we'd talked, he agreed to give me the manuscript to read but he still seemed a little suspicious. He brought out a loose-leaf manuscript that was a foot high and I carried it off upstairs to my room to begin reading. After a while, to my horror I found that I didn't understand a word. I didn't know whether it was me or the trip, so I took a Dexymil and stayed up for another 24 hours and kept on going and finished the book.

After I had read it twice, I *still* didn't understand a word of it and I didn't know what I was going to say to Nabokov. Eventually, I came down the next morning, 24 hours later, and he was sitting in the same place and I said solemnly: 'Mr Nabokov this is an extraordinary book but I must refer back to my associates at Paramount.' So I flew to New York to meet the board, wondering what I was going to tell them. But something helped me make up my mind. Years earlier on the east coast I had once been asked to back a play called *The Umbrella* with several big stars of the day: Geraldine Page, Tony Franciosa and Franchot Tone. I read this play twice at the time and I couldn't understand it. But I had shrugged it off and thought: 'Jesus what do I know? If Geraldine Page and the others want to do it, I'll raise the money.' When we brought the play to Philadelphia for its trial run, nobody understood it and it closed there and then. At that time I learnt the lesson that I may not be as literate

The Godfather *(far left) with Marlon Brando, the film that cemented Paramount's and Evans' success.*

Rosemary's Baby *(left) with Mia Farrow: the film helped to improve the studio's fortunes and marked the beginning of a close friendship between Evans and Roman Polanski.*

Henry Kissinger, Robert Evans *and* **Ali McGraw** *(right) at the première of* The Godfather.

as some people, but if I read a thing twice and I don't understand it, then the chances are that the public won't understand it either. So when I walked into the Paramount board in New York after flying from Lucerne I said: 'Gentlemen I've just come back from meeting Nabokov and I can't buy it because I don't know what I read.' They laughed but at least they were honest with me. Eventually the book was bought and there was some grumbling from my associates, but Columbia couldn't figure out a way to make it either. The film was never made.

Of course I had my disagreements with Paramount. I remember the first week of *Rosemary's Baby* (1968) when Roman was already a week behind the production schedule and they wanted to fire him. So I told them I would quit if they fired him. The same thing happened with *The Godfather* (1972). They wanted to cut it and I said: 'If you cut just one line of this picture, just one line, then I quit.' Then they wanted to put an intermission in it, because they thought nobody would sit for three hours without one. And I had to resort to the same tactic to stop them putting one in. Sometimes you have to put yourself on the line like that.

Love Story (1970) on the other hand had difficulties of a different kind. The script had been rejected by every major studio and when it came to me I couldn't find anyone who wanted to do it. I offered the male lead to Beau Bridges who turned it down: then Jon Voight turned it down, then Michael Sarrazin, then Michael York and then Michael Douglas. Nobody wanted to know. Ali finally came to me and said 'Do I have a disease or something?' I even offered these actors ten per cent of the gross because it was only a small budget, so each of them would have stood to make a fortune if they had taken it.

Eventually, after Ryan O'Neal was cast, I had to buy advertising for the book because the publisher just wanted to print 6000 copies and throw it away. I made an agreement with the publisher that I would give them $25,000 worth of book promotion on the understanding they would print 25,000 copies; then it had a chance. In fact when the film opened the book was a number one seller in hardback and softback, which I believe has never happened before or since. And in spite of everything I must admit that I got as much pleasure out of *Love Story* as any film I've ever been involved with. The picture turned out to be a kind of aphrodisiac; wherever it opened kids would walk out of the theatre arm in arm, in love! It was the 'make-out' picture of the decade.

I can take the credit for *Love Story*, but unfortunately like any other studio boss I have to take the blame for what we missed in those years. I read *The French Connection* and I thought it was rubbish and I turned it down. I also had the first crack at *Jaws* while I was working on *The Godfather* and my assistant read it for me and he said it was nothing. Another one that went through my fingers was *Airport* (1970): I read it and I wanted to buy it but the company wouldn't make it because we had someone from United Airlines on our board of directors who thought it was very anti-airline.

It's true that in the last couple of years at Paramount I wasn't a good administrator because I would tend to concentrate on certain pictures. At that point Paramount had offered me a deal whereby I could personally produce five pictures – and have a financial stake in them – and remain head of the company at the same time. But it caused chaos because the first of the five pictures, *Chinatown*, was a big success and all the other producers working for Paramount complained there was a conflict of interest. I was supposed to be looking after their pictures and I was spending all my time on *Chinatown*. So the Paramount board gave me a

straight choice: I could run the company for them or make my own individual films for them. In order to provide a financial incentive, if I chose to stay as head of the studio, they would give me a percentage of every film Paramount made. Imagine what that might have been worth with *Grease* and *Saturday Night Fever* on the way. But I just couldn't give up producing, so I gave up the company.

It was a fair outcome because *Chinatown* had been absorbing all my energies. I worked on it in such detail that even at the end I was grading the film to get the right colour. And as always there were problems: Roman Polanski and the screenwriter Robert Towne fell out, partly because Bob wanted one ending and Roman wanted another; Bob didn't want Faye Dunaway to be killed in the end. I decided to back Roman and consequently the two of them didn't talk for the whole of the picture. In fact there was so much animosity that Bob wasn't even allowed to look at the rushes: I had to show them to him over at my house. But the film got rave reviews and did very well: it cost \$3.8m. to make and ended up earning more than \$30m.

Chinatown made me immensely proud, but the catch is you can spend just as much time on a failure as you do on a success. One of my biggest disappointments as a producer was *Black Sunday* (1977), about a terrorist attack on the superbowl. I had a letter from the head of Loews, one of the biggest cinema chains in the US, predicting that *Black Sunday* was going to be bigger than *Jaws*. Then when I showed it to a thousand exhibitors, it had a much bigger reaction than *The Godfather*. But the public just didn't want to know. It was again partly a question of timing. The picture was held over for six months because of *King Kong*, and by the time it was released terrorism and mass disaster were not wanted by audiences. If I had romanticized it, it would probably have been a bigger hit.

If *Black Sunday* was my biggest disappointment, *Players* (1979), on which I spent two years, was my biggest personal flop, and it was a flop that went far beyond the realms of business. The project had originated when I looked at the best old sports films like *The Hustler* and *The Cincinnati Kid* and *Body and Soul*, and I decided I wanted to merge a very emotional love story into a dramatic tennis match. It proved to be a very difficult structure and we ended up having to cut away from the love story because it didn't hold up, but the film had some of the best sports footage ever.

Now, I was in Dallas at a special preview screening on a Sunday night shortly before the opening and it went down terrifically well. The following Monday I flew to New York where they were having a big press screening. I remember the phone was ringing as I got into my hotel room with Eddie Kalish our publicity chief on the line. I wanted to know how the screening was going. 'I don't know how to tell you this, Bob' he said. I couldn't understand what he meant. 'We're in the middle of the picture,' he went on, 'and every time Ali opens her mouth they begin laughing.' He didn't know what to do. First it had been ten people, but it grew from ten to twenty to fifty and by the end of the picture they were shouting at the dialogue. We had another showing the next night and the word must have spread like brushfire because from the first line they began laughing. Then came the reviews, which were not so much reviews as editorials: 'Bob Evans' revenge on Ali McGraw' was one of the headlines. It was personalized in a way that I considered completely unfair. I also felt terribly bad for Ali's sake because her part was difficult and we'd tried so hard to build it up. A short time later I had lunch with one of the top American critics and I said to her: 'Why did they go for me? What's wrong with a popcorn picture?' And she said: 'We expect a lot from you. You're one of the few producers who gives as much as the director, and, if you don't give it to us, we're going to give it to you. You can't do a popcorn film and expect to get away with it.'

I could see her point of view but it did seem unfair to me

Urban Cowboy *(far left), with John Travolta, proved to be Paramount's second most popular film of 1980, generating over $20m. in rentals.*

Players *(left), with Dean-Paul Martin, failed conspicuously badly at the American box-office.*

Robert Evans *and* **Faye Dunaway** *(right) at the opening of* Chinatown.

that everybody talks about Roman Polanski's *Chinatown* and John Schlesinger's *Marathon Man* and John Frankenheimer's *Black Sunday* but the minute I have a flop it's Bob Evans' *Players*. Anyway when the picture opened it did so badly that it was taken off almost at once. Even the 30 million active tennis players in America didn't go to it, but in a flop like that it's not the money side that I care about. With the receipts from overseas where it did fine and the sale to television *Players* will make money but I still feel badly about it.

The two films I'm currently completing are *Urban Cowboy* and *Popeye* and as far as I'm concerned they have the biggest audience potential of anything I've ever been involved with. *Urban Cowboy* is basically a story about young people in Texas who work in factories during the day and live out their fantasies at night. When John Travolta first came to the picture he was so timid about it that he wasn't going to do any publicity at all. Now he wants to go all over the world to promote it and I'm just as enthusiastic as he is.

Popeye began three years ago when I went to see the stage musical *Annie* on Broadway and loved it. I called Barry Diller of Paramount directly after the show and asked him to buy it for me, because I was dying to make it into a movie. They began negotiations and it turned out the owners wanted $10m. At eight and a half million I called a halt because my feeling is that at that kind of price you're damned if you succeed with the movie version and damned if you fail. I wanted to create comething, not just adapt a hit, and I was sitting in my office feeling very dejected when a fellow called Marvin Cane who runs Famous Music, which is Paramount's music subsidiary, called me and said: 'Bob I think you're crazy bidding for *Annie*. We get $75,000 of royalties over here just for the song "Popeye the Sailor Man". Why don't you do Popeye?' At that moment an alarm went off in my head. So I got Jules Feiffer in and he took two years writing the script. Robin Williams (from *Mork and Mindy* on TV) signed as Popeye and Robert Altman agreed to direct.

Nobody thought I would be able to get along with Altman, but in fact I have got along better with him than almost anyone else I've ever worked with. We shot the film in Malta because we needed a huge tank for the underwater footage, and we also needed to construct a sea-port city like San Pedro thirty years ago. Disney have agreed to co-distribute the film with Paramount. They came down to the set and saw three hours of film and all they said was: 'We wish Walt was alive to see it.'

It may sound egotistical but I would rather be remembered than be rich. I live in a rich way but I have no money; I am so bad at investments that if I had tried to lose money deliberately I could hardly have done any worse on the stock exchange than I have done. At this point I don't have a thousand dollars in my bank account and I have huge payments to meet, but I can't really pretend that I care. If I cared, then I would make six pictures in the next two years and live very well on the producer's fees. But I do not even want to think about what I will do next. Perhaps it's a terrible thing to gamble so much on two films but I think if both these pictures – *Urban Cowboy* and *Popeye* – flop then I will quit the movie business.* I would feel that I had lost my touch and I really wouldn't trust my own judgement as a film producer. I'm not afraid of that, because I quit being an actor and I've changed directions too many times to be frightened of it. But if these films work I want to stay with them, certainly throughout all of 1981.

Perhaps that approach is neither productive nor prudent, but I don't care. I have a passion for film rather than just the commercial appetite to see how many projects I can make. There's something that Popeye says that made me want to do his film in the first place. 'I yam what I yam and that's all that I am.'

*This statement was made before either film opened, while some observers were predicting their failure. In the event both films began uncertainly, but eventually proved successful.

'Independent' Producers, Independent Distributors

Today almost all producers are 'independent'. It has been well over a decade since any studio, except Universal, has had producers as permanent employees. But conversation with any producer quickly establishes how meaningless the term 'independent' is. At some point every producer has to accommodate to someone else even if it is only the people who are going to buy his or her picture and distribute it to the public. Top producer Saul Zaentz, who made *One Flew Over the Cuckoo's Nest* (1975), seasons his definition of independence, 'Getting to make the picture you want', with an anecdote: 'When I was in the army – just a kid, twenty, twenty-one – a colonel said to me, "Just remember one thing, sergeant: no matter how high you go, there's always somebody over you." The main thing is making the picture and hoping it will be successful commercially so you can live to fight again.'

Limitations on independent producers

Zaentz did not pursue 'traditional' financing methods on his first feature, the perhaps inaptly titled *Payday* (1973), because 'the more you got in with any company, the less control you had over the picture, and this picture could only work if it ended up as we envisioned.' Made with tax-shelter money assembled abroad, *Payday* was rejected by the majors; its original distributor, Cinerama, went out of business while exploiting it; its subsequent distributor, American International, did nothing with it. It languished. Such are the joys and privileges of total independence.

By contrast, Zaentz's second feature, *One Flew Over the Cuckoo's Nest* (1975), was an enormous hit. This time he did go straight to the majors for financing. Fifty per cent of budget was their best offer – and, on that, a contingency was imposed: he had to shoot the film on the studio backlot and rent the backlot facilities. 'I'm not faulting them. I'm not cheering them either, but I'm not faulting them.' Again, Zaentz purchased his independence from foreigners seeking American tax shelters; he shot the film in Oregon, bringing a completed film to United Artists for distribution.

Zaentz is welcome now at any of the majors, while in motion-picture parlance he remains an independent. *One Flew Over the Cuckoo's Nest* made it possible. 'It was like overnight. The day before we were those assholes from Berkeley, and then the picture came out. All of a sudden we got smart.' Independence *with* the majors means for Zaentz more money, less risk, more movies, less control.

Debra Hill, another independent producer (*Assault on Precinct 13*, *Halloween*, *The Fog*) has a rather different attitude: 'I know people who spend their lives trying to make deals with people capable of financing. We (she and John Carpenter) are independent film-makers. They buy our talent.'

Independent producer Sandy Howard (*A Man Called Horse*, *The Devil's Rain*, *Meteor*, *Terror Train*) finds his role difficult, but ultimately rewarding: 'Every film is a horror picture because it's a horror to get them made . . . Today I put myself in the position of being exposed for $1m. that I do not have.' In 1974 Howard announced ten pictures in the trade press, two years' worth of production with a total budget of $30.3m.; three were for Twentieth Century-Fox, two for Bryanston (a distributor now defunct), three were to star Richard Harris. In 1976 Howard announced eight pictures costing a total of $33.5m.; *Meteor*, at $10m., was one of them. In 1977 there were six pictures at a total of $25m.; *Meteor*, still unmade, was now estimated to cost $15m. In 1978 six to eight pictures were announced at a cost of $50m.; *Meteor* was now going to cost $16m. Of the twenty-one pictures he had named over the five years (each year there were titles held over from previous years), Howard actually produced eleven – plus another two, *Crunch* and *Terror Train*, that were never announced. In other words, he brought slightly more than half his projects to fruition.

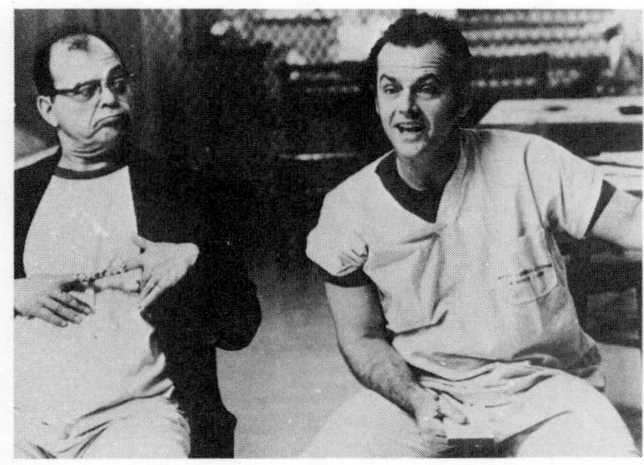

Saul Zaentz *(above)*

Sidney Lassick and Jack Nicholson *(above right) as fellow inmates in* One Flew Over the Cuckoo's Nest, *co-produced by Saul Zaentz and Michael Douglas for record-company offshoot Fantasy Films.*

Debra Hill *(above far right)*

Howard says: 'People are independent producers for different reasons. Number one, they can't get the pictures made with the American majors that they'd like to get made – an interesting small horror film, an interesting small romance, an interesting small science-fiction film. The American majors, in the normal course of events – and they're quite correct – are interested in the largest-grossing films they can possibly find. This is counter to the interests and the financial requirements of the independent producer, if he wants to make profits aside from his development fees. So, therefore, the independent who is truly independent, who has the ability to work with the majors or work alone, has to chart a course by which he can make the most money or make the films he wants to make.

'It's easy to do it when you have money. It's difficult to do when you don't. I lost a lot of money in 1979 on a couple of pictures that aborted. We took a beating on *Meteor* – too many goddamned partners – and on a couple of other pictures. But I've never failed to meet a commitment, although God knows I'm due to.

'I am independent. I don't know that I'm particularly proud of it. It's the way that I've gone in my life. There are some people who think I'm a *schmuck* because you're gambling every single day. Perhaps I'm a fool. I've made some very serious mistakes as an independent. I think I should have made more pictures with the American majors over the last few years. I think I'm welcome at every company if I have a fine script. I'm not welcome if I don't have a fine script. A lot of people think I should have been far more successful than I've been. I think they're probably right.

'Am I successful? No, I'm not successful. Am I active? Yes, I'm terribly active. Do I still have great potential? Yes, of course, I still have great potential, and I can't wait to see what happens in the last few chapters. My mountains are movies.'

These comments, including that of Debra Hill, make it fairly clear that a producer's 'independence' is at best qualified. James B. Harris, producer of films like *Lolita* (1962) and *The Bedford Incident* (1965) (which he also directed), sums it up: 'The best thing about independent production is being left alone to make your own movie. However it's not so great to be left alone when the picture is finished because it's very difficult to find honest, professional distribution. You could walk away with a film under your arm, and nobody gets to see it.'

This is the crucial point. Even if a producer is lucky enough to have private finance to make a picture without approaching the majors for production money, this does not enable him to get the picture shown. The pivotal function of the production-distribution-exhibition chain remains distribution, linking pictures with the theatres.

Independent distributors

Consequently the independence of an independent distributor, unlike that of the independent producer, has some substance, especially if that distributor produces his own films. Of course it is the majors who offer the fullest, most comprehensive distribution available, and the biggest films. But they do not always fill the market. Because they concentrate on high budget films and peak cinema-going seasons, such as summer holiday time and the Christmas period, and because their production methods are necessarily lengthy and inflexible, they can leave gaps in the system for smaller distributors to fill, cashing in either on a lull in successful majors' material or on a subject of topical or lurid appeal in which the majors are reluctant to invest.

American International Pictures

In the post-war period, despite the numerous small distribution companies who cater to the art-house audience, the notion of independent distributors in America has become inextric-

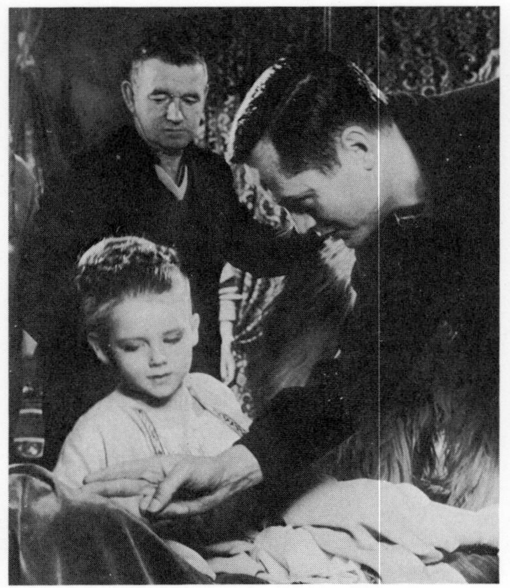

Roger Corman *(above left) gives direction to a young actor for* Masque of the Red Death.

Jack Nicholson and Sandra Knight *(above) in Roger Corman's* The Terror.

ably linked with the exploitation movie. The most famous post-war independent distributor, American International Pictures, dealt in low-budget horror, action and softcore sex movies, and their name conjures up images of crab monsters, hot rod girls, wasp women and things from beyond space. In the late 1950s and 1960s, the majors were reluctant to deal in these commodities, and the independents like AIP produced and distributed them to a small but lucrative market which centred around the drive-ins, catering to a substantially teenage audience. Roger Corman, a former post-graduate student at Oxford University and Twentieth Century-Fox messenger-boy, specialized in this kind of material and soon earned a reputation both as a skilful and speedy director and as an exceptional patron of young talent. In the early 1960s, when film courses were few and far between, numerous fledgeling film-makers and actors were working with Corman on pictures like *The Terror* (1963, starring the then unknown Jack Nicholson with Gary Kurtz, later producer of *Star Wars*, among its crew) and *Battle beyond the Sun* (1963, a Russian science fiction film, dubbed and re-edited by Corman for the American audience with a little help from an unknown director called Thomas Colchart, alias Francis Coppola).

But even Roger Corman could not have started out on this lucrative path if it had not been for American International, which had built up a distribution circuit for its double-bills as early as 1954. Its boss and presiding overlord was a cigar-smoking lawyer from Iowa called Samuel Z. Arkoff.

The notion of low budget semi-sensational features had of course existed long before AIP. The earlier independents, who were the distributors of 'B' pictures in the pre-television era, developed in tandem with the studios, providing the majors' theatre chains with second features all at fixed rates; that is, the total potential income of each film was known before release. A glance at the filmographies of directors like William Beaudine, Joseph Kane and Sam Newfield – who created 400 films between them – reveals the scale of the early independents' enterprise.

By contrast, AIP began only when that system was moribund, the studio production units almost dead, the contract lists of cast and crew dwindling. Television stalked the industry like the monsters in soon-to-be-marketed AIP chillers. Arkoff (and his partner, James Nicholson) were not creating 'B' pictures for the bottom half of the bill. Rather they had identified a distinct market which neither the majors nor television were satisfying – a market which is intriguingly delineated by the titles of some of their earliest successes: *I Was a Teenage Werewolf, Hot Rod Girl, Runaway Daughters, Naked Paradise, Teenage Caveman, She-Gods of Shark Reef, Twist All Night, Beach Party*. They responded to trends and may even have created them; but there was no question that most of their audience was young.

Few independents can afford to employ sales people on a permanent basis in each city and state as the majors do. They must therefore begin by using independent subdistributors known as states righters, who operate on a commission arranging distribution to the cinemas in their area, and who generally handle films from many independent companies at once. Of course, every independent distributor eventually hopes to buy up these states righters

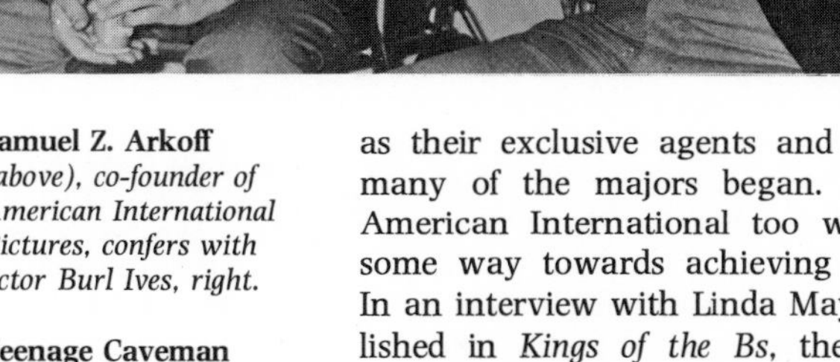

Samuel Z. Arkoff *(above), co-founder of American International Pictures, confers with actor Burl Ives, right.*

Teenage Caveman *(above right), directed by Corman and released by AIP, gave an early starring role to Robert Vaughn, centre.*

as their exclusive agents and this was how many of the majors began. In its heyday American International too was able to go some way towards achieving this ambition. In an interview with Linda May Strawn (published in *Kings of the Bs*, the indispensable reference book on the subject) Sam Arkoff recalls: 'The first couple of years we made only four or five pictures a year. So our franchise holders handled other pictures too. Then, gradually, they became more or less exclusive AIP distributors. They had to ask us and get our consent to take on some other producer's pictures. Finally we took them over.'

However, to start with, Arkoff recalled elsewhere, they had to scrape around to finance each film. Arkoff and Nicholson each contributed $3000 to start their distribution company. 'We got personnel to take $25,000 in salary deferments. We got $35,000 in advances from the subdistributors, $25,000 in advances from the film lab with the lab work itself deferred, plus $10,000 in advances from foreign distributors. That was enough to do a cheap picture. We did about 100 pictures that way.'

Eventually AIP attracted private investors. 'Of course,' Arkoff noted, 'there were always Texans.' This was a straight equity deal – nothing sophisticated – cash in exchange for percentages of incomes and perhaps a part for a former Miss Longhorn, who had classy lines but couldn't necessarily speak them. 'There were many enthusiastic local people with no picture business sense.'

In the independent film distribution business the market is the medium and the message is money. At bottom, a movie needs only an idea that is exciting and exploitable. Often the title and poster came first, something punchy like *The Phantom from 10,000 Leagues* (1955), and only afterwards the writer, script and director were hired. In its hunt for appealing material AIP established numerous genres: apocalyptic horror, teenage beach parties, motorcycles.

Roger Corman's New World

Roger Corman, having made many of AIP's genre hits including their commercially and critically successful adaptations from Edgar Allan Poe like *House of Usher* (1960, UK title *The Fall of the House of Usher*) and *The Tomb of Ligeia* (1964) and having flirted with 'important' films for Fox and United Artists, left AIP and the other independent distributors to found his own distribution company, New World, the success of which depended largely on his own formulae: lusty women in peril, lusty women in uniform, the car as weapon.

Women in prison had been marketable commodities since Cecil B. DeMille's *The Godless Girl* (1928). Sylvia Sidney spent half the Great Depression locked up on screen. Corman's brother, Gene, was film-maker Allan Dwan's agent at the time Dwan was producing admirable action movies, such as *Woman They Almost Lynched* (1953) and *Cattle Queen of Montana* (1954), prefeminist heroics (worthy of rediscovery). Besides Corman's earliest films for AIP his numerous other sensational subjects had included *Apache Woman, Swamp Woman, The Oklahoma Woman*, and *The Viking Woman and the Sea Serpent*. By the time he established New World in 1970, feminism was newsworthy. He therefore took a new look at this favourite

Barbara Stanwyck and Allan Dwan *(above far left) on the set of* Cattle Queen of Montana, *one of several fine '50s films made by the veteran director for independent producer Benedict Bogeaus.*

Joan Leslie *(above left) in* The Woman They Almost Lynched, *a low-budget western Dwan made for Republic.*

Lord Grade *(above), multi-national media mogul.*

movie theme. *The Big Bird Cage, The Big Doll House, The Hot Box, Caged Heat, Candy Stripe Nurses, Summer School Teachers, Big Bad Mama, Crazy Mama*: the women in these movies think. They make decisions that affect their lives, and once they have made those decisions, their resolve is strong. By shooting in the Philippines, Corman kept his early budgets almost as low as Arkoff had twenty years earlier. *The Big Doll House* cost $120,000 to produce. It grossed $10m. When budgets began to rise during the mid-1970s, Corman entrusted his very cheapest films to one person only, the resolute Mrs Corman. She is not a woman to waste money.

Like the majors, independent distributors imitate each other. AIP followed Corman into the women-in-action, or girl gangbusters, genre. Soon Pam Grier was their highest paid star after Vincent Price. Another independent, Dimension, jumped on the bandwagon with their star Cheri Caffaro.

Universal's *American Graffiti* (1973) provided the stimulus that another independent, Crown International, required: high school romance. *The Pom Pom Girls* was one of the top independently released features of 1976. Crown followed it with *The Van, Coach, Malibu Beach,* and *Van Nuys Blvd.* – with decreasing commercial impact. AIP's version was called *Cooley High,* New World's, *Rock and Roll High School.*

BBS and the youth boom

At times the independent distributors have played a crucial part in influencing Hollywood's mainstream production. For example the success of their motorbike and hells angel pictures led directly into the success of the youth-orientated bike picture *Easy Rider* (1969) which had started life as an AIP project. *Easy Rider* was the project of two enterprising film-makers, Bob Rafelson and Bert Schneider, who took the project to Columbia after they had quarrelled with Sam Arkoff. Together with a new partner, Steve Blauner, they formed BBS, and on the basis of *Easy Rider*'s mounting grosses (eventually totalling about $20m.) and the fact that Schneider's father was Abe Schneider, the chairman of the board of Columbia, and his brother Stanley Schneider was president of the studio, BBS got a six-picture deal, which included an artistic integrity clause: if budgets stayed in the semi-exploitation range – close to, but less than $1m. – Columbia had no right of project approval. BBS could deliver whatever cheap picture it pleased and Columbia, eager for the youth-market dollar, would distribute it. Dreams of 'Sons' and 'Daughters' and 'Grandchildren of Easy Rider' danced in their heads.

They employed writers of calibre such as Carol Eastman, usually credited as Adrien Joyce, writer of *Five Easy Pieces* (1970); their performers included Jack Nicholson, Dennis Hopper, Candice Bergen, Karen Black, and Luana Anders; and Peter Bogdanovich and Henry Jaglom were among their directors. In the centre of it all was the enigmatic Bert Schneider, an establishment anti-establishment figure with connections and political interests. He was the angel, the backer, the shrewd, bejewelled oracle in the cloud of pot smoke with the remarkably consistent taste in motion picture exploitation.

Every BBS film (with the possible exception of the self-consciously mythic *The Last Picture Show*) featured disaffected protagonists – traditional youth-market material – treading the exploitable narrows between straight America's assorted hypocrisies and an assortment of alternative life-styles: political, pharmaceutical, or delusional. *Five Easy Pieces, Drive, He Said* and *A Safe Place* all had the hallmarks of youth-market pictures except, increasingly, youth. Instead of being the Pepsi generation, they were the BBS generation.

Following the unreleasable (and expensive) *Last Movie* and the removal of Bert's father Abe from Columbia Pictures, which – despite the occasional hit like *The Last Picture Show* – was now losing money from BBS, this temporary burst of artistic freedom was soon brought to

Easy Rider *(above), with Dennis Hopper, Peter Fonda and Jack Nicholson, heralded a multi-picture studio deal for Bert Schneider's BBS Productions.*

The Exorcist *(above right) offered early evidence of the major studios' new willingness to embrace 'exploitation' cinema.*

an end. Columbia's new boss David Begelman terminated the arrangement.

Lord Grade's AFD

Some independent distributors have taken a different direction from AIP, New World and BBS (a production company rather than a distributor): instead of exploiting a market relatively untouched by the majors, they have aped the majors by trying both to create full-scale distribution systems from scratch and to make major movies to play them. The expense of such a full-scale assault is so colossal and the risks so great that only an individual or an organization of considerable wealth and experience has the remotest chance of success. The chief contender until recently was Britain's Lord Grade who was first a dancer (1927), then an agent (1933), then a very big agent (1947) and finally the boss of a British television empire and a film producer. Grade had been keen to break into the American movie market for many years and during the 1970s he assembled numerous big-budget movies with major stars, including *The Eagle Has Landed* (1976) for Columbia and *The Boys from Brazil* (1978) for Fox, only to see them fail at the box office. Convinced that this failure was partly the result of their distribution, Grade eventually established AFD, a brand new distribution company, to handle his (and the English company EMI's) product in America. But after heavy losses Grade made a distribution deal with Universal. Apart from *The Muppet Movie* (1979) AFD did not produce a really notable box-office hit, and they were very badly hurt by the total failure of the disco movie *Can't Stop the Music* and the hugely expensive *Raise the Titanic* in 1980.

The majors invade the market

In recent years even some of the older and more seasoned independent distributors have begun to face mounting problems. This is largely because the exploitation area has now been very successfully invaded by the majors themselves. There is less incentive for an audience to pay to see a low-budget thriller about possession by the devil when Warners' blockbusting *The Exorcist* (1973) with a full star cast and millions of dollars worth of effects is playing on the other side of the street. After the launching of the first Russian sputnik on 4 October 1957, Roger Corman needed only eight weeks to pump out the cheap science fiction movie *War of the Satellites*, but today such a film cannot compete with megabudget outer space pictures from Fox or Columbia. Once the majors attack a subject with any determination, the independents necessarily have to move on (or increase their budgets). Unfortunately for the independents, the majors are currently better attuned to the youth market and to sensation than they have ever been.

Daily Variety reported in June 1980 (in a special independent film issue) that independent distributors are alive and well worldwide. A few of the newer companies, like Sunn Classic, have done well by hard-selling pseudo-documentaries (*In Search of Noah's Ark*, 1977) and children's adventures (*The Wilderness Family*, 1976) to the family market with extensive television promotion. Yet the best known of the independents, the renowned purveyors of the *genres maudits* – AIP and New World – are troubled. Roger Corman's New World tried switching to higher budgets and made a short-lived attempt to expand its operations in England. AIP, chastened in the pursuit of loftier ambitions by costly flops like *A Matter of Time* and *Meteor*, has been absorbed by Filmways, who despite the success of *The Amityville Horror* (1979), parted company with Arkoff and faced a financial crisis in 1980. The words American International Pictures have been chiselled off the facade at 9033 Wilshire Boulevard in Beverly Hills, the house that *schlock* built. Samuel Z. Arkoff, for twenty-five years the archetypal independent distributor, has become just another independent producer.

Promotion and Release

The film industry rarely regards a movie as a major hit until it has been successful in America. Revenue from other countries is important but America represents about one half of the world market for a feature film. Therefore its 16,000 or so movie-theatres are the most obvious gateway to major box-office success. This explains the considerable attention devoted by the industry to America's exhibitors and the immense sophistication of the marketing techniques that are employed to fill their theatres.

Release

The Supreme Court Decision of 1948 (see p. 18) ensured that America's movie-houses ceased to be owned by the major studios. Nevertheless, there are still huge American theatre-chains controlled by single organizations. The biggest chain of cinemas in the United States, the General Cinema Corporation, has its headquarters in Boston and owns about 770 cinema screens. Other major circuits include United Artists Theatres based in Great Neck, Long Island, near New York, with 600 screens, and Commonwealth Theatres, serving mid-America, with more than 300. On the West Coast, Mann controls 200.

The studios hope that their major movies will at some stage be given what is known as a 'multiple break', a multiple booking in several hundred cinemas across the United States which can take full advantage of national media coverage. Because this process is extremely costly and usually very effective, it inevitably breeds intense competition between exhibitors for the most eagerly awaited films.

Long before a major film is scheduled for release, while it is still in production, its distributor will send a 'bid' letter to theatre-owners, giving specific conditions that the film's exhibitors will be expected to fulfill and asking for sealed bids. The conditions sought by the distributor might include a minimum length for the engagement, or a minimum advance payment, depending on how much the distributor thinks it can demand for this particular film.

Blind bidding for potential blockbusters

Because the law decrees that the movie companies must give all theatre owners the opportunity to bid for a film, each bid received is supposed to be opened publicly, without any deals being made behind the scenes. A producer cannot legally sign a contract with a single theatre chain giving it first choice of his movies, although accusations abound that this practice continues in secret. Certainly, if an exhibitor desperately wants a certain film from a major company, he may find it hard to resist their less saleable films in the hope that his tenacity will be remembered. But, in theory, the bidding system is supposed to eliminate any favouritism.

What it has not eliminated is cut-throat competition between exhibitors scrambling for the big, potentially money-making, films. On a major picture, 12 weeks minimum playing time may be demanded by the distributor and the exhibitor who accepts such terms will have to stick to them even if the film proves to be a flop. For the sequel to *Star Wars*, *The Empire Strikes Back* (1980), Twentieth Century-Fox reported that exhibitors were so eager to get the booking that some of them were offering as much as 28 week minimum runs. Such blockbusters are publicized well in advance, with news of major stars signed, colossal budgets, wonderkid directors and so on. But, generally speaking, they are not available for screening until a few days before their public opening, long after the bids have been made. The system is therefore called 'blind-bidding'.

In the case of *The Empire Strikes Back*, few people are complaining, but in recent years a series of big pictures attracted enormous advance bidding and then turned out, in the eyes of the exhibitors, to be very disappointing. *Exorcist II: the Heretic* (1977) was reputedly laughed off some New York cinema screens

King Kong: *the first major publicity campaign in RKO's history.*

when it opened and had to be hastily re-edited by Warners. Despite the teaming of Marlon Brando and Jack Nicholson, *The Missouri Breaks* (1976) did not live up to its ballyhoo, nor did Steven Spielberg's *1941* (1980) or Stanley Kubrick's *The Shining* (1979). Such films have fuelled demands by exhibitors that they should be able to see the films for which they are bidding and judge their audience appeal for themselves.

This feeling has been intensified by the amount of money the studios expect the exhibitors to pay for their best product. Most deals for major pictures call for 90 per cent of the box office gross to go to the distributor in the first week, after an agreed-upon allowance for house expenses (called the 'house nut') has been subtracted. That 90 per cent share is then reduced each week the movie plays. Usually the contract also stipulates that, regardless of the house nut, the distributor will receive no less than a fixed percentage of the box office gross – say 70 per cent, a 'fixed minimum floor'. To take an example: if a picture grosses $20,000 in its first week and the agreed-upon house allowance is $3000, the distributor will get 90 per cent of the difference, in this case $15,300. But, if the picture does not live up to its promise and takes only $6000 in the first week, then $3000, which is the income left after deducting the $3000 house expenses, is less than 70 per cent of the gross. The fixed minimum floor of 70 per cent will be $4200. So, because he has guaranteed this percentage to the distributor, the exhibitor has to pay the distributor the entire box office gross less expenses, and he has to reach further into his pocket and pay $1200 more. Hardly a profitable way to do business, especially when you had no opportunity to inspect the product, whose losses you now finance!

Intense lobbying from the theatre-owners has resulted in anti blind-booking statutes being passed in almost twenty states. For their part, the studios have sought to get around such restrictions, pointing out that in most cases their films are not ready to be seen by exhibitors at the time of bidding. If there are many more flops like *1941* in the 1980s, the pressure for change may become irresistible.

The *Cruising* controversy

In recent years American exhibitors have also been concerned not only about the quality of films provided by the majors but also by their sexual explicitness. In 1979 the General Cinema Corporation bid successfully (but blindly) for William Friedkin's gruelling thriller about the New York underworld *Cruising* which was rated 'R' by the Motion Picture Association of America's Board. When General Cinema's executives previewed the film they were so shocked that they refused to screen it altogether, claiming that it merited an 'X' rating and therefore could not be shown in one of their cinemas. ('X' in America has disreputable connotations, almost invariably denoting hard-core pornography, whereas in Britain 'X' is a respectable rating, accorded to the majority of adult movies.) Industry observers noted that even the publicity sparked by General's decision would be unlikely to make up for the loss of such a major cinema outlet.

Advertising and publicity

Back in the so-called Golden Years of Hollywood – during the 1930s and 1940s when the studios were all producing 50 or so pictures a year – the word 'marketing' had scarcely worked its way into the industry jargon. The studios owned their own chains of theatres, and their movies were automatically booked into those houses. Most of the advertising of individual movies was left to the exhibitors themselves, who used materials supplied by the distributor.

In those days there was much less competition for the entertainment dollar, because there was no television and people went to the movies regularly as a matter of course. However, there was competition between the

Ava Gardner *(far left) and Britain's* **Diana Dors** *(left) pose in typical examples of the early 1950s studio publicity shot.*

studios, and their publicity departments were intensely involved especially in grooming the stars each studio had under contract. It was a time when movie stars were glamorous, larger than life, and anything they did was news. There were more outlets for publicity, as distinct from advertising, not only big, slick magazines like *Life* and *Look* but many more newspapers and fan magazines. The studio publicity departments were horizontally structured, with specialists responsible for each area of the media. In the pecking order, the most important publicist handled the national magazines; next was radio, which in time became radio and television; then newspapers; the wire services; syndicated columnists; and so on down to the trade press.

However, in 1962, a survey by the Daniel Yankelovich company, which specializes in marketing research, concluded that publicity contributed little to the success of a motion picture, and that what really counted with audiences was advertising three days prior to the picture's opening. The news broke at the time when the studios were struggling to cut their overheads, and their reaction was prompt. They began dismantling their large publicity departments, and today a staff of only half a dozen or even fewer is commonplace.

Experience during the intervening years has, however, shown that strategically planned publicity can still be important to a picture's box-office success. As a result an enormous number of independent publicity companies and freelance publicists have set up in Hollywood. For any major movie, a unit publicist is usually assigned before filming begins, and his or her job is to provide a steady flow of publicity. Apart from preparing production notes and biographies of the stars and the film's production team, the publicist will try to drum up important news stories, searching for good news breaks like an international wire service story or a cover story in a nationally syndicated column, all aimed at making the public aware of the movie.

With regard to bought advertising, the exhibitor's share of the cost of a studio's national advertising campaign for a picture is today generally commensurate with the exhibitor's retained percentage of the box office receipts.

Marketing

The studios have been content to devolve much of the publicity work into freelance hands because so great a portion of their resources and energies is now devoted to the newly evolved science of marketing, which is simply the science of selling movies to the public. Each major movie has its own campaign tailor-made; the campaign may begin with a series of costly surveys to identify not only which are the film's most saleable traits but which are its least saleable traits. Every attempt will then be made to highlight the former and disguise the latter. At this early stage it is also vital to discover which particular advertising medium is most

Richard Zanuck *(right), producer of* Jaws, *with some of the omnivorous merchandise that made him a multi-millionaire.*

likely to reach the film's audience.

Marketing was undoubtedly one of the key factors behind Hollywood's remarkable success in the 1970s. Films like *Star Wars*, *Kramer vs. Kramer* and *10* have been sold in ways that the old moguls never anticipated. Marketing is the new art form at the majors, and the pay-offs can be tremendous. When a movie opens nationwide in the United States in 800 or 1000 theatres, or floods a specific city or region, accompanied by a brilliant marketing campaign, the box office take can be increased enormously. 'The real stars at the majors are the marketing people, not the production executives,' states a top production executive. 'People like Ashley Boone, Norman Levy, Pat Williamson, Hy Smith, Frank Mancuso. Producers are already beginning to say, they want their picture at Universal, or wherever, not because of Mr X, who is head of production, but because of Mr Y, who is this terrific marketing guy. Mr Y knows how to sell a movie, knows when and where to open it, knows audience demographics.'

One of the classic cases of successful marketing in the 1970s (detailed in an astute *New York Times* article by Richard Warren Lewis) was producer Peter Guber's 1977 campaign for *The Deep*. This began with hardback and paperback editions of Peter Benchley's novel on which the film was based. Then Guber himself published a 'behind-the-scenes book', entitled *Inside The Deep*, two days before the film's opening date, 17 June 1977 (chosen because 15 June was payday for most workers). The picture was booked into 800 theatres that week, as its director and stars made the rounds of the talkshow circuit, and supermarkets were saturated by 'Deep' merchandise and associated competitions. Columbia spent nearly $3m. on advertising, which had been specially researched to amplify the film's various crowd-pulling elements, and Guber's surveys showed that, by the time the film opened, his target audience would have been exposed to at least 15 different media pitches.

Of course this kind of campaign is so complex that a single misjudgement can seriously jeopardize a film's chances. In early 1980 Paramount found to their horror that their new John Travolta picture *Urban Cowboy* was attracting crowds of 18 years and over, while the kids – a vital part of the audience for most blockbusters – were staying away. The original poster featuring a close-up of Travolta was then withdrawn in favour of a picture of him dancing alongside his co-star. Paramount's research had told them that the under-eighteens were not as interested in Travolta as a moody cowboy as they were in seeing him dance. Around the same time, Clint Eastwood, who supervises much of his own promotional material himself, urgently rejigged the poster for *Bronco Billy*, replacing its western trappings with the more contemporary image of a motorized trailer. Such fine tuning, provided it is done in time, can mean the difference between success and failure.

Red River *(far left), one of the big successes of the 1940s. At a time when people went to the same movie-theatres regularly, trailers were crucial. This one was extremely successful.*

Ben Hur *(left) utilized its trailer to flaunt Oscars, long recognized as an important selling-point.*

Television and marketing

The larger the number of screens in a 'saturation' opening, the cheaper the per theatre cost if national network television is used. In the US the cut-off point for deciding whether the enormously expensive use of network television is cost-effective – instead of buying spots in local markets – is about 500 theatres. If there are fewer bookings than this, a campaign of television commercials on local stations in the cities where the film is showing is more cost effective. Network commercial costs are prohibitive – as high as $250,000 for a 30-second commercial on a special programme, such as the annual Super Bowl football game or during the baseball World Series. And, as Universal President Ned Tanen points out, your advertising spot has to compete with dozens of others: not just commercials for other theatrical movies, but also for television movies the networks are airing themselves. 'When we're buying these spots for a movie, whatever we do is literally a drop in the bucket compared to what the same station will do for its own hot "World Premiere Movie" which is mentioned on every soap, every prime time show, every station break. And can a viewer tell the difference between a "World Premiere", or whatever the station is calling it this week, and the big, hot, new theatrical movie?'

In the US, most advertisers have switched to using 30-second commercials because they are cheaper than the 60-second spots prevalent a few years ago – and this makes the TV screens more cluttered than ever with commercial messages. Occasionally, a studio will come up with an effective 10-second or 20-second commercial, but the norm is 30 seconds. Marketing men justify the cost by demonstrating that, used properly, a million dollars spent in television advertising can bring in three million or more extra box office dollars.

There are, of course, other ways of getting television coverage which are substantially cheaper than buying time for commercials. Sometimes a documentary is made of the filming of a feature. This is then sold or 'bartered' to television stations. 'Bartering' means exchanging the documentary for commercial air time. For example, Casablanca Record & FilmWorks was very successful in bartering a 30-minute disco programme it made for its disco feature *Thank God It's Friday* (1978).

The late Walt Disney knew how to use television as a marketing tool perhaps better than anyone else before or since. And Card Walker, head of the Disney operation today, was formerly a marketing man. For that studio's $18.5m. space spectacular, *The Black Hole* (1979), a straight documentary television film about black holes in space was produced for the 18 to 39 year-old market. The studio bartered the programme in the top 100 markets in the US in exchange for commercials to go on air between 21 and 30 December 1979. This is a period when independent television stations have difficulty selling advertising time – immediately before and after Christmas – and it was a perfect time for advertising *The Black Hole*, which was to open on 21 December.

The *Black Hole* documentary was aired by most stations in prime time in late November or early December, becoming a very economical way for Disney to whet the public's interest in the subject of its movie.

Walt Disney *(above), greatest of marketing men.*

Marketing research

'I think the first real national television buy for a motion picture was for a Clint Eastwood movie called *Dirty Harry*, somewhere around 1971,' marketing executive Dick Lederer says. 'At that time, the buy cost about $250,000. For the same rating points today, it probably would cost around $800,000. That is some difference, and the audience has not grown that much. So if you are going to take a picture out in a massive way, you had better be right. This is what is scaring many people in charge of film companies today. Marketing is more of a gamble than ever.'

Marketing budgets are often as high or

The Blue Lagoon *(right) cost $4.5m. to make and another $6.3m. to market. Its subject of pre-pubescent sexuality has long been recognized as highly saleable. Stanley Kubrick utilized a single image from his film* **Lolita** *(far right) to evoke the same subject.*

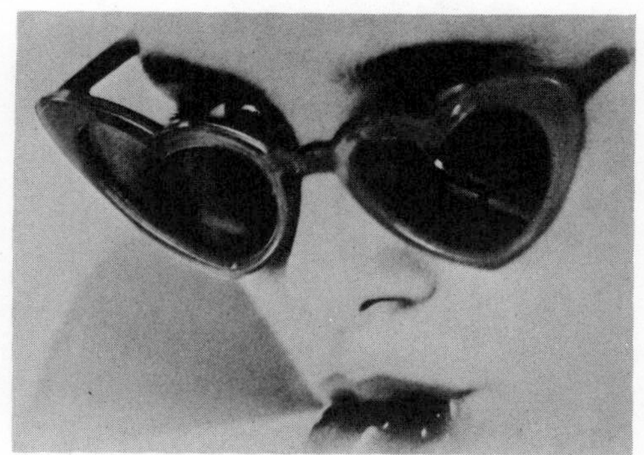

higher than production budgets. And Nat Fellman, former president of the National General chain of theatres, points out that 'just spending dollars won't always bring the public into the theatre. You have to have something that you are able to sell; you have to be sure you have a handle on your picture.'

Consequently, marketing research has come into its own. A relatively recent phenomenon in the marketing of motion pictures, it has evolved into one of the primary tools utilized in advertising/publicity/promotion campaigns.

Used properly, research can guide the companies into the best way of selling their films in the marketplace. How to 'position' the movie. Can the picture be categorized specifically as action/adventure? Comedy? Mystery? Love story? Thriller? Should the target audience be young people under 25, children, women, men, families, science-fiction buffs? What are the best media to use in reaching that target public?

An analysis must be made, as Fellman put it, of the picture's 'handle' to be exploited. Does it have star value in its cast? Is it based on a best-selling book with an exciting story? Is it about a subject in which the public is currently interested? And, actually, just how good a movie is it? How much would the film profit from a word of mouth pre-release campaign?

The marketing of *Kramer vs. Kramer*

A good example of sophisticated marketing is *Kramer vs. Kramer*, a hit for Columbia Pictures during the 1979 Christmas season which maintained excellent box-office figures well into 1980. Based on Avery Corman's 1977 novel, the film finished principal photography in December 1978. It is the simple story of an advertising executive in New York whose wife walks out to 'find her own identity' and leaves him saddled with their six year-old son. The title refers to the court case 18 months later when she tries to take the boy back.

'Because of its subject, the movie could have been perceived as a soap opera, the sort of thing that is done on television, or because of its title it could have been seen as nothing but a courtroom drama,' Marvin Levy, a top Columbia marketing executive comments. Research studies had indicated that women responded favourably to the subject, but men did not. So the studio felt it should at least try to neutralize young men's responses so they would not veto going to the theatre to see *Kramer vs. Kramer* if the women in their lives wanted to see it.

This is an example of what Richard Kahn, an MGM marketing man, has called using marketing research as an 'input' of information. 'The danger exists,' Kahn asserted, 'of elevating its findings to an unassailable pinnacle via misuse, misinterpretation, and over-confidence in its solution. The marketing of movies cannot be reduced to a computer science. Trained judgements, intuition and common sense must remain the hallmarks of motion picture marketing.' In other words, he's saying don't completely abandon that good old 'gut feeling' that has guided film-makers since the industry's early beginnings.

Kahn's warning is echoed by Dr Bruce Mallen, another marketing consultant: 'Whenever I move into a new product area as a consultant, people in that business always tell me that their business is different, that the usual marketing rules don't apply. And I have always found they were wrong and that their product could be marketed using the same basic methods. Until I reached the motion picture business. They were right about this business. It's crazy.'

In the case of *Kramer vs. Kramer* the film's producer, Stanley Jaffe, disagreed with research findings that its subject matter would not appeal to men. 'True, it's not an action-adventure film, but I don't think that those old guidelines about what men will go to see really hold any more,' he declared. And in the final analysis, *Kramer*'s box office success validated Jaffe's stand. Its audiences have not been exceptionally weighted towards women.

The studio strategists decided they should have an advertising campaign that stressed

Kramer vs. Kramer

There are three sides to this love story.

COLUMBIA PICTURES PRESENTS A STANLEY JAFFE PRODUCTION

DUSTIN HOFFMAN

IN

"KRAMER VS. KRAMER"

MERYL STREEP JANE ALEXANDER

Director of Photography NESTOR ALMENDROS

Based Upon the Novel by AVERY CORMAN

Produced by STANLEY R. JAFFE

Written for the Screen and Directed by ROBERT BENTON

Now A Best Selling Signet Paperback.

PG PARENTAL GUIDANCE SUGGESTED

SOME MATERIAL MAY NOT BE SUITABLE FOR CHILDREN

© 1979 COLUMBIA PICTURES INDUSTRIES, INC

THEATRE

International Velvet *(right) with Tatum O'Neal and horse proved impossible to sell. But Clint Eastwood and an orangutan in* **Every Which Way But Loose** *(far right) was a winning double.*

Kramer vs. Kramer *(left) starred Dustin Hoffman and Meryl Streep with Justin Henry as their son. It is interesting that at no point in the film do the Kramers live up to their publicity as a happy family. The advertisement featured in women's magazines (bottom left) reflected one aspect of the film.*

that the movie was about all three participants – not just about the mother and father, but also about the little boy. They also wanted to play down the inference of the title that conflict was the primary content of the story. And because *Kramer* did not contain what Levy referred to as the 'razzle-dazzle, the tremendous names, the instantly identifiable themes' of the blockbusters that were up against it in the marketplace, it was decided to 'position' the picture to appeal to adult moviegoers, not interested in the 'family' movies which normally dominate the Christmas period.

Kramer vs. Kramer would be bucking Paramount's *Star Trek – the Motion Picture* and Disney's *The Black Hole*, among others. As it happened, another 'non-family' movie was also a box office leader in that particular season – Universal's *The Jerk*, starring Steve Martin, hardly classifiable as 'adult' entertainment, but definitely not for the kiddies.

Columbia assigned two different advertising agencies, Diener/Hauser/Bates and Frankfurt Communications, to come up with a 'print ad' that would accomplish this positioning. Several were submitted before they found one that they felt would accomplish their purpose. One 'ad' was comprised of only the picture's title and the words 'An act of love'. It was felt that this was too austere. One candidate featuring childish lettering transposing the 'VS.' into 'loVeS' was considered too clever and too cute.

Two of the 'ads' submitted consisted of family photographs of the three stars, Dustin Hoffman, Meryl Streep and little Justin Henry. In one of them, a photograph of the wife had been partially removed from its frame; the studio executives in the end turned that one down because it might be too depressing. They finally went with the simple photograph of the three family members. The copy line chosen to accompany the picture read: 'There are three sides to this love story.' Another 'ad' designed especially to run in women's magazines showed the husband making breakfast for his son. That copy line read: 'Ted Kramer is about to learn what 10 million women already know.'

A three-week, $2m. television advertising campaign utilized three different 20-second commercials. Because the marketing research on *Kramer* indicated that Dustin Hoffman is a major draw, his scenes were featured in two of them. The scene featuring Meryl Streep pleading to keep her child was the focus of the commercial which ran during programmes with a high proportion of female viewers.

Because they believed they had an exceptional film, Columbia allowed magazine reviewers and editors to see it early. Their gamble paid off when *Time* magazine ran an eight-page story on *Kramer vs. Kramer* in its 3 December issue, two and a half weeks before the 19 December opening. Other favourable reviews followed in quick succession after the picture opened, and 'print ads' from then on featured a sampling of several laudatory reviews.

Kramer vs. Kramer was given an unusual release pattern for a Christmas holiday launch. Instead of opening in 600 or 800 or 1000 theatres nationwide, Columbia had booked it into only about 450 theatres – hoping to give an impression of being available but not *too* available. The ploy worked.

Word of mouth

International Velvet was a sentimental, beautifully-mounted movie with a story about a young girl's struggle to achieve a goal. But it did not fit into a specific category. As MGM marketing head Richard Kahn said before the picture was launched in July 1978, 'It's a family picture in the best possible sense, and audiences who have seen it have loved it – from 8 year-olds to 20 year-olds to 60 year-olds. All we have to do is get across its story elements, let people know that it is not *National Velvet* or *Lassie Come Home* updated.' Yet, in spite of a heavily publicized world premiere in Washington D.C. – with pictures of Tatum O'Neal and President Carter's daughter Amy getting national exposure in newspapers, magazines and on television stations across the country –

followed by an advertising campaign making heavy use of television, newspapers and radio, the picture did not do well at the box office.

There was no specific 'handle' to *International Velvet*, nor did it generate 'word of mouth'. Kahn had admitted before the premiere that *International Velvet* presented 'an interesting marketing problem. We have a film that satisfies all markets; all we have to do is get them in the theatre.'

'Usually the audiences in this country are fragmented,' Kahn observed. 'There are pictures that the under-13 set like, which are pretty much the province of Walt Disney. Then there is the 13 to 18 bubble gum, finger-snapping set, and their range of movie taste is eclectic. They go from *Goodbye Girl* to *Jaws*. Then there are the 18 to 25 year-olds, who look for thrills, sheer escapism or substance – not necessarily all in the same movie. And the over-25s who opt for the thought-provoking entertainment – good, not necessarily extreme, but nevertheless satisfying entertainment.' The fear was confirmed that *International Velvet*, by attempting to combine these audiences, ended up appealing to none of them.

In marked contrast *Every Which Way But Loose* had a very exploitable, two-pronged, 'handle': Clint Eastwood as the star and a lovable orangutan as his co-star. As Ned Tanen, president of Universal, so aptly put it: 'I don't think anyone in their right mind would think that *Every Which Way But Loose*, which is not our movie (it was released by Warner Brothers) would be half the smash it was without the brilliant television commercials of Clint Eastwood and the orangutan. He and the monkey are obviously having a good time together, and there's action, and they sold tickets.' (Enough tickets, in fact, to make the picture rank second only to Warner's *Superman* as the top grossing film of 1979 in the US.

'But when you get a relatively cerebral movie,' Tanen continued, 'it's very difficult within 30 seconds or 10 seconds or even a minute to say anything to an audience that's either watching a soap opera or "Happy Days" or the Super Bowl or whatever. How do you sell *An Unmarried Woman* on television?'

It remains true that the best thing a movie can have going for it is still strong, favourable 'word of mouth'. In an article reflecting lugubriously on the glut of product in 1980 and the numerous box office casualties, like *Xanadu*, *The Island* and *Bronco Billy*, *Variety* reported a leading distributor as saying: 'Things have gotten out of hand with endless national breaks for which the advertising campaigns alone cost as much as the films. The real thing that builds a picture is word of mouth.'

The Black Stallion provides an excellent example. In mid-December 1979, United Artists released this Francis Coppola production, an exquisitely photographed story of a boy and a beautiful horse shipwrecked together on an island, in only two theatres – one in New York and one in Los Angeles. About a month later, a Hollywood publicist, Murray Weissman, and his wife decided they would like to see the film because their friends had praised it so highly. When they arrived at the two-theatre Plitt complex in Century City, there was a line around the block. Disney's $18.5m. space extravaganza *The Black Hole* was also showing on one of the Plitt screens, so the Weissmans assumed the line was for *The Black Hole*. They were astonished on reaching the ticket window to learn that this long line was for *The Black Stallion*, a film which had had almost no publicity or advertising.

The Black Stallion *(left) had a deliberately muted but highly successful campaign.*

The Black Hole, backed by a $9m. advertising campaign and Disney's marketing know-how, had opened at the Plitt on 21 December, achieving a box office gross the first week of $62,922. *The Black Stallion* had opened a week earlier and had a first week's take of $27,600. Seven weeks later, still showing in the same theatre complex, *The Black Hole* took in a respectable gross of $7348 – but *The Black Stallion* had an eighth week total of $37,018. That kind of success alongside the failure of recent blockbusters like *1941* shows it's still true that even the most sophisticated and elaborate marketing strategy in the world cannot sell the public a product it doesn't want. If, on the other hand, a film catches on by word of mouth, the only thing people need to know is where it's playing.

THE CREATORS

Stars and Stardom

Robert Redford **Clint Eastwood** **Robert de Niro** **Warren Beatty** **Steve McQueen**

'The other day a man came up to me and kept saying "You're a star, you're a star." I thought: this year I'm a star, but what will I be next year – a black hole?'
Woody Allen

'One of the main things about being successful is that I stopped being afraid of dying. I was always obsessed with death, obsessed with things ending, my career being finished. Now I'm not so much. I couldn't understand why that was for a long time, and finally I realized it's because when you're a movie star you're already dead, you're embalmed.'
Dustin Hoffman

According to Ian Jessel, the marketing director of ITC, Lord Grade's production company, the top ten most bankable stars in 1980 were Robert Redford (whose box office value was estimated at $5m.), Clint Eastwood ($4m.), Robert de Niro ($3m.), Warren Beatty, the late Steve McQueen, Al Pacino, Woody Allen, Dustin Hoffman, Barbra Streisand and Paul Newman (the last two both estimated at $1½m.); Streisand, however, edges up to $3m. if she sings as well as acts. The only other women even close to Streisand are Jane Fonda and Diane Keaton, though Jill Clayburgh and Meryl Streep may be on their way into the top twenty.

Stardom is neither exclusive to America nor specifically cinematic – there are stars in several sports, in every entertainment medium and in almost all the developed countries of the world. But Hollywood stardom crosses all international boundaries; as Humphrey Bogart put it, 'You're not a star until they can spell your name in Karachi'. Hollywood has also evolved a star system of peculiar complexity – compared, say, to sport, which relies to a larger extent on measurable achievement.

Marilyn Monroe: *'only the public can make a star . . .'*

Until quite recently most writers on stardom have approached the subject in one or other of the following ways, Either, perhaps naively, they have considered stardom to be a direct consequence of what-the-people-want or, more cynically, they have seen it as a case of what-the-people-are-given. If we take the first attitude, film stars become a simple mirror of their social milieu: the film critic Alexander Walker, for instance, sees stars as 'the direct or indirect reflections of the needs, drives and dreams of American society'; similarly the critic and writer Raymond Durgnat describes them as 'a reflection in which the public studies and adjusts its own image'. But even if we accept that stars are mirrors, how and what they reflect remains unanswered. Do Greta Garbo, Joan Crawford, Jean Harlow and Mae West all mirror the same social milieu? Or only their specific audiences? Certainly Woody Allen offers the persona of a kooky critic to an urban intellectual audience, while Burt Reynolds' 'good ole Boy' image is a more southern, blue-collar phenomenon.

According to Sam Goldwyn, 'God makes the stars. It's up to the producers to find them.' Goldwyn later qualified this epigram: 'Producers don't make stars. God makes stars and the public recognizes his handiwork.' Marilyn Monroe put it another way when she announced that 'only the public can make a star . . . it's the studios who try to make a system out of it.' The question is, then, whether the world gets its stars directly from God (via Goldwyn) or, more democratically, from the people; whether stars are born or created.

The notion of the natural talent, the child prodigy, the born star has been challenged,

Al Pacino Woody Allen Dustin Hoffman Barbra Streisand Paul Newman

Clark Gable: *'I'm just a lucky slob . . .'*

rather surprisingly, by several stars themselves. Boris Karloff, who seems inseparable from the roles he made famous, once said, 'You could heave a brick out of the window and hit ten actors who could play my parts. I just happened to be on the right corner at the right time.' Similarly, with characteristic self-deprecation, Clark Gable admitted, 'I'm just a lucky slob from Ohio who happened to be in the right place at the right time.' Not all film stars are as modest. Nevertheless, such statements do suggest that stardom is less a matter of inevitability than of 'luck', less of 'talent' being discovered than of an actor or actress being in the right place at the right time. Though not just any actor or actress, Katharine Hepburn, echoing the notion of the 'star as a social mirror', has said that she was 'born with a set of characteristics that were in the public vogue'. But even this is not strictly true. Hepburn was by no means always in the public vogue; even she needed to be cast in appropriate roles, to find the right vehicles with the right collaborators. Without them, she could even be labelled box-office poison, as she was by a group of exhibitors in 1938.

The right 'characteristics' are obviously advantages to any would-be star. But no business has ever banked on such a lucky combination. The film industry is notorious for attempting to manipulate its market and produce its own public vogues, for fabricating film stars and launching them with a wave of press campaigns, pin-ups, leaked gossip, 'leapfrog' casting (where a new star is placed opposite an established star) and other such devices.

In the days of the studio system the stars were surrounded by teams of doctors and dentists, personal physicians and cosmeticians, psychiatrists and physical therapists, drama coaches and casting directors, elocutionists and lighting cameramen. They were paid huge salaries, attended by retinues of aides and admirers, and spoilt with little liberties (like the obligatory choice-of-hat clauses in James Stewart's contracts). In this way the studio bosses built up the necessary mystique of stardom, at the same time successfully disguising that in other respects stars were treated like children. Only occasionally could they choose roles for themselves, and they faced severe disciplinary measures if they refused more than two or three studio choices in a row.

But the studio bosses who so carefully promoted the stars' public image were wrong almost as often as they were right. The question therefore remains whether anything – be it publicity or skilful career guidance – can ever elevate a talentless or untimely performer to stardom. There are far too many cases of people given the full star-making treatment who failed to become stars (one of the best-known examples is Samuel Goldwyn's protegée Anna Sten); there are also any number of stars, especially in recent years, who have made it to the top without the benefit of such treatment. Clint Eastwood, for instance, who rose to stardom not via a Hollywood studio but in Italy, with low-budget westerns that ought to have been professional suicide, insists that 'I never had any promotions or big studio build-up. . . . There are stars who are produced by the press. I am not one of them.' Diane Keaton's agent, Arlene Rothberg, is adamant that: 'The only people who need publicity are people without talent.' In her first nine years in the business Keaton never even did a photo session.

Stardom, then, involves individual quality but also industrial commodity; thrives on public vogue but also on the right personal vehicles;

John Wayne *(far left) as* The Shootist: *a role that reflected his own battles with cancer.*

Diane Keaton and Woody Allen *(left) in* Annie Hall; *replaying their former off-screen relationship for laughs.*

demands the right material as well as the right medium. Together all these elements are associated with the word 'talent'. 'Top billing', 'top line talent' are common industry phrases, but exactly what the 'talent' of the stars is, or how they get to the top, is almost impossible to answer. 'Acting ability' is certainly not a condition for film fame. Neither is 'sex appeal' or what we might call 'photogenicity'. Nevertheless, these qualities are common to countless film stars and consequently have been harnessed in countless publicity campaigns. But more important than method, make-up or even vital statistics is the star's simultaneous function as both symptom and symbol of the time. Not just a mirror, but an embodiment of identifiable contemporary characteristics, an identification figure.

The star as symbol

Stars condense real characteristics in the lives of their audiences or, alternatively, compensate for their absence. For example, some early stars embodied inexpressible sexual energies and earned nicknames as evidence – the 'It Girl', the 'Oomph Girl'. Names have always been of the utmost importance. Both the image and the name of Cary Grant suggest debonair sophistication with an undercurrent of mischief; Grant's real name, Archibald Leach, hardly carries the same connotations. Similarly the name of Robert Taylor smacks of straightforwardness, whereas Spangler Arlington Brough, Taylor's real name, is damaging to the notion of classless America. Clark Gable's grin underlines an impudently self-conscious sexuality; Gary Cooper's slowness to speak and act tells volumes about his thoughtfulness, his thoroughness, his restrained reliability. Marie Dressler's size suggests a kindly, clumsy domesticity while Olivia de Havilland's sisterly sensitivity evokes goodness and asexual glamour.

There are any number of such 'types' – the tough guy, the wise guy, the good Joe, the rebel, the psycho, the boy next door, the girl next door, the dumb blonde, the femme fatale, the ingenue, the good/bad girl, the bitch, the kook, the whore with a heart of gold, the western-saloon-girl-who-sacrifices-herself-for-the-eastern-schoolteacher. For obvious reasons, certain types are more likely than others to attract actors and actresses at certain times. The rebel was an unlikely hero in the heyday of McCarthyist conformism, the prostitute an unusual heroine in the wake of the Hays Code; but teenage rebels were not just acceptable but sought after in the late 1950s when teenagers became a more significant proportion of Hollywood's audience, while in the 1970s the portrayal of prostitutes was realistic partly because of the impetus of American feminism.

Certain stars are remembered most for their roles in certain genres – Cagney and the gangster film, Bogart and the thriller, Wayne and the western, Davis and the deep south melodrama, Lombard and the screwball comedy, Heston and the epic. In the studio era a number of stars established relatively stable relationships with individual directors – John Wayne with John Ford and Howard Hawks, Humphrey Bogart with Hawks and John Huston. Today we might attribute some of Clint Eastwood's success to his collaborations with three good directors – Sergio Leone, Don Siegel and Eastwood himself.

Whatever types they are, however, stars must be larger than life; they must be extreme, extraordinary, idealized, even if simply extraordinarily ordinary (the director W. S. Van Dyke once attributed James Stewart's success in the cinema to his being 'so unusually usual'!). But many stars combine and condense what appear to be contradictory characteristics, so that each new star vehicle in a sense tells the star's story, the story of their achievement of that delicate balance.

Cary Grant *retired from the screen in the mid-60s, when still a major box-office draw.*

'Bankability'

If nothing else, we have established that stardom is an elusive quality. Today it is more un-

Sean Connery *(right) as James Bond, a role which elevated him to stardom but threatened to overshadow his subsequent career.*

Charles Bronson *(far right) changed his name from Buchinsky in mid-career, and became a star of the cinema of violence.*

James Stewart *made a successful transition from easy-going charmer to troubled introspective in the 50s.*

predictable than ever, for there is nothing that can guarantee a star success with an audience. And yet the notion of 'bankability' in relation to stardom is almost as old as Hollywood itself. In fact, the Bank of America pioneered the making of small loans to production companies as early as 1909, and from the beginning such loans were only made available on the strength of securities, conspicuous 'production values' of which stars were the most obvious example. Indeed, early production companies chose their names carefully to exploit this fact – Box Office Attractions and Famous Players-Lasky being two obvious examples. In 1918 the Bank of America made an unprecedented loan of $50,000 to Famous Players-Lasky, and the following year the same bank lent First National $250,000 to make *The Kid* for the simple reason that it starred Charles Chaplin. The loan was repaid with interest within six weeks. That same year Chaplin, Pickford, Fairbanks and Griffith formed United Artists in response to a series of 'combinations and mergers' which Fairbanks thought were 'controlling the stars as though we were chattels to be bought and sold'. Also in 1919, the Wall Street banking firm Kuhn, Loeb and Co. offered a $10m. issue of Famous Players-Lasky preferred stock. United Artists, on the other hand, refused to go public and instead turned to the exhibitors for assistance. In his history of United Artists, Tino Balio notes that at first:

> 'banks considered independent production a highly speculative enterprise . . . but slowly, the attitude of banks changed. Loan officers were beginning to discover what theatre owners had known all along, namely, that a Mary Pickford feature or a Chaplin comedy warranted a triple-A rating. So, in 1923, when United Artists did not have sufficient funds to advance Miss Pickford $150,000 for the completion of *Rosita*, she could turn to the Mutual Bank in New York.'

In 1927, an American investment company, Halsey, Stuart & Co., published an optimistic prospectus on The Motion Picture Industry as a basis for Bond Financing. In it its clients could read the following remarks on cine-stardom:

> 'the "stars" are today an economic necessity to the motion picture industry. In the "star" your producer gets not only a "production" value in the making of his picture, but a "trademark" value, and an "insurance" value, which are very real and very potent in guaranteeing the sale of this product to the cash customers at a profit.'

Compare this confidence in the 'bankability' of the stars on the eve of the depression with the remarks of two prominent bankers half a century later. Alexander Walker cites a top executive of California's Bank of America as saying, in 1969, that, 'Established stars no longer bring any insurance to a film production.' In 1976, another top film industry banker, William F. Thompson, Senior Vice President of Boston's First National Bank announced even more emphatically that 'stars don't bring the people to the box office . . . ' Between them these two banks are the major sources of investment capital for Hollywood.

But although these statements reflect the success of some recent films which do not include established stars and the failure of many which do, they do not mean that 'bankability' as a concept is dead. Ironically today it is not the banks who worry about 'bankability' but the studios. In a 1976 *Film Comment* interview Thompson of First National and his right-hand man George B. Bruns spelt out this distinction. The interviewer Patrick McGilligan had tried to draw them on the 'bankability' of Liza Minnelli. 'I wouldn't make that kind of judgement,' Thompson declared. 'I'd rather have Ted Ashley (head of Warners) tell me whether he wants her in a movie because I don't care whether she's in a movie or not.' Bruns spelt it out even more clearly: 'That use of the word "bankability" is unfortunate here . . . (It's) whether the *studio* thinks this person, for whatever reason, is a draw. For many years, John Wayne never made a film that was a total flop; he never made a *Jaws* either. The studio felt it could depend on John Wayne.

continued on page 112

The Most Profitable Stars Since 1932: the following lists are compiled on a strict points basis from information given in *Variety* and from *Motion Picture Almanac*'s annual surveys of money-making stars. Since US audience figures over the years are the prime source of measurement, the charts do not measure the continuing popularity of stars, like Warren Beatty, who enjoy periods of voluntary inactivity. It is not difficult to spot the movies which boost a star to number one in any given period but the keynote for success is these tables is consistency. Several big names score lower than might be expected, either because – as in the case of James Dean – they appeared in relatively few films, or because – like Marlon Brando or Jack Nicholson – they have not been content to standardize their screen image and their careers have been correspondingly erratic. In the All-Time List, compiled over 48 years from 1932–1980, John Wayne emerges far ahead of all other contenders, reflecting the sheer longevity of his popularity and therefore earning power. His only possible rival is Clint Eastwood, who may soon transcend Gable, Crosby and Cooper, but he will need many more years of major screen success to threaten Wayne. Doris Day is the only woman on the All-Time List. However, the runner-up is Betty Grable, and she is followed by James Stewart, Elizabeth Taylor, Shirley Temple, Steve McQueen, Spencer Tracy, Mickey Rooney, Robert Redford, Barbra Streisand, Humphrey Bogart and Julie Andrews.

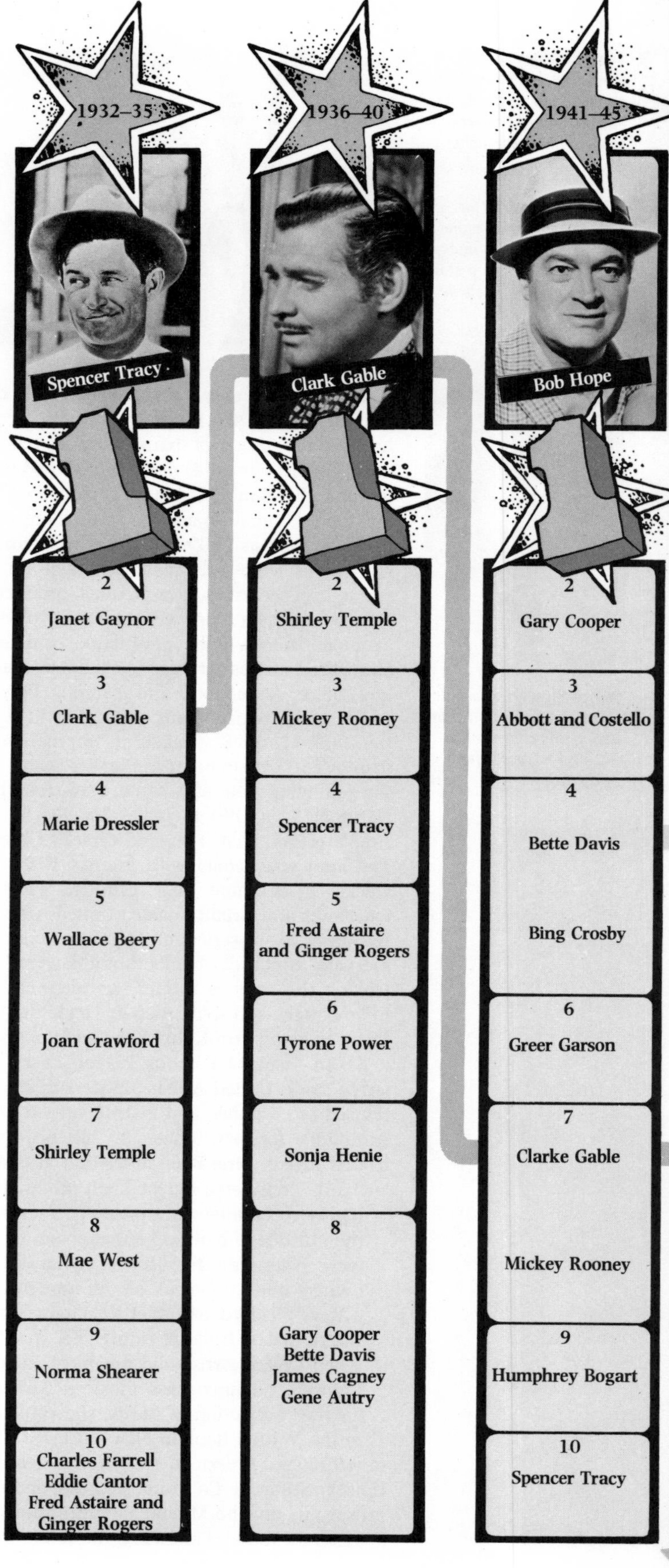

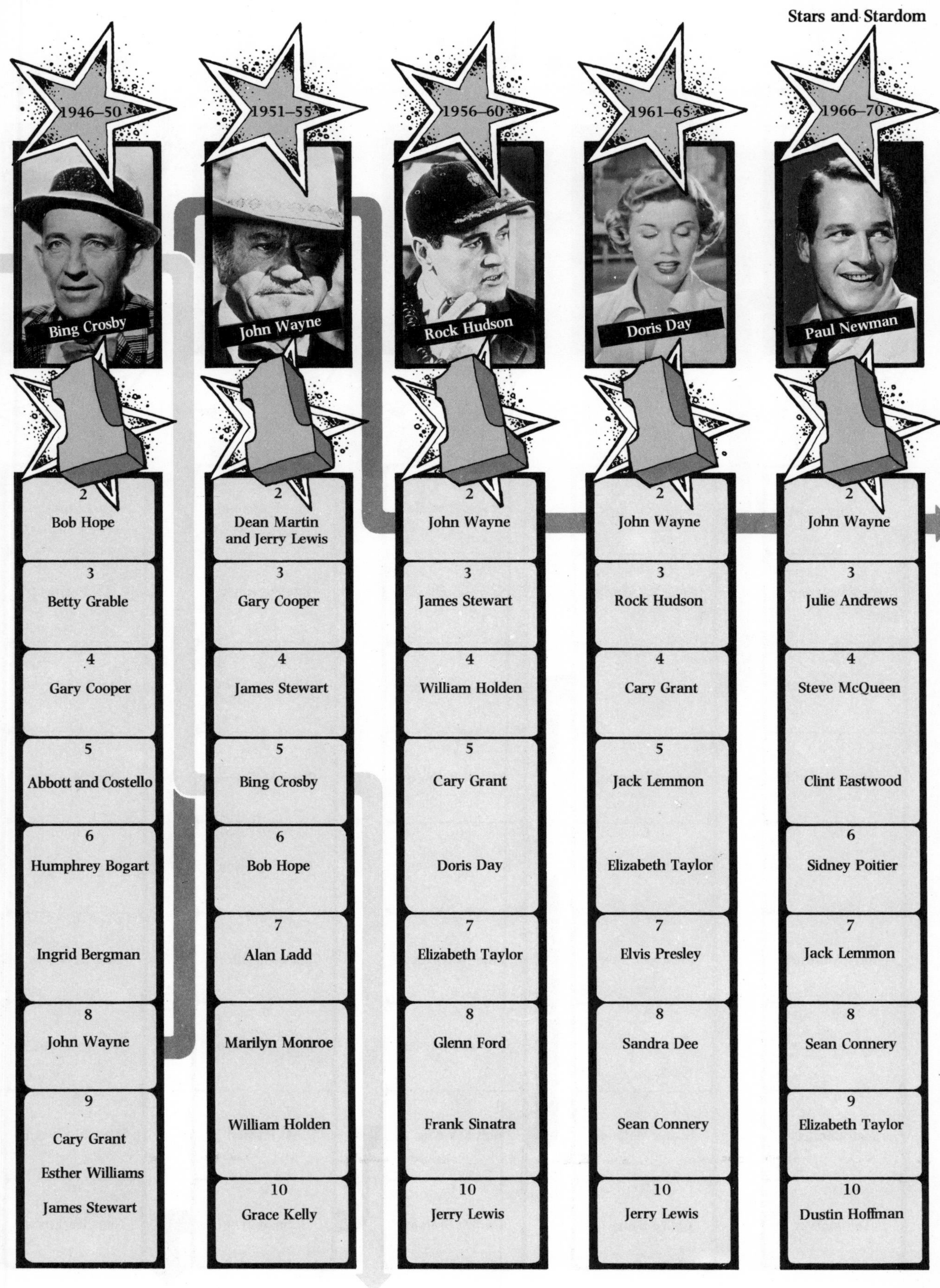
1946–50
Bing Crosby
2
Bob Hope
3
Betty Grable
4
Gary Cooper
5
Abbott and Costello
6
Humphrey Bogart
Ingrid Bergman
8
John Wayne
9
Cary Grant
Esther Williams
James Stewart
1951–55
John Wayne
2
Dean Martin and Jerry Lewis
3
Gary Cooper
4
James Stewart
5
Bing Crosby
6
Bob Hope
7
Alan Ladd
Marilyn Monroe
William Holden
10
Grace Kelly
1956–60
Rock Hudson
2
John Wayne
3
James Stewart
4
William Holden
5
Cary Grant
Doris Day
7
Elizabeth Taylor
8
Glenn Ford
Frank Sinatra
10
Jerry Lewis
1961–65
Doris Day
2
John Wayne
3
Rock Hudson
4
Cary Grant
5
Jack Lemmon
Elizabeth Taylor
7
Elvis Presley
8
Sandra Dee
Sean Connery
10
Jerry Lewis
1966–70
Paul Newman
2
John Wayne
3
Julie Andrews
4
Steve McQueen
Clint Eastwood
6
Sidney Poitier
7
Jack Lemmon
8
Sean Connery
9
Elizabeth Taylor
10
Dustin Hoffman

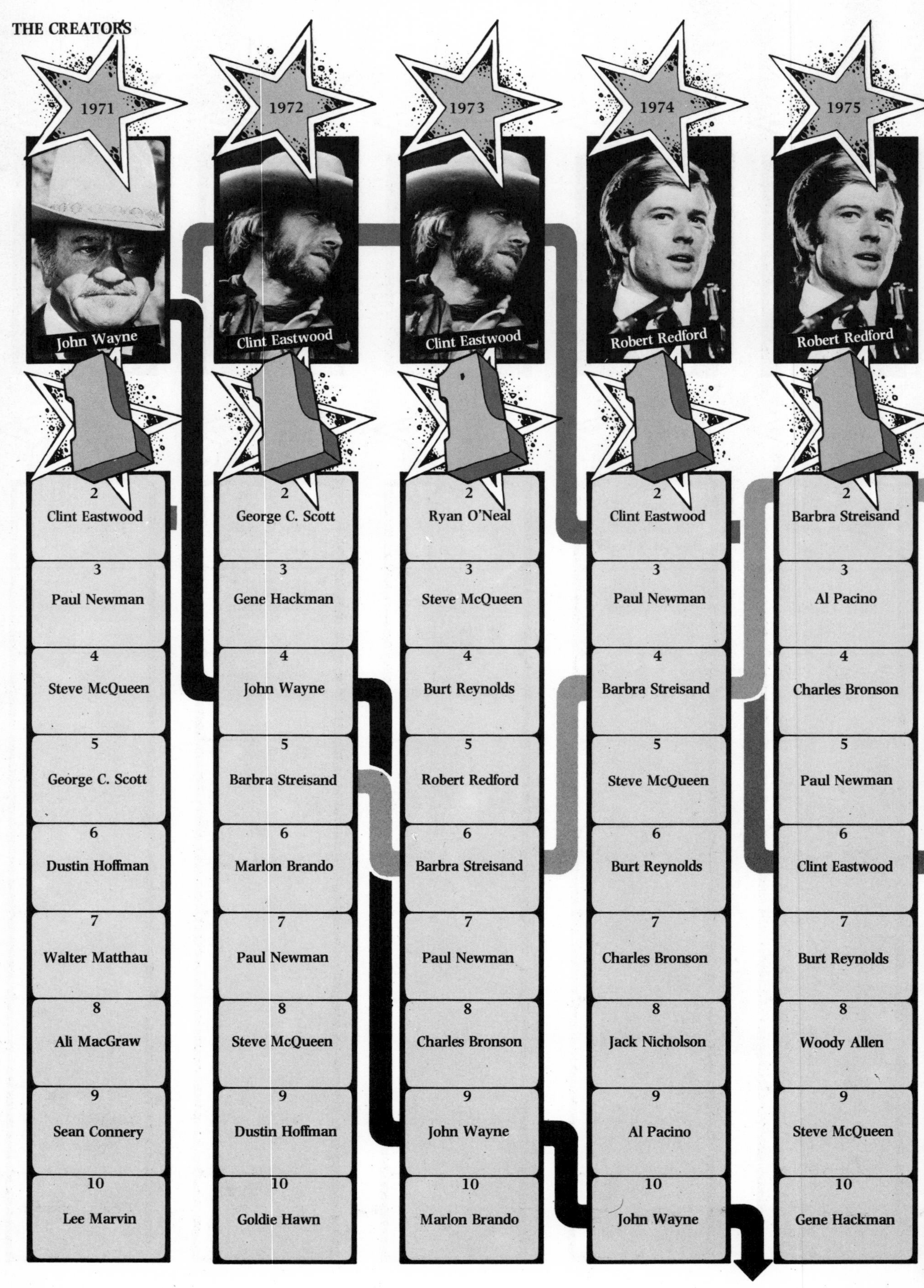
1971
John Wayne
2
Clint Eastwood
3
Paul Newman
4
Steve McQueen
5
George C. Scott
6
Dustin Hoffman
7
Walter Matthau
8
Ali MacGraw
9
Sean Connery
10
Lee Marvin
1972
Clint Eastwood
2
George C. Scott
3
Gene Hackman
4
John Wayne
5
Barbra Streisand
6
Marlon Brando
7
Paul Newman
8
Steve McQueen
9
Dustin Hoffman
10
Goldie Hawn
1973
Clint Eastwood
2
Ryan O'Neal
3
Steve McQueen
4
Burt Reynolds
5
Robert Redford
6
Barbra Streisand
7
Paul Newman
8
Charles Bronson
9
John Wayne
10
Marlon Brando
1974
Robert Redford
2
Clint Eastwood
3
Paul Newman
4
Barbra Streisand
5
Steve McQueen
6
Burt Reynolds
7
Charles Bronson
8
Jack Nicholson
9
Al Pacino
10
John Wayne
1975
Robert Redford
2
Barbra Streisand
3
Al Pacino
4
Charles Bronson
5
Paul Newman
6
Clint Eastwood
7
Burt Reynolds
8
Woody Allen
9
Steve McQueen
10
Gene Hackman

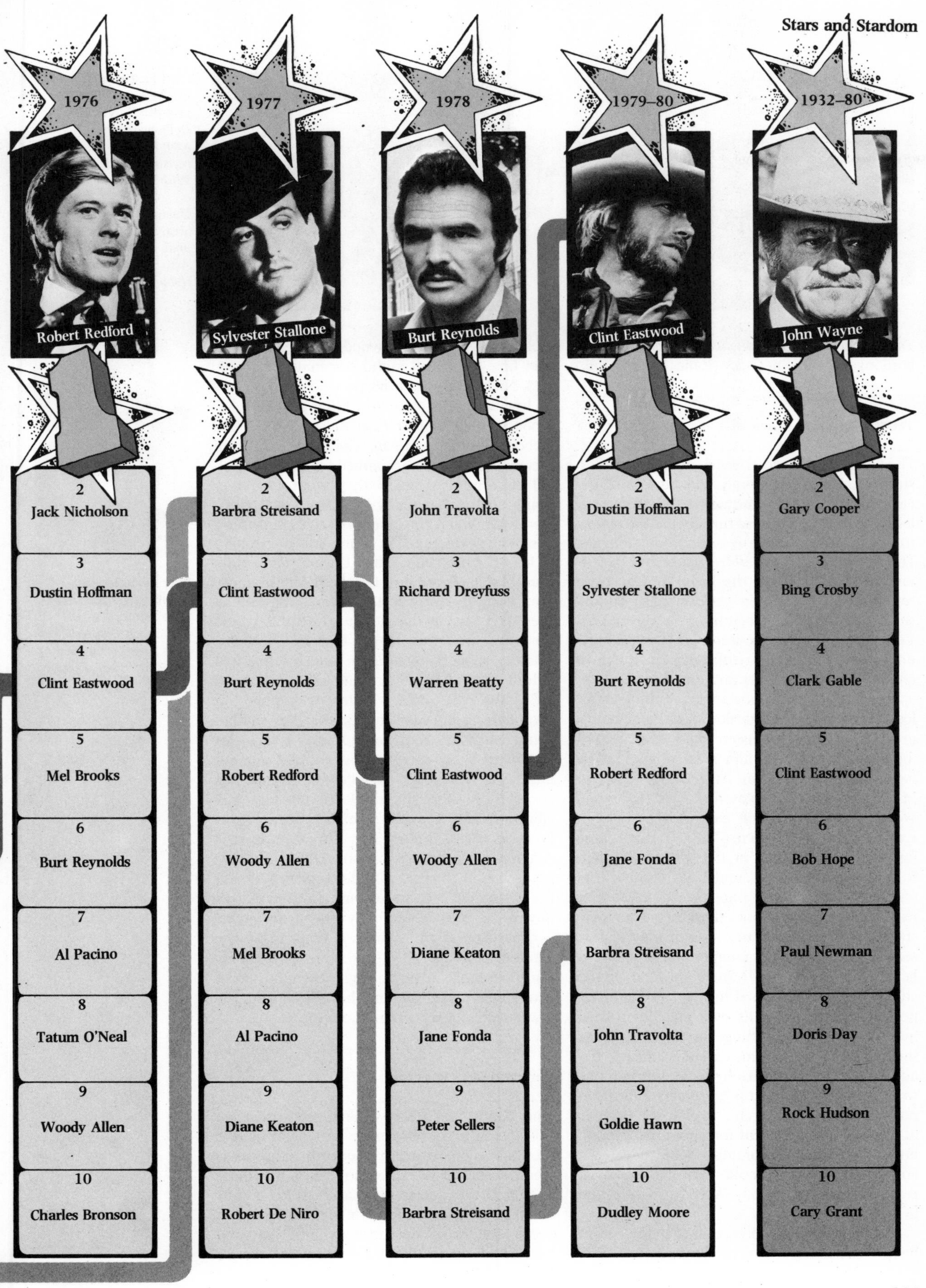
1976
Robert Redford
2
Jack Nicholson
3
Dustin Hoffman
4
Clint Eastwood
5
Mel Brooks
6
Burt Reynolds
7
Al Pacino
8
Tatum O'Neal
9
Woody Allen
10
Charles Bronson
1977
Sylvester Stallone
2
Barbra Streisand
3
Clint Eastwood
4
Burt Reynolds
5
Robert Redford
6
Woody Allen
7
Mel Brooks
8
Al Pacino
9
Diane Keaton
10
Robert De Niro
1978
Burt Reynolds
2
John Travolta
3
Richard Dreyfuss
4
Warren Beatty
5
Clint Eastwood
6
Woody Allen
7
Diane Keaton
8
Jane Fonda
9
Peter Sellers
10
Barbra Streisand
1979–80
Clint Eastwood
2
Dustin Hoffman
3
Sylvester Stallone
4
Burt Reynolds
5
Robert Redford
6
Jane Fonda
7
Barbra Streisand
8
John Travolta
9
Goldie Hawn
10
Dudley Moore
1932–80
John Wayne
2
Gary Cooper
3
Bing Crosby
4
Clark Gable
5
Clint Eastwood
6
Bob Hope
7
Paul Newman
8
Doris Day
9
Rock Hudson
10
Cary Grant

Clint Eastwood *(far left) in* The Good, The Bad and the Ugly: *his later Hollywood movies have often involved intriguing revisions of the Man With No Name persona.*

Dustin Hoffman *(left) in* Straight Time, *one of the final, acrimonious, First Artists productions, and a resounding box-office flop.*

They made that decision, *we* didn't. *They* were banking on him, not *us*.' (Italics in original.)

Technology and stardom

The film medium exercises its own influence on stardom. It was, after all, the advent of the close-up (sometimes known as the silent soliloquy) which first offered the cinema the opportunity to individualize its anonymous players. The coming of sound added vocal and instrumental possibilities to the facial and gestural repertoire of the screen performer, so ending some careers and beginning many others. Colour encouraged a new emphasis on costume and setting, and in particular placed an almost fetishistic value on hair and eye colours.

Ironically, most important of all the technological influences on stardom are the cinema's greatest rivals, television and the record industry. Several top film stars of the 1970s began their careers on American TV: Steve McQueen, Burt Reynolds and Clint Eastwood were all employed for extended periods in weekly series of their own. Similarly, three of the four top female stars of the 1970s – Diana Ross, Barbra Streisand and Liza Minnelli (the fourth is Jane Fonda) – are recording stars at least as much, if not more than they are movie stars. But it is not as curious as it may at first seem that the cinema's competition should also be its training ground. Since the end of the studio system Hollywood has lacked the facilities to groom stars of its own and has turned instead to adopting those of its competitor industries. This is to some extent because in the age of the blockbuster Hollywood does not like to take casting risks. 'It is extremely difficult to portray in the research', explains a former marketing vice-president for Columbia, 'how a given star would accomplish some new role. For example, how could you convey to a respondent what Woody Allen would be like in a dramatic role?'

For the same reason several of today's stars have their stellar origins in the cinema outside Hollywood – Clint Eastwood, Charles Bronson and Jane Fonda all found stardom in Europe; Jack Nicholson was a bit part player for years in low-budget exploitation films before Hollywood spotted him in *Easy Rider* (1969). And Robert Redford, Dustin Hoffman and Paul Newman had been acclaimed for their theatrical performances before they went into cinematic acting. But today it is American television with which the cinema draws its primary aesthetic distinctions, in acting and star quality as in everything else. James Garner, Peter Falk, Mary Tyler Moore and Elizabeth Montgomery are four of the top television stars, but none of them is a star in the cinema. And this works the other way too: in the late 1970s Henry Winkler of television's *Happy Days* has had two failures at the box office, while John Travolta of TV's *Welcome Back, Kotter* triumphed in *Saturday Night Fever* and *Grease*; the cinema could exhibit his body and not just his face, but becoming a big screen superstar did not enhance his small screen following. While his two film hits were still in release, breaking box office records, Travolta's final appearance in *Welcome Back, Kotter* was thrashed in the American TV ratings by an episode of *Little House on the Prairie*. The differences between the two media's stars are many. In Hollywood's heyday a star would play the same 'type' perhaps two or three times a year; today the small screen star plays the same 'part' thirty times a year. Not surprisingly, therefore, most actors who make the jump have been from the lower ranks of television stardom.

Burt Reynolds *in* Smokey and the Bandit Ride Again. *Reynolds has successfully straddled roles from macho hero to comic actor and director.*

The case of Jane Fonda

Jane Fonda is probably the most instructive example of a contemporary American actress who has become a star in an era when the movie world seems to be either unable or unwilling to control the species. Her career in the 1960s and 1970s has combined modelling (she was even 'Miss Army Recruitment' in 1962) and method acting (she studied with Lee Strasberg's

John Travolta *(right) in iconic pose from* Saturday Night Fever. *Even the poster campaign for* Urban Cowboy *was changed to accord with the star's public image.*

Jane Fonda and Donald Sutherland *(far right) teamed memorably in* Klute, *but neither* Steelyard Blues *nor* F.T.A. *repeated the popular success.*

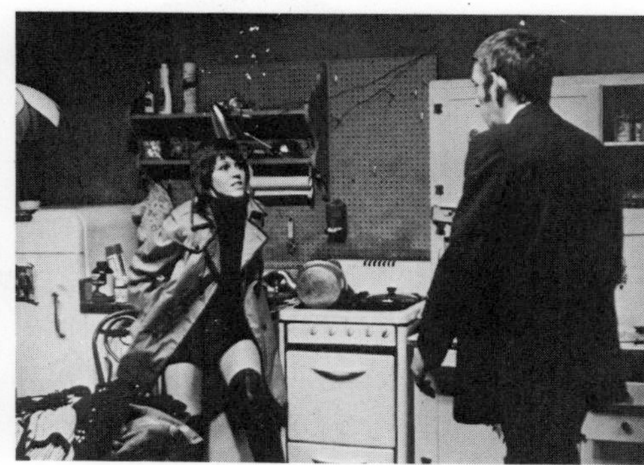

Actor's Studio between 1958 and 1961), softcore eroticism (like *Barbarella*, 1968) and screwball comedy (like *Barefoot in the Park*, 1967), literary adaptation (like Ibsen's *A Doll's House*, 1973) and left wing agit prop (like *F.T.A.*, 1972). The publicity machine has projected her variously as: Henry Fonda's daughter (the all-American girl) and Roger Vadim's mistress (the American girl gone to the bad); the Oscar-winner (for *Klute* and *Coming Home*) and the political outcast (for her trips to Hanoi, her support for the Vietcong, the Black Panthers and so on); both box-office star (*Cat Ballou, Barefoot, Klute, Coming Home, The China Syndrome, California Suite*) and box-office poison (*Steelyard Blues*). She has been celebrated as an American Bardot and berated as a cheesecake Che. She is an embodiment of the liberal left's opposition to sexual and other stereotypes and yet she herself has performed a number of such roles – and not only before her much publicized politicization. She is an actress who wants to use her stardom in as politically progressive a manner as possible, but who finds stardom itself hard to reconcile with radical cinema.

In 1965, 1967 and 1971 Jane Fonda's films had been among the top grossing films of the year; in 1972 she won an Oscar for *Klute*. She was a critical and commercial success, therefore, at the very moment that she felt unable to work either in mainstream Hollywood or in the margins of the political avant-garde. In Hollywood, Fonda complained, 'stories are always unravelled in the context of an individual's particular personality and psyche and in the events of one life, never against a social background'; in independent political cinema, on the other hand, attention to the social background seemed to leave little or no room for a star like Fonda, and to offer no attraction to the mass audience. Looking back, in 1977, she added 'I began to understand the role that movies play in making us feel a certain way about ourselves and placing us culturally within certain stereotypes'. She made two decisions: to form her own production company and to produce commercial political films, films combining positive 'strengthening' stereotypes with real social and historical backgrounds: 'I started to realize that if I was going to work, and if I wanted to remain in the context of the mass media, I was going to have to produce the films myself.' Turning down roles in *The Exorcist* and *Chinatown* she formed her own company, IPC, and began preparing story ideas herself. The first two highly successful films to emerge from the company were *Coming Home* (1978) and *The China Syndrome* (1979), the first about returning veterans of the Vietnam war and the second about a narrowly averted nuclear disaster.

Meanwhile she continued to make comedies, like *Fun with Dick and Jane* (1977) and *California Suite* (1980) – which were rather less successful in avoiding repressive stereotypes – a melodrama, *Julia* (1977) in which she played the writer Lillian Hellman, and two more mainstream 'death of the western' movies: *Comes a Horseman* (1978) and *The Electric Horseman* (1979). Fonda herself has criticized *Comes a Horseman*, which failed at the box office, because 'it's in the Hollywood tradition of the loner, the single hero against the bad guys' and she would have preferred the ending to show some form of small rancher solidarity. But her own star status acts against the likelihood of an end to the 'loner' convention.

Projects being prepared for Fonda's production company at the moment include a film about ordinary working people's experiences of the American war of independence. Fonda wants this to be about much more than 'just famous battles and famous names', but to what extent that is possible if she, or indeed any other film star, is in it remains to be seen.

Today's reluctant stars

The reluctance of contemporary film stars to accept the conditions of stardom is more and more apparent. Marlon Brando has rationed his recent appearances to quirky cameos – in *Superman, Apocalypse Now, The Formula* and

Marlon Brando *(far left) in* Last Tango in Paris: *the irresistible combination of stars and sex has sold movies since they began.*

Steve McQueen *(left) with Bibi Andersson in another First Artists indulgence,* An Enemy of the People, *which garnered neither profit nor much-sought prestige.*

Roots. Dustin Hoffman's first love seems to be live theatre. Jane Fonda's radicalism, her feminism, her French film-work, her ambivalence about stardom, her having her own company seem to mark her off from the likes of Redford and Eastwood, Streisand and the late Steve McQueen. In fact, though, Redford's politics are close to Fonda's, Eastwood's career (and Bronson's too) only took off, as Fonda's did, in Europe, and all of the above are or were rather reluctant stars, all with their own production companies. Even the characters Fonda plays are not all that different from those the others play, as she herself describes them: 'someone who fights back and doesn't stop and still survives' and, surprisingly, nor are her ambitions: 'trying to figure out how I can responsibly use what money I earn and what fame I have to improve the quality of people's lives.' The first statement could easily have been made by Clint Eastwood or Steve McQueen, the second by Marlon Brando or Robert Redford. Jane Fonda is not such an untypical star today, which is to suggest that all today's stars are radically different from those of the 1930s and 1940s.

In 1961 Redford received $500 for his first film role, in *War Hunt*; sixteen years later, in 1977, he earned $2m. for twenty days work on another war film, *A Bridge Too Far*, $100,000 a day. *A Bridge Too Far* starred Redford, Ryan O'Neal, Elliot Gould, Sean Connery, Michael Caine, and Gene Hackman but still proved disappointing at the box office. Paramount's publicity director, Larry Marks, describes it as 'the picture that proved that the public knows that when there are that many big stars in a movie each of them is going to be on for only a few minutes'. It also proved that when there are that many star cameos in a film there is time for very little else. And, with the exception of Brando, it's not cameos the stars want for their future film roles, it's 'good parts'.

Even Robert Redford admits to being a reluctant celebrity. 'I have no need to be a star', he says, and he is especially ambivalent about Hollywood. 'I look upon going to Hollywood as a mission behind enemy lines. You parachute in, set up the explosion, then fly out before it goes off.' Steve McQueen was equally antagonistic towards the industry: 'I only come back and make a movie when I need the money.' In the studio era, of course, the idea of 'coming back', of 'going to Hollywood', would have been incomprehensible – it was where the stars all lived. Today Redford has his own production company and is involved in political activities; Steve McQueen also had his own production company and appeared in an abortive Ibsen adaptation, *Enemy of the People* (1978), a project of his own. Warren Beatty, another top box-office star with political interests, is equally ambivalent about stardom: 'I'm not into leaving my footprints in the dust of time' he says. Beatty turned down starring roles in *The Way We Were*, *The Godfather*, *The Great Gatsby* and *The Sting*; he even refused an offer of $4m. for the role of *Superman*; so too did Robert Redford, Steve McQueen, Paul Newman and James Caan.

The uncertainty of today's stars arises partly from the fact that they have more money and more power than ever before. The lack of financial incentive to work can create neuroses as easily as it can happiness. Almost all of the major stars have tried directing (something that with few exceptions was unheard of in previous decades), but there has only been one concerted attempt by stars to create a mutual power-base within the industry, and that was in 1969, when Paul Newman, Sidney Poitier, Barbra Streisand and Steve McQueen were all among the top ten box-office attractions in the cinema. With considerable trumpeting they formed an alliance, based partly on the old United Artists model, called First Artists. Later they were joined by Dustin Hoffman.

The company based its activities 'on the underlying proposition that certain proven actors can and should exercise an inordinate amount of behind-the-cameras control over those projects in which they star' (though industry observers found it hard to see how a star like Streisand could exercise much more control than she already did), and on 'the

Sidney Poitier, *another partner in First Artists, has found more recent success as a director, with the likes of* Stir Crazy.

Gene Hackman, Liza Minnelli and Burt Reynolds *(right) were collectively unable to save the notorious '70s flop,* Lucky Lady.

Martin Sheen *(far right) finally transcended his type-casting as a second James Dean when registering the horror of* Apocalypse Now.

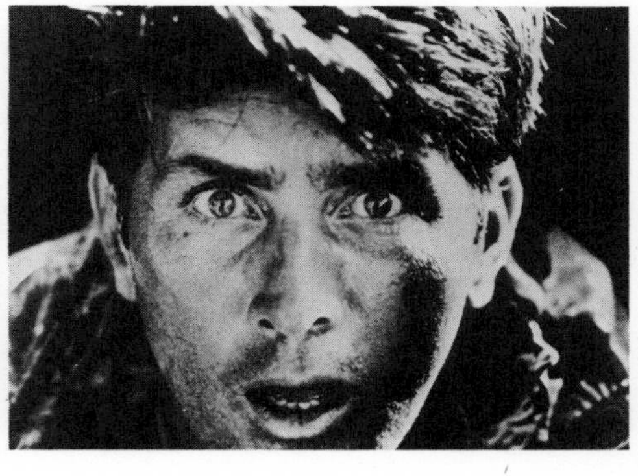

assumption that actors with established track records know intuitively which direction to go in and which films to make.' Every word of this statement (from the *Hollywood Reporter*, 12 September, 1972) would be mocked by First Artists' subsequent history. With \$3m. from London financiers (including the ill-fated Slater-Walker) First Artists put its shares on the market in 1969 at \$21 each. By 1973, despite the arrival of Dustin Hoffman, their value had slipped to \$4. With a few exceptions (*The Getaway* was one), most of the films produced by the company in the 1970s were sizeable flops: Steve McQueen in an adaptation of Ibsen's *Enemy of the People*, Barbra Streisand in *Up the Sandbox*, Paul Newman in *Pocket Money*, Dustin Hoffman in *Straight Time*, Sidney Poitier in *Warm December*. In 1980 First Artists went into liquidation amidst a flurry of litigation. *Variety* commented: 'however talented the group may be, their names alone apparently are no box-office insurance.'

But if no star is a guarantee of box-office success, stars are still considered by studios to be the best seal of quality available, especially when combined with other good elements. Star-power is seen at its worst in a film like *Lucky Lady* (1975), which took an entire year to cast because the production company Deluxe wanted three major stars and each of the three insisted on veto powers in the casting of the other two. Consequently the cast of *Lucky Lady* alone (Burt Reynolds, Gene Hackman and Liza Minnelli) cost in the region of \$5m.; the total budget was \$13m. but the total American gross was only \$12.7m.

The production of *Apocalypse Now* manifested many of the same problems. Francis Ford Coppola's original script was budgeted at \$13m. and required two stars in the roles of Willard and Kurtz. According to Eleanor Coppola's account of the making of the film, Coppola first offered the role of Willard to Steve McQueen who refused because the part 'wasn't right for him'. Coppola accepted the need for some rewriting but McQueen turned it down a second time because his children could not leave the country for the 17 weeks of location filming. Coppola now offered the role of Kurtz to Marlon Brando but he too was not interested. Al Pacino was then offered the Willard part but, although he was more interested in the role than McQueen, he was unable to do it. Coppola then returned to McQueen and offered him the three-week role of Kurtz instead. McQueen's agent agreed but only at the same \$3m. salary that had been offered for the 17-week role. Coppola considered this and called up James Caan to offer him the Willard role for \$1¼m.; Caan's agent refused to accept anything under \$2m. Coppola repeated his \$1¼m. offer and, when Caan turned it down, Coppola approached Jack Nicholson to play Willard. He got nowhere because Nicholson was busy on another film, so he then called up Robert Redford and offered him the Willard role. Redford too was involved in another film and in any case was only willing to consider the Kurtz role, because he didn't want extended periods on location. Coppola now cancelled the offer of the Kurtz part to McQueen and offered it to Nicholson but Nicholson was still too busy. Coppola completely rewrote the Kurtz part for Al Pacino but in Eleanor Coppola's diary the saga dragged on: 'Al says the part isn't right for him yet, Francis says that he needs a commitment before he can continue writing because the production date is closing in. Al says he can't commit. Francis says "Trust me, together we can make it great." Al finally says he can't commit.' Finally Coppola got a call from Brando's agent informing him that Brando was interested in the Kurtz role; meanwhile Harvey Keitel was employed in the role of Willard. A few days into shooting Keitel was sacked and Coppola cast Martin Sheen instead, an actor he bumped into in an airport lounge.

By 1980 the power of the legendary stars had turned casting into a nightmare. 'Us legends,' as Charles Bronson once said, 'tend to get picky in our twilight years.' However, luck still plays as big a part as it ever did. Boris Karloff's street corner has become Martin Sheen's airport lounge.

Reflections of a Star: Donald Sutherland

Donald Sutherland was born in Canada in 1935. He worked as a stage actor in England and had tiny parts in several films before he was rocketed to fame by Robert Altman's M*A*S*H *(1970). The success of* Klute *(1971) confirmed Sutherland's reputation as a key leading actor of the 1970s, whose laconic style would prove a perfect complement to Julie Christie in Nicolas Roeg's much acclaimed* Don't Look Now *(1973). Since then Sutherland has continued to star both in finely observed character roles like Fellini's* Casanova *(1976) and as the hero of successful Hollywood hits like* Invasion of the Body Snatchers *(1978), while the range of directors for whom he has worked reads a little like a pantheon of the post-war period from Fellini and Bertolucci to Altman and Pakula. Among his more recent films are Robert Redford's directorial debut* Ordinary People *(1980) and the screen adaptation of the best-selling spy story* Eye of the Needle *(1981). Below he talks about his own attitude to acting in the cinema and describes the background to his success.*

The Dirty Dozen *(left) was the first big break for Donald Sutherland, fifth from the left.*

Steelyard Blues *(right) was an anti-establishment comedy with Donald Sutherland as a tough ex-convict.*

I grew up in a small town in Nova Scotia in the days before television and I used to watch a lot of movies. The stars that I remember best are those for whom you could feel a definite kind of affection. They were the stars whose very performances seemed to embody a certain largesse, who were generous with themselves and with their audiences: Spencer Tracy, Robert Mitchum, Charles Laughton, John Wayne, Montgomery Clift, Kirk Douglas. They all seemed to be people you would want to go up to and hug. With regard to women I can remember finding something devastatingly desirable about June Allyson and wanting desperately to make love to her. But overall, amongst them all I think Robert Mitchum was *the* American actor for me. He seemed to have such a wonderful sense of character and precision, and also an amazing capacity for not seeming to care very much.

I had decided I wanted to be an actor as early as ten years old when I realized that I wasn't capable of becoming a sculptor or an artist, but I never thought of acting in terms of movies. It never entered my head because, in the place where I was brought up, the world of the cinema seemed completely beyond conception. This kind of feeling is illustrated quite well by what happened after *M*A*S*H* became a hit and some of the media went back to my home town to ask the people there what it was like to have known a famous actor. One guy they talked to said that I couldn't possibly be any good, because I used to sit behind him at school. That is exactly how I felt when I was there. It would have been stupid even to think about making movies because they were from another planet.

Consequently I thought of acting in terms of the theatre, but even so I did not perform in a play until I was seventeen and at university. I still remember persuading someone to bet me I wouldn't go and audition for a part in Thurber's *The Male Animal.* It was so I could go to the audition not to get a part but to collect on the bet, and in the event I got the part and it was a terrific experience: the audience laughed all the time I was on stage and applauded when I came on and applauded when I left. I expected the rest of life to be like that.

Following university I went to work in repertory theatre in Canada, and when I got a part in *The Tempest* I decided it was going to be the turning point. If I got good reviews, then I would be a professional actor, but if not I would give up. As it happened the reviews were good, so I travelled to England and enrolled in a school called LAMDA (London Academy of Music and Dramatic Art).

It turned out to be one of the worst experiences of my career. A woman at the drama school, who was considered the supreme voice teacher at that time, decided that my voice was too deep and that it should be raised an octave. As a result I could not speak for three months and, to this day, my voice has never entirely recovered. Eventually, after two years, they made it clear they thought I would be better off driving a truck and I left. It was a horrifying time of my life.

After that I found work at a Victorian repertory theatre in Perth in Scotland for a year, and around that time it began to dawn on me that, since the people who worked in films and TV were hardly gods, there was no reason why I shouldn't get work there. When I heard they needed a Danish Fortinbras for the BBC television *Hamlet* I went and learnt the role in Danish from a friend of mine, and then turned up for an interview with the director. I remember he was fairly indignant: 'What are you doing here?' he said, 'I don't want to see a Canadian.' I said I understood he wanted someone who could speak Danish and I gabbled some words in Danish and he gave me the role. Out of that came a TV play and from the TV play came my first movie, which was a horror film called *Castle of the Living Dead* (1964) in which I played a witch.

Shortly after that and a few other films, I got a small part in *The Dirty Dozen* (1967), and this changed my life. I had almost nothing to do in the film until one of the actors rebelled against the role he was playing because he thought it was beneath his stature. And the director Robert Aldrich, who didn't even know my name, simply said: 'You with the big ears do it.' And somehow or other that small part got me noticed.

At that point people started saying 'Come to America and we might be able to give you something.' But I had absolutely no money, and they just shrugged and said there was nothing they could do about that. Eventually in desperation I called up Christopher Plummer, who I hardly knew but had worked with on *Hamlet*, in the middle of the night and I pleaded with him and said I was in terrible trouble. Everything could go well for me if I could get to America, but I didn't have any money. He just asked 'How much do you need.' I said I needed $1500 and the next day his lawyer phoned and told me that the $1500 was ready for me. It took me five years to repay him.

In America I managed to get two films, *The Split* (1968) and *Start the Revolution without Me* (1970), but after that I was broke again. Then I happened to read a script which everyone said would finish my career. I thought it was very

funny, but no director was willing to do it and they were having considerable difficulty getting anyone else to play in it. I suggested James Coburn to act opposite me in it but he refused and eventually Elliott Gould was cast. The film turned out to be *M*A*S*H* and at that point everything in my life was turned upside down. I can still remember getting off an aeroplane in New York and walking into the terminal and suddenly people were kissing me. I was so green that I thought they must be people I knew. It was a delightful experience, but at the time I took it far too seriously. I know now that you should never look at it seriously and you certainly should not allow it to alter your life.

I think that first came home to me properly when I made *Don't Look Now* for Nick Roeg. He showed me that films are made by directors, and that a star's job is not to create a character for himself but to try and understand what character the director wants to create, and then help him flesh out his conception. The theatre is completely different because there the actor directly creates the emotional tension of the audience. In the cinema it's the director who will ultimately create the emotion and what you do is provide him or her with as much material as you can. The only way an actor can provide that material is by trying to understand what a director wants.

I phoned Nick Roeg from Florida after I had read the script of *Don't Look Now* and said that I wanted to sit down and talk to him about it. He said: 'What do you want to talk about?' I replied with this long speech about how I felt that ESP was a positive part of our lives and therefore we should make *Don't Look Now* a more educative sort of film, that the characters should in some way benefit from ESP and not just be destroyed by it. Nick said: 'That's not how I feel.' I said, 'Well what do you feel?' and he just said, 'What's in the script, do you want to do it or not?' I asked if we could talk about it and he said, 'No.' So I said, 'Well if you want to put it that way, yes I do.' and I just went and obeyed orders and I had a wonderful time.

The experience of making *Don't Look Now* was like living right on the edge of everything. Half the time it was hair-raising because I had vertigo, and the stuntman got vertigo so I had to do some of the tricks myself. We shot the climax last and I knew I was going to die in it and I became literally convinced that I would die, and dying began to feel almost like a sexual rite. I felt the same sort of intensity working with Fellini on *Casanova*. The collaboration between a director and a star in the movies can be so close and intense that you can only compare it to a love affair. And afterwards, as a consequence, the relationship becomes almost awkward. You have to break it off.

Naturally, like any actor, I've had my quarrels with directors and there have been times when the relationship hasn't gone well. On *Klute* for example I argued with Pakula, because I felt wrongly that not enough was being said about the character of Klute. Later when I saw the film I realized that everything that you need to know about the character is there and he appears as a passive, phlegmatic man who spends a lot of his time watching. In fact the film Pakula was making was much better than the film I would have been making, and I regret that I argued with him. The same kind of thing happened with Altman on *M*A*S*H*.

Of course some directors give you more physical directions than others. Perhaps because he is a brilliant actor in his own right, Robert Redford turned out to be one of the most physical directors I have ever worked with. On *Ordinary People* (1980) he was extremely precise about the tiniest detail: on the set he would come up and tell me very quietly where he wanted me to put my hand in a scene and it was always exactly right. I don't know what kind of a film-maker Redford will turn out to be, but he is a magnificent director of actors.

M*A*S*H *(far left): Sutherland and Elliott Gould in the film's football-game climax.*

Don't Look Now *(above left) with Sutherland and Julie Christie as the parents haunted by the memory of their drowned child.*

Klute *(below left) on location in New York. Sutherland with director Alan J. Pakula and Jane Fonda.*

Casanova *(right): Sutherland with Tina Aumont.*

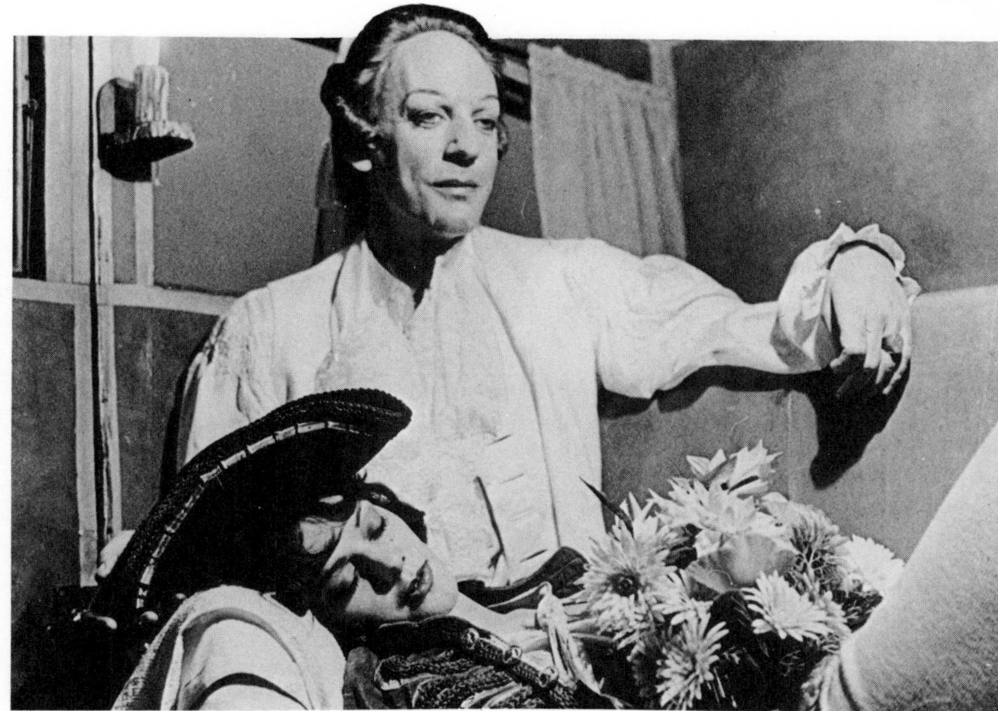

It's hard to define exactly what a star is, but I think of myself more as an actor. In some ways the difference between a star and an actor is like the difference between the French words *comédien* and *acteur*. A *comédien* is someone who plays himself and an *acteur* is someone who plays an assortment of people. Now Robert Redford is an excellent actor and, if you look at his work in *All the President's Men* (1976), *Jeremiah Johnson* (1972) and *The Electric Horseman* (1979), they are all different characters. But they're all honed round a very identifiable figure. It would be more difficult to pin down the connection between my roles in say *Casanova*, *The First Great Train Robbery* (1978) and *Klute*. But that may be because Bob works most often for Sydney Pollack, while I work with Fellini and Bertolucci and Chabrol and Altman and so many others.

It still gives me a lot of pleasure to do character roles and smaller parts. I can remember after *M*A*S*H* had become successful I happened to be playing an oddball in *Kelly's Heroes* (1970) and I thought that it would be the last time that I would be able to have fun in a character part. But then after I had made *Little Murders* (1971) I realized it was possible to do whatever you wanted. Currently I would love to make more films in Hollywood but nobody ever seems to offer them to me. The agents always call up and say they have a wonderful part for me in Timbuktu hanging by my heels in the jungle. It reminds me of years ago when I was in England and I desperately wanted a part in a film called *Four in the Morning* (1965). I thought I read it better than anyone could have, but they wanted a boy-next-door type; they said I didn't look as if I had ever lived next door to anybody.

I suppose one of the things I like best about film is the working environment. If I prefer to work in a studio rather than on location, it's because it's rather like working in a monastery; there's a very cloistered feel about the sound-stages; they echo with your own sound. This reverential atmosphere is possibly one of the reasons why movie-making is so boring for outsiders to watch. You might as well look at a watch-maker who takes half an hour off every five minutes: there is nothing to see. A Swedish director called Jan Troell illustrated this when he described his experience of working with Gene Hackman on a film. He had fought with Hackman all the time and was completely in despair because, to Troell on the set, Hackman's performance seemed completely inadequate. Then when he cut the movie together he was shocked to find it was all there: on film Hackman had built his role by a delicate series of sinews that the director had not even seen, and only the camera picked them up. Robert de Niro has the same kind of microscopic brilliance as a film actor. His precision and judgement are so fine that he will do the tiniest area of curve in his performance, and then another, and then another, until gradually he has defined the area of the curve and an aspect of the character he is playing. The kind of things I do tend to be a little more obvious by comparison.

There is a story that sums up just what that kind of acting discipline really is. A screen actor called Edmund Gwenn was destitute in New York in his eighties and someone brought him back to LA and put him in the actor's home and used to go to see him every Wednesday. One Monday he got a call from the home to say that Gwenn was dying and, if he wanted to see him, he should come before Wednesday because he was slipping into a coma. When he got there Gwenn was lying on the bed and he opened his eyes and asked what day it was. His friend told him it was Monday so Gwenn asked if he was dying. His friend said he was. And Gwenn said: 'It's not what I thought it would be like at all. It's hard. It's almost as hard as doing comedy.' And then he died. I think that story tells you what it feels like to be an actor.

Directors and Directing

The 1979 Academy Awards ceremony proved to be an evening in which nothing could resist the tide of *Kramer vs. Kramer*. If you treat a subject – divorce – so close to two-thirds of the members of the Academy, it is no surprise if they acclaim social responsibility and a sensitive treatment of modern emotional distress. Better still, even in this 'new', 'young' Hollywood, *Kramer* is a thoroughly old-fashioned film with a placid structure and a set of performances that looked admirable in the 1950s whenever Elia Kazan used them. Dustin Hoffman, at last, has been allowed to rival our memories of James Dean and Marlon Brando, instead of being asked to be a character actor. He and Meryl Streep took Oscars. *Kramer*'s director and writer Robert Benton won for adapted screenplay and for 'best director'. Then, as a climax to the evening, *Kramer vs. Kramer* won 'best picture'. There *is* something higher than direction.

Next day there were estimates that that last Oscar could add $25m. to the gross of *Kramer*. It was added that, even without the acting Oscars and the awards to Benton, the best picture accolade would have given the film fresh energy at the box office. All over America, new posters and new ads were singing out *Kramer*'s triumph, and 'best picture' was slapped across the middle, like the sash on a beauty queen. The old Hollywood faith, that a good director is a nice try but best picture is the fat cigar, held true. No one thought to re-issue *Bad Company* (1972) or *The Late Show* (1977), the earlier works of the year's best director. One day, perhaps, if there are Benton retrospectives, those films will be more honoured than the very effective but very calculated *Kramer vs. Kramer*.

Auteur or member of a team?

Benton still wore a big grin. He had knocked around too long without securing his place in the kingdom to be proud. In the early 1970s, in efforts to improve the reputation of the American screenwriter, because it had been negatively affected by the *auteur* theory which sought to establish the director as the pre-eminent creator of film, the critic Richard Corliss included Benton in a group of Easterners who 'may have composed a new Hollywood symphony, but it is still the conductor, the director, who takes the bow.' Benton had had successes: he wrote *Bonnie and Clyde* (1967) with David Newman, after which they went on to *There Was a Crooked Man* (1970), and *What's Up, Doc?* (1972) with Buck Henry, before writing *Bad Company*. It is still somewhat eccentric, or cultish, to call that picaresque, chilly Western one of the best American pictures of the 1970s.

Robert Benton

But on Oscars night, Benton was revealed as a fiftyish guy, bearded, happy and modest, with family in the audience charged with the relief that speaks of hard times and years when Dad was in a bad mood. Benton joined in with everyone else in admiring the 'family' atmosphere that had produced *Kramer*, no matter that it is about break-up and contested custody. He looked like a seasoned professional who had paid his dues and who was so utterly pleased to have the statuettes that he happily played the Hollywood game in which 'team spirit' disguises personal ambition. Even in the moment of triumph, he was less an *auteur* than a jolly, humble *patron*.

That very night, Hollywood had turned its back on the man who, more than any other, personifies the power, the glory and the mania of the new type of American director: Francis Ford Coppola. Not everyone admires or understands *Apocalypse Now* (1979). Hardly a soul has looked back fondly on the happy days and family atmosphere of its making – least of all Eleanor Coppola. But it was a work of dedication, independence, will and rampant ambition. It seemed to fulfil the hopes Hollywood often professes, but which actually frighten it, of amazing us with the force and scope of the medium. And in his own way, Coppola had paid his dues: he had made two very successful films in the 1970s; *The Godfather* had been a beguilingly slick meeting of genre entertain-

Kirk Douglas *(right) in* There Was a Crooked Man; *and* **Ryan O'Neal and Barbra Streisand** *(far right) in* What's Up, Doc?: *two films co-scripted by Robert Benton before he assumed the director's role.*

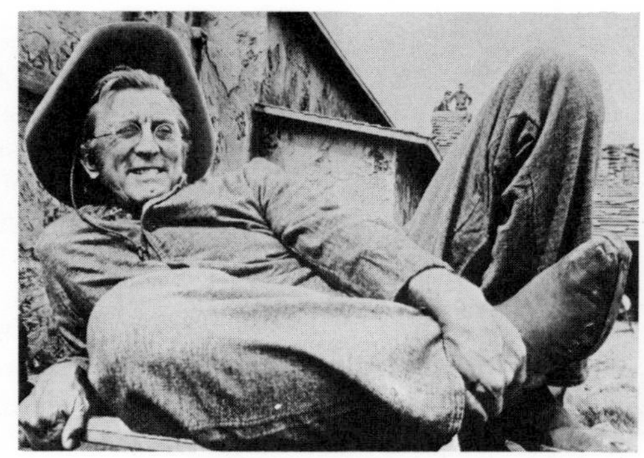

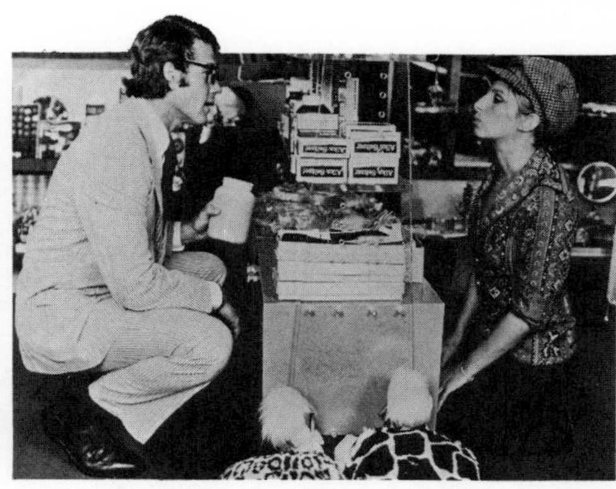

Francis Ford Coppola

ment and social commentary; and in Michael Corleone it had established a sinister role-model for every would-be Caesar in Hollywood. Last year on Oscars night Coppola had been on stage to rant and roar about momentous, but imprecise, things to come in the 80s; only weeks before Academy evening, 1980, Coppola had announced the purchase of the old General Services Studio and a dream of restoring the halcyon days of MGM's boy wonder producer of the 1920s and 30s Irving Thalberg with a 'family' enterprise. He said that there would be parks and companionship in his studio, and open house for the great directors of the world.

There is a constituency of film-makers for whom Coppola is the greatest hero. He is first among the 'movie brats' – that generation of whizz-kid film-makers like Steven Spielberg and George Lucas who came to fame in the 1970s – the one to whom they all look for sound advice and impetuous inspiration. He is also a ticket to the new world for such foreign film-makers as Wim Wenders, Hans-Jurgen Syberberg, Werner Herzog, Akira Kurosawa and Michael Powell, the difficult young and the stranded old, all being welcomed into the heart of the kingdom. If anyone could enable Jean-Luc Godard to make his long-cherished project *Bugsy Siegel*, it is Coppola; after all, he has backed Wenders on *Hammett* (1981), and must have a store of satanic American heroes for these foreign directors. Coppola is also a beacon for the thousands of film students who have a stairway to heaven in mind that includes Corman low-budget quickies, major screenplays, directorial breakthrough, Oscars enough to play skittles, millions, vineyards and the sweet pleasures of patronage.

But, in truth, Coppola is equal parts of Hollywood man and adventurous outsider, and no one in the kingdom quite trusts him or his goals. *Apocalypse Now* was regarded as a rogue film, just as any *auteur* has been, is now and always will be suspect in Hollywood, whatever splendour critics and academics see in him. We have lived through the notion, originally promoted in America by Andrew Sarris, of the director as *auteur*, and the golden legend of kids taking over the kingdom. The truth is muddier and bleaker: fewer films are made; technology is more encroaching and craft is less satisfactory; subject matter seems bolder, but exploitation has not faltered in its ingenuity or shamelessness; and the position of director is as complicated, uncomfortable and perilous as it was for Griffith, Stroheim, Welles, Nick Ray, or even for Red Ridingwood – the film director in F. Scott Fitzgerald's novel *The Last Tycoon* – that forlorn stiff who was coolly lifted off a film without the gracious producer Monroe Stahr breaking stride, and given his own coat – left on the set – as a limp going-away present:

> It was a sorry mess, Ridingwood thought. It meant he would have slight, very slight loss of position – it probably meant that he could not have a third wife just now as he had planned. There wasn't even the satisfaction of raising a row about it – if you disagreed with Stahr, you did not advertise it. Stahr was his world's greatest customer, who was always – almost always – right.

Scott Fitzgerald had mixed feelings about that power play, and the ambivalence is still with us today. He was moved by the authority of a producer like Irving Thalberg, even while he suffered from it. *The Last Tycoon* has as much love-hate for its hero as Coppola ever felt towards Michael Corleone – hero of *The Godfather*. Coppola, no doubt, means to provide opportunities for young talent, but he cannot resist the imperative of authority – that you must sometimes be a shit and a bastard. Not that Hollywood has ever lacked its share of righteous malice or neglected the sub-text that it is bliss to succeed, but downright cosy if your friends fail.

Fitzgerald could point to the subservient role of director Frank Borzage on the film Fitzgerald co-scripted for MGM, *Three Comrades* (1938), as proof that even the director had been ground down to the level of an employee. Similarly, it

is often argued that the heyday of the director was short: it lasted from D. W. Griffith's definition of the significance of the job in the early years before World War I to Thalberg's humiliation of Erich von Stroheim in 1924, when the producer supervised the cutting of Stroheim's *Greed*. Before about 1914, the movies had been a trade owned by exhibitors who were driven into production only to guarantee their own supply. After *Greed*, every studio copied Thalberg's search for efficiency and hired producers to regulate the 'artists' and ensure that the factory floor stayed active. As an historical outline, this is repeated in survey courses everywhere. But it relies too much on our allegiance to directors caught up in delusions of personal grandeur and the ideology of nineteenth-century melodrama. Just as Griffith is the spokesman for a generation of naive pioneers, and Stroheim a radiant self-destructive whose pride almost invited failure, so in the allegedly strict age of Thalberg there flourished John Ford, Howard Hawks, Ernst Lubitsch, Josef von Sternberg, Borzage, Frank Capra, George Cukor, Gregory La Cava, Leo McCarey, King Vidor and Raoul Walsh.

The 1960s: directors seen as *auteurs*

Those names come from the top two categories – Pantheon and the Far Side of Paradise – in Andrew Sarris's *The American Cinema*, published in 1968. That book was the culmination of an argument launched in 1962, the sum achievement of which was to promote the idea of the director as *auteur*; not just Bunuel or Truffaut, but Joseph H. Lewis or Cecil B. De Mille. Sarris always strove to avoid the wilder excesses of the approach: that because of, say, *Kiss Me Deadly*, any Robert Aldrich film, seen or not, must be extraordinary. (Realists rejoice that this inane law never deterred the boisterous Aldrich from going on to make quantities of junk, as well as a few more good films.) Sarris hoped that the theory of the director would never be built into a regime, but he knew that American experience of its own cinema was still warped by the tradition that cherished Fitzgerald's demise and the simplistic verdict that Welles had been driven out of work:

> Ultimately, the *auteur* theory is not so much a theory as an attitude, a table of values that converts film history into directorial autobiography. The *auteur* critic is obsessed with the wholeness of art and the artist. He looks at a film as a whole, a director as a whole. The parts, however entertaining individually, must cohere meaningfully. This mean-

Cecil B. De Mille *(left) shares a relaxed moment with the camera-strewn Yul Brynner during the production of* The Ten Commandments.

Alfred Hitchcock *(below left) in characteristic pose on the set of* Psycho: *as ever, his own best publicist.*

ingful coherence is more likely when the director dominates the proceedings with skill and purpose. How often has this directorial domination been permitted in Hollywood? By the most exalted European standards, not nearly enough. Studio domination in the thirties and forties was the rule rather than the exception, and few directors had the right of final cut . . . In retrospect, however, the studio system victimized the screenwriter more than the director. It was not merely a question of too many scribes spoiling the script, although most studios deliberately assigned more than one writer to a film to eliminate personal idiosyncrasies, whereas the director almost invariably received sole credit for direction regardless of the studio influences behind the scenes.

It has always been to Sarris's credit that he insisted on treating every film individually. Equally, the best – or maybe only the happiest directors – have been those who disregarded rules about what to expect and worked out their destiny from day to day. But the *auteur* theory soon leapt out of Sarris's control, its time was so ripe. The context of the movies was changing. The mass audience had already settled for television, and the old movie studios were in disarray. By the mid-1950s big stars had formed their own production companies, aware of the shrinking confidence of the studios and the vacuum that was developing at the centre of the business. As they carried the risk, and took more of the profits, so the studios were into a strategy that was already emotionally current – shooting in real places. That was one of the lessons of the new waves in Europe – not just the *nouvelle vague* in France, which spawned Godard and Truffaut, but the films of Antonioni, Fellini and Bergman, all of which impressed America at about the same time. Awkwardly and nervously, American movies entertained a little European influence.

That process succeeded least of all in Hollywood, a community so dependent on exiles and escapees from Europe that it has always been suspicious of un-American ways. The audience were the principal subscribers to the new intelligence. As more avid and knowledgeable filmgoers comprised a larger portion of the crowd in theatres, so they and their children began to receive an education in 'film studies'. That's where the *auteur* theory triumphed. For it appealed deeply to teachers who had grown stale or weary with Milton and George Eliot. They reckoned to increase their enrolments, prove their hipness and have fun in class, without compromising their own ideals about Great Artists, if they changed to Fellini and Hitchcock.

Hero worship had always energized the *auteur* theory. In France, above all, the young critics hailed distinguished veterans because they wanted to be like them: Howard Hawks, for instance, was not just an admirable filmmaker, but a dry manner and personal style to emulate. The definition of the role of director was the description of a task, and a splendour, that Truffaut, Godard and the others wanted for themselves. It was backed up with a very thorough defence of the potential of direction, despite restrictions of script, budget and odious producer. Thus, the French distinguished the narrative conventions from the plastic beauty in Anthony Mann, Vincente Minnelli or Nicholas Ray. The account of film as a heady audio-visual experience was vital and original; but it was clouded by a hero-worship which, in time, became respectable to academics.

In the 1960s, this critical argument was fought out against a background that prejudiced the result. The success of *Psycho* (1960), the mass of writing on Hitchcock and his own deft riding of the wave established a model hero for the new perception of film. His own dwelling on the engineered image encouraged viewers to bask in great moments of *mise-en-scène*. Lesser directors – in terms of visual brilliance and business *chutzpah* – took over their own films from the increasingly feeble studio system. Several European directors – Michelangelo Antonioni, Roman Polanski, François Truffaut, and then Milos Forman – ventured into the English language.

Film became an entertainment predicated on the names of directors. In the early 1960s, Otto Preminger followed the stately career of an independent producer-director and used elegant Saul Bass credits to establish a Preminger feeling. Jerry Lewis became for a few years the darling of some critics and the salvation of Paramount. Stanley Kubrick decisively abandoned America, as if to suggest the country was unworthy of him. John Boorman came the other way and, with *Point Blank*, revealed how far American genres had become international idiom. And a bevy of new directors lit up what was, in fact, a dull decade: Arthur Penn, Blake Edwards, John Frankenheimer, Sydney Pollack, Richard Lester and the several English directors, like Karel Reisz and John Schlesinger, who had a vague air of angry young men and/or swinging London. By the end of the decade, Coppola and Bogdanovich had begun. Bob Rafelson had made a film, *Head*, that no one noticed, and helped produce another, *Easy Rider*, that 'everyone' saw. Even the black-listed American writer/director Abraham Polonsky made a second film, and it was rumoured that Joseph Losey might return to America.

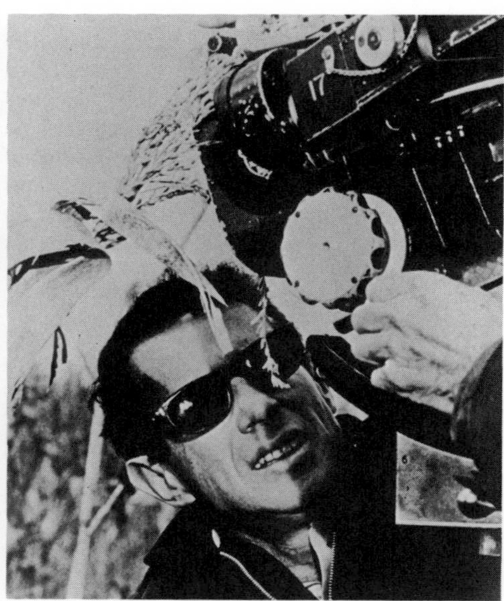

Meryl Streep and Alan Alda *(far left) in* The Seduction of Joe Tynan, *a political fable which re-established the Hollywood career of director Jerry Schatzberg.*

Arthur Penn *(left) on location with* Bonnie and Clyde.

Roman Polanski *(below) as he appears in his own film* Chinatown.

The 1970s: youthful audiences and directors

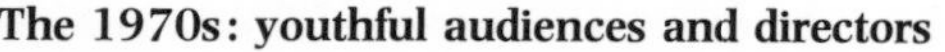

Bonnie and Clyde (1967) was the pivot of those changes: conceived and written by Robert Benton and David Newman, stimulated by the jostling proximity of laughter and pain in Trufaut's films. They offered the script to Truffaut and Godard – which only hints at how many youthful illusions have fallen from Benton like scales. But it ended up a producer's film, partially rewritten by Robert Towne, a vehicle for Warren Beatty who is one of the most reticent but prosperous figures of the 1970s, the star as producer, actor, writer and millionaire. He put himself in the film, along with the late 1960s anguish of the young. He got Penn to direct: together, a few years before, they had made one of the most glaringly European, financially disastrous and intriguing films of the decade, *Mickey One*. The 'French' script for *Bonnie and Clyde*, its jittery mix of 30s folklore and 60s mood, Penn's rapture and the chic bearing of the cast made a box-office coup. It promoted fashions, it challenged our feelings about violence, it launched Faye Dunaway, impressed one of the English champions of the *auteur* theory Robin Wood. It also profited Warner Brothers, convinced Warren Beatty to be more than an actor and augured a new phase of movies that dealt in the experience (i.e. the thwarted fantasies) of the predominantly young audience. Two years later, the youth boom was cemented by the huge success of *Easy Rider*. It initiated a spate of low-budget films by young directors, many of which proved unreleasable and contributed to the Hollywood studios' acute cash-flow crisis of the late 1960s. Joan Didion, in her essay 'In Hollywood', remembers 'the hangover summer of 1970 . . . when all the terrific 22-year-old directors went back to shooting television commercials and all the creative 24-year-old producers used up the leases on their office space at Warner Brothers by sitting out there in the dull Burbank sunlight smoking dope before lunch and running one another's unreleased pictures after lunch.'

Of course, after *Bonnie and Clyde* even Penn himself was never quite as striking again. He didn't cash in. He made movies more dismayed by Americana, stranger and more off-hand than the 1970s wanted. *Night Moves* (1975) and *The Missouri Breaks* (1976) have been condemned for obscurity and opportunism, respectively. They may well survive better than some films that were big hits in the 1970s. Penn is exactly the kind of man who deserves the new respect for directors, but in the 1970s his career faltered. He went back to the theatre and he was fired from *Altered States* (1980) before it had even begun to shoot.

You might not think it to hear the rhapsodies during the late 1960s and 1970s about Roger Corman's nurturing of new talent via low-budget exploitation films, or about the youth breakthrough after the success of *Easy Rider*, or about the creative association of young whizz-kids like George Lucas and Steven Spielberg, but directors were still fired, out of work and miserable. The talented Corman discovery, Monte Hellman, barely worked; Polonsky slipped back into oblivion; and even Bogdanovich, after three huge hits, had to start his career up again. Jerry Schatzberg tried to be experimental, then he had no work at all, then he settled for the glum safety of *The Seduction of Joe Tynan*. Even godfather Corman gave up directing to produce and distribute. It is likely

Faye Dunaway and Warren Beatty *(right) as the romantic gangsters of* Bonnie and Clyde.

Steven Spielberg *(below) frames a shot for* Close Encounters of the Third Kind.

that the average age of directors working in the 1970s was lower than at any time since the early 1920s. One can argue that more of those directors were their own screenwriters than ever before, and that they triumphed over problems and interference. When John Travolta dropped out of *American Gigolo* (1980), Paul Schrader was left with half a budget and the uncertain blessing of Richard Gere. But he went on with the film and made something more complex than Travolta could have sustained. Coppola was able to make *Apocalypse Now* (1979) on his own; any competent and conscientious studio executive would have cancelled or forbidden it. The system consented to Spielberg directing *Close Encounters of the Third Kind* (1977) secretly and *1941* (1979) expensively – for over $60m. between them – and seemed prepared to take the fat and the lean that resulted with equanimity. The 70s was a profitable decade for Hollywood: plenty of films flopped, but enough made fortunes, and the overall decline in attendance begun in the late 40s was reversed. Periodically, there were waves of euphoria, none greater than the years in which Coppola set Lucas up with *American Graffiti* (1973) and made such a triumph with *The Godfather* that he could offer *The Conversation* (1974) as a bonus – gravity and responsibility paid for with the profits of a blockbuster.

However, it's a self-deceiving and youthful mind that can be wholly pleased by the success of some of the young during the 1970s. No one should forget that young directors have also made adolescent films – lively and appealing, but shallow and inexperienced in terms of complicated lives, and camouflaged with technique. They may mature, if they can face failure as the most fruitful means to that end. They could just as easily come to resemble that other generation of elderly spoiled children, the founders of Hollywood: mini-tyrants like Mayer, Zukor, Cohn, Schenck, Laemmle. Coppola's wish to own a studio may involve the helping of friends and the easing of difficult and worthwhile projects. But it is also the wish to be a studio boss. On the west coast of America, pictures are still a business – in fact more a business than ever – and no one can survive there without devoting his energies to the acquisition of power.

The older generation out of work

Meanwhile, we should appreciate how far the changes in Hollywood practice that were proved in the 1970s have deprived us of an earlier generation. There is a terrible irony in the way belated critical acclaim, in France in the late 1950s and in America in the early 1960s, coincided with the withering of so many careers. It need not be tragic or surprising if old men work less: thus, Hitchcock, Hawks, Ford and Walsh went into semi-retirement. But King Vidor, I suspect, would still welcome the chance to direct if it came along. He remains one of the most socially active veterans in Beverly Hills. But *Solomon and Sheba*, his last picture, was made in 1959.

A slightly younger generation, who made their mark in the 1940s and 1950s, had a far sadder story to tell. Vincente Minnelli – creator of MGM musicals like *An American in Paris* and *The Band Wagon* – is still only 67, but he made just two films in the 1970s – *On a Clear Day You Can See Forever*, a calamity, and *A Matter of*

Billy Wilder *(far left), one of the few studio veterans still directing in the 80s.*

Sam Peckinpah *(left) surveys a location set-up in his beloved Mexico for* The Wild Bunch.

Time, worse. Nicholas Ray, of *Johnny Guitar* and *Rebel without a Cause*, finished nothing after 1963. Douglas Sirk, who made *Magnificent Obsession* and *Written on the Wind*, went back to Germany and teaching. Fred Zinnemann (*High Noon*) lost a major project. Joseph L. Mankiewicz (*All about Eve*) stagnated, Richard Brooks (*Blackboard Jungle*) seemed lost, and comedian Jerry Lewis' career came to depend on the annual muscular dystrophy telethon. Alexander Mackendrick (*Sweet Smell of Success*) gave up the business. Budd Boetticher (*The Man from the Alamo*) went south to become the sort of vagrant-poet that Sam Peckinpah might make films about. Elia Kazan (*On the Waterfront*) turned to writing. Orson Welles (*Citizen Kane*) roamed, yarned and mocked TV commercials with his flatulent dignity. George Cukor (*Philadelphia Story*) apparently lost confidence. Billy Wilder of *Double Indemnity* and *Some Like It Hot* worked on – *Avanti!, The Front Page* and *Fedora* – but with loss of heart and good humour. As he started making *Fedora* (1978), a testament that so few would appreciate, he told *American Film*:

> 'I am, I trust, off the hit parade only temporarily. I'm going through a dry spell, that's all. I did not suddenly become an idiot. I did not suddenly unlearn my craft. It's a dry spell. Occasionally the vineyards produce a bad vintage. They say Wilder is out of touch with his times. Frankly, I regard it as a compliment. Who the hell wants to be in touch with *these* times?'

That sounds alarmingly like Norma Desmond, Wilder's embittered heroine of *Sunset Boulevard* (1950), the past resenting the present because of its drab or lazy expectations. *Fedora* is not well made, though that need not be all Wilder's fault. It required a certain kind of grandiose star, and none was willing to risk it. But what could be more poignant than a senior director anxious to vindicate the well-made film, yet no longer able to make it all fit together? Samuel Fuller, the maker of superb action pictures like *Underworld USA* (1960), did nothing in the 1970s but *Dead Pigeon on Beethoven Street*, in Germany, and *The Big Red One*. It seemed wonderful that he should at last get that opportunity, in America, for Lorimar, one of the newer small independent production companies, through the help of Peter Bogdanovich, and with Lee Marvin in the central part. The film was shot, but nothing happened. Studio rumours reported that Fuller was unable to edit it. He asked for help, but no one could make it coherent. The picture was effectively shelved when one day a novice asked if she could try her hand at it. In the event, she turned that footage into the movie that was released. Youth gets a chance! Yes, but the pantheon crumbles, leaving the grim sight of old men less than they once were.

One could argue that Wilder's grievance and Fuller's dilemma were brutal evidence of their age, unkind time and the movies' interest in new subjects. But the thematic novelty of recent films may only be a matter of greater frankness, or extremism, with sex and violence, and less precision as far as intricate narrative mechanics are concerned. Is the medium as technically nimble as it once was? Lorimar, where both Wilder and Fuller sought help, rents studio and office space at Culver City and only employs technicians for TV series like *Dallas*. Cameramen, editors, art directors, gaffers are all free-lance now. They work less often than their forebears did in the 1930s and 40s, and teams stay together less than they did when the production studio factories had a body of craftsmen under contract. When you make a film today, you have to pick up your top technicians as best you can. The significant number of foreign cameramen on major American films – Vilmos Zsigmond, Laszlo Kovacs, Vittorio Storaro, Nestor Almendros, Guiseppe Rotunno, Sven Nykvist, Robby Muller, Bruno Nytten – suggests that uncertain movie work is less appealing to American cameramen. It has made for a gradual dilution of 'American style'. Studio house style died away in the 1950s; and in the 1970s it became harder to

John Travolta *(right) rides a mechanical rodeo bull in James Bridges'* Urban Cowboy, *produced by Robert Evans.*

Paul Newman and Robert Redford *(far right), both now directors in their own right, in* The Sting, *the movie which credited five producers.*

identify an American picture by its texture.

Very little study has been made of this, and it is not a thing Hollywood talks about, but it may well be that the quality of craft work in American film today is flattered by the technological advances in photography and sound. Walter Murch, at Coppola's company Zoetrope, is an artist, or magician, in sound, without whom *The Conversation* might never have been made. Dolby and digital sound permit new depths of clarity and density, as well as a more felt silence, yet it is harder to hear dialogue than it was in the 1940s. Photographic and processing expertise have reached such a stage of fidelity and ingenuity that 'life-like' colour has become an automatic, bland norm, while the laboratories can rescue all but the most devastating mistakes. Photography is more correct and more 'real'; but is it less expressive? Among editors, too, is it possible that younger, less experienced cutters, and directors allowed to supervise the editing, have contributed to slacker, longer films? I wonder whether the scripts of vintage comedies and thrillers of the 30s and 40s like *His Girl Friday*, *Laura* or *The Awful Truth* could be made today at the same running length.

That much is speculation. But the new vulnerability of the director cannot be questioned. He has to find his crew and then train it to his ways; whereas, the best studio directors of the old school like Anthony Mann or Mitchell Leisen had the advantage of a unit in which there were only occasional changes of personnel. They also had the studio's paternal administration, the cafeteria, pensions and producers. From 1943 to 1963, every film Minnelli made was at MGM; his decline happens to coincide with the need to scout around the town for work.

All those directors who fell by the wayside in the 1960s had been brought up in a system where the studio carried the weight of hack work on a film. If Fitzgerald saw Frank Borzage as a stooge, and if we treasure the personal tone that Borzage still put into *Three Comrades*, it may be because the director was free to direct. He had only to envisage the scene and handle the action. He did not struggle with the script, audition actresses and fight over casting. He did not argue for time and money, negotiate with every actor over terms, worry about lunch for the extras or have to handle anxious calls from investors in the company. Those tasks fell to the producer, a figure the director was able to despise, resent and blame, if need be.

The modern producer

There are still producers functioning, people who package, fund and sell others' films. They may be self-effacing admirers of their directors, or uninhibited profiteers. Their task may be to float all the money, resources and talent for a picture, or merely to take the administrative load off the director's back. They may be movie addicts, showmen or cold-blooded accountants. They are very seldom 'line' producers, the kind of people who rode steady, vigilant and even interfering herd on every stage of a picture. At best today they are sponsors or patrons. Charles Joffe has produced most of Woody Allen's later pictures and helped make Allen's 'seriousness' commercially viable. Clint Eastwood, an outstanding businessman, engaged in nearly as many areas of movie work as Allen, keeps Robert Daley as executive producer at his own company Malpaso. In the 1970s Irwin Winkler and Robert Chartoff brought *Rocky*, *Rocky II* and *Raging Bull* to the screen. Michael Douglas, a flimsy actor, seemed as dynamic as his father, Kirk, when it came to getting *One Flew Over the Cuckoo's Nest* or *The China Syndrome* made. Alan Pakula is one of the few directors who was a producer first. Robert Evans has ranged from *Chinatown* to *Black Sunday* and *Urban Cowboy*. Bert Schneider, once a crucial innovator via films like *Five Easy Pieces*, has put his name to only *Days of Heaven* recently. Frank Yablans has kept very firm control of *The Other Side of Midnight*, *Silver Streak* and *The Fury*. On that latter project, Brian De Palma seemed to be content with so rugged a producer, but he

Robert Redford *(far left) as the incognito prison governor in* Brubaker.

Gary Kurtz and George Lucas *(left), the team responsible for* American Graffiti *and, later, the* Star Wars *series.*

Marlon Brando and Francis Coppola *(right) discuss one of the former's scenes for* Apocalypse Now.

Robert Altman *(right), a prolific director whose Christmas 1980 hit,* Popeye, *was nonetheless his first box-office success since* M*A*S*H.

and Yablans later parted company and De Palma went back to the semi-underground pictures he made in the late 1960s. The shortage of hit material and the circling around of many would-be entrepreneurs can lead to the top-heavy credits of *The Sting*. That has five named producers – Tony Bill, Julia and Michael Phillips, David Brown and Richard Zanuck: as crowded a gamble as the movie itself describes.

The director as producer and businessman

More often than it might seem, however, directors do the work of producers. Since every film is now set up as a one-off deal, and since most films involve directors far earlier than was the case in the 30s and 40s, those directors need to be negotiators, businessmen and managers. Good evidence of this fact was offered recently in the pre-production arrangements on *Brubaker* (1980). It was a film placed at Twentieth-Century Fox, with pre-production working out of a bungalow on their lot. But it had originally been packaged and sold to Fox by its producer Ron Silverman, who had bought rights in the original book years before, advanced to a script and only then hired the director Bob Rafelson. As for Rafelson, he had directed two exceptional pictures, *Five Easy Pieces* (1970) and *The King of Marvin Gardens* (1972) for BBS, the company that he and Bert Schneider had founded with Steve Blauner. *Brubaker* was his first picture for a large studio, evidence of his own uncertain box-office record and of his famously aggressive integrity. But even under the cloak of a major studio, Rafelson, with a secretary and an assistant producer, was still working on scripts, budget and casting *and* making arrangements for the company's accommodations in Ohio. The panic and the excitement were not fulfilled. *Brubaker*, still with Robert Redford in its lead, became a Stuart Rosenberg film. Rafelson was fired after a week or so of location shooting because of an angry argument with a Fox executive who felt that the picture was already slipping behind schedule.

On most of the films discussed so far someone other than the director is credited as producer although as we have seen he may not give the director much help. But Paul Mazursky has been co-producer on his recent films including *An Unmarried Woman*, with Tony Ray, as part of his wish to operate from New York City, away from Hollywood pressures. Robert Altman is generally his own producer, and at Lion's Gate, his headquarters, he has fostered one of the closest bands of collaborators in front of and behind the camera. Director Michael Cimino was one of the producers on his film *The Deer Hunter* (1979). Warren Beatty is his own producer, his own secret empire. James Toback only made *Love and Money* (1981) because he held on to it against all delays and obstacles, including the departure of original owner Warren Beatty, the coming and going of notional producer Pauline Kael, the transfer of the project from Paramount to Lorimar, and his own eventual burden as producer when no one else was left.

You can deduce from this that the new film-maker must be not only capable and durable enough to handle that much paperwork, but actually inspired and aroused by it. Distributors and financiers are still very powerful, if push comes to shove, but they do recognize the extent to which the dynamic of the business has moved in favour of young hustler-artists. They have only contempt for and fear of a would-be director who cannot weigh his own film as a commercial operation.

Close friends Gary Kurtz (producer) and George Lucas (director) made *Star Wars* (1977)

together. Kurtz described his duties as 'line', or working producer to *American Film*:

> 'If you want to categorize the function of the *working* producer, it is to provide all the tools so the director can do everything he wants, or, at least, everything within the limits you are trying to work. I also function as a sounding board to discuss everything that comes up.'

But Lucas's own confession, or boast, shows how little scope that may leave for the producer beyond being a friend in need:

> 'I come up from the film-makers' school of doing movies, which means I did everything myself. If you are a writer-director, you *must* get involved with everything. It's very hard for me to get into another system where everybody does things for me, and I say "Fine". If I ever continue to do those kinds of movies, I've got to learn to do that. I have a lot of friends who can, and I admire them. Francis [Ford Coppola] is going through that now, and he's finally learning, finally getting to the point where he realizes *he* can't do it all. He's getting into the traditional system: "Call me when it's ready, and it better be right, and if it's not, do it again and spend whatever it costs to get it right." But you have to be willing to make *very* expensive movies that way.'

There are so many lessons of the 1970s in that: the near impossibility of low-budget films; the need to know and command everything, so reminiscent of old-time mogul David Selznick on *Gone with the Wind* (1939); the sense of film being for its creators a process of management (and gambling) as well as making. But even then, *Star Wars* was regarded sceptically by Fox, who had funded it; on first viewing, they thought they had a loser. It took critics and the public to persuade them they had the biggest grosser of all time. Even so, early hesitation meant a failure to get spin-off toys on the market by Christmas – a film is also tee-shirts, records and behaviour fads.

Lucas's assessment of himself did not exactly work out. So rich from *Star Wars*, he has set up his own special effects factory for producing sequels which he will not direct himself. He has become a tycoon, much like Coppola, who nevertheless appeared to be overwhelmed by the problems of delegation and organization that blurred creative decisions on *Apocalypse*.

The director as cultural hero

Now, as much as ever, the director is lured by the chance of making a compelling entertainment that will be a subject of conversation and the means of impact around the world. He can seem, to others and to himself, as titanic as the Coppola who made *The Godfather*; as passionate as the Scorsese of *Taxi Driver*; as diverse, tolerant and amused as Altman with *Nashville*; a boy wonder, like Spielberg with *Jaws* or Lucas with *Star Wars*. This is an eminence that very few Americans can hope to enjoy – even if it lasts but a week. At different times, Coppola, Woody Allen, Altman, and even Warren Beatty have been held representative of their country. Orson Welles was perhaps the first man to discover the glamour and the authority of being a movie director, and of doing it all himself.

But that strain can be killing. There were as many disappointments in the 1970s as there were promising debuts. It is harder than ever to build a career as gradually as art requires. Too often, a young man finds himself overwhelmed by the project of the year – make or break. One day during the near decade of *Apocalypse Now*, Eleanor Coppola found this message from the darkness in her husband's typewriter – it is a cry of dismay that suggests how far the beleaguered Kurtz would be a portrait of the film director at the end of his tether:

> 'My greatest fear – I've had for months – The movie is a mess – A mess of continuity, of style – and most important, the ending neither works on an audience or philosophical level. Brando is a disappointment to audiences – the film reaches its highest level during the fucking helicopter battle.
>
> 'My nerves are shot – My heart is broken – My imagination is dead. I have no self-reliance – But just like a child want someone to rescue me . . .'

The Movie Brats and Beyond

By the mid-1970s, Hollywood had undergone major changes. Although the studio moguls were not prepared to relinquish power, a sufficient number of cracks had appeared in the structure of the system to permit a group of determined young film-makers to penetrate the monolith. The key members of this group were Francis Ford Coppola, George Lucas and Steven Spielberg, with a penumbra grouping of Martin Scorsese, Brian De Palma and John Milius. Five of their films, *American Graffiti, Star Wars, Jaws, Close Encounters of the Third Kind* and *The Godfather*, have been among the top grossing films of all time. These men meet in both their public and private lives, as collaborators and friends, sharing both their profits and their ideas.

What unites them above all is their knowledge and love of film. With the exception of Spielberg, who emerged from the excellent nursery of the Universal-MCA studio making films for television, the other five were the products of film school. The key American film schools, of which this group were the alumni, were at the University of Southern California, The University of California, Los Angeles, and New York University; all of them developed in the 1960s. This background provided them with an impressive body of technical knowledge, a peer group of cineastes who would later become their collaborators, and the opportunity to view a vast selection of films not otherwise available, especially on the West Coast.

At the time that these men were emerging from their film schools, the studios were not prepared to take risks. Lacking capital, they preferred to invest in the spectacular, rather than the low-budget, feature. As opportunities for film-school graduates to enter the industry were minimal, the 'movie-brats' could not afford to nurse high aspirations. As George Lucas said, 'I thought I might be a ticket-tearer at Disneyland, or something.'

A major shift in the Hollywood industry resulted from the development of American International Pictures by Samuel Z. Arkoff and James H. Nicholson, in the late 1950s and early 1960s. This was the first company to orient itself towards the new market of suburban adolescents, a specialized market which was neglected by the major studios. Between 1963 and 1973, AIP was averaging twenty films a year, originating the beach-party cycle, the drag-race genre and introducing director Roger Corman's horror cycle. Working on low budgets and tight schedules, the company was prepared to hire untried directors. Through AIP and, later, through Roger Corman's own New World Pictures, were to emerge John Milius, Francis Coppola, Peter Bogdanovich, Martin Scorsese and, more recently, Walter Hill, Jonathan Demme and Jonathan Kaplan.

Since coping with finance is an indispensable part of the movie business, it is arguable that one of the reasons for the spectacular success of this new generation of directors is their rare combination of artistic ability and acute business acumen. To challenge Hollywood in the way they desire, film-making ability alone is not enough. They all share a healthy scepticism about the executives who control the studios, and an awareness of the dependence of the bureaucrat on the film-maker. 'We are the pigs,' George Lucas said. 'We are the ones who sniff out the truffles. You can put us on a leash, keep us under control. But we are the guys who dig out the gold. The man in the executive tower cannot do that.'

Francis Coppola was the architect of this generation, always in search of independence from the studio machinery. Out of *Rain People* in 1968 grew the friendships and organization that were to lead to the founding of a base in San Francisco. Although only a few hundred miles from Hollywood geographically, this base (which Spielberg was to christen Shangri-Coppola) represented the ideal of independence which this generation sought. On 14 November, 1969, a San Francisco attorney filed the papers for a new corporation, to be called American Zoetrope. Under George Lucas as Vice-President, and Francis Coppola as the sole shareholder, this group acquired its first studio.

Eleven years later, in March 1980, it was

Francis Ford Coppola

Steven Spielberg

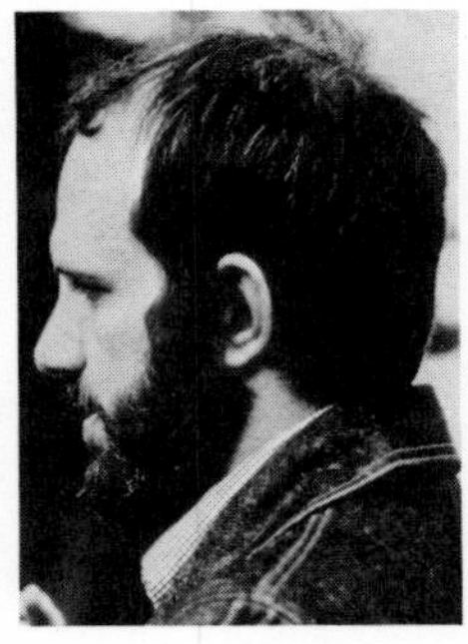

Brian De Palma

Close Encounters of the Third Kind *(right), with Richard Dreyfuss. This was one of Steven Spielberg's major successes.*

1941 *(far right): the jitterbugging scene. The film was Spielberg's first expensive failure.*

George Lucas

Martin Scorsese

John Milius

announced in Los Angeles that Coppola had acquired the Hollywood General Studios, on Santa Monica Boulevard. Coppola's ideal is to develop this studio as a base for a repertory company, with veteran directors participating as 'artists in residence'. He remains critical of current Hollywood practice. 'There are real opportunities now', he told *The L.A. Times*, 'for making the picture business succeed as both a business and an art form. Hollywood is missing it, and that's a pity.' As a result of his outspoken attacks on the film industry as presently constituted, he has attracted considerable hostility in Los Angeles. It is hard to resist a comparison with Orson Welles, whose aspirations and talents also antagonized Hollywood. (Added irony lies in the fact that Welles' first Hollywood film was to have been Joseph Conrad's *Heart of Darkness*, which provided the core of Coppola's *Apocalypse Now*.)

In the 1970s, it was suggested that the 'movie-brats' generation could revolutionize the film industry. Now, however, a question mark looms as the endless escalation of budgets again threatens. With the cost of *Apocalypse Now* reckoned to be $31m., and Spielberg's epic farce, *1941* at $26.5m., the emergence of a new kind of superstar-director economics has inevitably led to a backlash. Originally budgeted at $12m., the cost of *Apocalypse Now* spiralled as a result of typhoons, illness and mechanical problems.

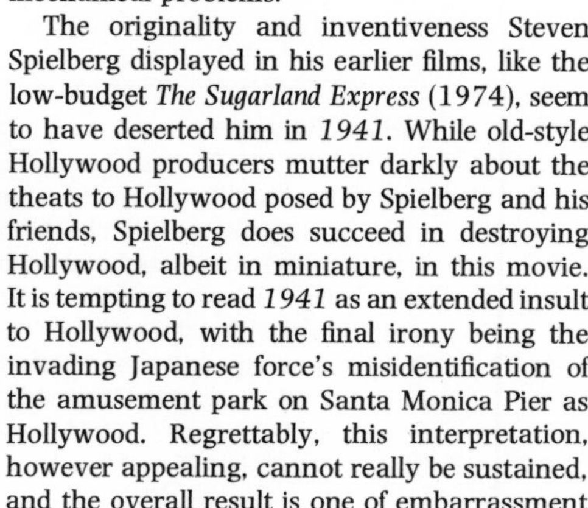

The originality and inventiveness Steven Spielberg displayed in his earlier films, like the low-budget *The Sugarland Express* (1974), seem to have deserted him in *1941*. While old-style Hollywood producers mutter darkly about the theats to Hollywood posed by Spielberg and his friends, Spielberg does succeed in destroying Hollywood, albeit in miniature, in this movie. It is tempting to read *1941* as an extended insult to Hollywood, with the final irony being the invading Japanese force's misidentification of the amusement park on Santa Monica Pier as Hollywood. Regrettably, this interpretation, however appealing, cannot really be sustained, and the overall result is one of embarrassment at the film's failure to generate amusement. Only the extraordinary jitter-bugging competition illustrates the impeccable timing and staging of which Spielberg is capable, suggesting the musical might be a genre at which he would excel.

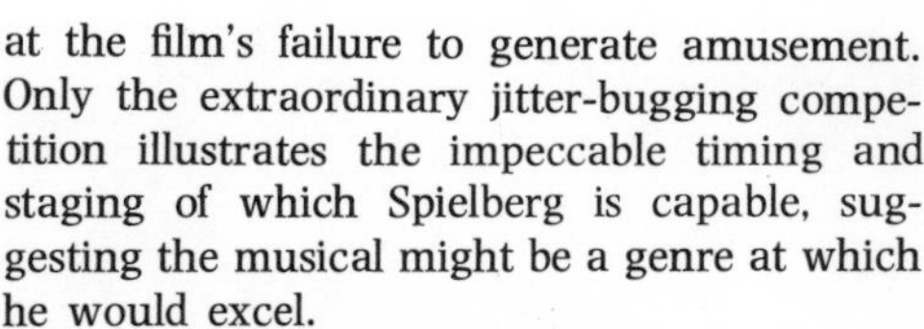

A *wunderkind* like Spielberg (whose films *Jaws* and *Close Encounters of the Third Kind* grossed $400m. and $200m. worldwide respectively) is under tremendous pressure from the industry to graduate to progressively higher budgets. Agents urge their successful clients to make more blockbusters, while studios compete to offer them increasingly higher budgets. Unfortunately large budgets and high quality entertainment do not always go together.

It would be ironical if the big-budget mistakes of the 1960s made in the wake of *The Sound of Music* were to be repeated by a new generation of film-makers who are consciously seeking to transform the industry. The example of *1941* serves as a warning that overspending on gadgetry, and special effects can be counterproductive. Arguably, many of 'the movie-brats' produced their finest work when operating under the constraints of low budgets, which forced them to evolve an economy of expression that generated extraordinary resonance.

At the moment, in spite of the success of cheap comedies like *Airplane!* (1980) any movement in the direction of lower-budget films seems to be unlikely, especially by film-makers who have a reputation for blockbusting. Steven Spielberg and George Lucas have collaborated on *Raiders of the Lost Ark*, currently budgeted at $32m., and John Milius, despite his commercially unsuccessful *Big Wednesday* (1978), has directed another epic, *Conan*.

The startling fusion of artistic and business ability that this group possesses could still result in the revitalization of the industry. If the mega-budgets could be used more judiciously, and Coppola's studio developed into an economically self-reliant and artistically self-sustaining group, this generation could still inject into the 1980s the energy and artistry they brought to the 1970s.

Confessions of a Movie Brat: Martin Scorsese

Martin Scorsese was born in Flushing, New York, the son of Italian immigrants. A movie fan from his earliest childhood, he ultimately abandoned his intention of becoming a priest to study film at New York University. After years of struggle, he directed his first feature Who's That Knocking at My Door? *in 1969, and by 1972 he was making* Boxcar Bertha *for Roger Corman. Between 1973 and 1976 Scorsese made three films that gained him a reputation as one of the world's leading film-makers. The autobiographical* Mean Streets *(1973) won critical acclaim and he followed it in 1974 with a big box-office success* Alice Doesn't Live Here Any More, *one of the first Hollywood hits in decades to feature a woman as its central subject. Two years later Scorsese became even more famous for the highly controversial* Taxi Driver. *Here Scorsese talks about his earliest memories of movies, his first and frequently desperate attempts to break into the industry and his work up to his most recent film* Raging Bull *(1980).*

One of the earliest things I can remember is watching the trailer of a Roy Rogers movie. The colour was beautiful: he was wearing fringes and sailing over a jump on his horse. And I remember my father saying, 'That's Trigger. Do you know what Trigger is?'

I said, 'The trigger of a gun?'

And he said, 'No, it's the horse's name. I'll take you to see it next week.'

I was about three years-old and I think that may be why I love trailers so much.

Until I was about seven or eight years-old we lived in a place called Corona in New York, in the suburb of Queens. It was a nice area; we had a backyard and a tree. But because of financial problems and illness we then had to move back to the tenement building in Elizabeth Street in Lower Manhattan where my parents were born. I grew up there and it was a rough area: you might be playing out in the sandbox when something fell behind you. You thought it was a bag of garbage but it turned out to be a little baby who fell off the roof. Little things like that! It could be terrifying playing in your own backyard.

We didn't have much money but, after essentials like food and clothes had been taken care of, the money was spent on television and movies. My father, who worked all his life in the garment district, was funny like that: he had been a big movie-buff himself in the 1930s and he used to take me every week. TV and movies were luxuries he would always afford even when there was no money for anything else. We were one of the first families in the area to get television. I remember in 1948 I was playing in the backyard and my cousin Peter rushed out, shouting, 'Come and see a television screen that's bigger than the whole house!' I ran in and there was a sixteen inch RCA Victor!

Earliest influences

Two films that played on television made an impression on me very early: one was Michael Powell's *The Thief of Baghdad* (1940) which for years I saw in black and white; and the other was Roberto Rossellini's *Paisa* (1946) because they used to show Italian movies. They also showed a lot of British films especially the Korda films, and years later my crowd would seek out arthouses playing British comedies like *Private's Progress* (1956) and we became big Terry Thomas and Ian Carmichael fans! They seemed totally insane to us! Two other British films that made a huge impression on me as a child were *Drums* (1938, UK: *The Drum*) and *The Four Feathers* (1939). Westerns and costume adventures were my other big favourites as a child: Gene Kelly in George Sidney's *The Three Musketeers* (1948) was one I loved, and I still like it.

The first thing I wanted to do in movies was act in them because that was the first thing I saw. I just didn't realize anything went on behind the cameras. Then I became fascinated by titles and credits. I drew a whole book of fictional titles and put my own combinations of stars in them and coloured the titles and created fictionalized posters. Then I began to draw cartoons to illustrate my own movies – a kind of storyboarding – and painted them in water colours, trying for Cinemascope and 3D. I remember planning this gigantic Roman epic because I loved anything with costumes. It was going to be in 75mm. – the biggest I'd ever heard of was 70mm. And I still have two coloured strips which get as far as the gladiatorial fights to mark the Emperor's home-coming after a war. In fact my wife had them framed because in retrospect they look exactly like the illustrations of Sicilian puppet shows. But eventually when I was twelve or thirteen I abandoned the storyboards and tried to make an 8mm. movie in black and white.

On the Waterfront (1954) was the first film I saw which seemed to relate to my own immediate experience of growing up. It was the closest thing to what I saw on the streets, and I saw it about twenty times straight, even though it doesn't seem nearly so accurate now as it did then. *East of Eden* (1955) had an equally big effect on me some months later.

One of the first directors I became aware of was John Ford. I quickly began to realize that the combination of John Ford and John Wayne on the credits meant something good. And on the night in 1956 when I graduated from my first school, I went with two friends to see *The Searchers* (1956) at a theatre called The Criterion. We walked in during the middle because in those days you never bothered to wait for the beginning, and it had an enormous effect on me. I went to see it over and over again: first run, second run, third and fourth. Eventually I knew every line by heart. Later on, three films – *Citizen Kane, The Seventh Seal* and *The Third Man* – made me realize what a film director did. After I saw *Citizen Kane* on television I'd go to the theatre to watch it over and over again, wherever it was playing in New York.

My first Catholic school was a crazy experience: you had Irish nuns teaching Italian kids with Puerto Ricans coming in. And in the neighbourhood where we lived there were fights all the time, many of them with the Puerto Ricans who were moving into the area. I had to have a kind of survival sense, and even now wherever I go, I try to sit with my back against the wall.

I used to hang out with a guy called Joey, on whom *Mean Streets* (1973) was partly based. Whenever there was a fight, everyone would tell us: 'Come on over, quick!' We'd say right and then we'd walk and take our time and by the time we got there it was all over. But Joey and I had a very close brush one night and I based the ending of *Mean Streets* on it. At one o'clock in the morning we were sitting in the back of this guy's red convertible – a big deal since none of us had cars. The owner had a young teenage kid with him in the front seat and he said he'd drive us around for a while. But we thought he was acting a little wise so eventually Joey and I got out on Elizabeth Street and went home. Three minutes after we left, there was a shoot-out. The wise guy in the red convertible had got angry with another driver blocking his path. He flashed his gun, but the other driver was a lot tougher than he was. He pulled alongside the red convertible and fired several bullets. And the teenage kid got it in the eye. So if we had decided to stay in the car it would probably have been us. Two months later John Kennedy was killed.

I first became interested in religion when I attended the Catholic school. I decided to become a priest so I went from there to a preparatory seminary in 1957 and I still wanted to become a priest right up to the time I made my first movie. But I failed a number of courses at the seminary and I had to go to High School in the Bronx. My first few years in High School were very bad. I was torn: there was the church and there was the street and there was also my earliest experience of falling in love. By my fourth year I was getting better grades and I wanted to go to the Jesuit University, Fordham, but my final grades couldn't make up for the first three years. I was rejected.

New York University

By this time I was reading a lot, and I thought of doing English at NYU. One day I was thumbing through their catalogue of courses when I noticed one on the history of motion pictures. They organized the course in such a way that maybe three or four people out of the 300 or 400 who enrolled would emerge at the end of four years to make a

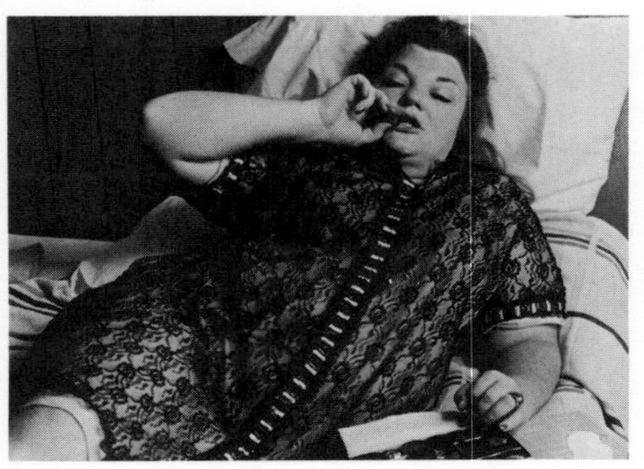

The Honeymoon Killers *(left and right) starring Tony Lo Bianco and Shirley Stoler was Scorsese's first assignment on a commercial feature, until he was fired and replaced by screenwriter Leonard Kastle.*

film. People thought I was crazy coming from my background and wanting to make movies, but I managed to figure out a way to afford the course, and I can remember attending the first lecture of the session along with about 300 others. The Professor came out onto a little stage and started talking. He went through movie history from the very beginning, talking very fast. And from the very first sentence he spoke I knew what I wanted to be. It didn't matter how many people were on the course. I was staying, and I was going to make films.

My time at NYU coincided with the French New Wave which redefined technique for all of us; and another film that affected me a good deal was John Cassavetes' *Shadows* (1959). It was after seeing that, I realized *we* could make films. The cameras were lightweight, they could be moved and nothing was forbidden anymore. We had learned the basic ground-rules on the course, but after *Shadows* and the New Wave, we felt free to break all of them, and the movies I made at school reflected this. In the first one, not one shot is a matched cut.

Another big milestone in my student days was the first issue of *Movie* magazine which lavished praise on American directors. I remember a guy bringing it into film class and we were all sitting round in amazement, realizing it was all right to like American movies after all. At that time, a lot of the guys I went to movies with had been starting to get a little nervous because I kept dragging them to see movies by people like Eisenstein. Because of *Movie* magazine and the writings of Andrew Sarris, it was OK to go to the triple features again.

Around 1964 I remember seeing Bertolucci's *Before the Revolution* (1964) at the New York Film Festival. It had an important effect on me. In fact it made me over-ambitious because shortly afterwards I started to make the first version of *Who's That Knocking at My Door?* We did it originally as a student film: my father got a student loan of $6000 for me and I shot it in 35mm. This turned out to be a big mistake because we couldn't move the camera and I couldn't really get the angles I wanted.

Early struggles

The whole thing turned into a disaster. By 1966 I was back on the street, desperately trying to make some money. I had teamed up with a writer called Mardik Martin, who I met at NYU after he had worked his way from Baghdad to America, and we had some horrible experiences. We had no money and we were killing ourselves to make movies. I had won some awards for my student films but by this time they were forgotten because *Who's That Knocking* in its first version had been universally hated. But the worse things got, the less I felt like giving in. I wouldn't even go to work as a writer. I was very determined and very angry. Mardik and I often ended up writing in his car in the snow, because the apartments were always so small and by now I was married with a small child and there would be constant quarrels. Mardik and I had no money; we were borrowing from everybody and seeing every movie that was playing. We would sit writing in the car with the snow outside, shivering and knowing we were mad. We tried to write absolutely everything from horror to sex movies which were then just beginning.

What eventually happened was that in 1967 I managed to get a producer to invest a little money in *Who's That Knocking* so that I could shoot some new scenes. The new version went to the Chicago Film Festival. I couldn't afford to go there, but it got a good review from Roger Ebert which helped considerably. I was invited to Europe to make some commercials, and I heard from New York that in spite of the review *Who's That Knocking* was still being turned down by every distributor except one. He specialized in sex films. And he was only prepared to take it if we added a nude scene. The actor Harvey Keitel flew over to Amsterdam to shoot the scene. There was no way of getting it back through the US Customs so I stuck the film in one pocket of my raincoat and the sound-track in the other pocket, and I shaved on the plane to look respectable and I got through. So my first feature ultimately opened in New York in September 1969.

Mardik and I had been working on a sequel to *Who's That Knocking* since 1966; it featured the same character, played by Harvey Keitel, several years later. But it was rejected everywhere. I couldn't even get in the front door of most producer's offices. And even my old professors at NYU, who had helped to put *Who's That Knocking* together, just said there's no market in Italian-American movies. So I put it away and some years later it was rewritten as *Mean Streets* (1973).

So after *Who's That Knocking* I was still looking round for work. I did a short for the USIA which they thought was so odd that they destroyed it unseen. Then I got a job directing a film called *The Honeymoon Killers* (1969) from a script by Leonard Kastle. I wanted to shoot it in colour but the pro-

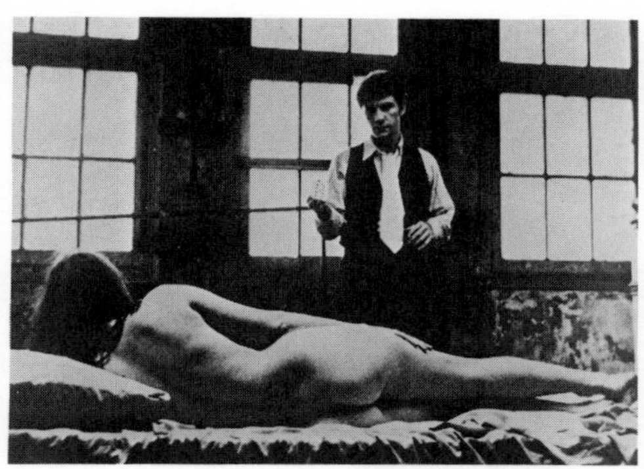

Who's That Knocking at My Door *(left)*: *Scorsese was forced by a distributor to add this nude scene which he shot in Amsterdam with Harvey Keitel.*

Boxcar Bertha *(right)* *was Scorsese's first commercial feature. It starred David Carradine and Barbara Hershey.*

ducer wanted black and white so we agreed on a kind of tabloid *National Enquirer*-type style. And then they fired me in the first week; this was because I felt that a director who really knows what he's doing does it in one take, and I was not keen on a lot of editing. But the script was over 175 pages long and the producers dreaded coming off the floor and finding it couldn't be put together. In some ways I never quite got over the fact that they fired me. Shortly afterwards I was offered a job teaching film in NYU; I got very involved in political films and the students were practically living in my house. Also I was away a lot of the time trying to set up projects on the outside. So I ended up getting fired from that as well.

Hollywood

Then a Hollywood producer called Fred Weintraub called me up and asked me to come to Hollywood to work on a feature-length rock documentary called *Medicine Ball Caravan* (1971). They had a ten hour rough-cut, parts of it in Techniscope, parts in 16mm. and some pieces of 8mm. too. It was meant to be a two week job, so when I got to Hollywood I bought a poster for Minnelli's *Two Weeks in Another Town* (1962) and hung it over my bed. But I ended up working on the picture for nine months.

At this point I got to know some of the other aspiring Hollywood film-makers, but all of us seemed to be involved in one disaster after another. Brian De Palma was working on the same lot doing *Get To Know Your Rabbit* (1972) which bombed. George Lucas had just made *THX1138* (1971) which the studio thought was terrible. Francis Coppola's programme to groom young directors had proved a disaster. In fact all of us felt we were going down the drain. *Medicine Ball Caravan* didn't work out either. I'd been in Hollywood nearly a year and I was boxed into another corner.

So I went to John Cassavetes who had become a friend and begged him for work. Just to keep me alive, he put me on *Minnie and Moskowitz* (1971) as a sound effects editor which basically meant that I held John while someone punched him. I was living in his house and my agent called his office, looking for me. John's secretary took the call and asked if it was anything important. 'Important?' my agent said. 'It's the biggest break of his life. He's gonna make a film. The script just came in.' And she said: 'Oh don't be silly', and hung up.

Boxcar Bertha

It turned out to be a script I'd been hoping to get for months. In my very first week in Los Angeles Roger Corman had said he would like me to do *Boxcar Bertha* (1972) which was the sequel to his very successful *Bloody Mama* (1970). Corman has given breaks to numerous young directors because he firmly believes that if you give some new kid with a little talent a chance he will cost very little, do his damnedest and deliver a much better picture than you ever get from a professional hack who costs much more money. I remember saying to him when he first talked to me about *Boxcar Bertha*: 'Does it have costumes? Does it have guns?' He said yes on both counts, so I said I would do it.

As it turned out I very nearly blew *Boxcar* the same way that I had blown *The Honeymoon Killers*. We were shooting in Arkansas and one of the cameramen kept begging me to take more coverage and not just to rely on the master-take; he wanted me to do more close-ups and short shots to help the editor. I was reluctant because I had drawn out every shot for *Boxcar* so I felt safe. But he turned out to be at least partly right. If I hadn't taken extra coverage then at least two or three sequences would have failed in the editing.

When we finished shooting I was pleased with *Boxcar Bertha* and as soon as I had a rough-cut I showed it to John Cassavetes. He said: 'Yes, it's very nice, it's technically terrific, so you've shown you can do that kind of action exploitation movie. But basically this isn't the kind of picture you should be doing. You don't want to leave your personal work behind and get caught up in the Corman AIP circuit. Haven't you got some project of your own you'd like to do?' So I told him that I'd got this movie about Italian Americans, but everybody just laughed at it and threw it away. He insisted that I should go back to work on it.

Mean Streets

I dug up the script and gave it to Sandy Weintraub who I was living with. She said that she thought a lot of the stories I told her about Little Italy were far funnier than anything in it. So I reworked *Mean Streets* completely and sent it to everybody I knew without any result. At that time I was still very keen on genre films and I was going to do either *The Arena*, a picture about gladiators that Corman was

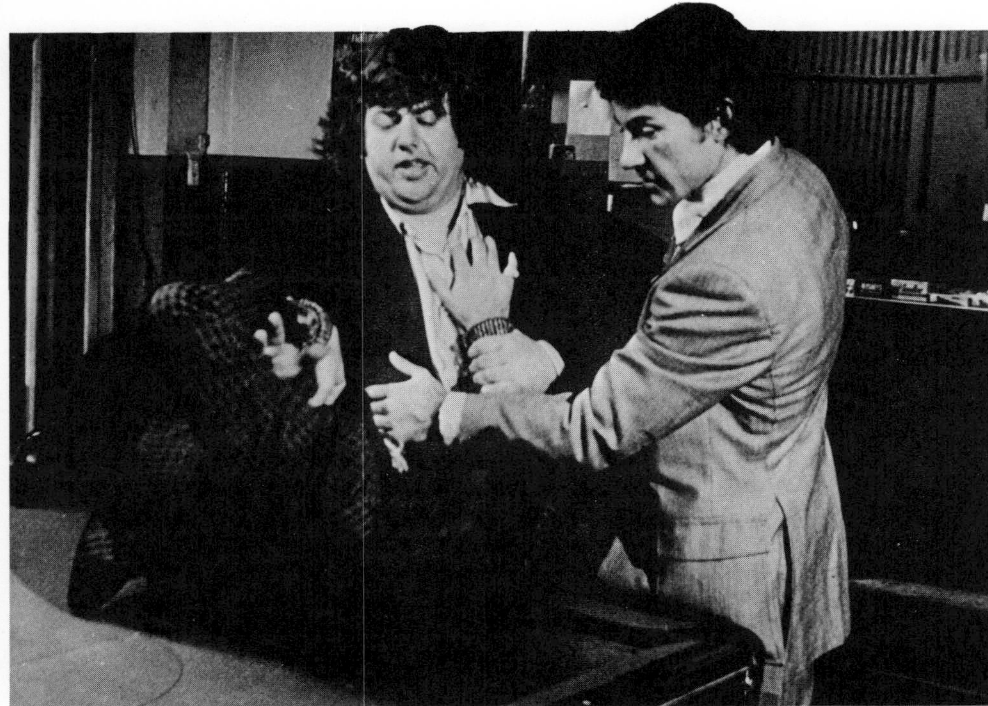

Mean Streets *(left) with George Memmoli, left, and Harvey Keitel attempting to settle a pool-room brawl.*

Alice Doesn't Live Here Any More *(right) with Ellen Burstyn and Kris Kristofferson.*

shooting in Spain, or *I Escaped from Devil's Island* in Costa Rica. But one night I happened to have dinner with John Taplin who had been Bob Dylan's road manager and was now interested in becoming a movie producer. He was keen to see the script of *Mean Streets*, but I really didn't think anything would come of it. However, he liked it, so I showed him *Who's That Knocking*, and he liked that as well. Then I took him to a preview of *Boxcar Bertha* at the Pantages Theatre: the audience loved the film and applauded; Roger Corman came out smiling; and even Sam Arkoff looked at me and said 'I've gotta tell you. It's almost good. That's the best preview we've had since *The Wild Angels*.'

I said, 'That's pretty good.'

He said, 'No, don't get too excited. That's almost good.'

So John Taplin had seen my movies and the preview reaction and he came up with some financial backing for *Mean Streets*, which promptly fell through. Afterwards we trailed around Hollywood trying to put the money together again from scratch. Inevitably one of the first people we tried was Roger Corman whose reader Frances liked the script.

I still remember the meeting I had with both of them. 'Frances here has told me that the script is very good,' Roger said. 'And it does have violence in it?'

Frances said yes.

So Roger said: 'And it does have sex in it?'

Frances said yes again.

So Roger said: 'And it does have gangsters?'

And she said: 'Oh yes.'

And he said: 'Well that's fine, lots of action?'

And she reassured him again.

So he said he was prepared to put up some money and shoot it very fast non-union in New York with my old students from NYU. But it so happened that around that time Roger's brother Gene was having some success with a black version of *The Asphalt Jungle* called *The Cool Breeze* (1972). So Roger said to me: 'Now there's just one thing. Would you think about making *Mean Streets* a black movie?' And I just looked at him. But I was so hungry to do the film that I would almost have done it.

As it turned out, Roger did help us a lot by giving us a slip saying he would distribute the film. And shortly afterwards the backer who had fallen through – a 23 year-old who had just come into an inheritance – came to LA and we had dinner with him and his wife. To this day I don't know what happened. As far as everyone was concerned the film was off, and we certainly didn't discuss it during dinner. But the next day the money was back in.

Mean Streets was shot mainly in Los Angeles, with most of the crew from *Boxcar Bertha*. The bar in the film is not an Italian bar at all in real life but a Chicano bar in a very rough section of Los Angeles. The everyday violence that goes on there is much worse than anything we showed. We rehearsed the cast for ten days in New York and shot a few days of exteriors on the East Coast, but all of the rest of the film, including the car-crash at the end, was shot in LA. Much of the improvisation in the film was taped at rehearsal and then scripted from the tapes before we shot it, but some scenes – like the one where Robert De Niro and Harvey Keitel fight each other with garbage pails – was improvised during shooting. I remember that at the end of one take Bobby threw the thing at Harvey, and Harvey threw it back and I said: 'Great we'll do that in the next take.'

We did the climactic scene where Bobby De Niro suddenly pulls a gun on Richard Romanus, on the next to last day of shooting. Something had happened between Bobby and Richard because the animosity between them in that scene was real, and I played on it. They had got on each other's nerves to a point where they really wanted to kill each other. I kept shooting take after take of Bobby yelling all

these insults, and the crew was getting very upset.

De Niro and I had known each other since we were about 15, but we were never close friends then – he just happened to know some people who lived a couple of blocks from me. Occasionally we'd find ourselves in the same group in a bar. Then in 1970 I met up with him again and I showed him *Who's That Knocking* and we both discussed making a film about our neighbourhood.

Alice Doesn't Live Here Any More

I remember a party on the New Year's Eve after I'd made *Mean Streets* where all of us Hollywood hopefuls seemed to be gathered: Brian De Palma, George Lucas, Steven Spielberg, Julia Philips, John Milius, Paul Schrader. Schrader had just sold his script for *The Yakuza* (1975) to Warners and he felt it was going to be the year for all of us. In some ways he was right: George had *American Graffiti* (1973), Brian made *Sisters* (1972, UK: *Blood Sisters*), Steven wasn't far away from *Jaws* (1975) and I was just about to make *Alice Doesn't Live Here Any More.*

I got a very positive critical reaction to *Mean Streets* and one day John Calley, head of production at Warners, rang up to tell me he had a script he thought I'd like to see. It had excited Ellen Burstyn who was then riding a wave on account of her success in *The Exorcist* (1973). Sandy Weintraub recommended the script and I read it and liked it. I thought it would be good to try and make a woman's film as honest as possible especially since a lot of people thought *Mean Streets* showed I couldn't direct women.

Alice was the first time in my movie career that I was able to build a proper set. It was the last picture to be shot on the old Columbia sound-stages on Gower Street and we even had the set decorator from *Citizen Kane.* For the opening sequence, showing Alice as a little girl, we tried for a combination of *Duel in the Sun* and *Gone with the Wind* in the William Cameron Menzies *Invaders from Mars* style. We painted a red sunset that went 180 degrees around the entire stage and we made up a little girl to look like Dorothy in *The Wizard of Oz* (1939) to stand in front of this incredible backdrop.

I also enjoyed working with Kris Kristofferson. At first we kept making each other nervous. In rehearsal he kept saying to me, 'Where do you want me to stand?'

And I would say, 'I don't know.'

And he'd say, 'You've gotta tell me where I'm supposed to stand.'

The poor guy had just done *Pat Garrett and Billy the Kid* (1973) which I loved, but a lot of people hated. So one day when we went off on our own to rehearse I kidded him and shouted stupid things and looned around, saying, 'I look funny in front of you and you look funny in front of me. So what? We'll look funny in front of each other.' It broke the tension, and after that it was great. I had learned something from him.

The idea of *Alice* was to use women in the crew and be as honest as possible, but we never intended it to be a feminist film. It was a film about self-responsibility and also about how people make the same mistakes again and again. There was some criticism of the ending – of the fact that Ellen Burstyn falls in love with a handsome man. But I thought there were plenty of lines to show that they would have their problems. Maybe Burstyn and Kristofferson would be together for the rest of their lives but it was going to be pretty stormy. And the film didn't end with them. It ended on her and the boy, walking away and talking.

After *Alice* I worked very hard with Marlon Brando trying to put together a film about the American Indians. It didn't work out and, after one last all-night attempt with

Taxi Driver *(left), with Robert De Niro in the title role, became Martin Scorsese's biggest commercial success.*

Brando to map out a script, I got very sick. But *Alice*'s success did change things and I was able to buy a house up in the mountain area away from the smog.

Taxi Driver

Around this time I wanted Paul Schrader to write a version of Dostoyevsky's *The Gambler* for me. He had written an outline, but one night while I was editing he went out to dinner with Brian De Palma and the two of them cooked up the idea for *Obsession* (1976). For three hours they made sure I couldn't find them, and by the time I tracked them down to Musso and Frank's grill, it was too late and the idea of *Obsession* was already born. So I couldn't get Paul to do *The Gambler* for me. But in a funny way it was a good thing, because I remember Brian said: 'Well look, read the script of *Taxi Driver*.'

Paul Schrader had written *Taxi Driver*, but at that point I didn't want to do it, because ironically I thought it was a labour of love which would not make a dime. So I went off and did some research for *New York, New York* which seemed much more commercial. But it happened that Robert De Niro's schedule had to be rearranged because he was due to film *1900* with Bertolucci, so I agreed to postpone *New York, New York* and do *Taxi Driver* instead.

Columbia were having big financial problems so they were not interested in laying out a lot of money to make *Taxi Driver*, especially since *The Yakuza* had done badly. So *Taxi Driver* was an economy picture – in fact there was even talk of doing it on videotape. But Julia and Michael Philips, the project's producers, had made *The Sting* (1973) and they were able to raise $900,000. Eventually it came out at $1,800,000.

Much of *Taxi Driver* arose from my feeling that movies are really a kind of dream-state, like taking dope. And the shock of walking out of the theatre into broad daylight can be terrifying. I watch movies the whole time and I am also very bad at waking up. I can be very nasty in the mornings even if I'm in good spirits when I go to sleep. The whole of *Taxi Driver* was about that sense of almost waking up – the twilight world between waking and sleeping.

There is something about what happens in summer in New York that is extraordinary. We shot the film in a very strong hot summer, and there's something in the atmosphere at night that is like a seeping kind of virus. You can smell it in the air and taste it in your mouth. It reminds me of the scene in *The Ten Commandments* (1956) portraying the killing of the first born where a channel of ice-green smoke seeps along the palace floor and touches the foot of a first-born son who falls dead. That's almost what it's like. A strange disease creeps along the streets of the city and, while we were shooting the film, we would slide along after it. Many times people threatened us, and we had to take off.

One night while we were shooting in the garment district, my father came out of work and walked by the set. The press of bodies on the pavement was so thick that in the moment I turned away from the lens to talk to him it was impossible to get back to the camera. That was typical.

As in my other films, there was improvisation in *Taxi Driver*: the scene between Robert De Niro and Cybill Shepherd in the coffee-shop is a good example. I didn't want the dialogue in the script so we improvised for about twelve minutes, then wrote it down and shot it. It was about three minutes in the end. Many of the best scenes – like the one in which De Niro blasts Harvey Keitel – were designed to be shot in one take, and every shot was drawn in advance.

Taxi Driver was my most successful film at the box office – its success completely amazed me. When I saw it with an audience everybody was screaming and yelling at the shoot-out, and though I admit to enjoying violence in movies, at times I've been upset by the audience reaction to that section of the violence. *Taxi Driver* is only one aspect of New York. On the other hand I do see it that way – it's

New York, New York *(right) concerned a post-war romance between a saxophone player, De Niro, and a big band vocalist, Liza Minnelli.*

my city, it's where I come from, I love it.

It wasn't easy getting Bernard Herrmann (who did the music for *Citizen Kane*) to compose for *Taxi Driver*. He was a marvellous crotchety old man. I remember the first time I called him to ask him to do the picture. He said it was impossible, he was very busy and asked what it was called. I told him and he said, 'Oh no. That's not my kind of picture title. No, no, no.'

I said, 'Well maybe if we can meet and talk about it.'

He said, 'No, no I can't. What's it about?' So I described it and he said, 'No, no, no. I can't, I can't. Who's in it?' So I told him and he said, 'No, no, no. Well I suppose we could have a quick talk.'

New York, New York

After the success of *Taxi Driver*, I was given a much bigger budget to do *New York, New York* which was almost a kind of Work In Progress and wasn't so successful. I wanted to capture a relationship between two people who were doing creative work and trying to live together. I knew that audiences might want a neat ending, but how can you put a conclusive wrap-it-up ending on a subject like that? The film was very autobiographical – it was about my second marriage, and I'm currently trying to see if I can edit another ending for the television version which might balance it better. I'm not sure if I can.

Raging Bull

My last film *Raging Bull* had been planned for a long time. But we kept on having problems with the script and I couldn't see how to do the central character – a boxer. Then one weekend in September 1978, I was taken seriously ill and I went into hospital. I don't know what happened but somehow during those four days alone in hospital I went through some kind of transformation and I came out of it. Afterwards Bobby De Niro came up to see me in hospital and we talked and somehow, because of what had happened, I not only knew how to do the character but also why I wanted to do it. The leading character in the film is very similar to me.

Raging Bull, which was co-written by Paul Schrader who wrote *Taxi Driver* and my old colleague Mardik Martin, has a lot of violence, but it's a completely different kind of violence from *Taxi Driver*. It's not only physical but psychological, and it doesn't build to a climax in the way *Taxi Driver* does. The climax of *Raging Bull* is something different altogether. I learnt a lot about myself from making the film. And at this point in my career, if I can't learn something from making a film – whether it's about myself or about history or just how the British serve tea – I'm not interested in doing the film. I suppose that if I had to fall back on my knowledge of craft and make an action/adventure or something I would do it to live. But I find it hard to see what you can do to top people like Hawks or Ford. Also we all seem to be agreed that making something like *Star Wars* is a murderous experience; with the use of blue screen as an effects background you can't even have people move an inch while they're talking so even shooting a simple dialogue scene becomes impossibly tedious. This is one reason why all of us are so involved in finding ways of simplifying, ways of making films faster and cheaper.

My next film *King of Comedy* is an attempt to cross over and give myself time to figure out the direction I'm going to move. I'm also keen to do something on the history of early christianity, and its links with paganism. I'm thinking in terms of ten or twenty hours of television, shot perhaps in video and in Europe. But I don't count on anything. Recently somebody was discussing some publicity tie-in on my latest movie and he said not to count on it. I said, 'Listen I don't count on anything except death.' And I don't.

Screenwriters and Screenwriting

It was in 1948 in *Ecran Francais* that Alexandre Astruc proposed 'this new age of cinema, the age of *camera-stylo* (camera-pen). This metaphor has a very precise sense. By it I mean that the cinema will gradually break free from the tyranny of what is visual, from the image for its own sake, from the immediate and concrete demands of the narrative, to become a means of writing just as flexible and subtle as written language.'

By 1980, Astruc's name was nearly forgotten, and his achievement as a director (*Une Vie*, 1958) had passed out of sight. But Paul Schrader surely still knew the name, and in 1980 he was one of the most prominent screenwriters in Hollywood. Schrader was trained in film school and had intense involvement as a critic in non-American film sensibility. He had been to UCLA, edited *Cinema* magazine, and written a book on Ozu, Dreyer and Bresson. Then he broke into the kingdom: he wrote *Obsession* for Brian De Palma, *Taxi Driver* for Martin Scorsese, *The Yakuza* for Sydney Pollack, *Rolling Thunder* for John Flynn, *Old Boyfriends* for Joan Tewkesbury, and three movies that he would direct himself – *Blue Collar*, *Hardcore* and *American Gigolo*.

In the first weeks of its release, it was reported that audiences were laughing at *American Gigolo* all over America, but the picture did remarkably well nonetheless. Of the films Schrader had directed, it was the first hit; and maybe in the nick of time. The man who startled Hollywood with his rapid rise, his intelligence and his personal abrasiveness, and the $300,000 fee for his least impressive script, *The Yakuza*, had been in trouble. *Gigolo* is a very serious picture; solemn, some would say. Yet it was laughed at. Did people find humour to enjoy in it? Was it a success because of public derision, or did that only signal how far Schrader had touched on a sensitive nerve – the separation of glamour and narcissism from love? *Gigolo* was patently authored; it attempted to reconcile the aesthetic and the spiritual. It lifted lines and scenes from the work of Robert Bresson. And it was written on the screen, in the air, on the wind – however we try to define it. *Gigolo* had a look and a sound. When I saw it, it seemed to me that people embarrassed by or scornful of the 'plot' were also disconcerted by the tawdry spirituality of the picture. On a literary level, *American Gigolo* is trash. But as an experience in the dark, drawing upon that especially zealous commitment to sight and sound that the dark demands, it was acute, awesome and more profound than either claims of trashiness or attempts at explanation.

All of which is commentary that horrifies an older school of screenwriters, and adds to their righteous indignation that for decades unscrupulous actors, producers and directors have been filching the credit for movies. Historically, the writers in Hollywood refused to see the mood and tone of pictures. They claimed to believe that directors simply transcribed their scripts onto celluloid. Gore Vidal has a reputation as an original wit, but he has interviewed out too often on the indignity of discovering *The Best Man* (1964) advertised in France as 'un film de Franklin Schaffner'. In an interview with *American Film* (1977) Vidal asserted that he could comfortably have directed the films made from his scripts, and that it was only an unfortunate and rather bored oversight that kept him out of the Pantheon:

> 'I had a chance to direct in the fifties, and I turned it down. In those days, nobody who was a serious novelist would have dreamt of directing. And a great many successful screenwriters felt the same. Directing was for the hustlers. Then along came the Europeans with their theories, and suddenly directors were ennobled. We novelists who had been central to the culture began to float out to the far perimeter where the poets live, and I now think that, perhaps, I missed a chance.'

It may be pretty for Vidal to reflect on the cinema's loss, but his languid superiority only exposes his aversion to the necessary vulgarity

Paul Schrader *(right), a prolific screenwriter who first turned to directing with* Blue Collar.

Gore Vidal *(centre right) shared script credit on* Is Paris Burning? *with the young Francis Ford Coppola.*

Raquel Welch *(far right) as* Myra Breckinridge *in the film adaptation of Vidal's satirical novel.*

of the movies. To bring a film to the screen is like wrestling with monsters dressed as clowns. It involves crawling, business mayhem, and persistent interference with fine ideas. Cut off from that far perimeter of poets, you can only dive in your pool to get clean. Vidal can observe that process from the outside, in his novel *Myra Breckinridge*, with scathing enjoyment. But he is squeamish about looking ridiculous himself – it is the one thing that keeps him from major achievement as a writer, too. Whereas the movie kingdom, rowdy and coarse, does not understand the fervent self-respect that Vidal is unwilling to risk.

That's why so many screenwriters once disdained directing and the squalid traffic of pictures. Vidal is only the last and most dandified figure in the line that has screenwriter Herman Mankiewicz cabling novelist Ben Hecht in 1926:

> 'Will you accept three hundred per week to work for Paramount Pictures? All expenses paid. The three hundred is peanuts. Millions are to be grabbed out here and your only competition is idiots. Don't let this get around.'

Just as William Faulkner pocketed the money and judiciously returned to Oxford, Mississippi, to get on with his 'real' work. Incidentally, Vidal believes that Faulkner could have directed Renoir's *The Southerner* (1945) without strain, an opinion that makes one wonder whether he can appreciate either the wilfully intransigent achievement of the novels Faulkner wrote or Renoir's enthusiastic ability for compromise.

The Hollywood writer was once a lowly and abused form of life, bemused that he could earn so much more holed up at the Garden of Allah or the Chateau Marmont than working on a novel, a play or an article for New York magazines. The bitterness he swallowed in the 1930s and 40s threw up as anger when in the 60s the *auteur* theory promoted the notion of the director as a movie's true creator and started assigning conceptual credit to people the writer had known as jerks. More recently, in the 1970s, the writer has been very highly paid by the movies, and he has found it easier to become a director and possible to own a piece of the project. Yet, perversely, the new status for the writer has coincided with a development away from the old script virtues of construction and dialogue. These are less rigid or evident than they were in, say, 1959 when Ernest Lehman wrote *North by Northwest* for Hitchcock. The two most vital words in *American Gigolo* – its literary triumph – may be the title itself.

The script as blueprint

Once upon a time, scripts were documents that had an internal use: they gave the studio hierarchy confidence to make a film in an era when planning had supplanted inspiration; they appealed to a star under contract to the studio; and they reassured the managerial forces that the project could be made on schedule and for the allotted budget. The script was a thorough blueprint, to be followed scrupulously in the shooting and to serve as a model for the editing. Of course, some films turned out very different from the script; and sometimes, if the script was lagging behind, the movie still had to be shot. But the approval of the script was the studio's ratification that the story 'worked' and that the product should be put together in its agreed numbered sequence. No matter who ended up with the credit, scripts removed blame – 'we filmed the script' was the defence when a picture flunked.

Films felt thoroughly constructed because of that systematic emphasis on sensible preplanning. Over a period of years, that made intricate plot construction one of the dominant characteristics of the American film. In the 1940s, and in *film noir* especially, there was an implicit ideal by which the system looked for plots as complicated as possible, but still under the control of accomplished lighting, tidy cutting and adroit performances. You can argue that it leads to a sterile ingenuity, exact but claustrophobic, which reaches its daft peak in *Sunset Boulevard* (1950) where the story is told by someone who is dead.

The script as idea

With the breakdown of the studio system, and the need to set up every movie individually, the script becomes a far more dynamic, external instrument. There is no factory now intent on stringent blueprint scripts. But there are distributors, financiers, agents and stars who need to be convinced about joining in a project. That's where the two words 'American Gigolo' may have been decisive, for they are an instant, commercial concept – like the name of a perfume or a restaurant. When you remember that, originally, Paramount had to say yes or no to 'John Travolta in *American Gigolo*', you can see how far movies may be summed up in a slogan. Those five words are enough to ring box-office bells – a current star of exceptional appeal well suited to a title as blatant as it is enigmatic. Paramount surely asked to see the script – the parent company, Gulf & Western, would tolerate only so much superstition. They may have read it carefully and suggested sensible changes as befits responsible entrepreneurs. But when Travolta dropped out of the project – leaving the script intact but vacant without his rubbery strut – and was replaced by Richard Gere, the budget and the expectations were cut in half. Moreover, the Paramount attitude was not so very different from the manner in which Paul Schrader had first conceived of the project as he recalled in *Film Comment*:

> 'Well, *American Gigolo* began in the screenwriting class at UCLA. In one of those roundtable discussions I was suggesting occupations for a character: What does this person do? Is he a salesman? Is he a writer? Is he a gigolo, an American gigolo? I made a joke and then said, "That's an interesting subject." Then, after class I thought, "Well, that *is* an interesting subject."
>
> 'The next day I was at the shrink's office, and we were talking about a problem of giving and receiving love, the difficulty of receiving . . . Sometimes it's easier to give than to receive. And as I was leaving the office, that little spark occurred, the crossing of two unlikes – which is Arthur Koestler's whole thing about the act of creation: two different things hit and spark, and bam! you've got something. The notion of the gigolo as a metaphor for the man who can't receive pleasure hit me, and from that moment on I had a metaphor that was uniquely representative of that problem. Then it was just a matter of plotting it out.'

Gloria Swanson *(above), as the faded movie queen of* Sunset Boulevard, *shoots the young screenwriter played by William Holden.*

'Bam!' is the give-away, even if it is dressed up as a Koestler synapse. Travolta plus 'American Gigolo' is one bam!, enough to excite Paramount, and it is entertaining to see how far for Schrader the bam bridges the classroom and the analyst's sanctum, a cute selling phrase that redeems a paining personal problem. (Did the shrink endorse the picture as therapy?) Schrader wrote five scripts in the year he wrote *American Gigolo*, so the need for an urgent bam! is more important than emotion recollected in tranquillity. Indeed, a screenplay laboured over is almost by definition unviable; the rapidity of writing is in direct relationship to the screened intensity. A movie writer ought to be able to write a script in a month, and still have time to kill at pinball. Most good movies are conceived as quickly as babies. The screenwriter John Milius, for example, has admitted (in an interview with *Film Comment* in 1976): 'I write longhand, six pages a day . . . in the evening I do about an hour and a half. . . . If I can do six pages in an hour and a half, think how much I could do writing all day, if I wasn't lazy. I could write a script in a week.'

The limitations of film

Now, *Gigolo* is the best picture Schrader has directed, as ambiguously touching and dis-

Richard Gere *(above) as the paid lover Julian Kaye in Paul Schrader's* American Gigolo: *a role first intended for John Travolta.*

tressing as *Taxi Driver*, as worldly and as adolescent. But it is hard to believe that it really clarifies the problem of receiving love. Perhaps that is too painful or too tangled to ride the celluloid slipstream. The movie only sketches or asserts its themes with the same kind of speed that makes 'American Gigolo' instantly fundable. This point is worth exploring, because it says a great deal about the role of the writer in movie-making and about the anatomy of a film.

You could argue that the problems of giving and receiving love are among the most serious and worthwhile of projects for an artist or a story-teller. (Though that claim does have the earnestness of someone proposing to eradicate typhus.) They are certainly novelistic, or worthy of the extended prose fiction that we categorize as the novel. They are all the more seemly material for novels if those books can manage to be about good sentences and paragraphs first. *Anna Karenina, The Portrait of a Lady, Mrs Dalloway* and *The Moviegoer* all worry away at them in one way or another. It might be feasible to propose that just about any novel ever written touches on them. Prose in itself describes and embodies the perplexities of thought. But how could anyone believe that the script of *American Gigolo* is not meretricious compared with those books, or that its aura and effects are not specious when measured against what a novel could do with the subject? No writer could leave Julian Kaye as emphatic and as vague as Schrader insists on making him. Words will not permit anything so nebulous, but pictures hint at the existence of deeper issues with the innuendo of a lewd wink at a marriage service.

American Gigolo does not inhabit that area of his own life that drew Schrader to the subject and title. It hovers around it like a gossip. Lack of tranquillity might explain that, but it could owe more to the slippery restlessness of movies as a medium. The picture actually presents a sleek, shallow character – the person as image, or as 'glossy', to use a photographic term – who is only agitated by the plot's cunning tricks. He has no inner life; he seems desperate to avoid any risk of it – when he is alone, he sculpts his muscles and studies shirts to avoid any form of reflection.

There is hardly ever an internal crisis – of spirit, mind or feelings – in film, though Schrader's idol Bresson comes as close to it as anyone, and in the process makes films that leave most people cold and uninterested. All the fret and agony is in the image, and *American Gigolo* is more a rhapsody to surface than its glib disapproval of modishness suggests. It has a tranquil narcissist as one character and a fashion model as its leading actress, and it is infatuated by its own recreation of Los Angeles interiors. The plot crisis is resolved by an action that implies a moral decision, and which borrows the language and gesture of Bresson's *Pickpocket*, but this is the dynamic of comic books or silent films in which every point must be spelled or mimed out in action. Schrader surely feels Julian's dilemma, and something of its dread is conveyed. Because the characters are so hollow, we can fill them out with our own imaginations. But there is a direct correlation between the instant enchantment of *American Gigolo* and the speed with which it fades. The picture is the terse conceptual novelty of the title plus Schrader's considerable success, cinematically, at giving it atmosphere. Real moral or psychological development has been sacrificed to the disco bam! of provocative password and suggestive ambience – like the use of the word 'Rosebud' in *Citizen Kane* and the palpable, deep-focus regret that fills Kane's extraordinary palace 'Xanadu' and makes us regard his self-pity as existential fatalism.

Schrader would not necessarily dispute this. In his *Film Comment* interview, the longer he talks the more you appreciate what the film has omitted:

> 'To be perfectly honest I didn't end up exploring the theme in the film the way I had hoped but just sort of became interested in the young man who had made something

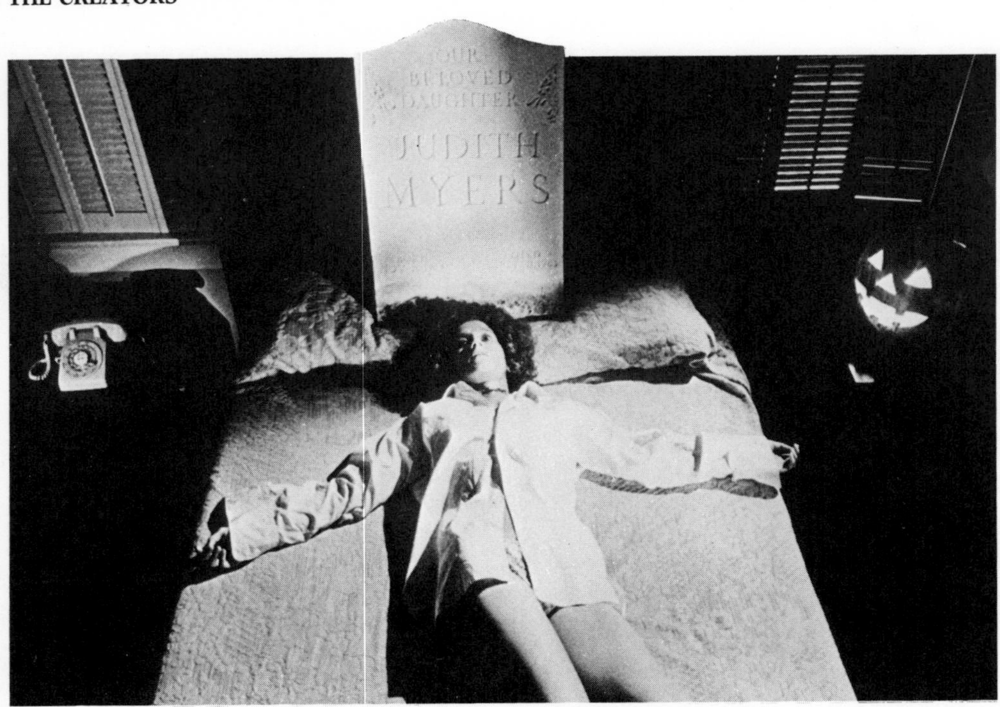

Halloween, *a script in one word. Nancy Loomis as one of the madman's victims in John Carpenter's movie.*

Peter Benchley *(right), responsible for adapting his own novels* The Deep *and* The Island. *He co-wrote the screenplay for his novel* Jaws *with Carl Gottlieb.*

of himself, a sort of Horatio Alger of sexual fantasy, who had made himself into this desirable object, and as a result of it had found an identity in pleasing others and had lost a sense of accepting anything real. And though it's not exactly a problem that many people face, it touches on a problem people do have. It's the whole problem of when you give something, you can distance yourself from it, just stand above it. When you receive something, it calls for more participation with the person who's giving, to deal with a one-to-one relationship, to show appreciation. It would be very easy for me to pick something off the wall and give it to you, but that is not an act of generosity, it's an act of ego. It's not an act of ego to take a gift from someone and relate to it. So that's really what it's about. It's about sex as ego on his part.'

However contradictory Schrader's comments are, no matter how few viewers would recognize the film from his description, he is unquestionably the *auteur*, the film's creator. It could be that his very volatility is what produces the unique and rather creepy ambivalence of the film. But his urgings and longings, his bams and dreams, have written a film in which the writing harnesses the straight-faced narcissism of the cast, that basking lizard called LA (Lies Allowed), the sumptuous production design whereby glamour verges on grace and chic seems sacramental, and the sensual nagging of the Giorgio Moroder music. *American Gigolo* was not hindered by two tracks from its score getting into the Top Ten, or by a look that beckoned and denied imitation just as surely as the poetic torture of fashion photography.

The film was the poster, an iconographically definitive design that combined ecstasy and anxiety in its silver-grey sheen and which thereby illustrated the title – one of the most suggestive the movies have known, with that faint hint of impossibility underlying everything – as if the public were hoping that one could not be both a gigolo and American.

The one-word script

It is not being dismissive to say that the title is the best piece of writing Schrader has done. Such packed simplicity is the essence of pictures. Steven Spielberg testified to the same thing when responding to a question at an American Film Institute seminar about whether his search for material favoured short treatments or finished scripts:

> 'What interests me more than anything else is the idea. If a person can tell me the idea in twenty-five words or less, it's going to make a pretty good movie. I like ideas, especially movie ideas, that you can hold in your hand.'

There are ideas and ideas, and anyone so desirous of having them all reduced to palmable size may only need ball bearings to play with. One can imagine the delicate dismay of Gore Vidal at that declaration of principles from

Roy Scheider and Lorraine Gary *(right) tend the victim of a shark attack in* Jaws.

Warren Beatty *(far right) as the libidinous hairdresser of* Shampoo, *with Goldie Hawn and Lee Grant. Beatty wrote the script with Robert Towne.*

a modern American in communications. But it's too good a game not to play, and you don't have to pursue it for more than half an hour to test its validity. I worked at it for ten minutes and came up with these – I don't think any readers will miss a title:

> Older guy comfortably in love meets perfect girl. Pursues her. Realises she is stupid as she shows no hesitation in going to bed with him.
>
> Man keeps stuffed body of mother. Believes she is inside him. Protects both of them from intruders. Keeps motel as trap.
>
> Taxi driver lives alone looking for love. Fails. Finds child whore and kills five to save her. Is he talking to us?
>
> Huge shark appears off resort coast. It eats people. Three men go out to fight it.
>
> Hairdresser screws around.
>
> Halloween.

All of those were substantial hits of the last two decades, and all of them had a novelty of plot that bordered upon impossibility or the liberation of dreams. Not even the last is intended as a joke. You could easily give a 25-word synopsis for John Carpenter's compulsive B picture. But the one word is all we need, and the brevity is always more intriguing. Halloween cannot promise anything unmenacing, and *Halloween* (1978) is to menace as sugar is to gratification. In the same way, I'm not sure that 'Shampoo' isn't better than 'Hairdresser screws around' because it is shorter and because it conjures up the froth of ejaculation – a sort of sperm rinse.

The significance of these short-form descriptions is that they capture the literary haste and impulse with which films are set up today. A movie script is generally a typescript that works out at about a page for every minute of screen time. Over the years, every effort has been taken to make them easy to read: their format provides a narrow, central area of type – hence the notion of reading down the middle of the page, the ease of falling as opposed to the effort of lateral scanning. You can speculate over the reasons for this, but if scripts are aimed at people who believe in speed reading, is it any wonder that a phenomenon of speed writing has evolved to accommodate them? Producers, stars and distributors have too many scripts to read. Therefore, they will be impressed by a script that reads quickly and fluently and in which crucial things happen early. There are decision-makers who like to boast that if they're not gripped by page 20 then they read no further. Another, rather scurrilous interpretation is that many of the people who have to read scripts do not read with comfort.

The nutshell idea can launch a blockbuster. David Brown and Richard Zanuck read Peter Benchley's novel for *Jaws* (1975) in manuscript. The novelist's agent may see film rights looming larger than any publishing deal, and in the last fifteen years more and more novels have

Robert Benton *(far left)*

William Goldman *(left)*

been written in a style-less style, about situations or locations that may appeal to the movies. Zanuck and Brown bought the book in twenty-four hours. They worked with Benchley on the first draft screenplay and then hired the two-fisted Spielberg to direct and to push the script into a tighter second draft. Far later in the day, John Milius added Robert Shaw's long speech about the sinking of the *Indianapolis* – the most 'eloquent' writing in the film, and a sequence that structures the picture by providing an extended, hallowed pause in which the mythic context of danger is deepened. But the mechanics of suspense on paper always depended on whether the shark could be made plausible on screen. *Jaws II*, a very much inferior film, suggests how much Spielberg's dynamic vision – his movie writing – and his identification with the two 'ordinary' men had to do with the success of the original. Nevertheless, there must have been an hour at which Zanuck and Brown decided that the essential scheme of the book – that the shark acts with intelligent malice – would work on screen. They fired one director on *Jaws II* to get what they wanted, and would surely have thrown Spielberg overboard if they had had to. Sharkishness is a trait that movie men understand.

Moreover, two years later, Spielberg himself wrote the screenplay for *Close Encounters of the Third Kind* more as a storyboard than a written script. When so much of a movie is in the fulfilment of visual wonder or the close-cutting of suspense, no wonder a 'script' turns into something a prospective buyer can see, spread out on the table and follow. It's like reading a comic strip. The influence of Alfred Hitchcock is enormous here, for he always preferred to spend months with his scriptwriters before emerging with a storyboard script that the actors and crew could simply execute. Spielberg might argue that the action of *Jaws* on the page could sound neutral. Its excitement lurks in the charged framing and editing, and in the Cassandra-like music, that encourages our involvement to transcend the fragile framework of impossibility.

So the script must be a means of selling a project, the thing that will stimulate investment confidence. There are writers so aware of that issue they will not trust reading when a more direct story-telling is available. James Toback had a script that several studios had turned down. He decided to let Warren Beatty have a chance at it – to hope that Beatty might read it would be negative thinking. But, he told Hollis Alpert in *American Film*, 'I know there is nothing harder than getting an unsolicited script read by people who have several hundred a day delivered to them. I knew Beatty's office was stacked with them. So I told him, "No, I've got to read it to you".' Beatty pulled back from such hustling, but then he conceded, and bought the script over dinner. For all he knew, there was nothing as yet on paper. If Toback waved paper in the air, that would only be a tactic pioneered by McCarthy.

That's not so far-fetched. A lot of scripts get talked up and contracted, long before they're written. Even beginners can sometimes get 'development money' to proceed with a five-page treatment. The few top writers can command large sums on the promise of a script, or a book, by the end of next year. There are people who have earned a living as screenwriters for ten years but who have had only one picture made in that time. The competition is intense: several hundred scripts in Beatty's office need not be an exaggeration. Most of them that are read come by way of the best-known agents. Scripts out of nowhere are sent back unopened, simply to protect the producers against legal charges that any film they do make owed something to a script they might have looked at years before. Beatty and Robert Towne had such a suit over *Shampoo* and they only reversed the first judgement (a six-figure damages fee) on appeal. It all confirms the adage that there are only seventeen stories and that all movies recycle them. And the old Hollywood still believes that you can't pull anything off without a sound script, while the new reckons that writing is the most promising route into the industry.

Michael Cimino *(right)*

Woody Allen *(far right)*

Neil Simon

Writing and directing

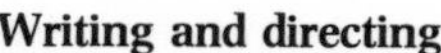

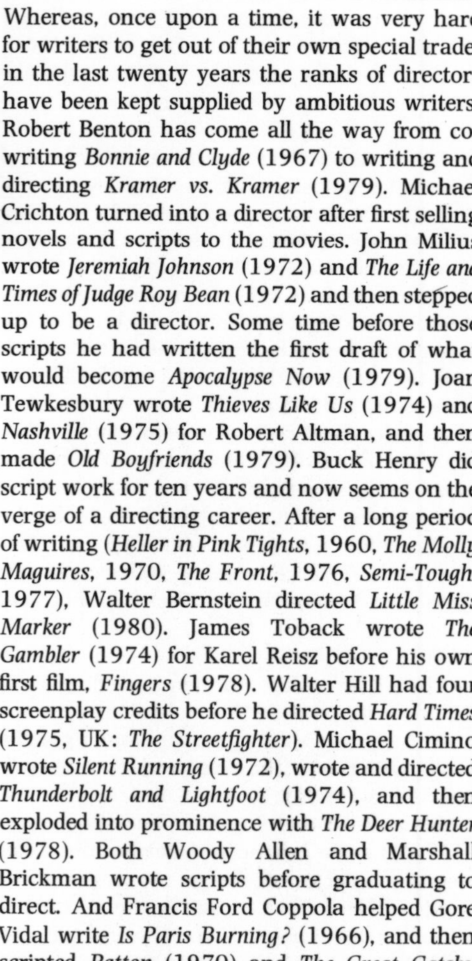

Whereas, once upon a time, it was very hard for writers to get out of their own special trade, in the last twenty years the ranks of directors have been kept supplied by ambitious writers. Robert Benton has come all the way from co-writing *Bonnie and Clyde* (1967) to writing and directing *Kramer vs. Kramer* (1979). Michael Crichton turned into a director after first selling novels and scripts to the movies. John Milius wrote *Jeremiah Johnson* (1972) and *The Life and Times of Judge Roy Bean* (1972) and then stepped up to be a director. Some time before those scripts he had written the first draft of what would become *Apocalypse Now* (1979). Joan Tewkesbury wrote *Thieves Like Us* (1974) and *Nashville* (1975) for Robert Altman, and then made *Old Boyfriends* (1979). Buck Henry did script work for ten years and now seems on the verge of a directing career. After a long period of writing (*Heller in Pink Tights*, 1960, *The Molly Maguires*, 1970, *The Front*, 1976, *Semi-Tough*, 1977), Walter Bernstein directed *Little Miss Marker* (1980). James Toback wrote *The Gambler* (1974) for Karel Reisz before his own first film, *Fingers* (1978). Walter Hill had four screenplay credits before he directed *Hard Times* (1975, UK: *The Streetfighter*). Michael Cimino wrote *Silent Running* (1972), wrote and directed *Thunderbolt and Lightfoot* (1974), and then exploded into prominence with *The Deer Hunter* (1978). Both Woody Allen and Marshall Brickman wrote scripts before graduating to direct. And Francis Ford Coppola helped Gore Vidal write *Is Paris Burning?* (1966), and then scripted *Patton* (1970) and *The Great Gatsby* (1974) in his early days.

There are times when it seems eccentric to want to do the one without the other. A few leading directors have no writing credits – Hal Ashby for one – but reports about the prolonged birth pains of *Coming Home* (1978) suggest that Ashby contributed several ideas and a great deal of scripting attention. Some directors are like Hitchcock in that they feel insecure without the presence of a writer and the opportunity of bouncing twists and lines back and forth.

Falling standards of dialogue

Still, a few directors remain content to make the films scripted by strong writers: Sydney Pollack, George Roy Hill, Herbert Ross and Sidney Lumet, who probably kept very quiet during the making of *Network* (1976). That diatribe against television was the personal triumph of Paddy Chayefsky, and one of the few films of the 1970s with which it was possible to sit back in the wash of elegant, rhetorical dialogue. That may only have constituted a crust of 'intelligence' on a soap opera film, but it reminded us of how seldom today's dialogue has wit or rhythm of its own. When people talk in pictures now, it is to promote the action and pocket-size ideas, not to revel in the rich sounds of language as sometimes seemed the case when Hawks, Sternberg, Lubitsch, Mankiewicz, Hecht, Raphaelson, Furthman and Wilder held sway. Woody Allen's dialogue is funny, to be sure, but I doubt if it would read better than a stream of one-liners, all the more desperate because of the lack of literary momentum. No one in pictures talks like Gore Vidal.

The best dialogue writer at work on film today is Neil Simon, alas. Alas because the films he works on are among the most depressingly safe, commercially cosy films made. Simon is an industry, or a genre, so successful that he has not had to alter or stretch his theatrical attitudes or exceed the veiled banter that passes for emotional seriousness. The limits of Simon as a screenwriter were made clear in the BBC TV presentations of Frederic Raphael's *The Glittering Prizes* and Alan Ayckbourn's *The Norman Conquests*. Their interplay of wit and real life, style and experience, farce and pain, revealed all the devices that cushion Simon against raw feelings. His people are always dialogue-smart. Too many writers are driven by a fear of upsetting audiences into movie conventions and away from experience.

The Last Detail *(far left), scripted by Robert Towne from Daryl Ponicsan's novel, starred, left to right, Otis Young, Randy Quaid and Jack Nicholson.*

Chinatown *(left), a Towne original screenplay for Roman Polanski and Robert Evans, starred Nicholson as L.A. private eye J. J. Gittes.*

Goldman, Sargent and Towne

Among writers who have not directed, or dominated a film – like Chayefsky and Simon – we should note William Goldman. His credits include *Butch Cassidy and the Sundance Kid* (1969) – a crucial mixture of Western genre and hip humour, apparently sufficient to crush the Western – *The Great Waldo Pepper* (1975), *All the President's Men* (1976) (a sly rendering of political mess as tidy *film noir*), *Marathon Man* (1976), *A Bridge Too Far* (1977) and *Magic* (1978). Alvin Sargent has written a body of films which illustrate his skill and human sympathy: *The Stalking Moon* (1968), *I Walk the Line* (1970), *The Effect of Gamma Rays on Man-in-the-Moon Marigolds* (1972), *Love and Pain and the Whole Damn Thing* (1973), *Paper Moon* (1973), and *Julia* (1977).

But probably the most respected among other writers is Robert Towne. He has been out of sight since *Chinatown* (1974), apparently working on a project about the infancy of Tarzan – literally being brought up by apes. Before that, Towne had several credits for scripts as economical and atmospheric as that for *Chinatown*. In addition, he was prized as the best script doctor, or rewrite man, in town. In that capacity, he worked extensively on *Bonnie and Clyde* and *The Godfather* (1971); among other things, he wrote the final conversation between Marlon Brando and Al Pacino. He also completely revised the script Schrader had written for *The Yakuza*, shared credit with Warren Beatty on *Shampoo* (1975) and wrote Hal Ashby's *The Last Detail* (1973).

The writer as collaborator

Towne's prestige does not appear to have inflated his very practical sense of how a writer on an American movie must endure rewrites in the process of collaboration and compromise. Towne argued with Roman Polanski over changes in *Chinatown*. No one can say who was right, but Towne acknowledges the decisive weight of responsibility and power that rests with the director. Like any writer, he knows that sometimes directors get the credit for things the writer invented. But, unlike Vidal, he doesn't sulk, or construct a theory whereby movies could dispense with directors:

> 'I don't know if it's true of any other kind of writing, but screenwriting has two levels, really. One is when you're initially working on the script, doing it in isolation, away from all the mechanics of the making of the movie, the presence of the actors, the production problems. Then you finish and bring it into the real world, the real-phoney world which is the movie world. That's a whole different process, and I think you've got to be schizophrenic about it. At one point you're more or less the creator, and then you're part of the group of people who are trying to bring something to life. It's difficult to make the distinction sometimes, but not all that difficult if you're working with people you trust and really care for. Then it can be very exciting.'

The writer in that situation is yielding his or her integrity (along with the loneliness), and if Towne is an outstanding example among Hollywood writers then he does seem to rate craft, conceptual vividness and on-screen workability above everything else. That is one way of saying that the American movie has not risked narrative structure in the last twenty years. The needs of the market, especially the pressure to be understood quickly, have restricted new possibilities. In Europe, occasionally, in the same period, the films of Jacques Rivette have encouraged a process of rehearsal and improvisation in which the players become the writers. Rivette has also broken through the supposed time limits and suspenseful rhythms of the feature film. His best pictures have been about fiction, duration and coincidence, not just machines for selling stories.

Jean-Luc Godard is another of the most radically innovative 'writers' of modern film,

Marlon Brando *(right) in* The Godfather, *co-scripted by novelist Mario Puzo and director Coppola with uncredited assistance from Robert Towne.*

The Discreet Charm of the Bourgeoisie *(far right), the most successful collaboration of fellow Surrealists Luis Bunuel and Jean-Claude Carrière.*

partly because he so rarely had anything resembling a script. He wrote with the camera and the dialectic of editing. In *The Discreet Charm of the Bourgeoisie* (1972) and *That Obscure Object of Desire* (1977), Luis Bunuel and Jean-Claude Carrière composed films that were satires upon the well-made film and profound celebrations of the clandestine shapes in life and dreams. Hans-Jurgen Syberberg, with *Our Hitler* (1977, UK title: *Hitler: a Film from Germany*), found a collage of fact and legend that makes every modern American picture seem old-fashioned.

The writer as director, or team member

Continental practice suggests that either the director must be the writer, or that the film may emerge from a new spirit of group enterprise. In America, too, we can see the roles of writer and director falling to the same person. But the Rivette approach, of liberty allowed to the actors, and the film being less a refined, finished toy than an 'attempt' at film, that has been tried in America only by Robert Altman. On *Nashville*, Joan Tewkesbury's script was the springboard for the actors' work on their parts. Many more hours were shot and edited than were ever released. Equally, Tewkesbury had written lives for the characters that never showed on film but which helped inform the performances. In her introduction to the published script – actually the cutting continuity – Tewkesbury gave this defence of the things in any film that are a matter of theatrical experience above and beyond literary comprehension:

> 'As you read the screenplay, remember this was written for a visual medium capable of giving assorted information to our perceptions on so many levels and in so many layers that we can't systematically record it. With that in mind, all you need to do is add yourself as the twenty-fifth character and know that whatever you think about the film is right, even if you think the film is wrong.'

Film as writer

It was more than twenty years ago that Nicholas Ray said if everything had really been in the script then there was no need to make the film. *Nashville* in script form is a dull read; as a film, it is hectic, confusing, random, musical, creative and an affirmation of the ordinary. But film tends to make everything extraordinary, and scripts are already tributes to the value of system. American movies have rated the sensational, organized image above ordinary experience – commerce has ordained that more than the minds of the film-makers. As a result, we have imbibed as an ideology a set of dramatic subjects, and a totally dramatic context that need not be exclusive. Film itself writes, with or without authors, with or without concepts or subjects. Film is a process, a sequential observation, more sensitive to time and change than susceptible to literary coherence. Large box-office movies show no sign of adapting to that, and they may find themselves farther and farther behind the sensibility of the time.

Film offends and disappoints our best writers and people who believe in literature. But that is because of its banal efforts to ape the novel, the play or the essay. It cannot match writing's ability to struggle with ideas, complex feelings or moral distinctions. But film is an atmosphere, a presence and a passage that reaches millions and affects them in ways they hardly notice. It is like air. The future is in films that write in that atmosphere. In an *American Film* interview with Harlan Kennedy, the English director, Nicolas Roeg, sees this task and opportunity, and it is one that will erase the distinction between writer and director:

> 'I believe film is an art. I believe it, I *truly* believe that. Thought can be transferred by the juxtaposition of images, and you mustn't be afraid of the audience not understanding. You can say things visually, immediately, and that's where film, I believe, is going. It's not a pictorial example of a published work. It's a transference of thought.'

A Screenwriter on Screenwriting: Robert Towne

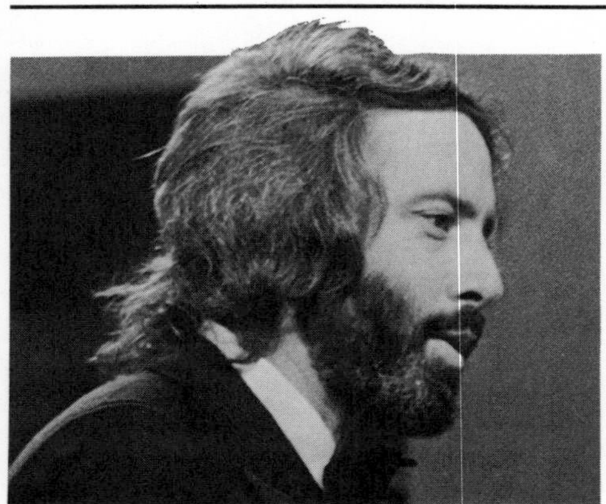

Robert Towne is one of the most prominent and respected of the new breed of Hollywood screenwriters who rose to fame in the 1970s. Producer Robert Evans' statement that 'I'd rather have the next five Bob Towne pictures than the next five Bob Redford pictures' has been widely quoted as a reflection of the new power of the Hollywood writer. It was men like Towne and William Goldman and Robert Benton who helped to build this power by creating original screenplays that enjoyed the kind of screen success normally obtained in the past only by adaptations of hit musicals and best-selling novels.

Robert Towne grew up in California and turned to screenwriting after working as a bank-teller, a fisherman and an actor. After two scripts for the ubiquitous Roger Corman, Towne became closely associated with Warren Beatty first as an uncredited writer on Bonnie and Clyde *(1967) and later on* Shampoo *(1975). He is also a friend and colleague of Jack Nicholson for whom he wrote* The Last Detail *(1973). Several other credits mark the decade but Towne's triumphant personal breakthrough was* Chinatown *(1974), a period detective story which ranks among the most sophisticated and intelligent Hollywood successes of the 1970s. Since* Chinatown, *Towne has been working on the long-awaited* Greystoke *for Warners, a marathon anthropological adaptation of Edgar Rice Burroughs' original* Tarzan of the Apes. *More recently Towne has made his debut as a director on* Personal Best *(1981). Below he recalls the evolution of his career and the long and subtle gestation of* Chinatown.

I was born in California, just before World War II, so I can remember Los Angeles before the war when it was an entirely different place. It had a beauty which is lost forever. After growing up in a little seaport town called San Pedro, I went to college as a liberal arts major and after that I did everything from selling real estate and serving in a bank to working as a commercial fisherman. Eventually I drifted into an acting class run by Jeff Corey.

Corey was one of the actors blacklisted during the McCarthy era and he was a terrific coach, especially for anyone who wanted to learn about movie writing. That class became a meeting-ground for a lot of very interesting people. It included Roger Corman, James Coburn, Sally Kellerman, Irving Kershner and Jack Nicholson. In fact it was at Jeff Corey's class that I first saw Jack Nicholson work, and I knew – from the first moment I saw him acting – that he was one of the most interesting people that I was ever going to see. In those days we shared a flat together for a year or so and became good friends and, like almost everyone else, we both got a break through Roger Corman.

When I was about 21, Corman was making two of his cheapies back-to-back in Puerto Rico and he persuaded me to take on a package deal in which I wrote a dreadful science fiction movie (*The Last Woman on Earth*, 1960) and worked as an actor as well. It was a deeply embarrassing experience, because I didn't know what I was doing and I can't act. But it was a start.

After that, I wrote for television for a couple of years on shows like *The Man from UNCLE* and *The Outer Limits* and a lesser known series called *Breaking Point*, which was probably the best TV show I ever scripted. But almost everything I did was fouled by continuity or editorial interference. My experiences there were not at all happy.

Bonnie and Clyde

By the time I left, Roger Corman had graduated to slightly bigger budgets with his Edgar Allan Poe series and I wrote *The Tomb of Ligeia* (1964) for him, though fortunately this time I didn't stick around while they shot it. My real chance occurred with something Roger was going to direct for Columbia. I did a rewrite which somehow got into the hands of Warren Beatty and Arthur Penn. On the strength of it I was asked to do a final draft on location for *Bonnie and Clyde*. Robert Benton and David Newman had done the original but I did a last version, aided and abetted by Arthur and

Bonnie and Clyde *(left), with Faye Dunaway and Warren Beatty. Robert Towne's contribution to the script was uncredited.*

Shampoo *(right) was co-written by Robert Towne and the film's star Warren Beatty.*

Warren. To work on critical and commercial successes like that is great, but finally there is something terribly capricious about it like shooting craps. Of course, all the really good movies like *Bonnie and Clyde* have a wealth of talented people behind them, but then the really bad ones do as well. In either case, you sweat and strain to make something turn out well and occasionally you succeed, but deep down you have to be aware of how capricious it all is. It may be great to shoot craps and win, but the experience isn't qualitatively different from shooting craps and losing. You're still shooting craps.

After *Bonnie and Clyde* I went to Spain to do another rewrite on something called *Villa Rides* (1968) with Robert Mitchum and Charles Bronson. It was one of those 'pay or play' situations (see page 56), meaning Paramount had to go ahead with the project and make the best of a bad job. After that, in the late 60s, I found myself in London. It was as far back as then that I began a first draft of my idea for *Shampoo*. But there was always so much to do in England in the late 60s that I never got much work done. It's probably because I like the country so much; nothing about it ever makes me feel angry or unhappy or passionate. So I didn't get very far with *Shampoo* until some years later when I came back to America and collaborated for the second time with Warren Beatty.

Learning from doing rewrites

It took a few years before projects that I had personally originated reached the screen. But you can learn a lot from rewriting. The first thing it teaches you is that there are two kinds of screenwriting. The first is the formative stage when you're starting from scratch with an original idea, and it's pure fiction like a novel. The second stage begins when the actors are cast. In a way it's no longer fiction, because there are real people involved. No matter how carefully you have worked on the first stage of the script, once it gets into the hands of a really good actor like Jack Nicholson then within a short time he's going to know the character better than you do. For that reason I think it's valuable that a certain kind of script revision begins at that point, in order to accommodate the actor's conception of a part and the accidents of shooting. Writing the first draft is a monastic, ascetic experience; during the second stage you're reacting to people and events.

Another thing I learned from the first part of my career, when I was engaged on several rewrites, is that dialogue should never spell out to an audience what a scene is about. There's a perfect example of this in a sequence I wrote between Marlon Brando, as the old mafia boss, and Al Pacino, as his son, in *The Godfather* (1972). Francis Coppola basically wanted a scene where the two men would say that they loved each other, because there was nothing like that in the book. It sounds simple; but you cannot write a love scene by just having two people say they love each other. I looked at the footage that had been filmed and talked to Marlon and Al; eventually I wrote the scene so that it was ostensibly about the succession of power, about youth taking over and the reluctance of the old to give way. The older man is telling his son to be careful in the future and mentions some of the people who might pose a threat, while the son reassures him with a touch of impatience – 'I can handle it.' And you can tell the father's obsessive concern for these details reflects his anxiety that his son is having to adopt a role that the old man never wanted him to have, as well as the father's reluctance to give up his power. Underlying all of this is the feeling that they care for each other. A scene like that takes a long time to write.

The Last Detail

After *The Godfather*, I adapted a book called *The Last Detail* for Jack Nicholson and Hal Ashby. Jack plays a petty officer in the Navy whose job is to escort a young recruit to prison where the kid faces a harsh jail sentence. It was part of my intention to show that horrible things can be done by very nice people. In my experience people *are* usually pretty nice, as long as it doesn't cost them too much. But when it really comes down to it and it looks as though it's going to cost somebody their job or something that's dear to them, they'll start shoving other people into the ovens. Now in *The Last Detail* Nicholson is flattered by the fact that this young, rather sick kid looks up to him as a surrogate father figure. So Nicholson takes him places and shows him things. But when it looks as though all of this might really cost Nicholson something, he just turns around and says 'It's my job.' Even though he is aware his attitude is fundamentally corrupt and cowardly.

Inevitably, while we were making the film, we considered changing the ending so that Nicholson *would* let the kid escape. But I thought that would really be letting the audience off the hook. The audience must be left with the

The Godfather *(left) was another major film on which Towne's contribution was uncredited. He wrote an important emotional scene between father and son, played by Al Pacino and Marlon Brando.*

The Last Detail *(right), with Otis Young and Jack Nicholson, right.*

problem, because ninety nine out of a hundred people in the audience – maybe a hundred out of a hundred – would have done what Nicholson did in the movie and taken the kid to prison, rather than risk their own skin. So I thought it would be completely dishonest of us to send the audience out of the theatre with a warm glow thinking: 'Gee the world is full of nice people.'

Chinatown

Chinatown began when I discovered I had a stronger feeling for Los Angeles than I had ever realized. Its genesis took place over a long period of time. I first became aware of it quite suddenly when I was walking up in the Santa Monica mountains. Like everybody else in Los Angeles, I had never thought of doing any walking until an old friend of mine talked me into it, and I found that I loved it. One day we were walking up in the Palisades when I suddenly felt as if I was about ten years old. It was an overwhelming feeling, and I couldn't understand where it came from. Until I realized that up there on the Palisades it was still like the city I remembered from childhood. Back then, you could smell the city: the pepper trees, the eucalyptus, the orange blossoms. It was a delight.

Rediscovering that feeling again drove me crazy, because it brought home to me that, before the war, Los Angeles had a kind of pastel beauty which was completely destroyed. I was filled with a sense of loss and longing, and I thought about it a lot. The city had changed because growth has always been considered good in western culture, and nowhere has it been considered more good than in Los Angeles.

These feelings were churning around in me, when I saw an article in the magazine section of the *LA Times*. It made me very angry but I didn't know what I could do about it. The article was about Raymond Chandler's Los Angeles and the writer had taken passages of his prose and put them beside photographs of the sections of the city he described. It jumped out at me at once that some of the places were still there unchanged, and a movie would be one chance of capturing the city for the last time, before they destroy it all completely. You could do it on location in a way that would be very surprising. I had read a little Raymond Chandler at that time, and I started reading him again. He wrote the best descriptions of the city I've ever read.

I still hadn't decided what I wanted to write, but I thought maybe I would do a detective movie. Around the same time I got involved in an ecological battle concerning some land in the Santa Monica mountains. There were pay-offs in City Hall, so we lost and the land went under. And this was very much on my mind when I went on location to Oregon for a small part Jack Nicholson had asked me to play in his first film as a director *Drive, He Said* (1971). Now in the Oregon library I happened to discover a book that was out of print. It was called *Southern California Country* by Carrie McWilliams and I couldn't believe how good it was. In fact I became obsessed with it. What particularly fascinated me was the description of how a local valley was raped to bring water to Los Angeles. The destruction of the valley community was so blatant I could hardly believe what I read. I was bowled over by it. It reminded me of our useless battle to save a part of the Santa Monica mountains. And at this point *Chinatown* began taking shape in my head. I began to write a story about a man who raped the land and his own daughter. One, at least, was in the name of progress.

As it turned out, Chandler was more of an inspiration in terms of his feeling for the city than anything else. His heroes tend to be tarnished knights whereas I wanted to make Gittes (played by Jack Nicholson) more vulgar and crass and venal than anything that had been done before – a guy who deliberately specialized in sordid divorce work and then rationalized his own seamy job. But then he gets involved with corruption on a level far beyond anything he can imagine. There was originally an exchange in the film between Gittes and the cop Escobar (Perry Lopez) which reflected that. It was cut out during the editing, and in some ways I regret that it's gone because of what it told you about Gittes as a character. Gittes is accused of extortion and he tells Escobar: 'I wouldn't extort a nickel out of my worst friend. That's where I draw the line.' And the exchange continued with Escobar saying: 'Yeah Jake I knew a whore once who for enough money would piss in the customer's face but she'd never shit on his chest. That's where *she* drew the line.' Gittes tried to get back by saying: 'I hope she wasn't too much of a disappointment to you.'

The point I was trying to make with that exchange was that, for all his apparent cynicism, Gittes is a rather naive person. He thinks there are limits to how bad people can be. I believe that, generally speaking, that was the kind of feeling which existed prior to World War II: a feeling that there were limits to human wickedness. The cynicism then had a kind of insane optimism about it – they knew everything was a scam but thought people were basically decent. And so in *Chinatown* Gittes really miscalculates how mons-

Chinatown *(left and right), written by Robert Towne and starring Jack Nicholson and Faye Dunaway, was one of the most creatively ambitious Hollywood screenplays of the 1970s.*

trous his enemy, played by John Huston, is capable of being; the enemy is, as Huston says, 'capable of anything.' Of raping the land and his own daughter. Gittes is quite used to catching people cheating on other people. It's easy to do that just as it's easy to unmask the isolated act of some social aberrant. But the crimes that can't be cut out of society are the really horrible crimes that are sane and come from greed. When corruption is as big as that, they can't punish it so they reward it and the names of those guys end up on plaques in City Hall, as pillars of the community. At times, during the writing of *Chinatown*, it all seemed so complicated that I almost despaired of it. And one of the things that was so difficult was to achieve this sense of a crime for which people would ultimately get rewarded.

The actual writing of *Chinatown* began in late August of 1972. Around that time I was asked by Jack Clayton to write *The Great Gatsby* (1974) but I was working on *Chinatown* and I just didn't want to stop. I went out for an Italian meal with Robert Evans, who was then in charge of Paramount. He was a little surprised I'd turned down *Gatsby* so I explained I was working on something personal that I wanted to finish. He drew me out and I told him about the notion of *Chinatown* as something dark and threatening and its link with the woman in a man's mind. Just a couple of sentences. And he said 'Jesus I'd like to do that.' I was pleased but I was reluctant to tie it up while I was still working on it. However, a month or two later I found I was broke and I called him up and he structured a deal which allowed me to finish the script without interference; after that he had a thirty day option to decide whether to go ahead. I can't say enough good about Evans; he's the kind of guy whose enthusiasm can really get you through a lot.

Roman Polanski was always in Evans' mind because of *Rosemary's Baby* (1968). Roman and I met briefly in March of 1973 after he had read the script's first draft. Then I did another draft and hammered out the third draft in about two weeks in August 1973. We started shooting the following October.

I think the single most valuable thing Roman suggested was the scene in which somehow Gittes had to get the information out of Evelyn that she had had her father's child. I tried it different ways, but I couldn't see how on earth he would get something so devastating and personal out of her. Roman said it should occur during a confrontation between the two of them and I agreed, but I said I just couldn't see any way to do it. And Roman just said: 'Oh it's easy. Have him beat it out of her.' It was such a simple solution.

At Roman's insistence there were alterations to *Chinatown* I'll always be uncomfortable with. For example, I felt at the time it would be more consistent with the tone of the film if it ended with Evelyn killing her father and being punished by the law. I felt that if there was a tiny ray of hope at the end then all the malevolence would stand out all the more sharply. It would underline the tragedy. I wanted it to be fatalistic but I was worried that Polanski's ending would be too overwhelming.

And I was always against setting the final scene actually *in* Chinatown. In my version Chinatown wouldn't have figured in any material sense at all because I wanted it to stand as a symbol. I felt the metaphor would sustain itself, and to bring in the location was heavy-handed.

The underlying theme of Chinatown itself had arisen because I bought my sheepdog from a Hungarian vice cop who had worked down in Chinatown in LA. He was filled with interesting vice stories, dating from his time in undercover as a phoney doctor in a massage parlour. And it was clear from his stories that the only people he was able to bust were petty idiots; the cops couldn't touch any of the big rackets.

That had stuck in my mind and it popped back out when I was working on the script. Because unlike any of the traditional Marlowe-type private eyes who would have outsmarted everyone in the end, Gittes in *Chinatown* believes that's what he's going to do, but instead he precipitates the whole tragedy. That's why he whispers that line at the end: 'As little as possible.' He knows that he's failed to remember that when you're in over your head, just like in Chinatown, you do as little as possible. And in his mind the psychological threat of Chinatown is intimately connected with the woman.

It seems to me that in this genre you can't any longer feel any real sense of physical danger for the hero. The real dangers are psychological; that the hero will go in over his head, that he will become emotionally involved and be led astray. And there is a strong tradition which identifies this psychological danger with the woman. The woman comes into the private eye's office and asks for help and turns out to be the villainess. I was trying to work against that tradition. Gittes instinctively mistrusts the woman, even after he's in love with her. But ultimately both he and the audience discover she's the most unselfish person in it. By then it's too late.

A Screenwriter on Screenwriting: Lorenzo Semple Jr.

If Robert Towne makes something of a speciality of original screenplays, Lorenzo Semple Jr. has up to now tended to work on adaptations and genre-oriented subjects. But his skill in creating fresh and witty approaches to old formulas has brought him considerable financial success and a growing critical acclaim, especially in Europe. The son of a prosperous New York family, Semple cut his teeth as script editor of the television series Batman *before graduating to film with a movie based on the series in 1966. He quickly gained a reputation in Hollywood as a writer of comedy (*Marriage of a Young Stockbroker, *1971) of thrillers (*Pretty Poison, *1968) and also as a fixer (he has done rewrite work on numerous screenplays including* Papillon, *1973). More recently he has worked with Dino de Laurentiis on blockbusters like* King Kong *(1976) and* Flash Gordon *(1980), to both of which Semple added his taste in genre-parody. But perhaps his most acclaimed script, co-written with David Rayfiel, is* Three Days of the Condor *(1975) which with its ingenious variations on the classic chase-thriller format has become something of a model for screenwriting text-books and film classes. Here Semple discusses the background to his films, giving his views on screenwriting, directors and the tangle of wheeling and dealing that inevitably surrounds the writing of popular cinema.*

I believe it was once said that the sole good reason for working in the theatre is that you can sleep in till eleven o'clock. The same applies to screenwriting. I originally majored in drama in New York and I wanted to go into the theatre, but like everyone else I was very attracted by movies and their so-called glamour.

After college I travelled around in Mexico and Spain, trying to write plays that either never got written or were not very successful. My movie and television career began with an out-and-out rejection. A producer called William Dozier has been commissioned by ABC Television in America to produce a pilot adventure for a series featuring the oriental detective Charlie Chan. Dozier asked me to write a script and both of us thought the result was pretty good until ABC said they couldn't use it because they didn't want anything with a Chinaman in it!

Even the criminals at ABC were a little bit ashamed about what had happened, and they promised to give us something else. I went off to Spain where I was living very cheaply, contemplating the idea of being a serious writer. One day I got a cable from Bill to say he was coming over with another project. He looked very sheepish when I met him at the airport and we went to the garden of the Ritz Hotel in Madrid to discuss it. He told me rather shamefacedly that they'd given him some character he knew nothing about called Batman. I had read Batman as a kid and the minute he told me I knew it couldn't fail.

It was all worked out in that garden. We decided to try and make it funny by seeming to take ourselves and the show seriously. It's difficult to do because the minute the show looks as though it's aware of being funny you've slipped into a tedious kind of farce. Ultimately that was what happened to *Batman* but to begin with it was a big hit, and I still think some of the early episodes are extremely funny. There was a line in the pilot that I used to tell writers was typical of what we wanted. Batman and Robin came into a night-club in full costume and the waiter asks if they want a ringside table. Batman says: 'No, we don't want to appear conspicuous.' Now a line like that is so routine in a detective series that you almost swallow it before you realize just how ludicrous it is. That was exactly what we wanted. But, by the end, the series was being done as all-out comedy and it just wasn't at all funny because it had no basis in reality on which to build. The original episodes were hard to duplicate and much of the writing just degenerated into hammy jokes.

Somehow ABC allowed me to be a story editor on *Batman*

from where I was living in Spain. In fact I didn't even see *Batman* until after it had been running for a while. I used to commission, edit and write scripts through the mail. They would have a fit if you even so much as suggested an arrangement like that now.

Sometime after *Batman* had been successful I came back to America and worked on one of the all-time stinkers – a Raquel Welch sky-diving picture called *Fathom* (1967). It was based on an adventure story by an English writer called Larry Forrester and Fox hired me to do the adaptation. At the time they were expecting *Modesty Blaise* (1966), starring Monica Vitti as the comic strip heroine, to be a big hit and they decided they wanted another female James Bond. It could even have been quite good. I wrote a sensational opening of 25 pages and gave them to the film's producer John Kohn, who had become a good friend. He asked me what happened next and like a damn fool I told him the truth: I didn't have the faintest idea. When he heard that, he said he thought we should plot it out fresh from the beginning. And that was where the whole thing started to collapse. I know I could have gone from one page to the next making it interesting even without a logical plot, because the story did not make rational sense anyway. But John and I now collaborated on the script in the most vile way you can: we would sit by the typewriter, I would say a line and he would veto it, he would say a line and I would veto it, until every line beaten out of the script was a compromise. Some script-teams apparently write like this, but I cannot imagine a less inspired method of writing. It guarantees a lumpen, leaden result and that is what we got. Not that we should take all the blame: I am told that Raquel Welch and the film's director hated each other so much they were communicating by notes from the first day. The whole thing was a shambles.

Pretty Poison

After *Fathom*, I moved further into the category of the Albanian-Renaissance man by writing *Pretty Poison* (1968). It began because the producer Lawrence Turman had just made a lot of money for Joseph E. Levine with *The Graduate*. So Levine had inaugurated a scheme to finance unknown interesting talents with low budget movies. My agent put me together with Turman and we talked about doing a book I liked very much called *She Let Him Continue* by Stephen Geller. I wanted to adapt the book and my agent asked for $12,000, but after his scheme produced two rotten movies, Levine lost interest and that was the end of our deal.

Then one day I ran into Larry Turman Christmas-shopping in Tiffanys. I told him I was sure the book would make a good saleable movie – why didn't I write it on spec and, if I sold it, we would split the money equally between the two of us. Larry said that it was a terrific idea so I wrote the script. And we sold it to Fox right away for a great deal of money. Afterwards, Larry's lawyers tried to sue me to get out of the agreement; I am sure his lawyers were responsible – they must have been appalled that instead of getting $12,000 I was going to get $110,000 or something. The production itself turned out to be pretty chaotic. It was Pauline Kael who made the film a small success.

Directors and directing

There are some very good things in *Pretty Poison*, but I think it would have been better if it hadn't been shot word for word from the script in the most literal-minded way. This is an unusual complaint coming from a writer but there are often times when directors should change things much more than they do. I have often thought there ought to be two separate words to distinguish someone who merely keeps the actors from bumping into each other from a film-maker who truly creates. Basically directing is a totally non-creative job and a few honest directors will admit that: it is a logistics post, a bit like being a supply sergeant with a mild skill in psychiatric counselling. On the one hand you have to answer every stupid question like telling the prop-man which gloves are to be worn in a scene, because no-one will ever do anything without the director's approval. On the other you have to be the psychiatrist and go over into a corner to listen to the whines and plaints of the actors, taking all of them very seriously, and being ultra-supportive. I am much too lazy to direct and I would be very bad at it because I'm not that fond of actors. I would just lose my temper and say: 'Come off it. Do the damn scene.' But I understand, from directors who've tried that, that it results in a total collapse of morale. Therefore besides being megalomaniacs, most directors are also thoroughly scared that the whole thing will fall apart around them. The job is naturally overrated. It's a system of cowards and incompetents.

Admittedly directing a film does demand energy because there is a very special quality of boredom on a film-set, unmatched in my experience anywhere else in the world.

Pretty Poison *(left), with Anthony Perkins and Tuesday Weld.*

Papillon *(right) starred Dustin Hoffman, left, and Steve McQueen, second left.*

I have seen people, whose life's ambition was to go on a film-set, become intolerably bored within three minutes of entering one, even if it contains Liza Minnelli and 400 people doing a huge production number. It takes somebody who thrives on that kind of boredom to direct a film and I have a relatively low opinion of directors. The creative part of it is in the ideas and a director can contribute to that. But it's noticeable that very few directors become successful writers while apparently anybody from James Caan to Burt Reynolds can make an adequate director. Some directors are, of course, very good with scripts. William Friedkin did a wonderful job on *The French Connection* (1971). Franklin Schaffner, with whom I worked on *Papillon*, has a wonderful story sense. In fact I think he is a better story editor than a director, not that he's a bad director.

Papillon

I became involved with *Papillon* in a very curious way. William Goldman had written an excellent screenplay from Henri Charrière's book. Steve McQueen signed a contract to do the picture and was paid half his money, but in the meantime he became involved with Ali McGraw and there was all that trouble between him and Robert Evans. Because of this he really didn't want to do the movie. He said Goldman's script was garbage and rejected it out of hand, but I don't think he even read it. Bill Goldman had written a script in the 'Butch Cassidy' vein which was very good – in fact it was far better than what was eventually shot. The rejection was probably a manoeuvre to gain time. They offered me a huge sum of money to do what was supposed to be a two week rewrite, in order to get it into a form which would be acceptable to McQueen. I started from scratch and worked on it for eight weeks. Eventually McQueen agreed.

Then they decided to bring Dustin Hoffman onto the picture, even though there was nothing for him in the script, just a small insignificant part. So another major rewrite was required. But because of the way my deal was structured it was impossible for them to afford me. I had originally been hired for a two week period and they had already paid a penalising amount to let me finish the script. So another writer was brought in. The resulting film was quite successful, but I found some aspects of it hard to take, especially the general implication that the scum of French society were all terrific people and the guards were all rotten. It has to be a little more complex than that.

The Parallax View

The production story behind *The Parallax View* (1974) was even more tortuous. Doubleday, the New York publisher, had the idea of getting into movies and making a lot of money. So they bought the novel of *The Parallax View* and hired me to write a script. The script I wrote was basically an original movie thriller, which developed one central idea from the book – in my opinion a very arresting idea. The idea was basically that a bureau exists which is concerned, not with assassinating people, but with fabricating evidence to *suggest* an assassination conspiracy, with the intention of using this evidence at some future date against whoever they want – blacks, jews, political opponents. The conspiracy is just a blank form with no name, a construction to implicate enemies in the future when required. A kind of Reichstag Fire held in suspension.

The script was sold outright and originally Michael Ritchie was going to do it. Then Alan J. Pakula came onto the picture and a firm deal was concluded. Alan said he thought the script was almost ready to shoot and he went off to Spain to make *Love and Pain and the Whole Damn Thing* (1973). By the time he came back he had decided that the whole premise of the script ought to be re-examined. He took the assassination thing seriously in political terms whereas I thought it was a witty premise for a genre picture. It seemed to me that doing it his way you might interest all assassination buffs but you lose all the intellectual interest as well as the complexity of the premise. Then they started talking about making the hero a reporter. One of the big problems of the movie industry is that, because its stars have a richly deserved sense of guilt about what they're being paid, we get an endless series of investigative reporter roles. I become enormously dispirited whenever I come across a reporter-hero because it seems so obvious and tiresome. In my version of *Parallax*, the hero was a small-town policeman.

So I said I wasn't interested in re-examining the central premise of the script and they would have to get someone else. Alan was furious and we still don't talk to one another. Paramount was even more furious. They said that I didn't care about the film and accused me of pure greed. In fact one of their executives, Peter Bart, sent me a telegram which I framed, saying he was shocked I would sell the project out for the sake of the almighty dollar. I couldn't get over the fact that any movie executive could actually say that with a straight face.

The Parallax View *(left) starred Warren Beatty, right, as a reporter battling against a vast assassination syndicate.*

Robert Redford *(right) as the CIA man on the run in* Three Days of the Condor.

At this point David Giler was hired to rewrite the script, and by chance shortly afterwards there was a writers' strike. It was a very important strike and enormous passions were generated; I happened to be co-chairman of the negotiating committee. David worked literally day and night, using coffee and heaven knows what but somehow he finished the rewrite. And I happen to know he did not write a line after midnight when the strike began. But afterwards, during the strike, the script was heavily rewritten by persons unknown. David was outraged at the fact that somebody had written extensively during the strike and, when the credits were being decided, he wanted it made clear that a lot of the script had not been written by him. I hadn't written any of it or very little, but I was responsible for it being made since I wrote the script that was originally bought. So in the end we decided to split the credits. I don't take credits very seriously but the credited writer gets 1.2 per cent of any sale to television; this money is paid by the studio to the guild and distributed to the credited writers.

There's no question that Alan Pakula did a wonderful visual job on *The Parallax View*. Its production design is superbly mysterious and it is a classic of confused genres. But I think its box office failure was deserved. Because basically it's a combination of the very obscure and the very obvious. I know there are people who love the film and think it's a true revelation of how things are in America, but frankly I think that's rubbish. The ending of my script of *Parallax* was not as strictly pessimistic as what they shot, but it certainly wasn't jolly. The hero did not get killed but a last-minute twist showed the audience that although he thought he'd escaped they were about to get him.

Three Days of the Condor

Like *Parallax*, the book of *Three Days of the Condor* had one marvellous idea. This one came right at the start and concerned a branch of the CIA that is exclusively employed with checking the plots of thrillers in case any of them correspond too closely to actual events. The rest of the book was virtually comedy, and its central character was facile. So I embroidered the central idea as much as I could, inventing things like translating machines that weren't in the book. I went through the numerous versions of it for Stanley Schneider, the producer, and David Rayfiel, who often works on Robert Redford's dialogue, came in at the end. I remember Stanley called me up in great embarrassment to say Redford wanted someone to polish up the dialogue but by then I had got so tired that I was relieved. They didn't change a great deal of my version, but they made just one major change which I thought was good at the time and probably helped the film's success. The premise of the book was basically that the heavies are involved in drug smuggling. We talked a number of times about getting something more timely, but I never could exactly come up with anything I liked. Under Redford's guidance they added a Middle East connection and oil. I wasn't opposed to it but now I think that the absolute banality of the original – that they were killing all these people and using an enormous government machine just to sell drugs and get rich – is more brutal and may even be more interesting. But I can't deny Redford's intelligence; he is excessively intelligent – in fact in my opinion he exceeds his brief!

King Kong

King Kong was another chaotic production, because there was such a terrible time problem. Universal wanted to do their own *Kong*. There were innumerable lawsuits pending and Dino de Laurentiis quite correctly said that the only way to beat them was to make our movie first. We had to start shooting before we should have, and then we shut down for three weeks because nothing else was ready. The huge mechanical ape, which got so much publicity, was never ready and did not appear in the movie at all apart from one terrible shot towards the end.

But it was a very friendly and cheerful movie to do, and on this occasion the chaos was fun. Dino de Laurentiis is very easy to get on with and he's good with scripts. We had a meeting lasting about ten minutes before I wrote *Kong* and I felt that, given the craziness of the subject-matter, we should try and meet the thing head-on. For example, rather than have the girl as a reporter or photographer who goes along on the trip in the usual utterly boring fashion, we would have her appear on a raft in the ocean in a magical way. It was an attempt at pastiche, but like *Batman* it needed to be played very low-key to get any humour out of it. I think John Guillermin is a good director and he did a good job, but to pull off this particular version in the circumstances you would have to be positively inspired. We had violated one major rule by not giving audiences what they expected – it was as if they had ordered fish and got meat. They wanted to be scared.

People like to talk about *Kong* as a big failure and it certainly wasn't up to expectations, but I thought it was a cheerful kind of movie and I'm pleased it did quite well worldwide. It's just that in those countries where it didn't do well, its distributors had put up big advances and got stung as a result.

Writing and production

It's impossible to enjoy writing for movies unless you can enjoy some of the business machinations that lie behind each project. Movies are so hard to make, and turn out so frequently to be bad that unless you can laugh at the wheeling and dealing, life would be absolutely intolerable. Deals are the real focus of movie-making. And I find that in order to preserve my sanity, it's necessary to make hit-and-run raids on the world of the deal. I tend to fly to Los Angeles, and stay three or four days; if you stay any longer, then you begin to experience various kinds of insanity like believing what you read in *Variety*.

My family had a certain amount of money and, though I didn't inherit a penny of it, it distanced me from the competitive urge that many writers have – the 'I'm gonna make it' or *What Makes Sammy Run* philosophy. It's often been said that anybody who truly wants to make a million dollars, can make a million dollars. But the catch is that you really must want to *make* it, which is quite different from wanting a million dollars to spend. If you genuinely want to accumulate, you can probably do it. I think I'd be the best producer in the world if I could stand talking on the telephone 100 times a day and waiting for calls. There are plenty of people in Hollywood in their forties and fifties who are struggling like that. You can't call it tragic because in a sense they deserve what they get in their quest for easy living. But there is a terrible degradation about it, especially for producers. I really don't know how anyone can bear the job of an independent producer today. There is nothing to do except wait for the phone to ring or make calls that pretend to be social but are in fact an attempt to sell something; creaking down the halls of Fox with three tennis rackets, pretending you're still young. It represents everything that is intolerable for a decent human being.

Currently I'm working on a couple of original scripts, but I enjoy doing adaptations more. I find my originals are often very poorly worked out and there's always the terror that I won't be able to finish them. On an adaptation I know where I'm going and my energies are freed to make improvements and invent new twists. I can approach the work savagely and really bring a critical sense to it without worrying that I'm going to destroy the whole thing. But if I do that to an original, I generally don't finish it.

I find it impossible to write at home so I write from an office, and I work morning hours for as long as I can. My writing method is based superstitiously around my typing and I was very pleased to read somewhere that Hemingway worked the same way. Every time I make a typo, I redo the page. I never write in a correction, so that each page invariably gets done ten or twelve times and I always rewrite it – I never just copy it. This way I never look at the page again once it is finished, and my scripts are never retyped. I may not be a writer but I really can type.

The knack of screenwriting

Increasingly in script construction I find that memory is everything. I have to hold things in my head in the knowledge that they may come in very useful later in the script. But the process has to be subconscious – it's no good making a list. And six weeks or so should be quite long enough to write a script of 120 pages, writing about four or five pages a day.

My basic view of movie-writing is that it is an elaborate form of games-playing. In the preface to *The Master of Santiago*, Montherlant makes an analogy between the playwright as the matador and the audience as the bull. I've always thought that was a wonderful description of movie-writing, which is manipulation in the most technical and literary sense. They come charging out and you deceive them, then you bloody them up a bit, finally you plunge the sword into them. And there is definitely a knack to it. Anybody can go to the movies and spot the absence of this knack, then come out and say: I could write better movies than this. But they quickly find it just can't be acquired overnight. At times I've hired kids to do things for me, very bright kids whom I respected in every way. And when they turn in their work I'm astonished; it's so poorly done. I think the knack can probably be taught but you have to have a ruthless teacher. Some of the worst movies and television have been written by ponderous and very serious writers dealing with heavy issues, who have no conception of the knack. The sad thing is that so many of them win EMMYs.

THE CRAFT

Movies in Production

If film-making were a more exact science than it is, a detailed production history of some recent films would convey the essential component steps of the commercial film-making process. The several skills of the film-crew on the studio floor can be outlined (p. 165), as can the general principles of film budgeting, but the film industry is unusual in that every single commodity that comes off its production line is custom-built. If Ford or British Leyland were to apply the same principles, then they would have to produce a different model every time they produced an automobile. Each of their production lines would be unique and used only once.

It's true that in the days before television, studios made every effort to standardize their product. Even then it was a losing battle because there were too many variables involved, and now that the more rigid schedules and formulae are reserved exclusively for television, feature films are more idiosyncratic than ever.

This makes it almost impossible to draw strict lessons from the study of individual films in production, although it is perhaps, paradoxically, the very elusiveness of the narrative film process which makes production history such a fascinating subject. The scrutiny of the ramshackle, haphazard and frequently nerve-racking jumble of events and people and interlocking skills behind a movie can only ever offer flashes of insight into the process as a whole. And this goes some way towards explaining why the results of the process are always unpredictable even to its most experienced practitioners.

'In pre-production'

Many of the trade-terms used so confidently by film-makers seem almost to be devised to camouflage the industry's lack of uniformity. 'Pre-production' for example sounds like a disciplined set-period of preparation before a film begins 'principal photography'. In fact it can mean almost anything: a studio may be tinkering with a script to which it is nominally committed before dropping it altogether, as Warners appear to have done with an early version of *The Omen* (1976). Sometimes a long and desperate search is being conducted to find a suitable bankable leading player; few films escape this unhappy hiatus but the classic example is *Love Story* (p. 61). Or the producers may even be temporarily reorganizing a production schedule for tax reasons; *Close Encounters of the Third Kind* (1977), for example, shot a couple of days at Los Angeles Airport in December of 1975 to claim tax relief for that year before closing photography down for several months. The film's immediate pre-production therefore technically took place after shooting had commenced!

So far as movies on the lower end of the budget scale are concerned, the favourite pre-production story is probably Roger Corman's account of the total preparation for the horror movie *Little Shop of Horrors*, which was supposed to have been shot in a matter of days in 1960 (a year in which Corman made five other films). 'We were going to play tennis that weekend,' he always claimed, 'but it was raining.'

Of course pre-production for any film that reaches photography must necessarily imply a period of intensive preparation after the deals are closed and the script written. The first more *passive* months of pre-production are spent tinkering with scripts and imaginary casting, the second *active* phase will include casting, location finding, the contracting of a studio (if studio based), set and effects design, hire of equipment, purchase of stock, detailed budgeting/scheduling, the arrangement of transport and (if a director is lucky) rehearsal. The pre-production period of two recent films, Orion's *Sphinx* and United Artists' *The Dogs of War*, present two very different case-studies.

The Hollywood company Orion – founded at the beginning of 1978 by the disenchanted former top executives at United Artists – bought the rights to Robin Cook's second novel *Sphinx* even before it reached galley-proof stage. Cook, a Boston surgeon, had had a bestseller with his

Stanley O'Toole *(right): producer of* Sphinx.

Director Franklin Schaffner *(centre right) on the set of* The Boys from Brazil *and (below right) demonstrating the gentle art of murder to Martin Benson before a take on* Sphinx.

Genevieve Bujold *(far right) in* Coma; *adapted – like* Sphinx *– from a Robin Cook novel.*

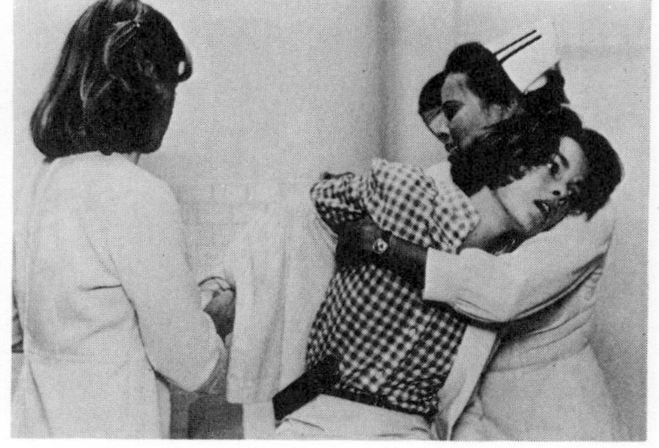

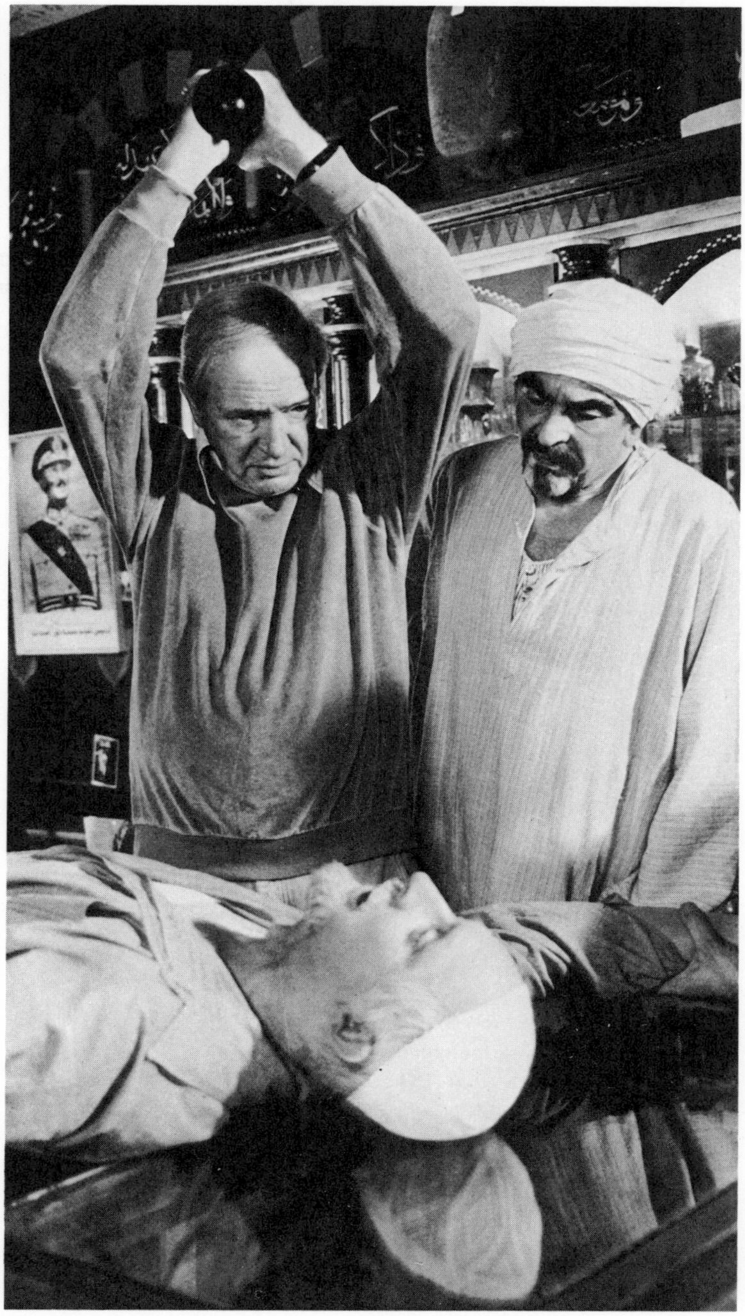

previous novel *Coma*, a thriller centring on the black market in human organs for transplant. *Coma* had been turned into an extremely skilled and successful motion picture by Michael Crichton in 1978; it starred Genevieve Bujold as a doctor trying to penetrate the mystery and deception she encounters in a large modern hospital. *Sphinx* also deals with an attractive female doctor, this time an Egyptologist, who finds herself embroiled in a conspiracy surrounding the black market in Egyptian antiquities. Cook was reportedly paid $1m. for the rights to his book because of the huge success of *Coma* both as a novel and a film. In fact the figure was probably nearer $700,000 plus various deferments and a chance to write the screenplay himself.

To direct the film, Orion asked the experienced Franklin Schaffner, who had been tinkering with a number of scripts since his previous assignment *The Boys from Brazil* (1978), from another best-selling thriller. Directors, like actors, tend to get type-cast and as a result of films like *Patton* (1970) (for which he won the Oscar for Best Director), *Papillon* (1973) and *Nicholas and Alexandra* (1971) Schaffner had naturally gained a reputation as a 'big budget, epic' man, with a penchant for adapting best-sellers. Coincidentally he has not made a film within the continental limits of the United States since *Planet of the Apes* in 1968.

As far as he was concerned *Sphinx* had two big things going for it: a well-defined female leading character and 'a stunning exotic location'. But everyone seemed agreed; Cook's original material ('though it did have some very good dramatic construction') and his screenplay were unworkable as a film.

Sphinx was due to be published by Putnams in the fall of 1979. Some months earlier, Schaffner and his producer for the project, the British Stanley O'Toole (with whom he had worked on *The Boys from Brazil* and on an aborted Warners film about the Entebbe raid) began their preparations. After a lot of discussion with Orion about writers, they settled on John Byrum.

Lesley-Anne Down *(far left) emerges from a cavern constructed for* Sphinx *in a Budapest studio.*

Running Scared *(left) was one of Stanley O'Toole's previous features. Ernie Day squats beside the camera; director David Hemmings and star Gayle Hunnicutt sit on the canal bank.*

When Byrum delivered his screenplay, it was clear he had vastly improved on Cook's original, creating in particular a spectacular climax for the film which was quite patently missing in the novel. O'Toole did his budget on that first screenplay, reckoning a $6.7m. below-the-line cost which proved a reasonable estimate. 'Below-the-line' refers to those areas of production cost directly related to the craft and organization of shooting – studio, technicians, bulk of cast, housing, catering and so on. 'Above-the-line' has to do with the more powerful individual 'elements' of the package: producer, director, stars and script as well as the cost of any source like a novel on which the project is based.

The producer of *Sphinx*, Stanley O'Toole, had been able to cut costs on one of his earlier films by shooting scenes in an East European country and at this stage in *Sphinx*'s history he decided to make a massive saving by shooting certain interiors in Hungary: 'I think the west has no choice but to look to the east, if you're going to try and make films for a price. I feel I have proved that by not going to somewhere like Pinewood studios I saved around two million dollars. The deal I've done here is about the best that could be done in this day and age. Over 100 people, 23 sets to build, all hotel and living expenses – the whole thing for a million dollars. The sets alone in England were going to cost two million. I reckon it is probably around two and a half times cheaper to shoot in the east.'

The imperative need to cut costs has recently led other producers to production decisions that are just as strange as O'Toole's plan to construct Egyptian caves in a large converted warehouse near Budapest with thick snow lying outside. Few locations in recent memory are as bizarre as those employed in Samuel Fuller's war film *The Big Red One* (1980). For this, a German concentration camp was constructed on a top security Israeli army base with young Israeli soldiers playing German guards, while a 20 kilometre stretch of coast north of Tel Aviv saw the North African campaign, the invasion of Sicily and D-Day.

The casting of *Sphinx* was a crucial problem. Frank Langella, who had made a hit on the Broadway stage as Dracula (besides starring in John Badham's screen adaptation in 1979) was always the choice for the mysterious Dr Ahmed Khazzan. To play the heroine Dr Erica Baron there were a number of options. In terms of bankability, Jacqueline Bisset seemed favourite and came within an ace of making the film despite an awesome asking price of well over $1m. Jill Clayburgh would have got a million too, but she opted not to do it.

In the end it appears to have been a toss-up between Candice Bergen and Lesley-Anne Down with the latter winning the day. Her price: somewhere around $400,000. With $1.5m. for the director and $250,000 for the producer, the final budget would be somewhere around $10.5m. Given how rarely above-the-line costs of recent films are made available and assuming these are accurate figures, the comparisons are quite revealing. The stars come abnormally far down the earnings tree because at the time of *Sphinx* neither had had a box-office success. Schaffner's large cut reflects the fact that, despite the comparatively modest earnings of *The Boys from Brazil*, he has been responsible for at least three major box-office hits (*Planet of the Apes*, *Patton* and *Papillon*). The producer's relatively modest cut would seem to relate directly to the questions raised in Chapter Two: The Deal; if *Sphinx* did extremely well, then O'Toole might expect to become quite wealthy even by Hollywood standards, but in the meantime he moves on as rapidly as he can to his next picture.

The original schedule for *Sphinx* drawn up by O'Toole called for five weeks of exterior shooting in Egypt, then a two week Christmas break followed by five weeks in Hungary. As so often happens, the problem of finding a star had delayed the process to a point where these dates could not be met, but the Hungarian studio was booked and could not be cancelled. It was therefore necessary to reverse the schedule and shoot the interiors first. This was the only answer,

John Irvin *(right) advises Christopher Walken, left, on his role in* The Dogs of War.

The Dogs of War *(far right) represented a return of sorts for director of photography Jack Cardiff (beside camera, in shorts) to the subject of his own earlier film,* The Mercenaries.

but it was not a popular one: for obvious reasons it is far easier to rearrange studio sets to match exterior footage than vice versa.

Further pre-production problems were to torment *Sphinx* right up to the eve of shooting. Even the most megalomaniac director will generally concede that the most important craftsman on the studio floor in respect of a film's overall appearance is its director of photography. Literally 48 hours before the studio start-date, *Sphinx*'s director of photography Claude Renoir (nephew of Jean) hurt his eye in an accidental fall. Shortly before, Renoir had damaged his other eye while making the James Bond film *Moonraker* where he had had to be replaced. Now he was forced to bow out of *Sphinx* and at remarkably short notice O'Toole managed to hire the accomplished but less experienced English photographer Ernie Day, who had done some superb work on one of the producer's earlier films *Running Scared* (1972).

The Dogs of War: six years in pre-production

Because *Sphinx* was based on a bestseller for which a good deal of money had been paid upfront against competition from other studios, Orion moved it into production comparatively rapidly, and its pre-production period was anguished but relatively short. By comparison John Irvin's *The Dogs of War* (1980) based on Frederick Forsyth's 1974 bestseller was in pre-production, at the passive stage, for all of six years.

The first two movies from Frederick Forsyth novels, *The Day of the Jackal* (1973) and *The Odessa File* (1974), were produced by Sir John Woolf, but the latter had flopped badly at the box office, and even *The Day of the Jackal* did not come up to expectations. Woolf had an option on *The Dogs of War* with development money from United Artists, but around that time UA noticed the similarity between *Dogs* and another project that producer/director Norman Jewison was developing for them called *Decline of the West*: both plots involved mercenaries in an emerging African country.

Larry De Waay, Jewison's production supervisor at the time, recalls the problems: 'John was having difficulties with *The Dogs of War* and we were having difficulties with *Decline of the West* and so it was agreed that since both were being financed in one form or another by UA it would make sense to go with just one and *Decline* was shelved.

'Norman became very enthused with the idea of *The Dogs of War* and in 1975 we made a trip to Africa with the writer Abby Mann who wrote *Judgement at Nuremberg* (1961). He wrote a script which Norman wasn't terribly happy with, so *Dogs* also kind of went on the shelf at that point and Norman went off to make *F.I.S.T.* (1978).'

The next writer to tackle *Dogs* was Michael Cimino, who was later to go on to direct *The Deer Hunter* (1978) and, more recently, *Heaven's Gate* (1980).

'Michael was involved for about seven months and wrote another screenplay and was also going to direct the film. However, he finally decided that it wasn't really the project for him because of the similarities – at least in the military aspects – between *Dogs* and *The Deer Hunter*.'

Meanwhile Sir John Woolf, after negotiations with UA, had bowed out of the project completely, leaving it with Jewison, as executive producer, and De Waay as producer. It was now 1979.

'After we completed . . . *And Justice for All* (1979) Norman and I had a long chat about *The Dogs of War* and he said that since I was going back to London I should try and run with it.' In London De Waay met up with John Irvin, a highly experienced British television and documentary director who was, as yet, untried in features, and the two discovered an immediate rapport.

'We got on very well and our own individual ideas about the concept of *Dogs* were very close. This coupled with the quality of his television material – and I hadn't yet seen his *Tinker, Tailor, Soldier, Spy* – as well as his experience

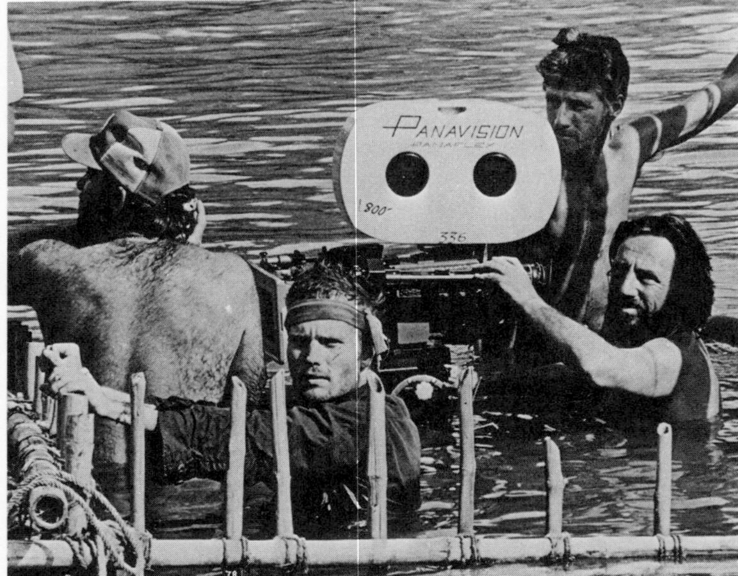

shooting documentaries in Vietnam all lent itself to this project.' So *Dogs* had a director, a producer but, as yet, no final script.

This was to be provided by a young American writer called Gary DeVore who had previously written a number of unfilmed screenplays. 'Gary wrote a screenplay which was getting close to what we wanted and UA liked it very much as well, so we then started location hunting. Locations had always been one of our major problems. We knew we would eventually conquer the screenplay, but whether or not we could find a country where we could shoot the piece was a different matter.'

The problem of location-finding is one of the most difficult and time-consuming aspects of pre-production. It is hard enough finding a building or a street or a field that has the necessary features and atmosphere and occasionally changes may have to be made in the script if the difficulties become too acute. But in the case of *The Dogs of War*, which was set in a fictitious African state, it was necessary to come up with an actual country. This is the sort of logistical problem which has been known to hold productions back for years, and sometimes to stop them being made at all. The budget of Cimino's epic study of the Vietnam war *The Deer Hunter* rose from $8m. to $13m., partly because of the appalling difficulty of finding and adapting a suitable location in which to restage scenes from the Vietnam war. Francis Coppola solved the problem on *Apocalypse Now* (1979) by simply building his own cities and supply centres in the Philippine jungle at a cost which most producers still find terrifying. De Waay was aware of the size of the task ahead and in 1976 he had taken the precaution of visiting the Seychelles and reaching a tentative agreement with the Prime Minister James Mancham.

Mancham may have come to regret his readiness to help. Eight months later he was ousted in a coup and there were rumours that local resentment against him had arisen partly because he was agreeable to the filming of *Dogs*. When De Waay wrote to the new regime he received no reply at all until a local hotelier informed him that, while he was quite welcome to holiday on the island, a film crew was out of the question.

De Waay had to start again. One step ahead of Hurricane David, he scoured the Caribbean in search of an island or state which could double as the West African country in Forsyth's book, a country whose wealth was based on platinum. Finally he landed at Belize on the Central American mainland.

'It turned out to be ideal for our purpose. We needed a country with a long coastline as our

The Sphinx crew *(left) on location in Egypt.*

Christopher Walken *(left) shares the discomfort of a riverside POW compound with the camera crew of* The Deer Hunter.

Kirk Douglas and Woody Strode *(left) commence combat before a gallery of technicians for Stanley Kubrick's* Spartacus.

mercenaries attack their target from the sea. Also we needed a building not far from the beach which we could use as the presidential palace. Belize had both. It also has a predominantly black population and the whole area looked very much like the West Africa of the story.'

Once De Waay had fitted this problematic piece into the puzzle, most of the other pieces fell into place quite smoothly. The six year hiatus meant that some of the content of Forsyth's original novel had to be updated. The star of *The Deer Hunter*, Christopher Walken, committed to *The Dogs of War* after reading the latest version of the script in October 1979. Arrangements were then made for 13 weeks of shooting to begin with a few days of New York locations in February 1979, followed by London, Miami and then the bulk of shooting in Belize. The script's final epic battle was estimated at 21 nights of filming. *The Dogs of War* total budget was finalized at $8.5m., which meant that by pure chance it conformed exactly to the average major motion picture budget (as estimated by the MPAA: the Motion Picture Association of America) for the year of 1979.

Principal photography

'Crewing up' a film is a bit like choosing specialized troops for a hard campaign. Almost as important as picking the best man or woman for each job is the necessity of gathering together a group of people who can work with each other in extremely close proximity for two months or more. Some producers will tell you it is better to have a good team man than a brilliant loner. To the uninitiated, feature film credits with terms like 'best boy' or 'key grip' may seem highly mysterious. But they become easier to interpret once you realize that each film unit is divided into several special departments; these include sound, camera, design, make-up, hair and wardrobe, and frequently each unit is made up of teams of people who have worked with each other previously.

The camera department is supervised by the director of photography. He will command an operator, a focus puller, a clapper-loader (who wields the clapper-board and loads the camera with film) and a grip (an assistant whose job is to push the camera). For commercial feature films the camera crew will always number at least four people, as will the sound crew: the sound mixer who is responsible for live sound on the studio floor (unlike the sound recordist who works in the dubbing phase of production), the boom operator, concerned with the movement and placing of the microphone boom, a sound assistant and a sound maintenance engineer.

The electrical department is run by a chief electrician, known as 'the gaffer', and his second-in-command is known either as a charge-hand electrician or (in America) as a 'best boy'. Many American crews also employ a technician called the 'key grip' who works partly as a construction manager and partly as a back-up to the camera crew. Inevitably, in setting up a shot, the chief electrician collaborates closely with the director of photography. Sometimes, if there is a close working collaboration between the two, the electrician may even rough out a lighting plan for the shot before discussion commences.

A movie's art department is run by the production designer or (on a small production) the art director, overseeing a set decorator as well as assistants, all responsible for the detailed planning of sets. Of course, on a major production involving considerable set construction an art department can expand enormously: Stanley Kubrick's *2001 : A Space Odyssey* (1968) lists three production designers *and* an art director. In every case though, the construction manager's team will have to realize all the art department's plan on the studio floor.

The overall day-to-day administration of the unit is generally undertaken by the production manager, but in addition there can be location managers who attend to the logistics of a particular location. On the set itself the first assistant director with two further assistant directors oversees the crew's interaction.

The 'first' is the director's right hand man, ensuring that there's quiet on the set and that everything is in its pre-determined position. There seems to be no natural progression from 'first' to fully-fledged director, indeed few ever become directors. Yet without a strong 'first', many a production would be in trouble.

The second and third assistant directors are concerned with more menial tasks; the 'second' supervises the comings and goings of the cast while the 'third' is perhaps the lowliest person on the set. He is best described as a 'runner' or, as he is called in the U.S., a 'gofer' – that is he 'goes for this, or goes for that.'

One other key person on the set is the continuity, or script, girl (the post has traditionally been occupied by a woman while, shamefully, all the other posts have been dominated by men). The continuity girl is charged with keeping the minutest details of the progression of the principal photography from take to take. In recent years the role of continuity has been maintained, even though with modern video equipment it's often possible to watch a scene as soon as it has been shot.

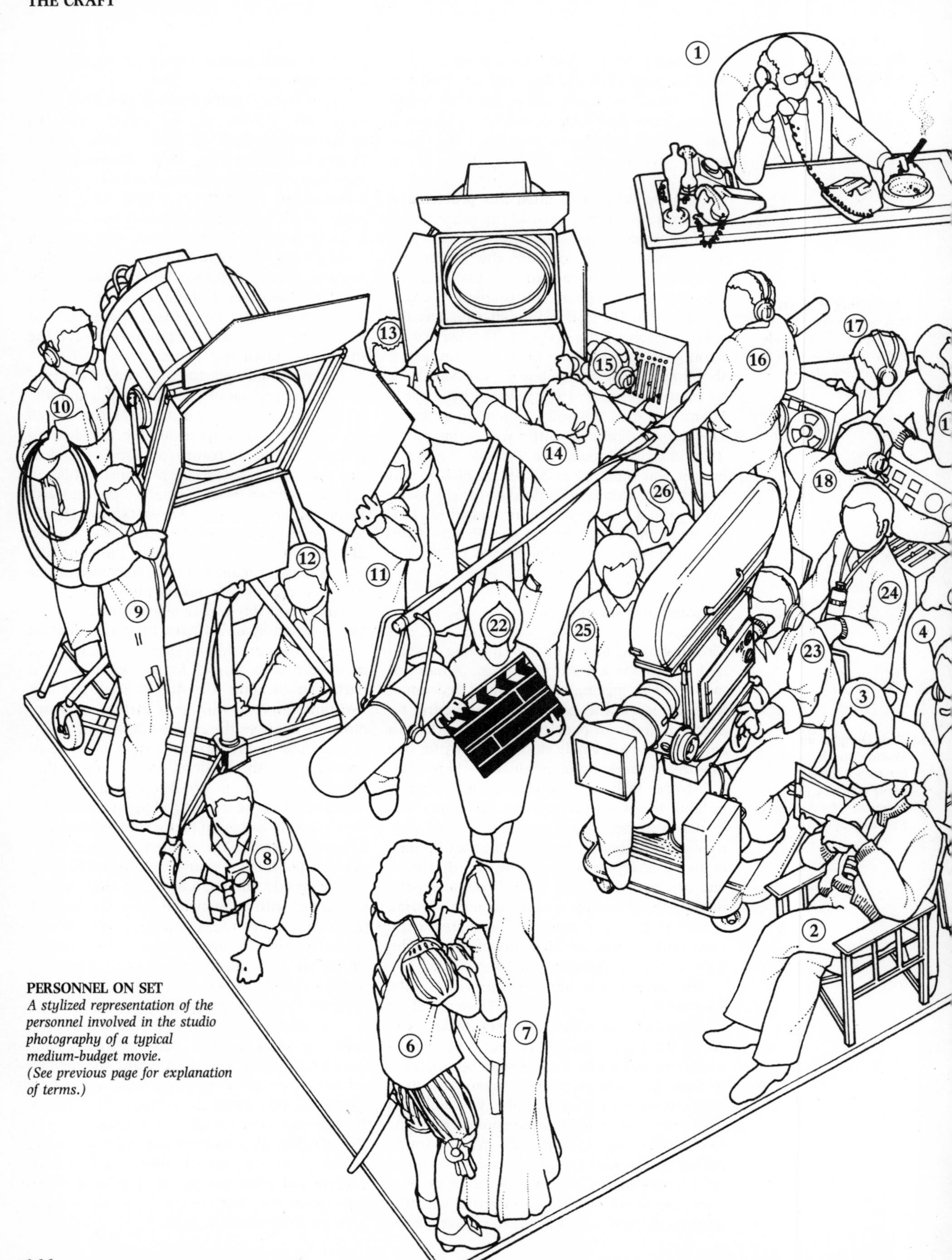

PERSONNEL ON SET
A stylized representation of the personnel involved in the studio photography of a typical medium-budget movie. (See previous page for explanation of terms.)

1 *Producer*
2 *Director*
3 *Continuity*
4 *First assistant director*
5 *Second assistant director*
6–7 *Actors*

ELECTRICAL DEPARTMENT
8–13 *Lighting crew*
14 *Best boy*
15 *Gaffer*

SOUND CREW
16 *Boom operator*
17 *Maintenance engineer*
18 *Sound mixer*
19 *Sound assistant*
20 *Composer*
21 *Music supervisor*

CAMERA CREW
22 *Clapper-loader*
23 *Operator*
24 *Director of photography*
25 *Focus puller*
26 *Grip*

PUBLICITY DEPARTMENT
27 *Publicity director*
28 *Publicity assistant*
29 *Stills photographer*
30 *Publicity assistant*

SCRIPT DEPARTMENT
31 *Writer*
32 *Script editor*
33 *Prompter*

34 *Production manager*
35 *Gofer*
36–37 *Prop assistants*

ART DEPARTMENT
38 *Production designer*
39 *Production buyer*
40 *Special effects supervisor*
41 *Draughtsman*
42 *Art director*
43 *Construction manager*
44 *Set director*

45 *Make-up artist*
46 *Hairdresser*
47 *Wardrobe*
48 *Accountant*

Jaws *(left) featured one of the most notoriously recalcitrant 'special effects' of recent years – Bruce, the mechanical shark.*

On the set

One of the first things that almost any visitor to a film-set notices is the interminable length of time it takes for the unit to set up even the briefest of shots. Screenwriter Lorenzo Semple Jr. (*Three Days of the Condor* 1975, *King Kong* 1976) describes the film-set as having 'a very special quality of boredom unmatched in my experience anywhere else in the world. I have seen people whose life's ambition is to visit a film-set become intolerably bored in just three minutes of walking on to it.' Inevitably this boredom is only enhanced if there are complicated special effects which constantly need to be overhauled like the mechanical shark in *Jaws* (1975). Jack Nicholson is on record as saying he would find it difficult to do a special effects thriller 'because making these films can get so excruciatingly boring. I talked to Robert Shaw and the other actors on *Jaws* and it turned out they just about went out of their birds.'

Directing

If boredom is one predictable part of film-making, its complement is anxiety or, at worst, panic. In a very famous account of what he regards as a typical first day's shooting, Sam Peckinpah described how he would always set up the very first shot of a picture and then go away to be sick. The experience of directing a film has been compared to flying a jumbo jet on a trans-continental flight: hours and hours of mind-numbing boredom occasionally interrupted by moments of pure terror.

The experience is beautifully conveyed by screenwriter William Goldman's account of one crucial day of filming on the multi-million dollar war film *A Bridge Too Far* (1977), as related in his book *Story of A Bridge Too Far*. Richard Attenborough and his crew of hundreds were shooting a particularly vital scene on the Nijmegen Bridge in Holland (which was only available between eight and nine on a Sunday morning). Tension was high because the weather had been bad and if anything interfered with the shot they would have to pay Robert Redford an extra half million dollars to stay around another week which, with additional costs, would probably have meant at least another million dollars on top of the production cost. The time comes to set up the shot:

> As well as being cold, it begins to look like rain. A lot like rain. And there is a terrible cutting wind. Personally I have never, on a movie set, felt anything close to such tension.
>
> Attenborough's feeling the tension too, more than the rest of us. But he can't show it. . . . A director on location is very much like a military leader and he has to behave in like manner so the men won't mutiny . . .
>
> Eight o'clock is coming nearer and nearer and things seem as if they're starting to break. Everything's got to work because there's no time to go back and do things over. But the weather seems as if it's going to be clear enough to shoot and now Redford's in position and the stunt men portraying German soldiers are climbing high in the girders of Nijmegen Bridge, roping themselves in, not for safety but because that's what the Germans did here in their final defense; and then the signal comes that all the stunt men are secured and you can begin to see the confidence flowing into Attenborough because even though there can't be anything wrong on this shot, he's thought so much about it, covered it from every angle the mind of man can come up with, and as crew members come running up to him with last minute questions he's snapping back the answers crisp and fast, 'Is the machine gun nest all right like that?' and 'Yes, fine' from Attenborough without a pause, and this questioner runs off while another comes up, going, 'Will you see the sentry box emplacement in this shot?' and the immediate 'We will, thank you,' takes care of that and 'Have the Sherman tanks been positioned properly?' and Atten-

A Bridge Too Far *(right), with Sherman tanks in position and smoke pots started.*

Richard Attenborough *(far right) – as director – in charge of co-ordinating the minutest logistics on* A Bridge Too Far.

borough quick takes a look, and says, 'The Sherman tanks are splendid as you have them,' and now an assistant director comes up behind with 'The corpses, Sir Richard,' and even though that's not a complete question, Attenborough knows precisely what to say and he says it, 'The corpses must keep their eyes shut at all times, all corpses will be visible in this shot,' and that cry echoes along the bridge as the assistant takes a megaphone and shouts to the extras playing dead Germans, 'Corpses – listen now you corpses – all corpses will keep eyes shut at all times while the cameras are rolling – you got that? – *not one bloody blink from one bloody corpse and that's final*!' and shooting time is almost on us now, and the rain *is* going to hold, and now another assistant runs up asking, 'What about the smoke pots?' and Attenborough, on top of his game, replies, 'You may start the smoke pots now, thank you very much,' and right then, this trusted aide comes roaring up, excitedly saying, 'What about the jeeps in the orchard, sir?'

I was standing by Attenborough and for a moment his eyes glazed over and he had to be thinking that suddenly the world had gone mad or was the world sane and the mistake his – had he forgotten – forgotten something vital? He was standing on a freezing bridge – what orchard? what jeeps? Was there some part of the shot that he'd neglected, something involving an orchard and jeeps, and here he was, with smoke pots going and high in girders, guys hanging and a star ready to shoot and two-hundred-seventy-five people waiting but this question must be answered because what if it ruins the shot and if the shot's lost a million dollars are lost and –

– then he smiled very sweetly to his aide and said, 'We will not require jeeps in the orchard at all, thank you so much for reminding me.' This, it turns out, referring to the last half of a later scene to be shot afterwards, the first half having been shot days before, all this in another location, and what this trusted aide had done was pick this particular moment to enquire if Attenborough's camera angle for this future sequence would require the placement of jeeps in the distant background in order to match with what had been done before.

The weather held, the shooting on the bridge went quickly, the last major disaster had been averted. As we left the bridge, there was a genuine feeling of exultation. Attenborough was cheery as usual, no more whistling needed that day. Later, perhaps, but not then. There are always 'laters' lurking in the lives of film directors, jeeps in the orchard that need tending to.

The 'jeeps in the orchard'; it is a good image to evoke the thousand and one things that can crop up in location or studio shooting to destroy a director's sense of confidence. Most backers are prudent enough to insert penal clauses into a director's contract so that if a film goes over schedule the director will suffer personally. The loss of a promised bonus is one obvious stick, but companies are aware that even this may not be enough of a disincentive if the film-maker becomes totally involved with the production. Consequently, some current contracts will remove editing rights when a director goes as little as ten per cent over budget. Because any good director is vitally involved with editing this is an awful prospect, especially since there are so many factors on the floor which can go wrong and cause delay.

Despite the increasing respect that directors have won from studios in the 1960s and 70s, it is still possible for them to be treated like hired hands. There is some evidence, for example, that certain executives at Universal regarded *Car Wash* (1976) as a 'piece of junk' to be done for as little money as possible and as quickly as possible, and that the studio were on the backs of its producer and director every day during a brutal shooting schedule. When the film went out and made about nine times what it cost, all the studio remembered was that the

Close Encounters of the Third Kind *(far left) climaxed in the luminous landing of the alien mother ship, 'a nightmare in lighting'.*

Ernie Day *(left), director of photography on* Sphinx*, checks a light reading with Lesley-Anne Down.*

director had gone ten days over!

But if the 'jeeps in the orchard' don't stem from studio interference, then you can often find them in a production's sheer physical difficulties. Steven Spielberg remembers *Close Encounters of the Third Kind* (1977) as 'a nightmare in lighting. We had more electricians and more lights than any film in Hollywood over the last decade. We had to light an area which was four times larger than the largest soundstage in the world.' Stanley Jaffe, who was overseeing the production for its backers Columbia echoes his sentiments: 'I never slept during that picture. I remember getting a call in the middle of the night saying they needed some more electricians. I said: "O.K. how many?" And they said: "Seventeen." SEVENTEEN! That is more than most whole crews. They had 60 arc lights strung out 80 feet above the ground and when I walked on to the set I just looked around saying "Holy shit!" It was all I could do. John Beech our production manager is good at keeping costs down, but the two of us would just look at each other and say "Ha ha!" What else are you going to do: go and kill yourself? Fortunately the picture made money. If it hadn't made money we would have jumped off the 80 foot catwalks!'

Other stories of directorial torment have sometimes centred round stars: Marilyn Monroe's last film had to be closed down altogether because she was never on time; on *Fathom* (1967) director Leslie Martinson and Raquel Welch are alleged to have been communicating by notes from the first day. But the 'jeeps in the orchard' can just as easily turn out not to be human. On *Sphinx* the 'jeeps' were bats.

Ten days after the production began shooting in Hungary, *Sphinx* ran into nearly insurmountable difficulties with live bats which were needed to lend authenticity to caves which had been constructed in the studio.

Production manager Ariel Levy explained: 'The idea was to gather up bats already in hibernation in cold caves, pack them into containers and bring them back to the studio. When we were ready for them we would put them in a room where for an hour they would become awake in a fairly ambient temperature. They would then be taken on to the stage, still in their containers, and spend another hour acclimatizing to the ambient stage temperature.

'By now they would be squawking, ready to fly and the moment you took the lid off the box, they'd go. We'd have the bats for a period of four hours after which time they would have to be returned to the containers, taken back into a room where the temperature could be dropped and thence returned to their cave and hibernation.

'Unfortunately our people didn't find the bats they were supposed to find. They then went to caves that were warmer and where the bats weren't yet hibernating, brought back live bats that were wide awake and flew them onto the stage where they proceeded to die all over the place. They originally gathered up 100 of which some 70 or 80 had actually died before even reaching the studio.'

The director of *Sphinx*, Franklin Schaffner, observed these farcical events with appropriate calm, betraying anxiety only when he paced up and down between takes with a cigarette tightly clenched between his lips. After much frantic activity, an attempt was made to make the bats fly by mechanical means. The wings of the dead bats were broken to give them mobility and then their bodies were suspended on nylon from a motorized boom which jiggled them about in a flying movement. This combined with pieces of torn brown paper thrown through a wind-machine seemed to produce acceptable results, but finally real bats were used in the scene. Inevitably precious hours had been lost, and a ludicrous heading on Call Sheet No. 12 (the call-sheets detail the logistics of each day's shooting) masked the anxiety in dry terms: 'Bats and handler required. Time to be announced (subject to bat availability).'

The bat problem as well as the illness of star Lesley-Anne Down was beginning to put *Sphinx* behind schedule. At this crucial point in a production the director is under strain and his or her own feelings of pressure are transferred

Apocalypse Now *(right) featured a visually and aurally stunning helicopter attack as its centrepiece, shot by ace European cinematographer Vittorio Storaro (far right, flanked by two colleagues). His work on this film won him an Oscar.*

straight to the next most important person on the set: the director of photography.

Cinematography

Cinematography is a careful exacting science and one which makes great demands on its exponents. The good director of photography must have the patience of a painter attempting to construct a masterpiece in the middle of a battlefield. On a film-set where time is so vitally important, the cinematographer preparing a shot is under constant pressure to work quickly, to give permission for the restless unit to go ahead and shoot. But if something is wrong with the director of photography's calculations or judgement and the results are flawed in any minor way, thousands of feet of rushes may have to be discarded and days lost. In this eventuality the blame will be placed squarely on his or her shoulders and instant dismissal is quite possible. Many cinematographers have been fired during the course of shooting a major feature; this happened recently on John Badham's *Dracula* (1979).

On *Sphinx* cinematographer Ernie Day was under great pressure especially since he was a last-minute replacement, and it was clear he was extremely nervous. Like the rest of the unit he hadn't been helped by the decision to shoot the film back-to-front. Normally the exteriors are followed by the interiors, making it easier for a cinematographer to match the artificial light to the natural light. *Sphinx*'s producer O'Toole was aware of the pressure but was still worried by his cinematographer's slowness:

'I know Ernie is capable of great things. The trouble is that I don't think any set of cameramen improvise and use their creative abilities as much as the French. They light from the front and then fill in towards the back. They can create atmospheres and moods to fit anything. And also, they're quick.

'British cameramen tend to light the back and take for ages to light up to the front where, of course, you have talking heads. I had to sack Ernie from *The Last of Sheila* (1973) because he had become a nervous wreck from working with the director Herbert Ross. He had become so intimidated by Ross that he just went to pieces: when we saw the rushes they were white. I took Ernie out and told him to ignore the man: "Don't you realise he's more frightened of you than you are of him?" I said. So Ernie went back to his hotel and next week we looked at the rushes and they were even whiter. In the end he had to go and in a way I was furious because I knew what he was going through. I think, for instance, he did a wonderful job on *Running Scared* which is still one of the most beautifully photographed movies that I've ever been involved with.'

Shortly after expressing these fears, O'Toole was horrified to find history repeating itself at the *Sphinx* 'dailies' (rushes are shown daily). Only this time the rushes were not too white but too dark. The editor Bob Swink, who was assembling some of the footage as the film progressed, spat his annoyance while Schaffner remained outwardly calm and Day continued to look nervous. It seemed as if history might repeat itself, but in fact Day would stay the course with some sharp reminders that the film was a 'big break' for him, that he 'should have more confidence in himself' and 'why not try and cut a few corners?' Ironically Day had the last laugh when, a few months later, he graduated to directing in his own right on the Ryan O'Neal picture *Green Ice* (1981). But cinematography is certainly not a pursuit for those with high blood pressure.

It is indeed partly because of their speed that in recent years European cinematographers have been a key feature of American movies. Three out of the five nominees for best cinematography in the 1980 Academy Awards – Giuseppe Rotunno for *All That Jazz*, Nestor Almendros for *Kramer vs. Kramer* and Vittorio Storaro (the eventual winner) for *Apocalypse Now* – were European. Their flair and a particular talent for improvisation has attracted the new generation of American

Marlon Brando and Catherine Allegret *(left) in* Last Tango in Paris, *shot for Bertolucci by Vittorio Storaro.*

film-makers. Storaro, who for much of 1979 and 1980 was directing photography on the Warren Beatty film *Reds: The Jóhn Reed and Louise Bryant Story*, points out how directors like Coppola, Scorsese, Spielberg and Lucas (and, he might have added, Beatty himself) were impressed by the energy and excitement of the European films of the 60s made by directors like Godard, Truffaut and Malle in France, Reisz, Schlesinger and Losey in England, and Fellini, Antonioni, Rosi and Bertolucci in Italy.

For example, before *Apocalypse Now* Storaro was best known for his association with Bertolucci, for whom he was cinematographer on *The Spider's Stratagem* (1970), *The Conformist* (1970), *Last Tango in Paris* (1972), *1900* (1976) and latterly *La Luna* (1979). It was the results of that collaboration – a style which denoted an extreme flexibility and mobility of the camera coupled with a highly stylized manipulation of both natural and artificial light – that particularly attracted the Americans. Of Bertolucci, Storaro says: 'For Bernardo, nothing is impossible!' Working with him demanded a continual solution of difficult technical problems. Coppola (a great admirer of *The Conformist* in particular) was aware of this when he recruited Storaro for *Apocalypse Now*. In addition to the sheer logistical difficulties encountered during *Apocalypse*'s immensely complex schedule in the Philippines, there was the experience of using seven or even ten cameras for scenes – some of which were set at night. Storaro refers to it modestly as a 'challenge'.

Another school of cinematography is represented by Britain's Douglas Slocombe who is nearly twice Storaro's age and whose countless major credits include *Julia* (1977), *The Lion in Winter* (1968) and *The Great Gatsby* (1974). Recently cameraman on Spielberg's *Raiders of the Lost Ark* (he also lit the Indian locations for *Close Encounters of the Third Kind*) Slocombe comes from a great photo-journalistic tradition. His father was the Paris-based correspondent of the *Daily Herald* and the *Evening Standard* and young Slocombe, after schooling in France and a degree at the Sorbonne, found he was equally interested in cinematography and journalism. When he came to London, he managed to place photographs in magazines like *Picture Post* and *Life* and eventually became a wartime news cameraman, providing action footage for films like *The Big Blockade* (1942), and *San Demetrio, London* (1943).

It was an unorthodox way of becoming a cinematographer, defying the usual route from clapperboy via focus puller and operator upwards. In fact Slocombe only worked once as an operator, on a film called *Champagne Charlie* (1944). 'I did the whole picture without realizing that the side-finder had to be adjusted at the beginning. In the compositions there must have been people with their heads cut off and, indeed, a lot of people who shouldn't have been in shot in the first place.

'Chick Waterson, who's been my operator for about 30 years (camera crews tend to stick together if possible), knows this is the only film I've ever operated on. Every now and then I'll hear, in the background, a quiet chorus of "Champagne Charlie" anytime I'm inclined to get a bit big-headed. I like to think they kicked me upstairs.'

Like most cinematographers Slocombe is quick to confess that the worst moments on a

Robert Redford and Mia Farrow *(right) in* The Great Gatsby, *a film distinguished by the camerawork of Douglas Slocombe.*

The Conversation *(far right) featured Gene Hackman as an electronic eavesdropper, demonstrating on film the offscreen advances in technique of sound editor Walter Murch.*

set arise when footage has to be retaken: 'I've always approached the few times I've had to do a retake with a sinking heart. Because it's a shot from, more often than not, the day before, you're therefore having to try and reproduce that day before.

'It's an awful thing to have to do. All the excitement has disappeared and that moment of real inventiveness has gone. At that moment you might as well be turning out sausages or motor car parts.

'But perhaps the most difficult thing to convey to the layman about cinematography is that it is a very insular art. I think many a cameraman going on another cameraman's floor would often find it difficult to tell what he's trying to do. Every cameraman is inclined to be his own master.'

Sound

Sound is a more flexible component of film than vision because it can be doctored, remixed and even added for the first time in the post-production stage. For this reason the sound crew on set cannot have quite the control demanded by the camera crew, but their importance may still be considerable, depending on the nature of the film. In improvised scenes of the kind featured in Pakula's *All the President's Men* (1976) – such as the electric moment where Bernstein (Dustin Hoffman) watches a minor employee of Nixon's Presidential campaign (played by Robert Walden) dissolve into tears – a director will generally want to use live sound provided he has the money to keep going until it is right, because everything is orientated towards the actors and their expression of emotion. In a crowded exterior this becomes less important and frequently impossible because of background noise.

Generally speaking, as dubbing techniques improve, the use of live sound has become rarer in features, while post-dubbing has become an extraordinarily subtle art with films like *American Graffiti* (1973) using their soundtracks as intricate mosaics of aural effect. Coppola's *The Conversation* utilized a suspense format to probe the mysteries and ambiguities in a few moments of recorded dialogue in such a way that its plot was almost an aural equivalent of Antonioni's film about a mysterious photograph: *Blow-Up* (1966). In the case of both *The Conversation* (1974) and *American Graffiti*, completely new techniques in sound were pioneered by the vastly talented sound editor Walter Murch.

Roy Baker, a veteran of sound editing who has worked on such films as Billy Wilder's *The Private Life of Sherlock Holmes* (1970) and *One Million Years B.C.* (1966) explains why sound recording on the set has to come second to the camera:

'Floor shooting is always the most expensive period for any film so they often have to sacrifice sound quality to get the day's work done. The sound recordist will sometimes object on the floor and say "Excuse me. If you move that, I'll get my mike in and I'll get a better result." Some directors will wait for that, but others will say "I'm sorry, no time, carry on." It may be expensive to post-synch but it's nowhere near as expensive as a few more days shooting.' ('Post-synching' is the technique of dubbing dialogue on to the film after shooting.)

King Kong *(far left) was shot in 1933 in accordance with meticulous pre-production drawings.*

Yvonne Blake *(left), a leading costume designer, worked on* Superman.

Franklin Schaffner *(below) in the Seti tomb for* Sphinx *with camera operator Alec Mills and assistant director Pepe Lopez, right.*

The art department

The production design for *Sphinx* was the work of Terry Marsh, a double Oscar winner (on *Doctor Zhivago* in 1965 and *Oliver!* in 1968). Together with the art directors Gil Parrondo and Peter Lamont they had gone to work in July of 1979 to reproduce Tutankhamen's tomb in the Budapest studio.

An exact reproduction was what Schaffner and O'Toole wanted: 'hieroglyphics, paintings, sarcophagus.' Parrondo recalls: 'None of us felt challenged until Schaffner's follow-up: "I mean," he said "with all the artefacts from the Tutankhamen exhibition which toured the world. I want the tomb the way Carter and Carnarvon discovered it in 1922. Exact replicas. You have six months!"'

That wasn't all. There is an undiscovered tomb in the story called Seti I which is supposed to put Tutankhamen's to shame with the lavishness of its furnishing. 'About eight or nine hundred artefacts in gold and jewels should do', Schaffner told Parrondo.

Working with English and Hungarian artists, they created the Seti I tomb on the main stage at the Mafilm studio in Budapest. The smaller Tutankhamen tomb nestled in another of Mafilm's studios, about eight miles outside the capital.

Inevitably once a designer has seen his designs executed there is less for him to do on the set, and it turned out that Marsh became a victim of *Sphinx*'s budget problems. By the time *Sphinx* had switched to Egyptian locations, producer Stanley O'Toole calculated they were around $375,000 over budget merely because they had shot eight days longer than planned, partly as a result of Lesley-Anne Down's illness. In order to try and bring the film back into line O'Toole had to move quickly: 'I came up with about thirty things and one of them was to lay off the production designer. Quite simply Terry Marsh had been on the movie for nine months and all his designs were done.' Marsh's $3000 a week salary was therefore saved for the rest of the shooting, and the art department team of Peter Lamont and Gil Parrondo were able to carry out the practical work that remained. But inevitably the parting of the ways was far from amicable.

Location filming

Although on *Dogs of War* in Belize, director John Irvin claimed to be shooting 14 set-ups a day ('which is actually faster than I shot *Tinker, Tailor, Soldier, Spy* for the BBC') location filming is generally even more painfully slow than working in a studio. Of the twelve-hour day his unit worked on *Jaws*, Steven Spielberg reckons only four hours were actively concerned with the process of filming. The other eight hours were spent anchoring boats, fighting the ocean and trying to get the mechanical shark to work.

One of *Sphinx*'s more difficult locations in Cairo was the National Museum which houses the Tutankhamen exhibition. This was the first time the exhibition had been photographed within the context of a feature film and a number of precautions had to be put into effect. A limit of brute lamp kilowattage (these are the big lamps used to light a set) was strictly observed so that rare enamelling and paint from the treasure cache would not deteriorate. Then, when cases along the corridor were in focus, the Panaflex camera had to operate at six frames per second instead of the normal 24 so that an infinity of reflections – movements from back-up tourists – would not show. Only normal security precautions, however, had to be taken and at the end of the week's shooting there was nothing broken, missing or out of place. This, despite a 100-man unit combing through the glass cases, thick cabling, massive booms, heavy light stands and cranes everywhere. Said the producer: 'They can stomp around as they like when we're out at the Pyramids, but here they walk on eggs.'

Despite enormous co-operation from both the Ministry of Culture and the Under-Secretary of State (they hadn't seen a copy of the shooting-script which portrayed aspects of their country

Omar Mukhtar – Lion of the Desert *(far right), like many films, required intricate story-boards from the art department before production began.*

Bruce Bushman *(right), assistant art director on Disney's* 20,000 Leagues Under the Sea, *examines miniatures for effects shooting.*

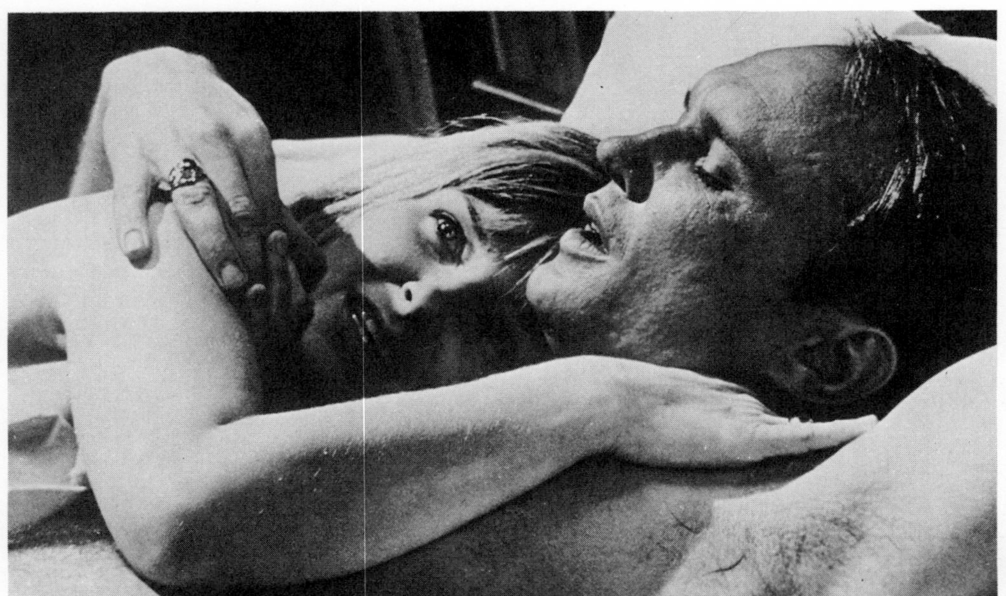

Joanne Woodward *(left) in* Rachel, Rachel, *her husband Paul Newman's directorial debut, which benefited immensely from the experienced editing of Dede Allen.*

John Trumper *(below), celebrated British film editor.*

in a fairly unflattering light), location filming on *Sphinx* got tougher and tougher as the unit moved upcountry. There were physical problems like sandstorms and scorpion bites. And there were problems of communication, especially in convincing the local labour force of the schedule's urgency.

In the event, like so many film-crews before them, *Sphinx* found it necessary to recruit a sort of local Godfather figure who was able to solve many of the problems of supply and labour supervision. But location crews can impose a real cultural burden on a foreign community, and even the local Mr Big couldn't prevent a near-riot when the time came for the crew to tear down a mosque that had been built specifically for the film. The villagers had been so impressed with the mosque that they had petitioned unsuccessfully for it to be presented to the local authority.

When *Sphinx* finally saw its last shot in the can at the beginning of April 1980, it was clear that the producer's stringent attempts to get the budget back into line had, at least for the moment, paid off. Despite the endless difficulties, the film had come in on schedule and a few hundred thousand dollars under budget. But, as the crew thankfully prepared to leave Egypt, they could hardly have known that their chosen location country was preparing a final unpleasant surprise.

Post-production: editing

Of the crafts associated with the movies, editing remains one of the most elusive and least appreciated by the public. While it is easy to judge elements such as photography and acting, editing is, for the most part, an unobtrusive craft. And despite the importance of the editor in shaping the finished film, the viewer can never really know exactly what role he played in structuring the narrative, establishing the relationships of the characters and otherwise contributing to the finished product.

'The trouble with editing is that it is so intangible,' says John Trumper, one of Britain's most experienced editors (*The Italian Job*, 1969, *Get Carter*, 1971, and many others). 'I would say Dede Allen did a beautiful job on the first film Paul Newman directed, *Rachel, Rachel* (1968), on the strength of Allen's other work and because Newman had never directed before. *Jaws* was beautifully cut by Verna Fields, almost an object lesson in how to edit. But who can say what contribution, say, Robert Wise made to *Citizen Kane* (1941) for instance? One never knows whether the director said "Cut there!"'

It's certainly true that many directors dictate exactly how their films should be edited. To them, the editor is merely a technician, carrying out their instructions. Several of the old Hollywood directors including Lewis Milestone, whose films included *All Quiet On The Western Front* (1930) and *Of Mice and Men* (1939), were renowned for their ability to cut *in the camera*. The result was not one shot more than was needed and the editor had merely to assemble this footage together. Alfred Hitchcock, too, was a walking compendium of cuts during principal photography.

But an editor can play a creative role if he or she is given a chance and may contribute much to the finished film. The majority of

John Coquillon *(right), a perfectionist of colour cinematography.*

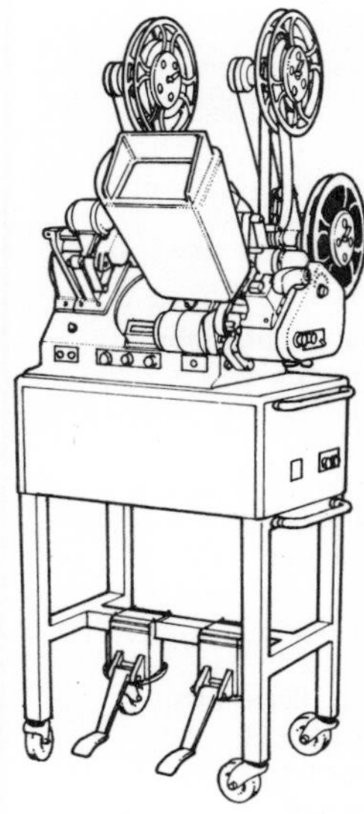

A moviola: *a commonly used aid to editing film. Picture and sound tracks can be run backwards and forwards at any speed, and stopped at any point for scrutinisation and marking.*

directors shoot a considerable amount of footage, covering scenes from various angles and in combinations of long, medium and close shots. While the director should obviously have a clear idea of what he wants the finished film to look like, the editor will make suggestions about pacing, atmosphere, use of reaction shots and so on. He can make a comedy funnier, increase the suspense in a thriller, double the excitement in a war picture. Good editing has saved many a poor film. On the other hand, poor editing can ruin an otherwise fine picture.

The editor tends to work very closely with the director. Throughout shooting he assembles each day's material (the rushes) for viewing by the director and other key members of the crew. These rushes are put together as the film progresses into an 'assembly', with the editor, more often than not at this time, working on his own, putting together what he thinks the director will want to see.

Ultimately, the director views the assembly with the editor and the two discuss what to take out, what to leave in, what to add and so on. The result of their discussions is the 'rough cut' of the film. Generally the 'rough cut' is somewhat longer than the completed film, but all the material is now in sequence and in very much the form the director wants. Further discussions between the director and editor result in the 'fine cut' after which the film is ready to go to the dubbing stage.

Dubbing

While the editor has been cutting the picture, the sound-editor has been cutting the soundtrack to match the visuals. Other tracks are now compiled, including music and effects; eventually all these tracks are mixed together to form the final soundtrack of the film.

Until now, the editor has been working with a rough print called a 'cutting copy'. The precious original negative has remained virtually untouched. Once the fine cut stage has been reached, however, the negative is cut to match this assembly.

Then a print is struck from the negative, complete with all the optical effects required, such as fade-ins and dissolves which, until now, have only been indicated on the cutting copy. The soundtrack is finally married to the print.

The first print of the film is viewed by the director and lighting cameraman, who will decide what work needs to be done on the film at the lab, especially in terms of its colour contrasts.

Cinematographer John Coquillon recalls this phase working with Sam Peckinpah on *Straw Dogs* (1971): 'I saw the film about eight times at the labs when I was grading the colour and I would see it through mute. It was an idea of Sam's. I had a message that the labs were to run off as many grading prints as were necessary to my satisfaction. There were no titles or opticals. I asked Sam why and he said, "When that happens it becomes a movie and you are here to grade that colour." So it really made one concentrate on shot for shot.' On another occasion the two men were in a huge bus used as a mobile cutting room and Peckinpah suddenly said that the two 'most beautiful machines in the world' were the movie camera and the moviola (a viewing machine for editing).

The long road to the screen: *the personnel required to transport an idea through pre-production, principal photography and post-production to the final print ready for distribution. No two feature films are made in the same way: some have more than one camera crew, many have several script writers, a few have as many as five producers. Those listed below will normally be involved in a major studio production.*

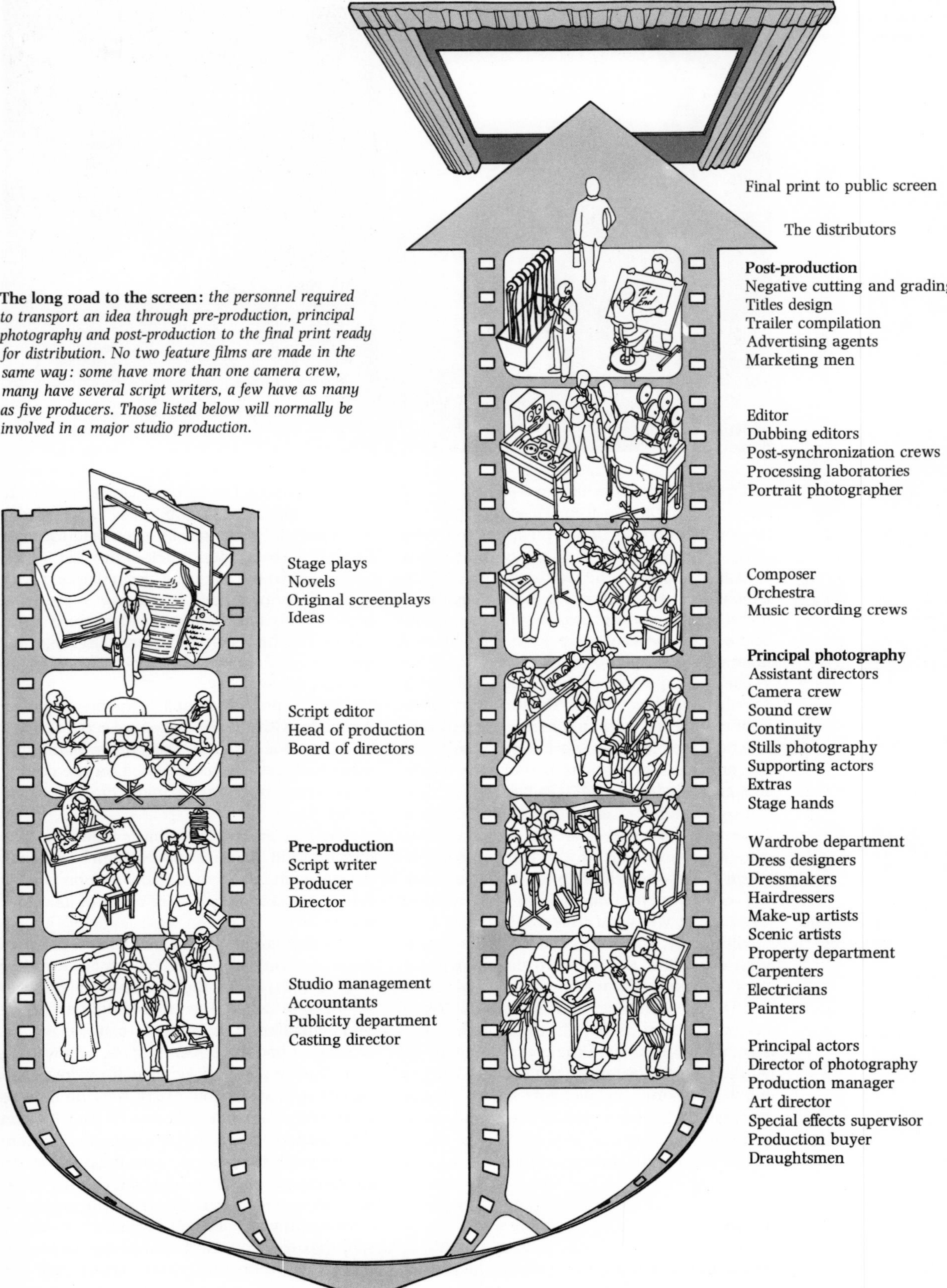

The Best Man *(right), with Henry Fonda, began a long working relationship between director Franklin Schaffner and editor Robert Swink.*

The Shining *(far right), with Jack Nicholson, represented a mammoth job of editing, and was still undergoing changes shortly after its release.*

'With one, you can create people, all types. With the other, you can make them beautiful or smash them into the ground!'

The shooting ratio

Because of the close working relationship between the editor and the director, most directors try to work with the same editor from picture to picture. Robert Swink who was editing *Sphinx* has worked with Schaffner on several of his films including *The Best Man* (1964), *Papillon*, and *The Boys from Brazil*. On *Sphinx* Schaffner shot between 250,000 and 300,000 feet of film which was edited down to around 11,000 for the finished picture, meaning four per cent of the footage was used.

Compared with many film-makers, that is a pretty indulgent shooting ratio. It's very little though compared with some; Stanley Kubrick, for example, is reported to have shot something like 1,300,000 feet for his film *The Shining* (1980). Kubrick even designed his own computer for the film which, at the press of a button, could recall instantly any particular piece of film.

It was in the editing stage of *Sphinx* that the production encountered its last and worst tribulation. It had taken a full three weeks for the cans of film to get through the Egyptian customs and arrive in Hollywood. There when a count was made, a number of reels were found to be missing including one full day's shooting – around 8000 feet. 'Good material too,' producer O'Toole admitted. 'Helicopter shots, establishing footage, even some first unit scenes with the stars.' The cost of re-shooting would be around $300,000, even if it were possible to return to Egypt and reassemble the cast. Both were out of the question.

This kind of theft is not without precedent in the world of high budget film-making. In 1975, $3m. worth of colour negative was stolen from the Technicolour laboratory in Rome, including irreplaceable material from Pasolini's *Salo* and the first three weeks' shooting of Fellini's *Casanova*. A 'conspiracy' of silence was said at the time to surround the case, which was never satisfactorily resolved. Three years later in August 1978 four masked men with guns burst into an editing studio in Boston and made off with 15 reels of raw footage from William Friedkin's movie *The Brinks Job*, later demanding a ransom of $600,000, which was never paid.

In the case of *Sphinx* the producers did not receive a ransom demand, although it was thought the film had been stolen by some disgruntled members of the local labour force. The makers had to send production manager Ariel Levy back to Egypt to negotiate for the film, offering an inducement of $15,000 for the cans. But his investigations yielded nothing. By then, said O'Toole, 'the cans were probably at the bottom of the Nile.' *Sphinx* would have to ride out the loss as best as it could.

Right up to the last, in ways over which even the film's publicity department could hardly rejoice, the traditional 'curse' against foreign interlopers (in itself perhaps a metaphor for local resentment against colonial plunder) seemed to surround *Sphinx*.

And like so many producers before him, O'Toole looked back on the experience of filming in an exotic location as something he never wanted to repeat: 'I'll never go there again' he said. 'We managed to surmount the problems but it was a question of dog eat dog.' Of course the producers of *Jaws* felt exactly the same way about nautical filming. Until it was time for the sequel.

Special Effects

Paradoxically some people in the special effects business think the worst thing that could have happened was the extraordinary success of *Star Wars* (1977) and *Close Encounters of the Third Kind* (1977). The major Hollywood production companies now link quality, budget and success. This has created a boom in special effects. But, with the high cost of shooting and marketing, it is unlikely that all the multi-million dollar effects movies produced are going to get their money back. When two or three $40m. movies crash badly, there may be a crisis of confidence.

Meteor (1979) is a good example of what can go wrong. The movie cost $17m. but looked cheap, with lines visible round a tidal wave sweeping through Hong Kong and insufficient detailing on models. There had been immense difficulties getting the initial finance. Then, after a year's work, optical effects expert Frank Van der Veer was fired and most of his work discarded. His replacement, Bill Cruse, said in an interview with *Starlog Magazine* that Van der Veer was just unlucky: 'So much of movie special effects work is risky: trial-and-error. This time, Frank just didn't pull it off.' After almost another year, Cruse was fired. So two years' work was effectively scrapped and, just two months before the planned release-date, two other effects men were brought in.

Similar problems dogged the *Star Trek* movie (1979). Robert Abel and his team reportedly promised to complete the effects for $4m. After a year, more than $4m. had been spent, not one foot of completed film had been delivered and the estimate for completion had risen to $16m. Abel claimed his main problem was a constantly-changing script. He and his crew of about 100 were fired and two new special effects supervisors brought in: Douglas Trumbull (of *Close Encounters*) and John Dykstra (of *Star Wars*). Producer Gene Roddenberry sent a memo to Paramount which highlighted one problem: 'The current state-of-the-art in optical effects has grown so technically complex and specialized that normal or even superior film-making experience is not a sufficient background for many of the optical effects decisions required of *Star Trek*'s producer and director'. One technician called *Star Trek* 'a political nightmare': no-one works in isolation on a movie.

On *Alien* (1979), large numbers of miniature sets had to be re-designed and several effects scenes re-shot because the concept changed during shooting. One member of the production team revealed that director Ridley Scott 'wanted very low-key lighting for his live-action scenes and so it was decided that there had to be low-key lighting for the model shots as well. A lot of the model work, that was filmed before Ridley Scott came down to Bray Studios, had regular space-type lighting. Virtually all this footage was scrapped, so they had to do it all over again in half the time they originally had. They were struggling for time and were filming up to the last minute and didn't actually complete. There was supposed to be a shot, at the very end, of the alien whirling off into space and exploding – actually seeing it die – but they didn't do it. And the explosion of the refinery at the end was very much of a mish-mash.' Nonetheless, the film won the Oscar for its effects.

The viewer is often only aware of the big set-piece special effects scenes like John P. Fulton's Oscar-winning parting of the Red Sea in *The Ten Commandments* (1956) or the appearance of Douglas Trumbull's mothership at the end of *Close Encounters of the Third Kind*. But the best effects are often the ones no-one notices, many in non-fantasy films. For example, much of the striking visual quality of *Citizen Kane* (1941) was the result of special effect work in the laboratory, and, according to the film's special effects man Linwood Dunn, up to 80 per cent of some reels carried special effects. Even the extent of the *Star Wars* effects is usually under-estimated. There is a much-quoted figure of 365 effects shots for the movie. But some shots contained 12 separate optical elements. The asteroid sequence in *The Empire Strikes Back* (1980) included over 40 shots. Some of these contained 28 separate optical elements, combined on an optical printer. The process of

Wally Veevers, *veteran special effects man whose career began in 1935. His films include* 2001 *and* Superman.

Douglas Trumbull: *after his success with* Close Encounters of the Third Kind, *he was called in to salvage* Star Trek: The Motion Picture.

Derek Meddings *(right), in white jacket, with director of photography Paul Wilson on the vast 'miniature' Metropolis set built for the model effects on* Superman II.

Black Narcissus *(left and right), set in the Himalayas, had many effects which the viewer takes for granted. A wind machine (left) helps to change the warm studio set to a cold Himalayan location. Director Michael Powell and cameraman Jack Cardiff shelter (right) as they shoot Deobrah Kerr through French windows and a fake rain-storm.*

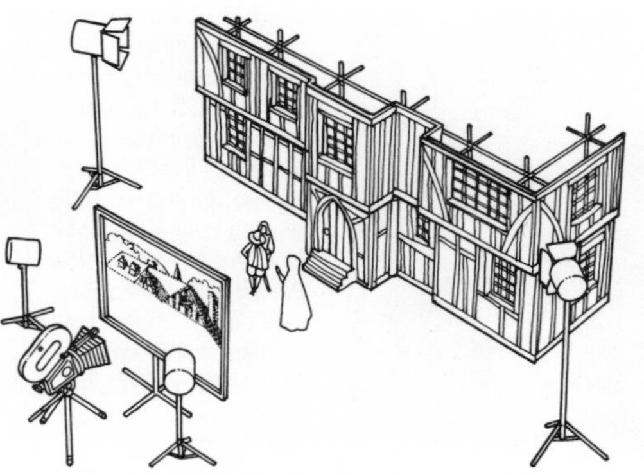

Glass-painting *can be used to reduce the cost of building a set. Roof and skyline (far left) can be painted onto a sheet of glass. This is placed between a half-built live-action set and the camera (left) so it appears that a full set has been built. As this prevents camera movement, the technique has been superceded by travelling matte systems.*

combining so many complex optical elements involved about 100 separate pieces of film passing through the printer for each shot. For *Close Encounters*, artist Matthew Yuricich created about 100 paintings on glass which were skilfully blended into scenes. In the sequence where a police car, chasing a UFO, crashes through railings at the side of a road, half the railings, the trees, the continuation of the road, the horizon and the clouds in the sky were all painted. Yuricich says: 'I ended up painting in almost every effects shot – tying together parts that either didn't work or they didn't have time to set up.'

Roy Field, the optical effects supervisor on *Superman* (1978) says, 'A lot of my work on other pictures is salvage work, where something has gone wrong in the original photography and you've got to remove people or objects and the audience probably doesn't even notice it's been done'. Wally Veevers, whose work stretches from *Things to Come* (1936) to *Raise the Titanic* (1980) agrees and says, 'Special effects is really a first aid department'. British special effects painter Doug Ferris also agrees: 'Most of my time is spent doctoring shots that other people have made a mistake with and, because they weren't originally shot with a special effect in mind, most of them really are a challenge.' As the illustrations on these pages show, the careful and considered use of special effects techniques can save money on a film, add greatly to its impact and be almost undetectable to audiences.

The techniques of special effects: mattes

The most common form of optical effect is a matte (from the French word for mask). This does just what its name implies; it blanks out part of the screen – as in shots of someone looking through binoculars, where part of the screen is black. At its simplest, a matte can be used to cut production costs. You can black out the top half of a picture and shoot live-action sequences in the bottom half – people in Roman togas, say, milling in front of the bases of vast columns. You can then paint on glass a top half for the picture which will match the live-action footage already filmed. By combining the two halves, you create a scene in which the Romans are seen milling around in front of a vast temple in a cityscape which it would have cost a fortune to build. Of course, because the live-action has to match a static painting, the live-action camera has to stay static too. But the matte can be of any shape in any part of the screen and, painted skilfully, it can be difficult to detect.

In the throne room scene at the end of *Star Wars*, only a few hundred extras were used to create the equivalent of a Nuremberg Rally. The extras were photographed three times at different distances from the camera, the three shots combined, the dividing lines camouflaged and the side ranks of men painted in by matte artist P. S. Ellenshaw. A similar scene at the rebel headquarters showed several fighter craft and their crews. That, too, was created by com-

Things to Come *made extensive use of foreground miniatures hung in front of the camera to blend into a live-action background. In this scene, ruins above the arches on the left and the top half of the buildings on the right are cleverly-shot foreground miniatures.*

Excalibur *(right and far right), on which mattes were used in many shots to provide atmosphere. Here an ordinary skyline has been transformed by the addition of a separate sunrise matted into the original. This technique means that film-crews no longer need to wait for hours or days to capture the required atmosphere on location shooting.*

bining several shots of a single craft and painting round the shots.

Travelling mattes

However, with the traditional static matte (one was used as far back as *The Great Train Robbery* in 1903), the two component parts of the picture are separate and this means that the actors cannot move out of the live-action area or they will disappear under the black matte. So, to jigsaw the live-action into a background, the travelling matte was developed. This changes its position, size and shape from frame to frame so that the matte corresponds exactly to the shape of the actor and he can move anywhere within the frame.

During the 1950s, the blue-screen travelling matte came into favour and it is still in wide use today – for example on *Flash Gordon* (1980) and *Dragonslayer* (1981). Basically, the action is shot in front of a blue backing. The colour negative film then undergoes a number of printings so that, when the specially-shot new background is added, it only shows on the blue parts of the picture. The action from the first shooting and the background from the second should then fit together exactly, like a jigsaw puzzle. This is done by 'optical printing' in the film laboratories. If there is a very slight error in the printing, a slight black line will be visible round the action as in *Meteor*, and there is also the danger of fringing caused by light reflecting off the blue backing on the foreground action. When a film frame only 35 mm across is projected on to a screen 100 feet across, the problem of matte-lines and fringing is acute.

The beam-splitting camera

The Rank Organisation in Britain produced a beam-splitting camera which was later refined by Disney in America and which, it is claimed, minimizes or eliminates matte-lines and fringing. The action is shot in front of a screen lit by yellow sodium vapour lamps. The live-action in the foreground is lit with separate lamps which filter out the yellow light. The camera has a prism behind the lens dividing the light into two identical images which fall on to two separate strips of film. One film records the shape of the yellow background, the other the shape of the separately-lit actors and foreground objects. By careful and complicated optical printing, a new background can be put into the shape recorded by the yellow film and combined with the live-action shape on the other film. The two separate components jigsaw together perfectly. Only Disney use this camera because, according to their matte artist P. S. Ellenshaw, 'nobody can make the damn prism. In fact, Disney tried to have another prism made and it was not as successful. Other people have tried, but not even the man who made the first prism has been able to do it again successfully.'

On the Double *was made possible by split-screen techniques. The split in this case runs down the right hand side of the grey vertical line and round the end of Danny Kaye's baton. One major problem is to ensure that the actors' eyelines are correct in separately-shot scenes.*

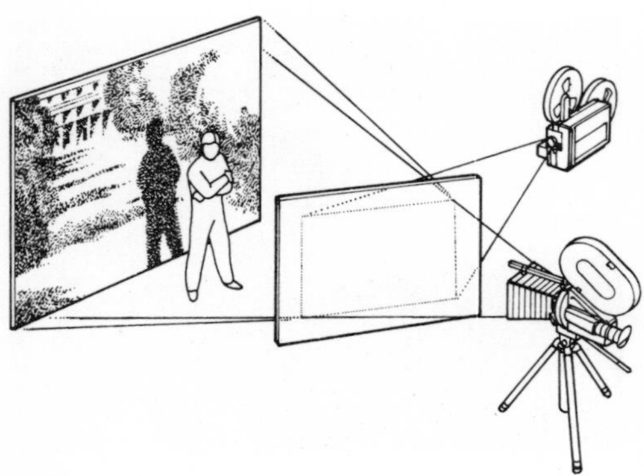

Front projection *(left) involves placing actors in front of a reflective screen, then shooting through a mirror which simultaneously reflects the image thrown by a projector. The simpler* **back projection** *system (right) places an actor before a translucent screen with an image projected onto it from behind. Both systems have their drawbacks.*

Front projection

However, *2001: A Space Odyssey* (1968) popularized another technique which is now very widely used. Director Stanley Kubrick wanted higher-quality visuals, so he decided to use 70 mm film rather than 35 mm. Because of the increased fringing which would have resulted on 70 mm, effects supervisor Wally Veevers did not use blue-screen or traditional travelling matte techniques. He used front projection.

Back projection, with the actors in front of a screen and a picture projected on to the screen from behind, dates back to the start of the film industry. It is still used today, principally for scenes shot through car windows. But, if used on a large scale, the effect is visible. The amount of light penetrating the screen from behind is less than the amount of reflected light from the well-lit live-action foreground.

In the front projection system, the actors stand in front of a screen made from a highly-reflective material which has the same effect as reflective roadsigns. The screen is made up of thousands of tiny beads which act like prisms. Only 2 per cent of light hitting the screen is absorbed – 98 per cent is reflected back in a straight line. The projector and camera must be in *exactly* the same position. So a front-surfaced mirror is used – a sheet of glass mirrored on one side, ordinary see-through on the other. The camera shoots through the clear side while the projector is pointed at the mirrored surface. By having both camera and projector at a 45 degree angle to the sheet of glass, the beam from the projector can be reflected off the mirrored surface to hit the front projection screen from the camera's exact line-of-sight. The screen reflects back the projected image in a straight line, through the glass, directly into the lens of the camera. Because actors' bodies and scenery are relatively non-reflective, and because they are brightly lit from another position by the studio lighting, the projected image does not show on them, only on the screen. The actors' shadows are hidden by their own bodies, because the

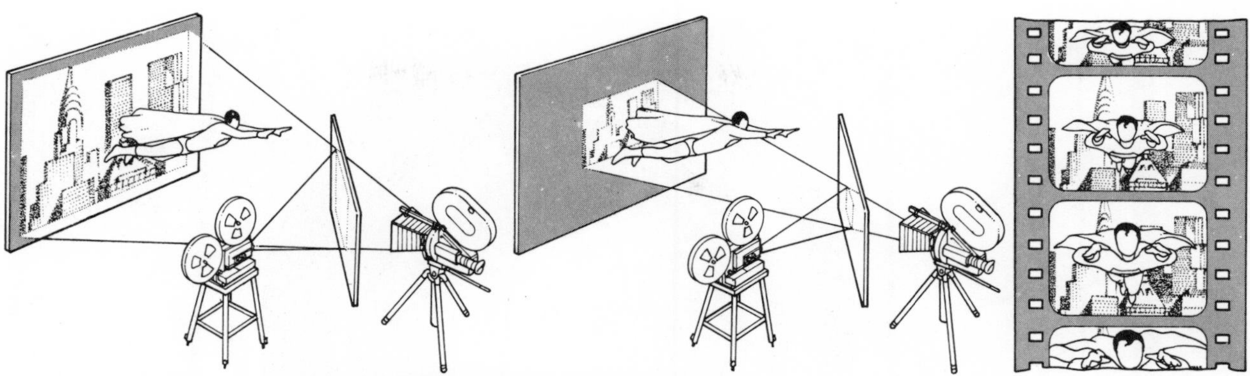

Superman (above) 'flew' in a few scenes by means of Zoptic front projection. Linked zoom lenses on camera and projector enabled Superman's size in the film frame to vary in relation to the background, giving the impression that he was moving.

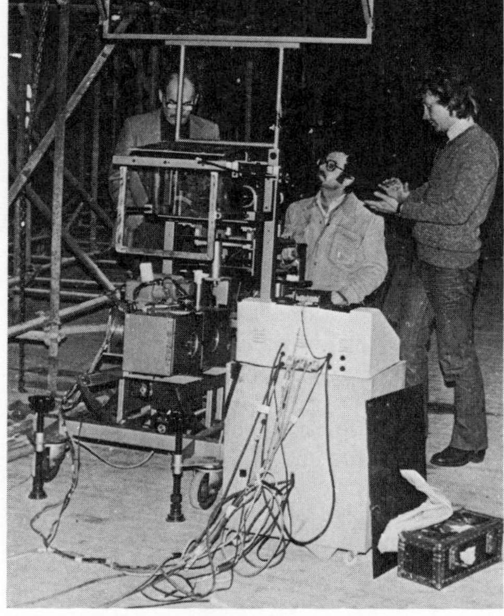

The Land That Time Forgot *(centre left) relied on the cheaper technique of back projection combined with live-action foregrounds.*

Zoran Perisic *seated at his Zoptic rig (above right) devised the system and supervised early tests (right).*

Superman *(left) also used travelling mattes. He was shot in front of a blue screen; a shape corresponding exactly to his body-outline was cut out of a skyline scene; and his body matted into the gap.*

camera and projector share the same viewpoint, and all light is being reflected back in straight lines. The end-result is a bright live-action foreground and an equally-bright background fitting together without any matte-lines. The director and effects man are also able to see what the result looks like at the time of shooting, rather than wait for the time-consuming laboratory work required with mattes.

In *Superman*, there is a scene in which Superman flies off Lois Lane's balcony, the camera follows Lois across the room and she opens the door to Clark Kent (i.e. Superman again). The action is seen in a single camera shot without cutting. Roy Field, the film's optical supervisor, explains how the effect (devised by Wally Veevers and executed by Charles Staffel) was achieved: 'It's a double front projection shot, actually. The head (first part) of that shot, with Superman flying off the balcony, was done in one pass on the front projection system. It was then re-projected and the camera panned off to the real set and tracked with Lois to the door.'

Making Superman 'fly'

One problem with front projection is that, if you want to move the camera, you have to move the projector and two-way mirror simultaneously. Zoran Perisic, who had been a special effects cameraman on *2001*, simplified this by developing his Zoptic (Zoom Optic) system, which includes synchronized zoom lenses on both camera and projector. It was used on the 1978 *Thief of Baghdad* and for some Superman flying scenes, but no single technique was used to make Superman fly. For some scenes, Superman was lying in a body mould attached to a pole, which penetrated the front projection screen, but which was hidden from the camera by the actor's body; a knuckle-joint at the end of the pole allowed the actor to be tilted and the camera itself could be rotated. (For *Superman II*, an improved Zoptic rig was coupled with a 90 by 30 foot front projection screen.)

In other sequences, Superman was flown by wires which were then individually hand-painted out on the film frames. At 24 frames per second, this means that a 10 second flying sequence could involve painting on 240 individual frames, each of which might have four wires supporting the actor – a total of 960 wires. Sometimes, the blue-screen system was used. In the movie Superman's costume is actually turquoise to allow this effect in the background; if it had been the blue of the comic strip, his costume would have become part of the matte. At still other times, Superman was actually a doll. And, on other occasions, the real Superman would stand on a front projection screen looking upwards at the camera, his hair blown back by an overhead fan and his cloak moved mechanically. When screened in the cinema, it looks as though he is flying horizontally because the audience assumes the bottom of the screen is 'down'. (By a reversal of this thinking, lift-shafts in films are often built horizontally with the camera looking along them because, if the audience is told it is looking into a lift-shaft, the unthinking assumption is that it is vertical.)

Using camera angles

Kubrick used unexpected camera angles to confuse the audience's visual senses in *2001*. In one scene, a stewardess carrying a tray walks up and round in a circle, exiting upside down. She was actually walking on a treadmill; the rest of the set, with camera attached, moved through 180 degrees while she remained in the same place. The viewer's eye assumes the camera is static. Kubrick avoided the wire problems which plagued *Superman* by refusing to use any wires unless the actor or props masked them from the camera. In one sequence, an astronaut is blown into an airlock, in another floats weightless in space as a mechanical pod approaches and catches him. In both cases, the scenes were shot with the camera looking upwards while the actor (and pod) was lowered on wires, hidden from the camera by the very object it was photographing. In the same way, the standard method of shooting space explosions is for the camera to look upwards at the explosion, which comes downwards and outwards towards it. The effect on screen is that the explosion radiates out equally in all directions unaffected by gravity. Miniature explosions for scenes involving models are shot on high-speed cameras so that, when projected, they will expand more slowly and therefore seem vaster.

Simulating blood

Realism has become more and more important – nowhere more so than in gore. The turning-point for non-Gothic gore was *The Wild Bunch* (1969), in which explosive squibs and small bags of blood were mounted on metal plates and attached to actors, then detonated either remotely or by a movement of the actor's arm. When the squib exploded, the actor was protected by the plate, but the force of the explosion burst the blood bag and ripped open a hole in the actor's shirt. With squibs front and back,

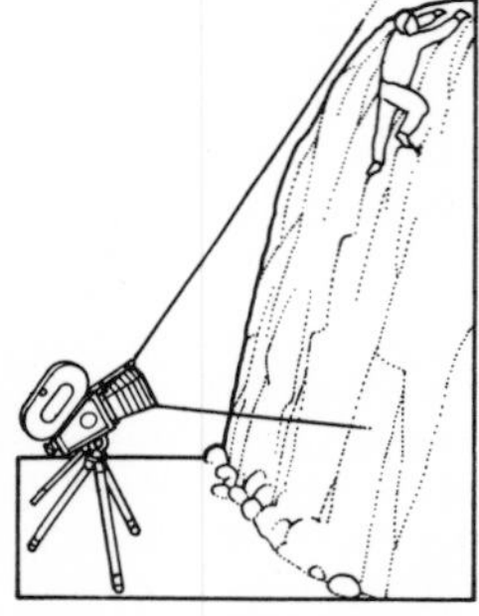

Camera angles *are used to confuse the eye. Low-angle and wide-angle shots give the impression of greater height.*

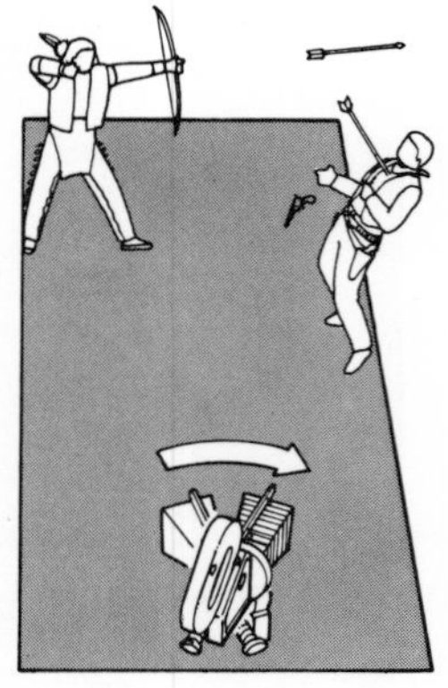

Fast pans *of the camera can be used to make an audience think they see an arrow travel from bow to body.*

2001 *(left): the stewardess apparently walks through 360 degrees. In fact she is standing on a treadmill on the ground, which is at the top of the screen. The camera and the entire set rotate together.*

Zombies – Dawn of the Dead *(above) included traditional horror film gore. Today even the 'documentary' approach of* **Victory at Entebbe** *(top right) gets the full gore treatment with actors rigged to spurt with blood on cue – thanks to explosive squibs and the special effects man's traditional standby, well-placed French letters.*

the audience saw the effect of a bullet ripping through a human body, with blood spurting from both entry and exit wounds. Usually meths is dabbed on the clothes to help the blood spread. The blood 'bag' is actually a balloon or contraceptive sheath. (In Britain, artificial blood is marketed under the name Kensington Gore.)

Creating blood on exposed parts of an actor's body is now relatively easy. The effects man can use a compressed air gun to fire a gelatin blood capsule which bursts open as it hits the actor. To slit an arm open with a knife, he can either use a real knife to cut open a false layer of skin attached to the actor's skin and covering artificial blood (as in *The Wild Bunch*'s full-frontal throat-slitting). Or a fake knife can be used which, as it touches real skin, releases a small amount of simulated blood from its hollow cutting edge. Arrows can be shot by compressed air along thin wires into a stuntman wearing a cork-covered and padded metal plate. In *Catch-22* (1970), a man was cut in half by a low-flying aircraft, his legs remained standing and then slowly fell. The top half of the image on screen was created with a dummy and good editing. But the buckling legs were visibly real. They belonged to a man whose upper body had been matted out.

Moon Zero Two *featured money-saving special effects by Les Bowie. The spaceship blows out talcum-powder.*

Cheap and simple effects

Often, though, the simplest effects are the best. For *One Million Years B.C.* (1966), the late Les Bowie, the father of modern British effects, created the world in six days for £1,200 using porridge for lava and water from taps to create a deluge. On *Flash Gordon* (1980), George Gibbs created a vapour trail for a rocket breaking through the upper atmosphere by spraying salt over the top and tilting the camera to create movement. On several films, rather than blow up houses, Les Bowie blew up photographs of houses and, with tight cutting on the flash of the explosion, no-one could tell. He also made extensive use of photographic cut-outs on the cheap Hammer movie *Moon Zero Two* (1969). More surprisingly, Wally Veevers used the technique on the multi-million dollar *2001*.

In-the-camera effects

'Kubrick insisted,' Veevers said, 'that there had to be live people inside all the spaceships. So we had to film people on different sets and insert them into our models.' There is, for example, a scene in which a spherical craft lands on the moon. Veevers stuck a 2 foot still of the craft onto a 14 by 9 foot glass screen: 'We had this still coming down and landing on the moon. Behind the glass, we had projectors that were projecting the live-action pictures into the still and we were tracking the camera back on a motorized track that moved very accurately as many times as I wanted to, so I could then put the background in behind the still on a second take with the still itself blacked out.' Veevers called his repeatable motion camera 'the sausage machine'.

The idea was taken much further by John Dykstra, supervisor of miniature and optical

Arthur C. Clarke *(above), author of* 2001. *His vision was realized thanks to some trail-blazing effects. The spacecraft (left) is not a model. It is a two-dimensional photograph with live-action scenes back-projected into the windows. The moonscape, stars and earth were added later, using the 'sausage machine' developed by Wally Veevers.*

effects on *Star Wars*. He developed the Dykstraflex camera system, which was linked to a computer memory and could repeat camera movements to an accuracy, he claimed, of two thousandths of an inch. Douglas Trumbull's similar Motion Tracking System for *Close Encounters* had, it was claimed, an accuracy of one ten thousandth of an inch. These memory-linked camera systems allow effects men to matte together different elements – spacecraft, starry skies, live-action etc – within a single frame. Shooting effects in the camera on the original negative is clearly preferable to laboratory work which involves the reprinting (and therefore degradation) of the film. Until the recent advent of memory-linked systems, in-the-camera techniques were very inflexible compared to lab-effects because the positioning and timing of every shot is so critical. The Dykstraflex allowed the *Star Wars* crew to use smooth, repeated camera movements rather than model movements much more than had been usual. And this saved a lot of time.

On *2001*, only nine years before, the model of the main spacecraft Discovery had had to be moved on a track 150 feet long. Shooting the entire movement took 4½ hours (to give a totally smooth result). This had to be done more than once, for matting purposes; and the craft had to travel at *exactly* the same speed each time. The wheel-shaped spacecraft in *2001* was nine feet in diameter and was shot by rotating it at ⅜ of an inch every minute. Douglas Trumbull has been quoted as saying: 'We thought at the time that *2001* would start a big trend. It didn't. The main effect it had is that people look at *2001* and say, "No-one's ever going to do this again – No-one's ever going to have the patience, the money or the talent to pull it together. . . ." However, it's possible now, with all the new equipment and techniques of our industry, to make the technical equivalent of *2001* in much less time, with much less effort.' Because of the new technology used on *Star Wars*, Dykstra's crew were able to show spacecraft crossing in front of planets – something not done in *2001*. And they were able to move their camera repeatedly to create realistic, fast-moving dog-fights.

The use of real camera movements also means that some individual frames of film will have blurred images, which the human eye accepts as natural. It is largely for this reason that stop-frame animation as used on the original *King Kong* (1933) and modern Ray Harryhausen films like *Clash of the Titans* (1981) tends to look unreal. (The technique is to shoot the film frame-by-frame, moving the models very slightly between each shot.) Even the smoothest stop-frame animation can *appear* to be jerky because the human eye is used to seeing, subconsciously, a slight blurring of movement in live-action photography. So, when it sees a clear, unblurred movement, it seems somehow unnatural. To overcome this, on *The Empire Strikes Back* and *Dragonslayer* Brian Johnson used a motion control system which automatically gave the animated object in each frame a realistic blur so that, paradoxically, the end result looks clearer and smoother. To get clearer pictures, he also used an improved version of the obsolete large-format Vista-Vision film which John Dykstra had returned to for *Star Wars*. This runs horizontally, not vertically, through the camera and gives increased picture clarity because it has roughly twice the negative area of a 35 mm frame. Disney, too, chose this format for their excursion into the space epic genre, *The Black Hole* (1979).

For *The Black Hole* they also developed mattescan, a system linking a computer to a camera crane, so that they could duplicate shots of simultaneously-moving live-action and matte paintings. There is one technically superb sequence in which humans are seen coming out of a lift. The camera pulls back and shows them entering an observatory, then tilts up to show the vast domed room. There was no such set. It was a composite of eleven separate live-action, model and matte elements. Disney also built a computerized camera system for *The Black Hole*'s model shots: ACES (Automatic Camera Effects System). This only had to be told two

Ray Harryhausen *(above) is known for his expert stop-motion animation, in which models shot one-frame-at-a-time are moved slightly between each shot. The system was used on such films as* **The Golden Voyage of Sinbad** *(above centre) and* Clash of the Titans. *The technique is also used by* **Roger Dicken** *(above right, with two creations from* Alien).

stationary points and it would find the smoothest way between them. Although not entirely successful, ACES went far further than the Dykstraflex – it was actually a computer-*controlled* camera system. But *The Black Hole* is an example of the sad fact that effects work cannot rescue an inferior script or a limited concept. Compare the original *Flash Gordon* and *Buck Rogers* effects (1936 and 1939) with the new ones (1980 and 1979) and the staggering technical advance is obvious. But compare the original *King Kong* (1933) with the re-make (1976), and you find that effects are not all that matters.

Too much technology?

The danger is that, with all this high technology available, the tail may begin to wag the dog. Until the big budgets came along, special effects men would often, successfully, create effects with basic equipment and a lot of ingenuity. They had to think of the cheapest, rather than the most obvious, way to create an effect. There is now a danger that sophisticated equipment may be used to achieve results which could be obtained more simply and cheaply.

One necessarily complex construction was Carlo Rambaldi's $30,000 alien for *Close Encounters*. It was controlled by fifteen flexible cables attached to mechanical joints or muscles. The cables ran through the alien's body and came out of his feet. By manually moving levers attached to seven of these cables, Rambaldi's assistants were able to push up or pull down a mechanical muscle next to the skin and create facial expressions including the famous smirk. Another five levers controlled the arm and hand movements. Throat and chest movements were achieved by pumping air into and out of the figure through tubes.

However, on some movies, technology may be used when it need not be. On *Alien*, a hatchway on a miniature craft was opened – fast – with a compressed air ram which needed electronic controls, air cylinders and back-up systems, all of which take time to set up, all of which can go wrong. The effect, one crew member revealed, could have been achieved just as effectively by a quick tug on a piece of cotton. One member of the crew on another recent big-budget effects movie has stated: 'There's more money in films now and so you've got to find some way to spend it. Each movie has to be more spectacular than the last and so they say they're going to be more expensive. But, in many cases, it's not necessary to spend money on more equipment and modern technology. You can achieve the effects very simply by cheaper methods.'

For example, on *Moonraker* (1979), John Dykstra was originally involved in shooting ninety flying shots. The deal fell through, so the remaining effects team fell back on an old-fashioned way of repeating shots without linking the camera to an expensive computer memory: they simply wound the film back in the camera. It meant a lot of detailed plotting and timing, and wouldn't have been feasible on an extremely complex sequence, but the result was good enough for Derek Meddings' effects to be Oscar-nominated.

British and American special effects

The difference between the British and American film industries is epitomized by their respective attitudes to special effects. British effects supervisor Roy Field says that 'the difference between us and the Americans, unfortunately, is that they have unlimited capital. We are never given any capital, so we're more inventive in that respect because we have to use existing machinery and, if we want something which isn't normal, we have a tremendous fight to get it from our producers because they say they can't afford it.'

Derek Meddings believes the problem arises from the very nature of the British system: 'The Americans still have a studio system, where a lot of people are employed by the studios. We're all freelance. A place like Pinewood will

Derek Meddings *(left) puts the finishing touches to his space station and shuttle for* Moonraker. *One of his least-noticed but most successful effects was a giant 'miniature' of the Golden Gate Bridge, with a model* **Superman** *(above) flying up to rescue the model school bus. Note the detail in the girders and the passengers in the bus.*

have a staff of plasterers and carpenters, but the technicians in the other fields are all freelance. So, when you go into Pinewood, you really have to take your own equipment. If you're making a big picture like *Superman*, they certainly will pay for a certain amount of equipment to be developed. But not in the way the Americans do. They will spend far more money because the people that are working there are actually employed by them.' An example of this is that Disney spent $100,000 simply developing matte-scan as a system of general use; it was not specifically designed for *The Black Hole*.

British supervisor Brian Johnson was obliged to go to California for model and optical filming on *The Empire Strikes Back* 'because there's a whole load of new equipment and it's fairly advanced technically and requires very knowledgeable operatives. The majority of those come from California because that's where all the electronic equipment originates from.' Universities on the West Coast turn out graduates not only experienced in film-making, but in using sophisticated computer techniques. It is an area in which British film-makers lag dangerously behind. The optical effects for the new *Flash Gordon* were created in America because the facilities and the trained personnel are there. *Flash Gordon*'s British model effects director Richard Conway says: 'The Americans have a terrific technical achievement because there's more investment but, as far as innovation's concerned, we seem to beat them.' However, Brian Johnson cautions: 'I think potentially we do have a lot to offer in the way of special effects in England. But we don't have the equipment to do an *Empire Strikes Back* type movie in its entirety. And we've got to get some equipment soon or we'll go under because of the motion control systems that are coming up in the States.' Investment is the problem, not talent; it is astonishing that so many of the world's top effects men are British.

The credit for their current success should really go to: the late Les Bowie, who employed and trained many of today's top talents on his Hammer films in the 1950s and 1960s; to the Gerry Anderson TV series like *Thunderbirds* (supervised by ex-Bowie Boy Derek Meddings) which created every conceivable kind of action effect with a series of puppets; to Stanley Kubrick who demanded perfection for *2001*. *2001* was especially influential because Kubrick chose a mixed team of British and American effects men, allowing a cross-fertilization of skills.

The influence of television

But several television shows have also had an influence on the new special effects. Les Bowie happened to pass by one day when BBC TV effects designer Ian Scoones was experimenting with silver paint, a cleaning agent and an oil-based aerosol paint. Viewed through a red filter, the vivid movement looked like the surface of the Sun. The effect was created for a *Dr Who* episode but, with Scoones' agreement, Bowie borrowed and developed the idea for the Krypton Sun at the start of the multi-million dollar *Superman*.

A less obvious example of the TV connection is *The Spy Who Loved Me* (1977) on which Derek Meddings faced an effects man's nightmare: lots of water. Many effects men refuse to work with water because it is impossible to 'scale'. The slightest movement will create a wave or droplet totally out-of-scale with a model. Meddings built a seagoing 'miniature' oil tanker for the film which was 63 feet long and weighed 12 tons. (The bigger the model, the more detail, the more in-scale the water

Shout at the Devil *(above right) had Meddings working on a different scale. The film climaxed with his destruction of a full-scale battleship, 300 feet long, made with 3 miles of tubular steel covered in wood and metal detailing. It was an expensive shot and there was no room for error. The explosion had to happen and had to be spectacular.*

and the greater the realism.) But even a 63 foot long, 12 ton craft does not displace the same amount of water and create the same bow wave as a supertanker. So Meddings attached water-disturbers to the hull below the waterline. It was a technique he had used on a much smaller scale on the Gerry Anderson series *Stingray*. The result in *The Spy Who Loved Me* is so realistic that few people realized they were watching a model until the tanker's bows opened.

Meddings confused the *Superman* audience by building a huge 'miniature' of the Golden Gate Bridge complete with fake San Francisco Bay beneath it. He filmed miniature cars travelling across the bridge, smashing into each other, a school bus swerving to avoid a crack in the road, then smashing through a railing to hang suspended on the edge of a parapet. The cars never touched the ground: they were run on horizontal wires to give smoother movement – another technique developed on the Anderson shows. In *Superman*, the model work and editing is so good in this sequence that many viewers assume they are watching a full-scale mock-up of the bridge with real vehicles.

The potential of videotape

'And they're a tough audience to fool,' Meddings says, 'Especially nowadays, because they're all armchair critics. They can watch television and, with these video recorders, they can record a film and run it back and see it again if they think something's not right.'

That's not the only way television could increasingly change the creation of film effects. There is the threatened disappearance of film altogether. If it becomes possible to transfer electronically-recorded effects on to film or to put electronically-recorded pictures directly on to cinema-sized screens *without noticeably losing picture quality*, that would pose an enormous threat to film as a medium for effects. Already, for the new *Flash Gordon*, Frank Van der Veer has used a 3000-line video system for some effects. (The current US TV standard is 525-lines; in Britain it is 625-lines.) He shot sequences on film, transferred them on to videotape to create electronic blue-screen effects and then transferred the results back on to film. Using this system, it is claimed, he was able to complete, in 25 minutes, travelling matte shots which could have taken two or three weeks if put through film laboratories. Even at 3000-lines, the definition is not perfect, but the future use of a 10,000-line or 20,000-line video system is a real possibility.

Until recently, as far as effects work was concerned, one big advantage of film over videotape was that its individual frames were readily accessible, whereas the electronic videotape system could only run at normal speed: there was no access to individual still frames of the videotape picture. But now there are various frame storage systems. These allow individual frames of the videotape picture to be recalled in any order and then manipulated, spun on their axes, squeezed, distorted, totally controlled. Almost anything which an optical printer can do to a film can now be done to a videotape recording. Electronic 'wipes' can rival mattes; the chromakey system is an electronic equivalent of blue-screen. And the main advantage of videotape, of course, is that the result can be seen as it is recorded, then immediately replayed, assessed and, if necessary, re-recorded on the same tape until perfect. All this is quite a few years off in terms of cinema usage, but it is an undeniable threat to those who have specialized in the use of film. When it comes, the change will be traumatic.

Film Music and Composers

One of the screen's greatest composers, the late Bernard Herrmann, once said: 'Music reaches people emotionally and links them in some mysterious way with what is taking place on the screen. It is the connecting link between celluloid and audience, reaching out and enveloping all into a single experience.'

Herrmann's view was fully understood in the silent days, when music played a key role in the success of a film. One leading director of silent movies estimated that nearly 50 per cent of a picture's emotional impact came from the music, whether it was played by a solo piano or a full orchestra. But with the advent of sound, a misunderstanding arose which dogged film music for several years. Quite simply, it was felt that the public would not accept music in films; they would want to know where it came from. Eventually, of course, this view proved to be false, but although music has been accepted in films for many years, even today its role is not fully understood.

For many people, film music means simply background music – something which is only noticed when the dialogue stops, and even then is dismissed as unimportant. This underestimates to an absurd degree the contribution music can make to a film. Sometimes composers are indeed asked merely to provide music which will create an atmosphere, reflect and highlight emotion, intensify or relax the pace of a film, and soothe or excite an audience.

Music can be used to achieve things which would otherwise be impossible in a film. For instance, scriptwriters are unable to use the novelists' device of interior monologue – references in the text to what the characters are thinking. However, in a film this can be conveyed by music.

Miklos Rozsa, a leading screen composer for over 40 years, put it this way: 'In films, music starts where words finish, when something can be telegraphed to the audience which neither action nor dialogue can express.' Rozsa speaks for many composers when he sums up his view of film music: 'Music should not illustrate a motion picture, but complete its psychological effect. I believe in foreground music. It is not salt or pepper to make the meat tastier or more palatable: it is one of the basic ingredients which form the art of film.'

The work of the composer

Although a composer has an important role to play, he is seldom involved in a film during shooting. He is usually hired during the course of production, and is brought in to start work when filming is completed. Occasionally, he may be given the opportunity to read the script in order to formulate some ideas. But many composers prefer to wait and see the completed film. John Williams, the foremost film composer in the world today, explains why: 'If I read a script, I cast it in my mind and imagine how it's going to look. I've been disappointed so many times at a finished film that I'd rather not read a script before it's made.'

Therefore the composer's work begins with a screening of a roughcut of the film. Often at this time, a 'temp-track' will be on the film. This consists of pre-recorded music (such as selections from albums of classical music) which the director and editor have been using to establish the mood of particular scenes. The film is then run again, with the producer, director, editor, and music editor in attendance. The composer discusses with the producer and director where music should be used in the film, a process known as spotting. The music editor notes where each music cue begins and ends, and then takes a print of the film to compile cue sheets.

To prepare these sheets, the music editor runs each reel of the film through a movieola which has a footage counter. This allows him to mark exactly where a cue begins and ends. He then lists all the dialogue and effects of the sequences which have been spotted, and the exact length of each cue.

At this point, the composer can begin writing the music for the film, having almost certainly sketched some themes from his first two view-

John Williams *(right), who has won Oscars for* Fiddler on the Roof, Jaws *and* Star Wars.

Brian Easdale *(far right) with the London Symphony Orchestra, recording the soundtrack for* Black Narcissus.

ings. Some composers run the film several more times; others work from the detailed cue sheets.

Orchestration

Because of the pressures of time, very few composers actually orchestrate their own scores. Instead, they write their music in an eight line sketch book, which is then passed to an orchestrator. With this system there is, inevitably, a danger that a score will emerge sounding rather different to the composer's intentions. But, as John Williams points out, it is possible through careful sketching to preserve a sound or a style. And as an additional protection, a composer usually works with the same orchestrator from picture to picture, thus ensuring that whoever completes the score is familiar with his work.

The need for an orchestrator becomes clear when one considers the work involved in a major film score. John Williams composed around 90 minutes of music for *Star Wars* (1977). The score ran to 900 pages; 500 of these pages were orchestrated by Williams' regular assistant, Herb Spencer, 100 by Williams himself, and the remainder by three other orchestrators. 'I sometimes think that as a musician, you don't have to be good, you just have to be strong,' says Williams, reflecting on the experience.

Recording

After the music has been orchestrated, it is ready to be recorded. Prior to the recording, the music editor will discuss with the composer whether he wants to use any devices to assist with the timing of the music. The most common timing aid is the click track. This is made by the music editor punching holes in the soundtrack of the film at regular intervals. The conductor and musicians hear on headphones resulting clicks from this track as it passes through the projector, allowing them to record music to a beat synchronized in advance with the timing of the film. The result is mathematically precise, but can produce a rather stilted performance.

Music in the Silent era

In order to see how film music has been used and has developed over the years it is necessary to return to the pre-talkie period. In those days, large theatres in the big cities boasted orchestras of up to 100 players, but in the majority of theatres, the musical accompaniment was the responsibility of one man, either a pianist or an organist. Most theatre organists had a tremendous repertoire, usually performed from memory, and the advantage over their piano-playing counterparts of having an instrument capable of imitating many orchestral colours.

The advent of the cue sheet revolutionized film music. Cue sheets were the earliest, crudest form of film scores, and consisted initially of selections from the popular classics, carefully timed to synchronize with the action on the screen.

As the popularity of the cue sheets grew, many of the music publishing houses employed staff composers to write appropriate mood music. Many were fast-working hacks who were not averse to plagiarizing the popular classics, but there were a number of serious composers at work. Outside America, classical composers such as Saint-Saëns and Shostakovich wrote scores for films, while in the United States composers like Mortimer Wilson were commissioned to write original scores for major productions such as Douglas Fairbanks' *The Thief of Bagdad* (1924).

The early years of sound

In 1926, synchronized sound was introduced to the public by Warner Brothers. Initially, the synchronized soundtracks consisted entirely of music and effects, as was the case with Warner Brothers' first Vitaphone feature, *Don Juan*. But within a year Al Jolson had told his mammy

Max Steiner *(far left) in his office at Warner Bros.*

Erich Wolfgang Korngold *(left) with fellow Warner Bros. contractee Bette Davis.*

and the audience that they ain't heard nothing yet, and dialogue was suddenly established in films. With it came a major problem: how to combine music and dialogue satisfactorily. Both had to be recorded at the same time in the early years, and the principal danger lay in drowning out long passages of dialogue with a full orchestra. The solution was provided by the addition of a new technician, the sound mixer. It was his job to control the various microphones used in sound recording. When music and dialogue were eventually recorded separately, his job became to combine the two on the final soundtrack.

The other problem concerning music in those early years was, as has been said, the belief that audiences would not accept music from an unidentified source. This notion led to some ludicrous results: in the Marx Brothers' first film *The Cocoanuts* (1929) 60 actors were hired to sit in a bandbox and pretend to play instruments whenever there was a musical number. In the end, they didn't even appear in the finished film, and it's safe to assume that audiences never bothered to consider where the music was coming from. Nevertheless, certain producers persisted in this attitude into the early thirties, so that in most films the only music derived from a clear source, such as a radio or record player.

Max Steiner

There was also a feeling that because dialogue was the primary novelty in films, background scoring was unnecessary. Just how wrong this view was would be demonstrated by a Viennese-born composer called Max Steiner.

Steiner had arrived in Hollywood in 1929 after an impressive musical career in Europe and New York. Initially, he worked on musical comedies, but within a very short time, he was appointed head of RKO's music department. His work consisted of writing music for the opening and closing credits of films, and occasionally some brief incidental music.

Steiner was encouraged to add more music to films when David O. Selznick took over as head of production at RKO. The result, in 1932, was a historic film score for the film *Symphony of Six Million*: for the first time in talkies, background music was used in almost half the picture, and from an unidentified source.

Steiner went on to pioneer the use of original scoring for films. *The Bird of Paradise* (1932), released a few months after *Symphony of Six Million*, included a Steiner score which ran throughout the film. Producers began to realize how effective music could be in a talking picture, and by the mid-thirties, a symphonic score was accepted as an integral part of a movie.

Steiner's first great film score of the early thirties was for *King Kong* in 1933. The most ambitious and elaborate score that had yet been attempted in Hollywood, *King Kong* remains an impressive achievement 47 years later. The composer's use of leitmotifs – individual themes associated with the various characters, locales, and dramatic events – was a traditional operatic device which transferred to film with great success. The score also catches much of the action on screen – mimicking aurally what is seen visually – and more importantly, it adds another dimension by revealing the emotions of the characters, particularly Kong himself. The music was also paced very accurately to match the tempo of the film.

This last point of co-ordinating the visual image with the musical pulse had interested Steiner from his earliest compositions. In 1935, while working on *The Informer*, a score which ultimately won him numerous awards, he pioneered the use of the click-track in features (the device had already been used in animation). With a few alterations, the techniques developed by Steiner are still in use today.

During the thirties and forties, Steiner became one of the most prolific composers in Hollywood. When he left RKO in 1936, he had written the music for about 135 films. In his next 30 years at Warner Bros. he wrote the scores for another 155. He won two Oscars – for *Now Voyager* (1942) and *Since You Went*

Franz Waxman

The Song of Bernadette *(right), for which Alfred Newman's score won an Oscar.*

Bernard Herrmann *(far right), whose scores include* Citizen Kane *and* Psycho, *was 'rediscovered' by the young directors of the 70s.*

Miklos Rozsa

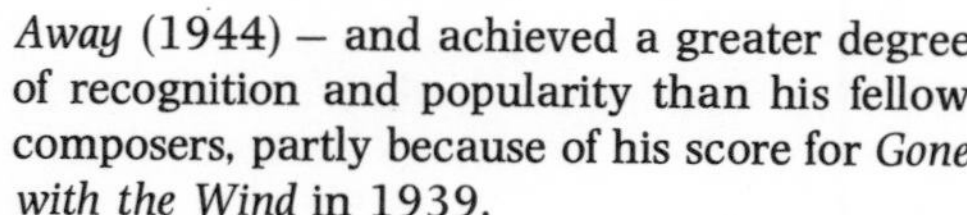

Away (1944) – and achieved a greater degree of recognition and popularity than his fellow composers, partly because of his score for *Gone with the Wind* in 1939.

Erich Wolfgang Korngold

It was another Viennese-born composer, though, who developed the symphonic film score to its highest level. Erich Wolfgang Korngold was a child prodigy who wrote many concert works before coming to Hollywood in 1934 to adapt Mendelssohn's music for *A Midsummer Night's Dream* (1935). He subsequently wrote the scores for pictures such as *Captain Blood* (1935), *The Adventures of Robin Hood* (1938) and *The Sea Hawk* (1940).

Korngold occupied a unique position. He chose his films with care, worked with a degree of freedom unknown to most composers, and developed the film score to an extraordinary degree. Even more than Steiner, he believed that the film script could be treated like an opera libretto. Thus his musical ideas were linked to characterization and the emotions expressed on the screen, and each idea was developed through the score as it would have been in concert music.

The late thirties and the forties

No other composer in Hollywood was in Korngold's position; but many impressive actors were produced in the late thirties and the forties, when the art of scoring was at its peak.

In Russia, Prokofiev was writing film music. His score for *Lieutenant Kije* (1934) eventually became a concert work in itself, as did his music for Eisenstein's *Alexander Nevsky* (1938). On the latter film, Eisenstein cut several sequences to music previously composed by Prokofiev. In England, composer Arthur Bliss wrote the score for *Things to Come* (1936), which became the first film to have its soundtrack released commercially. Another notable composer, William Walton, worked with Laurence Olivier on his films *Henry V* (1945) and *Hamlet* (1948), and Ralph Vaughan Williams contributed music to a number of films.

In America, composers such as Franz Waxman, Victor Young, David Raksin, Dmitri Tiomkin, Alfred Newman, Miklos Rozsa, and Bernard Herrmann produced outstanding scores. The latter three are particularly interesting. Newman, who was appointed musical director of Twentieth Century-Fox in 1940, was especially concerned to express the mood of a film, and was at his best writing highly emotional music. His characteristic sound, strings scored in their highest register, became permanently associated with Fox films right through to the fifties. His favourite score was for *The Song of Bernadette* (1943), which won him one of his nine Oscars, and showed at its peak his ability to translate intense emotion into music.

Miklos Rozsa and Bernard Herrmann

Hungarian-born Miklos Rozsa has written many memorable film scores in the past 40 years. Although distinctively Hungarian in many ways, his music has taken in the exotic qualities of *The Thief of Bagdad* (1940) and *The Jungle Book* (1967), the harshness of *The Killers* (1946) and *Brute Force* (1947), and the lush romanticism of *Madame Bovary* (1949) and *Lust for Life* (1956). In the fifties and early sixties, he composed the music for a series of historical and religious dramas, the most celebrated of which, *Ben-Hur* (1959), became the longest score ever written.

Like Rozsa, Herrmann came to prominence in the forties, and like Rozsa again, he had one of the most distinctive styles among film composers. This was largely to do with the fact that he insisted on orchestrating his scores himself: hence the 'Herrmann sound', often characterized by the woodwinds and brass playing in low registers. But Herrmann was the great individualist of film music; his combinations

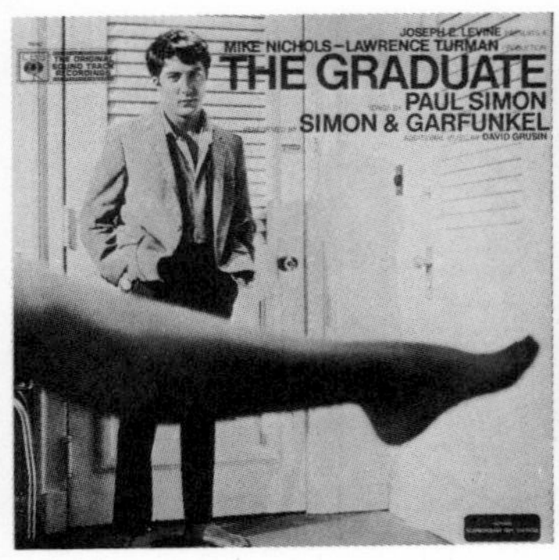

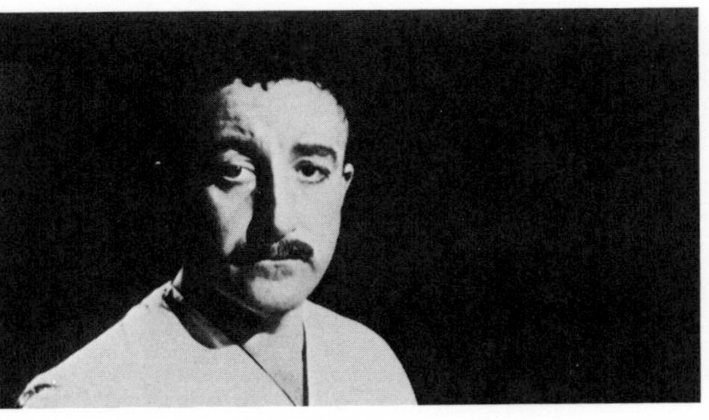

The Graduate *(far left), featuring the songs of Paul Simon, initiated a short-lived trend away from specially composed scores.*

Peter Sellers *(left) as Inspector Clouseau was one staple of the Pink Panther series; another was Henry Mancini's memorable theme tune.*

Leonard Bernstein

of instruments constantly altered, depending on what he thought a film required.

His first score was for Orson Welles' *Citizen Kane* (1941). Just as Welles created his masterpiece with this film, so Herrmann – who was just 30 at the time – produced one of the finest film scores ever, running through a remarkable gamut of styles: from the mysterious and atmospheric opening in the deserted grounds of Xanadu, through pastiche newsreel music, waltz themes, an aria from an opera . . . the list goes on and on. Rarely has a score been such an integral part of a film, and rarely has a composer worked with a director in the way Herrmann worked with Welles. Given 12 weeks to write the music, Herrmann could watch the film coming together with his music as an essential element in its construction.

Other memorable Herrmann scores from the forties and fifties include the Oscar-winning *All That Money Can Buy* (1941), the beautiful *The Ghost and Mrs Muir* (1947), and his films with Alfred Hitchcock, beginning with *The Trouble With Harry* in 1955. His finest work for Hitchcock was undoubtedly the score for *Vertigo* (1958), closely followed by *North By Northwest* (1959) and *Psycho* (1960). The latter demonstrated the excellence with which he could match a score to a film: Hitchcock having made a black and white film, Herrmann decided to create a 'black and white sound', using only the string section of the orchestra. The result is probably the most chilling score composed for a horror film, and it has been imitated innumerable times since, notably in the music for *Jaws* (1975).

Jazz and pop influences

By the early sixties, it was becoming clear that symphonic scores were falling out of favour. Composers such as Alex North and Leonard Bernstein had demonstrated the effectiveness of jazz music for films in the fifties with two important scores: North's *A Streetcar Named Desire* (1951), and Bernstein's *On The Waterfront* (1954). The latter in particular made a strong impact, combining the rhythms of jazz with the dynamics of the symphony orchestra. Other notable jazz scores included Elmer Bernstein's *The Man with the Golden Arm* (1955) and Leith Stevens' *The Wild One* (1953).

However, the jazz score which really changed the shape of film music in the sixties was written by Henry Mancini for the television series *Peter Gunn*. Released as an album, it sold over a million copies. Producers realized that music could be used to sell films, and began demanding 'marketable' scores. The result was that composers like Herrmann and Rozsa fell completely out of favour, while composers such as Francis Lai, Maurice Jarre and Michel Legrand, who wrote blander material which was more likely to sell records, flourished. The results were hit movie songs like Jarre's theme for *Dr Zhivago* (1965) and Lai's insidious score for *A Man and a Woman* (1966).

A number of fine scores were produced in the sixties, but largely by composers who tended to draw on jazz and pop influences, rather than the symphonic tradition. The British composer John Barry established his name with the Bond films, which typified much of the film music of the time: orchestral, but in a jazz idiom, and with a marketable theme song.

Theme songs had been popular with producers since the forties, when David Raksin's theme from *Laura* (1944) was released to astonishing success. But in the sixties, songs were used not just as theme music, but in many cases as the entire musical soundtrack of films. This practice, which was really started by the success of the Simon and Garfunkel songs on the soundtrack of *The Graduate* (1967), nearly rendered the art of film music obsolete.

Symphonic scores in the seventies

Then, in the early seventies, a resurgence began. A closely-knit group of young directors, who were establishing themselves in Hollywood, discovered the work of composers such as

Doctor Zhivago *(right) had Maurice Jarre's hit theme music as a distinct promotional bonus.*

John Barry

Herrmann, Korngold, and Steiner.

Brian De Palma was the first to act, hiring Herrmann – who had not worked in Hollywood since 1966 – to write the score for *Sisters* (GB: *Blood Sisters*) in 1972. Herrmann went on to write the scores for Larry Cohen's *It's Alive* (1974), De Palma's *Obsession* (1976), and Scorsese's *Taxi Driver* (1976), the last score he wrote before he died in 1975; Scorsese dedicated the film to his memory.

The face of movie music was changing again. Orchestral scores gew in popularity, and composers like Ernest Gold, an Oscar-winner for *Exodus* in 1960, once again found themselves in demand. Among the busiest composers of the seventies were: the late Jerry Fielding (*The Wild Bunch, Lawman, The Gauntlet*); Lalo Schifrin (*Dirty Harry, The Four Musketeers*); David Shire (*The Hindenberg, Farewell My Lovely, Old Boyfriends*); Bill Conti (*An Unmarried Woman*); Dave Grusin (*Three Days of the Condor, The Electric Horseman*); John Barry (*Robin and Marian, King Kong*); Marvin Hamlisch (*The Sting, The Way We Were, The Spy Who Loved Me*); Henry Mancini, whose music for films such as the *Pink Panther* series remained extremely popular; and the Italian composer Ennio Morricone, who made his name with Sergio Leone's spaghetti westerns, *A Fistful of Dollars* and *For A Few Dollars More*.

Perhaps the busiest composer throughout the sixties and seventies was Jerry Goldsmith, a graduate from television, at home with adventure films such as *The Blue Max, The Great Train Robbery*, and *Capricorn One*, spy films like the *Our Man Flint* series, war films, *Tora Tora Tora* and *Patton*, and science-fiction and horror films, *Planet of the Apes, Magic* and *Alien*.

By the end of the seventies, it was clear that the symphonic film score was once again important in Hollywood. Miklos Rozsa, for instance, who had only worked sporadically during the sixties, adapted his violin concerto for Billy Wilder's *The Private Life of Sherlock Holmes* in 1970, and then wrote the original scores for *The Golden Voyage of Sinbad* (1973), Resnais' *Providence* (1977), Wilder's *Fedora* (1978), and most recently, Nicholas Meyer's fantasy *Time After Time* (1979).

However, the composer who has become virtually a one-man industry in this field is a relatively young writer: John Williams. Another television graduate, he began writing for films in the early sixties. His projects ranged from the interesting – Don Siegel's version of *The Killers* (1964) – to the ridiculous – *Gidget Goes to Rome* (1963). He won the first of his three Oscars as musical director on *Fiddler on the Roof* (1971), and earned praise for scores like *The Reivers* (1969), *The Long Goodbye* (1973), *Earthquake* (1974) and *The Towering Inferno* (1974).

It was his collaboration with director Steven Spielberg that produced his first enormously popular score: *Jaws* (1975), for which he won his second Oscar. Williams' music added to the picture enormously, creating moments of great menace – particularly with the shark's theme, described by the composer as 'the thump-thump theme' – and moments of high excitement, with music in the mould of Korngold.

In fact, the two composers Williams most resembles, and whose influences he admits quite openly, are Herrmann and Korngold. The former can be heard clearly in Williams' scores for *Jaws, Close Encounters of the Third Kind* (1977) and *The Fury* (1978), while the latter is most apparent in *Superman* (1978) and Williams' third Oscar-winner, *Star Wars*.

The importance of this last score cannot be underestimated. It is no exaggeration to say that it single-handedly restored the traditional symphonic score to its old prominence. Not only was the film enormously popular, but so too was the score, selling over one and a half million copies in America soon after its release in 1977 – proof that symphonic film music can be commercially viable. Viable to such an extent, in fact, that Williams' music for the *Star Wars* sequel, *The Empire Strikes Back*, was actually issued before the film: a move which will be welcomed by anyone who believes that symphonic music is the finest way of forging what Bernard Herrmann described as that 'connecting link between celluloid and audience'.

Stunts

Times have changed. In the silent movie days, there were few veteran stuntmen. They either got injured, got killed or got out. Their average professional life was about five years. Stunting today is not exactly safer. But perhaps more care is taken. Recently, for *Highpoint* (1979), stuntman Dar Robinson was reportedly paid $100,000 to leap off the world's highest building, the 1822-foot CN Tower in Toronto. He jumped, reached a speed of 125 mph, then opened a hidden parachute only 375 feet from the ground. He had taken specialist advice from NASA, as well as a practice leap off the top of the Houston Astrodome and claimed he had been developing the jump for two years. Robinson escaped unhurt because he had taken precautions, but there is always an element of luck.

For *Hooper* (1978), his friend A. J. Bakunas had jumped out of a helicopter flying at 237 feet and landed safely in a crash pad, a large inflatable canvas bag filled with hydrogen. For *Steel* (1979), Bakunas jumped off a building over 350 feet high and again landed on a crash pad. Star Lee Majors remembers: 'He broke the top seam and went through the top of the bag and the second layer alone wasn't enough to save him. It was tough. He lived for about fifteen hours.'

Majors' cool attitude to the dangers of stunting is not shared by all film personnel. Veteran British stuntman Derek Ware recalls 'the novel experience, while hanging from a window cleaner's cradle 150 feet up the side of a building with the comedian Michael Crawford hanging from my feet, of observing the director on the ground below trying to direct the scene with his back turned. The poor man just couldn't stand heights. And the most ironic story concerns a stuntgirl, who having fallen 30 feet into a net which broke causing her to fracture her leg and nose, was unable to get into the first aid tent, because it was occupied by the director who had fainted.'

When other film technicians make a mistake, a retake is almost always possible though perhaps expensive. If a stuntman makes a mistake or runs out of luck, he can be dead or paralyzed. Any fall is dangerous. Crash pads can break. Water can be as hard as concrete if you hit it from the wrong angle. Stuntman Eddie Powell leapt just 40 feet into the ocean for *The Sea Wolves* (1980) and ruptured his spleen.

Derek Ware remembers a recent stunt which involved hanging by one hand from a loading bay, then dropping 72 feet into the River Thames. There were dangers other than the fall itself: 'I had to take the fall looking up because, if I tilted my head forward to try and see where I was falling, I might tip my point of balance and land on my side or, worse, my stomach. I was wearing a wetsuit and a cricket box (protecting the genitals) under my clothing, but no other padding. The wetsuit was protection against the impact of the water and any foreign bodies in it. The Thames is notorious for its pollution and I'd picked up a few grazes and abrasions in previous scenes, so I preferred not to run the risk of possible infection. (He has regular tetanus and typhoid injections.) My final preparation before the drop was to plug my ears with cotton wool and drink half a cup of milk laced with brandy. That helps keep the river water out of my system or at least cut the toxic content of it in half if I swallow any. . . . At least, that's what I tell myself.' When the scene was filmed, the cameras shot at a slightly higher speed than normal so that the jump, when projected at normal speed, would take longer and therefore look bigger.

Stunts may not always be what they appear. For the cliff-jumping scene in *Butch Cassidy and The Sundance Kid* (1969), the two stars jumped off the cliff on to a platform a few feet below the edge. The rest of the jump was made several weeks later by two stuntmen at the Fox Ranch in Malibu. They jumped off a 70 foot crane into water stirred up by a dozen outboard motors simulating rapids. The cliffs from the original location were painted on glass and their stunt shot through this fake landscape. Then their jump was cut on to the end of the stars' jump.

Shenandoah *(above right): the use of a concealed trampoline aids the illusion of a soldier blown up by cannon-fire.*

It's a Mad Mad Mad Mad World *(centre right): stuntmen propelled by air-rams on to fake telegraph wires rely on the air bags below for safety.*

Bullitt *(below right): stuntman Paul Nuckles crashes through a 'glass' door while doubling for Pat Renella.*

Fist fights

Stuntmen almost never actually hit each other when staging a fist fight. Derek Ware recalls: 'I was once asked by a young director if I would take a punch on the jaw, in the furtherance of the realistic drama he was producing. I agreed to do it for an extra £500. The director expressed surprise and muttered that he thought "stuntmen were supposed to be tough". I pointed out that it was Monday and I had work to do for the rest of the week and the week after, and that I wouldn't be able to do any of it with a split lip, let alone a broken jaw with contusions, or facial paralysis. Nothing looks sadder than an injured stuntman.'

Ware also describes 'the pleasure of watching the late Alan Ladd throwing a punch on a film set. His only direction to the actor he was aiming at was: "As my hand passes across your face, flick your head so that your hat flies off and hits that arc lamp over there." The director called "Action", the punch was thrown, the actor did as he was told and the shot was perfect, even though Alan Ladd's fist missed his opponent's jaw by 18 inches. So that's the secret of punch-ups. The whole thing is choreographed like a dance. The punches are masked deliberately or angled away from the camera. Sound effects are added afterwards. And the illusion is complete.'

Leaping and flying

Probably the most original stunting has been seen in the James Bond films, most of it devised and directed by the Briton Bob Simmons. He has achieved original effects with fire and explosives, using trampolines and air ramps to hurl the stuntmen into the air or across the set with the force of an explosion. An air ramp incorporates a platform which is activated by compressed air to hurl a figure upwards. Trampolines and air ramps are used to facilitate many of the leaps and dives in the 'Kung Fu' films, and they enable 'Wonder Woman' to make her remarkable vertical take-offs.

The current fashionable technique is flying on wires; this is used in *Superman* (1978), *The Empire Strikes Back* (1980) and *Flash Gordon* (1980). However, Derek Ware does not consider this to be stuntwork at all. 'I was doing it in theatrical productions of *Peter Pan* at the age of nine. It takes a bit of practice and good body control, depending on whether you're flying on a single wire, a hip harness (two wires) or a three wire rig, but there's nothing in it that a reasonably fit person couldn't pick up in a day.'

Shots which involve the breaking of glass are usually arranged by the special effects man.

'In the old days,' says Derek Ware, 'Fake "glass" was made of boiled sugar like a boiled sweet. The trouble was that it had to be kept refrigerated right up until you were ready to use it, otherwise it would melt under the lights and get tacky. The same with "resin" glass, which would powder rather than shatter. Today we've got "santalite", which is very brittle clear plastic quite like bakelite. It doesn't make a sound like glass shattering, but the sound effects department can add a smash sound afterwards. It's totally safe so long as you cover your face with your hands or forearms.'

British stuntman Ray Austin (now a TV director) was one of the few people who used to be prepared to jump through a genuine plate-glass window. 'The secret is,' he says, 'speed and the landing. You must beat the falling glass to the floor. It's much safer having glass fall on you than you on it.'

Stunting with horses

Getting animals to jump through glass is even more difficult. On *The Wind and The Lion* (1975), stunt co-ordinator Mickey Gilbert bolted a horse through a plate-glass window by taping two halves of ping-pong balls painted like eyes over the animal's real eyes.

In Britain and North America, such effects are carefully monitored by animal protection organizations. The carnage on films like *Ben-Hur* (1925) where over 100 horses were killed and, particularly, *The Charge of the Light Brigade* (1936) where several horses were also killed led to strict controls.

Particularly controversial was – and still is – the use of the 'Running W', a device for felling horses at the gallop. Design details can vary but, very simply, it involves a rope or wire attached to padding and rings on both front legs of the horse. This 'cable' runs through rings on a band round the horse's belly. The band is attached to the saddle. And the measured cable is anchored to a specific point on the ground, so that the fall will happen in front

Ben-Hur *(above far left): stuntman Joe Yrigoyen, working under the direction of Yakima Canutt, first crashes his chariot over a buried ramp, then (above left) is dragged around the arena on a sled hidden beneath him by the dust.*

The Wild Bunch *(below left): a horse is felled by a 'Running W' device.*

The Italian Job *(right): two sequence shots of a stunt devised by Remy Julienne in which a speeding mini-car is driven into a moving van – about a week's work ended up as a few seconds on screen.*

of the camera. When the galloping horse has run the length of the cable, the cable becomes taut, both the horse's front legs are automatically pulled up to its belly (with the strain of the jerk acting on the saddle, not the legs), the horse falls, the cable snaps (because of a special ring system), the horse somersaults, theoretically comes to his feet and continues running.

Doyen of American stuntmen Yakima Canutt is credited with the invention of this device and in John Baxter's book *Stunt*, he says: 'You hear stories about horses with their legs pulled off and all this stuff. Well, this is a load of nonsense. It's like anything else. If you did it right, it was all right. But, unfortunately, somebody will always see it done a few times, then offer to do it at half price and, if he didn't know how to do it, he would go out and cripple a horse. I myself, personally, rode 300 Running Ws and never crippled a horse.' (The stunt is now banned in North America and much of Europe.)

Canutt is also credited with the creation of the 'L' stirrup, open at one side, which allows a rider to fall or jump from his horse without trapping his feet. Of course, sometimes the plot requires that the rider's foot *is* trapped in the stirrup, dragging the stuntman along in the dirt. In this case, a 'drag leather' is used: a long leather strap (or wire) attached to the stirrup and saddle, then threaded up the trouser-leg to the hip, where it is either attached to a body harness or simply held by the stuntman. When he disconnects the strap, it whips down and out of his trouser-leg, leaving him behind. The strap is hidden in the dust as the horse rides off.

Stunting in cars

Nowadays, though, the car-chase has replaced the horse-chase and the car-crash has replaced the horse-fall. Doors are loosened if a car has to be blown up and welded if it has to roll over (to lessen the risk of a door buckling in on the driver). Bars strengthen the roof and a reinforced cocoon of metal may be built around the driving compartment. A crashing car will have its petrol tank emptied and replaced by a small container carrying only enough fuel for the sequence. But there is always the unexpected.

Peter Brayham, the man who jumped London's Tower Bridge in a car for *Brannigan* (1975) remembers having to drive an opened-top car up a ramp and over another moving car for *Sitting Target* (1972). He took off at 55–60 mph. 'When you jump a car,' he says, 'you have to get your engine back into second gear so that you've got traction to stop you. At first, all you see is the bonnet of the car. You don't see anything else because the car's pointing upwards. As I came down, I got my traction, the front dropped to the ground and the steering wheel snapped off in my hands. . . .' (After ploughing through a brick wall, he escaped with a couple of grazes on his forehead.)

Stunting with fire

There are always risks, even on big-budget movies. Experienced director Lewis Gilbert says, 'Really, you're very lucky if you don't have accidents on a Bond movie. It's pretty hair-raising stuff when you've got about 400 people running around with explosions going off all around them. However much you rehearse, someone is always going to do the wrong thing at the wrong time and run into a damned explosion.' On *The Spy Who Loved Me* (1977), Gilbert says, a stuntman was badly burned during explosions on the enormous set: 'Something hit him in the back of the neck and stuck there, burning away furiously. It was nasty. He got bad burns and he's had to have quite a lot of skin-grafting.'

Fire, again, can have unexpected dangers. Stuntmen wear fireproof underwear, suits and gloves, face-masks and miniature breathing apparatus designed for high-altitude parachutists. Derek Ware says, 'Fire is easy to work with, as long as you don't panic. But that's much easier said than done.' In a film studio, gas

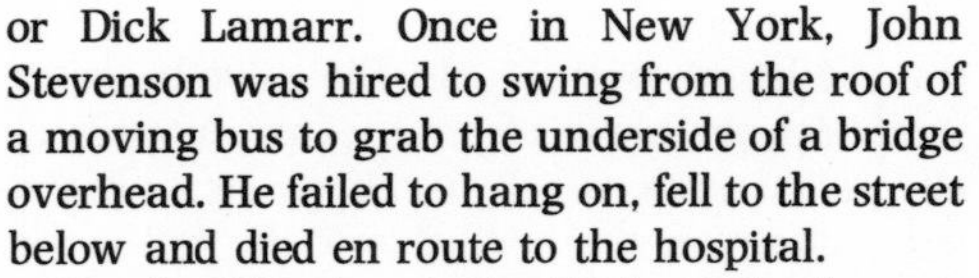

The Towering Inferno *(above far left): the 70s cycle of disaster movies demanded ever more sophisticated stunt-work.*

Witchfinder General *(above left): the fire is safely between the camera and the girl at the stake (above).*

pipes can be hidden round the sets, allowing controlled flames at the turn of a knob. On location work, petroleum jelly can be smeared on surfaces. 'It's like a very thick glue,' Ware explains, 'which burns brightly but doesn't give off a great deal of heat. When you smear it on thickly, it'll burn for a short time without the material it's stuck to catching fire at all. You can only keep this up for 30 seconds at most, but that's more than enough time on screen.' As the screen fire gets more and more out of control, a multi-facetted gas-jet can create flames safely between camera and stuntmen.

One aid for fire stunts is the Bowie Flame Harness developed by Les Bowie. This is a jacket and body-harness with a built-in gas burner connected to a pocket-sized butane gas bottle. The jacket is impregnated with petroleum jelly and, using a hand-held switch, the stuntman can set himself on fire and control the flames at will.

Stunt women

Female stunt artists have been fundamental to the development of stunting. The heroines of the silent film era, Pearl White and Ruth Roland, did more than anyone else to put stuntmen and stunt women on the map. Until 1914 any hazardous scenes in a film were considered part of the story line and the actors contracted to play the parts were expected to carry them out. The same principle applied to comic actors; knockabout and tumbling were their bread and butter. Mack Sennett's Keystone Kops have been described as 'the poorest paid stuntmen in Hollywood', because they took all those falls and car crashes for a basic rate as part of their performances. Additional fees for chases and tumbles were neither expected nor paid.

As Pearl White's scripts became more ambitious, the producers decided that a double should undertake the hazardous scenes. However, in 1915 the age of equality between the sexes had yet to come. The job usually went to small men: in Hollywood to Eddie Kelly or Dick Lamarr. Once in New York, John Stevenson was hired to swing from the roof of a moving bus to grab the underside of a bridge overhead. He failed to hang on, fell to the street below and died en route to the hospital.

Pearl White's rival, Ruth Roland, was doubled by Bob Rose, who is alive today and remembers running along the roofs of trains, being carried through burning buildings, and once transferring from a seaplane down a rope-ladder to a motor-boat: all activities then deemed unsuitable for a female.

Helen Holmes was the first serial star to boast a female double: Helen Gibson. The wife of Hoot Gibson, the silent cowboy star, Helen started out as a trick rider. But her abilities as the screen's first stunt woman came to surpass her feats on horseback, culminating with a stunt far ahead of its time, leaping a speeding motorcycle on to a roaring locomotive. She went on to replace Helen Holmes in the *Hazards of Helen* series (1915) and became a star in her own right.

With the coming of sound and the organization of Film Unions in Hollywood, stunt women also found their voice. Today the Sex Equality Act has made it mandatory that stuntmen cannot double for actresses unless the stunt has first been refused by a stuntgirl. Needless to say, such refusals are very rare.

Stunt women have been hard at work for decades. Audrey Scott's fifty-year career as a horsewoman saw her doubling everyone from Billy Dove in the silents, to Lucille Ball in the hunting scene in *Mame* (1974), and handling any form of horseflesh from a six horse stagecoach team to a bucking mule. Nowadays, the queen of stunt women is Kitty O'Neill, the deaf mute Cherokee Indian girl who can fall 180 feet and holds the women's land speed record of 618 mph.

Stuntmen and women are aware that it is the little, unexpected details, which the average filmgoer doesn't think about, that can be the killers and maimers. There's a saying in the stunt business: 'When they get to know your first name in hospital, you've made it.'

THE PRODUCT

Anatomy of the Movies All-Time Hit Lists

The Anatomy of the Movies All-Time Hit Lists have been compiled by Joel W. Finler and David Pirie in consultation with *The Economist* magazine. The aim has been to establish the best possible audience comparison between movies of different periods in cinema history. No figures are available which measure the audiences for individual films directly. However, a close assessment of a film's audience can be made from the earnings of the company which produced it (in trade terms, the film's 'rental'). The lists have been compiled from rental figures reported in *Variety*, *The Motion Picture Almanac* and from the records of the film companies themselves. Rentals from the US and Canada only have been considered; this is the biggest film market in the world, and often provides as much as two thirds of a film's total earnings. So that the lists are not weighted in favour of older films, only the sum made by each film on initial release has been considered; with very few exceptions films earn the bulk of their rental during this period. Re-release earnings are usually small.

Certain acclaimed box-office successes, like *My Fair Lady* and *West Side Story*, have had their rentals adjusted downwards by *Variety* some years after release. In such cases the lower figure has been adopted here.

Inflation

For a sensible comparison of the rentals of movies from different periods, the figures must be adjusted to allow for inflation. The most famous movie league table, *Variety*'s indispensable chart of 'All-Time Rental Champs', ignores inflation altogether. Well-acknowledged flops of the 1970s, such as *Myra Breckinridge*, appear on the *Variety* chart, while a 1940s success like *The Big Sleep* does not; if inflation is taken into account the older film earned more than five times as much. To provide a truer comparison an inflation factor is here awarded to each film, based on the period in which its rental was principally earned. Taking 1979, the most recent year for which rental figures are available, as the base year, a series of multiples has been compiled. These are calculated partly on the cost of living index, but principally on the rise in cinema ticket prices in the US and Canada. Ticket prices are the major element, because the intention is to compare the sizes of the audience for each film rather than the purchasing power of the producers' rentals. In those cases where a film was released late in the year prior to a jump in the inflation factor, it has been awarded the factor which applies to the succeeding year. (For this reason, in some cases the date against a film in the lists which follow will be different from the date given elsewhere in this book.)

The adjusted total is therefore the nearest possible approximation to the rental a film would have earned, had it been released in the base year of 1979.

Profitability

The lists do not reflect profitability. *Cleopatra* emerges as the twentieth biggest hit of all time, but so much was spent on its production that it was also one of the biggest flops, in terms of profit, in movie history. By the same token *Jaws II* achieves a substantial $55.7m. in inflation-adjusted rentals and scrapes into the top 50 just ahead of *Bonnie and Clyde*, which is in fact Number 51. *Jaws II* was certainly a hit picture, but it cost $25m. to make and so much was spent on national TV and poster campaigns that it was certainly less profitable than *Bonnie and Clyde*.

Hit movies by genre

The genre lists of hit movies, which appear at the beginning of each of the following nine chapters, necessarily include films which achieved much lower rentals than does the All-Time Top 50 and are consequently slightly less accurate where bunching occurs at the bottom of a category; in the case of horror – until recently the almost exclusive preserve of small companies looking for small profits on low budgets – it has been necessary to include rentals well below $10m. to complete the list. Sometimes it has proved impossible to arrive at a satisfactory rental figure for a well-known film: Universal's *Dracula* (1930) with Bela Lugosi, for example, appears to have enjoyed less success on first release than is supposed, partly because Universal was unable to book it into a sufficient number of movie theatres. Though no movie appears on more than one genre hit list, some movies bridge two genres and are mentioned in two chapters. For example, the 1950s cycle of science fiction/horror films, like *The Beast from 20,000 Fathoms*, *Invasion of the Body Snatchers* and *Them*, is inevitably discussed under both headings.

Selected runners-up

Appended to each genre list are 'selected runners-up'; these are movies which were unplaced but either came close or are sufficiently famous to be included for the sake of comparison.

1980 hits

At the time of going to press rental figures for 1980 have not been released. Those films which reliable reports already indicate would appear on the genre lists, if figures were available, are included beneath the appropriate list.

The All-Time Top 50 *(right)*: *Gone with the Wind* emerges so far ahead of its nearest rival, *Star Wars*, that there can be no question that it would appear as number one, no matter what form of adjustment for inflation was made and without considering its massive re-release earnings or the huge sums accrued from its sale to television. David O. Selznick's sale of the rights to MGM in the 1940s still ranks as one of the biggest business errors in Hollywood history.

But *Gone with the Wind*'s success does not detract from the enormous achievement of *Star Wars* which, after all, dates from the post-television era. And George Lucas's film is only the most spectacular example of the massive success of 1970s films on the list. One of the prime objects of producing a list adjusted for inflation is to see just how well the 1970s has performed as a movie decade once the bias of inflation is eliminated. In the event the 1970s stand out dramatically, contributing nearly 50 per cent of the top 50; the 1960s, 1950s and 1940s bunch together in descending order with 24, 20 and 14 per cent of the list respectively. The 1930s contribute only two films (4 per cent).

The relative strengths of the decades are quantified more accurately by breaking down the chart on a points basis, awarding 50 points for Number One, 49 for Number Two and so on down to 1 point for Number 50. On this basis the 1970s amass 523 points, while the 1960s and 1950s run each other very close with 288 and 282 points respectively. The 1940s trail with 106 and the two films from the 1930s total 83. The low figure for the 1940s may seem odd, since this was undoubtedly a decade of mass moviegoing, but only a few films stood out sufficiently far from the overall output to accumulate really huge audiences. It was a profitable period precisely because so many films made good money, even if few became massive hits. Conversely the success of the 1970s in terms of hits can be explained partly by Hollywood's increasing concentration on blockbusters – high budget films backed by massive advertising campaigns. But in itself the explanation is insufficient. *One Flew over the Cuckoo's Nest*, *Rocky*, *American Graffiti* or *Animal House* are not blockbusters in any recognizable sense – none of them cost very much and their success appears to have surprised the studios which made them almost as much as it surprised everybody else.

All-Time Box Office Hits

		Rental income from initial release period: $m.	Inflation factor	Adjusted total: $m.
1	Gone with the Wind, 1939	31	×10	310
2	Star Wars, 1977	164.8	×1.1	181.3
3	The Sound of Music, 1965	72	×2.5	180
4	The Ten Commandments, 1956	34.2	×5	171
5	Jaws, 1975	121.3	×1.25	151.6
6	Ben Hur, 1959	36.65	×4	146.6
7	The Godfather, 1972	85.7	×1.5	128.5
8	Around the World in Eighty Days, 1956	22	×5	110
9	Dr Zhivago, 1966	43	×2.5	107.5
10	Grease, 1978	93.3	×1.1	102.6
11	The Robe, 1953	17.5	×5.5	96.3
12	The Sting, 1973	68.45	×1.4	95.9
13	The Exorcist, 1973	66.3	×1.4	92.8
14	The Graduate, 1967	43.1	×2	86.2
15	Close Encounters of the Third Kind, 1977	77	×1.1	84.7
16	Superman, 1979	81	×1	81
17	Saturday Night Fever, 1977	73.5	×1.1	80.8
18	Snow White, 1938	8	×10	80
19	West Side Story, 1961	19.5	×4	78.2
20	Cleopatra, 1963	26	×3	78
21	Mary Poppins, 1965	31	×2.5	77.5
22	This is the Army, 1943	8.5	×9	76.5
23	Love Story, 1970	50	×1.5	75
24	South Pacific, 1958	16.5	×4.5	74.2
25	The Best Years of Our Lives, 1946	10.4	×7	72.8
26	One Flew Over the Cuckoo's Nest, 1976	59	×1.2	70.8
27	The Greatest Show on Earth, 1952	12.8	×5.5	70.4
28	Duel in the Sun, 1947	10	×7	70
	The Towering Inferno, 1974	50	×1.4	70
30	Animal House, 1978	63.5	×1.1	69.8
31	The Bridge on the River Kwai, 1957	15	×4.5	67.5
	Goldfinger, 1964	22.5	×3	67.5
	Thunderball, 1965	27	×2.5	67.5
34	From Here to Eternity, 1953	12.2	×5.5	67.1
	Smokey and the Bandit, 1977	61	×1.1	67.1
36	Airport, 1970	44.5	×1.5	66.7
37	Rocky, 1976	54	×1.2	64.8
38	The Longest Day, 1962	17.6	×3.5	61.6
39	Sergeant York, 1941	6	×10	60
	White Christmas, 1954	12	×5	60
41	The Poseidon Adventure, 1973	42	×1.4	58.8
42	Going My Way, 1944	6.5	×9	58.5
43	Butch Cassidy and the Sundance Kid, 1969	29.2	×2	58.4
44	Quo Vadis, 1952	10.5	×5.5	57.7
45	American Graffiti, 1973	41.2	×1.4	57.6
46	It's a Mad Mad Mad Mad World, 1963	19	×3	57
47	For Whom the Bell Tolls, 1943	6.3	×9	56.7
48	Bells of St Marys, 1946	8	×7	56
	Spartacus, 1960	14	×4	56
50	Jaws II, 1978	50.6	×1.1	55.7

1980 The Empire Strikes Back, Kramer vs. Kramer

Note: Some doubt surrounds the accuracy of the Dr Zhivago *figure which varies widely according to source.*

Westerns

The western, as we are all tired of being told, is *le cinéma Américain par excellence.* In fact, the failure of the 1970s to produce any consistent strain of western (despite some individual films as good as any ever made) to follow the 'psychological/social' model of the 1950s (*Shane, High Noon*) or the 'apocalyptic' breed of the 1960s (Sergio Leone, Sam Peckinpah) might be taken as proof that both film-makers and audiences have finally become too self-consciously 'aware' of the genre, too frozen in their attitudes ever to be able to create and respond to it freely again. Throughout film history, there have been critics ill-advised enough to grab a headline by announcing that they have just witnessed the death of the western. Although that continued in the 1970s (Pauline Kael, *New Yorker*, February 25, 1974), there seems to have been more a general assumption that – if not actually dead – it has been quietly put out to pasture, an attitude shared not only by critics: unless they starred Clint Eastwood, western projects have recently been finding finance hard to come by. This vague feeling that a funeral was somewhere taking place must also have had something to do with the subject of ageing and mood of elegy that overtook the genre as its most stalwart figures reached their twilight glory, from the supports (Ben Johnson in *The Last Picture Show*) to the stars (John Wayne in *True Grit* and *The Shootist*).

In retrospect, the 1970s may prove one of the western's most fascinating decades: a time when it continued to evolve creatively (albeit sporadically) while scarcely surviving commercially. The western still perhaps 'exemplifies' the American cinema, in a significantly perverse way. Where once it was the 'horse opera', the bread-and-butter of studio production lines (the industry even compiled separate annual lists of its top box-office stars and its top *western* box-office stars), it has now almost become Hollywood's underground art form, an endangered species of true cinematic invention in an age when the conglomerate packagers of entertainment might feel that it is too old-fashioned, or otherwise unsuited for galvanizing the mass audience. If the 'gimmick' has been the keynote of mainstream American production in the 1970s, then the western has gone the way of a lonelier, less merchandisable eccentricity (although the casting coup of *The Missouri Breaks* with Jack Nicholson and Marlon Brando must have seemed a good box-office idea). The decade saw a certain grizzled refinement of traditional themes and forms that has brought out the best in some veterans (Sam Peckinpah's *Pat Garrett and Billy the Kid*, Don Siegel's *The Shootist*). By the end of the 1970s, however, an unhealthily large responsibility for the future of the genre seemed to have devolved on Clint Eastwood – as one of the few certifiably 'bankable' stars left and a director of some promise, particularly in his westerns (*High Plains Drifter, The Outlaw Josey Wales*). Into the 1980s, even Eastwood's presence, behind and in front of the camera, has been unable to ensure the success of *Bronco Billy*, and the 'gimmick' of *The Long Riders* – actor brothers playing outlaw brothers – has failed to break the commercial curse on the western subject.

In retrospect, of course, something revolutionary seems to have happened to the western in every decade of its existence. It had just about atrophied in the 1920s before being revived by the epics *The Covered Wagon* and *The Iron Horse*; the 1930s was the great age of the B-western and of such popular offshoots as the singing cowboy; 1940, according to André Bazin, 'was a major milestone', the year when the classicism of *Stagecoach* began to tip towards the 'Super-western'; Philip French refers to 'the watershed year of 1950 when, in a mere four months, Hollywood released Delmer Daves' first western, *Broken Arrow*, Anthony Mann's first two cowboy movies, *Devil's Doorway* and *Winchester '73*, John Ford's thoughtful *Wagonmaster* and Henry King's *The Gunfighter*'. The fact that only two of the above-mentioned films, *The Covered Wagon* and *Broken Arrow*, make it into the list of all-time rental champs (although *Winchester '73* only just misses and was one of the top-grossing films of its year)

Jason Robards *(right) raises the flag over his desert water-hole – a private-enterprise oasis – in Sam Peckinpah's elegiac western,* The Ballad of Cable Hogue.

All-Time Hit Westerns

		Rental income from initial release period: $m.	Inflation factor	Adjusted total: $m.
1	Duel in the Sun, 1947	10	×7	70
2	Butch Cassidy and the Sundance Kid, 1969	29.2	×2	58.4
3	Shane, 1953	8	×5.5	44
4	How the West Was Won, 1962	12.2	×3.5	42.7
5	Unconquered, 1947	5.3	×7	37.1
6	The Outlaw, 1946	5.1	×7	35.7
7	The Covered Wagon, 1923	3.5	×10	35
8	Jeremiah Johnson, 1972	21.6	×1.5	32.4
9	The Alamo, 1960	7.9	×4	31.6
10	Red River, 1948	4.5	×7	31.5
11	Little Big Man, 1969	15	×2	30
12	The Tall Men, 1956	5	×5	25
13	True Grit, 1969	14.3	×2	28.6
14	California, 1947	3.9	×7	27.3
15	They Died with Their Boots On, 1942	2.55	×10	25.5
16	The Searchers, 1956	4.9	×5	24.5
17	The Virginian, 1946	3.35	×7	23.4
18	Cat Ballou, 1965	9.3	×2.5	23.3
19	Vera Cruz, 1954	4.6	×5	23
20	The Professionals, 1966	8.8	×2.5	22
21	Gunfight at the O.K. Corral, 1957	4.7	×4.5	21.2
22	San Antonio, 1946	3	×7	21
	Fort Apache, 1948	3	×7	21
	Broken Arrow, 1950	3.5	×6	21
25	Rio Bravo, 1959	5.2	×4	20.8
26	Hondo, 1954	4.1	×5	20.5
27	Pursued, 1947	2.9	×7	20.3
28	Cimarron, 1931	2	×10	20
29	Yellow Sky, 1949	2.8	×7	19.6
30	Shenandoah, 1965	7.8	×2.5	19.5
31	My Darling Clementine, 1946	2.75	×7	19.2
32	She Wore a Yellow Ribbon, 1949	2.7	×7	18.9
33	High Noon, 1952	3.4	×5.5	18.7
34	Across the Wide Missouri, 1951	2.75	×6	16.5
	Bend of the River, 1952	3	×5.5	16.5
36	The Iron Mistress, 1952	2.9	×5.5	16
37	Distant Drums, 1952	2.85	×5.5	15.7
38	The Outlaw Josey Wales, 1976	12.8	×1.2	15.4
39	One-Eyed Jacks, 1962	4.3	×3.5	15.1
40	Wells Fargo, 1937	1.5	×10	15
	Drums Along the Mohawk, 1939	1.5	×10	15
	Jesse James, 1939	1.5	×10	15
	Northwest Mounted Police, 1940	1.5	×10	15
	Northwest Passage, 1940	1.5	×10	15
	Santa Fe Trail, 1940	1.5	×10	15
	The Sons of Katie Elder, 1965	6	×2.5	15

Selected runners-up

Winchester '73, 1950	2.25	×6	13.5
Hang 'Em High, 1968	6.7	×2	13.2
El Dorado, 1967	6	×2	12
The Wild Bunch, 1969	5.3	×2	10.6

Note: It was impossible to arrive at an accurate rental figure for John Ford's Stagecoach, *but research indicates that it was not quite as financially successful as its huge reputation suggests.*

John Wayne *(right), as the dying gunfighter of Don Siegel's* The Shootist, *defies Harry Morgan's town marshal.*

The Great Train Robbery *(far right) was one of the first films to exploit the dime-novel popularity of the then not-so-Old West.*

suggests that popular cemand has not wholly supported the most vital developments in the genre, and has gravitated to critical 'classics' (*Shane*, for instance) where the veneration of art is bestowed on what is felt to be the essential simplicity and unchanging stereotypes of the form. One of the most vexed critical questions about the genre has in fact turned on this very point: whether it is better to speak of the seriousness 'of' the western or seriousness 'in' the western.

For every critic who has welcomed a new watershed in terms of changes in tone and content, there has been another to regret the passing of the archetypal simplicities that were held to define 'the' western. Bazin's suspicion of the post-war Super-western – 'a western which is ashamed of not being itself and seeks to justify its existence by a supplementary interest (which may be aesthetic, sociological, moral, psychological, political, erotic)' – does not mean that he was opposed to all change. He approved the evolution of the classicism of *Stagecoach* into the romantic 'personal' films of Nicholas Ray and Anthony Mann. But against the Super-western's straining for significance, he was led to assert that 'these superficial earthquakes have not shaken the economic core, the central block of ultra-commercial westerns, musicals or horse operas, whose popularity is being rediscovered by television,' which in turn leads him to the paradox of championing 'the Z-class westerns . . . of limited aesthetic interest' but whose presence 'is probably decisive for the general health of the genre'.

A metaphor for the commercial film industry

As an extension of this, Bazin's perception about the western that, 'Its phases do not deeply affect the existence of the genre', also encapsulates the dilemma of the critic when confronted by something which has perhaps always been a kind of super-genre: something outside the ordinary definitions and standards of cinematic merit, perhaps closer to being a metaphor for the whole commercial film industry. Critical frustration in the face of this leviathan might even be a mirror for the schizophrenia of the industry, which has often despised while capitalizing on this bread-and-butter product: 'The producers may have considered westerns lowly – they frequently did not think them important enough to list participants, although they were happy to supply credits for their society dramas, etc. – but westerns represented nonetheless a steady source of income. And they were made continuously, in especially heavy volume beginning in 1910.' (George Pratt, in *Image*, April 1958). As early as that, critics were complaining about the assembly-line formulas, the immutable repetition of situations and characters, and confidently predicting their imminent demise, for example a 1913 reviewer in *The Moving Picture World*: 'A closed season . . . may safely be declared on these overworked and senseless types: The Outlaw, The Sheriff, The Queen of the Ranch, The Half-Breed, The Bandit (Foreign and Domestic) . . .'

What has helped matters since then is that as our historical distance from the actual west has increased (only two years separated the groundbreaking *Great Train Robbery*, made in 1903, and the last such hold-up by Butch Cassidy and the Wild Bunch in the United States), and as the western has established its own mythic authority and fictional themes, so our notion of its relation to history and the 'real' west has been complicated. The western can no longer be dismissed with the simple complaint that 'it wasn't like that', although it is still liable to be treated with the contemptuous shrug of familiarity. But the continuing confusion as to what makes a 'good' western is bound up with its historical significance. Its exemplary quality as the kind of film-making that always kept the industry going results in Bazin's quandary: should one honour the ruck of undistinguished popular work or, stemming from that, some refined, idealized image (which seems to exist in every critic's mind) of what a true western is, or swim with the tide in which

Billy the Kid *together with Jesse James and the Younger gang have been western staples from the earliest silent pictures right up to the present day, although paradoxically it was Jane Russell who drew audiences to Howard Hughes' scandalous success* **The Outlaw** *(far left). Billy has been played by numerous*

the western becomes important according to what it picks up and reflects back of our changing conceptions of ourselves and our world.

The impossibility of classifying and assessing so protean a form has not, of course, prevented many commentators from attempting it, and the work of even the genre's foremost historian, William Everson, combines enthusiastic documentation with impatient assumptions about what a western should and should not contain. More complex attempts have been made not to judge the western but to explain its popularity, ranging from the most expansive account of its myths in terms of certain cultural/social/political events (Jim Kitses' *Horizons West*) to the most rigorous structural analysis of its narrative 'functions' (Will Wright's *Sixguns and Society*). The aim of both, in a sense, is to understand what validates the experience of westerns for their audience. Kitses invokes the literary legacy of nineteenth-century romance (from Fenimore Cooper to the 'dime novels'), the cultural as well as physical battleground represented by the frontier (freedom vs. progress, nature vs. civilization, individual vs. society), and the quest for identity on both a personal and a national level.

To this Wright objects: 'It is doubtful that many of us who enjoy westerns worry very much about progress versus freedom or Garden versus Desert, and the only source of evidence for the existence of these conflicts is the myth itself. An argument that attempts to explain a myth through a conflict that can only be found in the myth itself is necessarily suspect.' In order to understand more directly how westerns, like any myth, communicate a society's attitudes and concepts to its members, Wright breaks down a selection (the sixty-odd most commercially successful since 1930) into a limited number of story types and plot components. This, however, rather drastically reduces the meaningful elements of the films, as Wright cavalierly acknowledges: 'If the stories in a set of films are reduced to a single list of common functions, will not the unique characteristics of each film – the particular actors, scripts, settings – be lost? Not necessarily, since these characteristics provide realism and flavour to the stories. They embody the myth and are necessary for the communication of meaning; but they are extraneous to the analysis of that meaning.'

If one accepts the western's special function as an exemplary form of the American cinema, then it is a little rhetorical or naive to ask what makes it popular. The western embodies certain values and the kind of impetus – the pioneering spirit, entrepreneurial skill, economic exploitation and the thirst for vicarious excitement outside the everyday ('civilization') – which produced the commercial cinema in the first place. It has not always been unique in this respect – the gangster film in the 1930s was an interesting reflection of the Hollywood mentality (see Eugene Rosow's study, *Born to Lose*). But it did come first and it has been around longest. The cinema, perhaps, was the most natural medium of expression for the western, as either historical or ideal experience (it has certainly far outstripped its literary equivalent). In imaginative terms, one might even say that the western is both the inspiration and explanation of Hollywood, that the genre embraces the industry rather than vice versa. This chicken-or-the-egg formulation might seem a confusing way of reconciling genre and cinema, but in this case the historical growth and development of the two are so closely intertwined that it is possible to write about either one as a metaphor for the other.

The early years

The western 'movie' existed some time before the 'cinema' came fully of age. *The Great Train Robbery* (1903) has entered history as one of the first films to realize the dramatic possibilities of the medium; but before that, Thomas Edison's creative associate, W. K. L. Dickson, had made a simple, one-scene vignette, *The Cripple Creek Bar-room*, which was exhibited in Edison's kine-

actors including Kris Kristofferson in **Pat Garrett and Billy the Kid** *(left) in the 70s, and Audie Murphy in* **The Kid from Texas** *(right) in the 50s. In 1980 the Carradine brothers played the Younger brothers in* **The Long Riders** *(far right), but this clever casting failed to rekindle audience enthusiasm for the western.*

toscope parlours, penny-arcade predecessors of the first real cinemas, the nickelodeons. Among the 'stars' in the 1890s of Edison's prototype studio, the Black Maria, were 'Buffalo Bill' Cody and Annie Oakley, performing stunts in front of a cumbersome, immobile camera. This overlap of the 'real' west and its fictional equivalent suggests one reason why the western has lodged itself so centrally in the American film consciousness. The cinema appeared on the scene, technologically the most advanced myth-making apparatus and a 'socialised' form of entertainment soon to overtake the theatre, just as that crucial phase of the national experience, the winning of the west, was in the process of mythologizing itself through the dime novel and the Wild West Show.

To add to the confusion, the film-makers themselves could be described as the natural heirs of the nineteenth-century pioneer tradition: when threatened by the distribution monopoly which Edison attempted to impose with the Motion Picture Patents Company, the more enterprising independents abandoned the centres of film-making in New York and Chicago and went West. As many of them were already identified with Western product – co-founder of Essanay was 'Broncho Billy' Anderson, first of the cowboy personalities; Colonel Selig, who was to find his most valuable property in Tom Mix, had the highest output of westerns in pre-Hollywood days – the move seems to have been inevitable anyway. A final factor in the early pre-eminence of the western, and a further 'overlap' that explains its historical/metaphorical grip, is that the audience it catered to was largely drawn from the dispossessed, uprooted or simply restless tide that had heeded the mythical call to populate the West. Critics exasperated with the already ironclad clichés of the genre's first decade seem often to have been baffled as to who was watching westerns: 'Recently I visited five moving-picture houses in a Southern tour and five in a city in New England. The Indian was everywhere. The film-makers tell us that the demand for this sort of thing is overwhelming. I studied the audiences in the theaters visited . . . and noticed no such feverish enthusiasm . . . I sincerely believe they were tired of them, especially as the music with these pictures is always the same' (*The Moving Picture World*, quoted in 'The Posse Is Ridin' Like Mad' by George Pratt, in *Image*, April 1958).

Exhibitors, however, testified to the western's continued drawing power in the small towns and communities beyond the pale of the sophisticated East and in Europe, which had already begun turning out its own exotic versions of the American moviegoers' staple, and whose sustained admiration for the western has perhaps had something to do with the confusion (of industry and critics alike) as to whether this most homely popular entertainment is also the truest American 'art'. Reflecting this ambiguity, native film-makers have, in their hostility to the genre, often fluctuated between the cleansing outrage and the reforming ambitiousness of the righteous. Various early cinéastes took the western by the scruff of the neck and shook it to make something worthy of it: D. W. Griffith, Thomas H. Ince, W. S. Hart. After each of these creators had had his way, the western reverted to prolific mediocrity – the mundane continuity of Bazin's 'Z-Westerns'. Then, as in recent years, the reformer's mission was deceptively clear: to import more 'realism' into the genre. But realism has always been conditioned by the shifting ideology of the West, a vision of the Promised Land that connects one end of the realistic axis – Hart's Victorian tales of good overcoming evil in a strong man's soul – with the other, the aggressively amoral grubbiness of *Dirty Little Billy* (1972).

Epic westerns

More realistic detail has frequently meant simply more detail: Ince set out to transform the cheap and standardized westerns of his day by making them more authentic, but also by bringing to 'Inceville' the Miller Brothers' 101 Ranch Wild West Show to boost production

values. Throughout its history, in fact, the one overriding 'reality' to which the western has referred has been this quantitive physical one, a sense of potentially limitless space into which more or less action and detail, or to put it another way purely cinematic stimulation, can be poured according to dramatic rules and types which are so limited that their application is correspondingly broad and flexible. This expansiveness, combined with the genre's peculiar responsibility for reflecting the American historical 'adventure', would make the western natural material for the epic form.

Epic in this sense needn't mean a blockbuster in industry terms, although a predictable number of the latter have found their way into the top box-office list. Predictably enough, the western's intermittent resurgence after periods of lying fallow is usually marked by an intertwining of epic themes and box-office success: *The Iron Horse* and *The Covered Wagon* in the mid-1920s; *Cimarron* and *The Big Trail* at the beginning of the 1930s, when the 'serious' western was virtually to disappear for the first decade of sound; *Duel in the Sun* and *Red River* after the war; *The Alamo* and *How the West Was Won* at the beginning of the 1960s.

The western, however, can fulfil its epic role even in the absence of lavish production values. Ford's relatively modest *Stagecoach* (1939) is not as self-conscious in this respect as *The Iron Horse* (1924), and is even derived, at one remove, from a non-western source (Maupassant's short story *Boule de Suif*). But in its treatment of landscape (Ford's first sound western, this was also his first to make use of Monument Valley), its integration of a simple story-line with a richness of archetypal character and incident, its sense of the West as an arena for moral as well as physical struggle that is perhaps the first significant advance on the simple pieties of W. S. Hart, it seems a more resonant and 'authentic' western statement than the silent film. *The Iron Horse* is also episodic, but in the service of a rambling revenge plot – son hunts down his father's black-hearted (and black-faced) murderer – more out of place in its Victorian fashion than that of *Stagecoach*. The building of the transcontinental railroad provides a diffuse background of national achievement, although the film's main claim to fame was the exactness (and arduousness) with which it recreated the work of these pioneers. The 'physical' epic is the keynote of the 1920s – naturally enough, given the historical proximity of the real West, and the ease with which similar conditions could be encountered by film-makers bent on authenticity. By the time of *Stagecoach*, the winning of the West is already becoming more of an imaginative feat, subject to a more abstractly (or commercially) evolving mythology. Also in 1939, Ford burrowed further back into a recreated past for *Drums along the Mohawk* – which has made the chart even if *Stagecoach* hasn't – and a poeticised past for *Young Mr Lincoln*.

The 1930s

To each era, evidently, its own image of the West, and thus of America – and this applies even in those periods when the genre didn't

The Iron Horse *(far left) climaxed in the joining of the tracks of the Central Pacific and Union Pacific railroads.*

The Big Trail *(left) was Raoul Walsh's contribution to the cycle of epic westerns, marked by John Wayne's first starring role.*

Spencer Tracy *(right) leads a command of Rangers toward the* Northwest Passage. *Despite the success of this truncated epic, subtitled 'Book 1', no sequel followed.*

'take', either because its mythology was still undergoing revision or because it was displaced by a more immediate one (for instance, during World War II). In this respect, the 1930s is a fascinating puzzle: a time when the low-budget western, the flood of 'Bs' and serials, became the mainstay of the industry, while the epic (or serious, or mythological or otherwise historically minded) western apparently couldn't establish its credentials with the public. The handiest excuse for this dearth – the western wasn't thought suitable for the new medium of 'talkies' – is not really borne out by the fact that the genre seemed to adapt quite well to sound, and that in 1929/30 it managed to produce Victor Fleming's *The Virginian*, *Cimarron* and (going for wide-screen as well as sound) *The Big Trail* and King Vidor's *Billy the Kid*. William Everson even attributes the boom in low-budget westerns to the success of these major productions.

The disappearance of the 'real' western under the thundering hooves of the 'Bs' may have had more to do with studio economics, and with the horde of independent producers who jostled in the cheap western field with the major studios and presumably did much to create and sustain demand (even if their product was considerably cheaper and less expert). Paramount, whose Zane Grey westerns were one of the most profitable and best-made low-budget series, was virtually alone in essaying epic subjects in the mid-1930s, including Cecil B. De Mille's *The Plainsman* and King Vidor's *The Texas Rangers*, which stolidly carried on the making-of-the-west tradition of *The Covered Wagon* and *The Iron Horse* (De Mille later duplicating the Ford film for Paramount in *Union Pacific*). But the most spectacular, and spectacularly unsuccessful, throwback of this period was Universal's *Sutter's Gold* (1936), at different times in the hands of Sergei Eisenstein and Howard Hawks, but finally directed by *Covered Wagon*'s James Cruze, whose career as a major director was virtually finished by this financial disaster.

Conceivably, during the Depression, audiences weren't in the mood for the optimistic mythology of nation-building (as opposed to other forms of 'We're in the money' escapism), and westerns weren't yet mature enough to qualify that optimism. (Paradoxically, it was the winning of World War II that allowed the more troubled, pessimistic and inward-looking western to come into being.) But after *Stagecoach* and *Drums Along the Mohawk*, the genre briefly flowered in a revival of straight-faced but dubious historicity, with Warners, trendsetters in 1930s gangsterism, leading the way. Errol Flynn became the centrepiece of *Santa Fe Trail* (1940), as J. E. B. 'Jeb' Stuart fighting the crazed abolitionist John Brown (perfunctorily included was another epic of railroad construction, the Santa Fe), and of *They Died With Their Boots on* (1941) as a suitably ennobled General Custer. MGM, who rarely stooped to making westerns, produced the lavish *Northwest Passage* (1940), directed by King Vidor as a tale of trail-blazing and Indian-fighting that is red in tooth and claw. Also in 1940, De Mille weighed in with *Northwest Mounted Police* and William Wyler with *The Westerner*, more history-in-the-making to the extent that it involves the character of Judge Roy Bean, but closer to the neo- or

Henry Fonda *(far left), as Wyatt Earp, surveys a newly-peaceful Tombstone in John Ford's* My Darling Clementine.

Gregory Peck and Jennifer Jones *(left) exchange lustful glances in* Duel in the Sun.

Robert Mitchum *(right) in* Pursued, *a complex revenge western that positively invites psychological analysis.*

anti-western in terms of its downbeat, rather parched approach (according to Everson, 'its austerity and unglamorous picture of the West made it unpopular').

The post-war period

If such stirring tributes to the past helped to prepare America for war, the western was not a significant vehicle for helping to see her through it – always excepting the assembly-line of 'B' fodder, which only television could eventually halt (or co-opt). But when the western reappeared at war's end, two significant things had happened to its sense of history. One was the poeticizing, at a further remove from *Stagecoach*, of John Ford, who in *My Darling Clementine* (1946) could present 'his' West – Monument Valley as the location of Tombstone, Arizona, the friendship of Wyatt Earp and Doc Holliday, Earp's courtship of his sweetheart, and the gunfight at the O.K. Corral – as an image for 'the' West. A watershed western if ever there was one, *My Darling Clementine* combines the old epic energies and vision within a scaled-down, more 'realistic', domestic account of how the West was occupied. This is the western actively engaged in representing not just historical events but a theory of history – the film has become a focal point for discussion of garden vs. desert, civilisation vs. wilderness, etc. – and half-aware also that it now has its own history, to which evocative tradition belong those Fordian touches of character, landscape and social ritual.

The lengthening shadows of Ford's own history, in other words, are beginning to stand in for the ever-receding concept of the historical West. But the other immediate post-war trend is to take that history for granted, and to concentrate on the problems rather than the tradition to which it has given birth. Both Vidor's *Duel in the Sun* (1946) and Howard Hawks' *Red River* (1948) are epics, encompassing experiences which transformed the land (the arrival of the railroads again, democratizing the founding father's fiefdom; and the cattle drive which pioneers a way to the railhead, another link in the nation's food chain). In both, however, the epic accomplishments crystallize rather than resolve the dramatic problems: history-in-the-making, the focus in different ways of the 1920s and 1940s, becomes Americans-in-the-making. Once the challenge to fill the land has been met – once the call of the West has been silenced by the official closing (in the early 1890s) of the frontier – pioneer solidarity gives way to interest group divisiveness.

The first division is between father and son, establishing a new metaphor of the nation as family and the generation gap as the focus for competing idealisms: between a crusty, increasingly tyrannical conservatism and a newfangled faith in progress, democracy and the rule of law. Both films, of course, recreate the past in lavish detail, though not really to Fordian ends. Howard Hawks' *Red River* does its best to put the audience in the saddle, to convey what a cattle drive was like – picturesque to a degree, but probably the first nation-building epic to concentrate on daily, piecemeal labour. Characters are tested by the way they rise to the Puritan ethic rather than their manifest destiny: an ethic on its way to becoming the professional ethos which Hawks will ela-

borate completely outside history in *Rio Bravo* (1959).

Duel in the Sun does not so much set itself outside history as outdo it. As in *Red River*, the family is the crucible of western progress. But after the good son (Joseph Cotten) cuts the wire that separates his father's kingdom from that encroaching tide, and the bad son (Gregory Peck) atavistically carries on from where his hell-raising old man left off, the film proves temperamentally unsuited for the reconciliation that points to the future at the end of Hawks' film. Garden vs. desert is here a luridly primordial struggle. *Duel in the Sun* marks the passing of the oligarchical into the democratic West, the individualist into the collective, but is itself not inclined to witness the new dawn. The old imperialist longing is consumed in an equally unregenerative fury of sexual passion, and the film willingly follows into a land where it is forever sunset. (This last presumably courtesy of 'colour consultant' Josef von Sternberg, one of the many 'collaborators' with whom director King Vidor was surrounded in producer David Selznick's own epochal striving for another *Gone with the Wind*.) Comparison might also be made between Hawks' use of John Wayne, not ten years since *Stagecoach*, as representative of an unyielding, fossilizing West, and Lionel Barrymore's appearance in a similar role in *Duel in the Sun*, a theatrical figure in a rhetorical landscape.

Psychological westerns in the 1950s

The romantic deification of the demon lovers at its end might suggest that *Duel in the Sun* is itself an unregenerative extravaganza. But two important strains in the subsequent western seem to flow from this hot-house film – a situation which, by comparison with the discreetly developing classicisms of John Ford and Howard Hawks, interestingly reflects Vidor's position as *the* dramatist, in any context, of American energies and ambitions. The first is that group of 1950s films in which a range of psychological tensions and social problems suddenly seem to find their way into the western. Another shift takes place: from the pioneer hearth being the focus for the stresses of nation-building, it becomes a home like any other, its period context simply a foil for problems just as liable to crop up in the present. The past is no longer merely taken for granted, it is connected with the present. What is significant about the directors of these films (Delmer Daves, Anthony Mann) is that they are not identified primarily with westerns, although they often achieved a strength lacking in their other work.

These films are sadly unrepresented in the box-office chart, with the exception of Daves' *Broken Arrow* (1950) and a premonitory film from 1947, *Pursued*, in which the hero's demons are of the Freudian kind, directed by old western hand Raoul Walsh. The films which probably sum up the period in terms of popular recognition, *High Noon* (1952) and *Shane* (1953), embody less complicated statements and impress most by their formal qualities (dramatic unity and mythic purity, respectively). A further twist in film history's tail is that William Wellman's highly touted *Ox-Bow Incident* (1943), about lynch-mob injustice, should be an unpopular forerunner of social consciousness in the *High Noon* school, while the audience's fascination with violence, in the context of another collapse of patriarchal authority, in *Yellow Sky* (1948) earns him a place in the chart. Wellman's further experimentation in this field, the symbolic colour and metaphorical action of *Track of the Cat* (1954) is unsurprisingly absent.

The Freudian connections are there for the asking between Nicholas Ray's adolescent rebel without a cause and the hero of his extraordinary western *Johnny Guitar* (1954). In Anthony Mann's westerns, the politics of family and an epic scale of action combine in a mode pushing, more or less consciously, towards classical tragedy. One of the first of his 1950s series of westerns is called *The Furies* (1950), and the closest he came to fulfilling his ambition of making a western *King Lear* was that series' culmination in *Man of the West* (1958), in which the wide open spaces are the dark and brooding landscape of the monolithically stoic (Gary Cooper) and monomaniacally

Jane Fonda *(far left) in the parody western* Cat Ballou. *She made her mark in the genre proper in* Comes a Horseman.

Gary Cooper and Burt Lancaster *(left), as archetypal gringos in Mexico, lead the gun-play in Robert Aldrich's* Vera Cruz.

ambitious (Lee J. Cobb) westerner.

If there was one thing which *Duel in the Sun* contributed to the psychological liberation of the western in the 1950s, it was probably the image of Gregory Peck plainly lusting after the 'half-breed' Jennifer Jones. The cross-racial romance figures in *Broken Arrow*, necessarily more chaste because trying to be more 'positive': *Duel*'s heroine takes her mixed blood, and her irresistible sexual attraction to Peck's scapegrace son, as evidence of her 'bad blood'. But the casting of Peck, and the film's own formidable sensuality, cuts across the Manicheism of the good son/bad son split, and complicates the Hollywood rule whereby only out-and-out villains could be sexually aggressive. One precursor of eroticism out west was Howard Hughes' bizarre *The Outlaw* (1946), its release delayed for three years to allow publicity to build round reputed censorship trouble. But the film's mammary fixation, allied with a rampant misogyny, is less eroticism than camp gimmickry, and it should probably be aligned with those burlesque westerns, such as *Cat Ballou* (1965) and *Blazing Saddles* (1974), which have generally had an easier road to home (and the bank) than the formally more respectful comedy western, such as George Marshall's *Destry Rides Again* (1939) and *The Sheepman* (1958), and Delmer Daves' *Cowboy* (1958). Some directors (Burt Kennedy) straddle the two; the *ne plus ultra* of the burlesque western is probably Andy Warhol's *Lonesome Cowboys* (1968).

The western had always had a fascination for its badmen: outlaw biographies were one of the staples of the 1940s trend in historical westerns, tending variously to excuse, justify or glamorize their villainies. But in the 1950s, the historical badman as such disappears, because the heroes themselves are torn between positive and negative impulses, their psychological confusion a factor of the moral ambivalence that now infects the West as well.

Good son and bad son are one son in Joseph H. Lewis' *The Halliday Brand* (1957), and they are both Joseph Cotten. This suggests, and the plot closely follows suit, a revamp of *Duel in the Sun*; and the dream of empire just as explicitly, if less romantically, feeds on racial/sexual jealousies. In Arthur Penn's *The Left-Handed Gun* (1958), the outlaw, Billy the Kid (Paul Newman), is analyzed as a mixed-up, if not backward adolescent, troubled by the death, disappearance or betrayal of various father figures (Penn pellucidly depicts the emotional complications which Billy only sees 'through a glass darkly'). The one other, critically if not commercially, significant outlaw film of the decade, *The Gunfighter* (1950), was directed by Henry King, whose *Jesse James* (1939) was the most popular of the earlier cycle. Gregory Peck plays the gunfighter Johnny Ringo, who has aged into a disillusioned desire for respectability; Peck would complete a kind of trilogy – the good (or charming) badman of *Duel in the Sun* being the first stop – with the bad good man, a ruthless revenger, in King's *The Bravados* (1958). Along with psychological density, the 1950s western gains in moral weight and critical respectability simply through the mellowing of its major stars and the increased participation of many non-western ones. A maturity by association begins to overtake the callow 'oater' of yesteryear, and its long sunset years begin with Ringo trying to hang up his guns, and Marshal Kane (Gary Cooper) trying to turn in his badge in *High Noon*.

A second great western tributary springs more from the mood than the matter of *Duel in the Sun*. Be it with a sense of *Götterdämmerung*, apocalypse, elegy or cynical adventurism, these films accept that the pioneer trail has run out, the frontier is a closed option, and epic visions must be adjusted accordingly. It is the theme of the westerner who no longer has a place in the West, and whose alternatives seem to be either to move beyond it or to self-destruct. King Vidor himself takes up the subject in *Man without a Star* (1955), in which the wandering hero (Kirk Douglas) brushes with modernizing influences – a woman ranch boss; indoor plumbing – before heading out, possibly for Canada. But the most obvious direction to go is

James Stewart *(right) on the front porch he is later persuaded to leave by Richard Widmark in* Two Rode Together.

John Wayne *(far right) pauses briefly near the beginning of his obsessional pursuit in* The Searchers.

south, and a more significant western of the year before, Robert Aldrich's *Vera Cruz*, mixes American freebooters with idealistic revolution in Mexico. The theme of this loose-jointed, lighthearted adventure will become the more sardonically tight-lipped *The Wild Bunch* (1969), and Mexico as the last refuge or final resting place of America's drop-outs the ambivalent concern of Sam Peckinpah.

What the move also entails is contact with Europe – which was also coming in the opposite direction in the shape of the Spaghetti westerns, filmed in Italy with their generally Latinate casts and Mexican settings. Interestingly, the baroque stylization of Aldrich's *The Last Sunset* (1961) anticipates many Italian western mannerisms, and further defines the image of Mexico as the catch-all of America's human waste and betrayed ideals (in the romantic or wasted shape of unreconciled ex-Confederates). The European western returns the favour by emphasizing the Promised Land's purely mercenary incentives, draining it of those middle-ground figures (farmers, storekeepers, etc.) who peopled the pioneer dream. What it bequeaths to the American model, of course, is Clint Eastwood, who following the success of his Italian 'dollars' movies sneaked home through the back door in the pastiche Spaghetti western *Hang 'Em High* (1968), and then reclaimed the 'Man with No Name' to the pioneer experience and that middle-ground, farming community in *The Outlaw Josey Wales* (1976).

Given the failure of many of the westerns of Mann, Ray and Daves, both *nouveau* and neurotic, to catch on, John Ford's post-war successes are interesting. As the western's most personal *auteur* and traditional chronicler, he is not, however, immune to the tensions of the period. *Wagonmaster* (1950) sets an academic seal on *My Darling Clementine*, but a more adventurous line begins with *Fort Apache* (1948), which inaugurates a subject for a new age – the policing of the West. It takes refuge in militaristic nostalgia, unabashedly full-colour for *She Wore a Yellow Ribbon* (1949), more reservedly black-and-white in *Rio Grande* (1950), and resurfaces in the embittered histrionics of *The Horse Soldiers* (1959). The Civil War setting of the latter provides a conventionally 'safe' context for rendering internal conflict, but the fact that its squabbling humanitarian doctor and professional soldier are both northerners frees it from the debilitating romanticism that is frequently attached to the South (see the wistful *Rio Grande*, and the sentimental identification of the South with Mexico's Juaristas in *Vera Cruz*). That *The Searchers* (1956) should be Ford's most popular western of the 1950s suggests the drawing power of both his own and John Wayne's personal mythology, despite those harsh racist elements which the film – its reputation notwithstanding – throws up more problematically than critically.

Placidity in the early 1960s

The closest Ford comes to the bone in his treatment of white-Indian relations is in *Two Rode Together* (1961), reputedly made as a favour to Columbia boss Harry Cohn, which plays off savagery and civilization in the context of another mission, like that in *The Searchers*, to rescue 'Indianised' whites. *Cheyenne Autumn* (1964), Ford's attempt at a full-scale revision of his Indian history, is deadlocked by an epic (or rather, blockbusting) form that reflects his own and the industry's complacency. On the whole, the early 1960s represents a withdrawal from some of the interesting ground occupied by the western in the 1950s, a feeling for the nation's internal stresses and strains of which the Indian question was the most obvious symptom and symbol. There even seems to be an inverse principle at work here, by which the western reflects the pressures building up during the outwardly quiescent 1950s, but as Vietnam grows into an outwardly ever more disruptive issue in the 1960s, the western turns placid, becomes in popular terms the province of its 'amiable auteurs'. Andrew McLaglen doodles in the margins of Ford (*Shenandoah*,

Charles Bronson *(far left) blesses the cross-cultural marriage of Rod Steiger and Sarita Montiel in Samuel Fuller's* Run of the Arrow.

Dustin Hoffman *(left) awaits the death of his adoptive Indian grandfather, Chief Dan George, in Arthur Penn's* Little Big Man.

Gregory Peck and Eva Marie Saint *(below right) as the rescuer and the rescued in Robert Mulligan's haunting pursuit western,* The Stalking Moon.

1965) or puts himself at the service of the populist rallying of John Wayne (*McLintock!*, 1963). Reliable warhorse Henry Hathaway comes into his own: rediscovering in effective, if simplistic, terms the pioneering epic in his first two episodes of *How the West Was Won* (1962); by comparison with the ill-at-ease stylization of Ford's Civil War episode, doing a sound journeyman job on the Hawksian themes of professionalism and group responsibility in *The Sons of Katie Elder* (1965); and achieving a kind of classicism of his own with the expansive, quirky humanity of *True Grit* (1969), one of the few westerns to abandon the genre's rigidly schematized speech for the pleasures of vernacular. The Masters – Ford in *The Man Who Shot Liberty Valance* (1962), Hawks in *El Dorado* (1967) – meanwhile enter their own house justified.

New approach to the Indians: the late 1960s

In the latter half of the 1960s, as opposition to Vietnam ceases to seem a radical subversion and becomes a popular discontent, the western takes more fruitful shape. The ill-effects of the colonial experience come home, first as a new excuse for heroic individualism and romantic identification, once again with Mexico in revolt: Richard Brooks' windy *The Professionals* (1966). The experience is altogether harder to deal with, however, in a succession of westerns which take up the Indian dialogue of the 1950s, and the challenge of Sam Fuller's *Run of the Arrow* (1957), in which a white man swaps his own culture for that of the Indians. Ralph Nelson's *Duel at Diablo* (1966), Robert Mulligan's *The Stalking Moon* (1968) and Robert Aldrich's *Ulzana's Raid* (1972) share a disregard for liberal pretences of understanding the Indian, a ferociously plotted sense of the tactics of the chase, which keep the white men forever at a maddening remove from the 'hostiles', and the fact that – made by directors more urban than western – they fail, like the westerns of Mann, Ray, *et al.*, to make the box-office chart.

Self-denying epics in the 1970s

On the model of the 1950s, in fact, one might expect the post-Vietnam western, burrowing through the stagnant 1970s, to have become a lively and contentious form again. Perhaps only the new economics of the industry, chasing ever bigger blockbusters, have determined that the appearance of such moles should be sporadic rather than consistent. At the beginning of this essay it was suggested that the western looked so weak in the 1970s because it had failed to evolve into any significant new form. If it does have a new form, it is the self-denying epic, a revision of the outward-bound optimism of the 'quest' film in which the western setting was a natural arena for testing individual identity or national character. Now that test seems inevitably to result in self-deception, corruption and despair. Arthur Penn's *Little Big Man* (1970) is an absurdist extension of *Run of the Arrow*, in which the hero shuttles indecisively between white and Indian civilizations (the identity crisis and surrogate families of *Left-Handed Gun* played out in mock-heroic terms). In *Jeremiah Johnson* (1972), the mountain man is a drop-out who wants to retreat – not an adventurer who wants to advance – into the bleak grandeur of the West. Drop-out culture is also responsible for a revival of the historical outlaw, from the enormously successful *Butch Cassidy and the Sundance Kid* (1969) through various chic and violent identifications of the counter-culture then and now, to the commercial withering away of the form in *The Long Riders* (1980).

If the new epic western is not an odyssey but a stand-off, then its doyen is Sam Peckinpah. Part of the heroism of his most ambitious 1960s films, *Major Dundee* (1965) and *The Wild Bunch* (1969), is the struggle to reconcile contradictory energies. *Major Dundee* – for all its producer mutilations, perhaps the richer of the two – resumes the tensions and conflicts of two decades of Americans-in-the-making westerns. It is a search and destroy mission which barely manages to hold itself together, courting

Robert Redford *(right), bearded and bedraggled, as the eponymous mountain-man of Sydney Pollack's* Jeremiah Johnson.

Charlton Heston *(far right) as the arrogant cavalry officer of Sam Peckinpah's much-cut* Major Dundee.

disaster on the edge of more than one abyss – the gulf between North and South, black and white, red and white, Europe and America. *The Wild Bunch*, whose apocalyptic nihilism brought Peckinpah for the only time within sight of a commercial bonanza, is already beginning to give up on the search for home, country and freedom, and drifts south of the border to drown memories in a debauch of we'll-all-go-together-when-we-go. The theme is more serenely accommodated by his 1970s westerns: *The Ballad of Cable Hogue* (1970), in which the hero finds an illusory oasis over which to raise his country's flag, and *Pat Garrett and Billy the Kid* (1973), where the frustrated epic becomes a frozen one (characters forever on the move but never actually getting anywhere) and the questions of identity and freedom become a teasing conundrum (Bob Dylan's appearance as someone known as 'Alias').

Peckinpah exemplifies the troubled, outcast status of the western in the 1970s, and not only because his films have made that exile their theme. His production problems and peregrinations are legendary; he has officially become a citizen of Mexico, although like the characters of *Pat Garrett* (and, more closely, the hero of *Bring Me the Head of Alfredo Garcia*, 1974) he perhaps fears that expatriation is a dangerously negative freedom. The irony is all the greater considering that Peckinpah's background makes him one of the few genuine westerners to have taken the genre in hand. In this, as well as in the rigour of his moral vision, he is an appropriate heir of W. S. Hart – although that mantle more properly belongs to Clint Eastwood, whose reformation of Josey Wales is one of the current western's few optimistic moves. Peckinpah's other link with the past comes through the oft-ignored lyricism which accompanies his savagery: it is the Fordian vision of a home in the West, most consciously evoked as a moment of precarious harmony when the misfit company of *Major Dundee* are led in a graveside rendition of 'Shall We Gather at the River'.

Thrillers

The touchstone of comedy is laughter; of a horror movie, shock; of a musical, the release of joy; of a western, the sense of physical triumph. The touchstone of the thriller is tension. But in themselves none of these qualities is enough: without some moral dimension, a consciousness of man's relationship with society, laughter can become flat, shock mere sensation, joy perfunctory, triumph hollow. It follows therefore that there is a good deal more to the thriller than thrills.

There are also more variations to the thriller than to most of the other genres, save that equally loose one, 'action/adventure'. There's the gangster thriller, the psychological thriller, the chase thriller, the 'in the streets' thriller, the comedy thriller, the detective thriller and so on – few films fitting simply into one or other category but many with overlapping characteristics, while the genre as a whole shares several stylistic trappings with horror.

But as the years have passed, and many genres like the musical or the western have fallen on hard times, the thriller has grown in stature and complexity, remaining the most diverse, consistently popular and perhaps the most mature of genres, occasionally reaching a level of cinematic sophistication few other genres can match. Many of the thriller's most fascinating and money-spinning developments have taken place over the past two decades as the all-time rentals list indicates. But it is nonetheless relevant and interesting to see how the movie thriller began.

The first thrillers

Initially, the new medium of cinema itself was the thrill. The Lumières' documentary *Train Entering Station* (1895) reputedly made audiences flee or duck for cover, fearful for their lives; the cowboy in the final shot of *The Great Train Robbery* (1903) caused a gratuitously deliberate shock when he pointed his gun at the audience and fired at it. These famous examples of the primitive cinema's ability (conscious or otherwise) to cause a 'sensation', thrill the customers, illustrate how basic a cinematic genre the thriller is, but at the same time help to explain why the genre has taken so long to come of age.

The peepshows and nickelodeons which preceded the picture palaces promised cheap sensation, and such frank vulgarity remains deep in the medium's heart. The first decade of the cinema's commercial existence coincided with the rise of the tabloid press, with yellow journalism and lurid tales of sordid crime. The tabloids' readers were the people who went to the picture shows. Arthur MacEwan (the first editor of William Randolph Hearst's *San Francisco Examiner*) pronounced 'News is anything that makes the reader say "Gee Whizz",' and the new movie bosses echoed his sentiments.

Thrillers in the 1920s

Thus trying to trace the first real thriller is like trying to find the first English folk song. Edwin S. Porter's cross-cutting techniques were refined and made absolute by D. W. Griffith who is perhaps the first director to generate true 'suspense', in the climaxes of early 1920s movies like *Way Down East, Orphans of the Storm* and particularly *One Exciting Night*, which English critic David Robinson has cited as 'a pioneer murder-mystery drama'. *The Cabinet of Dr Caligari* (1919) and other Expressionist fantasies from Germany contain many elements of the thriller, but are more comfortably fitted into the story of horror movies.

A film like *The Penalty* (1920) illustrates the problem of assigning the thriller label. Lon Chaney would become a star three years later with *The Hunchback of Notre Dame*. In *The Penalty* he plays the legless king of the San Francisco underworld, having had his legs amputated as a boy after a street accident. But he now knows that the operation was not necessary. The surgeon, who has since become a master of his profession, operated in panic.

Clive Brook *(right) in Josef von Sternberg's* Underworld, *an early gangster thriller inspired by screenwriter Ben Hecht's experience as a newspaperman.*

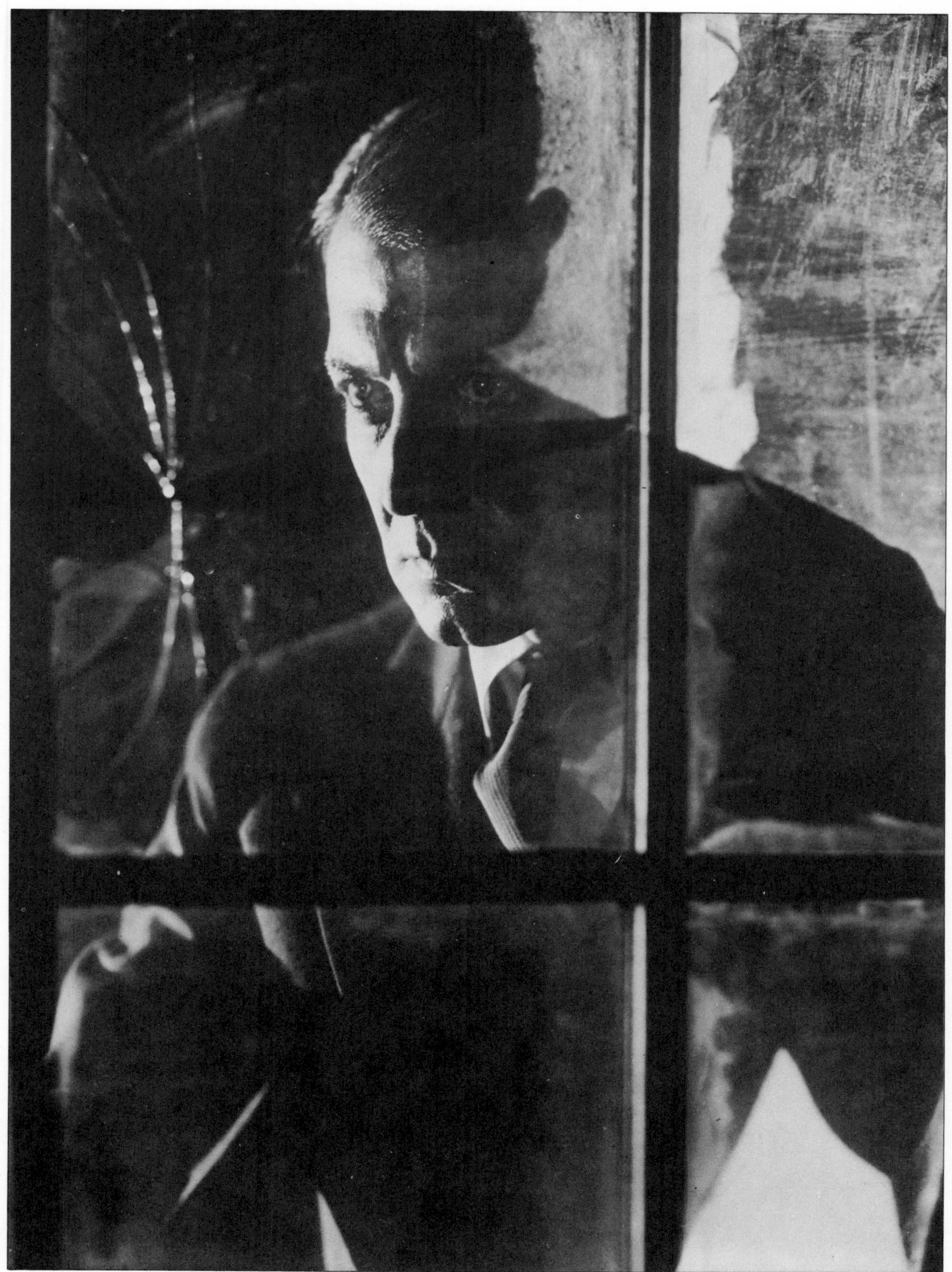

All-Time Hit Thrillers

	Rental income from initial release period: $m.	Inflation factor	Adjusted total: $m.
1 Jaws, 1975	121.3	×1.25	151.6
2 The Godfather, 1972	85.7	×1.5	128.5
3 Goldfinger, 1964	22.5	×3	67.5
Thunderball, 1965	27	×2.5	67.5
5 Jaws II, 1978	50.6	×1.1	55.7
6 Bonnie and Clyde, 1967	22	×2	44
7 The Godfather II, 1974	28.9	×1.4	40.5
8 The French Connection, 1971	26.3	×1.5	38.5
9 Bullitt, 1968	19	×2	38
10 You Only Live Twice, 1967	18	×2	36
11 Spellbound, 1946	4.9	×7	34.3
12 Moonraker, 1979	33.9	×1	33.9
13 Notorious, 1946	4.8	×7	33.6
14 Diamonds Are Forever, 1971	19.6	×1.5	29.4
15 Rear Window, 1954	5.7	×5	28.5
16 Magnum Force, 1973	20.1	×1.4	28.1
17 The Postman Always Rings Twice, 1946	4	×7	28
18 From Russia with Love, 1964	9.2	×3	27.6
19 Dirty Harry, 1971	17.8	×1.5	26.7
20 The China Syndrome, 1979	25.4	×1	25.4
21 The Getaway, 1973	18.1	×1.4	25.3
22 Three Days of the Condor, 1975	20	×1.25	25
23 The Spy Who Loved Me, 1977	22	×1.1	24.2
24 North by Northwest, 1959	6	×4	24
The Enforcer, 1976	20	×1.2	24
26 Dragnet, 1954	4.75	×5	23.75
27 Key Largo, 1948	3.25	×7	22.8
The Strange Love of Martha Ivers, 1948	3.25	×7	22.8
29 To Catch a Thief, 1955	4.5	×5	22.5
30 Live and Let Die, 1973	15.8	×1.4	22.1
31 Anatomy of a Murder, 1959	5.5	×4	22
32 In the Heat of the Night, 1967	10.9	×2	21.8
33 The Big Sleep, 1946	3	×7	21
Dark Passage, 1947	3	×7	21
Escape from Alcatraz, 1979	21	×1	21
36 The Man Who Knew Too Much, 1956	4.1	×5	20.5
37 Serpico, 1974	14.6	×1.4	20.4
38 Sorry, Wrong Number, 1948	2.85	×5	20
39 The Blue Dahlia, 1946	2.75	×7	19.3
The Spiral Staircase, 1946	2.75	×7	19.3
The Dark Mirror, 1946	2.75	×7	19.3

Selected runners-up

	Rental income from initial release period: $m.	Inflation factor	Adjusted total: $m.
Dr No, 1963	6.4	×3	19.2
On Her Majesty's Secret Service, 1969	9.1	×2	18.2
Suspicion, 1942	1.8	×10	18
Chinatown, 1974	12.4	×1.4	17.4
Torn Curtain, 1966	6.5	×2.5	16.3
Rebecca, 1940	1.5	×10	15

Lon Chaney *(above) as the legless villain of* The Penalty, *a bizarre and eccentric horror-thriller.*

The Lodger *(above right) was Hitchcock's first thriller, about a Jack the Ripper suspect; its title card was the work of artist Ted McNight Kauffer.*

Chaney wants revenge and plans, by seducing the surgeon's daughter, to force her father to graft on a new pair of legs which will be 'donated' by the girl's fiancé! Almost as a postscript, Chaney plans to commit a huge robbery, and intercut with all this are the activities of a lady undercover operator who, trying to get evidence against Chaney, falls in love with him instead.

In the end, the surgeon operates not on Chaney's legs, but on his brain. The 'beast' is tamed. He plans to use his mercurial mind for 'good' but is killed by his former cohorts before he can inform on them. 'Don't grieve – death interests me' are his dying lines before he pays 'the penalty'.

This weird film stands as a source of what we would now think of as three separate types of thriller – the underworld thriller with a bizarre gangland boss, gangsters and cops; the grotesque horror thriller with its lurid beauty, freakish poetry and sick shocks; and the classic melodrama with black villains, whiter-than-white heroes, secret passages, kidnappings and trapdoors. Because of his subsequent identification with the horror film, Chaney's presence would eventually postdate the film in that genre. It is however far more of a thriller than a horror movie, and it may be that among the many other virtually unknown Chaney films (not to mention the rest of Hollywood's unexplored output from this period) lurk equally fascinating works which we could call thrillers.

1926: the thriller comes of age

Effectively though, it is 1926 when the genre can really be said to have arrived. Appropriately enough, it is Alfred Hitchcock who ushers it in.

> 'We opened with the head of a blonde girl who is screaming. Then we cut to an electric sign advertising a musical play, "Tonight, Golden Curls", with the reflection flickering in the water. The girl has drowned. She's hauled out of the water and pulled ashore. The consternation of the bystanders suggests that a murder has been committed. The police arrive on the scene, and then the Press. The camera follows one of the newsmen as he moves towards a telephone. And now I proceed to show everything that happens as the news spreads around.
>
> First, the item is typed out on the wire-service machine so that we are able to read a few sentences. People in clubs learn the news. Then there is a radio announcement. Finally it is flashed on an electric news sign . . . And each time, we give additional information, so that you learn more about the crime. The man murders only women. Always blondes. He invariably strikes on a Tuesday. How many he has killed to date. Speculation on his motives. He goes around dressed in a black cloak and carries a black bag.
>
> What is in that bag?'

At last, we're on familiar ground. A shock opening shot; then the use of screen technique to impart information; the deliberate structuring of this information to build intrigue, suspense; even a plot device ('What is in that bag?'). Hitchcock is describing the opening sequence of *The Lodger*, his third film as director but, he claimed in an interview with François Truffaut, 'the first true "Hitchcock movie" . . . the first time I exercised my style'. The film concerns a lodger (Ivor Novello) who comes to stay with the Bunting family, and their suspicions that he is a murderer. Hitchcock was already in 1926 on his way to becoming the first director to make his reputation solely out of the study of what Robert Browning in 'Bishop Blougram's Apology' called that 'dangerous edge of things.'

1926 also saw another significant development within the thriller genre when Josef von Sternberg made *Underworld*, the first true gangster movie. Stylized, strange and romantic now, it caused a sensation when it first appeared. Americans had been breaking the Prohibition laws since 1920, the activities of Al Capone and his cronies were well known, and in 1925 F. Scott Fitzgerald's novel *The Great Gatsby* had drawn a seductive link between crime and the American Dream. The writer of *Underworld*, Ben Hecht, had once been a yellow press journalist, and claimed to know the film's milieu at first hand: 'As a newspaperman', he wrote 'I had learned that nice people – the audience – loved criminals, doted on reading about their love problems as well as their sadism'. But *Underworld* has more love than sadism, and doesn't look much like a gangster film today, concerned as it is with the triangular relationship between a gangster, a lawyer and

Little Caesar *(far left) with Edward G. Robinson, left. This was the first of the three seminal early thirties gangster movies.*

Humphrey Bogart *(left) as Dashiell Hammett's gumshoe Sam Spade in the John Huston version of* The Maltese Falcon.

a moll, while von Sternberg's slow, seductive rhythms are far removed from the frenetic world of screaming tyres and machine gun blasts now associated with gangster movies.

But of course, *Underworld* is a silent movie. Not until the coming of sound, the Wall Street crash and the St Valentine's Day Massacre did Hollywood seem truly interested in facing up to the gangster reality. But then it did so with a vengeance.

The early 1930s

The thriller element paramount in *Little Caesar* (1930), *Public Enemy* (1931), and *Scarface* (1932) – the most famous trio of gangster movies – is a sensational fusion of sound and fury. All three tell 'rise and fall' stories of their respective protagonists (Edward G. Robinson, James Cagney and Paul Muni – three actors virtually unknown to movie audiences before these films made them stars) and, with the true hypocrisy of yellow journalism, their violent activities are both celebrated and morally condemned. But the films were merely the tip of an iceberg: 300 gangster movies are estimated to have been made between 1929 and 1934.

Quick Millions (1931) has Spencer Tracy as its anti-hero, a sharp, wisecracking schemer who contrasts favourably with the almost inarticulate trio above, and – though Tracy's downfall is equally absolute – the film has a verve, a naturalism and a sense of witty honesty denied its more famous brethren (as does *Blood Money*, 1933, made by the same director, Rowland Brown, still an unjustly neglected figure). The most disturbing and unusual of all the gangster thrillers from this period is *Corsair* (1931). Its overall tone is robustly cynical, viewing gangsterism as the acme of the 'art' of capitalism while the plot's maritime bootlegging setting is a refreshing antidote to all those studio built city streets (some 50 per cent of the film was shot on location). The film's amoral sexuality is rancid, the world is seen to be a cruel, unloving place, and the fact that no major characters suffer any punishment is a further shock. More than most gangster thrillers of the period (excepting such images as the final shot in *Public Enemy* where the tortured, Mummy-like bandaged body of Cagney is left at his front door, to fall like a plank at his brother's feet), *Corsair* is genuinely alarming because of its acceptance of the twin worlds of Wall Street finance and racketeering.

This quality – the power to truly disturb – seems to be a crucial aspect of the thriller genre. Little of that power remains in the majority of 'classic' 1930s gangster films. And by 1934, the awesome censoring power of the Hays Office was ensuring that there would be few true thrillers made through the rest of the decade.

Indeed, the main developments in the thriller genre during the 1930s happened outside Hollywood. Many were in the field of literature. *Black Mask* had been founded in 1920 as a specialist crime and detection magazine, and by the 1930s Dashiell Hammett, an ex-Pinkerton agency detective, had ushered in the 'hard-boiled' school of detective fiction with *The Thin Man*, and *The Maltese Falcon* (1931) (for too long now overshadowed by the John Huston remake) had successfully adapted the Hammett world to the screen. But the concept of the tough, professional gumshoe, whose hands can get as dirty as his criminal opponents, could not long survive with the Hays Code. The film version of *The Thin Man* (1934), though breezily amoral, roots its interest in the society couple Nick and Nora Charles (who gave William Powell and Myrna Loy a new lease of screen life) and thereby helped to usher

Alfred Hitchcock *(above) had troubles with both the soundproofed camera booth and Czech star Anny Ondra's accent, but turned* Blackmail *into Britain's first talkie triumph.*

Peter Lorre *(far right) as the child murderer hunted by both police and underworld in Fritz Lang's* M.

in a new type of screen detective, upright, amateur and dilettante (Perry Mason, Philo Vance) or exotic (Charlie Chan, Mr Moto). The gangster was effectively replaced by this gallery of gumshoes, or by government agents, as in *G-Men* (1935) where Cagney used his machine gun on the side of law and order. The whodunit proved popular (though a writer like Agatha Christie who preferred puzzles to suspense would never be as popular in the cinema as on the printed page), but the real whiff of corrosion in Hammett's fictional world is rarely evident on the American screen in the 1930s.

Elsewhere, a broader sense of the genre was beginning to emerge. In Germany, films like Fritz Lang's *M* (1931) and *The Testament of Dr Mabuse* (1932) with its omnipotent master criminal and all but impotent forces of law and order, were taking a sideways look at the rise of Hitler and the moral decay of the nation. Lang's power to disturb remains strong. And in England, Hitchcock was continuing what at times resembled a one-man construction of the genre.

Hitchcock in the 1930s

Blackmail (1929), Hitchcock's (and Britain's) first sound film, carried his silent technique over to the new medium (and used an opening sequence similar to *The Lodger*). Concentrating firmly on the subject of a crime, the story is told through the eyes of a girl (Anny Ondra) who has killed the man who tried to rape her, and whose detective boyfriend (John Longden) is assigned to the case. Hitchcock's technique, constantly inspired by German silent cinema, makes *Blackmail* a milestone, for the film is constructed to ensure complete identification with the heroine and remains a revelation of how far the thriller can manipulate an audience's subconscious fears and desires.

The 1930s saw Hitchcock building from there. *The Man Who Knew Too Much* (1934), *The 39 Steps* (1935), *The Secret Agent* (1936), *Sabotage* (1936), *Young and Innocent* (1937) and *The Lady Vanishes* (1938) all vary in quality and ambition, but whatever the source material (John Buchan, Somerset Maugham, Joseph Conrad besides original screen stories) Hitchcock increasingly dispensed with literary storytelling and instead substituted his own visual and narrative logic. *The 39 Steps* in particular is a prototype of the thriller form: about an innocent man (Robert Donat as Buchan's Richard Hannay) who is on the run both from the police and a menacing spy-ring. Hitchcock's scenario is a series of virtually self-contained episodes of chase, threat, danger and escape, constructed carefully so that the audience shares the hero's experiences. Sober analysis of its construction reveals that many of its narrative and thematic links are essentially spurious or fantastic but the audience is never given the chance to reflect. The only reality, the only logic is that of the film. This picaresque structure, with its emphasis on speed and cunningly created set-piece scenes, which introduce new dangers with every shift in the action, was to become an important framework not only for many more Hitchcock movies, but for the genre as a whole. The chase thrillers now became an exemplary form which future films and film-makers could imitate, borrow and adapt.

But, like the book on which it was based, *The 39 Steps* was not merely an exercise in pyrotechnics. 'How thin is the protection of civilisation,' wrote John Buchan in *The Power House*, and this became a recurring theme for Hitchcock. Many of his British films of the 1930s involve ordinary people who accidentally find themselves pawns in powerful,

Gene Tierney *(far left) in the title role of* Laura, *Otto Preminger's* film noir *contribution to the vintage thriller year of 1944.*

Foreign Correspondent *(left) crossed a typical Hitchcock plot with a topical theme of pre-war espionage, and starred Joel McCrea.*

dangerous and destructive games which threaten their identities and their lives. And it was a theme he would develop in America.

The influence of *Citizen Kane*

But unexpectedly it was Orson Welles who eventually helped the Hollywood thriller to shift away from whodunits into a darker and more resonant vein via the landmark of *Citizen Kane* (1941). For out of this one film's style can be traced the rise of *film noir*, that extraordinary fusion of expressionism and melodrama which began to flourish in 1940s Hollywood. The complex flashback form of *Kane*, its mystery structure ('what is "Rosebud"?'), its eerie lighting and sombre visual tone offered a vivid new style and technique to the thriller as a genre. Indeed, much of Welles' later work falls into the thriller category: *The Stranger* (1946), *Lady from Shanghai* (1948) – with its climactic shootout in a hall of mirrors – *Mr Arkadin* (1955) and *Touch of Evil* (1958) all helped reinforce the fashionable notion that a thriller's style might almost be an end in itself. How a film created its suspense effects, how it came up with new, fresh methods of telling stories or shooting scenes, was for a time to become more important than what the story was about. Even Welles' adaptation of Kafka's *The Trial* (1962) can be seen as a kind of apocalyptic thriller. It is arguable that the genre's technical progress would have been seriously forestalled had *Kane*, in particular, not opened up so many cinematic possibilities.

Hitchcock in Hollywood

But if Welles was a somewhat peripheral father-figure of the thriller, Hitchcock remains its presiding genius. The 1940s saw him turn to Hollywood and employ the craft of American cinema – its enormous professionalism and technical skill – to reach artistic maturity. *Rebecca* (1940) could perhaps have been made in England, save for that technical excellence. But *Foreign Correspondent* (1940) could not. It is an adaptation of the picaresque form which is finally more disturbing than any of the British pictures. The famous shot of a group of windmills, one of which is revolving *against* the wind, is more chilling than anything in Hitchcock's previous work, where it would have merely seemed like an amusing *trompe d'oeil*. But war has darkened the tone. *Saboteur* (1942) looks at first like an updated *39 Steps*, allowing Hitchcock to stage his climax on the Statue of Liberty. But the web of intrigue uncovered by the innocent hero (Robert Cummings) is much more violent and unrelenting, as though the war had changed all games into unending matters of life and death.

The influence of war

Hitchcock's reputation as a master film-maker, and his new success in America, undoubtedly helped to make the thriller more respectable within the industry during the 1940s. But the trappings of war itself – its real-life spies and agents, its undercover work and physical danger, above all its threat to society – provided a new set of themes and characters to be explored within the thriller, as well as a sense of bitter reality. Authors of suspense fiction, like Graham Greene, Raymond Chandler, Eric Ambler and Geoffrey Household, had already proved that the genre could both entertain and provide a framework for more serious reflection. Household's compelling *Rogue Male*, about a man who is compelled to go to ground in the English countryside after attempting to assas-

Spencer Tracy *(right) fearfully watches the approaching lynch-mob in Fritz Lang's* Fury.

Barbara Stanwyck *(far right) as the archetypal* femme fatale *in Billy Wilder's labyrinthine thriller,* Double Indemnity.

sinate a foreign dictator, turned up, much altered, as *Man Hunt* (1941). But, despite some watering down, the film was given a haunting sense of malaise by Fritz Lang. The opening – with Walter Pidgeon stalking Hitler at Berchtesgarten, getting him in the cross-hairs of his rifle, then pulling the trigger on an empty chamber – is a heart-stopping moment to this day. As Pidgeon loads the rifle – too late, for guards pounce – we will him on, as though the film still had the power to alter history. Lang left Germany for Hollywood in the mid 1930s; his *Fury* (1936) and *You Only Live Once* (1937) are, perhaps, social thrillers – the former an anti-lynching drama, the other a tale of doomed lovers.

Graham Greene's novel *A Gun For Sale* became in 1942 *This Gun for Hire*, which made a star out of Alan Ladd, as Raven, the chillingly child-like hit man. The book is much altered and the bleak view of Britain in Greene's novel gives way to typical American backgrounds. But in the relationship between Ladd and Veronica Lake – two lost, almost arrested individuals – the film has a touching power, and Raven emerges as another archetypal character – the cold, spiritually bereft outlaw who is too old and too far past the point of no return to love or be redeemed. Greene purists scoff at the film, as they do at most American versions of his books, but perhaps they underrate Lang's adaptation of *Ministry of Fear* made in 1944 – arguably a key year for the thriller as the confusions, moral doubt and physical uncertainties of wartime found subconscious expression beneath its surface. *Laura* with its psychotic narrator, and splendid recreation of the 'dead' heroine, fuses detection and aberrant psychology into a bewildering web. *Gaslight*, a no-holds-barred melodrama with an unusually vicious edge as Ingrid Bergman is slowly destroyed by poisoner-husband Charles Boyer, is a project inspired by the success of *Rebecca* and Hitchcock's *Suspicion* (1941). Paradoxically Hitchcock falters with the turgid *Lifeboat*, but Billy Wilder's *Double Indemnity*, scripted by Raymond Chandler, was the epitome of black cynicism. Barbara Stanwyck's performance as a bored and bangled poverty-row *femme fatale* proved an inspiration for a myriad of sleazy goddesses later to prowl through the genre. Like *Laura*, this has a narration inspired by *Citizen Kane*, which establishes an overview of the sordid narrative for the audience.

In the same year: *The Mask of Dimitrios* – from Eric Ambler's novel – shares a similar device and a labyrinthine plot; *Dark Waters* finds Merle Oberon convinced that somebody is trying to drive her mad; Robert Mitchum made his thriller debut in *When Strangers Marry*; and Hitchcock's *The Lodger* was remade starring the roguishly rotund Laird Cregar as a possible Jack the Ripper. But two other films made in 1944 define the genre more absolutely than any of these.

Murder My Sweet was the first authentic adaptation of a Raymond Chandler/Philip Marlowe novel – and its opening shot, with a blindfolded Dick Powell being interrogated under a harsh white light (whether by police or villains is left unclear at first) propels the audience into a web of mayhem, crime and corruption in a heavily-mannered style which is the most obvious homage to *Citizen Kane* in any thriller yet made. *Phantom Lady* is even more visually extraordinary, because its director Robert Siodmak – like Lang, a German emigré – was seizing his first real chance to shine in Hollywood.

The thriller – in all its overlapping manifestations – had now definitely arrived, its mood – of dark pain, haunting enigma, serpentine mystery, and perverse motivation –

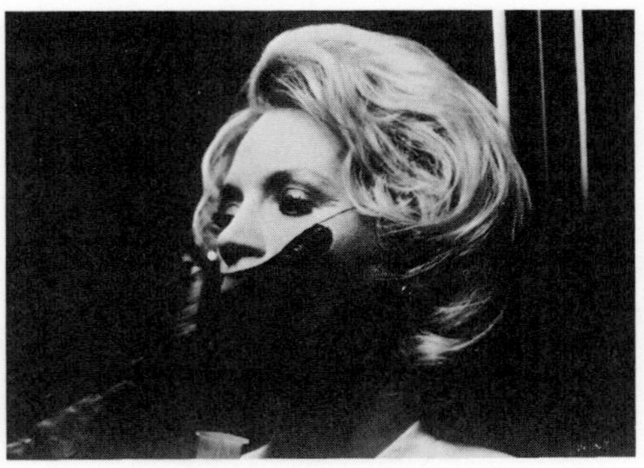

Cary Grant *(far left) on the run in the famous 'crop-dusting' sequence of Hitchcock's* North by Northwest.

Angie Dickinson *(left) about to meet a gory end in a lift in* Dressed To Kill, *a calculated homage to Hitchcock by Brian De Palma.*

perfectly reflecting the bewilderment of society as a whole.

But few of these films make it onto the best-seller list. The 1940s were still dominated by the Hollywood studio system. Profits were made from a totality of a year's output and only the biggest, most expensive films were singled out for special publicity or release treatment. Every studio had its 'B' pictures, a group of films made on low budgets and short schedules to be released in double-bills with 'A', first-feature, movies, ensuring that the production companies owned the whole programme in a cinema. Hitchcock apart, few thrillers were considered sufficiently prestigious to warrant major publicity and indeed many of the finest thrillers emerged from the 'B' category, which was something of a training ground for new, young talents, be they actors, directors, writers or producers. With the sole exception of *Rebecca*, it was not until the 1960s that the thriller became respected enough and lavish enough to win a Best Picture Oscar.

Mann, Huston, Siodmak and Lewis

'They say: "Give him fifteen days, give him no actors at all, only people who've never been in front of a camera before, God help him and let's see what happens". That's the way you generally start,' said Anthony Mann, whose series of second-feature thrillers made between 1942 and 1950 included some ground-breaking genre movies and enduring classics. *Desperate, Railroaded, T Men, Raw Deal, Reign of Terror, Border Incident* and *Side Street* are, when seen chronologically, an extraordinary progression. Mann was aided in most cases by cinematographer John Alton, whose book *Painting with Light* perfectly suggests the achievement of these films. Mann's world is defined totally by what the camera sees – and how it is encouraged to see it – a world of shifting allegiances, betrayals, confusions and bouts of almost motiveless violence. Mann also did some work on *He Walked By Night* (1948), an unjustly neglected mixture of police thriller and manhunt, with Richard Basehart as a psychopathic killer whose motives and character are never explained. He appears as nothing less than a force of evil, like a character from a ghost story.

By the late 1940s Mann's thrillers were illuminating one of the constant preoccupations of genre – how to find new ways of treating familiar material so that its very familiarity becomes a virtue. During this period other directors began to specialize in the thriller, sometimes – like Hitchcock and Lang – because their penchant for the darker side of cinema was encouraged by the commercial popularity of the genre. John Huston made his debut as a director with *The Maltese Falcon* (1941), which was faithful to the tone of the Hammett novel as well as to its plot. Later, Huston moved on to more consciously symbolic gangland stories like *Key Largo* (1948) in which a disillusioned war veteran encounters the threat posed by gangsterism to post-war America.

Siodmak followed *Phantom Lady* with psychological thrillers like *The Suspect, The Strange Affair of Uncle Harry* (both 1945) and *The Spiral Staircase* (1946) before he too moved on to more 'serious' crime movies like *The Killers* (1946), *Cry of the City* (1948) and *Criss Cross* (1949). *The Killers*, dark, arrogant, and extremely formal, is a superb piece, showing the *Kane* influence now perfectly integrated within the genre. Woody Brede's cinematography is every bit as complementary to Siodmak as Alton's was to Mann, notably in *The Killers* in a stunning sequence involving a payroll robbery which is shot entirely in one long take.

Joseph H. Lewis is still an obscure director compared to Huston, or even Siodmak. Graduating to major thriller projects via 'B' westerns in the 1930s, his *Gun Crazy* (1949) is one of the *tours de force* of the genre, deeply disturbing in its portrait of psychopathic lovers, brilliantly wilful in its technique. Lewis here outdoes Siodmak's payroll robbery sequence, by shooting a bank robbery entirely from the back seat

Henry Fonda *(above) as the innocent victim of mistaken identity in Hitchcock's* The Wrong Man.

Ingrid Bergman and Cary Grant *(right) explore the secrets of the wine cellar in* Notorious.

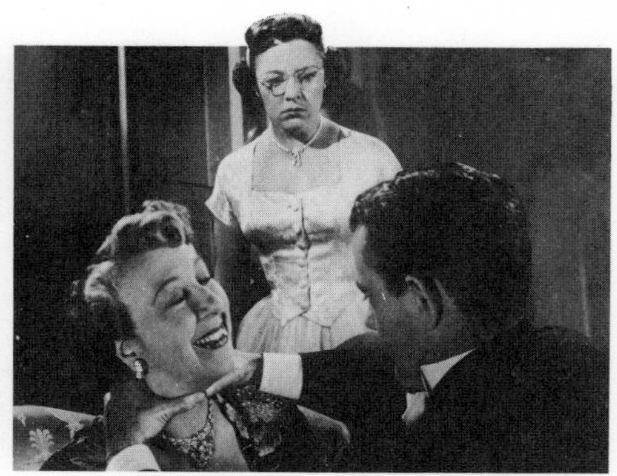

Robert Walker *(far right) is almost fatally distracted by Patricia Hitchcock as he demonstrates a stranglehold on Norma Varden in* Strangers On a Train.

of a car, which drives into a small midwest town, waits outside while the robbery is committed, and roars out the other side of town as the exultant robbers (who are also lovers) get away.

Gun Crazy certainly stands alone; on the other hand there were signs that the genre as a whole was beginning to affect mainstream movie-making. *The Postman Always Rings Twice* (1946), though a heavily censored adaptation of James M. Cain's violently erotic bestseller, made a huge impact. John Garfield and Lana Turner, as the murderous lovers, contributed to the atmosphere of sweaty, carnal crime.

But, while other film-makers were extending and developing the areas he had opened up, Alfred Hitchcock was still ahead of the field, and it is significant that *Spellbound* (1945) and *Notorious* (1946) should be two of the earliest films to figure on the All-Time Rental list. *Spellbound* derived from Hitchcock's wish to 'turn out the first picture on psychoanalysis'. With dream sequences based on designs by Salvador Dali, the film opened up another hitherto unexplored area for the thriller, making its characters' inner minds a subject of legitimate concern. *Notorious* however stands far higher in the Hitchcock pantheon, a spy thriller containing some of his most ingenious work.

The early 1950s

There is nothing really like the tumultuous kaleidoscope of 1940s thrillers in the next decade, as under threat from television, Hollywood began its search for new and spectacular subjects. A genre so familiar (and so inseparably identified with small screen monochrome) as the thriller, was bound to suffer from new attitudes in the age of cinemascope and colour. It is striking how few major American films are cast in the thriller mould at this time. Nonetheless, four major thrillers date from the early years of the 1950s. Otto Preminger's *Where the Sidewalk Ends* (1950), Joseph Losey's *The Prowler* (1951), Samuel Fuller's *Pickup on South Street* (1953) and Fritz Lang's *The Big Heat* (1954). All are linked to the politically intense atmosphere of America in the McCarthy era and the Cold War. Where public enemies had once been a threat to society, now society itself was seen as the threat, through the concept of 'The Organization' – a labyrinthine criminal syndicate based partly on realities like the Mafia, but also on fantasies of the 'red menace'. A clearly defined enemy now becomes an amorphous one, and the hero is unable to turn to the police, not because he will be presumed guilty, but because they may be part of the organization.

The new mood bred detective heroes as sadistic and amoral as Mickey Spillane's Mike Hammer. A film like *Kiss Me Deadly* (1955) seems to be saying that, given the awesome nature of the opposition, such a hero is the only possible saviour of the world. The overall tone of the thriller has become hysterical, as befits an apparently dying genre, but Hitchcock was able to keep it alive and healthy by going his own way. *Strangers on a Train* (1951), *I Confess* (1953), *Rear Window* (1954), a remake of *The Man Who Knew Too Much* (1956), *The Wrong Man* (1956), *Vertigo* (1958) and *North by Northwest* (1959) mix private concerns with cinematic spectacle to brilliant effect – *North by Northwest* proved to be a summation of all the chase thrillers which followed *The 39 Steps*, demonstrating conclusively that, with the right amount of spectacle and sophistication, the old formulas were well-suited to the post-television era.

Social thrillers

Parallelling Hitchcock's masterly return to the pure thriller form, the American cinema accepted the challenge of television by bringing out a wide variety of films on dramatic issues which used thriller and suspense techniques to involve the audience in a debate. Kazan's *On the Waterfront* (1954) is at least partly a thriller,

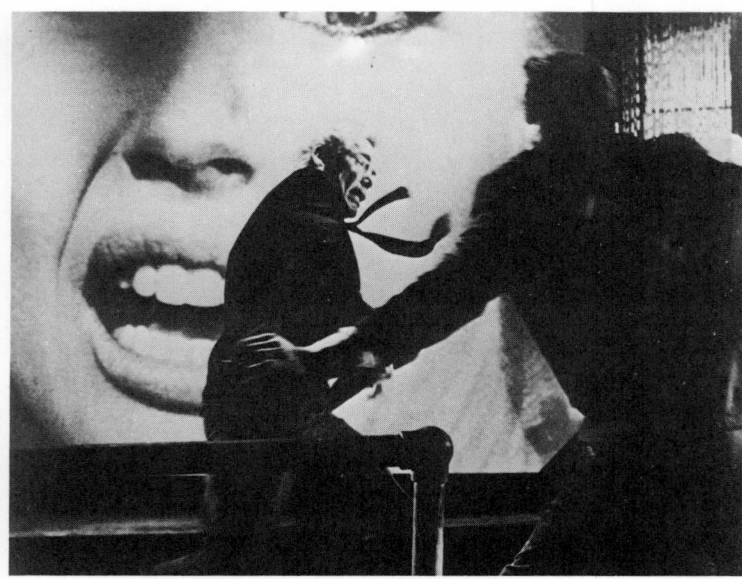

Bonnie and Clyde *(above left) exhibited European influences by way of its New Wave-inspired script by Robert Benton and David Newman: indeed it had first been offered to Truffaut and Godard.*

Point Blank *(above) also gained immeasurably from its cross-cultural inputs: it was director John Boorman's first American film.*

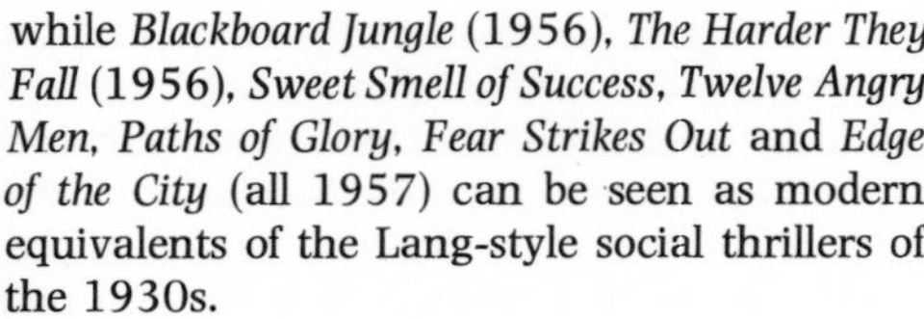

while *Blackboard Jungle* (1956), *The Harder They Fall* (1956), *Sweet Smell of Success*, *Twelve Angry Men*, *Paths of Glory*, *Fear Strikes Out* and *Edge of the City* (all 1957) can be seen as modern equivalents of the Lang-style social thrillers of the 1930s.

Europe, *Psycho* and James Bond

By the end of the decade, something even more important for the future was happening. In France, Jean-Luc Godard with *Breathless* (1960) and François Truffaut with *Shoot the Pianist* (1960) were making a radical series of movies, inspired by the Hollywood thriller. The form was at last achieving true status and acceptance, but Hollywood was still unsure which direction it would take. Boetticher's *Rise and Fall of Legs Diamond* (1960) and Fuller's *Underworld USA* (1960) are just about the last two traditional thrillers in the 1940s mould, made just at the point that Hitchcock turned everything upside down by killing off his leading lady in the first reel of *Psycho* (1960). The impact of this film has been felt ever since. Shocking, outrageous, structurally audacious, it remains the crucial signpost to the thriller's increasing merger with horror. A whole string of spin-offs followed, none worthy of it. But its success was almost a challenge. How could you out-do *Psycho*? It remained a goal for the film-maker to aim for, a treat for audiences to long for.

In the same way, the extraordinary success of the James Bond series established another central line of thrillers. Starting with *Dr No* (1962), the sexually promiscuous secret agent with his license to kill served twin fantasies of sex and violence. The unexpected box-office success led naturally to further Bond adaptations – and the need for each successive film to 'outdo' its predecessor, in gimmicky weaponry, plans for world domination and setpiece action sequences. Eventually they would become mindless exercises in logistics, with each new production increasingly like a private war.

The 1960s: a new pinnacle

The 1960s also marked the return of the private detective-cum-honest cop: *Experiment in Terror* (1962), *Harper* (1966), *Tony Rome* and *Gunn* (both 1967). But two other films from 1967 are of far greater importance. It took John Boorman with *Point Blank* and Arthur Penn with *Bonnie and Clyde* to show that the intellectualization of the thriller – filtered through the French new wave – had come full circle; the genre now reaches a new pinnacle.

Both films are excessively violent, both are ultra-conscious of style, both insisted on showing their killings in lurid detail, and, in killing off the old romantic innocence, invented a new romantic realism. *Bonnie and Clyde* became an event, a landmark, to set beside *Psycho* and the Bond films. In 1968, *Bullitt* fused the violence with 1960s cynicism and threw in the most stunning car-chase since *The Line Up* (1958) to create another precedent. And now the tone of the 1970s was set.

'Event' movies

Every film was now in commercial competition with every other film. There were no 'A' movies

Alfred Hitchcock *(above): undisputed and much-imitated master of the thriller genre.*

Dennis Weaver *(above) as the increasingly frantic prey of an anonymous, homicidal truck driver in* Duel.

Clint Eastwood *(above right) as the rebel cop Harry Callahan in Don Siegel's troubling urban thriller,* Dirty Harry.

Donald Sutherland *(above) as* Klute, *a small-town private eye out of his depth in the city and out of his element in the 70s.*

and 'B' movies. A film was an event or it was nothing. Thus there were the 'event' movies, vast and bloody tapestries of huge skill and energy, originating in 1971 with the biggest gangster movie of all time, *The Godfather*, a consummate epic chronicle of the Mafia. *The French Connection* (1971) set new standards of realism both in its observation of police routine and the special effects employed in its chases. Don Siegel's *Dirty Harry* (1971) was audacious enough to use western imagery in an urban setting and posed a host of embarrassing questions about society and the law.

Another noteworthy development of the 1970s was the increasing popularity of the conspiracy thriller which attempted to deal in realistic fashion with the notion of awesome and sinister networks of assassination. *The Parallax View* (1974) is an imaginative exploration of the conspiracy surrounding the Kennedy assassinations, but more successful commercially was a story of a maverick CIA hit unit *Three Days of the Condor* (1975).

The new Hitchcock?

Despite the event movie, some directors and writers remained free to make very personal thrillers. Altman explored the Raymond Chandler/Philip Marlowe legend in *The Long Goodbye* (1973), Roman Polanski and Robert Towne could make the masterpiece *Chinatown* (1974), while Sam Peckinpah even managed to finance a black comedy nightmare *Bring Me the Head of Alfredo Garcia* (1974), a film which undeservedly flopped. Another box-office failure was Arthur Penn's *Night Moves* (1975), which is nevertheless as stylish and extraordinary an exploration of the notion of detection as any film-goer could hope for.

Perhaps the saddest aspect of the decade was the final decline of Hitchcock himself. Having created the summation of the 'physical' thriller with *The Birds* (1963) and the psychological thriller with *Marnie* (1964), it was as if the director had nothing left to say or show. *Torn Curtain* (1966) and *Topaz* (1969) were hard to defend while *Frenzy* (1972) is a nadir, looking more like a film made by a Hitchcock admirer than the master himself. Hitchcock's last film *Family Plot* (1976), though more artistically ambitious and technically cunning, was empty of real imagination. It is interesting to speculate how crucial the death of Robert Burks may have been to the master. It was Burks who shot all Hitchcock's films from *Strangers on a Train* to *Marnie* (with the exception of the monochrome *Psycho*, which used John L. Russell, the regular cameraman on Hitchcock's TV series). All the mature works were visual collaborations with Burks, and what we recognize as Hitchcock may have been partly shaped by Burks.

But rebirth follows death, and a talent quite as intensely cinematic as Hitchcock's came to the fore in the 1970s with *Duel* (1971), *Jaws* (1975) and *Close Encounters of the Third Kind* (1977). Steven Spielberg may well have proved himself to be Hitchcock's heir (it is worth remembering in view of his flop, *1941*, that Hitchcock too had trouble with comedy). Though their concerns may be different, their approach to the medium is almost exactly the same, a stylistic dialogue with the audience which insists that the only reality is the reality of the screen. As long as Spielberg can stay in the ring, he seems as likely to inspire other film-makers to outdo him as Hitchcock himself.

Romance

Those pictures known generically as romance, 'weepies' or 'women's pictures' have enjoyed periods of overwhelming popular success, but with the passage of time have incurred considerable critical contempt. Their original detractors considered them a dilution of the powerful, purely sexual stature of the star, who became a drab, angst-ridden relative of the audience themselves. And more recently, despite some critical rediscovery of the films, especially those directed by Douglas Sirk, feminists have hammered the conventions promulgated by the genre as cheap propaganda – the 'rationalisations needed to reconcile women to marriage' after their increased mobility and war work in the late 1930s and early 1940s. The tears aroused by even the best weepies are never credited with an Aristotelian catharsis, because their genesis ('women's problems') is always construed as a diminished – and sometimes an entirely fabricated – world. A woman's picture is usually relegated to the status of a mere precursor of television's soap operas: 'a regular outlet for self-pity' which became less regular in the cinema as its function was appropriated by television.

The weepie genre began as a cinematic extension of popular romantic fiction, a market-proven success which worked according to fairly rigid conventions of feminine wishfulfilment and female-centred narrative. Fiction of this sort had in its own turn been influenced by changes in theatrical convention; by the 1880s and 1890s the domestic circle had been defined as a valid and respectable centre of dramatic interest and conflict. This was reflected in plays ranging from those of Ibsen and Chekhov down to the most populist stage dramas. Once authors had discovered the home as a focus for action, they often found the requisite tensions in the relationship between that home (formerly a more enclosed and self-sufficient community) and 'out there'. When fiction like Olive Higgins Prouty's *Stella Dallas* (1920) appeared, it was an outgrowth of those domestic stage dramas and their fictional equivalents – which showed families looking out from behind their drawing room windows and awaiting news of the world outside with mingled hope and dread. The home was still, in fact as much as in fiction, the centre of most people's universe. But at the turn of the last century, dramatic convention was freshly conscious of industrialization and technology, and of the fact that there was now an increasing number of forces beyond individual control determining individual lives. In this light, the re-assertion of individual choice became the most basic and obvious of dramas.

The themes of the genre

The woman's picture is so nicknamed because it is generally a woman who carries the themes of the film and therefore, goes the assumption, the action will be of interest mainly to women. The themes of the genre are: sacrifice and renunciation, service to the family, suffering and redemption, society and its pressures, and – that theme to which all others become a background wallpaper – romantic entanglement. All kinds of interaction between romance and reality are played out in women's pictures. And, within recognizable social boundaries (tacitly acknowledged by both the moviemakers and their audiences), the weepies conducted their own exploration of emotional boundaries. These were highly stylized: the laborious coincidences, telescoping of time, and postponements of passion in films like *Random Harvest* (1942) and *Valley of Decision* (1945) would tax the faith of the most fanatical SF stalwart if they had to be 'believed in'. Yet, if one looks beyond the cosmetics and the costumes, one can see in their intense interrogations of the heart the beginnings of an interrogation of the body. This was never overt – neither sociology nor the movie moguls stood to gain from any obvious portrayal of superior sexual or survival powers on the part of the second sex. But what the script often set out to show as feminine fragility or vulnerability

Belle Bennett *(right) as the self-sacrificing heroine of Henry King's silent version of* Stella Dallas. *Barbara Stanwyck took the role in King Vidor's 1937 remake.*

All-Time Hit Romantic Movies

	Rental income from initial release period: $m.	Inflation factor	Adjusted total: $m.
1 Love Story, 1970	50	×1.5	75
2 Mrs Miniver, 1942	5	×10	50
3 Sayonara, 1958	10.5	×4.5	47.2
4 Random Harvest, 1942	4.5	×10	45
5 Since You Went Away, 1944	4.9	×9	44.1
6 Stage Door Canteen, 1943	4.3	×10	43
7 Valley of Decision, 1945	4.5	×9	40.5
8 Valley of the Dolls, 1967	20	×2	40
9 Leave Her to Heaven, 1946	5.5	×7	38.5
10 Trapeze, 1956	7.3	×5	36.5
11 The White Cliffs of Dover, 1944	4	×9	36
12 Forever Amber, 1947	5	×7	35
Green Dolphin Street, 1947	5	×7	35
The Red Shoes, 1948	5	×7	35
The Way We Were, 1973	25	×1.4	35
16 Casablanca, 1943	3.7	×9	33.3
17 Picnic, 1956	6.3	×5	31.5
18 Summer of '42, 1971	20.5	×1.5	30.8
19 The World of Suzie Wong, 1961	7.5	×4	30
20 Romeo and Juliet, 1968	14.5	×2	29
21 Once Upon a Honeymoon, 1942	2.6	×10	26
Magnificent Obsession, 1954	5.2	×5	26
Imitation of Life, 1959	6.5	×4	26
24 To Each His Own, 1946	3.6	×7	25.2
Homecoming, 1948	3.6	×7	25.2
Little Women, 1949	3.6	×7	25.2
27 Three Coins in a Fountain, 1954	5	×5	25
28 Kitty, 1946	3.5	×7	24.5
Anna and the King of Siam, 1946	3.5	×7	24.5
30 Old Acquaintance, 1943	2.7	×9	24.3
31 This Above All, 1942	2.4	×10	24
32 Little Women, 1933	2.3	×10	23
33 Claudia, 1943	2.5	×9	22.5
Desirée, 1954	4.5	×5	22.5
35 Now Voyager, 1942	2.2	×10	22
Written on the Wind, 1956	4.4	×5	22
37 Ryan's Daughter, 1970	14.6	×1.5	21.9
38 Other Side of Midnight, 1977	18.4	×1.1	20.2
39 Love is a Many Splendored Thing, 1955	4	×5	20

Selected runners-up

The Turning Point, 1977	16.8	×1.1	18.5
Seventh Heaven, 1927	1.8	×10	18
Street Angel, 1928	1.7	×10	17
Splendor in the Grass, 1961	4.25	×4	17
Stella Dallas, 1925	1.5	×10	15
An Unmarried Woman, 1978	12.9	×1.1	14.2

1980 The Blue Lagoon

Russ Tamblyn *offers concerned sympathy to Diane Varsi in Mark Robson's* Peyton Place.

could become – when enacted in films from *Stella Dallas* (1937) to *Love is a Many-Splendored Thing* (1955) – the bravery of daring to lay yourself open knowing you have everything to lose. Greer Garson in *Random Harvest*, Ingrid Bergman in *Casablanca* (1942), Joan Fontaine in *Letter from an Unknown Woman* (1948): the best actresses in the better women's pictures turned defencelessness into the repetitive stubbornness of survival. Yet their more kitsch cousins (from Jane Wyman's *Johnny Belinda*, 1948, to Marie-France Pisier in *The Other Side of Midnight*, 1977) look more like victims and obsessional masochists than martyrs in any meaningful cause.

Because of their sex, all weepie heroines faced the double threat of both biology and sociology; unfulfilled desire was not merely frustration but a sure sign of social failure and a certain source of humiliation. And the genre's conventions were firmly middle class – with all the notions of cause and effect, decision and consequence, that entailed. To a large extent this was predetermined by the fact that many best-selling weepies owed their scripts to popular works of women's fiction. Henry King's *Stella Dallas* of 1925 was a scrupulous translation to the screen of the Prouty novel, and the formula was repeated with 'family classics' (*Little Women*, 1933), historical and costume drama-novels centred around the dilemmas of a single woman (*Forever Amber*, 1947 and *Desirée*, 1954), and popular novels about romance and its ramifications in domestic life (*Imitation of Life*, 1934 and 1959; *Love Story*, 1970; *The Other Side of Midnight*, 1977).

Sometimes the particular chemistry of a film (casting, direction, cinematography and catchy theme tune) would prove so potent at the moment of its public exposure that it became a sort of trailblazer. Joshua Logan's 1955 version of William Inge's play *Picnic* created one such sensation with its rising starlet Kim Novak, its ever-virile William Holden, and a popular theme song entitled 'Moonglow'. Its success spawned a series of imitators in the 1950s and 60s: *The Long Hot Summer*, *Peyton Place*, *A Summer Place*, *The Bramble Bush*, and *Splendor in the Grass* written by Inge himself. All were concerned to some degree with the melodramatic hothouse into which sexuality could transform a small town. *Peyton Place* (1957), a screen adaptation of Grace Metalious' best-seller, became so successful that its sequel (*Return to Peyton Place*, 1961) led directly to a television spin-off series. Originally two half-hours a week in 1964, by 1965 the TV *Peyton Place* was itself a popular phenomenon, promoted to three half-hour slots a week. A more recent example of the adaptation extracting and expanding the more romantic aspects of the original literary source is *Julia* (1977). Its script was fleshed out from a section of writer Lillian Hellman's memoirs.

Spectacle

When the purveyors of the woman's picture adapted a vehicle for the screen, they had to ensure spectacle as well as struggle in order to make full use of the medium. And the love of the poor or socially unacceptable girl for the rich, heroic fellow who was above her in social

Celia Johnson and Trevor Howard *as paragons of English reticence in David Lean's* Brief Encounter.

station was one mode of providing a banquet of costumes and set-piece extravaganzas. (Sometimes even the poor section of town from which she came, the 'other side of the tracks', was subject to elaborate over-design, as in *Valley of Decision*'s shanty town.) Another mode, developed after the genre had flowered in the 1940s, was the problematic love of a foreigner, which could occur in his or her native and exotic environment (*The World of Suzie Wong*, 1960 and *Love is a Many-Splendored Thing* are contrasting examples). Costume or period dramas (such as *Desirée*) were their own large-scale solution to the spectacle problem, but a visual carrot was generally dangled somewhere in the weepie – even if it was only a single party scene or a few new dresses.

Love and marriage

Above all else, the central concern of the woman's picture was the problem of love. And, because it was this genre which first followed love into marriage with some attention to reality, it is interesting to note that the weepie found all the risks and excitement and inherent meaning of love *outside* the marital relationship. The equations of erotic and exotic in such films as *Intermezzo* (1939, British title *Escape to Happiness*), *Casablanca* (1942), *Brief Encounter* (1945), *Ryan's Daughter* (1970), and *Mayerling* (1968) suggest that it is the illicit which holds the essence of romance. Those marital relationships to which lovers do sacrifice their passions and 'return' (as in *Brief Encounter* or *Intermezzo*) are by contrast deliberately homey and unerotic pairings, redolent at best of companionship and understanding. (A rare exception occurs with the re-make of *Intermezzo* as *Interlude*, 1968, where the dignity of Oskar Werner's betrayed wife is actually more attractive than the scatty sexuality of his young lover Barbara Harris). The dullest – and generally, the most problematically possessive – wives of all are those who remain resolutely offscreen while our heroines agonize over wounding them – as in *Love is a Many-Splendored Thing*.

Marriage is still a task and an aspiration in the weepie – the scriptwriters saw to that – but the spirit of the pictures remains with the illicit and ephemeral, whether or not there is a 'happy ending' at any altar or hearth. Affairs like those in *Intermezzo* and *September Affair* (1950) (both movies about adulterous idylls with famous pianists where the status quo is first shaken and then re-asserted through a renunciation) may have been intended first to challenge and then reassure the values of their viewers. In fact, the opposite occurs; the escape – however brief and doomed – into the forbidden romance is so satisfying and heightened an adventure that it leaves the audience ambivalent and disturbed.

The influence of World War II

Marriage in the weepie can be a stylistic coda – to a series of tests of true love. Or sometimes, when one or another of the real lovers is already married, marriage itself becomes the obstacle. For the woman's picture – with its

Love is a Many-Splendored Thing *especially if it takes place in an exotic locale like Hong Kong, where Jennifer Jones and William Holden find each other.*

disproportionate quota of disease, disaster, improper longings, ships passing in the night, and children tugging at all available heartstrings – reveals a high level of suspicion about marriage as an institution. These doubts were consonant with the period in which the weepie flowered: few other genre lists contain such a concentration of titles from the 1940s and early 1950s. It was a difficult, lonely, and confusing time for most individuals, and especially for women. During the war, they found themselves both entirely in charge of the home environment and at liberty to leave it to become involved in the war effort. Both the mood of patriotism and its propaganda stressed the ideal of war work – of a united devotion to an ideal nobler than the personal dreams of the single individual. Yet, at the same moment in time, uncertainty was all-pervasive: everything, not just the outcome of the war, seemed thrown into question. Emotions were heightened by nationalism, and by real partings, losses, deprivations, and fears. On the one hand, conventional rules and restraints seemed less important, as if they were relics of another life which might be lost forever. But on the other, they were also of extreme psychological importance – as the ideal, the way of life worth defending to the death.

Women were actually employed in almost every conceivable job left vacant by men while propaganda and sentiment enshrined them as waiting mothers, tender nurses, and patient guardians of the hearth. They themselves had to wrestle with all the ramifications of their new, very real mobility: a desire to cling to the securities of their traditional ideals did not always make sense in the face of those genuine but uncharted emotions which arose in this era of constant and drastic change. Thus the conflicts and fantasies and passions of the weepie. Its rationale is partly a tale of romantic ideals betrayed – the onscreen moments of unique, grandiose magic often stand in painful contrast to the drudgery and disillusion of marriage and real life which lurk outside the cinema. But it is also a genre whose real interest quite genuinely lies in the isolated and pure phenomenon of love: in the riddle of why men and women need each other at all. In the celluloid universe, it is love which brings order from chaos – love which makes momentary poetry of the world and confers meaning on lives which were previously dormant, if not entirely devoid of meaning. This transformation can be made explicit when love physically transforms a heroine, as it does in *Now, Voyager* (1942) – or the more esoteric *A Woman's Face* (1941), with a plot about a scarred and embittered woman which seeks to vindicate the equation of beautiful face and beautiful soul.

Time and time again in the woman's picture, love appears as a unique and 'pure' emotion which, in its urgency and compellingness, heightens the sense of time and the pressure of dilemmas. Because the sexual urge could never be explicitly portrayed onscreen (especially after the Hays Office edicts of the 1930s), a sense of breathlessness and haste stands in for it – as does the frequent lighting and sharing of cigarettes. Lovers rush between places, and positively whizz through duties and towards appointed meetings. 'I don't know what has happened to me,' gushes the erstwhile dignified lady doctor of *Love is a Many-Splendored Thing*, as she clambers all over the erring William Holden; 'I have such an *awareness*!'

Sacrifice and renunciation

Generally, the relationships of the weepies do represent heterosexual love as a challenge to the mind as well as the will: a chance to confront the unlike and to learn from it, to gain new perspective from the lover's 'otherness'. And there is a definite sense of equality in some of the love relationships; because sexual affinity is presented as a challenge, it calls for action and necessitates the taking of decisions. These decisions are almost always taken by the women and the men abide by them. Often when a man is romantically 'accepted' at last, it is because he has measured up to the woman's values – or because circumstances have altered to the point where her submission will entail no loss of personal integrity. The whole emotional construction of the weepie suggests that while men's ambitions (power, executive supremacy, affluence, vindication of family name or reputation, good character, pioneering feats) may be more worldly than the ambitions of women (endurance, self-sacrifice, a 'better future' for their children, the service of the family, integrity) they are never more real or more heroic.

A cold enumeration of the weepie's actual plot conventions – with their unrelenting emphasis on a domestic trauma – does make the form look like a logical model for the *reductio ad absurdum* it has reached on television. Many of the plots hinge on the sacrifice or renunciation of love: for family, in loyalty, or in payment for an emotional debt already incurred (Ingrid Bergman's sacrifice of Humphrey Bogart for her mentor and husband Paul Henreid in *Casablanca* is a convenient mixture of all three). Some sacrifice their offspring for their 'betterment' (*Stella Dallas; Madame X*, filmed in 1929, 1937 and 1966; *Kramer vs. Kramer*, 1979); some sacrifice a career for love (*Lady in the Dark*, 1944) or vice versa (*Morning Glory*, 1933). These sacrifice films may have tragic or 'happy' endings, but their emotions remain ambivalent, if not sometimes downright chaotic. As the dying Stella Dallas, standing in the rain, watches from afar the marriage of her daughter Laurel to a rich man, the audience feels for her sacrifice and understands that it *has* led to a better deal for her child. Yet we have already been made aware that Laurel is deeply unhappy on the eve of her wedding; she still hoped her mother would attend the rite, which lacks the true maternal blessing. Even more disturbing is the equanimity with which Helen, the more acceptable surrogate mother, accepts the necessity for Stella's sacrifice – leaving the curtains ajar so that Stella can come and see without being seen. The happy couple start life together looking out into the rain, as Stella ends hers looking in at them from behind the bars of an iron fence.

Tragic endings

The majority of the weepies end semi-tragically, especially the 'secret sorrow' pictures. These (like *Dark Victory*, made in 1939 and again, for TV, in 1975, *Love Story*, 1970, and *Letter from an Unknown Woman*) depict heroines struck down by illness or victimized by terrible mistakes, often of their own making, but sometimes (*Waterloo Bridge*, 1931 and 1940) by chance. The unlucky victims must usually face their trials (illegitimate offspring, mesalliances, and so on) alone, and sometimes in secrecy, if shame or a threat to someone else's feelings is involved. Such heroines unfailingly maintain a brave front for the world: from *Dark Victory* where Bette Davis mounts the stairs to die alone, through *Love Story*, where Ali MacGraw sits on the lap of the weeping Ryan O'Neal and instructs him to become a 'merry widower'.

The directors of romance

In many of the female-oriented weepies, as in the fiction and plays from which they were adapted, these rights and wrongs of choice were meant to represent inflexible social realities. But certain of those who effected their translation to the screen – together with the remarkable actresses they used – managed through commitment and sensitivity to do more than merely equate victimization and self-sacrifice with the lot of the 'average' women. The best romantic directors were men like John M. Stahl (responsible for the baroque 1935 version of *Magnificent Obsession* with Irene Dunne, for the original 1932 version of the seminal weepie *Back Street*, and for the first *Imitation of Life* in 1934), Max Ophuls (whose masterpiece came in 1948 with Joan Fontaine and Louis Jourdan in *Letter from an Unknown Woman*), and Douglas Sirk (*Magnificent Obsession*, 1954; *All That Heaven Allows*, 1955; *Written on the Wind*, 1956; *Imitation of Life*, 1959), who enjoyed his major success with romantic melodrama just as the genre's audience was changing its allegiance to television soap opera.

The real talent of these directors was in embracing the female sensibility not *as if* it were important but because they believed that it was. It took the sensitivity and style of Europeans like Ophuls (formerly Max Oppenheimer, of the German cinema) and Sirk (a German director, Detlef Sierck, who came to America in the early 1940s) – to create plots about women who were not vanquished victims but social outlaws, sometimes of an almost heroic stature. Both Ophuls and Sirk utilized the woman's capacity for romantic choice to epitomise her greatest conflicts: between children and freedom, duty and desire. They showed how the simplest of decisions – like the abnegation of the normal social responsibilities implied by 'love' – could be an act as radical as anything in a male-oriented genre. In *Letter from an Unknown Woman*, Ophuls confronts a woman's most dreaded humiliation – a love which remains forever one-sided – and transforms her degradation into a form of dignity: Joan Fontaine's obsession with the dissipated Louis Jourdan is balanced against his personal decline and a tragic equilibrium is therefore successfully established by the final scenes of the film.

Casablanca *features perhaps the most memorable of all renunciation scenes, with Humphrey Bogart's airport farewell to Ingrid Bergman.*

The importance of close-up

The close-up was an integral part of the weepie, yet the visual medium of cinema itself responded to the extraordinary female face with an almost chemical mystery, inevitably drawing a psychic beauty and suggestiveness from a physical one. Combined with the sheer energy, will, and charisma of the greatest actresses in the woman's picture (Greer Garson, Margaret Sullavan, Deborah Kerr, Joan Fontaine, Ingrid Bergman), the response of the medium itself to the feminine face and the play of emotions upon it was of major importance. It helped the women to tower over the mediocrities of many of the scripts and over their frequently inferior roles. The camera lingered on the face of woman much as it would have liked to linger on her body; but the face was never a passive encouragement to voyeurism. On the contrary, the faces of these women – today remembered as 'incandescent', 'transcendent', 'fragile, unbreakable icons' – could speak to the viewer in a specifically personal way. In their moments of doubt or pain or resolution, they could create great empathy with the viewer. And these faces also eloquently embodied the riddle of beauty and ephemerality, a riddle close to the heart of the film medium itself.

The images of renunciation, isolation, and lone dedication enshrined by these pictures (Belle Bennett staring through the rain-streaked bars at her daughter's wedding in *Stella Dallas*; Ingrid Bergman's last glimpse of Humphrey Bogart at the *Casablanca* airport; Jennifer Jones attempting to visualize the dead William Holden atop a deserted hill overlooking Hong Kong in *Love is a Many-Splendored Thing*; Greer Garson contemplating a growing pile of letters from Gregory Peck and deciding yet again not to answer them in *Valley of Decision*) are images heavily dependent on the close-up for their full emotional impact. In close-up these extraordinary women reveal a whole metaphysical world where the connections between feelings and conscience, hatred and love, embody a realization born out of conflict that love may be just as imprisoning as liberating, that the real test of the heart is the test of meeting another ego with integrity, of remaining able to give without losing one's own self.

Death-oriented weepies

With its tremendous box-office success in the 1940s, the woman's picture established an important place on the production schedules and in the minds of movie-makers. There have even been a lot of specifically death-oriented weepies surfacing in the late 1970s (deriving from the success of *Love Story* perhaps): *The Green Room*, *Moment by Moment* and *Promises in the Dark*. However, they have suffered a different fate to their predecessors – people have, as *New West* magazine's critic put it at the end of the decade, 'stayed away in droves'. Audiences no longer accept such depictions as illuminating or inspiring – they find them more depressing and frightening.

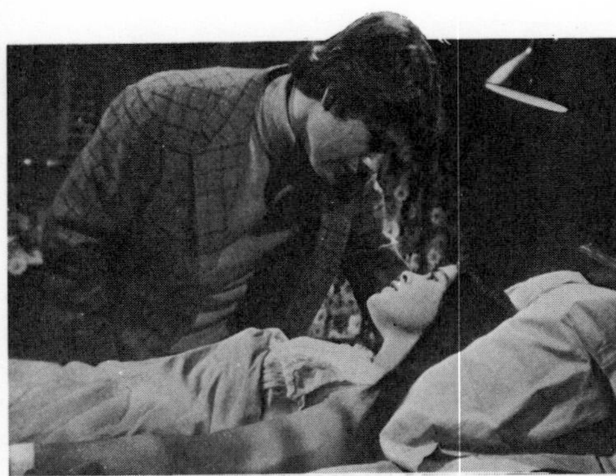

Ryan O'Neal *(far left) comforts the dying Ali MacGraw in Arthur Hiller's blockbuster weepie,* Love Story.

Trapeze *(left) played variations on the eternal triangle in a big-top setting, with Burt Lancaster, Gina Lollobrigida and Tony Curtis as the high fliers.*

The secondary female character

Yet there are certain facts of real life that the main cycle of weepies in the 1940s never ignored. They never pretended that the gifts of Nature were equally bestowed, nor did they espouse the 'propinquity' formula of the 1930s, whereby any two people stuck in an isolated situation find attractive qualities in one another and fall in love as a matter of course.

By the 1940s and 1950s, such behaviour could be described by Jennifer Jones in *Love is a Many-Splendored Thing* as 'mistakes in the name of loneliness'. *Valley of Decision* leaves us in no doubt that however strong the feelings of the main characters' respective childhood sweethearts (and their strength is emphasized rather than denied), they are not the genuine article. There is a similar mood in *Random Harvest* when Kitty, the infatuated cousin of amnesiac Ronald Colman, is forced to relinquish her love for him shortly before they are to be married because, despite their mutual affection she is not quite *the* one: 'I was grasping selfishly at my own happiness – I'm not the one. I'm nearly the one, Charles; so nearly the one that I shall always be proud of it. But nearly isn't enough for a lifetime.' This conventional wisdom is spoken rather unconvincingly by the very young Kitty, but it is with this secondary figure – the woman who can love and lose honestly and with no loss of dignity – that women viewers could identify most realistically.

The 'secondary woman', when she was not a rival or a relative, was often a girlfriend of the heroine, who could either provide a running commentary on the faults of men or exemplify by some misfortune of her own how men's baser desires put woman's precarious identity at risk. The Eurasian ex-convent school friend turned mercenary mistress in *Love is a Many-Splendored Thing* is a good example; like the black girl Sarah-Jane in *Imitation of Life*, she denies her birthright (already, as a Eurasian, that of a second-class citizen: something about which the script makes no bones), and tries to better herself in a 'whiter' world, but misapprehends the true values of that world.

Another commentator was frequently the older woman – a repository of wisdom to whom the heroine could turn in her hour of need for advice, acquired through years of decision-making and endurance. It is this sort of woman (the elderly Mrs Scott in *Valley of Decision*, Mrs Alcott in *Little Women*, Annie in *Imitation of Life*) that all of the heroines aspire to become. She of course represents the perfect mother, that Oedipal focus of many of the genre's male creators, and of its female novelist originators. The bland, blind husband who leaves Stella Dallas in the lurch in 1922 is bowled over by his second wife's compassionate, implicit understanding of her step-daughter's emotions. 'Helen, dear, you see with the eyes of an angel,' he says. 'No,' replies Helen, 'With the eyes of a mother.' The line was followed by thousands of scenes which made the same point: women cooking and serving food, women tending the sick, dressing the wounded, comforting the distressed, tucking children into bed, brightening up the home, 'making do' in difficult situations with ingenuity, pointing out the good from the bad and the right from the wrong.

Sex before romance

Womanly ambition not thus directed – like that of Gina Lollobrigida who desires star status in the circus in *Trapeze* (1956) – is pictured as both deviant and ultimately destructive. And the ambition of such erring women can always

Jill Clayburgh *(above), faced with involuntary liberation as* An Unmarried Woman *in Paul Mazursky's '70s romance.*

Picnic *(right), with William Holden and Kim Novak, profitably blurred the lines between romance and sexual melodrama in the '50s.*

be re-directed by a change of heart; Lollobrigida's Lola is (unconvincingly) transformed from scheming bitch to saviour when she 'listens to her heart' at last and admits that she loves crippled, ageing Burt Lancaster more than the spotlight. *Trapeze*'s coda also reveals how far the genre's conventions were slipping into kitsch after the 1940s as sexuality was allowed more overt expression. Lola, with her overtly displayed and decorated wasp-woman figure, is far more at home acting the perfidious *femme fatale* than she is attempting to persuade Lancaster and the audience that real feeling has been reborn in her ample bosom. Revealingly the more truly romantic relationship in *Trapeze* is between Lancaster and his young male disciple, Tony Curtis, a relationship which retains some concern for questions of caring, loyalty, and frankness about genuine feeling.

The romantic female lead of the 1950s grew in sexual mythology but shrunk in real status. By the 1960s there were few attempts to return to the old romantic formulas that had once proved so popular: the more successful romantic pictures were comedies with a faintly risqué undertone like the Rock Hudson/Doris Day series, inaugurated by *Pillow Talk* (1959). Despite the blockbuster success of *Love Story* at the end of the decade, few producers considered returning to women's pictures. But recently, in an attempt to capitalize on the evolving interest in woman as a theme (witnessed by numerous best-selling books), Hollywood has resurrected the woman's picture in a new liberated guise.

The liberated woman's picture

An Unmarried Woman (1978) contains scene after scene of classic woman's picture conventions: betrayal, loneliness, choice, the shock of rejection and the dilemmas of parenthood, vignettes of coping and failing to cope; and an ending packed with wish-fulfilment in which the hero awaits the heroine's decision and his happiness hangs in the balance. Yet its odd mixture of 1970s self-pity and Jill Clayburgh's interpretation of the woman's role – alternately presumptuous and demanding but somehow always grudging – was a million miles from the luminous, wounded faces of the original weepies universe. As the genre's popularity had shrunk, so had the universality of its problems. The *Unmarried Woman*'s only concern is being unmarried – she does not face poverty, death, disease, loss of offspring, or major social ostracism in addition. Yet she conveys less life than the faces of her forbears, who in bleaker conditions managed to suggest a boundless energy and hope. It was the energy and hope to go on valuing life and to transmute it, by sheer force

of will (and the creative force of belief) into something worthwhile. Beleaguered across the ocean from her lover and acting as a maid to his silly, thoughtless sister, the enterprising Mary Rafferty (Greer Garson) in *Valley of Decision* finds her grim consolation in designing and making the sister's beautiful frocks: a tiny but telling act of invention.

This was the less obvious but more honest side of the genre in its heyday; an insistence that courage exists as much in the daily grind of survival as it does in the boardroom and on the battlefield. The reasoning appealed to a large female audience but the truths were not just on display as a wailing wall of self-pity. In confronting them, women stars were able to enjoy for themselves as actresses an arena for action denied them in other, male-showcase genres – such as the thriller, the western, the adventure story, and the tales of front-line fighting. And to men the world they inhabited was sometimes equally exclusive and mysterious: 'I believe in so many things that you could never believe,' says Mary Rafferty to her lover Paul Scott (Gregory Peck). She means not just the superstitions and Irish Catholic guilt of which he has accused her; she means also that she adheres (perhaps involuntarily) to a female scale of values, familial and final and possibly more complicated than any male counterpart.

The images (resilience as well as resignation; reconciliation as well as humiliation) of the woman's picture endure because as well as re-asserting conventional ideas of social reality they also provided a glimpse of possibilities their first audience would have been unable to find anywhere else.

Comedy

Mae West and W. C. Fields *(right) acted together in only one film,* My Little Chickadee.

It all began, you might say, with comedy. Somebody turned the hose-pipe on the hoser, and there was cinema. And after their first astonishment the audience paid to laugh. Of course balance was essential. Beside the madcap chase, upsetting the fruit-stalls and sending the oranges flying, came the dramatic interlude: the old tramp asleep in the barn wakes up just in time to shin up the handy ladder and save the little girl from burning to death. Presently the condemned man's sweetheart would creep out to swing on the clapper of the bell, thus ensuring that curfew would not ring the signal for execution. But people still paid to laugh, and while the lions chewed up the Christians in the Roman arena, while Carver Doone sank slowly into the Lorna Doone bog, longer queues gathered outside the Electric Theatre (it was always the Electric Theatre) and the coins rang louder at the box-office if the spectator could be sure of coming out grinning.

Not that the cinema ever lost its love of confusion and the chase. But in its first two decades – if to keep things neat we may forget the tag-end of the nineteenth century, even if it means omitting some of the comic tricks of Méliès – comedy was busy disentangling the comedian from the joke: getting his silhouette clearly in the forefront of action, delineating him as the centre of laughter. The silent period produced the immortal comics.

Chaplin, Keaton and Lloyd

Between the beginning of World War I and the arrival of the talkies three figures disengaged themselves from the form: Chaplin, Keaton and Harold Lloyd – four if one may include the sad personality of Harry Langdon, a celebrity destroyed by the advent of sound. They disengaged themselves by a command of the medium which has never been outdone; only Jacques Tati in France thirty years later was to come near to it. They were stand-up comics in motion, in association, in narrative; they were simply themselves. The sophisticated cinema of today has little room for the individual who turns the opportunities of the screen to his own purposes. In the 1920s there was nothing between the comic and the spectator: no voice, no sound, only the arpeggios of the accompanying pianist; no elucidation beyond the hearty jokes of the titles. And those three pioneering exponents of silent comedy in the 1920s set about creating classical comedy.

Buster Keaton, to some of us the greatest (though regrettably his name does not appear in the list of the greatest money-makers), created an image of incomparable grace combined with imperturbability. He ran, and the simple action was both beautiful and funny; but the face (and that too was beautiful) betrayed no emotion. It froze; only the body was alight with hope, anxiety, elation, love. Difficult to understand why *The General* (1926) and *The Navigator* (1924) and *Sherlock Junior* (1924) don't get into the top financial bracket (though one must remember that Chaplin himself comes long after *Blazing Saddles*, 1974).

Harold Lloyd, a far less original comedian, does get in, and here one can see why. While Keaton wore an expression of no reaction, Lloyd was always buoyant; only when suspended from the hand of a clock high above the traffic in the street did he allow anxiety to cross that optimistic American face. Not the expression he displayed, but the position in which he displayed it was what counted. And the audience reacted: still, given the chance, reacts to the prodigies of cliff-hanging of a Harold Lloyd movie. With *The Freshman* (1925) something else was added: the hero, the cheerful guy who always comes out on top, begins with misplaced confidence. 'Step right up and call me Speedy!' he addresses his unwelcoming colleagues; self-assurance was set for a terrible fall before the final triumph. A shade of character crept into the story. *The Freshman* with its tale of University sports reflected the image of what every young American would have liked to be: the decent chap who wins through after troubles. Harold Lloyd stood for the small-town American of his day.

8

All-Time Hit Comedies

	Rental income from initial release period: $m.	Inflation factor	Adjusted total: $m.
1 The Sting, 1973	68.45	×1.4	95.9
2 The Graduate, 1967	43.1	×2	86.2
3 Animal House, 1978	63.5	×1.1	69.8
4 Going My Way, 1944	6.5	×9	58.5
5 American Graffiti, 1973	41.2	×1.4	57.6
6 It's a Mad Mad Mad Mad World, 1963	19	×3	57
7 The Bells of St Mary's, 1946	8	×7	56
8 Heaven Can Wait, 1978	47.6	×1.1	52.4
9 Tom Jones, 1963	16.95	×3	50.7
10 Blazing Saddles, 1974	35.2	×1.4	49.2
11 Every Which Way But Loose, 1979	48	×1	48
12 The Goodbye Girl, 1977	41	×1.1	45.1
13 M*A*S*H, 1970	30	×1.5	45
14 Welcome Stranger, 1947	6.1	×7	42.7
15 Mr Roberts, 1955	8.5	×5	42.5
16 The Love Bug, 1969	21	×2	42
17 Auntie Mame, 1958	9	×4.5	40.5
18 How to Marry a Millionaire, 1953	7.3	×5.5	40.2
19 The Odd Couple, 1968	20	×2	40
20 Young Frankenstein, 1975	30	×1.25	37.5
21 Operation Petticoat, 1960	9.3	×4	37.2
The Parent Trap, 1961	9.3	×4	37.2
23 Adventure, 1945	4.3	×8	36.4
The Absent-Minded Professor, 1961	9.1	×4	36.4
25 Irma La Douce, 1963	11.9	×3	35.7
26 Life with Father, 1947	5.1	×7	35.7
27 Those Magnificent Men in Their Flying Machines, 1965	14	×2.5	35
28 Oh, God, 1977	31	×1.1	34.1
29 What's Up Doc?, 1972	22	×1.5	33
30 No Time for Sergeants, 1958	7.2	×4.5	32.4
The Shaggy Dog, 1959	8.1	×4	32.4
32 California Suite, 1978	29.2	×1.1	32.1
33 Some Like It Hot, 1959	8	×4	32
34 Silver Streak, 1977	28.5	×1.1	31.7
35 The Bachelor and the Bobbysoxer, 1947	4.5	×7	31.5
36 The Seven Year Itch, 1955	6	×5	30
Pillow Talk, 1959	7.5	×4	30
38 Lover Come Back, 1962	8.5	×3.5	29.8
That Touch of Mink, 1962	8.5	×3.5	29.8
40 Up in Smoke, 1978	26.9	×1.1	29.6
41 Bob and Carol and Ted and Alice, 1969	14.6	×2	29.2
42 Foul Play, 1978	26.3	×1.1	28.9
43 Margie, 1946	4.1	×7	28.7
44 I Was a Male War Bride (UK title: You Can't Sleep Here), 1949	4.1	×7	28.7
45 Gentlemen Prefer Blondes, 1953	5.1	×5.5	28.5
46 The Great Race, 1965	11	×2.5	27.5
Shampoo, 1975	22	×1.25	27.5
Revenge of the Pink Panther, 1978	25	×1.1	27.5
49 The Apartment, 1960	6.7	×4	26.8
50 The Freshman, 1925	2.6	×10	26
51 Teahouse of the August Moon, 1957	5.6	×4.5	25.2
Father of the Bride, 1950	4.2	×6	25.2
53 The Kid, 1922	2.5	×10	25
The Gold Rush, 1925	2.5	×10	25
My Favorite Blonde, 1942	2.5	×10	25
56 Herbie Rides Again, 1974	17.5	×1.4	24.5

Selected runners-up

I'm No Angel, 1933	2.3	×10	23
She Done Him Wrong, 1933	2.2	×10	22

1980 Private Benjamin, Airplane, The Blues Brothers, Being There, Caddyshack, Stir Crazy, Any Way You Can, Nine to Five, The Jerk

Notes: Accurate rentals for It Happened One Night *(1934) are not available, but indications suggest the film did not achieve sufficient rentals to merit inclusion on our top 45 list of comedies. The Bob Hope and Bing Crosby* Road *movies appear on our musical list. Buster Keaton's most successful film with audiences appears to have been* The Navigator *(1924). Its rental was around $500,000, which multiplied by an inflation factor of 10, would give it a 1979 figure of only $5m.*

Buster Keaton *(right) as the cinema projectionist and amateur sleuth,* Sherlock Junior.

Charlie Chaplin *(far right) wrung equal measures of slapstick and sentiment out of his encounter with Jackie Coogan in* The Kid.

Harold Lloyd *(above) in unusually pensive mood in* Dr. Jack*: audiences knew him best as the king of thrill comedy.*

Keaton and Lloyd always won the game: not Chaplin. In his later films he added pathos to farce and presented a picture of physical defeat – but moral victory. In *The Kid* (1921) and in *The Gold Rush* (1925), where he was perfecting within the compass of narrative the tiny sketch – the dance with the rolls, for instance – of which he was master, he was still the all-round winner. Another thing he had in common with Lloyd and Keaton. All three were brilliant acrobats. All three employed the comedy of gesture, of attitude, of movement. And all three made attempts to move into the world of sound. Only Chaplin succeeded. And even he, with his forays into the sphere of the talkies, failed to win a place in the money-making league. Even his personality could not quite keep pace with the development of the screen.

Nevertheless it is from this beginning, this bold reduction of comedy to the personality and the physique of the individual that comedy was to grow into the complex we know today.

In no area of the cinema was the impact of sound, the human voice, felt more keenly than in comedy. In the cinema of action the addition of talk, at first almost a handicap, was rapidly accepted. With drama and romance it was a help to discard the interjections of explanatory titles. But with comedy, which had perfected the contribution of the individual mime or the acrobatic player, sound at first seemed a destroyer. Keaton did not need to speak, nor did Harold Lloyd; and though Chaplin, after long hesitation, took the decision to use his voice on the screen, he never again reached the flawless control which ravished the audience in *The Gold Rush*. By the beginning of the 1930s the cinema demanded not merely physical expertise, not merely the unflinching face; it needed a voice, a voice controlled, with range, an individual voice. Buster Keaton lacked that attribute; Harold Lloyd faltered. Chaplin went on to new triumphs – and yet, when one thinks of the final speech of *The Great Dictator* (1940) (for that, too, is comedy) there is a coarse veil between the sentiments and the sound which expresses them.

Mae West and W. C. Fields

Notable, then, that the comedy players famous in the 1930s, when the screen had rejected silence, owned distinctive voices. W. C. Fields, superb in *It's a Gift* (1934), spoke in wheedling tones which could have come from no other face. Mae West, who in 1933 moved into the ranks of the runners-up with *I'm No Angel* and *She Done Him Wrong* (six years later she joined W. C. Fields in *My Little Chickadee*) had a voice of cultivated impudence; disguising some outrageous suggestion as civil invitation, she dropped into a sensuous drawl; she ended the phrase with a vocal simper. She was the sex symbol of the 1930s, the first deliberate sex symbol of the talking cinema; after the chastity of the stars of the 1920s she made it her business to flaunt her appeal. The open sexuality was new; and then as now sex in the cinema meant money. Everybody, in the first half of the 1930s, talked about Mae West; her *double-entendres* became popular catchphrases. The fabulous bosom (it belonged, with a proper sense of proportion, to a tiny elegant figure) passed on its owner's name to a life jacket. Mae West at any rate deserved her share of the money-market.

Laurel and Hardy

But what about Laurel and Hardy? – the most economical and, in their flawless timing and delicacy of movement, the most refined clowns the cinema has produced. Their work began in the silent period but it flourished during the first two decades of the talkies; essentially they belong to the era of sound. They understood how to use sound: think of the battle to get a piano up a flight of stairs in *The Music Box* (1932). And they too had the advantage of voices one remembered: Laurel's plaintive, self-excusing; Hardy's aggrieved, forceful, a constant reproach to the errors of his partner. Their best work – though the feature films they made in ten years of association can't be ignored – was in short movies, in the anecdote, the single limited adventure. One can't expect, much as one deplores their absence, to find them in the list of best-sellers. But they are unique. They have no followers, they belong to no school.

Screwball

After the first traumatic shock of the death of the silent screen, the 1930s rallied to offer a comedy of absurdity and incongruity in social situations. It was a comedy of the irrational. It was crazy comedy; or, as at the time it was called, screwball. And in screwball the cinema of comedy experienced a kind of liberation.

One can say that Chaplin was the original genius who converted intellectual society to the screen, or that one laughs, really laughs, more at, say, Keaton in *Our Hospitality* (1923) than at director Frank Capra's *It Happened One Night* (1934). But Capra's film – it could be called the beginning of the great screwball period – has a range beyond the silent classic. It shows a remarkable narrative organization; a feeling for character independent of the leading players; a humane sense which controls the carefully devised extravagance of incident. It persuades the spectator that he is looking at a reflection of life.

Perhaps crazy comedy would have persisted until it had worn out its welcome. It attracted the most distinguished film-makers and the most gifted performers. Howard Hawks, for example, was the director of *Bringing Up Baby* (1938), and Katharine Hepburn and Cary Grant were the stars. The story of the pair in pursuit of an errant young leopard was accompanied by players of the highest order in minor parts (Charles Ruggles, for instance). The action made farce endearing; the dialogue was the more hilarious for being in its context perfectly rational (asked who is going to eat the huge slab of steak they are buying, the leopard-hunters reply: 'Oh, it's for Baby!').

Sentimental comedy

Why wasn't this irreproachable movie a great money-maker? Possibly its date was responsible: 1938, and war approaching. Perhaps the cinema could no longer afford the levity of crazy comedy. At any rate the 1940s brought a more sentimental mood. And the audience responded. In *Going My Way* (1944) Bing Crosby used his honeyed voice in the interests of comedy with a religious flavour. He assumed the uniform of a progressive priest and saved a party of young toughs from the New York streets. A year later he was again dressed in clerical attire (but with a straw boater) in *The Bells of St Mary's* (1945), this time dealing, in suitably distant manner, with Ingrid Bergman and a convent school. Again directing, Leo McCarey employed every dodge in the business to get a laugh in religious manner. And the coins clanged, or probably by this time the notes piled up, at the box office. There is money in religion when it is optimistic.

Whether at that time there was as much profit in straightforward witty comedy of character and situation is doubtful. Certainly, though, the first half of the 1940s was enlivened by the appearance of a genuine if brief-flowering talent: Preston Sturges. Brief-flowering because after a few years of success, first as a screenwriter, then as writer-director, the gift faded; and now probably few people think of Preston Sturges as among the important film-makers of the war years. But between 1940, when a modest but sparkling piece called *The Great McGinty* appeared and was followed by *Christmas in July* (the latter was about a slogan contest), and 1944, which brought *Hail the Conquering Hero*, a superbly timed war comedy about a soldier feted for fictitious action, one greeted with delight each Sturges film. *Sullivan's Travels* was among them, and *The Lady Eve*, *The Palm Beach Story* and *The Miracle of Morgan's Creek*; life blazed in them. Then the decline. The comedies lost the organization of their fun. Sturges's control over the timing of laughter weakened.

Perhaps his style, witty, sharp-edged, was not durable. At its best it had a tinge of destruction; it shied away from sentiment. True that no creator of comedy survives for ever, not even Chaplin. Capra, who was at the height of his powers during the best days of Sturges, faded

Ben Turpin *(top) in a Mack Sennett short: a distinctive face was no handicap for physical comedy.*

Harry Langdon *(above) left his public behind when he tried to break out of the persona created for him by his writers, who included the young Frank Capra.*

The Marx Brothers *(above right) – Harpo, Groucho and Chico – were and remain laugh-makers to an enthusiastic minority.*

Below Zero *(centre right) featured Stan Laurel and Oliver Hardy, and ended with a barrel of laughs.*

Cary Grant and Katharine Hepburn *(below right) armed with leopard-hunting gear in Howard Hawks's screwball comedy,* Bringing Up Baby.

in the end. But there was an element of sentiment in Capra's work which preserved it in public affection. When he attempted to soften his jokes, for instance in the treatment of anaesthesia in *The Great Moment* (1944), Sturges was never wholly successful. It was the joke, not the sentiment, which came out most strongly. And perhaps, looking at the history of film comedy for the first half-century of its life, one can say that with rare exceptions the most commercially successful works admitted romance.

The Marx Brothers

The reflection makes one think of the destructive, anti-romantic movies of the Marx Brothers, celebrities from vaudeville who erupted on the screen at the end of the 1920s and did their best work in the 1930s. Though one of their number, the beautiful, mute simpleton played by Harpo, never spoke, they belonged essentially to the talkies; at the heart of the joke was Groucho with his moustache and loping stride, offering insults all round. Groucho greeting some harmless character: 'They say I never forget a face, but I'll make an exception of yours'; Groucho responding to the threats ('You'll hear from me!') of some affronted stranger – 'Do that, if it's only a postcard!' – it is the dialogue, or often the monologue superimposed on the bizarre figures which brings the guffaws.

The Marx team presents one of the anomalies of the cinema. Everybody knows about the Brothers. There are books about them. The Groucho cracks have passed into the language. But their films don't rate with the huge money-makers. Groucho and Chico and Harpo were the creators of cult movies. They had and still have a faithful band of followers, spectators who see their films again and again, who collect and repeat their cracks. But their humour hasn't the popularity of, say, a Bob Hope.

Bob Hope

It has been said of Bob Hope that he is not funny in himself. One looked at Buster Keaton and laughed at gestures which were in themselves both beautiful and absurd. You laugh at the elongated body of Jacques Tati (who said that comedy resided in the legs). Bob Hope can arrange his features in shapes, in expressions which are risible; the humour, however, proceeds not from the visual performance but from the delivery of the lines. He has gifts developed by experience on the stage. He can sing and dance well enough to give background to his

comedy. He is entertaining in partnership: a good deal of his celebrity comes from his work with Bing Crosby and Dorothy Lamour in the 'Road' series – *Road to Singapore, Road to Zanzibar* and a list which ran from 1940 to 1962. And on his own he was to develop a character – the frightened hero of *The Paleface* (1948) and *The Lemon Drop Kid* (1951) and *Fancy Pants* (1950), who caricatured a gallant romantic original. At his best in the 1940s and the 1950s, he is one of the comedians who, unlike the majority of today's stars, succeeds by force of personality. The public went to see not a film with Bob Hope in the cast, but Bob Hope himself.

The 1940s and the 1950s continued to set the star above the movie. Looking down the catalogue of films financially distinguished, one repeatedly feels that much of the success is due not to writing or direction but to the mere presence of some favourite player; sometimes an actress.

Comediennes

Often the share in comedy of the female star is overlooked. Women are sacred, women – the sentiment dies hard – are not funny in action, in acrobatics. The great screen comedians have always been male. All the same there is a kind of comedy in which the female star can be supreme. The Marx Brothers themselves needed the imperturbable comic dignity of a Margaret Dumont. And there is a witty comedy which lives in the playing of women. Consider *How to Marry a Millionaire*, made in 1953 in CinemaScope (it was the first comedy to appear on the wide screen) with Marilyn Monroe, Lauren Bacall and Betty Grable. Think of *Gentlemen Prefer Blondes* (1953) with Jane Russell and Marilyn Monroe: it is a feminine comedy, a sexual comedy. Two years later came *The Seven Year Itch*: Marilyn Monroe again, this time without feminine support, as the girl innocently tempting the quiet married man who has decided to stay alone working in his New York apartment while his wife and family are on holiday. She was directed by one of the masters of comedy, Billy Wilder. The theme, drawn from a stage play by George Axelrod, promised success: the moral test of the middle-aged husband is one of the cinema's favourite comedy subjects. And Marilyn Monroe brought off superbly the joke of the naive girl and the man sorely tried.

Once more – it was in 1959 with *Some Like It Hot* – she was to work to Wilder's direction: and brilliantly, with her tenderly whispering voice, she held her own playing opposite Jack Lemmon and Tony Curtis, the two fugitive musicians, disguised in skirts and high heels, in flight from the gangsters they have seen at work. Monroe was at her most seductive; and the film, with Curtis assuming a Cary Grant accent and the incomparable Joe E. Brown joining in the happy confusion, still stands as one of the best comedies the screen has to offer. Impossible with such a director and such players to assign credit. Easy, though, to see why *Some Like It Hot* was a financial triumph. With its controlled farce, its thriller passages and its faint sexual suggestions it had everything the audiences of its period wanted.

Tony Curtis *turns on the secondhand charm to impress Marilyn Monroe in* Some Like It Hot.

War and extravagance

Times, though, were changing. The 1950s still held memories of the war, but the memories were softening, bringing reconciliation. Marlon Brando could still play the Nazi in *The Young Lions* (1958), but he was a repentant Nazi; and he could also play the smiling Japanese interpreter in *The Teahouse of the August Moon* (1956); it was one of his rare appearances in comedy and drew crowds to the box office. By the 1960s another kind of war, a future, a

Buddy Hackett and Mickey Rooney *(right) were among the multi-star cast of Stanley Kramer's juggernaut comedy,* It's a Mad Mad Mad Mad World.

Dustin Hoffman *was* The Graduate; *his degree tenderly bestowed by Anne Bancroft's Mrs. Robinson.*

doomsday war was occupying people's minds, and Stanley Kubrick was making a tragi-farce, *Dr Strangelove* (1964), about the possibility of a lethal error.

And the 1950s saw the beginnings of a shift away from the joke which depended on the individual star. *Around the World in Eighty Days* (1956) might follow the fortunes of the single adventurer played by David Niven, but for most people the fun was in identifying the scores of famous names whose owners flashed on the screen for perhaps a minute, in recognizing Frank Sinatra or John Gielgud, Fernandel or Beatrice Lillie or Noel Coward. Seven years later Stanley Kramer's *Its A Mad Mad Mad Mad World* employed another huge cast. But the wit of Mike Todd's extravagant joke was replaced by violence. Slapstick had come back; even Spencer Tracy at the end of his days (four years later he was dead) was involved in the savage fable about the pursuit of money. And audiences responded.

The audience wanted violence, they wanted irrational absurdity. Kramer's film was a commercial success. A year or so later *Those Magnificent Men in Their Flying Machines* with its caricature of early airplanes in an early race was a commercial success. And in the 1970s audiences were still getting the extravagance they craved. One remembers, for instance, Peter Bogdanovich, with his strong feeling for the past of the cinema, having a shot at the revival of farce in *What's Up Doc?* (1972): the chase, the confusion over the ownership of suitcases, everything attended by mishaps and adorned by references not literary but cinematic.

Sexual comedy

I am not saying that the comedy of the 1960s lacked wit, merely that these occasional essays in slapstick suggested a new mood in comedy. There was wit all right, but it snarled rather than smiled. Society itself was changing. Permissiveness, so-called, had set in. The hints of sexuality in the comedy of Marilyn Monroe, hints inseparable from her physical presence, had been replaced by frank invitation. Sex became a fact on the screen, not a secret, and with a sigh of relief the public settled down to enjoy the presentation.

Many successes in the cinema thus became easily explicable. Audiences might now and then respond to a romantic theme – as they responded to *Love Story* (1970) (though without its four-letter words they might have been less welcoming). But on the whole they wanted the sexual joke. In 1969 they wanted *Bob and Carol and Ted and Alice.* Bored couples had experimented with wife-swapping, and those who hadn't experimented were entertained by a fiction about it – even though on the screen the experiment ended in frustration and a burst of morality.

As it happened one of the best sexual jokes came fairly early, in 1967. *The Graduate* showed a young man just down from University who is taken to bed by a family friend, a woman considerably older than himself. The relationship between the two, the inexperienced boy and the experienced woman of the world, in spite of its intimacy preserved a superficial formality: in bed he always addressed her as Mrs Robinson. It was a good joke – and it was not wasted. Another thing: the tale had a romantic ending, and the public's taste for romance in comedy was gratified. Possibly the casting of a player at the time almost unknown, Dustin Hoffman, helped the movie. And *The Graduate* had a fourth advantage: surprise. It was impudently unexpected.

Not that commercial triumph in the cinema is ever predictable. But looking back – and enough time has passed for the full results to be known – one can see that the film had everything. A pleasure to be able to say, as one so

George Segal and Natalie Wood *(far left) as* The Last Married Couple in America, *bemused by the New Morality.*

Donald Sutherland and Elliott Gould *(left) as the last sane couple in Korea, in Robert Altman's anarchic war comedy,* M*A*S*H.

rarely can say, that a huge money-maker was a pleasure. For once the critics and the public were of the same mind.

One might pursue the subject of sexual comedy to a more recent example, *The Last Married Couple in America* (1980). A far cry from the days when divorce was almost taboo in the American cinema; here the entire cast are either separated or considering separation. Divorce becomes the fashionable practice; and a happy pair, after no more than a tiff, propose to follow the example of neighbours and friends and break up the home. The comedy, though, lies in the frankness with which the sexual situation is handled. An acquaintance demonstrates the liberal partnership he enjoys with his girl; at his request she strips naked in front of that last married couple. A friend who has broken with his wife describes in intimate detail his sexual difficulties; nothing is left imprecise. True that in the traditional fashion of cinema about marriage and divorce the 'last married couple' revert to marriage – a romantic solution which may well have contributed to the film's success. But the joke is in the frankness, in the open discussion of sexual problems – and I suppose in the nudity.

Irreverent slapstick

Reticence, in fact, is out of fashion. Even in slapstick the fun grows rougher. Interesting to compare the old type with the new. In the 1960s Kramer's *It's A Mad Mad Mad Mad World* took the public fancy with its cast of famous stars and its extras clustered high on a swinging fire-escape ladder. In 1979 Steven Spielberg, having won applause for a wide range of subjects from *Jaws* to *Close Encounters of the Third Kind*, experimented in the extravagant slapstick of *1941*. The film presented a state of chaos in Los Angeles after Pearl Harbour – everybody expecting attack, and panic heightened by the appearance offshore of a Japanese submarine with a German observer on board. Everything happens: anti-aircraft guns are installed in private yards, planes roar, motor-bikes race. And everything happens at once.

The old exponents of slapstick say that it needs precision, that it is an affair requiring handling far more delicate than is usually realized. Perhaps *1941* lacked that precision. Perhaps the timing of the film was wrong and people were not in the mood for a joke about Pearl Harbour. At any rate *1941* was a melancholy flop. The joke was too complex even for the public of the 1980s.

Of course there is the possibility that Spielberg's movie lacked the kind of violence which attracts modern audiences. Perhaps it needed also a fresh theme. Flouting authority has always been a cinema subject. It was used by Chaplin; it was at the heart of *A Clockwork Orange*: it reappears in the 1970s and the 1980s as a joke. A savage joke; it speaks to the young spectators who make up so much of today's audience. And it can make a movie a best-seller. *Animal House* (1978) is slapstick in the educational system: not the cheerful incongruousness of teacher and pupil in the British Will Hay classics, but rampage and riot, defiance out of control, John Belushi spitting out his lunch at his table companions. Some audiences may find it merely disgusting; to others *Animal House* can be a cult movie. For the rebellious young it satisfies a desire to humiliate authority.

Parody

The mood pervades other, less repellent forms of comedy. It is there in the ridicule of the martinet nurse in *M*A*S*H* (1970), where indeed the basic theme is one of irreverence – though duty hurries in at the end of the story to save face. And *M*A*S*H*, reverting in the 1970s to the theme of war (though it is war in a different theatre, in Korea, and with a different viewpoint) comes pretty high in the list of commercial successes.

The attitude of disrespect for discipline in

Ralph Bellamy and Donald Pleasence *(right) as a lawyer and a 'psychotheologist' recruited as an expert witness in Carl Reiner's religious satire,* Oh, God!

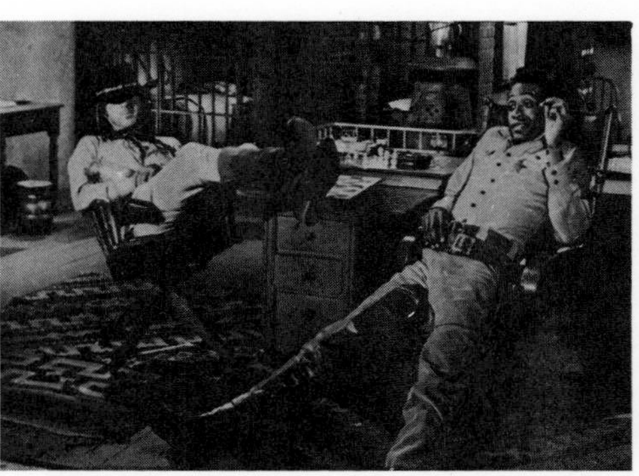

Gene Wilder and Cleavon Little *(far right) as improbable lawmen in Mel Brooks's burlesque western,* Blazing Saddles.

*M*A*S*H* verges on parody; and parody, again, is among the forms of comedy winning support in the cinema of the 1970s and 1980s. In the great days of romance and adventure, parody was rarely welcomed, though Disney in one of his short animated pieces brought off some splendid cartoon-jokes at the expense of the great stars from Garbo onwards. But in the anti-romantic mood of the new cinema nothing is safe. Mel Brooks joined the company of the money-makers in 1974 when he wrote and produced and directed *Blazing Saddles*, which took the clichés of the Western and made them absurd – the newly appointed sheriff, the threat of railway interests to the land, the battle – but fought this time with custard pies – between the virtuous and the villainous.

A year later the horror film was the target: *Young Frankenstein* took the old clichés and turned them upside down, with Peter Boyle as the Monster invited by the statutory innocent child to join her on the seesaw. But *Blazing Saddles* (sacrilege to Western fans) was the bigger money-spinner; and with a theme familiar to everybody who has ever set foot in the cinema the reason is clear enough.

An empty future?

It used to be said that comedy was conservative, the opponent of the new and the unfamiliar. True that from Aristophanes onwards the great comic writers have made fun of what they saw as the excesses of progress. But today we have a cinema which undermines the confidence of the past. No more of the pathos of Chaplin, the fearful acrobatics of Harold Lloyd or the David-versus-Goliath stance of Buster Keaton. Looking back over eight decades of the screen one sees the easy romantic optimism of Frank Capra overlaid by doubt. The effrontery of a Mae West is replaced by exhibitionism, the delicacy of Marilyn Monroe by consulting-room talk. The exquisite timing of Laurel and Hardy is forgotten; so is the verbal dexterity of Bob Hope. In one department of comedy, though, one can recognize an advance. The ageless George Burns of *Oh God!* (1977), presenting a friendly, homely deity in a cap, offers an image of religion a good deal more acceptable and more humane than the sentimentalities of the Bing Crosby movies of the 1940s.

For the rest we are left with a screen comedy which relies on extremes. Everything goes farther. In the effort to recapture the old pleasures film-makers resort to the tricks of slapstick – but exaggeration blunts the joke. Inhibitions have rightly been put aside, and the human body is no longer treated as a deadly secret to be kept hidden from its possessors; but one can have a surfeit of flesh. Still, the public is served. In his home the spectator can enjoy the uncluttered scene, action undisturbed by extravagant violence; television satisfies his need for domestic fun, domestic drama. In the cinema he wants more. It is his choice which selects the commercial winner.

Will he ever again, exercising his right of choice, revive the popularity of the single star, the individual comic? Much heralded, *The Jerk* arrived in London to introduce us to Steve Martin, who plays an incompetent, a butter-fingers, a man who, alone in charge of a garage, lets the visiting crooks get away with the building itself. The gags, though they may be cruder, are of the kind which endeared to us the famous silent comics. Perhaps they account for the success of the movie at the box-office. And for a moment one dreams of a future with a cinema comedy less complex, less uneasy, less violent, even less sex-ridden. But only for a moment; and I for one don't find Steve Martin very funny. I am haunted by the suspicion that in general comedy is no longer fashionable.

The public may applaud a Peter Sellers or a Dudley Moore. But what they really want is *Star Wars*. They want those space-figures without character and without passion. They want those enormous angular vehicles endlessly creaking about in the wastes of humanoid-infested nothingness. They want a future, and they want it empty.

Musicals

The Great Ziegfeld *(right), one of MGM's most lavish 1930s productions, was a musical biography, lasting nearly three hours, of Broadway impresario Florenz Ziegfeld. Here Virginia Bruce presides over the song 'A Pretty Girl is like a Melody'.*

'Wait a minute,' said an eager Al Jolson to amazed cinema audiences in between songs in *The Jazz Singer*, 'you ain't heard *nothin'* yet!' He was so right. A whole new genre lay before them once Warner Brothers' startling success at the film's New York premiere on October 6th, 1927 made it plain that the days of silents were numbered. Over the next decades audiences were treated to vast and varied quantities of music, from the sublime to the ridiculous. There were singing stars from nightclubs, vaudeville, Broadway revues, radio and the Metropolitan Opera. There were honey-voiced crooners, hot gospellers, raucous rock 'n' rollers, ballet troupes, circus acts, symphony orchestras, concert pianists, big bands, tap dancers, lady organists, singing cowboys, singing swimmers, singing (or at least barking) dogs. There were unique individuals like Fred Astaire, Judy Garland, Gene Kelly. Even within the confines of *The Jazz Singer* the range of music was big enough. Jolson went down on one knee to sing 'Mammy' with arms outstretched, tears in every note; he stood up reverently clothed in synagogue robes for the Jewish chant Kol Nidre, then he capered through breezy popular numbers like 'Toot, Toot, Tootsie, Goodbye'.

The Jazz Singer may seem terribly antiquated today, yet it isn't difficult to fathom the film's appeal to contemporary audiences. *The Jazz Singer* showcased a star of immense power and resonance, whose name on the cinema marquee would guarantee a crowd. Jolson had long electrified theatre audiences with his Broadway shows, one of which had provided dramatist Samson Raphaelson with the idea for the play on which the film was based. Raphaelson recognized in Jolson the emotional force of a Jewish cantor, and his plot dwelt to a melodramatic degree on the clashing claims of religion and show business. Even today *The Jazz Singer* can bring out handkerchiefs.

Hollywood later preferred to leave such heart-wrenching conflicts to their melodramas, but the subject of show business always remained a key element in musicals. For one thing, producers and writers quickly realized that, if you built stories around characters who worked in show business, you didn't have to think up logical explanations for their bursts of singing: you could simply cut from a plot scene to a musical performance. But more importantly, the world of show business presented cinema audiences with a seductive, glittering world of luxury, beauty and attainable riches – just the thing to clear away Depression nightmares for a few hours. For musicals have always provided the cinema's most clear-cut form of escapism – a trip to a brightly coloured world where everyone ultimately bubbles over with happiness. Significantly, it was only when audiences began to demand a radically different and harsher kind of escapism in the 1960s and 70s – car crashes, airplane disasters, all sorts of bloodbaths – that the musical genre seriously crumbled.

The late 20s and early 30s

But producers at the end of the 1920s had no time to analyze the appeal of their product; they were caught in a whirlwind trying to rush out films to meet the public demand. Studios embarked on massive spending sprees to acquire material and talent. Complete music publishing houses in New York were acquired. MGM, the studio which ultimately produced some of the greatest musicals in the 1940s and 1950s, had to build up its music department from scratch, taking over the entire staff and library of New York's Capitol Theatre.

The easiest way to make a musical film was to transfer a stage musical from Broadway to the screen: in 1929 Universal presented *Show Boat*, Paramount presented the Marx Brothers' musical comedy *The Cocoanuts*, RKO presented *Rio Rita*. Advertisements in the movie magazines made much of this Broadway link. 'The world's most famous thoroughfare is three thousand miles long now,' revealed a breathless page of advertiser's copy in *Photoplay*, October 1929, 'Warner Brothers and First National Vita-

All-Time Hit Musicals

	Rental income from initial release period: $m.	Inflation factor	Adjusted total: $m.
1 The Sound of Music, 1965	72	×2.5	180
2 Grease, 1978	93.3	×1.1	102.6
3 Saturday Night Fever, 1977	73.5	×1.1	80.8
4 West Side Story, 1961	19.5	×4	78.2
5 Mary Poppins, 1965	31	×2.5	77.5
6 This Is the Army, 1943	8.5	×9	76.5
7 South Pacific, 1958	16.5	×4.5	74.2
8 White Christmas, 1954	12	×5	60
9 The Jolson Story, 1946	7.6	×7	53.2
10 Fiddler on the Roof, 1971	34	×1.5	51
11 Funny Girl, 1968	24.9	×2	49.8
12 Yankee Doodle Dandy, 1942	4.8	×10	48
13 Meet Me in St Louis, 1944	5.2	×9	46.8
14 The King and I, 1956	8.5	×5	42.5
15 A Star is Born, 1977	37.1	×1.1	40.8
16 Anchors Aweigh, 1945	4.5	×9	40.5
The Thrill of a Romance, 1945	4.5	×9	40.5
18 The Singing Fool, 1928	4	×10	40
The Road to Morocco, 1942	4	×10	40
20 Blue Skies, 1946	5.7	×7	39.9
21 The Glenn Miller Story, 1954	7.6	×5	38
22 Hollywood Canteen, 1944	4.2	×9	37.8
23 Holiday Inn, 1942	3.75	×10	37.5
24 The Dolly Sisters, 1945	4	×9	36
My Fair Lady, 1964	12	×3	36
26 The Jazz Singer, 1927	3.5	×10	35
Oklahoma, 1955	7	×5	35
28 Guys and Dolls, 1956	6.9	×5	34.5
29 Star Spangled Rhythm, 1943	3.8	×9	34.2
30 Oliver!, 1968	16.8	×2	33.6
31 Sunny Side Up, 1929	3.3	×10	33
Hans Christian Andersen, 1952	6	×5.5	33
33 The Road to Utopia, 1946	4.5	×7	31.5
Till the Clouds Roll By, 1946	4.5	×7	31.5
The Road to Rio, 1947	4.5	×7	31.5
Easter Parade, 1949	4.5	×7	31.5
37 Show Boat, 1951	5.2	×6	31.2
38 The Harvey Girls, 1946	4.4	×7	30.8
39 Cabaret, 1972	20.3	×1.5	30.4
40 Gigi, 1957	6.7	×4.5	30.1
41 Broadway Melody, 1929	3	×10	30
A Star is Born, 1954	6	×5	30

Selected runners-up

Thoroughly Modern Millie, 1967	14.7	×2	29.4
High Society, 1956	5.8	×5	29
Ziegfeld Follies, 1946	4	×7	28
Seven Brides for Seven Brothers, 1954	5.6	×5	28
An American in Paris, 1951	4.5	×6	23
Love Me Tender, 1956	4.5	×5	22.5
The Wizard of Oz, 1939	2	×10	20
Singin' in the Rain, 1952	3.3	×5.5	18.1
Jailhouse Rock, 1957	4	×4.5	18
Rock Around the Clock, 1956	1.1	×5	5.5

1980 Popeye, Coal Miner's Daughter

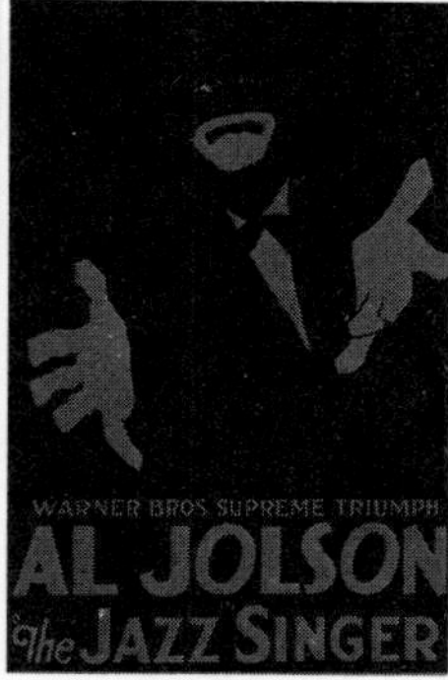

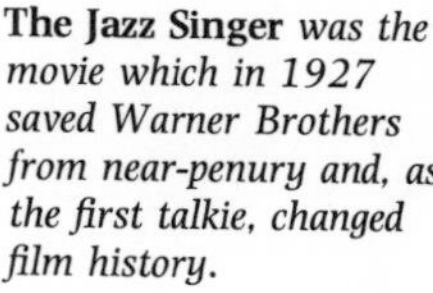

The Jazz Singer *was the movie which in 1927 saved Warner Brothers from near-penury and, as the first talkie, changed film history.*

42nd Street *(above centre) and* Gold Diggers of 1933 *(above right) continued Warners' highly successful adoption of the musical form. Both employ the distinctive style of designer Busby Berkeley.*

phone production will give you everything the stage can offer – its cyclonic dancing choruses, the flaming color of its glorified revues, its fabulous beauty ensembles in all their glory of costumes and settings.' Hollywood also got busy making their own glorified revues, with films like MGM's *The Broadway Melody* (1929), Universal's *King of Jazz* (1930), Warner's *Show of Shows* (1929), all of which offered a violently mixed bag of artistes hastily assembled.

Musicals thus began at a time of great turmoil in the industry, and the genre has remained perhaps the most volatile of all those developed in Hollywood, with constant fluctuations in its popularity, personnel and style. For to be commercially successful, the musical has to be geared to public taste in popular music, and that is always changing, almost with the frequency of hemlines and hairstyles. Also, given the genre's emphasis on physical beauty and athletic ability, it's hard, if not impossible, for a musical star to grow fat and old before the cameras the way John Wayne did in westerns. The musical demands reasonably young and vigorous performers to convince its audiences, and someone like Fred Astaire – who danced on screen from *Flying Down to Rio* (1933) to *Finian's Rainbow* (1968) – is very much an exception. The history of musicals is a history of small cycles at different studios, of different generations and styles, stars and writers rising and falling.

Busby Berkeley

The first switch in the musical's fortunes happened almost immediately. After just two years of them, public enthusiasm plummeted: the novelty of sound was no longer compensation for cardboard plots, sets and acting, or the tiresome repetition of dull songs. Production was cut back drastically: from over 70 musicals released in 1930, the level dropped below ten in 1931. But by 1933 three films, and one studio, changed the situation. With the release of Warner's *42nd Street, Gold Diggers of 1933* and *Footlight Parade*, musicals were once again back in favour.

Once again the world of show business was a central attraction. All three films described the trials and tribulations experienced by cast, producers and backers in putting on a lavish Broadway show, which finally materialized on screen in the form of amazing dance formations designed by Busby Berkeley. Berkeley had worked on many stage shows in the 1920s, but it was in the movies that he could really indulge his mania for making patterns out of pretty girls. His overhead shots showed them opening out like flower petals or forming the shape of a giant violin; in close-up his camera glided through rows of legs to find the romantic leads grinning idiotically at the end.

Today such moments are treasured as high camp, and the films' winsome leads Dick Powell and Ruby Keeler are almost as amusing. But to audiences at the time Berkeley's numbers simply provided musical escapism at its richest. The song titles alone provide evidence: 'We're in the money', 'Keep young and beautiful', 'With plenty of money and you'. No wonder Berkeley's chorus girls were always smiling. Yet if the musical numbers catered to the audiences' dreams, the plot lines took much more notice of their waking lives. After Ginger Rogers and company sing 'We're in the money' at the very start of *Gold Diggers of 1933* the show's props are impounded: the producer has no money at all and all the girls face unemployment. But everything was always all right on the night in the best theatrical tradition, and downtrodden audiences could take comfort in the amazing good fortune of Ruby Keeler's chorus girl, asked to deputize in *42nd Street* after the leading lady breaks her ankle.

Astaire and Rogers at RKO

The Warner brand of musical was peculiarly American. Continental practice was vastly different: many European musicals followed stage operetta conventions, but the early sound films of René Clair in France showed a new approach, with music flowing in and out of scenes and a satiric wit in the scripts. In America, Ernst Lubitsch used a similar approach for his films at Paramount, featuring Maurice Chevalier and Jeanette MacDonald. Such musicals enjoyed moderate success with audiences, though they were probably more popular with highbrow critics. But it was at RKO that Hollywood's own brand of sophisticated musical flourished. Again 1933 was the crucial year, with the release of *Flying Down to Rio*. Gene Raymond and Dolores Del Rio were the nominal stars, but the people who mattered were Fred Astaire and Ginger Rogers. With their next film *The Gay Divorcee* (1934), adapted from Cole Porter's stage show *Gay Divorce* (a title considered too permissive for the movies), they jumped to top billing, and provided seven more musicals for the studio before the cycle finished in 1939.

Broadway traditions were crucial for these films. If they weren't based directly on Broadway shows, they shared the same environments, the same plots, the same emotional ambience, the same top-flight composers (Porter, Irving Berlin, Gershwin). Audiences sat in the lap of luxury – or at least elegance – from beginning to end, watching the plots' tangled romances untangle themselves in nightclubs, parks, country estates, ocean liners and European hotels. There was also something of a theatrical air about the films' repertory company of supporting players: Edward Everett Horton's fusspots, Eric Blore's unctuous butlers, Erik Rhodes' excitable foreigners. Even the settings had the familiarity of theatre scenery: for *Flying Down to Rio* RKO instituted a structure called the B.W.S. (Big White Set), subsequently manipulated to form anything from the Venetian waterfront to a bandstand.

Where Warners clumped together their extravagant musical numbers for the finale, RKO spaced out their songs. And Hermes Pan, Astaire's choreographer, looked for human intimacy in his dances, not spectacle. The personalities of Astaire and Rogers, whether acting or singing, were vital to the films' appeal. Astaire had the effortless elegance of a man about town, yet there was a touch of light mockery to his attitudes that audiences relished. At RKO Ginger Rogers moved up the social ladder from the hardboiled show girls she had played elsewhere and acquired a high-class veneer, though a great deal of abrasiveness and grit remained. Both of them seemed highly sophisticated and highly down-to-earth – a unique combination. Equally unique was the quality of their songs; numbers like 'Night and day', 'The way you look tonight', and 'They can't take that away from me' were endlessly

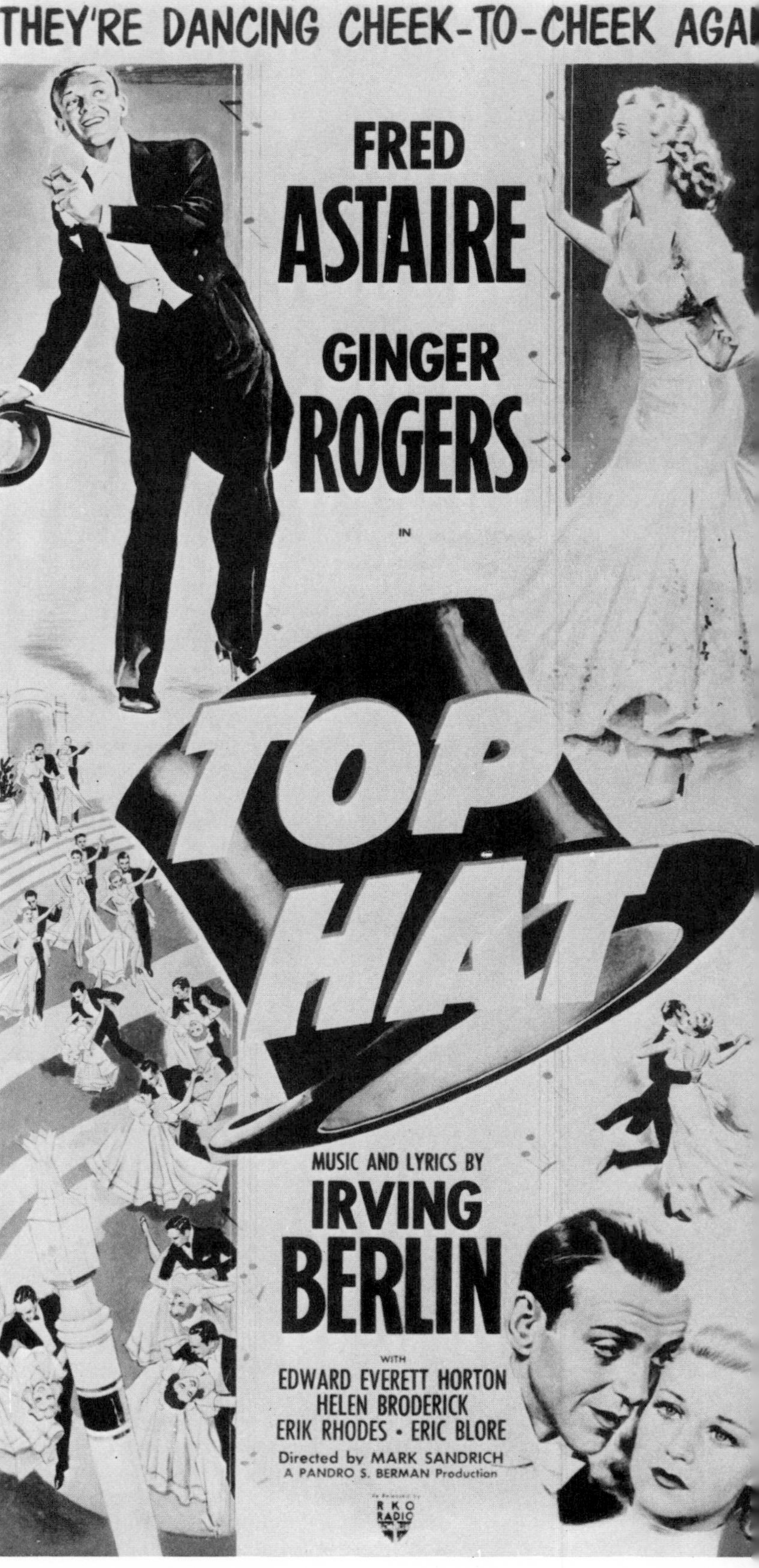

Top Hat *(left), one of the best remembered of all RKO's Fred Astaire/Ginger Rogers series, though interestingly the films do not rank as top money-makers.*

Nelson Eddy and Jeanette MacDonald *(right) in the lush* Maytime, *a film originally shown in sepia.*

Folies Bergère *(far right), Fox's attempt to emulate Warners' musical success. Dave Gould's choreography successfully emulated the Busby Berkeley style.*

performed on radio and records, contributing much to the films' popularity.

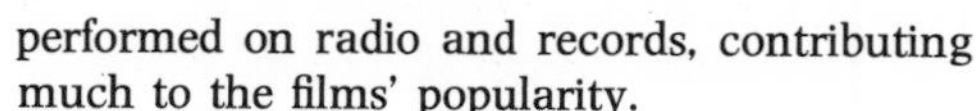

Eddy and MacDonald at MGM

The other chief musical duo of the 1930s – Nelson Eddy and Jeanette MacDonald – couldn't have been more different. They reigned at MGM, whose mogul Louis B. Mayer relished the old-fashioned and sentimental (and had a sizeable part of the American public behind him); when musical scores were played for his approval, the violin parts were given special prominence. For Eddy and MacDonald the studio resurrected some of Broadway's most popular operettas by Rudolf Friml and Victor Herbert. MacDonald duly replaced the mocking humour she displayed for Lubitsch with strait-laced earnestness. And Eddy, trained as an operatic tenor, proved an upstanding partner, forever wooing and rescuing his heroine in various historic and exotic climes, from New Orleans in *Naughty Marietta* (1935) to the Canadian pine forests of *Rose Marie* (1936). *Marietta* had a fresh air feel, partly due to the energetic direction of W. S. Van Dyke, but later the pace of the films slowed down and atmosphere was piled on to a claustrophobic degree. *Maytime* (1937) provided the epitome of the cycle – a film so relentlessly pretty that even the opening credits were spelled out in blossom leaves, floating on a stream. Some found it difficult to take the pair's posturing seriously even at the time, but they still had an audience devoted enough to justify the sums MGM spent on vast sets, crowds of extras and forests of may blossom. And, as in the Astaire series, the songs in the films were always individually popular, and their constant exposure on radio gained much free publicity.

Universal, Paramount and Fox

Elsewhere during the 1930s, Universal had the teenager Deanna Durbin as a star attraction: her singing had more class and more high notes than even Eddy and MacDonald, though her vehicles were much humbler; warm family stories like *Three Smart Girls* (1936) were the norm. Paramount had Bing Crosby, whose easy singing style and 'Mr Average' image kept him successful for many years in films with generally tedious scripts but, again, highly popular songs. Twentieth Century-Fox darted about among different performers and styles. *Folies Bergère* (1935), with Maurice Chevalier, achieved something of the Berkeley panache in its dance numbers; it also featured a story of triangular relationships and deceptions considered so suitable to musicals that it was remade twice officially (as *That Night in Rio*, 1941, and *On the Riviera*, 1951) and many more times unofficially. For the family market there was Shirley Temple, who enthusiastically tap danced, cried and ate chocolate cake in a stream of popular vehicles.

But by the end of the 1930s Fox had formed a house team of sorts – Alice Faye, John Payne, Tyrone Power, Jack Oakie – who appeared in unadventurous but pleasantly nostalgic films looking back to past times and tastes: *Alexander's Ragtime Band* (1938), *Tin Pan Alley* (1940), *Hello, Frisco, Hello* (1943). New songs were sprinkled among old songs in the public domain, for which no copyright payment was necessary. This helped ease production and reduce the budget, but it also chimed in with the public mood during the years of World War II: anything which reminded them of safer times was welcome. And the films' chief songstress, Alice Faye, had the fresh, uncomplicated appeal of the archetypal girl next door.

Moon Over Miami *(left) starred Betty Grable in a wafer-thin plot about husband-hunting in Florida.*

Lucille Ball *confronts a feline chorus in MGM's* Ziegfeld Follies.

Singin' in the Rain, *one of the most famous musical sequences of all time performed by Gene Kelly.*

Heyday in wartime

The 1940s, and the war, provided the Hollywood musical with its heyday, for never since the darkest days of the Depression had there been so much to escape from. For those in the forces starved of attractive female company, Fox provided the bubbly Betty Grable, whose lengthy legs and wholesome smile were pinned up in lockers and barrack rooms all over the world. She appeared in *Down Argentine Way* (1940), *Moon Over Miami* (1941), *The Dolly Sisters* (1945), often with gaudy Technicolor photography and gaudy supporting performers like Carmen Miranda.

Some of the very biggest commercial successes were linked directly to the war, and were heavily patriotic in flavour. Warners came back into the limelight with *Yankee Doodle Dandy* (1942), an exuberant biography of the Broadway personality George M. Cohan, impersonated with all possible panache by James Cagney. The soundtrack resounded with timely songs like 'Over there' (written for World War I) and 'You're a grand old flag'; the final moments saw an elderly Cohan receiving kind words from Roosevelt and watching the youth of America proudly marching off to the new conflict. Warners also scored a tremendous success with *This is the Army* (1943), based on Irving Berlin's stage show with three hundred soldiers forming the cast. Circumstances of war also allowed the studios to fall back on the revue format, which had languished since the early talkies. Warners rounded up usable performers in *Thank Your Lucky Stars* (1943) and *Hollywood Canteen* (1944); Paramount presented *Star-Spangled Rhythm* (1942).

Arthur Freed at MGM

But the studio which managed best to combine commercial with artistic success throughout the decade was MGM. A regular succession of polished, imaginative musicals was produced by Arthur Freed, a former songwriter who carefully assembled a unit of talented personnel, including directors Vincente Minnelli and Charles Walters, choreographers (and future directors) Gene Kelly and Stanley Donen, and Freed's musical associate Roger Edens. Other units operated under producers Joe Pasternak and Jack Cummings. And no other studio at the time could rival MGM's range of performers: Judy Garland, Mickey Rooney, Gene Kelly, Frank Sinatra, Jane Powell (a less classy Deanna Durbin), the sultry Lena Horne, quite apart from lesser period oddities like the operatic tenor Lauritz Melchior, classical pianist José Iturbi, grinning bandleader Xavier

On the Town *(right) with, left to right, Frank Sinatra, Gene Kelly and Jules Munshin as the three sailors with 24 hours leave in Manhattan.*

Meet Me in St Louis *(far right), Arthur Freed's huge 1940s success with Judy Garland, left, and Lucille Bremer. It was Garland's most popular musical.*

Cugat, the swimming star Esther Williams and the gimmick singer Virginia O'Brien (who sang completely without facial, or musical, expression). There was something, and someone, for everybody.

Freed hit his stride at the end of the 30s with a Garland-Rooney series brimful with homely fun; the two popular teenage stars were generally struggling to put on a show, against all parental advice. But Freed rapidly became more ambitious, and in almost every musical genre current during the 1940s managed to create the most lavish and sophisticated examples. None of Fox's essays in nostalgia proved as delightful or affecting as *Meet Me in St Louis* (1944), with Judy Garland as the daughter of a loving family in 1903 (the year of the World's Fair) threatened with a move to New York. At a time when so many American families were pulled asunder by war this had an obvious appeal. And none of the revue films proved as dizzily spectacular as *Ziegfeld Follies* (1946), where Astaire, Garland, Kelly and other luminaries were surrounded by sets of almost suffocating fancifulness. MGM also made its mark in the newly fashionable genre of biographical films about popular composers, which allowed studios to string together nothing but surefire songs, provided they could sort out the legal complications of ownership: it took two years' paperwork before MGM secured rights to the Jerome Kern material in *Till the Clouds Roll By* (1946). The studio also saluted Rodgers and Hart in *Words and Music* (1948) – though neither film had the fantastic success of Columbia's *The Jolson Story* (1946), which brought the star of *The Jazz Singer* bouncing back into the limelight even though he only sang on the soundtrack and left it to Larry Parks to act out his life.

But it was not all success. A few of Freed's productions were notable box-office failures: Vincente Minnelli's yen for artistic effects got completely out of hand in *Yolanda and the Thief* (1945), while Rouben Mamoulian's *Summer Holiday* (1948), another essay in Americana adapted from an O'Neill play, was too quiet in tone to arouse audience interest. But these were the penalties for trying to push the musical out of conventional patterns, trying to link plot, song and dance together as an integrated whole. Freed also proved receptive to Broadway's new creative talent: the most famous showcase for this was *On the Town* (1949), based on the musical by Leonard Bernstein with book and lyrics by the former nightclub entertainers Adolph Green and Betty Comden, and athletic choreography by Jerome Robbins. Following a perverse but well-established Hollywood tradition, MGM acquired this valuable property only to jettison most of the original music, and top management had cold feet about the whole project until the healthy box-office receipts came in. This was a musical with simple freshness and vigour: three sailors on leave, singing and dancing on location along Manhattan's sidewalks and roofs instead of being cloistered in some cluttered, unreal studio set. And they were also freed from the invisible proscenium arch that haunted so many musical numbers: the melodic and choreographic line of the songs were exhilaratingly scattered among different camera shots and angles. The film also provided further evidence of the appeal of Gene Kelly (one of the sailors along with Frank Sinatra and Jules Munshin). Kelly was the first male musical performer to match Astaire in stature, though his style was very different: where Astaire was suave, Kelly was almost butch, moving about with little grace but much restless energy and eagerness.

MGM continued to ride high in the early 1950s. From the Kern and Rodgers-Hart song catalogues they moved on to Gershwin's in *An American in Paris* (1951), supplying a far more sophisticated narrative and visual framework than usual. Arthur Freed's own song catalogue was used for *Singin' in the Rain* (1952), a satiric look at the early days of talkies written by Comden and Green. But despite such imaginative and popular films a decline began, for MGM as well as for other studios. One film, *It's Always Fair Weather* (1955), makes the change in public mood part of its subject. Three army

The King and I *(left) which, after* South Pacific *and* White Christmas, *was the third most successful musical of the 1950s. Deborah Kerr, seated centre, played the English governess to the Siamese court.*

Julie Andrews *(right) in* The Sound of Music.

Barbra Streisand *(left) with Michael Crawford in the unsuccessful* Hello Dolly.

buddies, inescapably recalling the three sailors of *On the Town*, reunite after ten years of civilian life. All in some way are failures and at first have to get drunk before they can summon the energy to sing and dance at all. The decline reflected the crisis facing the industry.

Rock 'n' roll

Characteristically, one of the few new developments in the 1950s musical output – the rock 'n' roll films – occurred in the low-budget market and involved a completely new audience. If MGM musicals were designed for plush theatres like Radio City Music Hall, *Rock Around the Clock* (1956) and *Don't Knock the Rock* (1956) were at home in drive-ins. When such films were shown in conventional buildings, their young volatile audiences often gave vent to their passions by attacking the fittings and ripping up seats; some local authorities in America and England banned certain films outright. But there was nothing worthy of censorship in the plots, which were further variations on the story about struggling teenagers putting on a show. Where Judy Garland's and Mickey Rooney's parents were terrified of swing, the older generation were now worried about rock 'n' roll and jiving, which they saw as the first steps to perdition. Low-budget specialists like Sam Katzman rushed their product out, crammed with big names like Bill Haley, Little Richard, Gene Vincent, The Platters, with disc jockey Alan Freed (no relation to Arthur) usually hovering in the background. The biggest name of all, Elvis Presley, starred in a total of thirty-one vehicles, beginning with a limp western *Love Me Tender* (1956). *Jailhouse Rock* (1957) was one of the few to use the singer's style sensibly; most of his other vehicles cast him adrift in plots of surpassing blandness. But Presley's name on any marquee guaranteed an audience of fans, who appreciated the songs if nothing else – though none of the films ever became substantial money-makers.

The Sound of Music: a false dawn

The only musicals which could now be guaranteed to succeed on a large scale were the Broadway transfers: *The King and I* (1956), *South Pacific* (1958), *West Side Story* (1961). When Fox turned to Rodgers and Hammerstein's *The Sound of Music* (1965), they had more of a success than anyone could possibly have imagined. But the film did have some highly potent ingredients. There were simple songs, easy to remember (if you didn't know them already); there was luscious Austrian scenery and a storyline which cannily involved such established heartstring-tuggers as children (seven of them) and a convent of nuns. And it was all set back in a time carefully identified in the opening credits as 'the last golden days of the Thirties,' before Europe was engulfed by World War Two. There was Julie Andrews, then riding the crest of her popularity, with all of the clean, radiant worthiness of Alice Faye in the 1940s (though her diction was too perfect for words). Emerging in the middle of the supposedly Swinging Sixties, *The Sound of Music* suddenly showed that there was still a vast market for simple, sentimental family entertainment – provided it was handled with taste and care (and Robert Wise's direction was meticulously tasteful).

Alas for Fox and other studios, *The Sound of Music* didn't prove that there was a new market for musicals as musicals. Hollywood read the

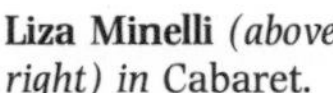

Liza Minelli *(above right) in* Cabaret.

West Side Story *(above far right): 'the Sharks' with, left to right, Jay Norman, George Chakiris and Eddie Verso.*

Grease *(right) with John Travolta and Olivia Newton-John, centre couple, the biggest musical of the 1970s.*

signs wrongly and geared itself up for a revival. Fox reunited Robert Wise and Julie Andrews for *Star!* (1968), a biography of Gertrude Lawrence, and produced a full-scale box-office disaster. Fox also poured its coffers into a version of the stage hit *Hello, Dolly!* (1969), which under its contractual terms could only be released after the Broadway run – and much of the public interest – was over. The result was another disaster. Then Columbia lost a fortune on *Lost Horizon* (1973), a colossally silly version of James Hilton's fantasy first filmed by Frank Capra in 1937.

As for MGM, that most musical of studios seemed to spend most of its time and talent in the 1960s preparing – and failing – to produce Arthur Freed's long cherished salute to Irving Berlin, *Say It with Music*; various stars and directors were announced at different times (including Julie Andrews), but it was plainly not the time for such extravaganzas. Once James Aubrey became company president in October 1969, MGM was gradually stripped of all those assets which had made it the cream of Hollywood. *Say It with Music* was promptly cancelled, and in May 1970 the studio's stockpile of sets, props and assorted memorabilia were auctioned off. Under the hammer went the massive title prop from their 1951 remake of *Show Boat*, the ruby slippers Judy Garland wore trotting down the Yellow Brick Road in *The Wizard of Oz*, even the swimming suits of Esther Williams.

Streisand, Liza Minnelli and Travolta

The event might seem to signal the musical's final demise, though the genre had been declining ever since studios stopped making musicals as a matter of course and switched to isolated versions of Broadway hits. Yet, new styles and new personalities continued to emerge. William Wyler directed *Funny Girl* (1968) in a fussily old-fashioned way, but its star Barbra Streisand created a deep impression with her manic exuberance. Bob Fosse's *Cabaret* (1972) likewise showcased the talents of Garland and Minnelli's daughter, Liza Minnelli; Fosse's direction of this and *Sweet Charity* (1969) had a feverish appeal.

Other kinds of spectacular mainstream entertainment returned to public favour in the 1970s, but very few people sang or danced: it was only at the end of the decade that a great success emerged in *Grease* (1978), which boasted vague but colourful 1950s nostalgia, the well-oiled charms of John Travolta and enough Hollywood veterans in the supporting cast for older viewers to feel welcome.

The musical's future is impossible to predict: it was volatile enough when there was a continuing tradition to nourish the studios. But the reliance on Broadway continues: versions of the latest smash musicals are in the pipeline – the modish *A Chorus Line* and the sugary *Annie*. And nostalgia for the immediate past is plainly still potent, but scarcely a guarantee of success. The massively ill-conceived *Sgt. Pepper's Lonely Hearts Club Band* (1978) was a box-office disaster, as was another 1960s classic *Hair* (1979), filmed with wild enthusiasm by Milos Forman. Now some film-makers have gone back much further into history; EMI's remake of *The Jazz Singer* (1980) had Neil Diamond in the part taken in 1927 by Al Jolson and an updated storyline (the Cantor and his son are the only family survivors from the Holocaust). If Hollywood has to return to *The Jazz Singer* for inspiration then plainly we still 'ain't heard nothin' yet.' But we might have heard most things worth hearing.

Horror

There are, basically, two sorts of horror: the kind you imagine, and the kind you experience. In one, a child huddles deliciously under the blankets, secure from the monster that haunts the darkness beneath the bed. In the other, a passer-by hurries to the scene of a street accident, dreading yet eager to catch a glimpse of blood and shattered flesh.

Both have played their part in the history of the tale of terror that stretches back to the folk tale and beyond. But words must always leave it to the reader or hearer to conjure a vision in his own mind; paintings, no matter how graphic, must carve out a moment in time, a static image to be animated as the viewer wills. It was not until motion pictures arrived that the horror story could, in theory, tell everything, leaving absolutely nothing to the imagination.

Few do, of course, since the purpose of a movie (to entertain) would be defeated if the audience were left literally terrified, vomiting with the uncontrollable nausea experienced by, say, a raw recruit spattered by fragments of human flesh on the battlefield, or by a detective stumbling for the first time upon evidence of the aberrations of a homicidal maniac. Such film-makers as do attempt to exploit horror on this level, increasingly numerous in recent years, in any case tend to come up against the stumbling-block of reality: simulated with the aid of make-up or camera trickery, the physical aspects of horror all too often simply engender disbelief.

Nevertheless, horror seen and horror imagined are both legitimate weapons for the artist, provided a certain balance is maintained. Familiarity breeds contempt, and yesterday's horror very often becomes today's cliché, or is at least subverted. Oblivious to the underlying emasculation symbolism of 'The Three Blind Mice', for instance, the childish imagination still responds delightedly to the magical nonsense-fun of the nursery rhyme, never for a moment experiencing any visceral reaction to the horror of those tails being cut off by a carving-knife. Revivify the scene by filming it with real mice and a real carving-knife, and the reaction would be very different. But what, with the magic gone, would be the point of the exercise?

All too often in recent years, as indifferent films become huge box-office successes largely on the strength of lurid details to which perfected technical skills lend increasingly graphic illusion – the possessed child spewing greenish bile in *The Exorcist* (1973), the decapitation by a sheet of glass in *The Omen* (1976), the man exploding as the parasite organism bursts out of his chest in *Alien* (1979) – one is tempted to ask that same question. After all, as Shelley suggested in his poem celebrating the 'tempestuous loveliness of terror', *On the Medusa in a Florentine Gallery*: '. . . it is less the horror than the grace/Which turns the gazer's spirit into stone'.

The history of the horror movie is littered with testimonials to the way exploiters have put a film's grace at risk by trying to accentuate the gruesome detail. To cite one example among many, producer Val Lewton's superb series of low-budget thrillers for RKO in the 1940s ran into constant interference from front office executives anxious to *show* what Lewton only suggested. *Cat People* (1942), the first and most successful of the series, beautifully directed by Jacques Tourneur, was about a young New York fashion designer (the marvellously feline Simone Simon) who falls in love and marries, but – troubled by a strange encounter which dredges up her secret fear that she is descended from a medieval Balkan sect whose women turn into raging felines when their passions are roused – refuses to consummate the marriage.

Subsequent events, escalating from the mortal terror of a caged bird in her presence to the unseen panther claws that menace a rival for her husband's affections, were deliberately calculated to suggest that while she might indeed be undergoing metamorphosis, she might equally well be no more than a lonely, neurotic, possibly lesbian woman driven to brute violence by her obsessive fears. But the terrifying ambivalence, charged by electric detail – her enigmatic smile as her hand bats

The Omen *(right) took the Devil's child theme of* Rosemary's Baby *a stage further, adding some spectacular violence and much arcane Christian scholarship. It spawned two sequels and paved the way for the boom in horror production at the end of the 1970s. Five-year old Harvey Stephens played Damien, son of the US Ambassador to Great Britain.*

All-Time Hit Horror Movies

	Film	Rental income from initial release period: $m.	Inflation factor	Adjusted total: $m.
1	The Exorcist, 1973	66.3	×1.4	92.8
2	Psycho, 1960	9	×4	36
3	The Amityville Horror, 1979	35	×1	35
4	The Omen, 1976	27.9	×1.2	33.5
5	Rosemary's Baby, 1968	15	×2	30
6	House of Wax, 1953	4.7	×5.5	25.7
7	Hallowe'en, 1978	18.5	×1.1	20.3
8	Exorcist II: The Heretic, 1977	13.9	×1.1	15.3
9	The Hunchback of Notre Dame, 1923	1.5	×10	15
	Frankenstein, 1931	1.5	×10	15
	Carrie, 1976	12.5	×1.2	15
	Coma, 1978	13.6	×1.1	15
13	The Phantom of the Opera, 1943	1.6	×9	14.4
	Omen II: Damien, 1978	13.1	×1.1	14.4
15	Whatever Happened to Baby Jane?, 1962	4	×3.5	14
	Willard, 1971	9.3	×1.5	14
17	Magic, 1978	11.9	×1.1	13.1
18	Dr Jekyll and Mr Hyde, 1932	1.3	×10	13
19	The Fury, 1978	11.6	×1.1	12.8
20	The Beast from 20,000 Fathoms, 1953	2.25	×5.5	12.4
21	The Invasion of the Body Snatchers, 1979	11.1	×1	11.1
22	Them, 1954	2.2	×5	11
23	Cat People, 1943	1.2	×9	10.8
24	Prophecy, 1979	10.5	×1	10.5
	Dracula, 1979	10.5	×1	10.5
26	It's Alive, 1974	6.9	×1.4	9.6
27	The Pit and the Pendulum, 1961	2	×4	8
28	The Fly, 1958	1.7	×4.5	7.7
29	The Phantom of the Rue Morgue, 1954	1.5	×5	7.5
	Race with the Devil, 1975	6	×1.25	7.5
31	Frankenstein, 1974	4.7	×1.4	6.6
32	The Creature from the Black Lagoon, 1954	1.3	×5	6.5
33	Homicidal, 1961	1.6	×4	6.4

Selected runners-up

Film	Rental income from initial release period: $m.	Inflation factor	Adjusted total: $m.
Invasion of the Body Snatchers, 1956	1.2	×5	6
The House on Haunted Hill, 1959	1.5	×4	6
Thirteen Ghosts, 1960	1.5	×4	6
The Time Machine, 1960	1.5	×4	6
Village of the Damned, 1961	1.5	×4	6
Gorgo, 1961	1.5	×4	6
Phantasm, 1979	6	×1	6
The Fall of the House of Usher, 1960	1.4	×4	5.6
The Revenge of the Creature, 1955	1.1	×5	5.5
Macabre, 1958	1.2	×4.5	5.4
The Blob, 1958	1	×4.5	4.5
Dracula, 1958	1	×4.5	4.5
Jack the Ripper, 1960	1	×4	4

1980 Friday the 13th, Dressed to Kill, When a Stranger Calls, The Shining, The Fog

Note: Reliable information on certain early Universal horror films is not available; it seems probable their initial rentals were much lower than is generally supposed. The original Dracula *(1930), for example, received only a limited release partly because cinemas were reluctant to book it. Conversely* Night of the Living Dead *certainly earned enough to be on the list, but reliable rental figures are not available.*

Simone Simon *with Kent Smith in* Cat People, *Tourneur's story of a haunted marriage which, after* The Phantom of the Opera *starring Claude Rains, ranks as the most successful horror movie of the 1940s.*

paw-like at the bird's cage; her long fingernails raking the velvet covering of a sofa in an access of rage – is very nearly denied by the unequivocal appearance, in a shot inserted at the studio's insistence, of a black panther during the final attack on the rival.

The film survives, of course, as does Tourneur's later *Night of the Demon* (1957), which attempts to show how fear can drive a man to believe anything. As directed by Tourneur, the film is a magnificent exercise in atmospherics in which a sceptical scientist is gradually persuaded through terror that the magician opposing him really does possess the power he boasts to raise the devil. But shots of an all-too-fleshly demon, inserted early in the film against Tourneur's wishes, reduce it to a much more pragmatic level, with the audience waiting sceptically for the reappearance of just another mock-up monster.

While both films remain high in the horror canon, it was this sort of interference, purely exploitative in intention, which gave the horror film a bad name. Even James Agee, one of Lewton's first apologists, felt obliged to explain, to excuse and to apply special pleading, entrenched in the common critical position that no serious attention would – or indeed, should – be paid to films with titles like *Cat People, I Walked with a Zombie, The Leopard Man.* Yet *Cat People,* while functioning as a splendidly full-blooded horror film, is also a subtle psychological study of the dangers inherent when an over-active imagination is fed by loneliness and fear, even if its strange, poetic delicacy is only fully apparent when considered together with Lewton's subsequent, and complementary, *Curse of the Cat People* (1944).

Although the 'grace' Shelley talks about is more likely to accompany evocation than demonstration of horror, it isn't necessarily a matter of discretion. A film like Mario Bava's *La Maschera del Demonio* (1961, known variously as *Black Sunday, Mask of the Demon* and *Revenge of the Vampire*), which begins with the chillingly evocative ring of a huge hammer being used to nail a spiked iron mask over the face of a girl about to be burned as a witch, could also encompass stomach-churning detail in its vision, as when slime and worms ooze from the eye-sockets of the witch's skull as her eyes re-surface and she prepares to rise again from the tomb.

In James Whale's *Frankenstein* (1931), the creation of the monster, stitched together from sectioned cadavers, is carefully elided. We see it for the first time in recuperation, as it were, with all operational scars healed, albeit grotesquely. But in Franju's *Les Yeux sans Visage* (1959, *Eyes Without a Face*), one scene opens with a scalpel tracing a bloody line on a girl's face in preparation for the removal of a section of facial tissue for a skin graft. Times change, and the frontiers of what is considered to be acceptable viewing are pushed back; but the shot is acceptable anyway in Franju's film, indeed essential to it, in that it offers a first intimation of the intolerable, pointless pain inflicted by a surgeon in his repeated, and invariably doomed, attempts to restore beauty to the daughter whose face he ruined in a car crash, and who ultimately rebels to make an end to his experiments. The context is all-important: without adequate dramatic or poetic justification, the moment of graphic violence tends to be devoid of grace.

Horror in the silent era

The earliest American horror films (those that have survived, at least) seem to be floundering

Lon Chaney *(far left) in his most famous role opposite Mary Philbin in the first* The Phantom of the Opera *(1925).*

Boris Karloff *(left) at his most avuncular, reading Jacqueline Wells' palm between takes of* The Black Cat, *and (right) in the original role of* Frankenstein.

in search of a genre. D. W. Griffith's *The Avenging Conscience* (1914), for instance, centres on a powerfully atmospheric adaptation of Edgar Allan Poe's 'The Tell-Tale Heart'; but as Griffith proceeds to orchestrate his narrative with themes from, and references to, other Poe stories ('William Wilson', 'The Black Cat') and poems ('Annabel Lee', 'The Raven', 'The Conqueror Worm', 'The Bells'), the film develops a literary rather than cinematic ambience.

The influence of German Expressionism

Even the best of these early efforts, the Lon Chaney *Phantom of the Opera* (1925), seems curiously tentative despite Chaney's superb performance, and despite some magnificent coups like the Phantom's majestic irruption into the masked ball at the Opéra costumed as the Red Death (a sequence originally filmed in colour). Ploddingly directed by Rupert Julian in an adaptation which simultaneously crams too much in and leaves too much out, the film completely misses the erotic element in the Beauty-and-the-Beast aspect of Gaston Leroux's novel. This was a mistake partially rectified in the otherwise much drearier 1943 remake. The spectacular Technicolor photography by Hal Mohr and W. Howard Greene probably accounts for this remake's surprising appearance in the best-seller charts; but there may have been another contributory factor. Where Chaney's Phantom concealed his hideous features behind a grubby linen cloth, Claude Rains wore a sculptured, exquisitely feline white mask. Apart from affording a handsome presence that made the anguish of wondering what lay underneath all the greater, this mask also lent the Phantom an ineffable whiff of sexuality well calculated to entrance his innocent protégée.

This touch of eroticism, combined with a masochistic post-war *angst* and with a revival of the dark romantic spirit of E. T. A. Hoffmann, was the mainstay of the silent, so-called 'Expressionist' cinema in Germany. By an unfortunate coincidence, just as this German influence began to impinge on America (chiefly by way of *The Cabinet of Dr Caligari* in 1919), Hollywood itself was bowing to the Broadway vogue for haunted house comedy-thrillers. Films like D. W. Griffith's *One Exciting Night* (1922), Roland West's *The Bat* (1926), Tod Browning's *London After Midnight* (1927), Paul Leni's *The Cat and the Canary* (1927), Benjamin Christensen's *The House of Horror* (1929) and *Seven Footprints to Satan* (1929), all revealed an impeccable absorption of Expressionist techniques in their stealthily prowling cameras, skilfully deployed shadows, and formalised acting styles; but all were obliged to throw away the ground gained by playing crassly for laughs in a parade of horrors that turned out to be spoofs.

Even Rex Ingram's *The Magician* (1926), a solemnly stylish adaptation of the Somerset Maugham novel inspired by the diabolist activities of Aleister Crowley, seems in two minds as to whether or not to encourage Paul Wegener to play for laughs in the leading role. One of the few exceptions, Tod Browning's *The Unknown* (1927), is unclassifiable, despite superficial resemblances to the same director's later *Freaks*. Here the circus ambience merely adds a few decorative thrills and frills; the kernel of the film is its acute psychological observation of a man (Lon Chaney), posing as an armless wonder in a circus, who falls in love with a girl possessed by a pathological fear of being touched, and who becomes so obsessed by his fear of losing her that, rather than run the risk, he has his arms amputated. A film of astonishing intensity, filled with a troubled malaise, *The Unknown* emerges less as a genre horror movie than as a case-book study of the crippling effects of masochism.

Caligari and *Frankenstein*

But with the coming of sound, and the emergence of James Whale's *Frankenstein* in 1931, it quickly became apparent that the lesson of the German silent cinema had not been wasted.

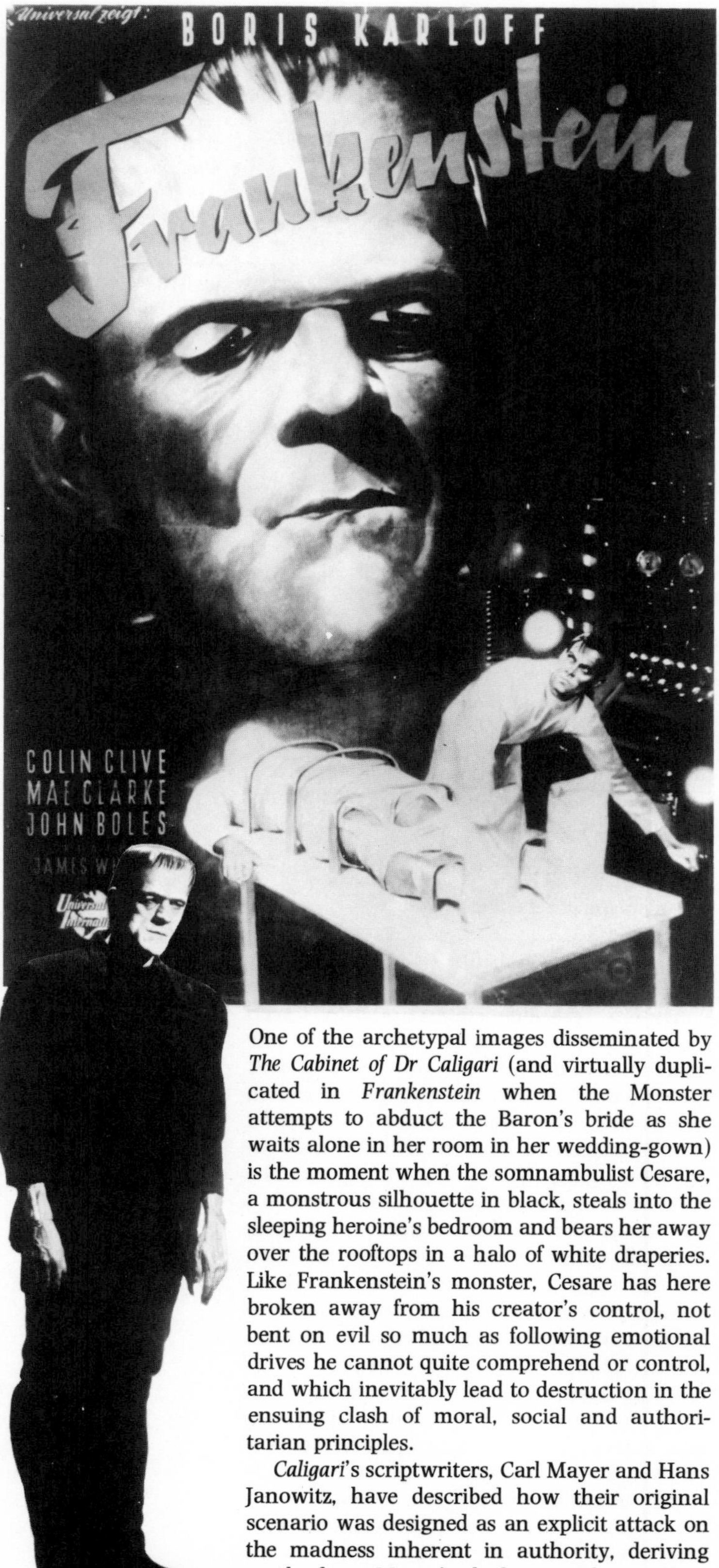

One of the archetypal images disseminated by *The Cabinet of Dr Caligari* (and virtually duplicated in *Frankenstein* when the Monster attempts to abduct the Baron's bride as she waits alone in her room in her wedding-gown) is the moment when the somnambulist Cesare, a monstrous silhouette in black, steals into the sleeping heroine's bedroom and bears her away over the rooftops in a halo of white draperies. Like Frankenstein's monster, Cesare has here broken away from his creator's control, not bent on evil so much as following emotional drives he cannot quite comprehend or control, and which inevitably lead to destruction in the ensuing clash of moral, social and authoritarian principles.

Caligari's scriptwriters, Carl Mayer and Hans Janowitz, have described how their original scenario was designed as an explicit attack on the madness inherent in authority, deriving partly from Mayer's dealings with an army psychiatrist who diagnosed his insubordinate attitude as mental instability, and partly from a strange experience suffered by Janowitz which left him convinced not only that he had witnessed a murder, but that undetected and unrepentant murderers, indistinguishable from any other passer-by, were roaming the streets by their thousands. Francis, the hero of their script, convinced that the sinister fairground showman Dr Caligari is manipulating Cesare to commit murder on his behalf, finally traces the somnambulist to an asylum where he unmasks the director as none other than Caligari, who promptly disintegrates into raving insanity.

Mayer and Janowitz were furious when their script was adjusted, at the instigation of director Robert Wiene, to include a prologue and epilogue revealing that, while Caligari is indeed in charge of the asylum, Francis himself is an inmate, and the murderous Caligari of the fairgrounds therefore merely a figment of his diseased imagination. Mayer and Janowitz felt that the film as it now stands, instead of being a subversive attack on authority, had been turned into a conformist argument for benevolent dictatorship. There is some justification for this view, although the ambivalent benevolence of Werner Krauss as the 'real' Caligari, trailing ineradicable echoes of his *alter ego*, leaves one in considerable doubt as to the fate likely to be accorded to individual liberties under his rule. But the point is that with *Frankenstein* as its first blueprint, the American horror film proceeded to coalesce the roles played by Francis and Cesare into one. The monster, in other words, became the hero.

James Whale was well qualified to effect this metamorphosis. A working class English youth who climbed socially (largely as the result of receiving an army commission during World War I), his films are full of upper class social graces, described with an affectionate elegance that simultaneously puts them mercilessly to the pillory. A homosexual condemned to lurk on the fringes of accepted normality, he made films full of marginal eccentrics treated with sympathy, understanding, and sometimes love. Small surprise, therefore, that his Frankenstein monster, marvellously played by Boris Karloff with virtually no expression but the mutation from candour to chill savagery mirrored in his limpid eyes, should be presented as 'growing up' in all-too-human terms. First he is the innocent baby, ecstatically reaching to grasp the sunlight that filters through the skylight into his cell; then the joyous child, playing at throwing flowers into the lake with a little girl whom he delightedly imagines to be another flower to be thrown in; and finally, as he finds himself progressively misjudged by the society that created him, the savage killer as whom he has been typecast.

Island of Lost Souls *(far left) with Charles Laughton, above, as the mad scientist destroyed by his own victims. H. G. Wells described it as a travesty of his original and the film was long banned in Britain.*

King Kong *(left); the original poster.*

Frederic March *(right) proved the screen's most popular* Dr Jekyll and Mr Hyde *in the version directed by Rouben Mamoulian.*

Tod Browning *(far right), one of the first successful horror directors, towers above the strange cast of* Freaks.

The sexual element

From *Caligari*, though reaching further back than that to the Beauty, Beast and wicked enchanter of fairytale, the horror film thus drew its three pivotal characters. Before long, mad geniuses in every conceivable guise were busily fabricating their ghouls, freaks, homunculi and living dead, while generally managing to harbour demure maidens (almost invariably dressed in the white of purity) to madden their monstrous creations with unrealizable desires. The resulting undertow of discreet eroticism informs most of the best horror movies of the early 1930s, from *Dracula* (1931) to *Murders in the Rue Morgue*, *White Zombie* and *Island of Lost Souls* (all 1932), not of course forgetting the immortal *King Kong* (1933), who dared to aspire to love and beauty and had to be exterminated by an outraged society; and it is the motive force behind Rouben Mamoulian's remarkable *Dr Jekyll and Mr Hyde* (1932), in which the sexual frustration that drives Jekyll to release Hyde is not only clearly adumbrated in the dialogue, but systematically stressed by cuts and dissolves linking Hyde's ecstasies and Jekyll's shame to the same root cause.

If *Dr Jekyll and Mr Hyde* stoutly defends the healthy normality of sex, Tod Browning's *Freaks* (1932) moved into the avant-garde of the contemporary horror movie mood by questioning the whole notion of *abnormal* sex. By no means the only film ever to have assembled a cast of genuine circus freaks, Browning's is surely unique in its treatment of its parade of appallingly mutated and malformed human beings. The simple story – a circus midget falls in love with a statuesque trapeze artist who plans to marry him for his money, murder him, and return to her strong-man lover, only to be caught and hideously mutilated by the vengeful freaks – is treated with an astonishing Grand Guignolesque flair by Browning, notably in the bacchanalian wedding sequence where the freaks ritually welcome the bride into their brotherhood, and the nightmarish final pursuit of the guilty pair through the mud and murk of a wildly stormy night. But what really astonishes about the film is the way, by the end, accepted values have been turned completely upside down. Normality here becomes abnormality, and vice versa.

The element of rebellion

This element of challenge to accepted norms was compounded by a further subterranean dimension – rebellion against authority – even more timely in its appeal to victims of the Depression years, who not only resented their material deprivations, but were all too willing to blame a system which appeared to thrive on an arbitrary suspension of the individual's inalienable right to the pursuit of happiness. The great classic creatures, from Frankenstein's monster to Carl Denham's giant ape in *King Kong*, all eventually threw down the gauntlet, but the horizons were often widened. Erle C. Kenton's *Island of Lost Souls* (1932, based on the H. G. Wells novel, *The Island of Dr Moreau*) features Charles Laughton as a fiendish, whip-cracking scientist whose experiments in surgical grafting and the cross-breeding of humans with animals have produced a pathetic series of bestial mutants, kept under hypnotic control by regular assemblies devoted to a liturgical chanting of the master's 'law'. The delirious final revolt, with the master dragged away to the 'House of Pain' in which he created his subservient brutes, leaves Orwell and *1984* far behind as it plunges into echoes of the wilder excesses

of the French and Russian revolutions.

In *The Most Dangerous Game* (also known as *The Hounds of Zaroff*, 1932), surely one of the most authentically Sadian films ever made, Count Zaroff (Leslie Banks) is a connoisseur of arcane pleasures, possessor of a remote island fortress to which he ensures that passing ships are attracted and then wrecked on the reefs. 'First the hunt, then the revels,' he purrs, delighted to discover that his latest victim is a big game hunter almost matching his own celebrity, as he suavely intimates the rules governing the sport he has devised to revive his jaded palate. Quite apart from the fact that the climactic hunt, with the human prey being forced to resort to bestial cunning to remain alive, is staged with eerily ferocious skill, it takes only a very short stretch of the imagination to see the fiendishly megalomaniac Zaroff as a prototype Führer.

Even more resonant in its implications, Edgar Ulmer's curiously plangent *The Black Cat* (1934) was originally planned as a version of the Poe story featuring the first co-starring duel between the box-office's two greatest monsters, Boris Karloff and Bela Lugosi. Abandoning Poe, Ulmer instead wove a highly literate web of torment out of the aura of mysterious, unimaginable evil that surrounded Aleister Crowley's infamous 'Abbey of Thelema', here brilliantly imagined as an elegantly modernist mansion of marble, glass and steel in which Karloff devotes himself to Satanic practices. Into this ominous eyrie, built over a mountain graveyard running with the blood of thousands of victims of World War I and with a forgotten cache of dynamite still serving as its precarious foundation stone, comes Lugosi in quest of the man who betrayed him during the war and annexed his wife and daughter to his own nefarious purposes. The mortal duel that ensues, epitomized in a chess game as minatory as the one in *The Seventh Seal*, gradually assumes metaphysical dimensions as it becomes apparent that, with both men left morally dead by their experiences, one having passed the limits of cruelty, the other of suffering, questions of remorse and retribution are already beside the point. Rarely has the cinema presented quite such a resolutely bleak indictment of war and its spiritual aftermath.

The genre in decline

It is no accident that all these films were made before 1934, when the Hays Office cracked down with a strict implementation of its Code. Censorship knocked the heart out of the horror movie, muffling its subversive qualities and condemning it to decline for the next twenty years. Although Val Lewton's RKO series in the 1940s struck a richly resonant vein by combining traditional themes with the mood and manner of the contemporary *film noir*, the best that can be said of the rest is that they were either half-hearted elaborations of earlier themes distinguished by excellent trick-work (*Devil Doll*, 1936 and *Dr Cyclops*, 1940, both capitalized on Whale's delirious *The Bride of Frankenstein* of 1935), or clever exercises in style with brilliant *mise en scène* masking the emptiness (Rowland V. Lee's *Son of Frankenstein*, 1939, Robert Siodmak's *Son of Dracula*, 1943).

Censorship was only one contributory cause, however. Another was that key creative figures only slummed in the horror movie, and all too quickly came to be replaced by second-rate directors, actors and writers. The most important factor, though, was that the films tended to feed on each other, either repeating the last success or resorting to desperate excess in the hope of going one better. The spiral of diminish-

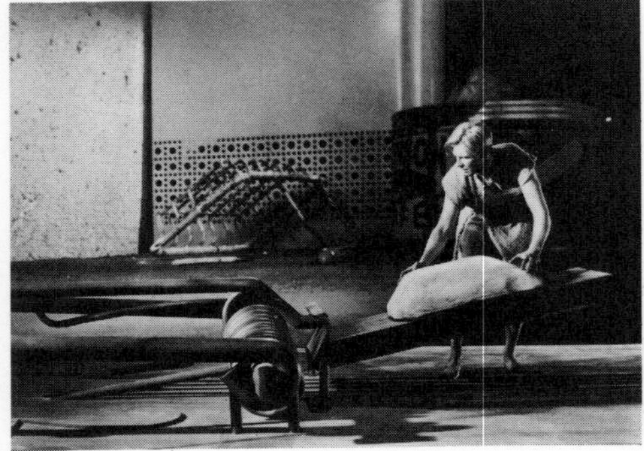

The Incredible Shrinking Man *(above left) from Richard Matheson's story was one of the most anxiety-ridden of all the SF/horror movies of the 1950s.*

The Pit and the Pendulum *(above) saw its box-office take boosted by a typically strident publicity campaign from American International.*

ing returns is amply illustrated by the dreary absurdity of the string of sequels which strained inadequate inventive resources in a bid to rival Whale's superb *The Invisible Man* (1933), or by the way in which Universal's monsters were eventually lumped together, three or four to a bargain package.

Hammer horror

It seemed to occur to no one to go back for inspiration to such seminal novels as Mary Shelley's *Frankenstein*, Bram Stoker's *Dracula*, Gaston Leroux's *The Phantom of the Opera*, Guy Endore's *The Werewolf of Paris*, or A. Merritt's *Burn, Witch, Burn*, all of which had at worst been butchered or travestied, at best truncated, when originally adapted, and none of which has ever been fully realized. And when Hammer Films launched their highly profitable programme of classic resuscitations with *The Curse of Frankenstein* (1957) and *Dracula* (1958), they made the same mistake of producing scripts that were reductions of what were already reductions. But given lush colour, superb sets (especially in *Dracula*) and explicitly gory detail, Hammer coasted sensationally to success.

Roger Corman

There was a crudity about much of Hammer's work (Dracula's bloodshot eyeballs, for instance, or the risible greenish make-up inflicted on Frankenstein's monster) which contrasted unfavourably with Roger Corman's analogous modernization of the old horror movie, first in a series of vividly violent, self-mocking quickies (the best of which was *Bucket of Blood*, 1959), then more lavishly and languorously in a series of Poe adaptations that began with *The Fall of the House of Usher* (1960) and *The Pit and the Pendulum* (1961). Elegant, civilized, witty, and remarkably sensitive to the spirit of Poe (despite the element of camp that so often mars the work of that otherwise excellent actor Vincent Price), these films are nevertheless no more than nostalgic *tableaux vivants*, extremely enjoyable exercises in style like the *Son of Frankenstein* and *Son of Dracula* mentioned earlier.

Science fiction influence in the 1950s

At around the same period, however, under the impetus of a worldwide concern about the possibility of nuclear disaster, the stagnant genre was given a new lease of life by graftings, more specifically scientific in nature than the horror film had hitherto been accustomed to, from science fiction. In *Them!* (1954), atomic tests in the New Mexico desert produce a species of 15-foot ant that threatens to wipe out the human race; in *The Incredible Shrinking Man* (1957), a radioactive mist causes the hero to shrink gradually in size until he is reduced to battling against a domestic spider with a pin as his sword; in *The Fly* (1958), serving as his own guinea-pig in his attempts to transpose atoms so that solid matter can be transmitted through space, a scientist reintegrates himself with the head of a fly which intruded upon his experiment.

The common denominator behind these films – the possibility of monstrous mutation resulting from nuclear experiment – first hit the box-office in *The Beast from 20,000 Fathoms* (1953), a coarsened adaptation of Ray Bradbury's charmingly fairytale story, 'The Foghorn', in which a prehistoric sea monster answers what it takes to be a mating call from a foghorn, only to disappear back into the depths when its desire remains unsatisfied. The storyline was predictably altered so that the monster was roused from its slumbers by atomic tests, and proceeded to establish a pattern of

Piper Laurie *(above) made an unexpected return to the screen as the religious maniac mother in Brian De Palma's* Carrie.

The Texas Chainsaw Massacre *(above right) proved one of the most unrelenting and influential of all late 1970s horrors. Its very basic killer-on-the-loose theme was emulated many times.*

behaviour for its countless successors by launching an all-out attack on Manhattan.

Such antics, though generally much inferior, fell into the old *King Kong* category, minus the motivation of rebellion. But *Them!* touched a rawer nerve of possibility, not least because for much of the time its menace was provided, not by clumsily articulated models, but by real ants, enormously magnified. In *The Incredible Shrinking Man*, similarly, it is very noticeable that the climactic duel with a property department spider is much less effective than the shrunken man's earlier clash, by way of trick photography, with a real cat. And in Don Siegel's classic *Invasion of the Body Snatchers* (1956), it is the sense of reality dominating the action that makes the horror all too real: the quiet little town, carefully established in its utter ordinariness, where people are attacked not by fang and claw but by an alien duplication that leaves them as mindless, empty shells.

It was around this time, curiously enough, that horror films began making regular appearances on the box-office charts. People who had previously looked upon Gothic horrors and Grand Guignol as beneath contempt flocked in their millions to see *Psycho* (1960) and *What Ever Happened to Baby Jane?* (1962). Showmanship had a good deal to do with it, of course, arousing a widespread curiosity to see the shower-bath murder in *Psycho* or the acting duel between Bette Davis and Joan Crawford in *Baby Jane*.

Janet Leigh *as featured in the poster (but not the film) of Hitchcock's* Psycho.

Looking back at the phenomenal success of *Psycho*, however, it seems evident that the film was something of a watershed. Where horror movies had normally either distanced their preoccupations by masking them in guises borrowed from fairytale and Gothic fantasy, or presented them directly through a heightened realism, Hitchcock sought a more visceral effect. He achieved it, firstly, by making his heroine, the identification figure whom the audience expects to win through to the end, a murder victim at a disorientatingly early stage of the plot; and secondly, by presenting the murder in graphic detail that seems to show everything (while in fact showing very little).

Indulgence in the 1970s

The general trend in horror movies over the past decade – the financially successful ones, at least – has been to accentuate both of Hitchcock's ploys. Hence, on the one hand, the emphasis on blood and guts, shown with a gratuitous indulgence that is exploitative rather than necessary (as it was in *Psycho*), and which mars not only the work of Hitchcock's imitator, Brian De Palma (*Carrie*, 1976, *The Fury*, 1978), but *The Exorcist, The Omen, et al.* And on the other, the persistent attempt to 'domesticate' horror, to make it more shocking by decorating traditional themes with current traumas. *Rosemary's Baby* (1968) and *It's Alive* (1974) both play skilfully on the fear of drug-aborted pregnancies through old-fashioned plots; the haunted house phenomena of *The Amityville Horror* (1979) are predicated on the peculiarly modern motiveless urban terrorism of the opening murder of an entire family; and in *Prophecy* (1979), an ursine King Kong rides again, somewhat absurdly, to a tune called by ecological concerns.

The modern horror film may be strong on effects, but for that same reason it is all too often low on grace. Time will have to have the last word, but it is a fairly safe bet that films like *The Exorcist* and *The Amityville Horror*, or even *Rosemary's Baby*, will not retain the power to enthral after forty years, as Whale's *Frankenstein* still does today. Not for nothing do the old myths and legends survive in their chameleon forms: mysterious, timeless, magical, they always leave something to the imagination in their appeal to half-forgotten tribal fears and fancies.

Science Fiction

Of all the great cinematic genres which have evolved in Hollywood none has taken so long to lose its low-budget status and become a real commercial force as science fiction. For nearly 40 years after the introduction of sound, the form was clearly defined and prolific but lacked even marginal respectability. Movie science fiction in the public's eye meant monsters, ray guns, aliens and robots. It lagged decades behind written science fiction and, in spite of the occasional gem, its ability to suspend disbelief was severely restricted by its resources; invariably science fiction was at the bottom end of the market, accorded the lowest budgets and having to make do with the most obscure casts.

Occasionally there were ambitious and expensive science fiction films such as MGM's *Forbidden Planet* (1956) and *2001: A Space Odyssey* (1968), but almost invariably these appear to have been undertaken with immense reluctance by the studios as special prestige productions. Indeed even *2001* is reputed to have taken seven years of theatrical release to recoup its costs.

It is only since the huge success of *Star Wars* in 1977 that science fiction has become a truly important feature of commercial cinema, acceptable to the studios as a subject worthy of stars and large budgets. Ten years ago there was not a single science fiction film in any list of all-time top-grossing movies. Now there are several.

The sudden success of the form has come about partly because of improved technical capabilities, but there are other more revealing reasons. Until a short time ago science fiction was considered by most film investment analysts to be too sensational and youth-orientated for the mass market. Even as late as the early 1970s investors still pined for middle-of-the-road success from films like *The Sound of Music*, aimed at the over-thirty-five age group. It was obvious there was a market for science fiction but it was considered too small to justify a significant outlay of money. The major producers therefore happily consigned the bulk of science fiction production to the smallest independent companies, who had to find ways of portraying space monsters and extraterrestrials with pitiful resources. In the circumstances it is hardly surprising that most of these companies fell back on promotion: the promotional campaign and poster for films like *The Beast with a Million Eyes* and *Invasion of the Saucer Men* were usually produced long before the script; the films themselves were almost secondary considerations. Several small companies like American International grew fat on their profits. Then, in the late 1960s, the majors saw the failure of several 'safe' family musicals like *Star!* and *Dr Dolittle*, followed by the success of the 'disaster' movies, which had once been the domain of the smaller production companies. In 1974, *The Exorcist* became the first 'horror' movie ever to gross more than \$20m.: another 'B' movie genre had hit the big time. It was only a matter of time before the majors turned their attention to science fiction.

When they did, they found that, with a budget to match its immense visual demands, science fiction ceased to be the pulp fodder of teenagers and became exactly the kind of universally-appealing, middle-of-the-road spectacle they sought. There was even a bonus in the form of a degree of intellectual respectability. One of the strangest spectacles of 1970s Hollywood was the sudden gold-rush by major companies to buy up the re-make rights to long-forgotten 'B' features of the 1950s, like *The Thing from Another World* and *Invasion of the Body Snatchers*.

But in order to understand the success of the new films, it is necessary to appreciate the work of film-makers once regarded by their contemporaries as hacks. They toiled seven days a week in places like Gower Gulch in Hollywood (an area now known in movie legend as Poverty Row) to entertain the teenage audiences which the rest of Hollywood had neglected. All categorizing of movies is fraught with problems. *Frankenstein* should be a definitive science fiction film – misguided scientist conducts well-meaning experiment which goes wrong – but its

Attack of the 50 Foot Woman *(right) used a typically exploitative publicity approach, but many of the more respectable science fiction films used equally memorable campaigns, including* War of the Worlds *(top right),* Forbidden Planet *(centre right) and* Metropolis *(bottom right).*

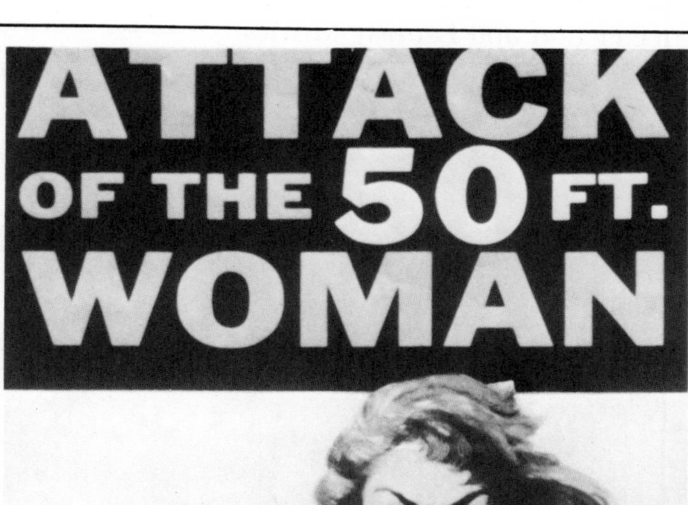
ATTACK
OF THE 50 FT.
WOMAN

H.G. WELLS' THE WAR OF THE WORLDS
Color by Technicolor
A MIGHTY PANORAMA OF EARTH-SHAKING FURY !
A PARAMOUNT PICTURE

M·G·M PRESENTS
FORBIDDEN PLANET
AMAZING!!

METROPOLIS
MANUSKRIPT
THEA VON HARBO
REGIE FRITZ LA

All-Time Hit Science Fiction and Fantasy Movies

		Rental income from initial release period: $m.	Inflation factor	Adjusted total: $m.
1	Star Wars, 1977	164.8	×1.1	181.3
2	Close Encounters of the Third Kind, 1977	77	×1.1	84.7
3	Superman, 1979	81	×1	81
4	Snow White, 1938	10	×8	80
5	2001 : A Space Odyssey, 1968	21.5	×2	43
	King Kong, 1976	35.8	×1.2	43
7	Alien, 1979	40.1	×1	40.1
8	20,000 Leagues Under the Sea, 1954	8	×5	40
9	Star Trek, 1979	35	×1	35
10	Planet of the Apes, 1968	15	×2	30
11	A Clockwork Orange, 1971	15	×1.5	22.5
12	King Kong, 1933	2	×10	20
13	Journey to the Center of the Earth, 1959	4.8	×4	19.2
	On the Beach, 1960	48	×4	19.2
15	The Thief of Bagdad, 1924	1.5	×10	15
	Dr Strangelove, 1963	5	×3	15
17	The Island at the Top of the World, 1974	10.2	×1.4	14.3
18	The Birds, 1963	4.6	×3	13.8
	Fantastic Voyage, 1966	5.5	×2.5	13.8
20	Mighty Joe Young, 1949	1.95	×7	13.6
21	The Lord of the Rings, 1979	13.5	×1	13.5
22	The Lost World, 1925	1.3	×10	13
23	Beneath the Planet of the Apes, 1970	8.6	×1.5	12.9
24	The Seventh Voyage of Sinbad, 1959	3.2	×4	12.8
25	The Andromeda Strain, 1971	8.3	×1.5	12.5
26	Buck Rogers, 1979	11.8	×1	11.8
27	The Thing, 1951	1.95	×6	11.7
28	Logan's Run, 1976	9.5	×1.2	11.4
29	The Day the Earth Stood Still, 1951	1.85	×6	11.1
30	The War of the Worlds, 1953	2	×5.5	11
	Barbarella, 1968	5.5	×2	11
	Rollerball, 1975	8.8	×1.25	11
33	When World's Collide, 1951	1.6	×6	9.6
34	Wild in the Streets, 1968	4.6	×2	9.2
35	It Came From Outer Space, 1953	1.6	×5.5	8.8
36	This Island Earth, 1955	1.7	×5	8.5
	It Came from Beneath the Sea, 1955	1.7	×5	8.5
38	Escape from the Planet of the Apes, 1971	5.6	×1.5	8.4
39	Forbidden Planet, 1956	1.6	×5	8

Selected runners-up

Destination Moon, 1950	1.3	×6	7.8
Sinbad and the Eye of the Tiger, 1979	7.7	×1	7.7
Westworld, 1973	5.2	×1.4	7.3
The Incredible Shrinking Man, 1957	1.43	×4.5	6.4
Rocketship X-M, 1950	1	×6	6

1980 The Empire Strikes Back, Flash Gordon

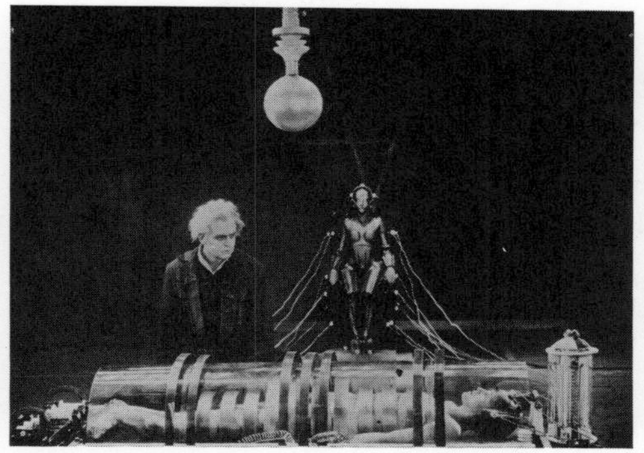

Flash Gordon *(above), the 1936 version starring Buster Crabbe and Jean Rogers.*

Metropolis *(above right) with Rudolf Klein-Rogge as Rotwang, the mad scientist creating a humanoid robot.*

Things To Come *(above, far right) made imaginative use of foreground miniatures.*

style and approach make it a horror movie. *Invasion of the Body Snatchers*, undoubtedly science fiction, has no scientific element. The term science fiction (SF), more correctly, covers science fantasy and speculative fiction.

Definition and history

As far back as 1902, French film pioneer Georges Méliès shot Jules Verne's *Trip to the Moon*. But the first major SF movie production was Fritz Lang's spectacular *Metropolis* (1927) with eight leading players, 1500 supports and thousands of extras for the crowd scenes. Shot over 310 days and 60 nights, this futuristic allegory of contemporary society retains its impact today, although H. G. Wells thought it 'Quite the silliest film!'. Its influence was long-lasting: the artificial hand of the evil scientist Rotwang influenced Peter Sellers' Dr Strangelove and the film's robot-woman inspired the design of C3PO in *Star Wars*. However, *Metropolis* was so costly it nearly bankrupted Germany's UFA Studios. That and the massive box-office failure of Fox's SF musical-comedy *Just Imagine* (1930) effectively dissuaded other major producers from entering the SF field until 1936.

That was the year H. G. Wells had a chance to show how it could be done when Alexander Korda produced his social prophecy *Things to Come*. (Earlier working titles had included *Whither Mankind?*) The film is now regarded as a classic. At the time, Wells said, 'This picture is not intended as an indictment of civilization so much as an evening's entertainment,' and the *Sunday Times* wrote: 'It makes Armageddon look like a street row.' But it cost almost £300,000 ($1.5m.) and failed to make a profit. If Britain's *Things to Come* failed because it was too up-market, Hollywood did not make the same mistake.

The serial *Flash Gordon* (1936) was shot in six weeks with 85 set-ups a day and cost an expensive $500,000 at a time when the most important 'A' features were being made for $1m. On being told the script outline, star Larry 'Buster' Crabbe's response was apparently 'They're goddam nuts!' But it was Universal's second biggest money-maker of the year. There were sequel serials *Flash Gordon's Trip to Mars* (1938) and *Flash Gordon Conquers the Universe* (1940) as well as Universal's other popular serial *Buck Rogers* (1939) and Republic's *Adventures of Captain Marvel* (1941), *Captain America* (1943) and *King of the Rocket Men* (1949). The message got through to Hollywood producers: big-budget SF films like *Metropolis, Just Imagine* and *Things to Come* will lose money, but cardboard sets, wooden acting and trite plots will make a profit. The SF movie was now solidly trapped in the 'B' feature mentality.

That it could make money was proved in 1950, with the US release of producer George Pal's *Destination Moon*, based on Robert Heinlein's novel *Spaceship Galileo*. The $600,000 film did unprecedented business across the country. *Rocketship X-M*, started after *Destination Moon* but released a month before, also made a financial killing for independent Robert L. Lippert in the wake of *Destination*'s success. Costing just $94,000 and shot in three weeks, it took a million dollars within months. With potential profit-margins like this, the other Hollywood studios saw a bandwagon and prepared to jump on it with their own cheap 'sciencer' movies – *The Thing from Another World* at RKO, *The Day the Earth Stood Still* at Fox and *Flight to Mars* at 'Poverty Row' Monogram (all 1951).

The 1950s SF boom seems to have been caused initially by the fact that space travel had now become a real possibility because of Wernher von Braun's rocket work during World War II. There was also the effect on the public imagination of the spate of UFO sightings which started in 1947, and the positive memories of those movie serials of the 1940s. There was also another element: paranoia. Along with the hope of space travel came a realization of man's insignificance in the universe and the prospect of imminent annihilation if the bomb fell. It was also the start of the Cold

War and the era of the McCarthy witch-hunts. The 1950s SF boom spans the period between *I Married a Communist* (1949) and *I Married a Monster From Outer Space* (1958). The SF movie has always been open for allegory and, in the fearful 1950s, stories of invasion or infiltration by aliens struck a chord with the American public who were constantly being bombarded with news of threats from without and within. The epitome of wish-fulfilment in SF films is perhaps *Red Planet Mars* (1952) in which a scientist discovers an advanced Martian civilization ruled by God. Earth is swept by a religious revival. The Russian people overthrow their godless communist government.

The paranoid mood of the time posed a problem for Julian Blaustein. He had just produced *Broken Arrow* (1950), one of the very first films which treated the Red Indian sympathetically. He wanted to build on this success with a story whose theme was 'that peace is no longer a four-letter word'. This was risky because of the McCarthy HUAC Hearings and the outbreak of the Korean War. But Fox chief Darryl F. Zanuck backed the project. Blaustein had found a 1940 story *Farewell to the Master* by Harry Bates and, from this, scriptwriter Edmund H. North constructed a movie outline called *Journey to the World* about a man who comes from above, assumes the name of Carpenter, preaches a gospel of peace, is betrayed, rises from the dead and returns to where he came from.

North says, 'It was my private little joke. I never discussed this angle with Blaustein or (director Robert) Wise because I didn't want it expressed. I hoped the Christ comparison would be subliminal.' And, apart from having to tone down the resurrection scene for the Breen (censorship) Office, no one seems to have noticed the parallel on initial release because the film was just another 'B' feature 'sciencer' with a down-market title *The Day the Earth Stood Still* (1951). It was seen as an unexceptional fantasy movie about a humanoid alien and a robot landing in Washington. But it typifies the best SF movies of the 1950s for several reasons. It could be enjoyed on more than a superficial plot level. Vast studio overheads were included in the $960,000 budget. The spaceship was said to have cost $100,000 although the actual basic construction cost was $20,000. And the lead character was an unknown, Michael Rennie. (Zanuck had wanted Spencer Tracy and Wise wanted Claude Rains, but both were unavailable.) Unknowns are almost traditional in SF movies – the only 'names' in *Star Wars* were Peter Cushing and Alec Guinness in relatively minor roles. This is partly because SF movies could never afford big names and partly because audiences might be less likely to believe in fantastic plots if they were peopled with familiar faces: Robert Redford reportedly turned down the role of Superman because 'no one would believe Robert Redford flying'.

First Men in the Moon: *a crane had to lower the space craft on to the lunar set.*

George Pal: initiator of a cycle

In 1951, producer George Pal returned to box-office success with Paramount's $963,000 *When Worlds Collide*, basically the story of a scientific Noah with a rocketship, referred to as the Ark of Space. The project had a long history. Paramount had bought the story in 1932 for Cecil B. De Mille (who preferred to make *Cleopatra*). In 1950, George Pal bought the rights from Paramount. After the success of Pal's *Destination Moon*, Paramount bought the rights back and then offered it to him as a producer. He accepted and had another success.

A similarly tortuous story lay behind Pal's equally-successful *War of the Worlds* (1953). Paramount had bought the H. G. Wells novel for Cecil B. De Mille in 1925 and had offered it to Sergei Eisenstein in 1930. In 1932, De Mille became interested and, at around the same time, Hitchcock wanted to direct it. In 1934, Alexander Korda wanted to produce it but, finding Wells had sold the rights to Paramount 'in perpetuity', made *Things to Come* instead. So, in 1952, George Pal began production with a $2m. budget. Three days into shooting, production almost collapsed when Paramount found they had only bought *silent* movie rights. After sorting this out, production continued with 70 per cent of the budget being spent on special effects – by no means an exceptional proportion.

H. G. Wells *lived to see many of his ideas as films. Here with producer Alexander Korda, left, he discusses sketches for* Things to Come.

George Pal's successes had started a cycle. In 1953, there were 27 SF features, documentaries, serials and shorts produced and released in the US. And now SF film-makers had another spectacular effect: 3D. In 1952, United Artists had made a financial killing with their 3D *Bwana Devil*. In 1953, Warners successfully released *House of Wax* in 3D. So Universal bought a Ray Bradbury treatment *The Meteor* because, says director Jack Arnold, 'they thought it could be successfully adapted to make a 3D picture'. Having bought it, Universal did the Hollywood thing and largely threw out Bradbury's outline, commissioning Harry Essex to write a new storyline which was filmed as *It Came from Outer Space* (1953). Like *The Day the Earth Stood Still*, it was unusual in that the alien who landed on Earth was largely sympathetic. Director Jack Arnold says, 'I wanted to have some kind of meaning to it all . . . It said that we as people are afraid of anything that is different from us. If it's different, we hate it, we want to destroy it. That's our failing as human beings . . . I think science fiction films are a marvellous medium for telling a story, creating a mood and delivering whatever kind of a social message should be delivered.' But the sympathetic alien was unusual at the time because the paranoid strain of SF films was holding sway. *Invaders from Mars* (1953) told of a group of Martians preparing the way for a full-scale invasion by kidnapping humans, whom they turned into saboteurs of military installations. *The Twonky* (1953) even had an alien living inside a TV set: more a case of Hollywood producers' paranoia than anything else.

When 'they' were not attacking from the skies or from TV sets, they were rising from the depths. *The Beast from 20,000 Fathoms* (1953), revived by the radiation from atomic tests, started a whole new monster cycle. This time it was Warners who bought a Ray Bradbury story which had appeared in the *Saturday Evening Post* titled *The Beast from 20,000 Fathoms*. Having bought the story and title, Warners proceeded to throw out both and have a script written called *The Monster from Beneath the Sea* with some ideas contributed, uncredited, by special effects man Ray Harryhausen. The Bradbury title eventually resurfaced but little of his plot – and one of the film's verbal highlights is a reference to the famous Loch Lomond Monster (sic). Nonetheless, the film was a success, a $5m. return on a $250,000 outlay. This was largely thanks to Harryhausen's effects and the direction of Eugène Lourié, who had previously worked with Jean Renoir but who now became, with Jack Arnold, one of the 1950s' most efficient SF directors.

The mid-50s monster cycle

Seeing the success of *The Beast*, Warners rushed out *Them!* (1954), which they had originally intended as their first 3D movie. This time, atomic testing created giant ants. Screenwriter Ted Sherdeman, who adapted George Worthing Yates' original story, says: 'The idea appealed to me very much because, aside from man, ants are the only creatures in the world who plan and wage war – and nobody trusted the atomic bomb at the time.' *Them!* was hated by Jack Warner and became his company's highest-grossing picture of the year. For George Worthing Yates, it led to script assignments on *Conquest of Space* (1955), *It Came from Beneath the Sea* (1955) and *Earth vs the Flying Saucers* (1956). In the 1980s, SF films can be said with some justification to be special effects men's or directors' movies; back in the 1950s, due to lack of budget and shooting time, they were really writers' movies – although, of course, no one person is ever completely responsible for the impact of a film.

While making *It Came from Outer Space*, producer William Alland (a former assistant to Orson Welles; he played the reporter in Citizen Kane) had developed a story by Maurice Zimm, partly re-written by Harry Essex, which featured another monster. A $12,000 rubber suit was designed by Jack Kevan of the Universal make-up department and tested in a 20-minute 1953 short *Abbott & Costello Meet the Creature*. The following year, Universal released the full 3D feature *Creature from the Black Lagoon* which again teamed producer Alland and director Jack Arnold. It was a box-office smash. Originally, the Creature was to have been played by

The Creature from the Black Lagoon *advances on Richard Carlson and Julie Adams.*

Glenn Strange, a former Frankenstein monster, but lack of aquatic ability sank his chances. Instead, the Creature was played on land by Ben Chapman and underwater by student Ricou Browning who says, 'It was like swimming in an overcoat.' Essentially, the film is *King Kong* underwater, with the sympathetic Creature falling for a lithe girl who enters his secluded domain with a scientific expedition. Arnold says, 'I set out to make the Creature a very sympathetic character. He's violent because he's provoked into violence.' However, the sympathetic nature of the Creature was deftly undercut by the posters with their selling line 'CENTURIES OF PASSION PENT UP IN HIS SAVAGE HEART!'

The Quatermass Trilogy

The Creature from the Black Lagoon spawned two sequels: the 3D *Revenge of the Creature* (1955), notable for Clint Eastwood's movie debut as a lab assistant with a rat in his pocket, and *The Creature Walks among Us* (1956). In Britain, too, 1954 saw the start of a movie trilogy. Nigel Kneale's *The Quatermass Experiment*, a BBC TV series in 1953, became a big-screen success the following year.

Unfortunately, little of Kneale's unique television work has been faithfully transferred to the cinema. Of *The Quatermass Experiment* (US title *The Creeping Unknown*, 1955), he says, 'There was the usual hurried deal by Hammer with some American people (Robert L. Lippert) and they insisted on having an American actor and an American adapter. So this writer came over who worked out some nonsense which turned my poor old Quatermass into a screaming, shouting person – probably like the last film producer he'd worked for.' *Quatermass II* (1957, *Enemy from Space* in US), says Kneale, 'was about the evil of secrecy. It was a time when mysterious establishments were popping up in England: like Harwell atomic research and Porton Down germ warfare.' The third Hammer adaptation *Quatermass and the Pit* (US title *Five Million Years to Earth*, 1967) was the most effective of the trilogy because it was more closely based on Kneale's original BBC TV series of 1963. (Thames TV's 1979 series *Quatermass* was released as a theatrical feature *The Quatermass Conclusion* in some territories.)

Coinciding with the start of the intelligent British Quatermass series and the competent American Creature series came a tacky Japanese answer to *The Beast from 20,000 Fathoms*. In 1954, Toho Studios produced their film about a monster awakened by the detonation of The Bomb. Called *Gojira* (reputedly after a huge member of staff on the Toho lot) it was released in the US two years later under the title *Godzilla, King of the Monsters* with additional footage featuring Raymond Burr. Over the course of more than 15 features, Godzilla gradually changed from evil monster to Earth's protector with actor Haruo Nakajima wearing the 100 pound Godzilla suit from 1954 until 1972. The strain on audience credulity grew ever greater. While the Japanese were discovering that cheap films could make fast money, so were Roger Corman and American International Pictures with interesting but appallingly bad films like *The Day the World Ended* (1955), in which the seven survivors of Armageddon include a gangster and a stripper. Such films were nicknamed 'Z' movies but had their own devoted following.

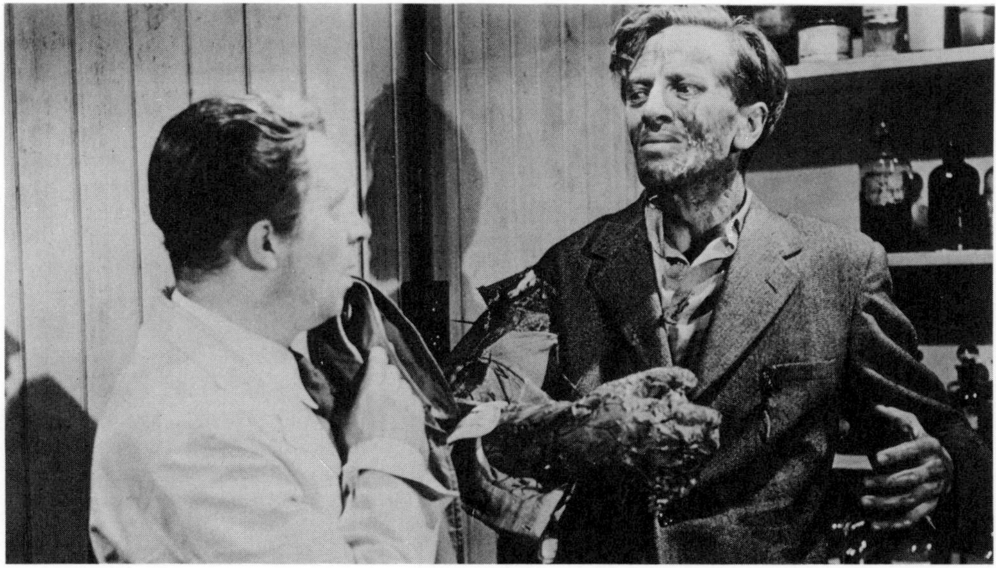

The Quatermass Experiment *(US:* The Creeping Unknown) *with Richard Wordsworth, right, as the astronaut who returns to earth to find he is being taken over by an alien life-form.*

Jack Arnold

By 1955, Universal was short of money and, according to director Jack Arnold, 'They were looking for some exploitation films. They didn't want to spend much money. So I sat down and wrote a story called *Tarantula*.' The movie, based on a TV play Arnold had directed, was shot cheaply in under 20 days, using desert locations, models and real spiders kept under control by air jets. 'The more I did this type of film,' Arnold told John Brosnan in *The Horror People*, 'the better I liked it, because the studio left me alone.' He had been a cameraman making wartime documentaries with director Robert Flaherty and, on his SF movies, Arnold tried 'to make the locale a part of the atmosphere. The first thing I did was establish the atmosphere . . . I think the only way you can get an audience to accept the impossible is to get them involved in a mood. That's why I made a lot of use of actual physical locations'.

One of the key creators of 1950s science fiction, Arnold had realized as early as his first science fiction movie *It Came From Outer Space* in 1953 that studio budgets would simply not sustain the element of strangeness and alienation these films needed. Looking around for something to augment their meagre special effects, he eventually settled on a forbidding stretch of desert near Dead Man's Curve about twelve miles north of Hollywood. And it was this desert, more than anything else, that came to symbolize the bleak tone of American 1950s science fiction in the world's imagination: 'Most of *It Came From Outer Space* was shot out on the desert . . . *Tarantula* was shot in the same area . . . where there was an outcropping of rocks that I particularly wanted to use. I would just go into the desert and look for something that looked eerie and if it gave me the shivers I would say right – we'll shoot here.' *Tarantula* brought director Arnold and producer Alland together again and, in the same year, so did *This Island Earth*.

One studio noticeably absent from the movie space race was MGM who made up for it with *Forbidden Planet* (1956), their translation of *The Tempest* to outer space with good special effects and a touch of Freud stirred in. Now remembered as a classic hit, it was regarded at the time as a financial disappointment – a reminder that hindsight can distort. On first release, even a film as exceptional as Don Siegel's *Invasion of the Body Snatchers* (1956) was looked upon as an unexceptional programmer. Today, *Invasion* is regarded as a compelling comment on the McCarthy era and an intelligent allegory on loss of identity in contemporary society. The theme of aliens taking over human bodies certainly goes back to *It Came From Outer Space* and *Invaders From Mars* and can, perhaps, be traced back to medieval fears of possession. But a simpler explanation for Allied Artists' interest in the project is that it meant cheap aliens: they were just ordinary human beings. Similarly, 1950s science fiction films often dealt with post-holocaust scenarios: this may partly have been because of audience preoccupations with the threat of The Bomb, but it also meant you could make a film with only six or seven people in it. Amid the modern analyses of science fiction themes, it is easy to forget that *Variety*'s original review of *Invasion of the Body Snatchers* read: 'Occasionally difficult to follow due to the strangeness of its scientific premise'. By and large, audiences for SF films were and are out for uncluttered entertainment. Jack Arnold

Planet of the Apes *(far left) generated several spin-offs and probably made more profit for Fox than the bigger box-office hit* 2001: A Space Odyssey *did for MGM.*

Star Wars *(left) with Alec Guinness, left, as Ben Konobi battling Dave Prowse as Darth Vader.*

says: 'My objective was primarily to entertain but I also wanted to say something. If ten per cent of the audience grasped it, then I was very successful.'

Author Richard Matheson says of *The Incredible Shrinking Man* (1957): 'The book was written in the form of flashbacks but, at that time, movies were very conventional. I feel it lost something by being presented in straight narrative.' If Matheson felt himself handicapped then so was Jack Arnold, employed to direct *The Incredible Shrinking Man* with a leading actor who was six foot one inch tall. The special effects were a nightmare: giant raindrops had to be created using water-filled condoms and Arnold was later called into the front office to justify his purchase of 100 gross of contraceptives. (He said there was a post-production party.) The movie cost Universal $800,000 and, regarded by many including Arnold himself as his best film, made a profit. Matheson scripted a sequel called *The Fantastic Little Girl*; Arnold turned it down (under the subsequent title of *The Incredible Shrinking Woman*) and it was never made. However, exploitation experts American International leapt in with *The Amazing Colossal Man* (1957) and little Allied Artists tried to make it big with *Attack of the 50 Foot Woman* (1958) directed by an embarrassed Nathan Juran, who had himself credited as Nathan Hertz. Both movies were written by Mark Hanna and are an example of that supreme Hollywood genre The Bandwagon. The posters for *The Amazing Colossal Man* had tempted fate by asking 'WHEN WILL IT STOP?'

By now the market was getting swamped with cheap exploitation products; 1959 saw the arrival of *Teenagers from Outer Space* and Robert Vaughn as *Teenage Caveman*. To worsen matters the cheap Japanese monster films had caught on, and with a glut of 'Z' movies, the McCarthy era over, the Red scare lessening and the Kennedy era dawning, the bubble finally burst and the science fiction boom was over. Possibly it was also killed by America's move into the real world of space: the period from 1958 to 1968 is devoid of any notable trend in SF movies. Possibly during the ten years between man's first step into space and his first step onto the moon producers were shy of SF: science fact was outstripping science fiction.

There were, of course, notable individual exceptions like *The Time Machine* (1960), *Village of the Damned* (1960), *The Man With The X-Ray Eyes* (1963), *Seconds* (1966), *Fahrenheit 451* (1966) and *The Sorcerers* (1967). But there were no genuinely influential SF movies until 1968, when two appeared.

Planet of the Apes and *2001*

Planet of the Apes gave rise to four sequels and two TV series. It showed that a children's adventure can also be an adult fable and that an adult fable can be fun – well-made fantasy would still sell to a wide market. The second major SF movie of the year was MGM's *2001: A Space Odyssey*. The space race had made some science fiction concepts more easily acceptable and also changed the look of SF – gone were the sleek, featureless rockets and in came lots of detail. *2001* also showed that the technology existed to create a visually astounding movie, although *2001* itself was so obscure, expensive, complicated and initially unprofitable that it probably deterred many producers from entering the field until *Star Wars*. Effectively, *2001* gave screen SF artistic respectability and *Star Wars* gave it commercial respectability. *Star Wars* director George Lucas and producer Gary Kurtz learned another lesson from 1968: that if you combined the entertainment of the *Planet of the Apes* series with the technology of *2001* you had a recipe for box-office success.

2001 was also interesting because of HAL the homicidal computer. In the 1950s, the threat to humanity came from 'out there' – whether Russia or outer space. Now the movie audience had 'Learned to Stop Worrying and Love the Bomb' and post-holocaust films did

The Empire Strikes Back *(right), the* Star Wars *sequel, proved one of 1980's biggest hits. Here Harrison Ford silences the talkative robot C3PO.*

The Black Hole *(far right), whose stars were its sets and models; this mile-long vessel, USS Cygnus, was rediscovered after 20 years lost in space.*

not have the drawing-power they once had. In the 1960s, the new and growing threat to humanity – the source of paranoia in SF films – was not aliens or communists, it was technology. This strand developed from *2001* through films like *Colossus: The Forbin Project* (1970), *Westworld* (1973), *The Stepford Wives* (1975) to *Coma* (1978) and *The China Syndrome* (1979).

Star Wars (1977) was another matter: a technically brilliant though thematically shallow achievement which was unique in that it was designed, in producer Gary Kurtz's words, as 'an homage to all the action adventure fantasies' of the movies – in particular the science fiction serials of the 1930s like *Flash Gordon*.

Star Wars and after

Star Wars finally convinced producers and studios that in SF films, unlike many other genres, you probably have to spend money to make money. *Star Wars* cost $11m. Columbia spent $21m. on *Close Encounters of the Third Kind* (1977) – an audacious and visually splendid story of the first contact with UFOs, which reworked elements of *Invaders from Mars* and *It Came from Outer Space*. They then took the unprecedented step of allowing director Steven Spielberg to shoot additional sequences for a re-issue (1980). The two *Superman* films (1979 and 1980) finally duplicated the world of the fantasy super-hero with astonishing exactitude and probably cost between $50m. and $60m. between them.

The plot of *Alien* (1979) was an ingenious combination of *It! The Terror from beyond Space* (1958) and *Planet of the Vampires* (1965) with some elements from *Dark Star* (1974), and its scene of a monster erupting from someone's chest was similar to one shot for, but cut from the release print of, Hammer's *To the Devil a Daughter* (1976). Scriptwriter Dan O'Bannon originally conceived *Alien* as a low-budget movie costing 'no more than half a million dollars'. Eventually, the budget rose to nearly $11m. but it remains at heart a 'B' or 'Z' movie.

Gradually the science is lessening and the fantasy is increasing. *Star Wars* was followed by *The Empire Strikes Back* (1980), a more complex and spectacular film mixing SF with Tolkien's *Lord of the Rings*, adding better relationships and better pacing.

The remake of *Flash Gordon* (1980) tried to add overt humour to SF, always a dangerous thing and seldom successful: *Dark Star* (1974) and *A Boy and His Dog* (1975) are notable exceptions. With the rising cost of fantasy movies, *Dragonslayer* (1981) marks an interesting development in which two studios (Disney and Paramount) combine to finance a film. And *Clash of The Titans* (1981), although more fantasy than science fiction, was interesting because of its impressive cast list. As producer Charles Schneer pointed out, 'Half a dozen years ago, stars would have thought twice about competing with Gorgons, Medusas and Krakens, but we're living in a world of splendid visual effects pictures.'

This is fine for producers and audiences but can cause headaches for actors and directors. Maximilian Schell said after completing *The Black Hole* (1979) that 'in these sci-fi pictures, it is practically impossible for an actor to play against the special effects and win.' And, if actors have problems on the new breed of SF movies, so too do directors. Irvin Kershner, talking about his work on *The Empire Strikes Back*, points out: 'There were many shots where I would shoot the live-action (in England) and then send the scene back to the studio in San Francisco for the optical effects to be added. There were shots where we had to use the Vista Vision camera, it had to be exactly 4½ feet off the ground, it had to be pointed no more than 15 degrees up, the light had to come from the right, it had to be orange – all because of the special effects that would be added later – and then I would be as free as I wanted within that frame.' It's a long way from the days when Roger Corman shot *Creature from the Haunted Sea* (1961) in six days and *Monster from the Ocean Floor* (1954) for $12,000. But then, it is far-removed only in scale, not in content.

Action-Adventure

In its many guises – from swashbuckler to war film, from biblical epic to modern disaster movie – the action-adventure picture has commanded big budgets and big box office returns throughout the history of Hollywood. The prominent position of the action-adventure film in Hollywood's repertoire predates even the establishment of the studio system which began to dominate American film-making during the middle and late 1920s. Of the dozen or so top grossing pictures during the 1915–31 period, half fall into the action-adventure or war film category including *The Four Horsemen of the Apocalypse* (1921), *The Ten Commandments* (1923) and *The Birth of a Nation* (1915).

Griffith, DeMille, Ingram and Fairbanks

These films reflect the prominent position occupied at that time by a small group of leading producer-directors including Rex Ingram, Cecil B. DeMille and especially D. W. Griffith.

Influenced by the success of such early Italian feature-length epics as *Quo Vadis?* (1912) and *Cabiria* (1913), Griffith directed his first feature, *Judith of Bethulia*, in 1913. (Four reels in length, the film was about twice as long as the average film of the period.) Griffith followed it with *The Birth of a Nation* (1915) and *Intolerance* (1916), thereby establishing his undisputed supremacy in the epic genre at a time when production in Europe was severely affected by World War I.

The Birth of a Nation had such a phenomenal success with film audiences all over the world, that one can only estimate how much the film earned. Iris Barry suggests world-wide rentals of $18m., and Louis B. Mayer apparently made his first million from the New England rights (excluding Boston) alone. With a negative cost of about $100,000, the picture was certainly one of the most profitable ever made. *Intolerance*, on the other hand, cost over $2m. to produce and, with its four interlocking stories, was a more difficult picture for audiences to appreciate. Although it represented the peak of Griffith's achievement as a director, particularly in the Babylon and modern stories, the film lost money, and Griffith was never again able to produce a picture on the same lavish scale.

As for DeMille, although his name today is generally associated with the biblical epic, his first major entry in this genre, *The Ten Commandments*, appeared in 1923 after he had been directing for ten years. The picture was more notable for its extended biblical prologue than for the melodramatic and old-fashioned moralizing of its modern story, which perhaps reflects the influence of *Intolerance*. *The Ten Commandments* was a big hit at the box office, in contrast to DeMille's independent production of *King of Kings* in 1927, a considerably more expensive film which scarcely made any profit on rentals of $1.5m.

At about the same time, during the early 1920s, Rex Ingram had emerged as the leading producer-director at Metro with the success of *The Four Horsemen of the Apocalypse*, which turned Rudolph Valentino into a major star. The film echoed *The Birth of a Nation* with its theme of members of a family fighting on opposing sides in a war. Later Ingram pictures included a lavish production of *The Prisoner of Zenda* (1922) and *Scaramouche* (1923), both starring Ramon Novarro, while Valentino, too, made a notable swashbuckler, *Monsieur Beaucaire* (1924). But none of these matched the success of *The Four Horsemen*.

The actor-producer who effectively dominated the swashbuckling genre during the 1920s was Douglas Fairbanks. He covered a wide range of literary classics from *The Mark of Zorro* (1920) to *The Iron Mask* (1929) via *Robin Hood*, *The Three Musketeers* and others, all of them released by United Artists. His biggest hit was *The Thief of Bagdad* (1924) directed by Raoul Walsh. At this time, a pattern of competition and imitation first became a familiar part of the American film scene, for virtually every major studio had released at least one swashbuckler of note featuring their leading male star between 1923 and 1927.

The Towering Inferno *(right) was easily the most successful of all the disaster movies at the box-office. The well-orchestrated teaming of Paul Newman and Steve McQueen was coupled with impressive effects. Here, Richard Chamberlain is in the cage.*

Birth of a Nation *(above), the most successful box-office film of the cinema's early years.*

All-Time Hit Action and Adventure Movies

	Title	Rental income from initial release period: $m.	Inflation factor	Adjusted total: $m.
1	The Ten Commandments, 1956	34.2	×5	171
2	Ben-Hur, 1959	36.65	×4	146.6
3	Around the World in Eighty Days, 1956	22	×5	110
4	The Robe, 1953	17.5	×5.5	96.3
5	Cleopatra, 1963	26	×3	78
6	The Towering Inferno, 1974	50	×1.4	70
7	The Bridge on the River Kwai, 1957	15	×4.5	67.5
8	Smokey and the Bandit, 1977	61	×1.1	67.1
9	Airport, 1970	44.5	×1.5	66.7
10	Rocky, 1976	54	×1.2	64.8
11	The Longest Day, 1962	17.6	×3.5	61.6
12	Sergeant York, 1941	6	×10	60
13	The Poseidon Adventure, 1973	42	×1.4	58.8
14	Quo Vadis, 1952	10.5	×5.5	57.7
15	For Whom the Bell Tolls, 1943	6.3	×9	56.7
16	Spartacus, 1960	14	×4	56
17	Samson and Delilah, 1950	9	×6	54
18	The Guns of Navarone, 1961	13	×4	52
19	Earthquake, 1974	36.1	×1.4	50.5
20	Lawrence of Arabia, 1963	16.7	×3	50.1
21	Birth of a Nation, 1915	5	×10	50
22	Billy Jack, 1971	32.5	×1.5	48.8
23	El Cid, 1961	12	×4	48
24	Rocky II, 1979	43	×1	43
25	Patton (UK title: Patton – Lust for Glory), 1970	27	×1.5	40.5
26	The Dirty Dozen, 1967	20.1	×2	40.2
27	Ben-Hur, 1926	4	×10	40
	Reap the Wild Wind, 1942	4	×10	40
	Battle Cry, 1956	8	×5	40
30	Hooper, 1978	34.9	×1.1	38.4
31	Thirty Seconds over Tokyo, 1944	4.2	×9	37.8
32	The Big Parade, 1925	3.5	×10	35
	Wake Island, 1942	3.5	×10	35
34	The Deep, 1978	31.3	×1.1	34.4
35	Easy Rider, 1969	16.9	×2	33.8
36	Deliverance, 1972	22.4	×1.5	33.6
	The Trial of Billy Jack, 1974	24	×1.4	33.6
38	Exodus, 1960	8.3	×4	33.2
39	Ivanhoe, 1952	6	×5.5	33
40	The Longest Yard, 1974	23	×1.4	32.2
41	The Wilderness Family, 1976	26.6	×1.2	31.9

Selected runners-up

Title	Rental income	Inflation factor	Adjusted total
The Sands of Iwo Jima, 1950	5	×6	30
The Sea Chase, 1955	6	×5	30
Strategic Air Command, 1955	6	×5	30
To Hell and Back, 1955	6	×5	30
The Three Musketeers, 1948	4.2	×7	29.4
King Solomon's Mines, 1950	4.8	×6	28.8
David and Bathsheba, 1951	4.72	×6	28.3
Midway, 1976	22.3	×1.2	26.8

1980 Smokey and the Bandit Ride Again, The Electric Horseman

The Thief of Bagdad *(right) with Douglas Fairbanks.*

Ben Hur *(far right): the original, 1926, version starring Ramon Novarro, centre.*

Rudolph Valentino *dances to stardom in* The Four Horsemen of the Apocalypse, *his first major role.*

Charlton Heston *as Moses in Cecil B. DeMille's* The Ten Commandments, *the most successful action-adventure of all time.*

The influence of the studios

Eventually, the concentration of power in the hands of a small number of major studios during the middle and late 1920s restricted the activities of the independent producer-directors like Griffith, DeMille and Ingram, as did the arrival of sound and the onset of the Depression which limited the number of large scale productions.

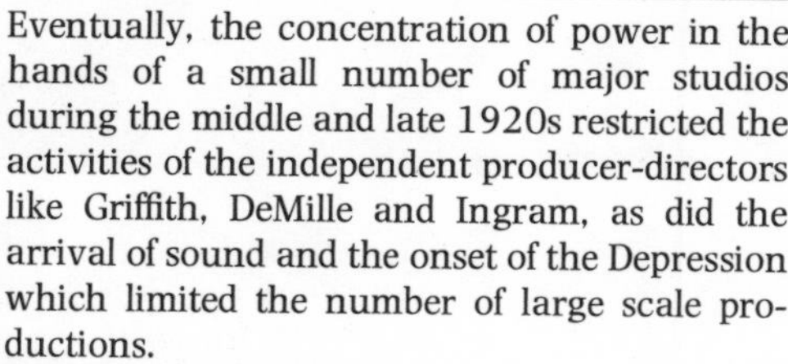

The success of *Ben-Hur*, starring Ramon Novarro, and *The Big Parade*, directed by King Vidor and starring John Gilbert, in 1925 helped to make MGM's name. Both did exceptionally well at the box office, but *Ben-Hur*'s rentals of $4m. were cancelled out by the excessive production costs, while *The Big Parade* at $3.5m. was far more profitable, having cost only $250,000. MGM was less successful with its few big action pictures of the late 1920s – *Bardelys the Magnificent* (1926), *The Cossacks* (1928) and *The Viking* (1929), the studio's only major venture into early Technicolor.

The war films of the period provide an example of how the new studio system operated. The success of Laurence Stallings' play, *What Price Glory?* prompted MGM to hire him to script *The Big Parade*; this proved to be a big hit and stimulated Fox in turn to make a film version of his play in 1926 (rentals of $2m.). Fox then made a sequel, *The Cockeyed World* (1929), with the same cast and director (Raoul Walsh), which was an even bigger hit with rentals of $2.7m.

Meanwhile, William Wellman at Paramount had begun a cycle of World War I flying pictures in spectacular fashion with *Wings* (1927), the first winner of the Oscar for Best Film. And independent producer/director Howard Hughes was close behind with *Hell's Angels* which was not completed and released by United Artists until 1930. Other flying pictures of the period included: *The Dawn Patrol* (1930) and *The Last Flight* (1931) from Warners; *Hell Divers*, one of the first pictures to star Clark Gable at MGM in 1931; and *The Lost Squadron* (1932) from RKO. Universal had its one big prestige success of the period with *All Quiet on the Western Front* (1930) which won the Best Film Oscar. For an expensive, prestige production, however, the picture made only a small profit.

Whether through good commercial practice – jumping on the bandwagon when a successful picture appeared to be establishing a new trend – or simply through fear of being left behind, the game of 'follow the leader' has been played regularly by American film-makers from the silent days up to the current cycle of science fiction epics.

Costume pictures in the mid 30s

During the worst years of the Depression the studios were forced to cut back on the production of expensive costume pictures, although Cecil B. DeMille continued to turn out popularized depictions of the ancient world: *The Sign of the Cross* (1932) was followed by *Cleopatra* (1934); neither was very successful. However, between 1935 and 1937 the studios revived their interest in large-scale costume pictures and a more lavish style of filming in order to satisfy the increased demand for escapist entertainment in a world which saw war approaching.

There was, for example, a short-lived series of British Empire movies beginning in 1935 with Paramount's *The Lives of a Bengal Lancer* starring Gary Cooper, followed by Warner's *The Charge of the Light Brigade* (1936) starring Errol Flynn, Fox's *Wee Willie Winkie* (1937) and RKO's *Gunga Din* (1939). Clearly the majority of action-adventure pictures of this period were designed by each studio to spotlight their male stars.

At MGM Clark Gable's new stature was reflected in 1935 productions like *China Seas* and *Mutiny on the Bounty* followed by *San Francisco* (1936), and *Test Pilot* (1938). After starring in *Captain Blood* (1935) Errol Flynn followed Douglas Fairbanks as the screen's leading swashbuckler and played in *The Adventures of Robin Hood* (1938), the first Technicolor swashbuckler, followed by *The Sea Hawk* (1940) and *The Adventures of Don Juan* (1948). Meanwhile, DeMille at Paramount had a hit with *The Crusades* in 1935 and followed it with *The Buccaneer* (1938) starring Fredric March.

Surprisingly, the team of Ernest B. Schoedsack and Merian C. Cooper, which had been responsible at RKO for the production of *King Kong* (1933), initiated the most successful action-adventure cycle of the late 1930s. They found their inspiration in the early Italian epic cinema with an effective remake of *The Last Days of Pompeii* (1935), combining costume spectacle with disaster. MGM responded with Gable, Spencer Tracy and Jeanette MacDonald in *San Francisco* (1936), recreating the famous Californian earthquake of 1906; the film became one of the biggest hits of the 1930s. John Ford directed *The Hurricane* for Samuel Goldwyn and United Artists in 1937, while Fox countered with *In Old Chicago* (1938) climaxing with the great Chicago fire of 1871. Similar disasters were prominent in such pictures as *The Good Earth* (MGM, 1937) and *Suez* (Fox, 1938) starring Darryl F. Zanuck's latest discovery, Tyrone Power, who also appeared in *In Old Chicago* and the lavish production of *The Rains Came* (1939). It was therefore no surprise that even *Gone with the Wind* (1939) climaxed with the burning of Atlanta in vivid Technicolor.

War movies in wartime

However, by 1938 World War II seemed increasingly likely, and a new war cycle was under way. Quickest off the mark was Warners with a remake of *The Dawn Patrol* (1938) starring Errol Flynn, followed in 1939 by *Wings of the Navy*, *Espionage Agent* and *Confessions of a Nazi Spy* with Edward G. Robinson, and *The Fighting 69th* (1940) starring James Cagney. With an unrivalled group of action directors like Michael Curtiz and Raoul Walsh under contract and a notable roster of gangster stars and character actors, Warners was well placed to make the switch from crime and adventure films to wartime spy stories and battlefield heroics. The studio had its biggest hit since *The Singing Fool* (1928) with *Sergeant York* (1941) directed by Howard Hawks and starring Gary Cooper who won an Oscar for his performance as a farmer who becomes a World War I hero.

But once again the other studios were not far behind. Clearly, Hollywood was well equipped to depict the Nazi menace on the screen as many leading writers and directors were themselves refugees from Nazi Germany. The production of war pictures peaked during

Captain Blood, *with Errol Flynn and Olivia de Havilland, became one of the most celebrated pirates in screen history. His fame proved so enduring that in the 1960s Flynn's son Sean was starring in a sequel,* Son of Captain Blood.

1943–44, when Technicolor was becoming more popular, and the cycle not surprisingly evaporated after 1945 although there was a revival during the late 1940s. In 1949 MGM had an unexpected success with *Battleground*, directed by William Wellman, while the small studio Republic had the biggest hit in its history with Allan Dwan's *The Sands of Iwo Jima* (1949) starring John Wayne.

Swashbucklers post-war

A revival of interest in the swashbuckler, in Technicolor, developed towards the end of the war: *The Spanish Main* (1945) was RKO's first stylish venture into colour and was followed by Douglas Fairbanks Jr in *Sinbad the Sailor* (1947). At Columbia, Cornel Wilde, a skilled fencer, starred in *A Thousand and One Nights* (1945) and *Bandit of Sherwood Forest* (1946), and Larry Parks in *The Swordsman* (1947). Errol Flynn starred in Warners' *The Adventures of Don Juan* in 1948, and Tyrone Power, who had appeared in Fox's colourful version of *The Black Swan* in 1942, was rather less effective as *The Captain from Castile* in 1947. At MGM Gene Kelly followed his musical swashbuckling role in the delightful Vincente Minnelli production of *The Pirate* (1948) with a lively performance as D'Artagnan in the studio's hit version of *The Three Musketeers* (1948).

The Adventures of Robin Hood *featured classic villain Basil Rathbone, left, and classic hero Errol Flynn crossing swords for the second time. Their first encounter was in* Captain Blood.

There were few other costume epics of note during the immediate post-war period when the studios were hit hard by falling box-office receipts and declining profits. During the fifties the industry adjusted to the new climate, largely created by television, in a number of ways: an increase in the production of 'A' features; a substantial growth in colour filming which rose from only 15 per cent of the total in 1949 to 29 per cent in 1952 and 43 per cent by 1953; in America, the expansion of drive-in cinemas, which accounted for 30 per cent of the total by the late 1950s; and the studios began to look to the action-adventure spectacular in colour to provide the film-going public with that special experience which would attract them away from television and back into the cinemas.

Epics in colour

Again DeMille led the way with his hit version of *Samson and Delilah* (1949) which earned $9m. in rentals and marked his return to the ancient world for the first time since 1934 (*Cleopatra*). Fox followed with *David and Bathsheba*, the top-grossing picture in 1951, and MGM spared no expense to produce *Quo Vadis* in the same year at the Cinecitta studios in Rome. The final cost was estimated at $7m., set against rentals of $10.5m.

Dawn Patrol, *the story of World War I flying officers with, left to right, Basil Rathbone, David Niven and Errol Flynn in the 1938 remake.*

MGM initiated a new African adventure cycle in 1950 with *King Solomon's Mines* filmed on location in Technicolor, and Fox had an even bigger hit two years later with a loose adaptation of Hemingway's story, *The Snows of Kilimanjaro*. Horizon Pictures, a new independent production company set up by John Huston and Sam Spiegel, provided the newly reorganized United Artists with its first big hit that same year with *The African Queen*, the first colour film for director John Huston, featuring Humphrey Bogart and Katharine Hepburn. The mounting demand for action to be filmed on location sent John Ford to Africa to direct a highly successful remake of *Red Dust* (1932) called *Mogambo* (1953) with Clark Gable bringing an added maturity to the role which he had played 22 years before.

Wide-screen processes

The studios' continued decline after 1951 was reflected in a substantial fall in the number of films being produced and released, in the new independence of many stars and directors who were forming their own production companies, and in a major trend towards shooting the pictures themselves on location and abroad, away from the Hollywood back lots. It was no longer possible to rely on studio mock-ups to represent any setting in the world, and the various wide-screen processes, which became popular after 1953, introduced audiences to exotic and foreign settings never before seen on the large screen in colour. The Cinerama Corporation was successful with its glorified travelogues – *This is Cinerama* (1952), *Cinerama Holiday* (1955) and *The Seven Wonders of the World* (1956) – while Michael Todd had a big hit with *Around the World in Eighty Days*, filmed in Todd AO and winner of the Best Film Oscar in 1956, with rentals of $22m.

MGM initiated a new cycle of knighthood pictures in colour with the highly successful *Ivanhoe* in 1952 followed by *Knights of the Round Table* (1953), the studio's first production in CinemaScope, and *Quentin Durward* (1955). All three were filmed in Britain and France to take advantage of picturesque locations and authentic castle settings never before filmed in colour; they drew on the talents of leading British actors and technicians like cameraman Freddie Young and designer Alfred Junge, although the director (Richard Thorpe) and star (Robert Taylor) were both American. (Rival entries in the knighthood stakes released in 1954 included *The Black*

Moonfleet: *Stewart Granger shoots the elegant smuggler, George Sanders, in Fritz Lang's film of J. Meade Faulkner's novel set in 18th-century Devon.*

Knight from Columbia, Fox's *Prince Valiant*, Universal's *The Black Shield of Falworth* and *King Richard and the Crusaders* from Warners.)

There was also a cycle of costume adventure pictures at MGM starring Stewart Granger; these included in 1952 remakes of a pair of early Metro successes, *Scaramouche* and *The Prisoner of Zenda* along with *Beau Brummel* (1954) and *Moonfleet* directed by Fritz Lang in 1955. During the mid-1950s the studios made an unexpected but successful return to the war film, including a few in CinemaScope and colour from Warners – *Battle Cry* (1955) and *The Sea Chase* (1955). Two other big successes were Paramount's *Strategic Air Command* starring James Stewart, and war hero Audie Murphy starring in his own story, *To Hell and Back*, at Universal. Most successful of all was the Sam Spiegel production, for Columbia, of *The Bridge on the River Kwai*, British-American co-production directed in CinemaScope by David Lean; this was the top Oscar-winning picture in 1957 and it turned out to be one of the top grossing films of the decade.

Biblical epics in the 1950s

However, three of the top four grossers of the 1950s and the vast majority of the big budget epics continued to be set in ancient times, many of them with biblical themes. As Foster Hirsch noted (in *The Hollywood Epic*), 'Stories set in ancient Greece, Rome, Jerusalem and Egypt, subjects taken from the Bible and screenplays based on slick, best-selling novels with biblical characters became hot commercial properties.' A prime example was Fox's first CinemaScope production, *The Robe* (1953), from the novel by Lloyd C. Douglas. Its premise, the effect of Christ's robe on various individuals after the crucifixion, was a useful peg for the spectacular and the salacious – and the film became a big money-earner. A similar mixture gave DeMille a big hit with his last picture, *The Ten Commandments*, filmed in Paramount's VistaVision process in 1956 and earning $34.2m. in rentals. But the biggest grossing picture of the decade was the MGM remake of its first blockbuster silent film from thirty years before, *Ben Hur*. Filmed in the 65 mm widescreen format during 1957–58, the picture was the top Oscar-winner for 1959 and highly profitable with rentals of $40m., although the costs and problems in filming had been immense.

In retrospect, the 1950s can be seen as the boom period for the costume epic, a time when the major Hollywood companies apparently thought that this type of picture would provide the panacea to revive the declining industry.

Paul Newman *(far right) makes his screen debut in 1955 as the slave desired by Virginia Mayo in Warners'* The Silver Chalice.

The Bridge on the River Kwai *(right), the most successful war movie of all time.*

Charlton Heston *(right) watches Christ's agony in William Wyler's immensely successful remake of* Ben Hur. *Only* The Ten Commandments, *which also starred Heston, was more successful in its genre. The women are played by, left to right, Cathy O'Donnell, Martha Scott and Haya Harareet.*

The almost endless list of biblical blockbusters included some strange pairings: a thirty-five year-old Rita Hayworth played *Salome* (1953) at Columbia; Paul Newman made his film debut as a slave freed by St Luke in *The Silver Chalice* (1955) at Warners; the same studio persuaded director Howard Hawks and novelist William Faulkner to try their hands at recreating the world of ancient Egypt in *Land of the Pharoahs* in 1955, and in the same year director Robert Wise ventured into the costume epic with *Helen of Troy*.

MGM's entry in the 'forgettable epic' stakes was Richard Thorpe's *The Prodigal* (1955) featuring Lana Turner as a pagan high priestess who seduces the son of a Hebrew farmer. Directors Michael Curtiz (with *The Egyptian*) and Delmer Daves (*Demetrius and the Gladiators*, a sequel to *The Robe*) were marginally more successful at Fox in 1954. The same year Douglas Sirk directed Universal's *The Sign of the Pagan* with Jack Palance giving a surprisingly likeable performance as Attila the Hun and stealing the picture from Jeff Chandler; Richard Burton starred as *Alexander the Great* for producer-director Robert Rossen (United Artists, 1956). All these were, of course, in colour and CinemaScope. American stars even appeared in a number of the Italian action costumers of the period – Anthony Quinn as *Attila* (1955) and Kirk Douglas as *Ulysses* (1954).

The decline of the epic

By the end of the decade the seam was almost worked out. Two veteran directors ended their careers in distinctly anti-climactic fashion with biblical flops: Frank Borzage made *The Big Fisherman* for Disney and King Vidor made *Solomon and Sheba* for United Artists, both expensive productions filmed in 70 mm in 1959. The same year Stanley Kubrick was hired to replace Anthony Mann and was given what was then the largest budget of his career, $12m., to direct *Spartacus* in Spain in 70 mm. Aided by a talented group of collaborators, including scriptwriter Dalton Trumbo and cameraman Russell Metty, and a star-studded cast, the resulting film was distinctly superior entertainment and did reasonably well at the box office, but not well enough to be profitable in view of the substantial costs involved.

A serious fall in profits for most of the Hollywood majors during the early 1960s contributed to the rapid demise of the epic cycle. This was reflected vividly in the decline and fall of independent producer Samuel Bronston. He had a big success in 1961 with *El Cid* starring Charlton Heston as the eleventh-century knight who drives the Moors from Spain. (This was effectively the culmination of the 1950s knighthood cycle.) Bronston's return

Exodus *with Paul Newman, left, was Otto Preminger's extremely lengthy adaptation of Leon Uris's novel about the early years of Israel. The legend persists that comedian Mort Sahl was invited to a private screening and stood up in the middle pleading: 'Otto, let my people go!'*

to the life of Christ for *King of Kings* in 1961 was moderately successful, but his *55 Days at Peking* (1963) was disappointing at the box-office in spite of a cast led by Charlton Heston and David Niven. And Bronston's last two epics, *The Fall of the Roman Empire* and *Circus World/The Magnificent Showman* (both 1964) failed dismally at the box office, as did George Stevens' $20m. production of *The Greatest Story Ever Told* (1965) with rentals of only $7m.

Of all the major companies only Fox continued to have a substantial stake in the ancient world, releasing *The Story of Ruth* and *Esther and the King* in 1960 and Robert Aldrich's weak production of *Sodom and Gomorrah* in 1962. Some of the more interesting biblical epics like Columbia's *Barabbas* (1962), boasting a script by dramatist Christopher Fry, were made in the cycle's dying days, but the costume epic finally and irreversibly overdid itself with the ill-starred Elizabeth Taylor vehicle *Cleopatra* in 1963. The film was a major box-office disappointment. World-wide rentals and leasing to television might eventually recoup its unprecedented production cost of about $44m. (still an industry record), but Hollywood could never forget.

Action-adventure films continued on a large scale after *Cleopatra*, following the pattern of American producer, director and star, British featured players and technicians, with European locations, especially Italy or Spain. But, in marked contrast to the 1950s, there is a notable absence of costume drama, aside from the literary adaptation of *Dr Zhivago* (1965). As if *Cleopatra* had not already made the point, the total failure of *The Bible* (1966) provided a final warning to producers.

War movies in the 60s

On the other hand, the war picture in its many guises now made a notable comeback. It explored World War I themes, *Lawrence of Arabia* (1962) and *The Blue Max* (1966), the 1948 Israeli war of independence, *Exodus* (1960) and even Vietnam, *The Green Berets* (1968). But the vast majority of these movies concentrated on World War II which was recent enough to have affected the lives of a large proportion of film-goers, while far enough in the past to have acquired a certain nostalgia and to qualify for up-dated treatment. A loosening of censorship restrictions, particularly during the late 1960s, allowed a greater realism in portraying the horrors and violence of war, which was exploited, for example, in Robert Aldrich's *The Dirty Dozen* (1967), the most profitable war picture of the decade.

Although British-based writer-producer Carl Foreman had a big hit with his production of *The Guns of Navarone* in 1961, it was Fox which dominated the war film revival. Darryl Zanuck produced his large-scale, star-studded

The Dirty Dozen, *Robert Aldrich's war movie in which Lee Marvin, standing, leads a team of renegades including Donald Sutherland, left, and Telly Savalas, second left, on a violent World War II mision.*

re-creation of *The.Longest Day* (1962), followed by *Von Ryan's Express* (1965), *The Blue Max, The Sand Pebbles* (1966), *Patton* (1970, UK title *Patton – Lust for Glory*) and *Tora! Tora! Tora!* (1970). However, most of these pictures were expensive to produce, and a few even lost money (*Sand Pebbles* and *Tora!*). Ironically, Fox had its biggest and most unexpected success with the black comedy, *M*A*S*H*, set in the Korean war, as director Robert Altman made effective use of his tiny budget, free of studio interference while the bosses were preoccupied with the major problems of filming two blockbuster war pictures at the same time (*Patton* and *Tora!*).

Disaster movies

The beginning of the 1970s marked a major turning point for the film industry which was going through one of its periodic crises. Between 1969 and 1971, five of the seven majors had at least one disastrous year, with losses of $30m. or more, and the writing-off of pictures which would never recoup their costs. The companies began to search for a new formula to meet the expectations of the modern, sophisticated, film audiences of the 1970s. This took the form of an upgrading of a number of genres formerly associated with cheaper, black-and-white filming such as the gangster film, science fiction, horror and sports, with an emphasis on contemporary settings and the occasional venture into the recent past.

These new developments were reflected in completely new forms of successful action-adventure pictures which fell into three main categories: disaster movies, sports films and a successful series of male-oriented action pictures. The most conspicuous home of the third category was Warner Brothers, who distributed much of the work of action stars like Tom Laughlin (*Billy Jack* earned $32.5m. in rentals in 1971), Clint Eastwood (*Every Which Way But Loose* made $48m. in 1978) and Burt Reynolds (*Hooper*, $35m. in 1978).

But overall, Universal was most successful with action-adventure during the 1970s, although the studio had not previously been associated with this type of film. Their successes included a sports picture (*Slap Shot*, 1977) and war films like the highly profitable and cheaply produced *Midway* (1976) which made liberal use of stock footage. But most important was the new cycle of disaster movies beginning in 1970 with the smash box-office hit, *Airport*, the first big blockbuster hit in the long history of Universal.

Apart from *Airport* and Fox's *The Poseidon Adventure* (1972), the peak of the disaster cycle was concentrated in the years 1974–75 when Universal released *Earthquake*, followed by *Airport 75*, *The Hindenburg* and *Jaws* (rental income: $133m.), and Fox and Warners released their joint production of *The Towering*

Airport 77 *(far left) with Joseph Cotten, second right.*

Hurricane *(left), with Dayton Ka'ne threatening Mia Farrow, cost $22m. to make and only recouped $4.5m.*

North Dallas Forty *(below), with Nick Nolte, centre, reflected the new success of sports movies.*

Rocky *(right) with Sylvester Stallone, left, and Burgess Meredith was the most successful sports picture of all time.*

Smokey and the Bandit *(far right) was packed with every imaginable car stunt. Here Mike Henry straddles the hood of Sheriff Jackie Gleason.*

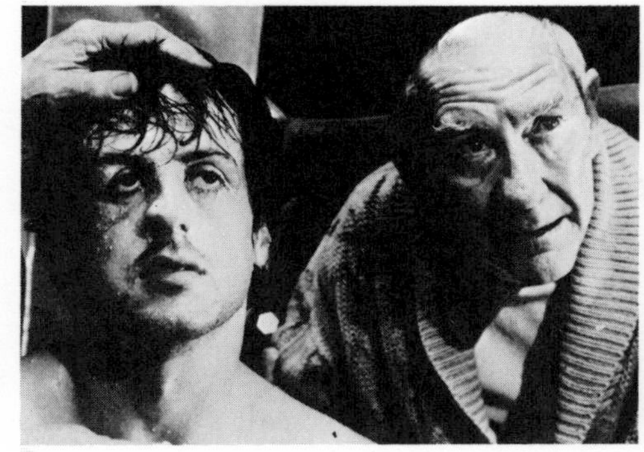

Inferno. Universal alone continued to turn out disaster sequels through the late 1970s as if determined to squeeze the last bit of revenue out of the cycle. The company had a surprisingly big hit with *Jaws II* (1978), but the *Airport* series provides a perfect demonstration of the way the law of diminishing returns generally applies to sequels: *Airport*, \$44.5m.; *Airport 75*, \$26m.; *Airport 77*, \$16m.; *Airport 79 – The Concorde*, \$6.5m. A similar lack of impact at the box office was experienced by most of the other belated entries in the disaster stakes which include flops like Paramount's *Black Sunday* (1977), Irwin Allen's productions of *The Swarm* (1978) and *Beyond the Poseidon Adventure* (1979) and Dino de Laurentiis' remake of *The Hurricane* (1979).

The success of the disaster movies reflected a new fascination with the mechanics of film-making and with elaborate special effects; not surprisingly therefore, disaster movies were replaced by the science fiction cycle of the late 1970s. And a number of directors had no difficulty making the switch: John Guillermin from *The Towering Inferno* (1974) to *King Kong* (1976); Steven Spielberg from *Jaws* (1975) to *Close Encounters of the Third Kind* (1977); and Robert Wise from *The Hindenburg* (1975) to *Star Trek* (1979).

Sports movies

Perhaps it is no accident that the successful upgrading of the sports film genre exactly paralleled the disaster/science fiction cycle. For the emphasis on the skills and accomplishments of the individual in sport provided film audiences with the kind of personalized stories on a smaller scale, which were lacking in the big budget blockbusters where characters were often dwarfed by the machinery and effects.

Robert Aldrich's successful picture about American football played by convicts, *The Longest Yard* (GB: *The Mean Machine*) starring Burt Reynolds, initiated the trend in 1974. This was followed in 1976 by United Artists' smash hit boxing picture, *Rocky*, and the baseball movie, *The Bad News Bears* from Paramount, followed by two less successful *Bears* sequels.

The hits in 1977 were *Semi-Tough* with Burt Reynolds on the football field again (directed by Michael Ritchie who made *The Bad News Bears*), *Slap Shot* with Paul Newman as an ageing ice hockey star, and *One on One*, the story of a college basketball star. The sports cycle appeared to be going strong through the end of the decade. There was the surprisingly successful appearance of *Rocky II* (1979) although the picture was less a sequel than a *remake*, another football hit with Nick Nolte starring in *North Dallas Forty*, while Peter Yates directed a successful cycling picture, *Breaking Away*. In addition, there was a large number of successful sports-related comedies and dramatic pictures, including *The Other Side of the Mountain* (UK: *A Window to the Sky*), *Heaven Can Wait*, *The Main Event* and *The Champ*.

The 1980s

By 1980, as the boom of the 1970s began its inevitable decline, there were indications that the film companies were once again looking around for new directions in which to extend the action-adventure genre. Their ability to bounce back from the creative crises of the 1960s provides hope that this will be possible, but many of the more recent experiments have proved negative. Attempts to revive swash-buckling and pirates via *Swashbuckler* (1976, UK title *The Scarlet Buccaneer*), *Royal Flash* (1975) and *The Island* (1980) have failed. A more logical development is the combination of science fiction and action adventure into a 'sword and sorcery' genre which features knights, monsters and magic. But, in any case, the big American film companies have proved many times in the past their ability to attract audiences with ventures into new and profitable areas. And the action-adventure film, in all its guises is likely to make a come-back during the 1980s as it has done so many times before.

Drama

It was often by fully assuming the strictly limited measure of artistic freedom afforded by genre movies that Hollywood directors produced their most durable work. Although the logistics of the old studio system seemed to demand that any outsize maverick talents be either homogenized or eliminated, the studios were remarkably astute at accepting cinematic innovations if these could be justified by narrative or 'atmospheric' requirements. Thus, the looming shadows and warped perspectives of German Expressionism – the cinema of Robert Wiene, and Fritz Lang – became, when enlisted into 1930s horror movies, the tone of the supernatural, which was to be transformed in its turn – refined and urbanized – into the more subtle angst of 1940s *film noir*. Again, within the framework of musical comedy, directors like Vincente Minnelli, Rouben Mamoulian and Stanley Donen were to enjoy freedom of a kind denied them in their 'straight' movies (except in so far as these resembled musicals): freedom in décor and costume, of course, but also, significantly, in camera movement and the exploration of filmic space. It is not overimaginative to detect, in the showbiz surrealism of Kathryn Grayson's 'Beauty' number from Minnelli's *Ziegfeld Follies* (1946), the influence, however trivialized, of French avant-gardism of the 1920s; whereas in Europe such visual delirium could be accommodated only by resolutely non-genre art movies like Alain Resnais's *Last Year at Marienbad* (1961) and Federico Fellini's *Juliet of the Spirits* (1965).

Genre, then, was not a straitjacket but a uniform; and, like all uniforms an unrealistic, and occasionally poetic, surface was the mark of its conformity.

A genre of adaptations

Most of the films in the drama all-time rentals list are adaptations of novels or plays; and almost all those which are not may be considered 'adaptations', nevertheless: of a news item (*Dog Day Afternoon*, 1975), or a life (*I'll Cry Tomorrow*, 1955). All are representative of Hollywood's periodic attempts to come to grips with attitudes that seem to resist *a priori* genre classification. However, these films do belong to a single, clearly definable genre, even if what they share tends to be camouflaged by an unusually wide range of source material.

Since, in virtually every case, the films were produced because of the success or prestige of their sources, the adaptive process has to remain, in a sense, *incomplete*. Because the original property is a genuine production value often acquired at considerable expense, it is not merely adapted, but must be seen to be adapted and the factors most crucial to the original's success have to be displayed as conspicuously as possible within the film, whether or not they lend themselves to cinematic expression. *Gone with the Wind* (1939), for example, posed few problems: the novelistic 'sweep' of Margaret Mitchell's best-seller, with its Civil War backdrop, its intimate dramas caught up in the march of history and its proliferation of minor characters, suffered little in translation to the screen and, in a set-piece like the burning of Atlanta, probably gained. But even the theatricality of *Cavalcade* (1933), taken from the famous and successful play by Noel Coward, far from being a conceptual flaw in the film version, constituted an essential residue of cultural respectability, a guarantee of vulgarization without vulgarity, which in no way impaired its box-office returns.

Although audiences today are no longer so conditioned by the normative notion of a ninety-minute movie, films lasting well over two hours were once extremely rare, their excessive length invariably contingent on literary origin: for example, *Gone with the Wind* (220 minutes), *For Whom the Bell Tolls* (168 minutes), *The Best Years of Our Lives* (172 minutes), *Dr Zhivago* (193 minutes plus 4 minutes overture and 2 minutes intermission music). And as if to forestall any inopportune directorial tampering, to this kind of prestigious production were assigned such stalwart studio employees as Victor Fleming, Sam Wood,

Gone with the Wind, *David O. Selznick's adaptation of Margaret Mitchell's novel, is far and away the most successful movie in film history.*

All-Time Hit Drama Movies

	Title	Rental income from initial release period: $m.	Inflation factor	Adjusted total: $m.
1	Gone with the Wind, 1939	31	×10	310
2	Dr Zhivago, 1965	43	×2.5	107.5
3	The Best Years of Our Lives, 1946	10.4	×7	72.8
4	One Flew Over the Cuckoo's Nest, 1976	59	×1.2	70.8
5	The Greatest Show on Earth, 1952	12.8	×5.5	70.4
6	From Here to Eternity, 1953	12.2	×5.5	67.1
7	Guess Who's Coming to Dinner, 1968	25.5	×2	51
8	The Song of Bernadette, 1943	5	×10	50
9	Peyton Place, 1957	11	×4.5	49.5
10	The Carpetbaggers, 1964	15.5	×3	46.5
11	The Four Horsemen of the Apocalypse, 1921	4.5	×10	45
12	The Caine Mutiny, 1954	8.7	×5	43.5
13	Hawaii, 1966	15.5	×2.5	38.8
14	The Lost Weekend, 1945	4.3	×9	38.7
	Weekend at the Waldorf, 1945	4.3	×9	38.7
16	To Sir, with Love, 1967	19.1	×2	38.2
17	The Bible, 1966	15	×2.5	37.5
18	The Yearling, 1947	5.2	×7	36.4
19	Who's Afraid of Virginia Woolf, 1966	14.5	×2.5	36.3
20	All the President's Men, 1976	30	×1.2	36
21	The Snows of Kilimanjaro, 1952	6.5	×5.5	35.8
22	Cat on a Hot Tin Roof, 1958	7.8	×4.5	35.1
23	Cavalcade, 1933	3.5	×10	35
	The Razor's Edge, 1946	5	×7	35
25	Midnight Cowboy, 1969	16.3	×2	32.6
26	The Green Years, 1947	4.6	×7	32.2
27	War and Peace, 1957	6.3	×5	31.5
28	Not as a Stranger, 1955	6.2	×5	31
29	The Hucksters, 1947	4.4	×7	30.8
30	The High and the Mighty, 1954	6.1	×5	30.5
31	The Country Girl, 1955	6	×5	30
	I'll Cry Tomorrow, 1955	6	×5	30
33	The Deer Hunter, 1978	26.9	×1.1	29.6
34	Saratoga Trunk, 1946	4.2	×7	29.4
	Pinky, 1949	4.2	×7	29.4
36	Hitler's Children, 1943	3.2	×9	28.8
37	Johnny Belinda, 1948	4.1	×7	28.7
	Cass Timberlaine, 1948	4.1	×7	28.7
	The Snake Pit, 1949	4.1	×7	28.7
	Joan of Arc, 1949	4.1	×7	28.7
41	Dog Day Afternoon, 1975	22.5	×1.25	28.1
42	How Green Was My Valley, 1941	2.8	×10	28
43	Island in the Sun, 1957	5	×5.5	27.5
44	Gentleman's Agreement, 1947	3.9	×7	27.3
45	San Francisco, 1936	2.7	×10	27

Selected runners-up

Title	Rental income from initial release period: $m.	Inflation factor	Adjusted total: $m.
Tales of Manhattan, 1942	2.6	×10	26
Sea of Grass, 1947	3.65	×7	25.6
A Man for All Seasons, 1967	12.8	×2	25.6
A Streetcar Named Desire, 1951	4.25	×6	25.5
East of Eden, 1955	5	×5	25
King's Row, 1942	2.35	×10	23.5
Moulin Rouge, 1953	4.2	×5.5	23.1
Grand Hotel, 1932	2.3	×10	23
The Nun's Story, 1959	5.7	×4	22.8
A Man Called Peter, 1955	4.5	×5	22.5
Watch on the Rhine, 1943	2.5	×9	22.5
Suddenly Last Summer, 1960	5.5	×4	22
To Kill a Mockingbird, 1963	7.2	×3	21.6
Man With the Golden Arm, 1955	4.1	×5	20.5
The Bad Seed, 1956	4.1	×5	20.5
The Great Gatsby, 1974	14.2	×1.4	19.8
Some Came Running, 1959	4.3	×4	17.2

1980 Kramer vs Kramer

Omar Sharif *(right) rails against the ignorance and poverty around him in David Lean's* Doctor Zhivago.

Hoagy Carmichael *(far right) shares his piano stool with Harold Russell as he entertains the war veterans of* The Best Years of Our Lives.

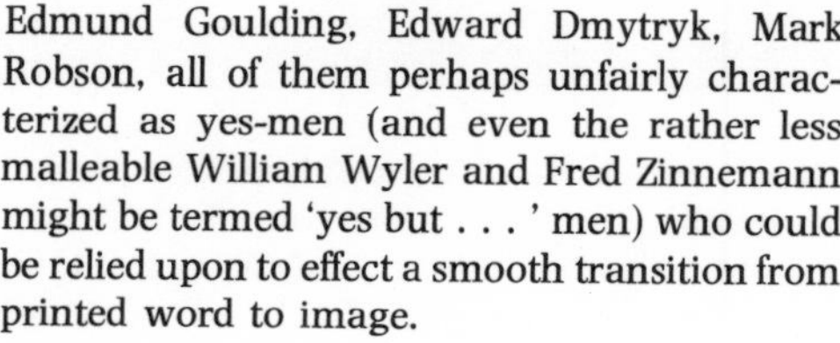

Edmund Goulding, Edward Dmytryk, Mark Robson, all of them perhaps unfairly characterized as yes-men (and even the rather less malleable William Wyler and Fred Zinnemann might be termed 'yes but . . . ' men) who could be relied upon to effect a smooth transition from printed word to image.

The Best Years of Our Lives

The ideal, which was no doubt of some seamless union of 'cultural' integrity and familiar movie raciness, was achieved most notably by Victor Fleming (plus the uncredited George Cukor and, of course, producer David Selznick) in *Gone with the Wind* and, at the cost of greater abuse to a more distinguished original, by David Lean in *Dr Zhivago*. But the most useful example is Wyler's *The Best Years of Our Lives* (1946), based on a verse novel by MacKinlay Kantor, *Glory for Me*, about three discharged World War II servicemen – from the army, navy and air force – and their difficult readjustment to civilian life.

Wyler's direction was in his best soberly efficient manner and scenarist Robert Sherwood, a well-known playwright, handled the multiple narrative strands with remarkable skill, plausibly interweaving the lives of the three protagonists – played by Fredric March, Dana Andrews and the armless war veteran Harold Russell – without ever smudging or losing sight of the whole design. Basically, however, when these various strands are disentangled and held up for individual inspection, they prove to be rather trite and even dishonest. March, as vice-president of the local bank in charge of G.I. loans, meets increasing opposition from his board of directors whenever he tries to aid some ex-serviceman lacking collateral, proving once again that Hollywood could countenance social change only if accomplished through the quasi-charitable initiative of a few men of good-will; since the wife he married just before being sent overseas (Virginia Mayo) is so obviously a slut, her pretty head filled with night-clubs and mink coats, Andrews is permitted to turn almost righteously to March's daughter – sweet, understanding, middle-class Teresa Wright – for comfort; and even the very moving and tasteful (for once the critic's cant word is justified) scenes involving Russell and his fiancée (Cathy O'Donnell) are motivated by the timeworn movie rhetoric of disablement: does she love him or does she just pity him?

What makes it superior to such a resumé and vindicates the admiration of no less a critic than André Bazin is that much of what is interesting in the film occurs in the interstices of these novelettish situations. It is in its transitional scenes, its liaisons, those moments when plot-lines converge like two men meeting unexpectedly at a street corner, that one has the sense of an authentic community existing not merely behind but all around the central trio, and this is never wholly subsumed by the close-up treatment accorded their own personal predicaments. Because of its length, moreover, the film has time to breathe properly; and Gregg Toland's photography, underpinning the dramatic scenes with an almost claustrophobic use of deep-focus, loosens up for the freer, more documentary features of small town life. Although it cannot have been much inspired by Kantor's novel, the film does paradoxically convey the impression of a brilliantly distilled novel, a 'good read', an impression which is

Christopher Walken *(left) as a captive of the Viet Cong and unwilling participant in a 'game' of Russian Roulette, in* The Deer Hunter.

reinforced by the solid, if transparent, 'prose' of Wyler's visual style.

The Deer Hunter

In this respect, an instructive comparison may be drawn with a more recent movie drama, Michael Cimino's *The Deer Hunter* (1978). The two works present some striking symmetries: both deal with the psychological effects of war on three friends (even if the war's aftermath, which occupies the whole of *The Best Years of Our Lives*, constitutes only the third panel of *The Deer Hunter*'s triptych form); in Cimino's film, too, one finds the theme of physical mutilation, with the John Savage character having his legs amputated and refusing absolutely to see his wife; and both end with a ritualized affirmation of American values emerging (relatively) unscathed from the ordeal.

But there are also significant differences. In Wyler's film the unseen war remains an abstraction, its necessity never questioned, its hurts those inflicted by any war, indeed, by War itself. If Cimino was obliged to adopt an overtly ideological position towards Vietnam, it was not just because much of *The Deer Hunter* is actually set there: the degree to which public opinion was divided over the war may be gauged, if from no other source, from the reluctance with which Hollywood has finally begun to tackle the question and the tacit understanding that genre 'war movies' cast in a straightforward adventure mould would be an inadequate response. In fact, the bad conscience concerning American involvement that permeates *The Deer Hunter* (in the bar-room encounter with a disillusioned Green Beret, for example) is just as geared to confirming the audience's prejudices as anything in *The Best Years of Our Lives*: the unspoken question hovering over the film is less 'Why are we in Vietnam?' than 'How could the President allow our boys to be contaminated by gooks?'

But if Vietnam is represented by Cimino as an oriental hell on earth (the implication being that its hellishness predated the descent into it of American soldiers and weaponry) and the Viet Cong as congenitally malevolent – the 'wily yellow devils' of colonial mythology – he proves considerably subtler in his depiction of the home ground. Since, in view of the increasing fragmentation of American society after the upheavals of the 1960s, it was no longer admissible to paint small town existence in purely symbolic terms, with the broad, generalizing brush-strokes employed by Wyler and Sherwood, the Pennsylvania steelworking community of *The Deer Hunter* is particularized to the point where its inhabitants are mostly of Russian Orthodox stock; but, apart from the fact that the presence of immigrants from a Communist country neatly mirrors the dispatching of second- or third-generation American sons to another country which threatens to become Communist, Cimino domesticates the more alien aspects of his setting by devoting the whole first hour-long section of the film to one of the codified celebrations of Americanness, a white wedding (precisely the ritual that ends *The Best Years of Our Lives*).

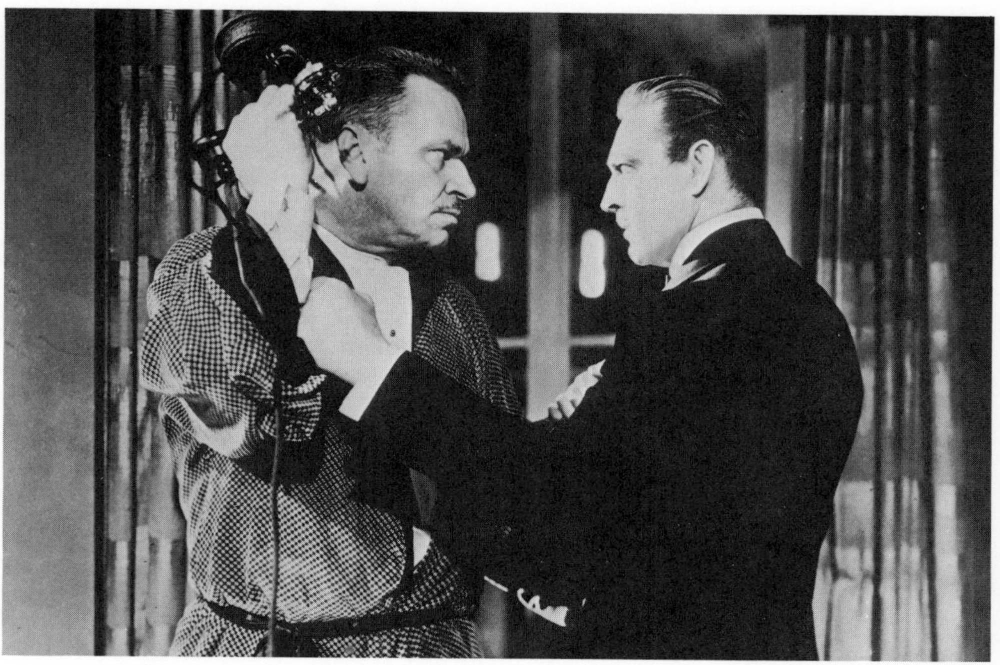

Wallace Beery and John Barrymore *(right) as two of the guests whose destinies become entwined in* Grand Hotel.

The two films, then, function in similar fashion, the mood only having changed; and if *The Deer Hunter* differs by being an original script, it was naturally 'adapted' for paperback publication.

Episodic drama

Occasionally a novel is adapted to the screen so seamlessly that it is able to break free of the 'drama' category and launch a new movie cycle. Set almost entirely inside a hotel (whose model was reputedly the Adlon of pre-war Berlin), *Grand Hotel* (1932) from Vicki Baum's international best-seller, recounts several interlocking stories involving its divers clientele: a temperamental ballerina (Greta Garbo) falls in love with a jewel thief (John Barrymore); a terminally ill clerk (Lionel Barrymore) embezzles from his firm to enjoy one last, expensive fling, etc. While the film's episodic framework encouraged the kind of starry casting which was practically a guarantee of box-office success in the 1930s, its narrative paths criss-crossing within the confines of the glamorous decor made the spectators feel they had been given access to a world of power and wealth and beauty, however briefly, while the very brevity of each episode conspired to render it even more real, as if 'overheard'. Other films belonging to this category are *Weekend at the Waldorf* (1945), virtually a remake of *Grand Hotel*, and William Wellman's *The High and the Mighty*, based on a tense novel by Ernest K. Gann about a motley selection of passengers and crew on board an aircraft whose wings begin to ice over. It was the latter film, made in 1954, that helped to alert Hollywood to the possibility of dispensing with a cumbersome portmanteau construction in the manner of *Grand Hotel* in favour of a single plotline centred around some vast, heuristic crisis, testing character as it revealed it. Although spasmodic attempts were made to revive the original concept (as, for example, Anthony Asquith's British film of 1963, *The VIPs*), the combination of a natural catastrophe with a multiplicity of characters eventually proved irresistible and the 'disaster movie' was born.

Biopics

Hollywood's quest for respectability and prestige is at its most overt in the adaptation of biography. Films like Daniel Mann's *I'll Cry Tomorrow* (1955, on the life of actress Lillian Roth) and John Huston's *Moulin Rouge* (1952, about Toulouse-Lautrec), can be traced to a cycle of Warner Brothers 1930s productions in which a heavily made-up Paul Muni impersonated the faces that are found on French banknotes. He starred in *The Story of Louis Pasteur* in 1935 and *The Life of Emile Zola* two years later, both directed by the German emigré William Dieterle. Their pompous historicism together with Muni's stiffly pedantic performances renders them virtually unwatchable today, but they were huge critical and commercial successes in their time. Soon however, the lives of bourgeois intellectuals were accounted insufficiently 'cinematic' (Zola's significance, for example, had been predicated almost solely on his involvement in the Dreyfus case) and the succeeding films focused more and more on two related species of celebrity: the fine artist and the showbusiness artiste. The former were generally treated romantically and trivially, with artists depicted as superhuman beings scorching paper or canvas with their genius and descending from ivory towers only to enmesh themselves in what invariably proved to be doomed love affairs.

No less romantic in their fashion, if on a less grandiose scale, were the showbusiness biographies, whose heroes and, more often, heroines struggled to overcome such various afflictions as alcoholism (*I'll Cry Tomorrow*), physical disability (Curtis Bernhardt's *Interrupted Melody*, 1955, whose subject was the crippled soprano Marjorie Lawrence), undesirable mobster connections (Charles Vidor's *Love Me or Leave Me*, 1955, about the torch singer Ruth Etting) and, in a general way, the intoxication of fame itself.

Alcoholism as a theme

I'll Cry Tomorrow is mediocre stuff, directed without style and gratingly played by Susan Hayward in her most Oscar-grabbing manner; but the heroine's dark secret is interesting. The theme of alcoholism has seldom been of primary importance in Hollywood movies, its admittedly limited possibilities being usually confined to minor characters, younger brothers or first husbands (not forgetting those seedy doctors perennially employed as tragi-comic relief in Westerns). Its predominance in biopics, however, would seem to intimate that its representation on the screen could only be sanctioned and made acceptable to the public, if enshrined in the dual celebrity of character and performer, the former long since redeemed or dead, the latter, it is clearly understood, playing courageously against type.

The most memorable treatment of the theme remains Billy Wilder's multi-Oscar-winning *The Lost Weekend* (1945), based on the novel by Charles R. Jackson. Although the screenplay by Wilder and Charles Brackett softened the original (notably by the appendage of an implausible redemption scene at the end), the film actually added a few punches for those that it pulled, such as the famous visualization of the protagonist's d.t.s and the leeringly snide male nurse played by Frank Faylen. Its triumph at the box office appeared to demonstrate that even such glum material – which had caused Paramount considerable apprehension during the shooting – could mobilize the public if presented with impeccable credentials: an estimable novel, a downbeat performance by an actor more at home in light comedy, Ray Milland, and a grippingly realistic approach to the subject-matter. Another such success, George Seaton's *The Country Girl* (1954) boasted a Clifford Odets play, Bing Crosby as an alcoholic actor on the skids and, as a bonus, Grace Kelly in dowdy cardigans and 'plain' make-up as his long-suffering wife. On the other hand, the commercial failure of Blake Edwards' *Days of Wine and Roses* (1962) no doubt derived from its quite subtle modulation of tone from comedy to drama.

The portrayal of sexuality

Cinema has often trailed far behind the other arts in the treatment of 'adult' themes, and the safety-net of pre-sold literary respectability sometimes enabled it to stray – with obvious timidity – into territory that had formerly been off-limits. A case in point is Tennessee Williams, one of the most filmed of contemporary writers. His plays were a boon to Hollywood, because their rejection of realism in favour of the poeticization of moral and physical squalor was not difficult to sensationalize in film publicity but bowdlerize in practice. The theme of homosexuality, for example, finally surfaced in mainstream American cinema in Richard Brooks' glossy adaptation of Williams' *Cat on a Hot Tin Roof* (1958), but the references to the hero's repressed desires, which in the original were unambiguous enough for the play to receive its English première at a theatre club, became in the film version so oblique as to be almost impenetrable. Brooks has been one of the most persistent offenders at raising serious issues only to recoil from them. In a subsequent adaptation of the same dramatist, *Sweet Bird of Youth* (1962), about an ageing actress (Geraldine Page) and the sturdy young gigolo (Paul Newman) who tags along with her, his decision to have the stud facially disfigured instead of castrated effectively emasculated the material.

Homosexuality also figured, a shade more graphically, in Joseph L. Mankiewicz's version of Gore Vidal's adaptation of another of Williams' sickly psychodramas, *Suddenly, Last Summer* (1959), with its flashback of the notorious, but otherwise unseen, Sebastian Venables being chased (and, presumably, eaten) by a horde of urchins. But even more candid treatments of the theme continued to associate it with disease or abnormality, like Dustin Hoffman's tuberculosis in John Schlesinger's *Midnight Cowboy* (1969), based on the novel by James Leo Herlihy, or the sex-change operation for Al Pacino's boyfriend that triggers

Kirk Douglas *as the increasingly distraught Van Gogh in Vincente Minnelli's superior biopic of the artist,* Lust for Life.

Ray Milland *as the hallucinating alcoholic in Billy Wilder's* The Lost Weekend.

Burt Lancaster and Deborah Kerr *in the once notorious, now clichéd, love scene of* From Here to Eternity.

off the heist in Sidney Lumet's *Dog Day Afternoon* (1975).

One of the unexpected results of the suspended state of sexual repression in which the Hays Code kept the American cinema for over three decades was its reversal of the natural evolution of any art-form from crudity to refinement. In their attempts to circumvent the censors, Hollywood directors and cameramen were obliged from the start to find ways of conveying sexuality without crudely exposing it: which might almost be a definition of eroticism. As a substitute for sheer physicality, shots were erotically sensitized by the widespread use of filters, gauzes and shadows; and innuendo in dialogue was raised to a fine and subtle art, as with Lauren Bacall's 'If you want me, just whistle . . .' exit line from the William Faulkner and Jules Furthman script for Howard Hawks' adaptation of Ernest Hemingway's *To Have and Have Not* (1944). Such niceties more or less disappeared when, from the mid-1950s on, the rigid corset of censorship was progressively unlaced and – again, often via popular literature – sex was accorded more direct treatment.

Zinnemann's *From Here to Eternity* (1953), an ill-digested condensation of James Jones' mammoth chronicle of life on a Hawaiian military base just before Pearl Harbor, is best remembered, perhaps, for its love scene on the beach between Burt Lancaster and Deborah Kerr, which became for a while (as numerous parodies bear witness) the movie equivalent of a well-thumbed page in some slightly risqué best-seller. What is most striking about the scene when viewed with hindsight is not its 'torrid' semi-nudity, relatively tame by present standards, but the fact that, in the organization of its visual elements, it set a style in romantic soft-core eroticism for years to come (Henry King's *Love is a Many-Splendored Thing*, 1955, for example) before – supplemented by slow-motion, soft-focus and open air musak – it became a standard ingredient of television commercials. The elements were: the beach itself as an erotic space, both open and (if deserted) closed, public and intimate, a 'feminine' landscape of undulating dunes interspersed with pubic tufts of grass; sand and sea forever in motion, merging, clinging, highlighting different areas of the body; and, of course, the waves, that vague, all-purpose metaphor towards which the camera will pan, discreetly but suggestively, at the appropriate moment.

For its time, however, this sequence was an exception. Though in apparent violation of the medium's predominantly visual status, sex in the cinema remained until recent years rigorously unphysical; and what meagre advances were made derived almost exclusively from the utilization of language which, however explicit,

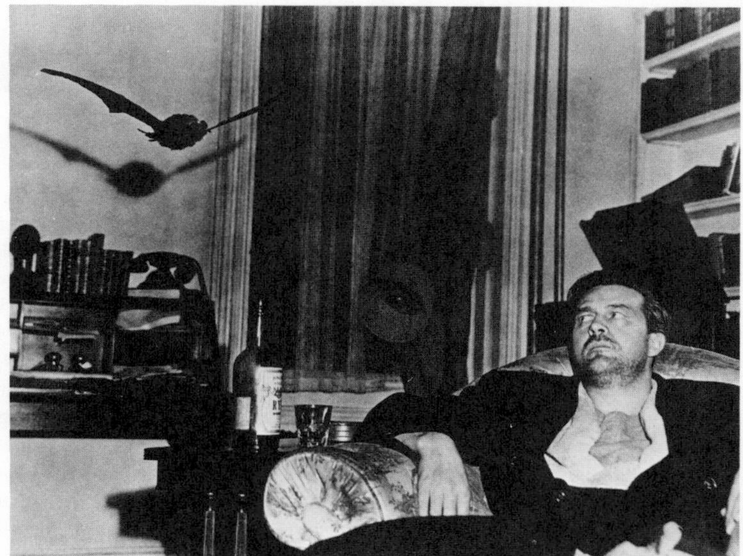

Elizabeth Taylor and Richard Burton *(left) were virtually type-cast by their off-screen image for the domestic verbal hostilities of* Who's Afraid of Virginia Woolf?

Olivia de Havilland *(right) as the hapless inmate of a nightmarishly conceived asylum in* The Snake Pit.

Gregory Peck *(far right) dominates the courtroom proceedings of* To Kill a Mockingbird, *as a liberal lawyer defending a black man in the American South.*

had been 'laundered' by previous literary usage. Such adaptations, in short, provided Hollywood with a golden opportunity to pass the buck. In Mark Robson's *Peyton Place* (1957), from the novel by Grace Metalious, and in Edward Dmytryk's version of Harold Robbins' *The Carpetbaggers* (1964), sex was verbalized rather than visualized (when in the latter movie Carroll Baker performs a drunken striptease, the camera does not linger, thus adding an extra layer of 'tease'). These films both illustrated and pandered to a taste for low- or high-grade gossip, often masquerading as 'adult themes frankly aired', and they too have found their true level on television, respectively in the unashamed soap opera of *Dallas* and the more ambitious (if less diverting) *Best Sellers* series.

The theme of insanity

Mike Nichols' *Who's Afraid of Virginia Woolf?* (1966) stands slightly apart. Its immense commercial success would appear to have been due less to the intrinsic prestige of Edward Albee's play than to the promise of Richard Burton and Elizabeth Taylor engaged in a no-holds-barred histrionic duel; and also to a fundamental misunderstanding at the level of genre classification: with its adults-only certificate, with Elizabeth Taylor cosmetically aged for her role and even sporting a fright wig, and with a title that for the average movie-goer was a little mystifying, it is very possible that audiences categorized the movie with Robert Aldrich's *What Ever Happened to Baby Jane?* (1962) and the cycle of geriatric 'shockers' which it inspired.

Hollywood wilfully manipulated just this type of ambiguity when dealing with the theme of insanity. In Anatole Litvak's *The Snake Pit* (1948), where Olivia de Havilland is incarcerated in the high-security ward of an asylum at the mercy of a pack of demented harridans pawing obsessively at her, and *Suddenly, Last Summer*, where a similar fate befalls Elizabeth Taylor, both the imagery and the sadistically melodramatic angles at which it is framed were appropriated from horror movies. Milos Forman's *One Flew Over the Cuckoo's Nest* (1975), from Ken Kesey's novel, functioned in a related manner, even if the focus of sympathy had significantly altered. Viewed thus from the outside, madness (and especially collective madness) was transformed into a horrific or sad but reassuringly alien spectacle, the condition itself invariably reduced to its most uncommon denominators: lunatics playing ping-pong without bats or balls, taking themselves for Napoleon or Teddy Roosevelt, and so on. At best, they were capable of inspiring pity, the kind of pity one extends to Frankenstein's monster when played by Boris Karloff. Although attempts had been made (Fritz Lang's German *M* of 1931) and would be made (Martin Scorsese's *Taxi Driver*, 1976) to dismantle the very precise mechanism of anti-identification operating in such films, to credit the mentally disturbed with those 'normal' human contradictions denied by more monolithic archetypes, Hollywood during its 'golden age' could not envisage them except as personifications of abnormality, of difference, of the Other.

Race as a theme

But this whole notion of 'otherness', all but excluded from the simple mythical structures of genres like the western, can be shown to underlie most of the films under review. They were stories and subjects that Hollywood would not normally have attempted. And since part of Hollywood's reluctance – its sense of us and them – was undoubtedly racist in origin, it is not surprising that a sense of taboo is nowhere stronger than in works dealing with racial tension itself. After decades of offensive if endearing stereotypes (typified by Hattie McDaniel's resilient mammy in *Gone with the Wind*), the question, when finally broached, emerged as one of Us in relation to Them: essentially a question, as with *The Deer Hunter*'s treatment of the Viet Cong, of contamination. In Robert Rossen's *Island in the Sun* (1957), from a novel by Alec Waugh not set in the United States at all but in the British West Indies, the implication was clear: the two races might co-exist harmoniously though unequally on condition that they never intersect, but it scarcely constituted an adequate response to the lived experience of the vast majority of black Americans. More traditionally, in Robert Mulligan's adaptation of Harper Lee's Pulitzer Prize-winning *To Kill a Mockingbird* (1962), the black was presented as one of nature's intended victims, harmless and hapless, whose only salvation lay in the courageous and lonely defence of a good, liberal and white lawyer (Gregory Peck) amid the picturesque bayous and lynchings of that comfortably exotic habitat of racial feudalism, the Deep South. When, in the 1960s, the American Dream acquired its first true-blue black hero in Sidney Poitier, the times they were a-changin' but not so inescapably as at first sight: in James Clavell's *To Sir, With Love* (1967) Poitier was a schoolmaster whose patience with unruly pupils and obtuse colleagues verged on saintliness; in Stanley Kramer's *Guess Who's Coming to Dinner* (1967) he was a Nobel Prize laureate.

No ordinary heroes or villains

In less generic terms, such disparate figures as Bernadette of *The Song of Bernadette* and the nun of *The Nun's Story*, the Welsh miners of *How Green Was My Valley* and the Quakers of *Friendly Persuasion*, Bogart's schizophrenic sea-captain in *The Caine Mutiny* and Patty Duke's child murderess in *The Bad Seed* were all freaks in precisely the sense that the cast of Tod Browning's exemplary horror film *Freaks* (1932) were not, larger-than-life Balzacian monsters who could be viewed only through the double glazing, as it were, of literature and cinema and would not be found amongst the more ordinary heroes and villains of the other genres. They invited awe or admiration rather than sympathy. Even Scarlett O'Hara proved no ordinary heroine, being cast only after a much-trumpeted nationwide search for talent; and it is equally indicative of *Gone with the Wind*'s pretensions that its relatively short title was nevertheless considered too grand merely to materialize on the screen: instead, it solemnly traversed it from right to left, almost in a parody of the act of reading.

Flops

It is fair to say that the cinema's first failure was Thomas Alva Edison, the man who claimed he invented it in 1892 (he didn't; the kinetoscope, or peep show, the first apparatus to achieve persistence of vision by means of perforated strips of celluloid, was the sole creation of his British employee William Kennedy-Laurie Dickson). Edison failed to see the commercial potential of moving pictures. He intended his films to be accompanied by synchronized sound, but never got round to perfecting the process. Failing to apply for European patents, he left Dickson's invention unprotected, and consequently R. W. Paul in England and the Lumière brothers in France were able to build their own kinetoscopes and reap the benefits. Edison couldn't see the need for projecting his pictures on to a screen; it was the selfsame Lumières who first achieved this in 1896. And when it had become obvious, after the success of *The Birth of a Nation* in 1915, that the future of the film industry lay in the feature film, not the short, Edison continued making shorts. His company went out of business in 1918.

But at least Edison made a substantial contribution to motion picture history, which is more than can be said for William Friese-Greene, who, thanks to chauvinistic British journalism and a 1951 biopic called *The Magic Box* (a failure, incidentally), is still thought of, quite erroneously, as the Father of the Cinema. Certainly he was there inventing cinematographic gadgets alongside the rest of the pioneers; whether any of them worked, however, is very much open to dispute. Other losers active during the dawn of the cinema include Woodville Latham, who failed to demonstrate a workable projector in New York in 1895, and David Devant, who made an abortive attempt to film Queen Victoria's Diamond Jubilee Procession in 1897.

Down the years we have been led to believe that each new development in the technology of the cinema was greeted with gasps of delight and pandemonium at the box office. This is not strictly true. The first attempts to make pictures move had the contrary effect. Reviewing a programme of films projected by R. W. Paul in 1896, one critic wrote: 'The introduction of the Cinematographe at the Canterbury [a London theatre] on Monday evening was attended only with partial success. Difficulties of working had hardly been overcome, and one of the pictures was so blurred and indistinct that the audience did not hesitate to express their disapprobation.' Such teething troubles took years to rectify. Early movie-goers regularly barracked the lack of illumination on the screen, or the incorrect speed of projection.

Sound, colour and gimmicks

The birth of the sound film was equally painful. This is hard to credit today because the success in 1927 of *The Jazz Singer*, the first feature film with synchronized dialogue, has passed into legend. The fact remains, however, that during the months leading up to that auspicious premiere, audiences were actually driven out of cinemas by the atrocious quality of many of Warner Brothers' Vitaphone shorts: tinny speakers producing whining, distorted noises were a poor substitute for the glorious pit orchestra.

Experiments with colour were generally enjoyed from the time hand-colouring was first introduced in 1896, although it's seldom remembered that the first feature in three colour Technicolor, *Becky Sharp* (1935), was another box-office failure, the reason being perhaps that it was an adaptation of Thackeray's *Vanity Fair*, not the sort of subject-matter to appeal to the masses. It was the success of the second Technicolor feature, *The Trail of the Lonesome Pine* (1936), a popular melodrama, that persuaded producers to persevere with the expensive Technicolor process.

Of the gimmicks introduced to revitalize the cinema during its post-1946 slump, only the letter box shaped screen has survived. The biggest disaster was Smell-o-Vision, used for one film, *Scent of Mystery* (GB: *Holiday in Spain*),

Dr Dolittle, *the $20m. musical flop, starring Rex Harrison, that nearly sank Twentieth Century-Fox just as it was recovering from the horrific losses of* Cleopatra.

Forty Major Flops

	Negative cost: $m.	Rental from U.S. and Canada: $m.	Loss: $m.
1 Waterloo (1969)	25	1.4	23.6
2 Darling Lili (1970)	22	3.3	18.7
3 The Fall of the Roman Empire (1964)	20	1.9	18.1
4 Cleopatra (1962)	44	26	18
5 Hurricane (1975)	22	4.5	17.5
6 Sorcerer (1977)	22	5.9	16.1
7 Meteor (1979)	20	4.2	15.8
8 Dr Dolittle (1967)	20	6.2	13.8
9 The Greatest Story Ever Told (1965)	20	6.9	13.1
10 The Island (1980)	22	9.6	12.4
11 Star! (1968)	15	4.2	10.8
12 Tora! Tora! Tora! (1970)	25	14.5	10.5
13 The Wiz (1978)	24	13.6	10.4
14 Mutiny on the Bounty (1962)	20	9.8	10.2
15 Battle of Britain (1969)	12	2	10
16 The Molly Maguires (1970)	11	1.1	9.9
The Brinks Job (1978)	15	5.1	9.9
18 The Red Tent (1971)	10	.9	9.1
19 The Private Life of Sherlock Holmes (1970)	10	1	9
20 Hello Dolly (1969)	24	15.2	8.8
The Prisoner of Zenda (1979)	12.5	3.7	8.8
22 The Only Game in Town (1970)	10	1.5	8.5
23 The Lost Horizon (1973)	12	3.8	8.2
24 Paint Your Wagon (1969)	20	14.5	5.5
25 The Long Riders (1980)	11	5.9	5.1
26 55 Days at Peking (1963)	10	5	5
27 Dracula (1979)	15	10.5	4.5
28 Hair (1979)	11	6.8	4.2
29 Nicholas and Alexandra (1971)	11	7	4
30 Sweet Charity (1969)	7.5	4	3.5
31 The Bible (1966)	18	15	3
A Bridge Too Far (1977)	24	21	3
33 Chitty Chitty Bang Bang (1968)	10	7.1	2.9
34 Barry Lyndon (1975)	12	9.2	2.8
35 New York, New York (1977)	8.5	6	2.5
36 Xanadu (1980)	12.5	10.3	2.3
37 Casino Royale (1967)	12	10.2	1.8
38 Camelot (1967)	15	14	1
39 Myra Breckinridge (1970)	5	4.3	.7
40 Lucky Lady (1975)	13	12.7	.3

When a film fails to recover its negative cost in the American market, its producers very often face considerable losses, whether on paper (they may have had substantial non-returnable advances from exhibitors) or in practice. They still have to meet the huge cost of promotion – often as much as or more than the cost of the film itself – and their film will be regarded a failure until additional income from TV sales or the world market proves otherwise. Where the loss is large, the figures very rarely return to the black and few of the films below ever did. Indeed in certain rare cases like *Hello Dolly* where the studio has provided details of losses on individual films, the shortfall turns out to be nearly *twice as high* as our estimate (in Dolly's case $13.7m!). This list has not been adjusted for inflation.

Note: Accurate negative costs are not available for many movies which should undoubtedly appear on this list. Sergeant Pepper's Lonely Hearts Club Band, Rough Cut, Crossed Swords, Times Square, Quintet, Swarm *and numerous others fall into this category.* Raise the Titanic (1980), *with a potential loss on American earnings of $29.2m., would easily beat* Waterloo *to first place, but since the film is still playing as this book goes to press it has not been included.*

The Door in the Wall *(right), Glenn Alvey's rarely shown film from the H. G. Wells short story, shot in Dynamic Frame.*

Stop the World – I Want to Get Off *(far right), Philip Saville's film of Anthony Newley's hit stage musical, with, left to right, Tony Tanner, Neil Hawley and Millicent Martin.*

in 1960. 'It was almost instantaneously rejected by the public', admitted its promoter, Mike Todd Jnr. Another one-off experiment was Dynamic Frame, a process in which the screen changed its shape to suit the action. Few people were aware of the innovation because of the limited exposure given to the only film in Dynamic Frame, *The Door in the Wall* (1955), by its sponsor, the British Film Institute. In its original form, Electronovision, which allowed a film to be shot with the speed and economy (and consequent dullness) of a video production for TV, lasted only a few months in 1964. None of the three main Electronovision films – *Hamlet, Harlow* and *The TAMI Show* (in UK: *Gather No Moss*) made money, but while the technique still promised to revolutionize movie-making, a British counterpart, Mitchell System 35, was utilized for the shooting of the highly-stylized and cheap-looking *Stop the World – I Want To Get Off*, still recalled with pain by British cinema managers as the most unsuccessful British film of 1966.

The flashiest flash-in-the-pan, however, was stereoscopy. As long ago as 1938, *Three Dimension Murder*, a black-and-white 3-D film directed by George Sidney, had proved that the public did not like wearing special glasses in order to watch movies. But in 1952, when crowds flocked to see *Bwana Devil*, the first feature in 'Natural Vision' (3-D and colour), Hollywood threw caution to the wind and began churning out stereoscopic films. Only one, *House of Wax*, made a fortune before the novelty wore off. By the end of 1953 *Kiss Me, Kate*, a flop in 3-D, had been re-released flat with the announcement 'See it without special glasses!' The public responded, and that was the end of Natural Vision.

Films with a message

It goes without saying that not every film that makes money deserves to. Though by no means a rule of thumb, it could be said that a film will do well if it makes no great intellectual demand on its audience, and features well-liked players behaving in a sympathetic fashion. This is the diehard legacy of the cinema as it was at the turn of the century, a popular, cheap art with its roots in music-hall in Great Britain and the nickelodeon in America. Occasionally, and very occasionally, a frustrated film-maker with something to say and a financier willing to let him say it, will break with tradition, and, by dint of inspiring performances, or a gripping story, or sometimes unanimous critical approval, will succeed.

Examples of this kind of success are well-known because of their rarity. King Vidor's *The Crowd* attempted social realism at a time – 1928 – when it must have seemed like madness to do so; but the film struck a chord. John Ford's sombre tragedy *The Informer* was doomed until it received official approval in the shape of several of the 1935 Academy Awards; takings immediately improved and the film ended up in the black (a pattern often repeated since). Set in the slums of New York's Lower East Side, *Dead End* (1937) was a tremendous risk for the post-Depression era, but its characters (the Dead End Kids) proved so likeable that they were still featuring in spin-off comedies twenty years later. The artistry of *Great Expectations* (1946) made Charles Dickens a box-office draw. The fluke British success of *Lord of the Flies* (1963) probably surprised no one more than its director Peter Brook, who, along with a handful of film-makers such as Joseph Strick and Orson Welles ('It is hard to imagine a movie career more littered with sensational catastrophes than mine'), has been allowed to spend most of his career in splendid isolation from the demands of the front office. Without a major star or any obvious selling angle, *The Graduate* had been written off as a no-hoper before it was released; its comparative frankness and Dustin Hoffman's cute mannerisms turned it into the top grosser of 1967. Controversy also tipped the balance in favour of *Sebastiane* (1976), still one of the few examples of male homosexuality being used as the subject of a hit film (*Staircase, The Boys in the Band, Fortune and Men's Eyes* and *Nijinsky* were calamities).

Miraculously the isolated victory of the outsider has always been sufficient for a dozen idealists to risk their own foolhardy projects, presumably in the sanguine expectation that the public is eager to have its taste re-educated. This, of course, is hardly ever the case, although one hopes this realization will be a long time dawning: without the gambler and the often indirect influence he exerts, the cinema would have gone long ago the way of big city theatre.

Nijinsky, *with the title role played by George De La Pena, was Herbert Ross's brave but unrewarded attempt to pursue the unexpected success of his earlier ballet film* The Turning Point.

Three causes of failure

Apart from a few recurring phenomena, which we'll come to later, there are three main causes of failure in the cinema: most importantly – to borrow Nicolas Slonimsky's phrase from the *Lexicon of Musical Invective* – 'non-acceptance of the unfamiliar'; then a dislike of star players (and to a lesser degree directors) who are out of touch with what their public expects; and finally refusal to accept the cinema as a medium of culture or education.

Whether the film is good or bad has little relevance. What is 'bad' anyway? The definition varies from decade to decade, country to country. Monogram Pictures, American rubbish of the 1930s, were eulogised in France in the 1950s. *The Rocky Horror Picture Show* (1975), rejected in Britain as inferior to the stage show it was adapted from, achieved unprecedented cult status in America (where the stage show flopped!). Only the tiniest proportion of movies fail to please some of the people some of the time: they're usually comedies featuring comedians past their prime and directed by men with no sense of comic timing, comedies which commit the cardinal sin of being unfunny. Most of Buster Keaton's sound films come into this category, particularly *The Invader* (US: *An Old Spanish Custom*), which he made in Britain in 1935. Laurel and Hardy's entire output during the 1940s was, to use Stan Laurel's own description, 'garbage'. It's said that the movies were made deliberately carelessly because Fox and MGM felt the comics had lost their public appeal. These pitiful films are truly among the world's worst.

The ingredients of success

During the cinema's infancy, exhibitors learned that the public would stay away from films unless they were romantic, comic, or built around a chase. In America films were also supposed to lose the audience's attention if they were longer than a reel (ten minutes) or two at the maximum. This was in fact a mistaken assumption. Films of much greater length were gaining wide popularity in Europe, but when American producer George Kleine imported the five reel *Life of Moses* in 1910, his distributor would only allow it to be screened a reel per week. Needless to say, it was a failure. Pioneer director D. W. Griffith came up against the same obstinacy when he produced the four reel *Judith of Bethulia* in 1913. The same distributor hired it out to cinemas at the standard rate for four reels of film, and since *Judith* was a biblical spectacle which had gone one hundred per cent over budget into the bargain, it didn't make a profit.

Kleine finally struck out by organizing an independent screening of the Italian epic *Quo Vadis?* in 1913, an immediate success which paved the way for *The Birth of a Nation* in 1915 and subsequently the rapid switch-over to feature film production. But for the next fifty years – incredibly enough – audiences demanded much the same kind of romantic escapism in their features as they'd come to expect from shorts. It was a long time before they would even accept an unhappy ending. The chief reason for the failure of *A Woman of Paris* (1923) was not that its director, Charles Chaplin, chose to stay behind the camera for the first time, but that its hero committed suicide. Practically anything that suggested life was less than a bowl of cherries was asking for trouble. Josef von Sternberg's first film, *The Salvation Hunters* (1925), depicting life in a poor ghetto, was greeted with total apathy, and it's likely that von Sternberg's career would have never got off the ground had not the film's star and main financier George K. Arthur pulled strings to get distribution from the influential United Artists. Victor Sjöström's *The Wind* (1928), now one of the classics of the silent

Mary Pickford *made a determined, but unsuccessful, attempt to broaden her screen image in* Stella Maris.

screen, made no money in 1928.

Horror was acceptable only under the guise of a fairy tale, certainly not as a flesh-and-blood reality, as in *Freaks* (1932). Negroes, the source of a more Freudian kind of fear, were still being presented as harmless, singing and dancing caricatures in the 1950s; an all-black film such as *Hallelujah* plainly stood no chance in 1929 – it was one of the first flops of the talkie era. Even the presentation of comedy had severe limitations. The Marx Brothers well and truly exceeded them, and in the early 1930s had little more than a cult following. Paramount couldn't see their comedy appealing to a wider audience and let them go to MGM in 1935. Black comedy was an outrage in 1942 when *To Be or Not to Be* seemed to be making fun of the Nazi occupation of Warsaw.

Most forms of experimentation failed. There was Robert Montgomery's totally subjective camerawork in *The Lady in the Lake* (1946) and Hitchcock's ten minute takes in *Rope* (1948). Attempts to revive the silent film were cold-shouldered: *The Thief* (1952), starring Ray Milland, had trouble getting screenings; *Silent Treatment* (1967) got none at all – it remains unreleased.

No amount of conniving on the part of publicists would get the public to turn out for a film it considered too bleak. Nicholas Ray's *They Live by Night* (1948) was subjected to a string of title changes during a year of sneak previews, but none of them made a grim story of two lovers on the run from the police any more attractive. When *The Ox-Bow Incident* (1943), a sombre re-enactment of the lynching of three innocent men in 1885, began to slump at the box office, posters appeared daring patrons to endure its rigours. This kind of challenge has been made in connection with many films since, sometimes with success, but on this occasion the challenge was declined.

As late as the 1960s, the more sordid side of life was not to the average cinemagoer's liking. Kitchen sink drama – a trend which produced *Look Back in Anger*, *Saturday Night and Sunday Morning* and *The Entertainer* and is now considered the pinnacle from which British cinema has since declined – had little popular success, and although Lindsay Anderson's *This Sporting Life* (1963) is now thought of as one of the finest British films of the 1960s, it was also one of the most downbeat and consequently fared worst of all.

When a star steps out of role

Having previously looked upon the movies as a form of prostitution, stage actors began prostituting themselves in 1912. To their chagrin, the public generally resented Broadway sophisticates being foisted on them (exceptions included Douglas Fairbanks, George Arliss, the Barrymores and Marie Dressler); they'd already begun to create their own, more spellbinding, screen idols, to dictate their images, and – still common practice today – to protest at the first sign of their creations failing their simple duties.

Mary Pickford was the first screen goddess thus created. She was her public's 'Little Mary' and was still having to adopt this role when she was over thirty. She railed only once or twice: in *Stella Maris* (1918) her character was a serene little girl who was not all she appeared to be; she played an adult role in *Dorothy Vernon of Haddon Hall* (1924). Audiences would not accept either film. Charles Ray was a male version of Mary Pickford, very popular in hayseed roles from 1912 to 1920. This was not how he pictured himself, however, and he finally got his chance to play in 'artistic, uplifting, psychological drama' by producing *The Courtship of Miles Standish* (1923), a lavish period piece involving a $65,000 full-size reconstruction of the 'Mayflower'. The film was a catastrophe and led eventually to Ray's bankruptcy. Theda Bara also lost a battle with public opinion, but under precisely the opposite circumstances. In 1916 she was the premiere femme fatale: it was she who was photographed hunched over a male skeleton. Naturally she came to grief when Fox cast her in *Heart and Soul* (1917) as a fine, upstanding woman.

Harry Langdon was a sad case. One minute he was a clown spoken of in the same breath as Keaton and Chaplin, the next minute he was a bankrupt, lucky to find work stooging in low budget comedies. A single film had changed his life, *Three's a Crowd* (1927), a slow, maudlin romance he'd insisted on directing himself. The rapidity of Langdon's downfall was unequalled by another comedian until 1969, when Norman Wisdom, Britain's top film comic for twelve years, stripped off in a sex comedy called *What's Good For the Goose*. His film career stopped dead.

Audiences have also balked at films which promise one thing (escapism) and deliver another (drama). '*Farewell My Lovely* (1944) starring Dick Powell' sounded like a musical. People were very disturbed to find Powell playing his first straight role as private eye Philip Marlowe, and when the inevitable happened and takings fell off, RKO had to come up with a more descriptive title (*Murder My Sweet*). *The Treasure of the Sierra Madre* (1948) was boycotted because it came out at a time when Humphrey Bogart was topping popularity polls, and yet it had no love interest.

Great mistakes have been made by studios that have overestimated their stars' versatility. Bette Davis knew she was too old at forty to play a girl looking for excitement in the big city in *Beyond the Forest* (1949), but Jack Warner insisted she should do it. The result was a disaster, which ended many successful years for Davis at Warner Brothers, although, ironically, the film was later immortalised by playwright Edward Albee, who quoted one of its lines ('What a dump!') in *Who's Afraid of Virginia Woolf?* The name of *Parnell* (1937) has also lived on purely because it was one of the very few Clark Gable pictures to lose money: no one was prepared to accept the King of Hollywood as an Irish politician. Paul Muni, on the other hand, was a rare example of the star who was rebuffed when he tried to give the public what it wanted. Best known from *Scarface* (1932), Muni was also fond of appearing in 'worthy' biopics, giving rise to Hal Wallis' remark, 'Every time Paul Muni parted his beard and looked down a telescope Warner Brothers lost a million dollars'. Trying to recapture the old magic, Muni returned to the Scarface mould in *Angel On My Shoulder* (1946), but his time had passed, and the film's failure left Muni so embittered that it was thirteen years before he made another Hollywood movie.

Great artistic follies

The very instant movies became fashionable in 1915, studios fell over themselves to cater for the intelligentsia, a policy which, though frequently self-defeating, has continued ever since. Triangle, a company which achieved the unlikely alliance of D. W. Griffith and 'the king of comedy' producer Mack Sennett, was the first studio to sign up a roster of stage luminaries, nearly sixty of them in this case including Sir Herbert Beerbohm Tree, whose unpopular production of *Macbeth* (1916) led to Sir Herbert tearing up his Triangle contract. Triangle collapsed in 1919 (only the Mack Sennett productions had been making money). Undeterred by this calamity, the Goldwyn company bulldozed into the culture business in 1917, contracting so many veteran Broadway actresses that the studio became known as 'The Old Ladies' Home'. The acquisition of opera singer Mary Garden caused much excitement, but only because the public thought she was Mary Gardener, a nickelodeon queen. Not content with his distinguished thespians, Goldwyn also signed up twelve 'Eminent Authors' to pen high class screenplays. One of them was Maurice Maeterlinck, who spoke no English, but dutifully set to work on an adaptation of his *Life of a Bee*. Between them, the Eminent Authors produced only one successful film (*The Old Nest*, 1921, written by Rupert Hughes). Goldwyn went bankrupt in 1922, later merging with Metro Pictures, who were themselves reeling from the losses sustained on a series of 'Screen Classics'.

What's Good for the Goose *starring Norman Wisdom, second from left, as an assistant bank manager who falls for a teenage girl.*

MGM were appalled when they saw Gene Kelly's *Invitation to the Dance* (1956); it was a ninety minute *mime*. The film was shelved for months and never given a proper release. One of the first movie philanthropists was Edwin Thanhouser, who made silent adaptations of Shakespeare because he wanted to. Alexander Korda, one and only saviour of the British film industry, knew that *Rembrandt* (1936) wouldn't make money, but thought it only fitting that the first film to be shot completely in his grand new Denham studios should

Invitation to the Dance, *Gene Kelly's fusion of live action and animation.*

be a 'prestige' production. *Wilson* (1944), starring Alexander Knox as the President, was the pet project of producer Darryl F. Zanuck. He threatened that if it failed he'd never make another film without Betty Grable. It did fail, and he was heartbroken. Four years later, when accepting an oscar for *Gentleman's Agreement*, he said, 'Many thanks. But I should have won it for *Wilson*'. *Fantasia* (1940) was also the realization of a dream for Walt Disney, who thought he had found a way of introducing the masses to classical music. He hadn't; *Fantasia* has always preached either to the converted, or, in later years, to camp followers, and it was decades before the film recouped its costs. Disney, his fingers burned, never again mixed art and entertainment, and did very well.

Surprisingly, Shakespeare is by no means box-office poison. There have been more misses than hits – notable failures include: the Pickford-Fairbanks *Taming of the Shrew* (1929), Max Reinhardt's all-star *Midsummer Night's Dream* (1935), Olivier's *Hamlet* (1948, only a succès d'estime), Orson Welles' *Macbeth* (1948), Renato Castellani's *Romeo and Juliet* (1954), Polanski's *Macbeth* (1971), and Charlton Heston's *Antony and Cleopatra* (1972). But the cinema has the occasional knack of making the bard a box-office smash. Olivier's *Henry V* was an international moneyspinner despite costing £500,000 in 1944. Zeffirelli's *Romeo and Juliet* (1968) was a three-handkerchief weepie that grossed $17.5m. in the USA alone.

For consistent unpopularity the work of George Bernard Shaw is hard to beat. *Pygmalion* (1938) excepted, films of Shaw plays have emptied cinemas since *How He Lied to Her Husband* was brought to the screen in 1931. When *Major Barbara* (1941) went down the drain, £20,000 of the lost investment was Shaw's own. And it was a Shaw play that was the subject of Britain's biggest movie fiasco, *Caesar and Cleopatra* (1945), the £1,278,000 nightmare that helped cripple the Rank Organization.

Sequels and re-makes

Down the years the film industry has thrown up certain areas of no man's land into which producers wander at their peril. The most notorious of these has its own warning sign: no sequel is ever equal. Recent examples of unequal sequels are enough to send shudders up the spine: *Alfie Darling, Exorcist II – the Heretic, Look What's Happened to Rosemary's Baby, Beyond the Poseidon Adventure.* It goes without saying that no sequel is ever superior, although a borderline case is *The Bells of St Mary's* (1945), which was as successful as its predecessor, *Going My Way* (1944). But there are positive rewards to be derived from sequels, as *Rocky II* (1979) and the sequel to *Star Wars, The Empire Strikes Back* (1980) demonstrate.

The re-make can also be dangerous territory, dangerous enough, anyway, to make it difficult to remember more than a handful of re-makes that have done better business than their originals: these include *The Dawn Patrol* (1938), the second re-make of *The Maltese Falcon* (1941), the second re-make of *Show Boat* (1951), *House of Wax* (1953) and *The Man Who Knew Too Much* (1956). A list of ruinous re-makes would have to be topped by the 1963 *Cleopatra* ($10m. alone spent on unusable footage shot before the transfer from Britain to Italy), the 1962 *Mutiny on the Bounty* (cost $20m., lost $10m.), the 1977 *Wages of Fear* (originally known as *Sorcerer*, cost $22m., lost $16m.), and would then continue downwards almost ad infinitum.

It is obviously very silly to plough into a production if rivals have already begun shooting their own versions of the same subject. And yet this recklessness occurs quite often. There were two life stories of Oscar Wilde in 1960, two of Jean Harlow in 1965. One film of Ibsen's *A Doll's House* (1973) was enough of a gamble; when it was joined by a second later the same year, one could only admire its nerve. Wastefulness reached a new height, however, in 1976 with the *three* (almost identical) accounts of the Israeli raid on Entebbe airport.

The point is, of course, that all these films suffered by dividing the available market. Even movies with similar subjects have to fight to the death if they arrive around the same time: many people gave *A Walk in the Sun* (1945) a

Charles Laughton *(far left) in the title-role of Alexander Korda's* Rembrandt, *described by Graham Greene as 'reverent but pompous'.*

Cleopatra *(left), starring Elizabeth Taylor and Richard Burton, still holds the record for the highest Hollywood budget of all time.*

miss because they'd just seen the same sort of thing in *The Story of G.I. Joe*. *Fail Safe* suffered because nuclear destruction had so recently been made the subject of a comedy, *Dr Strangelove* in 1963.

Nepotism

As we have noted, audiences have not been prepared to give movie celebrities much leeway, and so it's scarcely to be wondered at that producers, with a whim to promote as actresses their wives or mistresses, have been given particularly short shrift. William Randolph Hearst was the most monomaniac star-maker. He bought a film company to make pictures starring his girlfriend Marion Davies, supervised all of them himself, and wouldn't release them if he didn't like them. He later admitted that they all had to be written off as tax losses. Vera Hruba Ralston was another pretty girl with an influential friend. She appeared in no films other than those produced by her husband Herbert J. Yates, boss of Republic Pictures. Darryl F. Zanuck 'discovered' a bevy of young actresses, none of whom amounted to anything and one of whom, Bella Darvi, had the misfortune to become a laughing stock. Today, when a movie is on the drawing board, one of the most formidable stumbling blocks is still the producer's lady, although the actor who thinks he can direct can be another unwelcome intrusion. If proof were ever needed that actors are not in touch with the real world, one could cite the number of stars who have directed one flop and never again been allowed behind the camera: Marlon Brando, John Mills, Peter Sellers, Roddy McDowall, Charles Laughton, Anthony Quinn, Burgess Meredith, Albert Finney, Frank Sinatra, Kirk Douglas, James Caan and dozens more. Some actors are allowed to make one flop after another: David Hemmings and Richard Attenborough are still at it.

In recent times unfashionable genres have produced many a surefire failure. Following the heyday of the biblical epic, the bottom fell out of the movie religion market to such an extent that the genre is now virtually extinct: brave revival attempts such as *The Shoes of the Fisherman* and *Pope Joan* have met with complete antipathy. And as a result of the diminishing family audience, the musical is now a high-risk venture. Huge sums were lost on *Star!*, *Dr. Dolittle*, *Hello Dolly!* and *Mame*, and more recently even multi-million dollar advertising campaigns and hit soundtrack albums could not draw audiences to the likes of *Sgt. Pepper's Lonely Hearts Club Band*, *Can't Stop the Music* and *Xanadu*.

Contemporary stars out of character

Despite the supposed collapse of the star system, the failure of a number of recent films can be attributed directly to the 'failings' of their stars. Barbra Streisand stepped way out of line to play a daydreaming housewife in an offbeat fantasy *Up the Sandbox* (1972). She hurriedly returned to romantic comedy in *The Way We Were*. John Travolta nearly ruined his career by attempting to play a straight romantic lead in *Moment By Moment* (1978). On the strength of *Rocky*, Sylvester Stallone was allowed to write himself

Lucille Ball *in* Mame *had little luck with the public and even less with the critics. The latter complained that the singers were tone-deaf and that close-ups of Lucille Ball were blatantly out-of-focus.*

roles in two uncommercial subjects, *F.I.S.T.* and *Paradise Alley*. His public instantly forgave him when he reappeared as *Rocky II*. The case of Farrah Fawcett-Majors is not so straightforward. It seems unaccountable that such a popular TV actress could fail so dismally as a movie star (she has to date suffered three flops in a row, *Somebody Killed Her Husband, Sunburn* and *Saturn 3*). All there exists to enlighten the mystery is the surprisingly long line of TV favourites before her (Raymond Burr, Carol Burnett, Dick Van Dyke, Sid Caesar, Mary Tyler Moore, Rowan and Martin, *et al*) whose appeal somehow went astray in transit from the small screen.

Failures in the 1970s

The failure that comes completely out of the blue has been a rarity lately, but *The Great Gatsby* (1974) was one such surprise. During production the film was confidently expected to outgross *The Godfather*, and arriving as it did at the peak of the nostalgia boom, its success seemed assured. As it turned out, the clothes caught on, the film didn't. Robert Redford proved miscast as Gatsby, and the story buckled under the weight of *Cleopatra*-style extravagance. A year later *Lucky Lady*, which featured the 'infallible' teaming of Gene Hackman, Liza Minnelli and Burt Reynolds, also bit the dust. And in 1979 the World War II comedy *1941*, directed by whizz-kid Steven Spielberg, became a landmark flop.

It's hard to see why *Lucky Lady* and *1941* were so widely disliked. In both cases literally nothing was spared (the budgets were astronomically high, $26.5m. for *1941*) in the attempt to give the public what it had found thoroughly enjoyable on previous occasions. One could point out, of course, that the bigger they are the harder they fall, an adage that may well become increasingly apt as far as the movies of the 1980s are concerned.

The implication now to be drawn is of a multi-million dollar industry grinding away for the sole delectation of fickle philistines, and casting aside like old boots anyone who shows a spark of individuality. But this is not the case. To answer the first point, the public will hardly ever accept pure rubbish, except in sex films which have their own unique standards. Secondly, the movie business generally looks after its own. During the heyday of the studio system contract players would often be crowded together in all-star jamborees. These films were cheap, but still unsuccessful: audiences resented watching a number of stars, who were obviously friends, coming together and having a good time without communicating that fun to those in the stalls. The studios with their stables of stars are long gone, but all-star productions are still an occasional feature on production schedules: *The Story of Mankind, Jet Storm, Pepe, Casino Royale, The Madwoman of Chaillot, Scavenger Hunt*. Why are these films made? They're almost guaranteed to bring in paltry returns, and it's a cast iron certainty they will do if, like *The Phynx* or *Won Ton Ton, the Dog who Saved Hollywood*, they rely heavily on old-timers in the cast. It's almost as if somebody periodically says, 'I know two men and a dog who will love this picture. Who cares about the money?' It would be nice to believe that that was true.

Index

Bold numerals indicate photographs or illustrations.

A

B

C

G

H

I

J

K

L

M

N

O

P

Q

R

S

T

U

V

W

X

Y

Z

Shuckburgh Reynolds Ltd would like to thank the following: Takashi Ishikawa of Dai Nippon Printing Co.; Mike Jarvis, Alan Norris and Peter Brealey of SX Composing Ltd.; Arthur Windsor for the index; Vincent Porter; Sybil del Strother; Lesley Gilbert; Kate Caute; Nigel O'Gorman.